Lecture Notes in Computer Science

Vol. 88: Mathematical Foundations of Computer Science 1980. Proceedings, 1980. Edited by P. Dembiński. VIII, 723 pages. 1980.

Vol. 89: Computer Aided Design - Modelling, Systems Engineering, CAD-Systems. Proceedings, 1980. Edited by J. Encarnacao. XIV, 461 pages. 1980.

Vol. 90: D. M. Sandford, Using Sophisticated Models in Resolution Theorem Proving.
XI, 239 pages. 1980

Vol. 91: D. Wood, Grammar and L Forms: An Introduction. IX, 314 pages. 1980.

Vol. 92: R. Milner, A Calculus of Communication Systems. VI, 171 pages. 1980.

Vol. 93: A. Nijholt, Context-Free Grammars: Covers, Normal Forms, and Parsing. VII, 253 pages. 1980.

Vol. 94: Semantics-Directed Compiler Generation. Proceedings, 1980. Edited by N. D. Jones. V, 489 pages. 1980.

Vol. 95: Ch. D. Marlin, Coroutines. XII, 246 pages. 1980.

Vol. 96: J. L. Peterson, Computer Programs for Spelling Correction: VI, 213 pages. 1980.

Vol. 97: S. Osaki and T. Nishio, Reliability Evaluation of Some Fault-Tolerant Computer Architectures. VI, 129 pages. 1980.

Vol. 98: Towards a Formal Description of Ada. Edited by D. Bjørner and O. N. Oest. XIV, 630 pages. 1980.

Vol. 99: I. Guessarian, Algebraic Semantics. XI, 158 pages. 1981.

Vol. 100: Graphtheoretic Concepts in Computer Science. Edited by H. Noltemeier. X, 403 pages. 1981.

Vol. 101: A. Thayse, Boolean Calculus of Differences. VII, 144 pages. 1981.

Vol. 102: J. H. Davenport, On the Integration of Algebraic Functions. 1–197 pages. 1981.

Vol. 103: H. Ledgard, A. Singer, J. Whiteside, Directions in Human Factors of Interactive Systems. VI, 190 pages. 1981.

Vol. 104: Theoretical Computer Science. Ed. by P. Deussen. VII, 261 pages. 1981.

Vol. 105: B. W. Lampson, M. Paul, H. J. Siegert, Distributed Systems – Architecture and Implementation. XIII, 510 pages. 1981.

Vol. 106: The Programming Language Ada. Reference Manual. X, 243 pages. 1981.

Vol. 107: International Colloquium on Formalization of Programming Concepts. Proceedings. Edited by J. Diaz and I. Ramos. VII, 478 pages. 1981.

Vol. 108: Graph Theory and Algorithms. Edited by N. Saito and T. Nishizeki. VI, 216 pages. 1981.

Vol. 109: Digital Image Processing Systems. Edited by L. Bolc and Zenon Kulpa. V, 353 pages. 1981.

Vol. 110: W. Dehning, H. Essig, S. Maass, The Adaptation of Virtual Man-Computer Interfaces to User Requirements in Dialogs. X, 142 pages. 1981.

Vol. 111: CONPAR 81. Edited by W. Händler. XI, 508 pages. 1981.

Vol. 112: CAAP '81. Proceedings. Edited by G. Astesiano and C. Böhm. VI, 364 pages. 1981.

Vol. 113: E.-E. Doberkat, Stochastic Automata: Stability, Nondeterminism, and Prediction. IX, 135 pages. 1981.

Vol. 114: B. Liskov, CLU, Reference Manual. VIII, 190 pages. 1981.

Vol. 115: Automata, Languages and Programming. Edited by S. Even and O. Kariv. VIII, 552 pages. 1981.

Vol. 116: M. A. Casanova, The Concurrency Control Problem for Database Systems. VII, 175 pages. 1981.

Vol. 117: Fundamentals of Computation Theory. Proceedings, 1981. Edited by F. Gécseg. XI, 471 pages. 1981.

Vol. 118: Mathematical Foundations of Computer Science 1981. Proceedings, 1981. Edited by J. Gruska and M. Chytil. XI, 589 pages. 1981.

Vol. 119: G. Hirst, Anaphora in Natural Language Understanding: A Survey. XIII, 128 pages. 1981.

Vol. 120: L. B. Rall, Automatic Differentiation: Techniques and Applications. VIII, 165 pages. 1981.

Vol. 121: Z. Zlatev, J. Wasniewski, and K. Schaumburg, Y12M Solution of Large and Sparse Systems of Linear Algebraic Equations. IX, 128 pages. 1981.

Vol. 122: Algorithms in Modern Mathematics and Computer Science. Proceedings, 1979. Edited by A. P. Ershov and D. E. Knuth. XI, 487 pages. 1981.

Vol. 123: Trends in Information Processing Systems. Proceedings, 1981. Edited by A. J. W. Duijvestijn and P. C. Lockemann. XI, 349 pages. 1981.

Vol. 124: W. Polak, Compiler Specification and Verification. XIII, 269 pages. 1981.

Vol. 125: Logic of Programs. Proceedings, 1979. Edited by E. Engeler. V, 245 pages. 1981.

Vol. 126: Microcomputer System Design. Proceedings, 1981. Edited by M. J. Flynn, N. R. Harris, and D. P. McCarthy. VII, 397 pages. 1982.

Voll. 127: Y. Wallach, Alternating Sequential/Parallel Processing. X, 329 pages. 1982.

Vol. 128: P. Branquart, G. Louis, P. Wodon, An Analytical Description of CHILL, the CCITT High Level Language. VI, 277 pages. 1982.

Vol. 129: B. T. Hailpern, Verifying Concurrent Processes Using Temporal Logic. VIII, 208 pages. 1982.

Vol. 130: R. Goldblatt, Axiomatising the Logic of Computer Programming. XI, 304 pages. 1982.

Vol. 131: Logics of Programs. Proceedings, 1981. Edited by D. Kozen. VI, 429 pages. 1982.

Vol. 132: Data Base Design Techniques I: Requirements and Logical Structures. Proceedings, 1978. Edited by S.B. Yao, S.B. Navathe, J.L. Weldon, and T.L. Kunii. V, 227 pages. 1982.

Vol. 133: Data Base Design Techniques II: Proceedings, 1979. Edited by S.B. Yao and T.L. Kunii. V, 229–399 pages. 1982.

Vol. 134: Program Specification. Proceedings, 1981. Edited by J. Staunstrup. IV, 426 pages. 1982.

Vol. 135: R.L. Constable, S.D. Johnson, and C.D. Eichenlaub, An Introduction to the PL/CV2 Programming Logic. X, 292 pages. 1982.

Vol. 136: Ch. M. Hoffmann, Group-Theoretic Algorithms and Graph Isomorphism. VIII, 311 pages. 1982.

Vol. 137: International Symposium on Programming. Proceedings, 1982. Edited by M. Dezani-Ciancaglini and M. Montanari. VI, 406 pages. 1982.

Vol. 138: 6th Conference on Automated Deduction. Proceedings, 1982. Edited by D.W. Loveland. VII, 389 pages. 1982.

Vol. 139: J. Uhl, S. Drossopoulou, G. Persch, G. Goos, M. Dausmann, G. Winterstein, W. Kirchgässner, An Attribute Grammar for the Semantic Analysis of Ada. IX, 511 pages. 1982.

Vol. 140: Automata, Languages and programming. Edited by M. Nielsen and E.M. Schmidt. VII, 614 pages. 1982.

Vol. 141: U. Kastens, B. Hutt, E. Zimmermann, GAG: A Practical Compiler Generator. IV, 156 pages. 1982.

Lecture Notes in
Computer Science

Edited by G. Goos and J. Hartmanis

172

Automata, Languages and Programming

11th Colloquium
Antwerp, Belgium, July 16–20, 1984

Edited by Jan Paredaens

Springer-Verlag
Berlin Heidelberg New York Tokyo 1984

Editor

Jan Paredaens
Department of Mathematics and Computer Science
University of Antwerp, UIA
Universiteitsplein 1, B-2610 Antwerp

CR Subject Classifications (1982): 4.1, 4.2, 5.2, 5.3

ISBN 3-540-13345-3 Springer-Verlag Berlin Heidelberg New York Tokyo
ISBN 0-387-13345-3 Springer-Verlag New York Heidelberg Berlin Tokyo

Library of Congress Cataloging in Publication Data. Main entry under title: Automata, languages and programming. (Lecture notes in computer science; 172) Proceedings of the 11th Colloquium on Automata, Languages and Programming. 1. Machine theory–Congresses. 2. Programming languages (Electronic computers)–Congresses. 3. Programming (Electronic computers)–Congresses. I. Paredaens, Jan, 1947-. II. International Colloquium on Automata, Languages and Programming (11th: 1984: Antwerp, Belgium) III. Series.
QA267.A9215 1984 511 84-10577
ISBN 0-387-13345-3 (U.S.)

Printed in Germany

ICALP 84 was the Eleventh Colloquium on Automata, Languages and Programming in a series of meetings sponsored by the European Association for Theoretical Computer Science (EATCS). The previous meetings have been held in Paris (72), Saarbrücken (74), Edingburgh (76), Turku (77), Udine (78), Graz (79), Amsterdam (80), Haifa (81), Aarhus (82) and Barcelona (83).

ICALP 84 was organized by the Universitaire Instelling Antwerpen (UIA) and the Rijksuniversitair Centrum Antwerpen (RUCA). The Organizing Committee consisted of L. Janssens, W. Kuijk, J. Paredaens and R. Verraedt.

The conference covered the main theoretical and fundamental aspects of computer science, such as automata theory, formal language theory, analysis of algorithms, computational complexity, computability theory, mathematical aspects of programming language definition, logic and semantics of programming languages, program specification, theory of data structures, theory of data bases, cryptology and VLSI structures.

From a total of 141 submitted papers, 46 have been accepted by the Selection Committee, that consisted of G. Ausiello (Rome), A. Blikle (Warsaw), J. De Bakker (Amsterdam), H. Edelsbrunner (Graz), H. Ehrig (Berlin), P. Flajolet (Le Chesnay), H. Genrich (Bonn), M. Nielsen (Aarhus), M. Nivat (Paris), J. Paredaens (Antwerp), A. Paz (Haifa), G. Rozenberg (Leiden), A. Salomaa (Turku), J. Thatcher (Yorktown Heights), A. Van Lamsweerde (Namur) and J. Van Leeuwen (Utrecht). The other members of the Program Committee were A. Aho (Murray Hill), M. Havel (Prague), C. Papadimitriou (Athens) and M. Paterson (Warwick).

There were two invited lecturers: R. Fagin (IBM, San Jose) with "Topics in Database Dependency Theory" and A.L. Rosenberg (Duke Univ., Durham) with "The VLSI Revolution in Theoretical Circles".

I gratefully acknowledge the economic support from Agfa-Gevaert, Bank Brussel Lambert, Bell Telephone Mfg. Company, IBM Belgium, IBM Europe, Ministerie van Nationale Opvoeding en Nederlandse Cultuur, Nationaal Fonds voor Wetenschappelijk Onderzoek, Rijksuniversitair Centrum Antwerpen RUCA, Sabena Belgian World Airlines, Stad Antwerpen and the Universitaire Instelling Antwerpen UIA.

I also thank all those who made this conference possible, especially the members of the Program Committee and of the Organizing Committee, the staff and the students of our university who collaborated anonymously.

March 31, 1984 Jan Paredaens

Conference Chairman

11th International Colloquium on
Automata, Languages and Programming

ICALP 84
July 16–20, 1984
Antwerp, Belgium

TABLE OF CONTENTS

Referees for ICALP-84

A. Aalbersberg
I. Aalbersberg
S. Abiteboul
A. Aho
L. Aiello
Y. Ali
P. Ashveld
F. Aurenhanner
G. Ausiello
L. Barachowski
J. Bergstra
J. Bermond
E. Best
W. Beynon
A. Blikle
S. Bloom
A. Borodin
P. Branquart
M. Broy
J. Bruno
M. Bruynooghe
J. Brzozowski
W. Bucher
B. Ceslebus
M. Chytil
A. Cohn
A. D'Atri
S. Dahlhaus
P. Darondeau
D. De Baer
J. De Bakker
P. De Bra
P. Decansart
J. Denef
P. Deransart
W. de Roever
F. Des
R. Devillers
H. Edelsbrunner
H. Ehrig
J. Engelfriet
P. Enjalbert
Z. Esik
M. Fantzen
W. Fellner
C. Fernandez
J. Finance
P. Flajolet
N. Francez
G. Frandsen
J. Gallier
R. Gandy
N. Gaudel
H. Genrich
R. Gerth
A. Gibbons
U. Goltz
P. Gorlacik
M. Grabowski
M. Gyssens
J. Hagelstein
J. Harjie
M. Harrison
D. Haussler
I.M. Havel
M. Heydemann
H. Hoogeboom
G. Huet
M. Hybri
A. Itai
R. Janicki
D. Janssens
J. Jaromczyk
F. Jensen
J. Karhumaki
H. Kleyn
J. Klop
B. Konikowska
V. Koubek
D. Kozen
I. Kramosil
H. Kreowski
L. Kucera
P. Kurka
L. Kyzousis
C. Lautemann
L. Le Charlier
H. Lenstra
P. Lescanne
J. Leszcwylowski
M. Linna
G. Louchard
G. Louis
B. Mahr
J. Makowski
H. Mannila
A. Marchetti
B. Mayoh
A. Mazurkiewicz
W. McColl
J. Meyer
B. Monien
M. Moscarini
P. Mosses
S. Mozan
J. Nesetril
M. Nielsen
M. Nivat
C. Nourani
F. Oles
H. Olivie
E. Orlowska
M. Overmars
P. Padawitz
C. Papadimitriou
I. Parberry
J. Paredaens
D. Park
M. Paterson
A. Paz
M. Penttonen
A. Peyrat
C. Peyrat
R. Pinter
A. Pirotte
J. Pittl
G. Plotkin
A. Poigne
L. Pomello
A. Proskurowski
M. Protasi
C. Puech
J. Quisquater
K. Raiha
Y. Raz
J. Remy
H. Rirri
B. Robinet
M. Rodek
A. Roscol
G. Rote
G. Rozenberg
K. Ruohonen
W. Rytter
D. Sacca
N. Saheb
A. Salomaa
A. Salwicki
G. Sarvusi
E. Schmidt
R. Seidel
B. Serlet
M. Sintzoff
S. Sippy
S. Skyum
J. Sokol
D. Stanat
J. Staunstrup
M. Steinby
J. Stogerer
S. Szpakowicks
M. Talamo
A. Tang
J. Tarhio
J. Terlouw
J. Thatcher
A. Thayse
P. Thiagaraja
E. Ukkonen
P. Van Emde Boas
A. Van Lamsweerde
J. Van Leeuwen
R. Verraedt
A. Verroust
P. Vitanyi
K. Voss
H. Wagener
E. Wagner
M. Wand
E. Welzl
J. Winkowsi
M. Wirsing
D. Wood
A. Yaghi
S. Zak

Author Index

THE THEORY OF DATA DEPENDENCIES - AN OVERVIEW[1]

Ronald Fagin and Moshe Y. Vardi
IBM Research Laboratory
San Jose, California 95193

Abstract: Dependencies are certain sentences of first-order logic that are of special interest for database theory and practice. There has been quite a bit of research in the last decade in investigating dependencies. A selective overview of this research is presented. In particular, the focus is on the implication problem for dependencies, and on issues related to the universal relation model.

1. Introduction

In the *relational database model*, conceived by Codd in the late 60's [Co1], one views the database as a collection of relations, where each relation is a set of tuples over some domain of values. One notable feature of this model is its being almost devoid of semantics. A tuple in a relation represents a relationship between certain values, but from the mere syntactic definition of the relation one knows nothing about the nature of this relationship, not even if it is a one-to-one or one-to-many relationship.

One approach to remedy this deficiency is to devise means to specify the missing semantics. These semantic specifications are often called *semantic* or *integrity constraints*, since they specify which databases are meaningful for the application and which are meaningless. Of particular interest are the constraints called *data dependencies*, or dependencies for short.

The study of dependencies began in 1972 with the introduction by Codd [Co2] of the *functional dependencies*. After the introduction, independently by Fagin and Zaniolo [Fa1,Za] in 1976, of *multivalued dependencies*, the field became chaotic for a few years in which researchers introduced many new classes of dependencies. The situation has stabilized since 1980 with the introduction, again independently by various researchers, of *embedded implicational dependencies* (EIDs). Essentially, EIDs are sentences in first-order logic stating that if some tuples, fulfilling certain equalities, exist in the database then either some other tuples must also exist in the database or some values in the given tuples must be equal. The class of EIDs seems to contain most previously studied classes of dependencies. (Recently, De Bra and Paredaens [DP] considered *afunctional dependencies*, which are not EIDs.) We give basic definitions and historical perspective in Section 2.

Most of the papers in dependency theory deal exclusively with various aspects of the *implication problem*, i.e., the problem of deciding for a given set of dependencies Σ and a dependency τ whether Σ *logically implies* τ. The reason for the prominence of this problem is that an algorithm for testing implication of dependencies enables us to test whether two given sets of dependencies are equivalent or whether a given set of dependencies is redundant. A solution for the last two problems seems a significant step towards automated database schema design, which some researchers see as the ultimate goal for research in dependency theory [BBG]. We deal with the implication problem in Section 3.

An emerging application for the theory of dependencies is the *universal relation model*. This model aims at achieving *data independence*, which was the original motivation for the relational model. In the universal relation model the user views the data as if it is stored in one big relation. The data, however, is not available in this form but rather in several smaller relations. It is the role of the database management system to

----

[1]An expanded version of this paper, which deals also with the role of dependencies in acyclic database schemes, appears in the Proceedings of the AMS Short Course on the Mathematics of Information Processing, Louisville, Kentucky (Jan. 1984) under the title "The theory of database dependencies - a survey".

provide the interface between the users' view and the actual data, and it is the role of the database designer to specify this interface. There have been different approaches to the question of what this interface should be like. We describe one approach, the *weak* universal relation approach, in Section 4.

A survey like ours of a rich theory necessarily has to be selective. The selection naturally reflects our tastes and biases. A more comprehensive, though less up to date, coverage can be found in the books [Ma,Ul].

2. Definitions and historical perspective

We begin with some fundamental definitions about relations. We are given a fixed finite set U of distinct symbols, called *attributes,* which are column names. From now on, whenever we speak of a set of attributes, we mean a subset of U. Let R be a set of attributes. An *R-tuple* (or simply a *tuple,* if R is understood) is a function with domain R. Thus, a tuple is a mapping that associates a value with each attribute in R. Note that under this definition, the "order of the columns" does not matter. If S is a subset of R, and if t is an R-tuple, then $t[S]$ denotes the S-tuple obtained by restricting the mapping to S. An *R-relation* (or a *relation over R*, or simply a *relation,* if R is understood), is a set of R-tuples. In database theory, we are most interested in *finite* relations, which are finite sets of tuples (although it is sometimes convenient to consider infinite relations). If I is an R-relation, and if S is a subset of R, then by $I[S]$, the *projection* of I onto S, we mean the set of all tuples $t[S]$, where t is in I. A *database* is a finite collection of relations.

Conventions: Upper-case letters A,B,C, ... from the start of the alphabet represent single attributes; upper-case letters $R,S,...,Z$ from the end of the alphabet represent sets of attributes; upper-case letters $I,J,...$ from the middle of the alphabet represent relations; and lower-case letters $r,s,t,...$ from the end of the alphabet represent tuples.

Assume that relations $I_1,...,I_n$ are over attribute sets $R_1,...,R_n$ respectively. The *join* of the relations $I_1,...,I_n$, which is written either $\bowtie \{I_1,...,I_n\}$ or $I_1 \bowtie ... \bowtie I_n$, is the set of all tuples t over the attribute set $R_1 \cup ... R_n$, such that $t[R_i]$ is in I_i for each i. (Our notation exploits the fact that the join is associative and commutative.)

Certain sentences about relations are of special practical and/or theoretical interest for relational databases. For historical reasons, such sentences are usually called *dependencies.* The first dependency introduced and studied was the *functional dependency* (or FD), due to Codd [Co2]. As an example, consider the relation in Figure 2.1, with three columns: EMP (which represents employees), DEPT (which represents departments), and MGR (which represents managers). The relation in Figure 2.1 obeys the FD "DEPT→MGR", which is read "DEPT determines MGR". This means that whenever two tuples (that is, rows) agree in the DEPT column, then they necessarily agree also in the MGR column. The relation in Figure 2.2 does not obey this FD, since, for example, the first and fourth tuples agree in the DEPT column but not in the MGR column. We now give the formal definition. Let X and Y be subsets of the set U of attributes. The FD $X \rightarrow Y$ is said to hold for a relation I if every pair of tuples of I that agree on each of the attributes in X also agree in the attributes in Y.

The original motivation for introducing FDs (and some of the other dependencies we discuss) was to describe database *normalization.* Before giving an example of normalization, we need to define the notion of a relation scheme. A *relation scheme* is simply a set R of attributes. Usually, there is also an associated set Σ of sentences about relations over R. A relation is an *instance* of the relation scheme if it is over R and obeys the sentences in Σ. Thus, the sentences Σ can be thought of as "constraints", that every "valid instance" must obey. Although we do not do so, we note that it is common to define a relation scheme to be a pair $\langle R,\Sigma \rangle$, where the constraints Σ are explicitly included.

We now consider an example of normalization. Assume that the attributes are {EMP,DEPT,MGR}, and that the only constraint is the FD DEPT→MGR. So, in every instance of this scheme, two employees in the same department necessarily have the same manager. It might be better to store the data not in one relation,

EMP	DEPT	MGR
Hilbert	Math	Gauss
Pythagoras	Math	Gauss
Turing	Computer Science	von Neumann

Figure 2.1

EMP	DEPT	MGR
Hilbert	Math	Gauss
Pythagoras	Math	Gauss
Turing	Computer Science	von Neumann
Cauchy	Math	Euler

Figure 2.2

EMP	DEPT
Hilbert	Math
Pythagoras	Math
Turing	Computer Science

DEPT	MGR
Math	Gauss
Computer Science	von Neumann

Figure 2.3

as in Figure 2.1, but rather in two relations, as in Figure 2.3: one relation that relates employees to departments, and one relation that relates departments to managers. We shall come back to normalization in Section 4.

It is easy to see that FDs can be represented as sentences in first-order logic [Ni1]. Assume, for example, that we are dealing with a 4-ary relation, where the first, second, third, and fourth columns are called, respectively, A, B, C, and D. Then the FD $AB \rightarrow C$ is represented by the following sentence:

$$(\forall abc_1c_2d_1d_2)((Pabc_1d_1 \wedge Pabc_2d_2) \Rightarrow (c_1 = c_2)). \tag{2.1}$$

Here $(\forall abc_1c_2d_1d_2)$ is shorthand for $\forall a \forall b \forall c_1 \forall c_2 \forall d_1 \forall d_2$, that is, each variable is universally quantified. Unlike Nicolas, we have used individual variables rather than tuple variables. Incidentally, we think of P in (2.1) as a *relation symbol*, which should not be confused with an *instance* (that is, a *relation*) I, for which (2.1) can hold.

Let X and Y be sets of attributes (subsets of U), and let Z be U-XY (by XY, we mean $X \cup Y$). Thus, Z is the set of attributes not in X or Y. As we saw by example above (where X, Y, and Z are, respectively, the singleton sets {DEPT}, {EMP}, and {MGR}), the FD $X \rightarrow Y$ is a sufficient condition for a "lossless decomposition" of a relation with attributes U into two relations, with attributes XY and XZ respectively. This means that if I is a relation with attributes XYZ that obeys the FD $X \rightarrow Y$, then I can be obtained from its projections $I[XY]$ and $I[XZ]$, by joining them together. Thus, there is no loss of information in replacing relation I by the two relations I_1 and I_2. We note that this fact, which is known as Heath's Theorem [He], is historically one of the first theorems of database theory.

It may be instructive to give an example of a decomposition that does lose information. Let I be the relation in Figure 2.4, with attributes STORE, ITEM, and PRICE. Let I_1 and I_2 be two projections of I, onto {STORE, ITEM} and {ITEM, PRICE}, respectively, as in Figure 2.5. These projections contain less information than the original relation I. Thus, we see from relation I_1 that Macy's sells toasters; further, we see from relation I_2 that someone sells toasters for 20 dollars, and that someone sells toasters for 15 dollars. However, there is no way to tell from relations I_1 and I_2 how much Macy's sells toasters for.

The next dependency to be introduced was the *multivalued dependency*, or MVD, which was defined, independently by Fagin [Fa1] and Zaniolo [Za]. It was introduced because of the perception that the functional dependency provided too limited a notion of "depends on". As we shall see, multivalued dependencies provide a necessary and sufficient condition for lossless decomposition of a relation into two of its projections. Before we give the formal definition, we present a few examples. Consider the relation in Figure 2.6, with attributes EMP, SALARY, and CHILD. It obeys the functional dependency EMP→SALARY, that is, each employee has exactly one salary. The relation does *not* obey the FD EMP→CHILD, since an employee can have more than one child. However, it is clear that in some sense an employee "determines" his set of children. Thus, the employee's set of children is "determined by" the employee and by nothing else, just as his salary is. Indeed, as we shall see, the multivalued dependency EMP↠CHILD (read "employee multidetermines child") holds for this relation. As another example, consider the relation in Figure 2.7, with attributes EMP, CHILD, and SKILL. A tuple (e,c,s) appears in this relation if and only if e is an employee, c is one of e's children, and s is one of e's skills. This relation obeys no nontrivial (nontautologous) functional dependencies. However, it turns out to obey the multivalued dependencies EMP↠CHILD and EMP↠SKILL. Intuitively, the MVD EMP↠CHILD means that the set of names of the employee's children depends only on the employee, and is "orthogonal" to the information about his skills.

We are now ready to formally define multivalued dependencies. Let I be a relation over U. As before, let X and Y be subsets of U, and let Z be U-XY. The multivalued dependency $X \twoheadrightarrow Y$ holds for relation I if for each pair r, s of tuples of I for which $r[X] = s[X]$, there is a tuple t in I where (1) $t[X] = r[X] = s[X]$, (2) $t[Y] = r[Y]$, and (3) $t[Z] = s[Z]$. Of course, if this multivalued dependency holds for I, then it follows by symmetry that there is also a tuple u in I where (1) $u[X] = r[X] = s[X]$, (2) $u[Y] = s[Y]$, and (3) $u[Z] = r[Z]$.

Multivalued dependencies obey a number of useful properties. For example, if U is the disjoint union of X, Y, Z, and W, and if I is a relation over U that obeys the MVDs $X \twoheadrightarrow Y$ and $Y \twoheadrightarrow Z$, then it follows that I

STORE	ITEM	PRICE
Macy's	Toaster	$20.00
Sears	Toaster	$15.00
Macy's	Pencil	$ 0.10

Figure 2.4

STORE	ITEM
Macy's	Toaster
Sears	Toaster
Macy's	Pencil

ITEM	PRICE
Toaster	$20.00
Toaster	$15.00
Pencil	$ 0.10

Figure 2.5

EMP	SALARY	CHILD
Hilbert	$80K	Hilda
Pythagoras	$30K	Peter
Pythagoras	$30K	Paul
Turing	$70K	Tom

Figure 2.6

EMP	CHILD	SKILL
Hilbert	Hilda	Math
Hilbert	Hilda	Physics
Pythagoras	Peter	Math
Pythagoras	Paul	Math
Pythagoras	Peter	Philosophy
Pythagoras	Paul	Philosophy
Turing	Tom	Computer Science

Figure 2.7

obeys the MVD $X \twoheadrightarrow Z$ [Fa1]. So, MVDs obey a law of transitivity. We shall discuss more properties of MVDs in Section 3, where we give a complete axiomatization for MVDs.

Note that MVDs, like FDs, can be expressed in first-order logic. For example, assume that $U=\{A,B,C,D,E\}$. Then the MVD $AB \twoheadrightarrow CD$ holds for a relation over U if the following sentence holds, where P plays the role of the relation symbol:

$$(\forall abc_1c_2d_1d_2e_1e_2)\ ((Pabc_1d_1e_1 \wedge Pabc_2d_2e_2) \Rightarrow Pabc_2d_2e_1). \tag{2.2}$$

Embedded dependencies were introduced (Fagin [Fa1]) as dependencies that hold in a projection of a relation (although, as we shall see, for certain classes of dependencies they are defined a little more generally). We shall simply give an example of an embedded MVD; the general case is obvious from the example. Assume that we are dealing with 4-ary relations, where we call the four columns $ABCD$. We say that such a 4-ary relation I obeys the *embedded MVD* (or *EMVD*) $A \twoheadrightarrow B \mid C$ if the projection of R onto ABC obeys the MVD $A \twoheadrightarrow B$. Thus, the EMVD $A \twoheadrightarrow B \mid C$ can be written as follows:

$$(\forall ab_1b_2c_1c_2d_1d_2)((Pab_1c_1d_1 \wedge Pab_2c_2d_2) \Rightarrow \exists d_3Pab_1c_2d_3). \tag{2.3}$$

As a concrete example, assume that the relation of Figure 2.7, with attributes EMP, CHILD, and SKILL, had an additional attribute BIRTHDATE, which tells the date of birth of the child. Then this 4-ary relation I would obey the embedded MVD EMP$\twoheadrightarrow$CHILD | SKILL. Note that I need not obey the MVD EMP$\twoheadrightarrow$CHILD (although it does obey the MVD EMP$\twoheadrightarrow$\{CHILD,BIRTHDATE\}).

Several dependencies were defined within a few years after the multivalued dependency was introduced; we shall mention these other dependencies later in this section. Of these, the most important are the *join dependency*, or JD [ABU,Ri2]), and the *inclusion dependency*, or IND [Fa2]. Assume that $\mathbf{X}=\{X_1, ..., X_k\}$ is a collection of subsets of U, where $X_1 \cup ... \cup X_k = U$. The relation I, over U, is said to obey the join dependency $\bowtie [X_1, ..., X_k]$, denoted also $\bowtie [\mathbf{X}]$, if I is the join of its projections $I[X_1],...,I[X_k]$. It follows that this join dependency holds for the relation I if and only if I contains each tuple t for which there are tuples $w_1, ..., w_n$ of I (not necessarily distinct) such that $w_i[X_i] = t[X_i]$ for each i $(1 \le i \le n)$. As an example, consider the relation I in Figure 2.8 below.

A	*B*	*C*	*D*
0	1	0	0
0	2	3	4
5	1	3	0

Figure 2.8

This relation violates the join dependency $\bowtie [AB, ACD, BC]$. For, let w_1, w_2, w_3 be, respectively, the tuples (0,1,0,0), (0,2,3,4), and (5,1,3,0) of I; let X_1, X_2, X_3 be, respectively, AB, ACD, and BC; and let t be the tuple (0,1,3,4); then $w_i[X_i] = t[X_i]$ for each i $(1 \le i \le n)$, although t is not a tuple in the relation I. However, it is straightforward to verify that the same relation I obeys, for example, the join dependency $\bowtie [ABC, BCD, ABD]$.

Let us say that the join dependency $\bowtie [X_1, ..., X_k]$ has *k components*. Join dependencies are generalizations of multivalued dependencies; thus, each multivalued dependency is equivalent to a join dependency with two components, and conversely. Assume now that $X_1 \cup ... \cup X_k \subseteq U$, and denote $X_1 \cup ... \cup X_k$ by X. A relation I with attributes U is said to obey the *embedded join dependency* $\bowtie [X_1, ..., X_k]$ if its projection $I[X]$ obeys the join dependency $\bowtie [X_1, ..., X_k]$. We shall see soon that join dependencies can be written in first-order logic. Embedded join dependencies, too, can be so written, but they require existential quantifiers, just as embedded multivalued dependencies do. Note that our notation, the set U of attributes does not appear, and so the same syntactical object $\bowtie [X_1, ..., X_k]$ is used to represent a join dependency over X and an embedded join dependency over U. However, the two would be written in distinct ways in first-order logic. This is actually a nice convenience, especially in the case of functional dependencies, where a similar comment applies.

The intuitive semantics of *multivalued* dependencies were fairly well understood at the time they were first defined. However, it was not until several years after *join* dependencies were defined that their semantics was adequately explained (by Fagin et al. [FMU]). Let us consider an example (from [FMU]). Assume that the attributes are *C*(ourse), *T*(eacher), *R*(oom), *H*(our), *S*(tudent), and *G*(rade). The informal meaning of these attributes is that teacher *T* teaches course *C*, course *C* meets in room *R* at hour *H*, and that student *S* is getting grade *G* in course *C*. If we were to define a single "universal" relation over these attributes, it would be

$$\{(c,t,r,h,s,g)\text{: } t \text{ "teaches" } c\text{; } c \text{ "meets in" } r \text{ "at hour" } h\text{; and } s \text{ " is getting" } g \text{ "in" } c\}.$$

This relation is of the form

$$\{(c,t,r,h,s,g)\text{: } P_1tc \wedge P_2crh \wedge P_3sgc\}, \tag{2.4}$$

for certain predicates P_1, P_2, and P_3. The fact that a relation with attributes c,t,r,h,s,g is of the form (2.4) for for some predicates P_1, P_2, and P_3 is a severe constraint. In fact [FMU], this constraint is precisely equivalent to the join dependency $\bowtie [TC,CRH,SGC]$. The obvious generalization of this observation to arbitrary join dependencies explains their semantics. Before we leave join dependencies, let us note, as promised, they, too, can be written as sentences in first-order logic. For example, if we are dealing with relations with attributes c,t,r,h,s,g, then the join dependency $\bowtie [TC,CRH,SGC]$ can be written as

$$(\forall ctt_1t_2rr_1r_2hh_1h_2ss_1s_2gg_1g_2)((Pctr_1h_1s_1g_1 \wedge Pct_1rhs_2g_2 \wedge Pct_2r_2h_2sg) \Rightarrow Pctrhsg) \tag{2.5}$$

So far, each of the dependencies we have discussed has two properties: (1) each is *uni-relational*, that is, deals with a single relation at a time, rather than with inter-relationships among several relations, and (2) each is typed. By *typed*, we mean that no variable appears in two distinct columns. For example, the sentence $(\forall xy)((Pxy \wedge Pyz) \Rightarrow Pxz)$, which says that a relation is transitive, is *not* typed, since the variable y appear in both the first and second columns of P in the sentence. The next dependency that we shall discuss violates both (1) and (2) above, that is, is neither uni-relational nor typed. This dependency is the *inclusion dependency*, or IND [CFP]. As an example, an IND can say that every MANAGER entry of the P relation appears as an EMPLOYEE entry of the Q relation. In general, an IND is of the form

$$P[A_1...A_m] \subseteq Q[B_1...B_m], \tag{2.6}$$

where P and Q are relation names (possibly the same), and where the A_i's and B_i's are attributes. If I is the P relation and J is the Q relation, then the IND (2.6) holds if for each tuple s of I, there is a tuple t of J such that $s[A_1...A_m] = t[B_1...B_m]$. Hence, INDs are valuable for database design, since they permit us to selectively define what data must be duplicated in what relations. INDs are commonly known in Artificial Intelligence applications as *ISA* relationships (cf. Beeri and Korth [BK]). Not surprisingly, the inclusion dependency, too, can be written in first-order logic. For example, if the P relation has attributes ABC, and the Q relation has attributes CDE, then the IND $P[AB] \subseteq Q[CE]$ can be written

$$(\forall abc)(Pabc \Rightarrow \exists dQadb). \tag{2.7}$$

After multivalued dependencies were defined, there was a period where a large number of other dependencies were defined. We have already discussed the classes of join dependencies, embedded join dependencies, and inclusion dependencies. Others (many of which were introduced before join dependencies) include Nicolas's *mutual dependencies* [Ni1], which say that a relation is the join of three of its projections; Mendelzon and Maier's *generalized mutual dependencies* [MM]; Paredaens' *transitive dependencies* [Pa], which generalize both FDs and MVDs; Ginsburg and Zaiddan's *implied dependencies* [GZ], which generalize FDs; Sagiv and Walecka's *subset dependencies* [SW], which generalize embedded MVDs; Sadri and Ullman's and Beeri and Vardi's *template dependencies* ([SU], [BV4]) which generalize embedded join dependencies; and Parker and Parsaye-Ghomi's *extended transitive dependencies* [PP], which generalize both mutual dependencies and transitive dependencies. We remark that the last 3 kinds of dependencies mentioned were introduced to deal with the issue of a complete axiomatization (see Section 3): subset dependencies were introduced to show the difficulty of completely axiomatizing embedded multivalued dependencies; extended transitive dependencies were introduced to show the difficulty of completely axiomatizing transitive dependencies; while template dependencies were introduced to provide a class of dependencies that include join dependencies and that can be completely axiomatized. Inclusion dependencies, which had been used informally for databases by many practitioners, were not seriously studied until relatively late [CFP].

Various researchers finally realized that all of these different types of dependencies can be united into a single class, which we shall call simply *dependencies*. Before we can define them formally, we need a few preliminary concepts. We assume that we are given a set of *individual variables* (which represent entries in a relation of a database). The *atomic* formulas are those that are either of the form $Pz_1...z_d$ (where P is the name of a d-ary relation, and where the z_i's are individual variables), or else of the form $x=y$ (where x and y are individual variables). Atomic formulas $Pz_1...z_d$ we call *relational formulas*, and atomic formulas $x=y$ we call *equalities*. A *dependency* is a first-order sentence

$$(\forall x_1...x_m)((A_1\wedge...\wedge A_n)\Rightarrow\exists y_1...y_r(B_1\wedge...\wedge B_s)), \tag{2.8}$$

where each A_i is a relational formula and where each B_i is atomic (either a relational formula or an equality). We assume also that each of the x_j's appears in at least one of the A_i's, and that $n\geq 1$, that is, that there is at least one A_i. We assume that $r\geq 0$ (if $r=0$ then there are no existential quantifiers), and that $s\geq 1$ (that is, there must be at least one B_i.) Note that because of all these assumptions, each dependency is obeyed by an empty database with no tuples. Furthermore, our assumptions guarantee that we can tell if a dependency holds for a relation by simply considering the collection of tuples of the relation, and ignoring any underlying "domains of attributes". Intuitively, in considering whether a dependency holds for a relation, the quantifiers can be assumed to range over the elements that appear in the relation, and not over any larger domain. This property is called *domain independence*. See Fagin [Fa4] for a much more complete discussion of domain independence.

If each of the formulas B_i on the right-hand side of (2.8) is a relational formula, then we call the dependency a *tuple-generating dependency*; if all of these formulas are equalities, then we call the dependency an *equality-generating dependency*. Of the dependencies we have focused on above, the (embedded) multivalued dependency, the (embedded) join dependency, and the inclusion dependency are each tuple-generating dependencies; thus, each of the first-order sentences (2.2), (2.3), (2.5), and (2.7) above represent tuple-generating dependencies. Tuple-generating dependencies say that if a certain pattern of entries appears, then another pattern must appear. Functional dependencies, as we see by example in the sentence (2.1) above, are equality-generating dependencies. Equality-generating dependencies say that if a certain pattern of entries appears, then a certain equality must hold. A *full* dependency is one in which r=0 and s=1 in (2.8), that is, one in which there are no existential quantifiers and in which there is only one atomic formula B_i on the right-hand side. Thus, a full dependency is of the form

$$(\forall x_1...x_m)((A_1\wedge...\wedge A_n)\Rightarrow B), \tag{2.9}$$

where each A_i is a relational formula, where B is atomic. Functional, multivalued, and join dependencies are all full dependencies. We may refer to a dependency (2.8) as an *embedded dependency*, to emphasize that we are allowing (but not requiring) existential quantifiers. Note that in the case of full dependencies, we would not gain anything by allowing the possibility of having several atomic formulas on the right-hand side, since such a sentence is equivalent to a finite set of full dependencies as we have defined them.

The class of dependencies was defined independently by a number of authors, who usually focussed on the uni-relational case. (Note that the only special case of a dependency that we have mentioned so far that is not uni-relational is the inclusion dependency.) Beeri and Vardi [BV7] refer to this class as the class of all *tuple-generating* and *equality-generating dependencies*. Fagin [Fa4] focused on the typed, uni-relational case, which he called *embedded implicational dependencies* (with the full dependencies being called *implicational dependencies*). Yannakakis and Papadimitriou [YP] defined *algebraic dependencies*, which are built out of expressions involving projection and join, and which, on the surface, look very different from our first-order definition. It is somewhat surprising that their class (which is typed) turns out [YP] to be identical to our typed, uni-relational dependencies. Paredaens and Janssens [PJ] defined *general dependencies*, which are full, typed, uni-relational dependencies. Also, Grant and Jacobs [GJ] defined *generalized dependency constraints,* which are full dependencies.

An often heard claim is that in the "real world" one rarely encounters dependencies in their most general form. According to this claim FDs, INDs, maybe MVDs are the only kinds of dependencies that earn the title "real world dependencies". We have two answers to this claim. First, we believe that there are real-world situations that do require the more general dependencies. Even when the database itself can be specified by FDs, user views of this database may not be specifiable by FDs [Fa4, GZ]. Furthermore, even if only simple dependencies arise in practice, the more general dependencies are very useful theoretically. For example, statements about equivalence of queries can be expressed by dependencies [YP]. We refer the reader to [Hu, Va3, Va5] for more examples of the latter argument.

3. The Implication Problem

3.1. Implication and finite implication

Logical implication is a fundamental notion in logic. Let Σ be a set of sentences, and let τ be a single sentence. We say that Σ *implies* τ, denoted $\Sigma \models \tau$, if every model of Σ is also a model of τ. In our context, $\Sigma \models \tau$ if every database that satisfies all dependencies in Σ satisfies also τ. For example $\{A \rightarrow B, B \rightarrow C\} \models A \rightarrow C$.

The relevance of implication to database theory became apparent in Bernstein's work on synthesis of database schemes using FDs [Ber]. Let Σ_1 and Σ_2 be sets of dependencies. We say that Σ_1 is *equivalent to* Σ_2, denoted $\Sigma_1 \equiv \Sigma_2$, if every database that satisfies all dependencies in Σ_1 also satisfies all dependencies in Σ_2 and vice versa. We say that Σ_1 is *redundant* if $\Sigma_2 \subset \Sigma_1$ and $\Sigma_1 \equiv \Sigma_2$. (We use $\subseteq$ to denote containment and $\subset$ to denote proper containment.) Clearly, Σ is redundant if there is some $\tau \in \Sigma$ such that $\Sigma - \{\tau\} \models \tau$. Since Bernstein's synthesis algorithm requires eliminating redundant FDs , and since the problem of eliminating redundant dependencies can be reduced to the problem of testing implication of dependencies, the notion of implication became a central notion to dependency theory. The significance of implication was reconfirmed in later works, e.g., [BMSU,Ri2].

In database theory we often like to restrict our attention to finite databases, since in practice databases are finite. We say that Σ *finitely implies* τ, denoted $\Sigma \models_f \tau$, if every finite database that satisfies Σ satisfies also τ. Clearly, if $\Sigma \models \tau$ holds then $\Sigma \models_f \tau$ also holds. But it is possible that $\Sigma \models_f \tau$ holds while $\Sigma \models \tau$ does not. That is, it is possible that every finite database that satisfies Σ satisfies also τ, but there is an *infinite* database that satisfies Σ but not τ. Implication and finite implication lead to two decision problems. The *implication problem* is to decide, for a given set Σ of dependencies and a single dependency τ, whether $\Sigma \models \tau$. The *finite implication problem* is to decide, for a given set Σ of dependencies and a single dependency τ, whether $\Sigma \models_f \tau$.

Let $\Sigma = \{\sigma_1,...,\sigma_n\}$. Then $\Sigma \models \tau$ $(\Sigma \models_f \tau)$ if and only if $\sigma_1 \wedge ... \wedge \sigma_n \wedge \neg \tau$ is (finitely) unsatisfiable. (A sentence is (finitely) satisfiable if it has a (finite) model. It is (finitely) unsatisfiable if it has no (finite) model.) Since unsatisfiability is known to be recursively enumerable (Gödel's Completeness Theorem), and finite satisfiability is clearly recursively enumerable, it follows that the relationships $\models$ and $\not\models_f$ are recursively enumerable. Suppose now that for some class of dependencies $\models$ and $\models_f$ are the same. Then $\models$ and $\not\models_f$ complement each other and they are both recursively enumerable. It follows that they are both recursive [Ro]. Indeed, the standard technique for proving solvability of the implication problem is to show that implication and finite implication coincide.

Dependencies are $\forall^*\exists^*$ sentences, i.e., they are equivalent to sentences whose quantifier prefix consists of a string of universal quantifiers followed by a string of existential quantifiers. Thus, $\sigma_1 \wedge ... \wedge \sigma_n \wedge \neg \tau$ is a $\exists^*\forall^*\exists^*$ sentence. When Σ, however, consists of full dependencies, then $\sigma_1 \wedge ... \wedge \sigma_n \wedge \neg \tau$ is an $\exists^*\forall^*$ sentence. Thus, the (finite) implication problem for full dependencies is reducible to the (finite) satisfiability problem for $\exists^*\forall^*$ sentences. This class of sentences is known as the *initially extended Bernays-Schönfinkel class.* For this class, satisfiability and finite satisfiability coincide, and therefore both are recursive [DG]. Thus, for full dependencies, implication and finite implication coincide, and are recursive. Unfortunately, the satisfiability problem for the Bernays-Schönfinkel class require nondeterministic exponential time [Le], and hence is highly intractable. Since the class of full dependencies is a proper subset of the class of universal sentences, one may hope that the implication problem for full dependencies is not that hard. We study this problem in Section 3.2.

For simplicity we restrict ourselves in the sequel to uni-relational dependencies, i.e., dependencies that refer to a single relation.

3.2. The implication problem for full dependencies

Since for full dependencies implication and finite implication coincide, everything we say in this section about implication holds, of course, for finite implication as well.

Even though the significance of implication was not yet clear in 1974, it was studied by Armstrong [Arm], apparently just out of mathematical interest. Armstrong characterized implication of FDs using an *axiom system*. An axiom system consists of *axiom schemes* and *inference rules*. A *derivation* of a dependency τ from a set Σ of dependencies is a sequence $\tau_1, \tau_2, ..., \tau_n$, where τ_n is τ and each τ_i is either an instance of an axiom scheme or follows from preceding dependencies in the sequence by one of the inference rules. $\Sigma \vdash \tau$ denotes that there is a derivation of τ from Σ. An axiom system is *sound* if $\Sigma \vdash \tau$ entails $\Sigma \models \tau$, and it is *complete* if $\Sigma \models \tau$ entails $\Sigma \vdash \tau$. Armstrong's system, denoted $\mathcal{FD}$, consists of one axiom and three inference rules:

FD0 (reflexivity axiom): $\vdash X \rightarrow X$.
FD1 (transitivity): $X \rightarrow Y,\ Y \rightarrow Z \vdash X \rightarrow Z$.
FD2 (augmentation and projection): $X \rightarrow Y \vdash W \rightarrow Z$, if $X \subseteq W$ and $Y \supseteq Z$.
FD3 (union): $X \rightarrow Y,\ Z \rightarrow W \vdash XZ \rightarrow YW$.

Theorem 3.2.1. [Arm] The system $\mathcal{FD}$ is sound and complete for implication of FDs. □
(In fact, Armstrong proved a somewhat stronger result, which we shall not discuss here. See [Fa3].)

Armstrong did not consider the algorithmic aspects of his axiom system. This was done by Beeri and Bernstein [BB], who were motivated by the fact that one of the steps in Bernstein's synthesis algorithm [Ber] is a test for implication. They were the first to phrase the implication problem. (Beeri and Bernstein called it the *membership problem*. In some papers it is also called the *inference problem.)*

Let Σ be a set of dependencies, and let X be a set of attributes. The *closure* of X with respect to Σ is the set of all attributes functionally determined by X, that is, $\{A: \Sigma \models X \rightarrow A\}$. Clearly, once we know the closure of X with respect to Σ, we can find out easily whether $\Sigma \models X \rightarrow A$. Beeri and Bernstein showed that the system $\mathcal{FD}$ can be used to construct closures very fast.

Theorem 3.2.2. [BB] The implication problem for FDs can be solved in time $O(n)$, where n is the length of the input. □

A large part of dependency theory since 1976 was devoted to studying these two aspects of implication, i.e., axiomatization and complexity of the implication problem. For example, shortly after the introduction of MVDs in 1976, they were axiomatized by Beeri et al. [BFH], and Beeri proved that implication problem is solvable [Bee]. Both works tried to get results analogous to the results for FDs.

The axiom system $\mathcal{MVD}$ consists of one axiom and three inference rules:

MVD0 (reflexivity axiom): $\vdash X \twoheadrightarrow Y$, if $Y \subseteq X$.
MVD1 (transitivity): $X \twoheadrightarrow Y,\ Y \twoheadrightarrow Z \vdash X \twoheadrightarrow Z - Y$.
MVD2 (augmentation): $X \twoheadrightarrow Y \vdash XW \twoheadrightarrow YZ$ if $Z \subseteq W$.
MVD3 (complementation): $X \twoheadrightarrow Y \vdash X \twoheadrightarrow Z$, if $XYZ = U$ and $Y \cap Z \subseteq X$.

Theorem 3.2.3. [BFH] The system $\mathcal{MVD}$ is sound and complete for implication of MVDs. □

We note that Beeri et al. [BFH] also present a sound and complete axiomatization for FDs and MVDs taken together. This axiomatization contains all of the axiom schemes and inference rules for FDs and MVDs separately that we have already seen, along with two "mixed" rules, that account for the interaction of FDs and MVDs.

The analogue of closure of an attribute set X is now not an attribute set but rather a collection of attribute sets: $rhs_{\Sigma}(X) = \{Y: \Sigma \models X \twoheadrightarrow Y\}$. Now $rhs_{\Sigma}(X)$ can contain exponentially many sets, and hence is not very useful algorithmically. However, using the system $\mathcal{MVD}$ it is not hard to verify that $rhs_{\Sigma}(X)$ is a Boolean algebra. Furthermore, since it is a field of finite sets, it is an *atomic* Boolean algebra, and every every element is the union of the atoms it contains. The set of atoms of this Boolean algebra is called the *dependency basis* of X with respect to Σ, denoted $dep_{\Sigma}(X)$. Thus

$$dep_{\Sigma}(X) = \{Y: Y \neq \emptyset, \Sigma \models X \twoheadrightarrow Y, \text{ and if } \Sigma \models X \twoheadrightarrow Z, Z \subseteq Y, \text{ and } Z \neq \emptyset, \text{ then } Z = Y\}.$$

Lemma 3.2.4. [BFH] $dep_{\Sigma}(X)$ is a partition of U. Furthermore, $\Sigma \models X \twoheadrightarrow Y$ if and only if there are sets $W_1,...,W_m$ in $dep_{\Sigma}(X)$ such that $Y = W_1 \cup ... \cup W_m$.

Beeri [Bee] has shown how $dep_{\Sigma}(X)$ can be constructed efficiently using the system $\mathcal{MVD}$.

Theorem 3.2.5. [Bee] The implication problem for MVDs can be solved in time $O(n^4)$, where n is the length of the input. □

Beeri's algorithm was improved by Hagihara et al. [HITK], Sagiv [Sag1], and finally by Galil [Ga]. Galil's algorithm runs in time $O(n \log n)$. These papers and [Bee,BFH] discuss also the interaction of FDs and MVDs.

It is easy to see that Lemma 3.2.4 does not depend on Σ being a set of MVDs. Thus, testing whether an MVD $X \twoheadrightarrow Y$ is implied by a set Σ of dependencies can be done efficiently as long as $dep_{\Sigma}(X)$ can be constructed efficiently. This was shown in [MSY,Va4] to be the case when Σ is a set of JDs and FDs, and in [Va1] for the case when Σ is a set of typed full dependencies.

Theorem 3.2.6. [Va1] Testing whether an MVD or an FD is implied by a set of typed full dependencies can be done in time $O(n^2)$, where n is the length of the input. □

Let us refer now to implication of JDs. Aho et al. [ABU] described an algorithm, called later the *chase,* to test implication of JDs by FDs.

Theorem 3.2.7. [ABU] Testing whether a JD is implied by a set of FDs can be done in time $O(n^4)$, where n is the length of the input. □

More efficient implementations of the chase were described by Liu and Demers [LD] and by Downey et al. [DST]. The latter algorithm runs in time $O(n^2 \log^2 n)$.

The ideas in [ABU] were generalized by Maier et al. [MMS] to deal with arbitrary implication of FDs and JDs.

Theorem 3.2.8. [MMS] The implication problem for FDs and JDs is solvable in time $O(n^n)$, where n is the length of the input. □

The question then arose whether the exponential upper bound of the above theorem can be improved. Unfortunately, Theorems 3.2.6 and 3.2.7 probably describe the most general case for which an efficient decision procedure exists. Recall that a problem is NP-hard if it is as hard as any problem that can be solved in nondeterministic polynomial time. A problem is NP-complete if it is NP-hard and it can be solved in nondeterministic polynomial time. It is believed that NP-hard problems can not be solved efficiently, i.e., in polynomial time. ([GJ] is a good textbook on the theory of NP-completeness.) Thus, proving that a problem is NP-hard is a strong indication that the problem is computationally intractable.

Theorem 3.2.9.
1) [FT] Testing whether a set of MVDs implies a JD is NP-hard.
2) [BV3] Testing whether a JD and an FD imply a JD is NP-complete. □

Thus, we know how to test implication of FDs and JDs in exponential time, and we know that the problem is NP-hard. We do not know, however, how to pinpoint the complexity of this problem. We do not know for example whether testing implication of a JD by a set of MVDs can be done in nondeterministic polynomial time. One approach to the problem was to try to find a axiom system for FDs and JDs. Surprisingly, even for JDs alone finding a axiom system is extremely difficult (see [BV1,BV5,Sc3]).

NP-completeness strongly suggests, rather than proves, that a problem is intractable (i.e., it proves intractability under the assumption that there are problems that can be solved in nondeterministic polynomial time but not in deterministic polynomial time). In contrast, EXPTIME-completeness is a proof that a problem is intractable. A problem is EXPTIME-complete if it can be solved in exponential time and it is also as hard as any problem that can be solved in exponential time. Since it is known that there are problems that can be solved in exponential time and in fact do require exponential time, it follows that EXPTIME-complete problems require exponential time.

Theorem 3.2.10. [CLM2] The implication problem for typed full dependencies is EXPTIME-complete. □

Interestingly, Beeri and Vardi presented an elegant axiom system for typed full dependencies [BV4]. This demonstrates that there is no clear relationship between having an axiom system for a class of dependencies and the complexity of the implication problem for that class.

In conclusion of this section, the reader should keep in mind that the above lower bounds describe a worst-case behavior of the problems. It is not clear at all that this worst-case behavior indeed arise in practice.

3.3. The implication problem for embedded dependencies

While for full dependencies the implication problem is clearly solvable and the questions to answer involve upper and lower bounds, this is not so with embedded dependencies, since satisfiability and finite satisfiability do not coincide for the class of $\exists^*\forall^*\exists^*$ sentences, and the corresponding problems are both unsolvable [DG]. Thus, we have to deal here with both implication and finite implication and their corresponding decision problem. Since the class of dependencies is a proper subset of the class of $\forall^*\exists^*$ sentences, one may hope that the (finite) implication problem for embedded dependencies is solvable.

The first disappointing observation is that implication and finite implication do not coincide for embedded dependencies.

Theorem 3.3.1. [CFP,JK] There is a set Σ of FDs and INDs and a single IND τ such that $\Sigma \models_f \tau$, but $\Sigma \not\models \tau$.

Proof: (a) Let Σ be $\{A \rightarrow B, A \subseteq B\}$, and let τ be $B \subseteq A$. We first show that $\Sigma \models_f \tau$. Let I be a finite relation satisfying Σ. We now show that I satisfies τ, that is, $I[B] \subseteq I[A]$. Since I satisfies $A \rightarrow B$ it follows that $|I[B]| \leq |I[A]|$. Since $I[A] \subseteq I[B]$, it follows that $|I[A]| \leq |I[B]|$. Thus, $|I[A]| = |I[B]|$. But since $I[A] \subseteq I[B]$ and since both $I[A]$ and $I[B]$ are finite, we than have $I[B] = I[A]$, so $I[B] \subseteq I[A]$. This was to be shown.

To show that $\Sigma \not\models \tau$, we need only exhibit a relation (necessarily infinite) that satisfies Σ but not τ. Let I be the relation with tuples $\{(i+1,i): i \geq 0\}$. It is obvious that I satisfies Σ but not τ. □

One may think that this behavior is the result of the interaction between tuple-generating dependencies and equality-generating dependencies, but an example in [BV7] shows that even for tuple-generating dependencies the two notions of implication and finite implication differ.

The simplest instance of embedded dependencies are the EMVDs. The (finite) implication problem for EMVDs has resisted efforts of many researchers, and is one of the most outstanding open problems in dependency theory. A significant part of the research in this area has been motivated by this problem. For example, underlying the search for bigger and bigger classes of dependencies was the hope that for the larger class a decision procedure would be apparent, while the specialization of the algorithm to EMVDs was too murky to be visible. Also, underlying the work on axiomatization was the hope that an axiom system may lead to a decision procedure just as the axiom systems for FDs and MVDs led to decision procedures for these classes of dependencies.

Maier et. al [MMS] suggested an extension of the chase to deal with EJDs, and this was further generalized by Beeri and Vardi [BV2] to arbitrary dependencies. Unfortunately, the chase may not terminate for embedded dependencies. It was shown, however, that the chase is a *proof procedure* for implication. That is, given Σ and τ, the chase will give a positive answer if $\Sigma \models \tau$, but will not terminate if $\Sigma \not\models \tau$. Furthermore, Beeri and Vardi [BV4] also presented a sound and complete axiom system for typed dependencies. Nevertheless, all these did not seem to lead to a decision procedure for implication. In 1980 researchers started suspecting that the (finite) implication problem for embedded dependencies was unsolvable, and the first result in this direction were announced in June 1980 by two independent teams.

Theorem 3.3.1. [BV6,CLM1] The implication and the finite implication problem for tuple-generating dependencies are unsolvable. □

This result is disappointing especially with regard to finite implication, which is the more interesting notion. As we recall, $\not\models_f$ is recursively enumerable. Thus, if $\models_f$ is not recursive, then it is not even recursively enumerable. That means that there is no sound and complete axiom system for finite implication.

Both proofs of Theorem 3.3.1 seem to use *untypedness* in a very strong way, and do not carry over to the typed case. Shortly later, however, both teams succeeded in ingeniously encoding untyped dependencies by typed dependencies.

Theorem 3.3.2. [BV7,CLM2] The implication and the finite implication problem for typed tuple-generating dependencies are unsolvable. □

As dependencies, EMVDs have four important properties (see for example (2.3)):

(1) they are tuple-generating,
(2) they are typed,
(3) they have a single atomic formula on the right-hand side of the implication, and
(4) they have two atomic formulas on the left-hand side of the implication.

Dependencies that satisfy properties (1), (2), and (3) above are called *template dependencies,* or TDs [SU]. Thus, EMVDs and EJDs are in particular TDs. Since Theorem 3.3.2 covers properties (1) and (2), the next step was to extend unsolvability to TDs.

Theorem 3.3.3. [GL,Va2] The implication and finite implication problems for TDs are unsolvable. □

In fact, both papers prove unsolvability for the class of *projected join dependencies.* A projected join dependency (PJD) is of the form $\bowtie [X_1,...,X_k]_X$, where $X \subseteq X_1 \cup ... \cup X_k \subseteq U$. It is obeyed by a relation I if $I[X] = \bowtie \{I[X_1],...,I[X_k]\}[X]$. For an application of PJDs see [MUV]. PJDs extend slightly JDs, since if $X = X_1 \cup ... \cup X_k$, then the PJD $\bowtie [X_1,...,X_k]_X$ is equivalent to the JD $\bowtie [X_1,...,X_k]$. Thus the class of PJDs lies strictly between the classes of EJDs and TDs. The implication and finite implication problems for EJDs are, however, still wide open.

Even though the existence of an axiom system for a certain class of dependencies does not guarantee solvability of the implication problem, finding such a system seems to be a valuable goal. In particular attention was given to *k-ary* systems. In a *k*-ary axiom systems, all inference rules are of the form $\tau_1,...,\tau_n \vdash \tau$, where $n \leq k$. It is easy to verify, for example, that the systems $\mathcal{FD}$ and $\mathcal{MVD}$ in Section 3.3 are 2-ary.

Theorem 3.3.4. [PP,SW] For all $k>0$, there is no sound and complete k-ary axiom system for implication and finite implication of EMVDs. □

We refer the reader to [BV4,Va2] for a discussion regarding the existence of a non-k-ary axiom system for EMVDs.

Let us refer now to what some people believe are the only "practical" dependencies, FDs and INDs.

Recall that FDs are full dependencies, so implication and finite implication coincide and both are solvable (and by Theorem 3.2.1, quite efficiently). INDs, on the other hand, are embedded dependencies, so a straightforward application of the chase does not yield a decision procedure. A more careful analysis, however, shows that the chase can be forced to terminate.

Theorem 3.3.5. [CFP] The implication and finite implication problem for INDs are equivalent and are PSPACE-complete. □

(PSPACE-complete problems are problems that can be solved using only polynomial space and are hard as any problem that can be solved using polynomial space. It is believed that this problems can not be solved in polynomial time [GJ].)

Let us consider now implication of arbitrary dependencies by INDs. Since containment of tableaux [ASU] can be expressed by dependencies [YP], a test for implication of dependencies by INDs is also a test for containment of conjunctive queries under INDs. We do not know whether implication and finite implication coincide in this case. We have, however, a positive result for implication.

Theorem 3.3.6. [JK] Testing implication of dependencies by INDs is PSPACE-complete. □

The finite implication problem for this case is still open.

Casanova et al. [CFP] investigated the interaction of FDs and INDs, and they discovered that things get more complicated when both kinds of dependencies are put together. First, they showed that implication and finite implication are different (Theorem 3.3.1). In addition they showed that there is no sound and complete k-ary axiom system for implication and finite implication of FDs and INDs. (Mitchell [Mi1], however, has shown that in a more general sense there is a k-ary axiom system for implication of FDs and INDs.) In view of their results, it did not come as a surprise when Chandra and Vardi and, independently, Mitchell proved unsolvability.

Theorem 3.3.6. [CV,Mi2] The implication and the finite implication problems for FDs and INDs are unsolvable. □

Some people claim is that in practice we encounter only INDs that have a single attribute on each side of the containment, e.g., MANAGER⊆EMPLOYEE. Such INDs are called *unary* INDs (UINDs). Reviewing the proof of Theorem 3.3.1, we realize that even for FDs and UINDs implication and finite implication differ. Considering our experience with dependencies, this looks like a sure sign that the problems are unsolvable. The next result by Kannelakis et al. comes therefore as a refreshing surprise.

Theorem 3.3.7. [KCV] The implication and the finite implication problem for FDs and UINDs are both solvable in polynomial time. □

For other positive results for INDs see [KCV,JK,LMG].

In conclusion to this topic, we would like to mention an argument against the relevance of all the above unsolvability results. The assumption underlying these results is that the input is an arbitrary set Σ of dependencies and a dependency τ. The argument is that the given set Σ is supposed to describe some "real life" application, and in practice it is not going to be arbitrary. Thus, even if we concede that TDs arise in practice, still not every set of TDs arises in practice. The emphasis of this argument is on "real world sets of dependencies", rather than on "real world dependencies". For further study of this argument see [Sc1,Sc2]. While we agree with the essence of this argument, we believe that the results described above are useful in delineating the boundaries between the computationally feasible and infeasible. This is especially important, since we do not yet have robust definitions of real world sets of dependencies.

4. The Universal Relation Model

4.1. Motivation

A primary justification given by Codd for the introduction of the relational model was his view that earlier models were not adequate to the task of boosting the productivity of programmers [Co1,Co3]. One of his stated motivations was to free the application programmer and the end user from the need to specify access paths (the so-called "navigation problem"). A second motivation was to eliminate the need for program modification to accommodate changes in the database structure, i.e., to eliminate access path dependence in programs.

After a few years of experience with relational database management systems, it was realized [CK] that, though being a significant step forward, the relational model by itself fails to achieve complete freedom from user-supplied navigation and from access path dependence. The relational model was successful in removing the need for *physical navigation*; no access paths need to be specified within the storage structure of a single relation. Nevertheless, the relational model has not yet provided independence from *logical navigation*, since access paths among several relations must still be satisfied.

For example, consider a database that has relations *ED*(Employee, Department) and *DM*(Department, Manager). If we are interested in the relationship between employees and managers through departments, then we have to tell the system to take the join of the *ED* and *DM* relations and to project it on the attributes *EM*. This is of course an access path specification, and if the database were to be reorganized to have a single relation *EDM*, then any programs using this access path would have to be modified accordingly.

The *universal relation model* aims at achieving complete access path independence by letting us ask the system in an appropriate language "tell us about employees and their managers", expecting the system to figure out the intended access path for itself. Of course, we cannot expect the system to always select the intended relationship between employees and managers automatically, because the user might have something other than the simplest relationship, the one through departments, in mind, e.g., the manager of the manager of the employee. We shall, in a universal relation system, have to settle for eliminating the need for logical navigation along certain paths, those selected by the designer, while allowing the user to navigate explicitly in more convoluted ways.

Unlike the relational model, the universal relation model was not introduced as a single clearly defined model, but rather evolved during the 1970's through the work of several researchers. As a result, there have been a significant confusion with regard to the assumptions underlying the model, the so-called "universal relation assumptions". We refer the reader to [MUV], where an attempt is made to clarify the situation.

In this and the next section we restrict ourselves to finite databases.

4.2. Decomposition

The simplest way to implement the universal relation model is to have the database consist a *universal relation*, i.e., a single relation over the set U of all attributes. There are two problems with this approach. First, it assumes that for each tuple in the database we always can supply values for all the attributes, e.g., it assumes that we have full biographic information on all employees. Secondly, storing all the information in one universal relation causes problems when this information needs to be updated. These problems, called *update anomalies*, were identified by Codd [Co2]. The solution to these problems is to have a conceptual database that consists of the universal relation, while the actual database consists of relations over smaller sets of attributes. That is, the database scheme consists of a collection $\mathbf{R} = \{R_1,...,R_k\}$ of attributes sets whose union is U, and the database consists of relations $I_1,...,I_k$, over $R_1,...,R_k$, respectively.

A principal activity in relational database design is the decomposition of the universal relation scheme into a database scheme that has certain nice properties, traditionally called *normal forms*. (We shall not go here into *normalization theory*, which is the study of these normal forms, and the interested reader is referred to [Ma,Ul].) More precisely, starting with the universal scheme U and a set of dependencies Σ, we wish to replace the universal scheme by a database scheme $\mathbf{R} = \{R_1,...,R_k\}$. The idea is to replace the universal relation by its projection on $R_1,...,R_k$. That is, instead of storing a relation I over U, we *decompose* it into $I_1 = I[R_1]$, ..., $I_k = I[R_k]$, and store the result of this decomposition. The map $\Delta_{\mathbf{R}}$ defined by $\Delta_{\mathbf{R}}(I) = \{I[R_1],...,I[R_k]\}$ is called the *decomposition map*.

Clearly, a decomposition cannot be useful unless no loss of information is incurred by decomposing the universal relation. (This is called in [BBG] the *representation principle.*) That is, we must be able to reconstruct I from $I_1,...,I_k$. More precisely, the decomposition map has to be *injective*. For our purposes it suffices that the decomposition map is injective for relations that satisfy the given set Σ of dependencies. In this case we say that it is injective with respect to Σ. When the decomposition map is injective it has a left inverse, called the *reconstruction map*. The basic problems of *decomposition theory* are to formulate necessary and sufficient conditions for injectiveness and to find out about the reconstruction map.

The natural candidate for the reconstruction map is the join, i.e., $I = I_1 \bowtie \ldots \bowtie I_k$. The naturalness of the join led many researchers to the belief that if the reconstruction map exists then it is necessarily the join. This belief was refuted by Vardi [Va3], who constructed an example where the decomposition map is injective, but the reconstruction map is not the join. It is also shown in [Va3] how to express injectiveness as a statement about implication of dependencies. Unfortunately, even when Σ consists of full dependencies, that statement involves also inclusion dependencies. It is not known whether there is an effective test for injectiveness.

If we insist that the join be the reconstruction map, then we can get a stronger result.

Theorem 4.2.1. [BR,MMSU] Let Σ be a set of dependencies, and let $\mathbf{R}$ be a database scheme. $\Delta_{\mathbf{R}}$ is injective with respect to Σ with the join as the reconstruction map if and only if $\Sigma \models \bowtie [\mathbf{R}]$. □

Thus, if Σ consists of full dependencies then we can effectively test whether the decomposition map is injective with respect to Σ.

Another desirable property of decompositions is *independence* [Ri1]. Intuitively, independence means that the relations of the database can be updated independently from each other. For further investigation of the relationship between injectiveness and independence see [BH,BR,MMSU,Va3].

A point that should be brought up is that decomposition may have some disadvantages. Essentially, decomposition may make it easier to update the database, but it clearly makes it harder to query it. Since the join operation can be quite expensive computationally, reconstructing the universal relation may not be easy even when the reconstruction map is the join. In fact, even testing whether the relations of the database can be joined without losing tuples is NP-complete, and hence, probably computationally intractable. Let the database consists of relations $I_1,...,I_k$ over attribute sets $R_1,...,R_k$. We say that the database is *join consistent* if there is a universal relation I such that $I_j = I[R_j]$, for $1 \leq j \leq k$. (Rissanen [Ri1] calls a join consistent set of relations *joinable*. A join consistent database is also called *globally consistent* [BFMY], *join compatible* [BR], *valid* [Ri3], *consistent* [Fa5], or *decomposed* [Va3].) It is easy to verify that the database is join consistent if $I_j = \bowtie \{I_1,...,I_k\}[R_j]$, for $1 \leq j \leq k$.

Theorem 4.2.2. [HLY] Testing whether a database is join consistent is NP-complete. □

Thus there is a trade-off between the ease of updating the database and the ease of querying it. The smaller the relation schemes, the easier it is to update the database and the harder it is to query it. Recognizing this trade-off, Schkolnick and Sorenson investigated what they called *denormalization* [SS]. The idea is to decompose the universal scheme with both the ease of updating and the ease of querying in mind. The result of the decomposition depends in this approach on the predicted use of the database.

4.3. The Universal Relation Interface

Suppose now that decomposition has been achieved. That is, assume that, starting with the universal scheme U and a set Σ of dependencies, we have designed a database scheme $\mathbf{R} = \{R_1,...,R_k\}$, and we now have a database $\mathbf{I} = \{I_1,..,I_k\}$ over $\mathbf{R}$. Two questions have now to be resolved: how to determine whether the database is semantically meaningful, i.e., satisfies the given dependencies, and how to respond to the users' queries that refer to the universal relation. If the database is join consistent, then we can construct the universal relation I such that $\Delta_{\mathbf{R}}(I) = \mathbf{I}$. But if the database is not join consistent, then there is no corresponding universal relation.

We outline here one approach to the problem, called the *weak* universal relation approach. (This approach was suggested by Honeyman [Ho] and further developed in [GM,GMV,MUV]. For other approaches and their relationship to the weak universal relation approach see [GM,GMV,MRW,MUV].) According to this approach, a universal relation exists at least in principle, even though it may not be known. The database is seen, from this viewpoint, as a partial specification of the universal relation. More precisely, the relations $I_1,...,I_k$ are partial descriptions of the projection of the universal relation I on the relation schemes $R_1,...,R_k$. Thus a universal relation I is considered to be a *weak universal relation* for $\mathbf{I}$ with respect to Σ if it satisfies Σ and $I_j \subseteq I[R_j]$, for $1 \leq i \leq k$. $\mathbf{I}$ is *consistent* with Σ i.e., semantically meaningful, if it has a weak universal relation with respect to Σ.

The above definition is existential in nature and does not lend itself to an effective test. The *consistency problem* is to decide, for a given set Σ of dependencies and a database $\mathbf{I}$ over a database scheme $\mathbf{R}$, whether $\mathbf{I}$ is consistent with Σ.

Theorem 4.3.1.
1) [GMV] The consistency problem for embedded dependencies is unsolvable.
2) [GMV] The consistency problem for full dependencies is EXPTIME-complete.
3) [Ho] The consistency problem for FDs is solvable in polynomial time. □

Thus, for embedded dependencies there is no effective test for consistency, for full dependencies there is an effective though intractable test, and the good news is that for FDs there is a polynomial time test for consistency. We note that the presence of the independence property, mentioned is Section 4.2, may make it easier to test for consistency. We refer the reader to [CM,Gr1,GY,Sa] for the study of independence in the context of the weak universal relation approach.

We now refer to the issue of query answering. For simplicity we restrict ourselves to queries of the form "give me the relationship between employees and managers". More precisely, the query is a set X of attributes, and the desired answer is the so-called *basic relationship on* X. If we had a unique universal relation I, then answer would undoubtedly be $I[X]$. But in our case we have only weak universal relations, and we clearly have infinitely many of those. Since we cannot know which of the possible universal relations actually represent the "real world" at a given moment, we assume that the only facts that can be deduced about the universal relation from the database are those that hold is all weak universal relations. This motivated researchers ([MUV,Ya] following [Sa]) to adopt the following definition. Let $weak(\mathbf{I},\Sigma)$ be the set of all weak universal relations of $\mathbf{I}$ with respect to Σ. We can see this set as the embodiment of the information represented by the database [Me]. The answer to the query X, denoted $\mathbf{I}[X]$, is therefore taken to be $\cap \{I[X] : I \epsilon weak(\mathbf{I},\Sigma)\}$. Note that the answer is with respect to Σ.

The above definition does not seem to lead to an effective procedure for computing $\mathbf{I}[X]$.

Theorem 4.3.2.
1) [GMV] Computing answers with respect to embedded dependencies is unsolvable.
2) [GMV] Computing answers with respect to full dependencies is EXPTIME-complete.
3) [Ho] Computing answers with respect to FDs can be done in polynomial time. □

We refer the reader to [Gr2,MRW,MUV,Sag2,Sag3,Ya] for further study of query answering.

We conclude this section by considering again the questions raised in the previous section. There we started with a universal relation I and applied the decomposition map $\Delta_{\mathbf{R}}$, to get the database $\Delta_{\mathbf{R}}(I) = \{I[R_1],...,I[R_k]\}$. Suppose now that we pose the query U to this database. In this case we would expect our query answering mechanism to be the desired reconstruction map, i.e., we would expect $I = \Delta_{\mathbf{R}}(I)[U]$.

Theorem 4.3.3. [MUV] The following two conditions are equivalent:
1) $\Sigma \models \bowtie[\mathbf{R}]$.
2) $I = \Delta_{\mathbf{R}}(I)[U]$, for every universal relation I that satisfies Σ. □

In other words, if our query answering mechanism happens to be the reconstruction map, then for join consistent databases it is actually the join.

BIBLIOGRAPHY

[ABU] A. V. Aho, C. Beeri, and J. D. Ullman, The theory of joins in relational data bases. ACM Trans. on Database Systems 4,3 (Sept. 1979), 297-314.

[ASU] A. V. Aho, Y. Sagiv, and J. D. Ullman, Equivalences among relational expressions. SIAM J. Computing 8,2 (May 1979), 218-246.

[Ar] W. W. Armstrong, Dependency structures of database relationships. Proc. IFIP 74, North Holland, 1974, 580-583.

[Bee] C. Beeri, On the membership problem for functional and multivalued dependencies in relational databases. ACM Trans. on Database Systems 5,3 (Sept. 1980), 241-259.

[BB] C. Beeri and P. A. Bernstein, Computational problems related to the design of normal form relational schemas. ACM Trans. on Database Systems 4,1 (March 1979), 30-59.

[BBG] C. Beeri, P. A. Bernstein, and N. Goodman, A sophisticate's introduction to database normalization theory. Proc. Int. Conf. on Very Large Data Bases, 1978, Berlin, 113-124.

[BFH] C. Beeri, R. Fagin, and J.H. Howard, A complete axiomatization for functional and multivalued dependencies in database relations. Proc. ACM SIGMOD Conf. on Management of Data, 1977, Toronto, 47-61.

[BFMY] C. Beeri, R. Fagin, D. Maier, and M. Yannakakis, On the desirability of acyclic database schemes. J. ACM 30,3 (July 1983), 479-513.

[BH] C. Beeri and P. Honeyman, Preserving functional dependencies. SIAM J. Computing 10,3 (Aug. 1981), 647-656.

[BK] C. Beeri and H. F. Korth, Proc. 1st ACM SIGACT-SIGMOD Symp. on Principles of Database Systems, 1982, Los Angeles, 51-62.

[BMSU] C. Beeri, A. O. Mendelzon, Y. Sagiv, and J. D. Ullman, Equivalence of relational database schemes, SIAM J. Computing 10,2 (June 1981), 352-370.

[BR] C. Beeri and J. Rissanen, Faithful representation of relational database schemes. IBM Research Report, San Jose, California, 1980.

[BV1] C. Beeri and M. Y. Vardi, On the properties of join dependencies. In Advances in Database Theory (H. Gallaire, J. Minker, and J. M. Nicolas, Eds.), Plenum Press, 1981, 25-72.

[BV2] C. Beeri and M. Y. Vardi, A proof procedure for data dependencies. Hebrew University of Jerusalem Technical Report, Dec. 1980.

[BV3] C. Beeri and M. Y. Vardi, On the complexity of testing implications of data dependencies. Hebrew University of Jerusalem Technical Report, Dec. 1980.

[BV4] C. Beeri and M. Y. Vardi, Formal systems for tuple and equality-generating dependencies. SIAM J. Computing 13,1 (Feb 1984), 76-98.

[BV5] C. Beeri and M. Y. Vardi, Formal systems for join dependencies. Hebrew Univ. of Jerusalem Technical Report, 1981. To appear in Theoretical Computer Science.

[BV6] C. Beeri and M. Y. Vardi, The implication problem for data dependencies. Proc. XP1 Workshop on Relational Database Theoery, Stony Brook, NY, June 1980.

[BV7] C. Beeri and M. Y. Vardi, The implication problem for data dependencies. Proc. 8th Int. Colloq. on Languages Automata and Programming, 1981, Acre Israel. Appeared in: Lecture Notes in Computer Science - Vol. 115, Springer-Verlag, 1981, 73-85.

[Ber] P. A. Bernstein, Synthesizing third normal form relations from functional dependencies. ACM Trans. on Database Systems 1,4 (Dec. 1976), 277-298.

[CFP] M. A. Casanova, R. Fagin, and C. Papadimitriou, Inclusion dependencies and their interaction with functional dependencies. Proc. 1st ACM SIGACT-SIGMOD Symp. on Principles of Database Systems (1982), Los Angeles, 171-176. To appear in J. Computer and System Sciences.

[CM] E. P. F. Chan and A. O. Mendelzon, Independent and separable database schemes. Proc. 2nd ACM SIGACT-SIGMOD Symp. on Principles of Database Systems, 1983, Atlanta, 288-296.

[CLM1] A. K. Chandra, H. R. Lewis, and J. A. Makowsky, Embedded implicational dependencies and their inference problem. Proc. XP1 Workshop on Relational Database Theoery, Stony Brook, NY, June 1980.

[CLM2] A. K. Chandra, H. R. Lewis, and J. A. Makowsky, Embedded implicational dependencies and their inference problem. Proc. 13th ACM Symp. on Theory of Computing, 1981, Milwaukee, 342-354.

[CV] A. K. Chandra and M. Y. Vardi, The implication problem for functional and inclusion dependencies is undecidable. IBM Research Report RC 9980, May 1983.

[Co1] E. F. Codd, A relational model of data for large shared data banks. Comm. ACM 13,6 (June 1970), 377-387.

[Co2] E. F. Codd, Further normalization of the data base relational model. Courant Computer Science Symposia 6: Data Base Systems, 1971, Prentice Hall, 33-64.

[Co3] E. F. Codd, Relational databases: a practical foundation for productivity. Comm. ACM 25,2 (1982), 109-117.

[DP] P. De Bra and J. Paredaens, Conditional dependencies for horizontal decompositions. Proc. 10th Int. Colloq. on Languages Automata and Programming, 1981, Barcelona. Appeared in: Lecture Notes in Computer Science - Vol. 154, Springer-Verlag, 1983, 67-82.

[DST] P. J. Downey, R. Sethi, and R. E. Tarjan, Variations on the common subexpression problem. J. ACM 27,4 (Oct. 1980), 758-771.

[DG] B. S. Dreben and W. D. Goldfarb, The Decision Problem: Solvable Classes of Quantificational Formulas. Addison Wesley, 1979.

[Fa1] R. Fagin, Multivalued dependencies and a new normal form for relational databases. ACM Trans. on Database Systems 2,3 (Sept. 1977), 262-278.

[Fa2] R. Fagin, A normal form for relational databases that is based on domains and keys. ACM Trans. on Database Systems 6,3 (Sept. 1981), 387-415.

[Fa3] R. Fagin, Armstrong databases. Proc. 7th IBM Symp. on Mathematical Foundations of Computer Science, Kanagawa, Japan, May 1982. Also appeared as IBM Research Report RJ3440 (April 1982), San Jose, California.

[Fa4] R. Fagin, Horn clauses and database dependencies. J. ACM 29,4 (Oct. 1982), 952-985.

[Fa5] R. Fagin, Degrees of acyclicity for hypergraphs and relational database schemes. J. ACM 30,3 (July 1983), 514-550.

[FMU] R. Fagin, A. O. Mendelzon, and J. D. Ullman, A simplified universal relation assumption and its properties. ACM Trans. on Database Systems 7,3 (Sept. 1982), 343-360.

[TF] P. C. Fischer and D.-M. Tsou, Whether a set of multivalued dependencies implies a join dependencies is NP-hard. To appear in Theoretical Computer Science.

[Ga] Z. Galil, An almost linear-time algorithm for computing a dependency basis in a relational database. J. ACM 29,1 (Jan. 1982), 96-102.

[GJ] M. R. Garey and D. S. Johnson, Computers and Intractibility: A Guide to the Theory of NP-Completeness. Freeman, 1979.

[GZ] S. Ginsburg and S. M. Zaiddan, Properties of functional dependency families. J. ACM 29,4 (July 1982), 678-698.

[Gr1] M. H. Graham, Path expressions in databases. Proc. 2nd ACM SIGACT-SIGMOD Symp. on Principles of Database Systems, 1983, Atlanta, 366-378.

[Gr2] M. H. Graham, Functions in databases. ACM Trans. on Database Systems 8,1 (March 1983), 81-109.

[GM] M. H. Graham and A. O. Mendelzon, Notions of dependency satisfaction. Proc. 1st ACM SIGACT-SIGMOD Symp. on Principles of Database Systems, 1983, Los Angeles, 177-188.

[GMV] M. H. Graham, A. O. Mendelzon, and M. Y. Vardi, Notions of dependency satisfaction. Stanford University Technical Report STAN-CS-83-979, Aug. 1983.

[GY] M. H. Graham and M. Yannakakis, Independent database schemes. Proc. 1st ACM SIGACT-SIGMOD Symp. on Principles of Database Systems, 1982, Los Angeles, 199-204. To appear in J. Computer and Systems Sciences.

[GJ] J. Grant and B. E. Jacobs, On the family of generalized dependency constraints. J. ACM 29,4 (Oct. 1982).

[GL] Y. Gurevich and H. R. Lewis, The inference problem for template dependencies. Proc. First ACM SIGACT-SIGMOD Principles of Database Systems (1982), Los Angeles, 221-229.

[HITK] K. Hagihara, M. Ito, K. Taniguchi, and T. Kasami, Decision problems for multivalued dependencies in relational databases. SIAM J. Computing 8,2 (May 1979), 247-264.

[He] I. J. Heath, Unacceptable file operations in a relational data base. Proc. 1971 ACM-SIGFIDET Workshop on Data Description, Access, and Control, 1971, San Diego.

[Ho] P. Honeyman, Testing satisfaction of functional dependencies. J. ACM 29,3 (July 1982), 668-677.

[HLY] P. Honeyman, R. E. Ladner, and M. Yannakakis, Testing the universal instance assumption. Inf. Proc. Letters, 10,1 (1980), 14-19.

[Hu] R. Hull, Finitely specifiable implicational dependency families. Univ. of Southern California Technical Report, 1981. To appear in J. ACM.

[JK] D. S. Johnson and A. Klug, Testing Containment of Conjunctive Queries under Functional and Inclusion Dependencies. Proc. 1st ACM SIGACT-SIGMOD Symp. on Principles of Database Systems, 1982, Los Angeles, 164-169. To appear in J. Computer and Systems Sciences.

[KCV] P. C. Kannelakis, S. S. Cosmadakis, and M. Y. Vardi, Unary inclusion dependencies have polynomial-time inference problems. Proc. 15th ACM SIGACT Symp. on Theory of Computing, 1983, Boston, 264-277.

[LMG] K. Laver, A. O. Mendelzon, and M. H. Graham, Functional dependencies on cyclic database schemes. Proc. ACM SIGMOD Symp. on Management of Data, 1983, San Jose, 79-91.

[Le] H. Lewis, Complexity results for classes of quantificational formulas. J. Computer and Systems Sciences 21,3 (Dec. 1980), 317-353.

[LD] L. Liu and A. Demers, An algorithm for testing lossless join property in relational databases. Information Processing Letters 11,2 (1980), 73-76.

[Ma] D. Maier, The Theory of Relational Databases. Computer Science Press, Rockville, Maryland, 1983.

[MMSU] D. Maier, A. O. Mendelzon, F. Sadri, and J. D. Ullman, Adequacy of decompositions of relational databases. J. Computer and Systems Sciences 21,3 (Dec. 1980), 368-379.

[MMS] D. Maier, A. Mendelzon, and Y. Sagiv, Testing implications of data dependencies. ACM Trans. on Database Systems 4,4 (Dec. 1979), 455-469.

[MRW] D. Maier, D. Rozenshtein, and D. S. Warren, Windows on the world. Proc. ACM SIGMOD Symp. on Management of Data, 1983, San Jose, 68-78.

[MSY] D. Maier, Y. Sagiv, and M. Yannakakis, On the complexity of testing implications of functional and join dependencies. J. ACM 28,4 (Oct. 1981), 680-695.

[MUV] D. Maier, J. D. Ullman, and M. Y. Vardi, The revenge of the JD. Proc. 2nd ACM SIGACT-SIGMOD Symp. on Principles of Database Systems, 1983, Atlanta, 279-287.

[Me] A. Mendelzon, Database states and their tablueax. Proc. XP2 Workshop on Relational Database Theory, June 1981.

[MM] Mendelzon, A. O. and D. Maier, Generalized mutual dependencies and the decomposition of database relations. Proc. Int. Conf. on Very Large Data Bases, (A. L. Furtado and H. L. Morgan, eds.), 1979, 75-82.

[Mi1] J. C. Mitchell, Inference rules for functional and inclusion dependencies. Proc. 2nd ACM SIGACT-SIGMOD Symp. on Principles of Database Systems, 1983, Atlanta, 58-69.

[Mi2] J. C. Mitchell, The implication problem for functional and inclusion dependencies. MIT Technical Report. To appear in Information and Control.

[Ni] J-M. Nicolas, First order logic formalization for functional, multivalued, and mutual dependencies. Proc. ACM SIGMOD Symp. on Management of Data, 1978, 40-46.

[Pa] J. Paredaens, Transitive dependencies in a database scheme. MBLE Research Report R387, 1979.

[PJ] J. Paredaens and D. Janssens, Decompositions of relations: a comprehensive approach. In Advances in Data Base Theory - Vol. 1 (H. Gallaire, J. Minker, and J-M. Nicolas, eds.), Plenum Press, 1981, 73-100.

[PP] D. S. Parker and K. Parsaye-Ghomi, Inference involving embedded multivalued dependencies and transitive dependencies. Proc. ACM SIGMOD Symp. on Management of Data, 1980, 52-57.

[Ri1] J. Rissanen, Independent components of relations, ACM Trans. on Database Systems 2,4 (1977), 317-325.

[Ri2] J. Rissanen, Theory of relations for databases - a tutorial survey. Proc. 7th Symp. on Math. Found. of Comp. Science, 1978, Lecture Notes in Computer Science - Vol. 64, Springer-Verlag, 537-551.

[Ri3] J. Rissanen, On equivalence of database schemes. Proc. 1st ACM SIGACT-SIGMOD Symp. on Principles of Database Systems, 1982, Los Angeles, 23-26.

[Ro] H. Rogers, Theory of Recursive Functions and Effective Computability. McGraw-Hill, 1967.

[SU] F. Sadri and J. D. Ullman, Template dependencies: A large class of dependencies in relational databases and their complete axiomatization. J. ACM 29,2 (April 1981), 363-372.

[Sag1] Y. Sagiv, An algorithm for inferring multivalued dependencies with an application to propositional logic. J. ACM 27,2 (April 1980), 250-262.

[Sag2] Y. Sagiv, Can we use the universal instance assumption without using nulls? Proc. ACM SIGMOD Symp. on Management of Data, 1981, 108-120.

[Sag3] Y. Sagiv, A characterization of globally consistent databases and their correct access paths. ACM Trans. on Database Systems 8,2 (June 1983), 266-286.

[SW] Y. Sagiv and S. Walecka, Subset dependencies and a completeness result for a subclass of embedded multivalued dependencies. J. ACM 29,1 (Jan. 1982), 103-117.

[SS] M. Schkolnick and P. Sorenson, The effects of denormalization on database performance. The Australian Computer Journal 14,1 (Feb. 1982), 12-18.

[Sc1] E. Sciore, Real-world MVDs. Proc. ACM SIGMOD Symp. on Management of Data, 1981, 121-132.

[Sc2] E. Sciore, Inclusion dependencies and the universal instance. Proc. 2nd ACM SIGACT-SIGMOD Symp. on Principles of Database Systems, 1983, Atlanta, 48-57.

[Sc3] E. Sciore, A complete axiomatization of full join dependencies. J. ACM 29,2 (April 1982), 373-393.

[Ul] J. D. Ullman, Principles of Database Systems. Computer Science Press, Rockville, Maryland (1982)

[Va1] M. Y. Vardi, The implication problem for data dependencies in relational databases. Ph.D. Dissertation (in Hebrew), The Hebrew University in Jerusalem, Sept. 1981.

[Va2] M. Y. Vardi, The implication and finite implication problems for typed template dependencies. Proc. 1st ACM SIGACT-SIGMOD Symp. on Principles of Database Systems, 1982, Los Angeles, 230-238. To appear in J. Computer and Systems Sciences.

[Va3] M. Y. Vardi, On decomposition of relational databases. Proc. 23rd IEEE Symp. on Foundation of Computer Science, Chicago, 1982, 176-185.

[Va4] M. Y. Vardi, Inferring multivalued dependencies from functional and join dependencies. Acta Informatica, 19(1983), 305-324.

[Va5] M. Y. Vardi, A note on lossless database decompositions. To appear in Information Processing Letters.

[Ya] M. Yannakakis, Algorithms for acyclic database schemes. Proc. Int. Conf. on Very Large Data Bases, 1981, 82-94.

[YP] M. Yannakakis and C. Papadimitriou, Algebraic dependencies. J. Computer and System Sciences 25,2 (1982), 3-41.

[Za] C. Zaniolo, Analysis and design of relational schemata for database systems, Ph.D. Dissertation, Tech. Rep. UCLA-ENG-7669, UCLA, July 1976.

THE VLSI REVOLUTION IN THEORETICAL CIRCLES

Arnold L. Rosenberg

Department of Computer Science
Duke University
Durham, NC 27706 USA
and
Microelectronics Center of North Carolina
Research Triangle Park, NC 27709 USA

Presented in these pages are personal observations concerning the effect that Very Large Scale Integrated circuit technology (VLSI) has had on the Theoretical Computer Science field and community, together with some guesses as to why this technological advance has had so much more profound an effect on the Community than have had numerous earlier technological advances. The tale spun includes some sociology, some technology, and some history -- as well as some theoretical material, mostly as illustration.

1. INTRODUCTION

Theoretical Computer Science (henceforth, "Theory") can be argued to be generally unresponsive to changes in computer/computing technology. Typically, a new technological advance is ignored completely (e.g., the advent of time sharing and the development of memory hierarchies). A very few advances engender some number of Theory papers, but little beyond this level of attention (e.g., the emerging "science" of compiler construction). Fewer advances yet capture the imagination of theoreticians enough to lead to the development of an identifiable new branch of Theory (e.g., the areas of programming language semantics, databases, and distributed computing). But, there has been one technological development that has countered the general insouciance of the Theory community, that has so captured the attention of a number of long-time theorists that they have shed their theoretician's jeans for the suit and tie of the practicioner, and that has induced many other theorists to commit themselves to a special branch of Theory devoted to studying this new area. As my title indicates, it is the advent of integrated circuit technology that I refer to here, most especially in its incarnation as Very Large Scale Integrated circuit technology, VLSI.

I have been asked to discuss here the impact of this new technology on Theory. I have taken this charge quite literally, so the reader should expect much of what follows to be of quite an untheoretical nature. There will be some technology, some sociology, and some history -- although some theoretical material is included, mostly as illustration. What I have tried to present in these pages are my observations concerning the effect that VLSI has had on the Theory community, together with some guesses as to why this technological advance has had so profoundly different an effect on the Community than have had numerous earlier advances.

2. "WHAT'S IT ALL ABOUT, ALFIE?"

In order to understand what VLSI is, one must understand what an integrated circuit is and what the "scale" of integration is.

2.1. What Is An Integrated Circuit?

You are sitting at a table on which sit a small (about 60 mm on a side) square made of glass (call it a "chip") and three pens, marked *D*, *P*, and *M*, respectively. You begin to draw lines on the chip with the *P* pen, never allowing lines to cross. Once happy with your *P* lines, you start drawing lines with the *D* pen, again never allowing lines to cross, although you may (and, indeed, are encouraged to) draw *D* lines just up to, and perpendicular to *P* lines. Finally, you draw whatever lines you wish with the *M* pen; these lines may cross *P* and *D* lines, but not each other. When crossing a *D* or a *P* line, you can press hard, to cause the *M* ink to mix with the other ink. To a very crude approximation, you have just created an MOS (Metal-Oxide-Silicon, a name that harkens back to an earlier era) integrated circuit.

How do your lines create a circuit? We present just enough explanation to prepare you to consult texts. The ink in the *M* (Metal) pen consists of metal, usually aluminum. The ink in the *P* (Poly) pen consists of polycrystalline silicon, highly doped with negative ions. The ink in the *D* (Diffusion) pen consists of heavy negative doping, which gets absorbed by (diffuses into) the glass substrate as you draw lines. Hence, all kinds of lines conduct electricity, though the *M* lines do so much more efficiently than the *P* lines, which in turn do so much more efficiently than do the *D* lines (because of differences in resistivity). When *D* lines abut *P* lines (as you were encouraged to make them do), the juncture forms a Field

Effect Transistor (FET), which can be viewed as a switch that responds to changes in voltage levels; FETs are the only active devices in an MOS circuit. The wires that you have drawn interconnect the switches to create the circuit.

We have, of course, grossly simplified here, but the imagery is not misleading. The major surprise in viewing an integrated circuit is the absence of discrete transistors or resistors or capacitors. One sees only lines.

2.2. What Is (Very) Large Scale Integration?

One major impact of circuit integration is the ability to pack dense circuits in very small areas: basically, one needs only equip his pens with very small nibs. Indeed, technologists are now talking about producing lines of submicron (i.e., $< 10^{-6}$ m) width. Chips with roughly $.5\times10^6$ transistors have been produced, and chips with twice this density are certain to appear within a few years. Yet more chip capacity is imminent as improvements in technology allow chips to expand without excessive sacrifice in yield (= the percentage of usable chips).

As chip capacity expands, one refers to increased *scale of integration*, measured roughly in orders of magnitudes of transistors on a chip: Roughly 10^4 transistors on a chip is often referred to as LSI (Large Scale Integration), while VLSI begins at 10^5 transistors on a chip. The successor to VLSI, at 10^6 transistors on a chip, will likely be termed ULSI, replacing "very" with "ultra". Who knows what comes thereafter?

2.3. Where Does Theory Come In?

Theory plays three "standard" roles in the VLSI picture, in addition to the nonstandard roles we shall emphasize.

In its classic role, Theory explores the limitations and potential of the new computing environment. This role was initiated by Thompson [75] in his seminal dissertation, wherein he proposed the model that is still used with only minor modifications. The circuit to be implemented is viewed as a graph; the chip is viewed as a grid. One lays out the circuit by embedding it in the grid so that graph edges map onto edge-disjoint paths in the grid. The major measures of the efficiency of an implementation are: the Area of the implementation, measured by the area of the smallest rectangle that encloses the circuit layout, and the

Time, which is measured in standard circuit-theoretic fashion, often enhanced by assessing logarithmic time for traversing long runs of wire [14]. A perusal of the bibliography attests to the robustness of this avenue of exploration.

Theory's second role has been to study computational structures that fill specific needs in the new computational environment. These structures are often close relatives of known ones. For instance, most of the many special-purpose "VLSI engines" in the literature (e.g., [32,33,48]) are close cousins of the cellular automata and iterative arrays of finite automata of earlier years. More exciting, perhaps, are the new "general-purpose" structures that have emerged, such as Leighton's mesh of trees [35]. Although invented for quite different purposes, the mesh of trees turns out to be a very interesting computational network. In quite a different direction, the author [15, 61] has discovered a way to organize a bus of wires as a stack, as an avenue toward fault-tolerant implementations of arrays of processors.

The third major role for Theory has been in the development and analysis of algorithms that aid in the design process. Traditionally, (integrated as well as ordinary) circuits have been designed with the human designer being at least an equal partner of the computer. This is no longer possible, since increases in scale of integration have permitted designs of complexity beyond the capabilities of the human designer. Indeed, we are now seeing chips that contain entire systems. As in most complex computational areas, the major contributions of algorithm theorists are either in the arena of small subproblems (e.g., [3]) or in the arena of well-motivated heuristics for large problems (e.g., [57]). No contribution of Theory is more important to the world of integrated-circuit design than is the design and analysis of algorithms.

2.4. The Remainder of the Paper

The roles in the previous subsection are those that Theory plays (at least to some extent) in every application area that it visits in more than a cursory way: distributed computing, databases, or programming languages, for example. But, there has been interplay between integrated circuit technology and Theory that has been different in either kind or extent from other application areas. This is the subject of this paper. In Section 3 we illustrate the sociological impact of VLSI on Theory by enumerating theorists who have taken an extended leave from Theory to participate in the construction of (hardware or software) VLSI systems. Section 4 is devoted to the role of VLSI in resurrecting two areas that had all but disappeared from mainstream Theory, switching theory and logical design. Section 5 discusses a unique effect of VLSI (all the moreso of ULSI) among application areas: it has rendered (at least almost) feasible -- hence respectable in the eyes of practicioners -- large segments of what were viewed as blue-sky Theory, mainly having to do with unlimited parallelism. Indeed, it is the promise of massively parallel computing structures that has seduced many theorists from their ivory towers. Finally, Section 6 presents an important moral of the tale we relate: many of the notions that are needed for the study of VLSI are old notions, developed for studying (apparently) quite unrelated issues. Thus, as in other sciences, theoreticians in computer science often identify notions and issues whose importance transcends the motivating application. This is why Society has found theorists good guys to have around, even when it's not quite clear how they earn their salaries.

3. "NO, YOU DON'T KNOW ME"

Perhaps G. H. Hardy started it, the avoidance by theorists of practical issues. Even among our own number, there were theoretical computer scientists who not too many years ago expressed great pride in never having written a nontrivial program.

Perhaps VLSI has changed it, at least temporarily. A glance at the VLSI literature indicates that many from our midst have made serious commitments to this application area. Indeed, if my vision has not been distorted by being so close to the action, VLSI's sociological impact on Theory may well be its greatest. There has been a sizable at-least-temporary migration by a large number of visible theorists from Theory to VLSI systems work. I do not refer here to younger people who have been raised as VLSI theorists, nor to theorists who have dabbled in VLSI but have made no major commitment to the area, but rather to people who have been visible in the world of "standard" Theory, who have made major commitments to the study and development of VLSI systems. It is worth noting that the list of researchers who have begun their careers as VLSI theorists is quite substantial and impressive; moreover, the dabblers in VLSI theory have often left a mark for posterity. But, it is not they we want to focus on. Let us look at some of the serious migrants. (The References list samples of their VLSI work.)

Brenda Baker (Bell Labs) has done considerable work lately on problems related to routing wires on chips.

Len Berman (IBM, Yorktown) has been working for the past few years on a system that will permit the high-level specification of an integrated circuit.

Donna Brown's (U. Illinois) recent work has focussed on chip routing.,

Larry Carter (IBM, Yorktown) has moved from studying hashing to work on both theoretical and practical aspects of the problem of testing circuitry on chips.

H. T. Kung (Carnegie-Mellon U.) began, roughly six years ago, to study systolic arrays, a class of highly parallel special-purpose architectures that are well-suited to VLSI technology. He continues to study and refine these arrays and is building some both at CMU and at a company in California.

Tom Lengauer and Kurt Mehlhorn (U. Saarlandes) are presently designing and implementing the HILL design system. As part of this development, they are studying design algorithms relating to routing, compaction, and logic simulation.

Dick Lipton (Princeton U.) has been working on both testing and high-level design aids, most notably via the ALI language.

Franco Preparata's (U. Illinois) interest in VLSI-oriented problems has been manifest in work on chip-routing and on the use of the cube-connected-cycles structure in designing optimal VLSI circuits for a variety of tasks.

Ron Rivest (MIT) has been the mastermind behind the PI placement and routing system, in addition to working on theoretical aspects of the routing problem.

Arny Rosenberg (Duke U. and MCNC) has been working for the past five years on a variety of problems related to VLSI circuit layout, most recently concentrating on the problems of multilayer circuit realization and the design of fault-tolerant processor arrays, the latter via the DIOGENES methodology.

John Savage (Brown U.) made a gentle transition from circuit complexity to VLSI circuit complexity. This has been followed by a sharper transition, to the development and refinement of the SLAP design system, which allows one to proceed interactively from a specification of a circuit via Boolean equations to a layout of the circuit.

Larry Snyder's (U. Washington) interests in parallel computation have combined with his interest in VLSI to spawn the development of the Blue CHiP, a Configurable Highly Parallel machine design; he is also directing a comparative study of VLSI design tools.

Tom Szymanski (Bell Labs) has recently moved away from work on the complexity of VLSI design algorithms to the direction of a project that will develop sophisticated VLSI design tools.

Jean Vuillemin (U. Paris) has studied VLSI complexity theory, has collaborated on much of Preparata's optimal circuit work, and is currently developing a VLSI design-aid system.

Any list such as we have attempted is doomed to incompleteness. I apologize to any whose contributions I have inadvertently omitted or misclassified. But, incomplete though the list may be, it is impressive in its population. It will be interesting to see as time passes whether the sheep will return to the fold or will seek the greener pastures (?) of more applied work.

4. "GOOD MORNING, YESTERDAY"

The 1960's saw a sharp decline of interest on the part of the Theory community in a variety of topics that can loosely be grouped under the rubric switching circuit theory and logical design. The older among the readers might recognize this as the original name of the Theory conference that has evolved from

Switching Circuit Theory and Logical Design

to

Switching and Automata Theory (SWAT)

to the present (hopefully permanent)

Foundations of Computer Science (FOCS).

The changes in name have reflected changes in Theory. A fascinating effect of VLSI has been to reawaken interest among theorists in several of these abandoned topics. Indeed, so intense has been the renewed interest that the past two FOCS Symposia have seen (not altogether frivolous) suggestions that the Meeting revert to its original name.

Testing. Among the topics that have experienced renewed popularity is the crucial issue of *circuit testing.* In many respects, this topic is not the same one that was studied in decades past. Circuit testing in the 1950's envisioned a world of relays that were easily accessible via probes and that had the nasty habit of sticking in open or closed position. The problem of testing was basically that of trying to detect a small number of sticky relays in combinational (= memoryless) and sequential (= memory-ed) circuits having hundreds, or at most thousands of relays. VLSI has changed the picture in at least three respects. Firstly, the circuits that one now needs to test have tens (or hundreds) of thousands of transistors (which play the role of yesterday's relays). Secondly, aggrevating this change in scale, chips can generally be probed only from their peripheries, so a chip with n devices can usually be probed at only roughly $n^{1/2}$ positions. Thirdly, the single stuck-at fault models of the past are of questionable validity now, both in terms of the *single* -- one must now expect fault numbers to increase with increased densities -- and the *stuck-at* -- VLSI devices have many nasty ways of failing.

Somewhat counteracting these ways in which the testing problem has become harder are two new avenues for solving the problem. Firstly, certain popular VLSI design styles obviate testing sequential circuits. Disciplines such as LSSD (level-sensitive scan design) [22] impose on the designer a register-to-register design format in which the registers can be converted to shift registers for the purposes of testing. This style allows all logic to be tested as combinational logic (after the registers have been tested). Secondly, the vastly increased densities of devices on chips allow one to contemplate *self-testing circuitry (STC)*: one places on the chip a moderate amount of extra circuitry whose role is to test the other circuitry. The STC, being much less massive than the working circuitry, can comfortably be tested via external probes. One popular scenario is the following. The STC controls the LSSD registers on the chip. When the TEST signal is presented to the chip, all registers are reconfigured to shift registers. The STC begins to generate tests locally (in a distributed fashion) for the working circuitry. As the tests are completed, the STC collects and analyzes the results. (There is, of course, the question of how to respond to detected faults, but that falls under the aegis of fault-tolerant computing, which is not our concern here.) How can such a scenario be realized? This entails two related questions, How does one generate tests? and, How does one analyze tests?

One promising approach to test generation is to follow the lead of workers on error-correcting codes and use primitive polynomials over GF(2) to supply the LSSD registers with linear feedback so that they "automatically" generate test vectors when "seeded" with a suitable constant vector. The power of this approach is that it gives rise to very small test-generating circuitry. The difficulties with the approach are: it requires either partitioning of the combinational logic, to permit exhaustive test generation, or some form of sophisticated circuit analysis that permits choosing a polynomial that tests the circuit in question. We briefly illustrate the exhaustive generation scenario. Say that (perhaps after partitioning one's circuitry by introducing new registers) one has a block of combinational circuitry between an input- and an output-LSSD register, that has the property that each output position of the circuit depends on at most roughly 20 input positions. Such a block is a candidate for exhaustive testing, since current on-chip speeds render some small multiple of 2^{20} a reasonable number of cycles for testing. The problem now becomes the following. One has an n-bit input LSSD register, and one is given some family $S_1, S_2, \ldots, S_r$ of subsets of $\{0,1,\ldots,n-1\}$; the set S_i is the set of input positions affecting output position i. One wants to find a primitive polynomial over GF(2)

$$P(x) = a_0 + a_1 x + \cdots + a_k x^k$$

of as small a degree k as possible (perforce $k \geq \max |S_i|$) such that the linear recurrence

$$y_{m+k} = a_0 y_m + a_1 y_{m-1} + \cdots + a_{k-1} y_{m-k+1},$$

($m > 0$) in GF(2) will, when "seeded" with the initial values

$$y_0 = y_1 = \cdots = y_{k-1} = 0, \quad y_k = 1$$

generate a length-($2^k + k - 1$) string whose substrings sampled at the positions indicated by each set S_i consist of all $2^{|S_i|}$ binary strings. [6] presents a partial solution to this problem.

The most studied approach to the test collection/analysis problem is *signature analysis*, which basically amounts to "hardware" hashing the results of applying the test vectors to the circuit by "collecting" the results in the output LSSD register, also outfitted with linear feedback. The power of this approach is that it requires very little circuitry. The difficulty with the approach is that it requires, for its success, an assurance that the faults in the circuit-under-test are uncorrelated so that simultaneously occurring faults will not mask one another. Such assurance is hard to come by with VLSI circuits; indeed, no good model of VLSI faults has appeared in the literature. And, until the technology "cools down" some, no company is likely to share its proprietary fault data in the near future. Carter [12] has shown that an approach analogous to that of the Carter-Wegman universal hash functions [13] will yield an effective solution to the problem (as in [13], one wants to take the dice into one's own hand instead of leaving them with Nature); but such an approach leads to excessive amounts of circuitry (to remember all of the functions). He has some yet-unanalyzed heuristics that hold some promise.

Logic Design. By the mid-1960's, the theoretical excitement had left the world of logic design. There was no lack of challenges, but the problems that logic designers were working on lacked the fundamental nature that attracts the Theory community. The advent of VLSI has added an ingredient to these problems that has reawakened the theoreticians' interest, an uncompromising quest for regular structure. What VLSI excels at is the construction of systems that have very large numbers of instances of a very few types of objects; understanding such regularity is what Theory excels at. Examples of such regular structures abound, ranging from the parallel adder of Brent and Kung [8] to the pattern recognizer of Foster and Kung [25] to Preparata's multiplier [50]. Space limitations preclude our describing any of these.

Switching Theory (for MOS). The design of truly sophisticated VLSI design systems, ranging from high-level specification languages to logic-level simulators requires an accurate yet simple model of the behavior of VLSI circuits, playing much the role that conventional switching theory plays for relay circuits. Bryant [11] began to develop such a theory, and recently, Lengauer [43] has joined the development effort. Several factors make the development of a switching theory for MOS circuits significantly harder than for relay circuits. (1) Wires and switches in MOS are bidirectional. (2) Since switches in MOS respond to changes in voltage levels, one must be able to model levels intermediate between logic-0 and logic-1, which correspond to partially open switches. But, perhaps the greatest impediment to such a theory is that certain aspects of timing that can be ignored with impunity in the world of relays (where one can look at a circuit's state only at settled moments) must be modeled explicitly in an MOS environment. (3) In many situations, switching from logic-1 to logic-0 is much faster than switching from logic-0 to logic-1. (4) There exist MOS circuits whose functional behavior depends on timing. (5) Issues of transistor size are crucial to the correct operation of an MOS circuit; and mistakes in sizing usually manifest themselves in timing problems. Thus, charge *strength* as well as charge value must be modeled in an MOS-oriented switching theory. Lengauer's [43] theory adopts Bryant's notions of charge and strength assignment, but also builds in timing considerations (delay independence) by formulating an axiomatic model of circuit behavior rather than a deterministic state-transition model. This is a very important and active area that is crucial for the development of VLSI design systems.

5. "TO DREAM THE IMPOSSIBLE DREAM"

For decades, theoreticians have studied computing devices that incorporated massive parallelism. As early as the 1950's, researchers were studying so-called cellular automata and iterative arrays of finite automata, though often for their biological rather than computational implications. By the 1960's, many of these devices were studied as serious computational devices, and attempts were made to compare their efficiency with that of serial computing devices [2,18,19]. Interest in massive parallelism grew in the 1970's with the change of focus of work on circuit complexity from circuits *per se* to circuits as exemplars of parallel computing devices. In an attempt to understand the nature of parallel computation, the powers of circuits were enhanced, even to the point of allowing circuits to alter their inter-device connections [21].

Possibly the major computational contribution of VLSI has been to render feasible the blue-sky speculations of the parallel-computation theorists. Work on special-purpose VLSI processor arrays is now commonplace, and many such devices have actually been fabricated [25]. And, most of these arrays are modeled after the iterative arrays of finite automata of an earlier day. More interesting is that many of the designs of yesteryear that were genuine intellectual *tours de force* can now be derived algorithmically from much simpler designs [38]. With the understanding of how to design such machines has also come increased understanding of the limitations of parallelism; this theme recurs in the next Section, under "Information Flow". Most exciting of all, recent work on reconfigurable VLSI systems spawned by realization of some of the limitations of parallelism [73] and by concerns about fault tolerance in processor arrays [15, 61] have rendered feasible self-modifying machines such as those posited in [21].

6. "I'VE GROWN ACCUSTOMED TO HER FACE"

For a theoretician, one of the most exciting experiences when studying VLSI is the recognition of an old friend, a question or a technique that arose earlier for other purposes. Examples are so common that discipline is needed to keep within allotted space.

Information Flow.

Since the late 1950's, the role of information flow as a limiting factor in computation was recognized. Shepherdson [71] used an information flow argument to prove that two-way head motion does not enhance the power of finite automata; Rabin [54] began the more common use of such arguments, to obtain negative results, proving that 2-tape Turing machines were often faster than one-tape ones; Hennie [29] used a similar argument to bound the time required for a classical Turing machine to recognize certain formal languages; and Cobham [17] used information flow to prove perhaps the first time-space tradeoff result: Let M be any bounded-action machine with a read-only input tape that recognizes the palindromes. The product of the maximum time that M expends when processing a word of length n and the number of bits required to specify the distinct configurations attained when processing such words must be proportional to n^2. When Thompson began his study of computational complexity in a VLSI environment, it became clear quickly that flow of information was close to being the whole story. To illustrate the role of information flow on chips, we sketch the simplest of all such arguments, a bound on the area-time^2 product for any layout of an n-input permutation network. (Area-time^2 is the complexity measure that arises naturally in VLSI problems.) Say we have an n-input permuter laid out in a rectangular region of a grid, of dimensions $H \times L$, with $H \le L$: the permuter's devices occupy unit-side squares, and its wires have unit width (the standard idealization of the VLSI setup). By a now-standard device of Thompson, we can pass a line (possibly having a unit-length jog) along the shorter dimension of the rectangle, that segregates half of the circuit's inputs from the other half; some $n/2$ outputs are thereby segregated from some $n/2$ inputs. Now, some permutation demands that these isolated input and output terminals communicate with each other. Since the separating line has length $\le H+1$, and since wires have unit width, such communication must take at least $\frac{n}{2(H+1)}$ units of time; this must, therefore, also be a lower bound on the TIME required to compute the permutation. We thus have the two inequalities

$$\text{AREA} \geq H^2$$

and

$$\text{TIME} \geq \frac{n}{2(H+1)}$$

which combine to prove that

$$\text{AREA}\times\text{TIME}^2 \geq (const)n^2.$$

Vuillemin [76] has refined this genre of argument to include circuits for any transitive function (roughly, any vector-input, vector-valued function that can compute "shifts" of its arguments), and Lipton and Sedgewick [44] have refined information-flow arguments to yield area-time^2 bounds for certain binary-valued functions.

Formula Size.

A major reaction to the increasing scale of integration has been the attempt to automate (at least partially) the process of designing and implementing circuits. One of the earliest sophisticated developments in this direction was ***array logic*** [24]. In rough terms, array logic allows one to realize logic functions using memory-like (hence, regular) structures: one builds a standard array that is "personalized" to compute the desired function. The most familiar example of array logic is the ***programmable logic array (pla)***, which takes as input any collection of Boolean expressions in sum-of-products form; the functions specified are realized by setting the transistors/switches in two "matrices", an AND matrix (to realize the products) and an OR matrix (to realize the sums). A major problem with pla's is that the matrices are often huge, even for rather simple functions, which tends to lead to rather sparsely used matrices. Theoreticians quickly noted that this problem had its roots in the issue of formula size. Lupanov [45] had noted in the 1960's that certain functions admit only enormous sum-of-products (SOP) formulas. Specifically, any SOP formula for the n-input parity function must have length $n2^{n-1}$: each product in the formula must contain n literals, or else the function will be erroneously TRUE on some TRUE setting of an even number of variables; all 2^{n-1} products containing an odd number of uncomplemented variables must appear in the formula, or the function will be erroneously FALSE on some TRUE setting of an odd number of variables. (See also [28].) Practicioners had already intuited the inherent limitations of pla's and had begun using them only for small control-logic functions.

Others.

Network Flow. Among wire-routing problems, one of the thorniest is *switchbox routing*. One is given fixed terminals on the periphery of an empty rectangle, and one must run wires to establish certain specified electrical equivalences. Frank [27] has discovered a nonobvious algorithm to solve this problem, based on a nonobvious way of viewing switchbox routing as a network flow problem.

Computational Geometry. An important facet of VLSI design is to check that wires and devices are spaced properly in relation to one another, to maintain desired electrical equivalence and distinction. Such *design-rule checking* can be viewed as a class of computational geometry problems. Indeed, algorithms and data structures from that area are common in sophisticated design-rule checkers.

Space limitations have limited us to only a very few examples of a wide and varied topic here. For instance, we have not even mentioned the relevance of Tarjan's 1972 work [74] on sorting for the study of fault-tolerant processor arrays [16], nor the relevance of Even and Itai's [23] work on circle graphs for multilayer circuit realization, and on and on.

7. A MORAL

The moral of our tale is two-sided. On the one hand, good Theory transcends its immediate application. It predicts, it prods, and it helps to analyze. On the other hand, good applied areas transcend their apparent boundaries. They supply new problems for Theory, and they also give Theory a chance to look its progeny in the eye.

ACKNOWLEDGMENT.

This research was supported in part by NSF Grant MCS-83-01213.

REFERENCES

In addition to illustrating points in the text via citation, this list of references is intended to give the reader an entry into the world of VLSI through the eyes of theorists.

1. R. Aleliunas and A.L. Rosenberg (1980): On embedding rectangular grids in square grids. *IEEE Trans. Comp., C-31*, 907-913.
2. A.J. Atrubin (1965): A one-dimensional real-time iterative multiplier. *IEEE Trans. Elec. Comp., EC-14*, 394-399.

3. B.S. Baker, S.N. Bhatt, F.T. Leighton (1983): An approximation algorithm for Manhattan routing. *15th ACM Symp. on Theory of Computing*, 477-486.

4. B.S. Baker and R.Y. Pinter (1983): An algorithm for the optimal placement and routing of a circuit within a ring of pads. *24th IEEE Symp. on Foundations of Computer Science*, 360-370.

5. Z. Barzilai, J.L. Carter, A.K. Chandra, B.K. Rosen (1983): Diagnosis based on signature testing. IBM Report RC-9682.

6. Z. Barzilai, D. Coppersmith, A.L. Rosenberg (1983): Exhaustive bit-pattern generation, with applications to VLSI self-testing. *IEEE Trans. Comp., C-32*, 190-194.

7. G.M. Baudet, F.P. Preparata, J.E. Vuillemin (1983): Area-time optimal VLSI circuits for convolution. *IEEE Trans. Comp., C-32*, 684-688.

8. R.P. Brent and H.T. Kung (1980): The chip complexity of binary arithmetic. *12th ACM Symp. on Theory of Computing*, 190-200.

9. M.L. Brady and D.J. Brown (1984): Arbitrary planar routing with four layers. *1984 MIT Conf. on Advanced Research in VLSI*, 194-201.

10. D.J. Brown and R.L. Rivest (1981): New lower bounds for channel width. *VLSI Systems and Computations* (ed. H.T. Kung, B. Sproull, G. Steele) Computer Science Press, Rockville, MD, pp.178-185.

11. R.E. Bryant (1981): A switch-level model of MOS logic circuits. *VLSI 81: Very Large Scale Integration* (ed. J.P. Gray) Academic Press, London, pp. 329-340.

12. J.L. Carter (1982): The theory of signature testing for VLSI. *14th ACM Symp. on Theory of Computing*, 66-76.

13. J.L. Carter and M.N. Wegman (1979): Universal classes of hash functions. *J. CSS 18*, 143-154.

14. B. Chazelle and L. Monier (1981): A model of computation for VLSI with related complexity results. *13th ACM Symp. on Theory of Computing*, 318-325.

15. F.R.K. Chung, F.T. Leighton, A.L. Rosenberg (1983): DIOGENES -- A methodology for designing fault-tolerant processor arrays. *13th Intl. Conf. on Fault-Tolerant Computing*, 26-32.

16. F.R.K. Chung, F.T. Leighton, A.L. Rosenberg (1984): Embedding graphs in books: A layout problem with applications to VLSI design. Typescript.

17. A. Cobham (1966): The recognition problem for the set of perfect squares. *Proc. 7th IEEE Symp. on Switching and Automata Theory*, 78-87.

18. S.N. Cole (1969): Real-time computation by n-dimensional iterative arrays of finite-state machines. *IEEE Trans. Comp., C-18*, 349-365.

19. S.A. Cook and S.O. Aanderaa (1969): On the minimum computation time of functions. *Trans. AMS 142*, 291-314.

20. J.A. Darringer, W.H. Joyner, C.L. Berman, L. Trevillyan (1981): Logic synthesis through local transformations. IBM Report RC-8748.

21. P.W. Dymond and S.A. Cook (1980): Hardware complexity and parallel computation. *Proc. 21st IEEE Symp. on Foundations of Computer Science*, 360-372.

22. E.B. Eichelberger and T.W. Williams (1978): A logic design structure for LSI testability. *J. Design Automation and Fault-Tolerant Comp. 2*, 165-178.

23. S. Even and A. Itai (1971): Queues, stacks, and graphs. In *Theory of Machines and Computations* (Z. Kohavi and A. Paz eds.) Academic Press, NY, pp. 71-86.

24. H. Fleisher and L.I. Maissel (1975): An introduction to array logic. *IBM J. Res. Dev. 19*, 98-109.

25. M.J. Foster and H.T. Kung (1980): The design of special-purpose VLSI chips. *Computer 13*, 26-40.

26. M.J. Foster and H.T. Kung (1981): Recognize regular languages with programmable building-blocks. In *VLSI 81: Very Large Scale Integration* (ed. J.P. Gray) Academic Press, London, pp. 75-84.

27. A. Frank (1982): Disjoint paths in a rectilinear grid. *Combinatorica*, to appear.

28. M. Furst, J.B. Saxe, M. Sipser (1983): Parity, circuits, and the polynomial-time hierarchy. *Math. Syst. Theory*, to appear.

29. F.C. Hennie (1965): One-tape, off-line Turing machine computations. *Inform. Contr. 8*, 553-578.

30. R.M. Karp, F.T. Leighton, R.L. Rivest, C.D. Thompson, U. Vazirani, V. Vazirani (1983): Global wire routing in two-dimensional arrays. *24th IEEE Symp. on Foundations of Computer Science*, 453-459.

31. H.T. Kung (1983): Systolic algorithms and their implementation. Typescript.

32. H.T. Kung and C.E. Leiserson (1980): Systolic arrays (for VLSI). In Chapter 8 of (Mead-Conway, 1980).

33. H.T. Kung and R.L. Picard (1984): One-dimensional systolic arrays for multi-dimensional convolution and resampling. In *VLSI for Pattern Recognition and Image Processing*, Springer-Verlag.

34. A.S. LaPaugh and R.J. Lipton (1983): Total stuck-at fault testing by circuit transformation. *20th ACM-IEEE Design Automation Conf.*

35. F.T. Leighton (1984): Parallel computation using meshes of trees. *1983 Workshop on Graph-Theoretic Concepts in Computer Science*, 200-218.

36. F.T. Leighton and A.L. Rosenberg (1983): Automatic generation of three-dimensional circuit layouts. *1983 IEEE Intl. Conf. on Computer Design*, 633-636.

37. F.T. Leighton and A.L. Rosenberg (1984): Three-dimensional circuit layouts. Submitted for publication.

38. C.E. Leiserson, F.M. Rose, J.B. Saxe (1982): Digital circuit optimization. *3rd Caltech Conf. on VLSI.*

39. T. Lengauer (1982): The complexity of compacting hierarchically specified layouts of integrated circuits. *23rd IEEE Symp. on Foundations of Computer Science*, 358-368.

40. T. Lengauer (1983): On the solution of inequality systems relevant to IC-layout. *J. Algorithms*, to appear.

41. T. Lengauer (1984): Efficient algorithms for the constraint generation for integrated circuit layout compaction. *1983 Workshop on Graph-Theoretic Concepts in Computer Science*, 219-230.

42. T. Lengauer and K. Mehlhorn (1984): The HILL system: a design environment for the hierarchical specification, compaction, and simulation of integrated circuit layouts. *1984 MIT Conf. on Advanced Research in VLSI*, 139-149.

43. T. Lengauer and S. Naeher (1984): Delay-independent switch-level simulation of digital MOS circuits. Typescript.

44. R.J. Lipton and R. Sedgewick (1981): Lower bounds for VLSI. *13th ACM Symp. on Theory of Computing*, 300-307.

45. O.B. Lupanov (1961): On the realization of functions of logical algebra by formulae of limited depth in the basis [AND, OR, NOT]. *Probl. Kibernetiki 6*, 5-14.

46. C. Mead and L. Conway (1980): *Introduction to VLSI Systems*, Addison-Wesley, Reading, MA.

47. K. Mehlhorn and F.P. Preparata (1983): Routing through a rectangle. Typescript.

48. Th. Ottmann, A.L. Rosenberg, L.J. Stockmeyer (1981): A dictionary machine (for VLSI). *IEEE Trans. Comp., C-31*, 892-897.

49. F.P. Preparata (1981): Optimal three-dimensional VLSI layouts. *Math. Systems Theory 16*, 1-8.

50. F.P. Preparata (1983): A mesh-connected area-time optimal VLSI multiplier of large integers. *IEEE Trans. Comp., C-32*, 194-198.

51. F.P. Preparata and W. Lipski (1982): Optimal three-layer channel routing. *23rd IEEE Symp. on Foundations of Computer Science* 350-357.

52. F.P. Preparata and J.E. Vuillemin (1980): Area-time optimal VLSI networks for multiplying matrices. *Inf. Proc. Let. 11*, 77-80.

53. F.P. Preparata and J.E. Vuillemin (1981): The cube-connected cycles: a versatile network for parallel computation. *C. ACM 24*, 300-309.

54. M.O. Rabin (1963): Real-time computation. *Israel J. Math. 1*, 203-211.

55. S.P. Reiss and J.E. Savage (1982): SLAP -- A methodology for silicon layout. *IEEE Int'l. Conf. on Circuits and Computers*, 281-285.

56. R.L. Rivest, A.E. Baratz, G. Miller (1981): Provably good channel routing algorithms. *VLSI Systems and Computations* (ed. H.T. Kung, B. Sproull, G. Steele) Computer Science Press, Rockville, MD, pp.153-159.

57. R.L. Rivest and C.M. Fiduccia (1982): A "greedy" channel router. *19th ACM-IEEE Design Automation Conf.*, 418-424.

58. A.L. Rosenberg (1981): Three-dimensional integrated circuitry. In *VLSI Systems and Computations* (ed. H.T. Kung, B. Sproull, G. Steele) Computer Science Press, Rockville, MD, pp. 69-80.

59. A.L. Rosenberg (1981): Routing with permuters: Toward reconfigurable and fault-tolerant networks. Duke Univ. Tech. Rpt. CS-1981-13.

60. A.L. Rosenberg (1983): Three-dimensional VLSI: A case study. *J. ACM 30*, 397-416.

61. A.L. Rosenberg (1983): The Diogenes approach to testable fault-tolerant arrays of processors. *IEEE Trans. Comp., C-32*, 902-910.

62. A.L. Rosenberg (1984): Fault-tolerant interconnection networks: a graph-theoretic approach. *1983 Workshop on Graph-Theoretic Concepts in Computer Science*, 286-297.

63. A.L. Rosenberg (1984): On designing fault-tolerant VSLI processor arrays. *Advances in Computing Research 2*, to appear.

64. W.L. Ruzzo and L. Snyder (1981): Minimum edge-length planar embeddings of trees. *VLSI Systems and Computations* (ed. H.T. Kung, B. Sproull, G. Steele) Computer Science Press, Rockville, MD, pp. 119-123.

65. M. Sarrafzadeh and F.P. Preparata (1983): Compact channel-routing of multiterminal nets. Typescript.

66. J.E. Savage (1981): Area-time tradeoffs for matrix multiplication and related problems in VLSI models. *J. CSS*, 230-242.

67. J.E. Savage (1981): Planar circuit complexity and the perfoprmance of VLSI algorithms. In *VLSI Systems and Computations* (ed. H.T. Kung, B. Sproull, G. Steele) Computer Science Press, Rockville, MD, pp. 61-68.

68. J.E. Savage (1982): Multilective planar circuit size. *20th Allerton Conf. on Commun., Control, and Computing.*

69. J.E. Savage (1983): Three VLSI compilation techniques: PLAs, Weinberger arrays, and SLAP, a new silicon layout program. In *Algorithmically-Specialized Computers* (ed. L. Snyder, L.J. Siegel, H.J. Siegel, D. Gannon) Academic Press, NY.

70. J.E. Savage (1983): Heuristics in the SLAP layout system. *1983 IEEE Intl Conf. On Computer Design*, 637-640.

71. J.C. Shepherdson (1959): The reduction of two-way automata to one-way automata. *IBM J. Res. Dev. 3*, 198-200.

72. L. Snyder (1980): A synopsis of the Blue CHiP Project. Purdue Univ. Dept. of Computer Science Tech. Rpt.

73. L. Snyder (1981): Overview of the CHiP computer. In *VLSI 81: Very Large Scale Integration* (ed. J. P. Gray) Academic Press, London, pp. 237-246.

74. R.E. Tarjan (1972): Sorting using networks of queues and stacks. *J.ACM 19*, 341-346.

75. C.D. Thompson (1980): A complexity theory for VLSI. Ph.D. Thesis, Carnegie-Mellon University; see also Area-time complexity for VLSI. *11th ACM Symp. on Theory of Computing*, 1979, 81-88.

76. J. Vuillemin (1983): A combinatorial limit to the computing power of VLSI circuits. *IEEE Trans. Comp.*, *C-32*, 294-300.

TUPLE SEQUENCES AND INDEXES

Serge Abiteboul
Institut National de Recherche en Informatique et Automatique,
78153 Rocquencourt, France

and

Seymour Ginsburg
University of Southern California
Los Angeles, California 90089-0782

ABSTRACT

The concept of tuple sequence is introduced in order to investigate structure connected with relational model implementation. Well-known problems like decomposition and duplicates are addressed for tuple sequences. The lexicographical ordering of tuple sequences is studied via the notion of index (dependency). Certain properties of index families are shown, and two algorithmiques questions related to indexes considered. Also, a sound and complete set of inference rules for indexes is exhibited. Finally, indexes and functional dependencies in combination are studied.

1. INTRODUCTION

It is widely acknowledged that the relational model offers a simple and uniform logical view of data. Nevertheless, there are certain shortcomings of the model due to the lack of structure in a relation. One of the major deficiencies is that implementation requires more structure. In particular, information is often recorded sequencially. Furthermore, accessing and updating techniques make use of this structuring. The purpose of the present paper is to incorporate this notion of sequencing into the classical model and examine the resulting structure, here called tuple sequence, with respect to several implementation problems.

---

[1]This work was supported in part by the National Science Foundation under grant MCS-7925004.

Since tuple sequences are introduced primarily to investigate mechanisms connected with relational model implementation, a major theme in the paper is the translation (and study) of prominent relational concepts into analogous notions for sequences. In particular, analogues are presented for the operations of projection, join and selection, as well as two fundamental dependencies (FDs and JDs). Some well-known results about relations, e.g., decomposition, turn out to be surprisingly different for sequences.

The underlying concept of a tuple sequence is that of sequencing tuples. In general, such a sequencing is arbitrary. However, it is sometimes the case that the sequencing is determined by the content of tuples. This leads to the other major theme of the paper, that of an index. (An index is a sequence of attributes such that the tuples are lexicographically ordered by the attribute sequence.) The notion of index presented here should not be confused with the classic concept of an index mechanism [AS,S]. However both notions are concerned with falicitating access.

A system which includes this idea via the term "ordered relation" is presented in [SK]. Data sequencing is also considered in [ACGV]. However, these two investigations are not concerned with indexes.

Organizationally, the paper is divided into four sections. Section 1 introduces tuples sequences and several operations on such sequences. The decomposition of sequences and the existence of duplicates are briefly discussed. Section 2 presents the index dependency. A complete and sound system of inference rules is exhibited for indexes, and the interaction between index and functional dependencies is examined. In Section 3, two algorithmic questions related to index satisfaction are investigated. Finally, Section 4 considers the projection of arbitrary index families.

This extended abstract is based on [AG]. The proof and a more detailed discussion can be found there.

2. TUPLE SEQUENCES

In this section, we present the notion of tuple sequence and a number of operations on these sequences, as well as some related concepts such as duplicate free and join dependency.

We shall assume throughout an infinite set of abtract symbols called *attributes*, and for each attribute A a set dom(A), called the *domain* of A, of at least two elements. To simplify the discussion, we shall also assume that dom(A) is a subset of the integers, and is thus totally ordered. (Without this assumption, we should add the condition that indexes, which occur in Section 3, are defined only over totally ordered domains.)

Definition: Let U be a finite set of attributes. A *tuple* (over U) is a function u from U such that u(A) is in dom(A) for each A in U. For each U, let tup(U) denote the set of all tuples over U.

Our interest in this paper is with (finite) sequences of tuples over the same set of attributes. Motivated by the classical relational operations, we consider four operations on sequences of tuples, namely projection, concatenation, selection and join. Let us first consider an example:

R	A	B	C
	0	1	0
	0	0	1
	3	0	0

R′	B	C	D
	0	1	1
	1	0	0
	0	0	0

Figure 2-1: Two Tuple Sequences

Example: Consider the tuple sequences R and R′ given in Figure 2-1. Then one *projection* of R (namely S), one projection of R′ (namely T), the *concatenation* of S and T, the *join* of R and R′ and a *selection* on R can be found in Figure 2-2.

The formal definition of projection and concatenation are straight-forward and therefore omitted. The definition of selection is now given.

Definition: Let U be a finite set of attributes, $W \subseteq U$, and w a tuple over W. Then for each tuple over U, let $\text{select}_{W=w}(u) = u$ if $u[W] = w$, and[2] $\text{select}_{W=w}(u) = \emptyset_U$ otherwise. For each tuple sequence $S = u_1 \ldots u_n$ over U, the *selection* of S by w, denoted $\text{select}_{W=w}(S)$ is the sequence, $\text{select}_{W=w}(u_1) \ldots \text{select}_{W=w}(u_n)$.

We now define the join operation.

Definition: Let u and v be one-tuple sequences over U and V, respectively. If $u[U \cap V] =$

[2]For each set U of attributes, $\emptyset_U$ denotes the empty sequence over U.

S	B	C
	1	0
	0	1
	0	0

T	B	C
	0	1
	1	0
	0	0

S T	B	C
	1	0
	0	1
	0	0
	0	1
	1	0
	0	0

$R \bowtie R'$	A	B	C	D
	0	1	0	0
	0	0	1	0
	3	0	0	0

$select_{B=0}(R)$	A	B	C
	0	0	1
	3	0	0

Figure 2-2: Operations on Those Sequences

$v[U \cap V]$, let $u \bowtie v$ be the one-tuple sequence over UV defined by $(u \bowtie v)[U] = u$ and $(u \bowtie v)[V] = v$. If $u[U \cap V] \neq v[U \cap V]$, let $u \bowtie v$ be the empty sequence. Let $S = u_1 ... u_n$ and $S' = v_1 ... v_m$ be sequences. Then $S \bowtie S' = (u_1 \bowtie S) ... (u_n \bowtie S)$ where $u_i \bowtie S = (u_i \bowtie v_1) ... (u_i \bowtie v_m)$ for each i.

Note that duplicates are allowed in sequences. Therefore, tuple sequences provide a natural formalism to study duplicates. It is easily seen that join and selection can't introduce duplicates. (A more detailed discussion on duplicates can be found in [AG].) Note also that join, as defined here, is not commutative.

To conclude this section, the decomposition of sequences is considered via the notion of join dependency.

Definition: Let U be a finite set of attributes. A *join dependency* over U is an expression of the form $<U_1, ... U_k>$, where $k>0$, $U_j \subseteq U$ for each j in [1,k], and $\{U_j \mid 1<j<k\}$ covers U.

By similarity with the definition of join dependency in the relational model, we have:

Definition: A sequence S over U *satisfies* the *join dependency* $<U_1, ... U_k>$ if $S = S_1 \bowtie S_2 ... \bowtie S_k$ for some sequences $S_1, ... S_k$ over $U_1, ... U_k$ respectively.

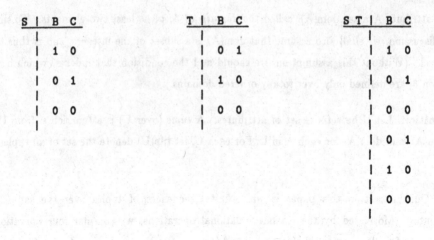

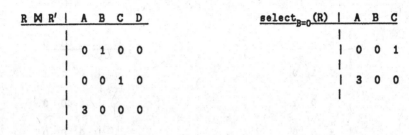

In the relational model, a relation satisfies a join dependency if this relation is equal to the join of its projections on the different blocks of the join dependency. The analogous result for sequences is not true. Indeed a characterization for when a sequences satisfies a join dependency is more complicated and is not resolved here. However, a characterization can be found in [AG] for the case when the join has exactly two components. An algorithm to check whether a join dependency is satisfied is given there, and it is shown that it takes polynomial time.

3. INDEXES

As mentioned in the introduction, the notion of tuple sequence leads to the concept of index. In this context, an index (dependency) is a string of attributes. A given tuple sequence "satisfies" a particular index if the tuples are lexicographically ordered in the sequence according to these attributes. In this section, the notion of index is formally introduced, and a sound and complete set of inference rules for indexes exhibited. Finally, the interaction between index and functional dependencies is investigated.

Definition: Let U be a finite set of attributes. An *index (dependency)* over U is a nonempty string $A_1...A_k$ of attributes in U.

An index serves as a dependency in the following way:

Definition: A tuple sequence $S = u_1...u_n$ over U *satisfies* the index $A_1...A_m$ over U, denoted $S \models A_1...A_m$, if for all u_i and u_j in S, $i<j$, there exists k in $[0,m-1]$ such that $u_i[A_1...A_k] = u_j[A_1...A_k]$ and $u_i(A_{k+1})<u_j(A_{k+1})$. A sequence S satisfies a set Γ of indexes if S satisfies each index in Γ.

Clearly, if S satisfies $A_1...A_m$, then the tuples in S are sequenced lexicographically (in the order $A_1,...A_m$) by the content of the tuples.

S	A	B	C
	0	0	3
	0	1	3
	1	0	4

Figure 3-1: A Tuple Sequence

To illustrate the previous definition, consider the sequence S in Figure 3-1. Then S satisfies the indexes AB and ACB. However, S does not satisfy the index AC.

We now study the implication problem for indexes. First though we need the notion of the "shuffle" of two strings.

Notation: Let X= $A_1...A_m$ and Y= $B_1...B_n$ be strings of attributes. Let p= m+n. Then *shuffle(X,Y)* denote the set of all strings Z= $C_1...C_p$ for which there exists two subsequences $i_1,...,i_m$ and $j_1,..j_n$ of 1,...p such that X= $C_{i_1}...C_{i_m}$, Y= $C_{j_1}...C_{j_n}$ and $\{i_1,...i_m\} \cup \{j_1,...,j_n\} = \{1,...p\}$.

We now have:

Definition: Let IR be the following set of rules.

I1: **If X is an index, then XA is an index;**

I2: **If X and Y are indexes, then shuffle(X,Y') is a set of indexes for every prefix Y' of Y; and**

I3: **If XAYAZ is an index, then XAYZ is an index.**

Our soundness and completeness result is:

Theorem 3.1: IR is sound and complete for proving implication of indexes. □

Functional dependencies play a major role in database design. It turns out that functional dependencies and indexes interact in various ways.

We start by presenting the concept of FD within the context of tuple sequences.

Definition: Let U be a finite set of attributes. A *functional dependency* (FD) over U is a formal expression X->Y where X and Y are subsets of U. A sequence S over U satisfies an FD X->Y over U, denoted S $\models$ X->Y, if for all tuples u and u′ in S, u[X] = u′[X] implies u[Y] = u′[Y]. An FD X-> U over U is also called a key dependency.

We now exhibit a strong connection between indexes and key dependencies.

Proposition 3.2: Let S be a duplicate-free sequence over U. Then S satisfies the key dependency X->U iff there exists a permutation of S which satisfies the index X. □

We next turn to inference rules for FDs and indexes taken together.

Besides the three classical inference rules for FDs (F1,F2,F3) [BFH] and the three rules for indexes, we need three "mixed rules".

IF1: If X is an index, then X->U;

IF2: If X' ->A, X'⊆X and XAY is an index then XY is an index; and

IF3: If X' ->A, X'⊆X and XY is an index then XAY is an index.

Now we have:

Theorem 3.3: The set {I1,I2,I3,F1,F2,F3,IF1,IF2,IF3} is sound and complete for proving implication of FDs and indexes. □

We conclude this section with a result which states the existence of the analogue for tuple sequences of Armstrong relation.

Theorem 3.4: Let Γ be a set of indexes and FDs. Then Γ is closed under {I1,I2,I3,F1,F2,F3,IF1,IF2,IF3} iff there exists a sequence S which satisfies each index and FD in Γ and no other index or FD. □

4. INDEX SATISFACTION

We briefly examine two algorithmic questions related to indexes. The first one is: How difficult is it to check whether a given sequence satisfies a particular index? The second is: How difficult is it to find a minimal index for a sequence?

The answer to the first question is given by:

Theorem 4.1: Let U be a set of attributes, S a sequence over U and X an index over U. Then the problem of whether or not S satisfies X can be solved in $O(|S|.|X|.|U|)$.

Proof: (sketch) We first show that a sequence S satisfies an index X iff uu' satisfies X for each two consecutive tuples u and u' in S. Then we prove uu' $\models$ X, if the word X belongs to the regular expression E^*LU^* where E= {A in U/ u(A)=u'(A)}, and L= {A in U/ u(A)<u'(A)}. □

We proved that index satisfaction can be decided in polynomial time. However finding a minimal index is NP-complete as shown in the next theorem. First we define the notion of minimal index.

Definition: Let S be a sequence. Then an index X is *minimal for* S if S $\models$ X, and $|X| \leq |Y|$ for each index Y such that S $\models$ Y.

Now we have:

Theorem 4.2: The problem of finding a minimal index for a sequence is NP-complete.

Proof: (sketch) The proof that it is NP involves some regular language manipulation, and uses the result [SM] that the problem of determining whether two regular expressions represent the same language is in NP.

The proof that it is complete is done by reduction to the Hitting Set Problem [K]. □

5. INDEX FAMILIES

In this section, we examine the effect of projection and join on sequences which satisfy a given set of indexes. To do this, we use the concept of an index family.

Definition: Let Γ be a finite set of indexes over U. Then the index family defined by Γ, denoted SAT(U,Γ), is the set of all sequences over U satisfying Γ.

In Section 2, projection and join were defined for sequences. Those mappings are now extended to families of sequences.

Notation: Let F, G be families of sequences over U, and W, respectively, and V⊆U. Then $\Pi_V(F) = \{\Pi_V(S) \mid S \text{ in } F\}$ and $F \bowtie G = \{S \bowtie S' \mid S \text{ in } F, S' \text{ in } G\}$.

It is easily seen that the projection of an index family is not, in general, an index family. (For instance, let F= SAT(AB,{AB}). Then $\Pi_A(F)$ is not an index family.) Indeed, to characterize the projection of an index family, we need to introduce the concept of weak index.

Definition: A *weak-index* (*dependency*) over U is a (possibly empty) string X of attributes in U, and is denoted w(X).

The corresponding notion of satisfaction is given by:

Definition: Let S be a sequence over U and w(X) a weak-index over U. If $X = \epsilon$ (the empty string) then S *satisfies* w(X). If $X \neq \epsilon$ then S *satisfies* w(X) iff for all tuples u_i and u_j in S, $i<j$, either $u_i[X] = u_j[X]$ or $u_i u_j \models X$ (i.e. $u_i u_j$ satisfies the index X).

The concepts of implication and SAT are extended to sets of indexes and weak-indexes together, in the obvious way.

Now we have:

Theorem 5.1: The projection of a family defined by a set of indexes and weak-indexes is also a family defined by a set of indexes and weak-indexes. □

We now consider the join of two index families. We shall restrict our attention to the join of two index families, each of which is defined by one index. (The general case is more complicated, and will not be addressed here.)

It turns out that the join of two index families SAT(U,X) and SAT(V,Y) satisfies the join dependency $\bowtie\langle U,V\rangle$, and the index dependency XY. Indeed we have:

Theorem 5.2: Let F= SAT(U,X) and G= SAT(V,Y) be two index families. Then $F \bowtie G$ is a family defined by index and join dependencies iff

a. $U \cap V \subseteq \{A \text{ in } X\} \cap \{A \text{ in } Y\}$, or

b. $\{A \text{ in } X\} = \{A \text{ in } Y\}$.

Furthermore, if $F \bowtie G$ is a family defined by index and join dependencies, then $F \bowtie G = \{S \text{ over } U \mid S \models \bowtie(U,V) \text{ and } S \models \ XY\}$. □

REFERENCES

[ACGV] S. Abiteboul, M-O Cordier, S. Gamerman and A. Verroust, Querying and Filtering Formated Files, Proceedings of Intern. Conf. on Database Machine (1983).

[AG] S. Abiteboul and S. Ginsburg, Tuple Sequences and Indexes, University of Southern California, Technical Report #83-205.

[Ar] W. W. Armstrong, Dependency Structure of Database Relationships, Proceedings IFIP74, North-Holland (1974), p. 580-583.

[AS] M. M. Astrahan et al., System R: A Relational Approach to Data Base Management, ACM TODS, Vol. 1 (1976), p. 97-137.

[BFH] C. Beeri, R. Fagin and J. H. Howard, A Complete Axiomatization for Functional and Multivalued Dependencies in Database Relations, ACM SIGMOD International Symposium on Management of Data (1977), p. 47-61.

[DKG] U. Dayal, N. Goodman and R. Katz, An Extended Relational Algebra with Control over Duplicate Elimination, Proceedings of the ACM Symposium on Principles of Database Systems (1982), p. 117-123.

[K] R. M. Karp, Reducibility among Combinatorial Problems, in Complexity of Computer Applications, ed. R. E. Miller and J. W. Thatcher, Plenum Press, New York, 1972, p. 85-104.

[Sh] D. W. Shipman, The Functional Data Model and the Data Language DAPLEX, ACM TODS, Vol. 6 (1981), p. 140-173.

[SM] L. J. Stockmeyer and A. E. Meyer, Word Problems Requiring Exponential Time, Proceedings of the Fifth Annual ACM Symposium on Theory of Computing (1973), p. 1-9.

[S] M. Stonebraker et al., The design and implementation of INGRES, ACM TODS, Vol. 1 (1976), p. 189-222.

[SK] M. Stonebraker and J. Kalash, Timber: A Sophisticated Relation Browser, Proceedings of the Eighth International Conference on Very Large Data Bases, Mexico City (1982), p. 1-10.

THE COMPLEXITY OF CUBICAL GRAPHS
(Extended Abstract)

Foto Afrati, Christos H. Papadimitriou *, and George Papageorgiou
National Technical University of Athens

1. Introduction

Suppose that we are given a finite automaton, such as the one shown in Figure 1. We may wish to assign a *bit vector* of some fixed length to each state of the automaton; such encoding of the states is desirable in connection to applications of finite automata to communication protocols, for example [Pa]. We may encounter the following problem, though: If we assign bit vectors to states arbitrarily, we may end up with an automaton in which transitions from one state to the next entail the change of several positions in the bit vector (e.g., to go from state 0010 to 1001 in Figure 1, three positions must be changed). Ideally, we would like to obtain an assignment in which adjacent states differ in *only one* position. This is not always possible, though. For example, the automaton in Figure 1 can have no such assignment (for a variety of reasons to become evident soon). In particular, for such an assignment to be possible, the underlying graph of the automaton (with directions and labels ignored) must be a subgraph of some *cube*. Recall that a cube C_n is the graph with nodes the elements of $\{0,1\}^n$, and an edge between two nodes whenever the Hamming distance of the corresponding bit vectors is one.

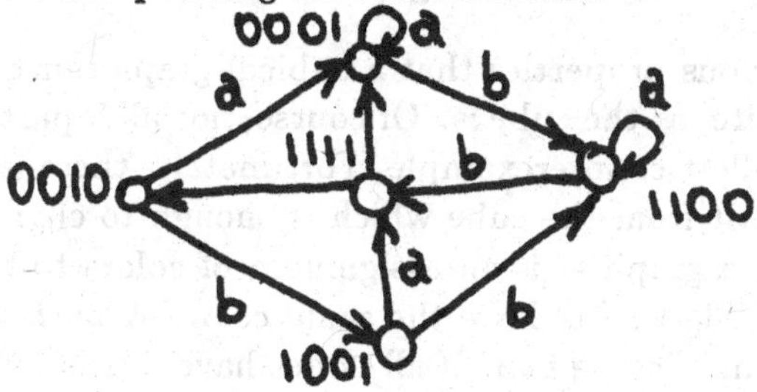

Fig. 1

We call a graph *cubical* if it is the subgraph of some cube C_n. If G is cubical, then the *dimension* of G is the smallest n such that G is a subgraph of C_n. Cubical graphs have been studied in the past [GG] in relation to isometric embeddings (see also [Dj]). Also, Czechoslovakian researchers had been independently attacking this problem [HL1, HL2, HM, Ha, Ne]**. These latter papers deal mainly with embedding trees in the cube (a question considered in our Section 4).

* Also, Stanford University

** These references were pointed out to us by the referee. We had no chance to look them up, and thus our reporting on these references is based on the information given to us by the referee

In the next section we establish a connection between cubical graphs and a restricted form of edge coloring. (A version of the same, rather straight-forward, characterization appears in [HM].) It follows from this characterization that a graph is cubical if and only if its biconnected components are. We also establish an upper bound for the dimension of a biconnected cubical graph. For general graphs, Garey and Graham had shown that the dimension is at most $|V|-1$, and that this is the best possible (the star is an example establishing this). We show that, for *biconnected* graphs, the bound is $\lfloor |V|/2 \rfloor$ and it is the best possible.

Can we test whether a graph is cubical in polynomial time? In section 3, we show that testing for cubicality is NP-complete, thus verifying a suspicion implicit in [GG]. Our proof involves a rather complicated reduction from the problem of exact cover with sets [GJ].

We also study the special case of trees. All trees are cubical, but calculating the dimension is non-trivial. We can calculate the dimension of full binary trees, and generalize to any full regular tree. These results were first proved in [HL1, HL2]. For general trees, however, there is no obvious way for calculating the dimension. In fact, there is an alarmingly exponential gap between the lower bound ($\log |V|$) and the upper bound ($|V|-1$) for the dimension of a tree. We give an approximation algorithm which embeds a tree into a cube with dimension at most the *square* of the true dimension of the tree. We conjecture that calculating the dimension of a tree is NP-complete.

2. Cubical Graphs and Edge Coloring

There are some obvious properties that a cubical graph must have. For example, it must be bipartite, as the cube is. Of course, not all bipartite graphs are cubical $-K_{2,3}$ is the smallest counterexample. Fortunately, there is one property that cubical graphs inherit from the cube which is enough to characterize them.

An *edge coloring* of a graph G is an assignment of colors to the edges of G so that no two adjacent edges of G have the same color. A *path* is a connected set of edges with maximum degree two. If all nodes have degree two or zero, the path is called a *cycle*. Given an edge coloring and a path, we call the path *even* if all colors appear an even number of times in the path. Finally, call an edge coloring *proper* if it has the following property: A path is even with respect to it if and only if it is a cycle. A version of the following characterization of cubical graphs was first shown in [HM]:

Theorem 1. A graph is cubical iff it has a proper coloring.

Sketch. Think of the color of an edge e as the direction of e when seen as an edge of the cube. The "only if" part follows. For the "if" part, any proper edge coloring suggests an embedding.•

Corollary. A graph is cubical iff all its biconnected components are.

Proof. Consider proper colorings of all biconnected components. Now change the names of the colors so that none appears in two different components. Since no cycle contains two edges from different components, this is a proper coloring.•

In [GG] it was shown that any cubical graph $G(V, E)$ has dimension at most $|V| - 1$. We improve this for biconnected graphs —of interest because of the Corollary . The new bound is $\lfloor |V|/2 \rfloor$. It is the best possible (see Figure 2).

Theorem 2. Let $G(V, E)$ be a biconnected, cubical graph. The dimension of G is at most $\lfloor |V|/2 \rfloor$.

Proof. We assume that the cubical graph has already been edge-colored as per Theorem 1. If we delete any color of a cubical graph (that is, delete all edges colored this way in the edge coloring of Theorem 1), it is easy to see that the graph is disconnected (since the cube is). Also, none of the components formed can be trivial, i.e., a single point (this is because the coloring is proper and the graph biconnected).

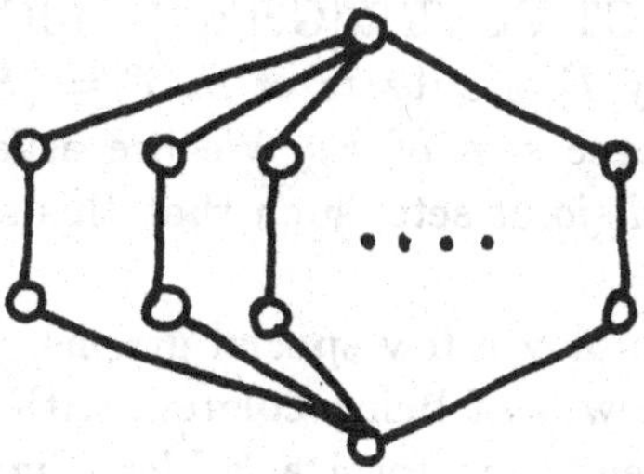

Fig. 2

So, after deleting one color, we have two nontrivial components. We shall continue deleting colors so that (a) two new components are formed with each deletion, and (b) there are at least two nontrivial components. More specifically, we choose a component C. Since the graph is biconnected, and C is, by induction, not the only nontrivial component, we can find a cycle (in the original graph) visiting C and some other component. In fact, unless all components are stars (which case is handled separately below), we can find a cycle such that its intersection with C is a path that is not a *twig* (a twig is a path of length two whose endpoints have degree one in C). This is done simply by picking an edge that is not adjacent to a degree-one node, and a cycle through this edge and an edge of another component. If the cycle re-enters C, we can pick the first and last point of C visited, and replace the intermediate path by a path in C.

Now, there must be a color that appears an odd number of times on that path. If the path has length three or more, we can assume that this color is not at one of the ends. Deleting this color creates at least two new components (it splits C, and it splits the other component on which this color must appear to balance its odd occurrences on C), and at least two of them are nontrivial. The latter fact follows from the fact that, if the path is longer than three, then the two outermost undeleted edges are in different components, and if it has length two, it is not a twig.

If all components are stars, then a simpler argument works. There has to be more than one nontrivial component, because the edges of the star all have different colors, and thus the necessary cycle through each must pass through another star. Certainly two new components are formed with each color deletion.•

3. NP-Completeness

We are interested in the complexity of the following problem:

CUBICAL GRAPHS: "Given a graph, is it cubical? "

Theorem 3. CUBICAL GRAPHS is NP-complete.

Sketch. We reduce EXACT COVER [GJ] to CUBICAL GRAPHS. In this problem we are given a family F of subsets of S, $F = \{S_1, \ldots, S_n\}$, with each element in S appearing in three sets of F. We are asked whether there is a subfamily of F consisting of *disjoint* sets, such that this subfamily covers all of S.

In our construction we employ a few special graphs. For example the *rectangle* (Figure 3a) has a single way of being colored, with opposite sides having the same color. It can be extended to form a *ladder* (Figure 3b), which can be colored using one color on each "step", and using some combination of colors on the remaining edges, as long as edges at the same height are colored the same. Ladders will be used to propagate colors across the graph. We represent a ladder with, say, five steps as in Figure 3c. On the other hand the *hexagon* (Figure 3d) has three essential ways of beeing colored, depending on whether edge x, y or z will agree with edge a. Three colors must be used.

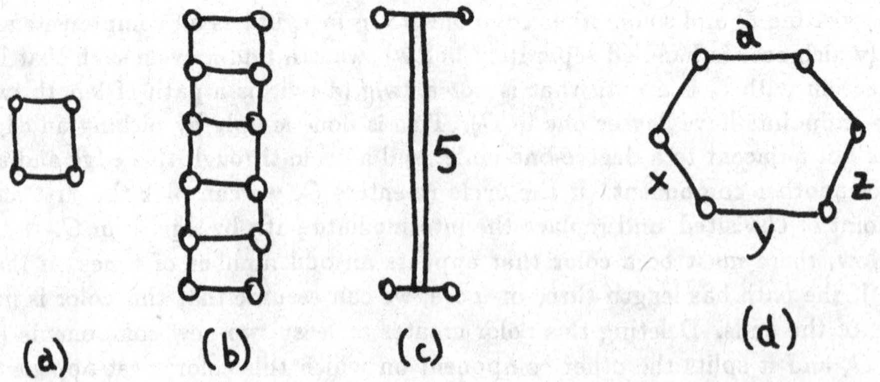

Fig. 3

Our construction uses these graphs (the reader may want to follow the illustration in Figure 4). For each element of S in the EXACT COVER problem we have a separate copy of the hexagon. The upper edges of the hexagons are connected by rectangles as shown in Figure 4, and thus all have the same color. Suppose that a hexagon corresponds to an element x; the three lower edges of the hexagon corresponds to the three sets to which x belongs. If two such edges, belonging to different hexagons, correspond to the same set S_j, then they are connected by ladders, so that they get the same color. The lengths of these ladder graphs are prescribed in detail in the following way. Consider any two such edges to be connected (the edges marked in Figure 4). There are two paths connecting a vertex of one to a vertex of the other, and not passing through the two edges in question, nor through any of the top edges of the hexagons (the heavy line in Figure 4). The length of the ladder is going to be the length of one of these paths, plus two. Once all thses ladders are placed, the construction is complete.

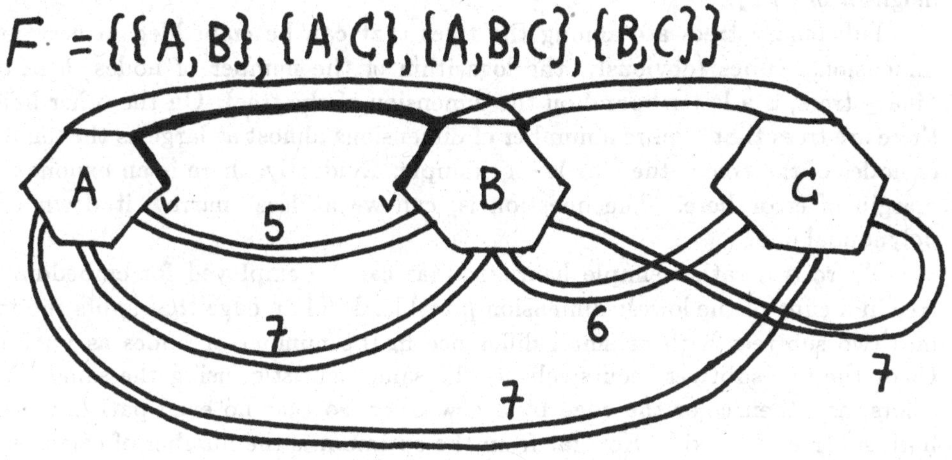

Fig. 4

The argument is that the given instance has an exact cover iff the graph constructed is cubical. Suppose that the graph is cubical. Then the top edges of the hexagons all take the same color, say 0, and so does one of the three lower edges of the hexagon. We say that a set S_j is in the cover iff its edges get the 0 color (because of the ladders, if one does, then all do). It follows that all elements are contained in one set in the cover, and so this is indeed an exact cover.

Suppose now that an exact cover exists. We shall construct a proper edge-coloring based on this exact cover. If set S_j is in the cover, then all edges corresponding to S_j take color 0, otherwise, they take color j. The remaining edges of the hexagon are colored accordingly, except that the top edges are all colored 0. It is very non-trivial, however, to show that the coloring is proper, with respect to cycles in which more than one ladder participates. The details will be supplied in the final version.•

4. The Dimension of Trees

All trees are cubical (since they have no cycles, give each edge a different color). The problem here is to minimize the dimension. This does not seem easy to do, and we conjecture that it is also NP-complete. For full binary trees however, the following result can be obtained by an explicit non-trivial construction.

Theorem 4. A full binary tree with height h has dimension $h + 2$.•

This result was first shown in [HL1]. Mike Paterson has an interesting extension of this Theorem [Pat]; namely, one can embed *two* full binary trees of height h in C_{h+2}.

Full binary trees are among the trees that can be embedded in very low-dimensional cubes (obviously, the logarithm of the number of nodes, h in full binary trees, is a lower bound on the dimension of the tree). On the other hand, there are trees that require a number of dimensions almost as large as the number of nodes of the tree —the star is an example. Evidently, there is an exponential margin of error here. The question is, can we at least narrow it down to a polynomial one?

There is a rather simple heuristic that can be employed for embedding a tree in a cube of the lowest dimension possible: Find an edge that splits the tree into two subtrees with as small difference in the number of nodes as possible. Color the two subtrees recursively by the same heuristic, using the same set of colors, and then color the edge by a new color, so that no even path involving both subtrees can exist. How far from the optimum is the number of colors used this way?

Theorem 5. The above heuristic applied on a tree with dimension k uses at most k^2 colors.

Sketch. There is always an edge that divides the tree into two subtrees of sizes with ratio at most $d - 1$, where d is the maximum degree of the tree. If $C(n)$ is the worst-case behavior of the heuristic on trees with n nodes, $C(n)$ obeys the following equations:

$$C(2) = 1$$

$$C(n) < C\left(\frac{n \times d}{d+1}\right) + 1$$

where d is the largest degree of the tree, and thus,

$$C(n) < d \times log(n)$$

However the dimension is upper bounded by both factors at the right hand side of the latter inequality.•

REFERENCES

[Dj]: D. J. Djocovic, Distance-preserving subgraphs of hypercubes, *J. Combinatorial Theory Ser. B 14* (1973), 263-267.

[GG]:M. R. Garey & R. L. Graham, On cubical graphs, *J. Combinatorial Theory 18* (1973), 263-267.

[GJ]: M. R. Garey & D. S. Johnson, *Computers and Intractability : A guide to the theory of NP-completeness*, Freeman, San Francisco, 1979.

[Ha]: I. Havel, Embedding graphs in undirected and directed cubes, *Proc. Conf. Lagow* (1981), Poland.

[HL1]: I. Havel & P. Liedl, Embedding the dichotomic tree into the cube, *Cas Pest. Mat. 97* (1972), 201-205.

[HL2]: I.Havel & P. Liebl, Embedding the polytomic tree into the n-cube, *Cas Pest. Mat. 98* (1973), 307-314.

[HM]: I. Havel & J. Moravel, B-valuation of graphs, *Czech. Math. J. 22* (1972), 338-351.

[Ne]: L. Nebesky, On cubes and dichotomic trees, *Cas. Pest. Mat. 99* (1974), 164-167.

[Pa]: G. Papageorgiou, PH. D. Thesis, National Technical University of Athens, in preparation.

[Pat]: M.S. Paterson, Private Communication, March 1984.

P-GENERIC SETS.

Klaus Ambos-Spies
Hans Fleischhack
Hagen Huwig
Lehrstuhl Informatik II
Universität Dortmund
D-4600 Dortmund 50

ABSTRACT. We introduce the notion of a p-generic set. P-generic sets automatically have all properties which can be enforced by usual diagonalizations over polynomial time computable sets and functions. We prove that there are recursive - in fact exponential time computable - p-generic sets. The existence of p-generic sets in NP is shown to be oracle dependent, even under the assumption that $P \neq NP$.

1. INTRODUCTION.

In recent publications structural properties of recursive sets like p-immunity, non-p-selectivity, non-p-mitoticity have been studied. These properties have in common that no polynomial time computable set has any of these properties. So the existence of a set with one of these structural properties in the class NP of non-deterministically polynomial time computable sets would separate P from NP. The existence of recursive sets which enjoy some of these properties has been proved by diagonalization arguments. In some cases it has been shown that the existence of such sets in NP is oracle dependent.

In this paper we formally characterize a class of diagonalizations over the classes P and PF of polynomial time computable sets and functions, respectively, called p-standard diagonalizations. Usual diagonalization arguments, like those employed for ensuring the above mentioned properties, prove to be covered by our formal notion. As we show there exist - in fact exponential time computable - sets, here called p-generic, which automatically have all properties enforcable by p-standard diagonalizations.

It turns out that the question whether p-generic sets exist inside NP is oracle dependent: We prove this by constructing recursive oracles A and B such that $P^A \neq NP^A$, $P^B \neq NP^B$ and there is a p^A-generic set in NP^A but NP^B contains no p^B-generic set. For properties Q enforcable by diagonalization over P this yields a new method for proving the existence of an oracle A such that some set in NP^A fulfills Q^A: to ensure this it will suffice to show that in the unrelativized case Q is enforcable by a p-standard diagonalization and that this fact relativizes.

Finally, we show that p-standard diagonalizations in general do not suffice for diagonalizing over polynomial time bounded Turing reductions. Our diagonalization concept can be extended, however, to cover such diagonalizations too. Again we can construct recursive sets having all properties enforcable by these more general diagonalization arguments. Due to the more involved diagonalizations here, however, the sets we construct can be recognized only in double exponential time.

Caused by lack of space most of the proofs are dropped throughout this paper. They can be found (together with further results) in [2].

Our study of p-generic sets has been inspired by genericity notions for recursively enumerable sets introduced by C.Jockusch [5] and W.Maass [7].

2. PRELIMINARIES.

Lower case letters k,m,n,x,y,z stand for elements of $\mathbb{N}$, the set of nonnegative integers. $\Sigma = \{0,1\}$. $\sigma,\tau,\ldots$ denote strings i.e. elements of Σ^*, capital letters A,B,C,... stand for recursive subsets of Σ^*. A set A is called tally if $A \subseteq \{0\}^*$. $|\sigma|$ is the length of σ, and, for $n < |\sigma|$, $\sigma(n)$ is the (n+1)st component of σ, i.e. $\langle i_0,\ldots,i_{k-1}\rangle(n) = i_n$. $\sigma * \tau$ is the concatenation of σ and τ. We say σ extends τ if $\sigma = \tau*\eta$ for some $\eta\varepsilon\Sigma^*$.

We identify a set and its characteristic function; i.e. $\sigma\varepsilon A$ iff $A(\sigma) = 1$ and $\sigma\notin A$ iff $A(\sigma) = 0$. $A{\upharpoonright}n = \{\sigma:\sigma\varepsilon A \& |\sigma|<n\}$ denotes the restriction of A to arguments of length $<n$. For tally A, we interpret $A{\upharpoonright}n$ as string, i.e. we let $A{\upharpoonright}n = \sigma$ where $|\sigma| = n$ and $\forall k < n(\sigma(k) = A(0^k))$. We write $A \overset{*}{=} B$ iff $(A-B) \cup (B-A)$ is finite.

P(NP) is the class of subsets of Σ^* which are (non)deterministically computable in polynomial time. PF is the class of deterministically in polynomial time computable functions from Σ^* to Σ^*. $\{P_n: n\varepsilon\mathbb{N}\}$ and $\{f_n:n\varepsilon\mathbb{N}\}$ are effective enumerations of P and PF, resp. $\{M_n^X:n\varepsilon\mathbb{N}\}$ is an effective enumeration of the deterministic polynomial time oracle machines (with oracle X). We also use M_n^X to denote the set accepted by M_n^X.

A is polynomial time many-one (p-m) reducible to B, $A \leq_m^p B$, if, for some n, $\forall\sigma(A(\sigma) = B(f_n(\sigma)))$. A is polynomial time Turing (p-T) reducible to B, $A \leq_T^p B$, if $A = M_n^B$ for some n. We write $A =_{m(T)}^p B$ iff $A \leq_{m(T)}^p B$ and $B \leq_{m(T)}^p A$. The p-m(T)-degree of A is denoted by $\deg_{m(T)}^p A$. P^A is the set of deterministic polynomial time sets relative to A, i.e. $P^A = \{B:\exists n(B = M_n^A)\}$.

3. DIAGONALIZATIONS OVER POLYNOMIAL TIME COMPUTABLE SETS AND FUNCTIONS.

The goal of this section is to give a formal characterization of a class of diagonalization arguments over polynomial time computable sets and functions, which subsumes the common diagonalizations over P.

For this sake we analyze three typical constructions by diagonalizations, namely that of

i) a recursive set A_1 which is not in P,

ii) a recursive *p-immune* set A_2, i.e. an infinite set A_2 which does not contain an infinite subset which is in P([3],[4]), and

iii) a recursive *non-p-m-autoreducible* set A_3, i.e. a set which cannot be non-trivially p-m-reduced to itself ([1]; to be more precise:

$\forall f \varepsilon PF(\forall \sigma(f(\sigma) \neq \sigma) \Rightarrow \text{not } A_3 \leq^P_m A_3 \text{ via } f))$.

The sets A_i, i = 1,2,3, are effectively constructed in stages, where at the end of stage s $A_i \uparrow s$ is determined. The latter and effectivity of the construction imply that A_i is recursive. The constructions have in common that the condition we have to satisfy is broken down in to an infinite list of simpler requirements, namely

R^1_e: $A_1 \neq P_e$,

R^2_e: $|P_e| = \infty \Rightarrow P_e \not\subseteq A_2$, and

R^3_e: $\forall\sigma(f_e(\sigma) \neq \sigma) \Rightarrow \text{not } A_3 \leq^P_m A_3 \text{ via } f_e$

($e \varepsilon \mathbb{N}$), respectively. (In case of A_2 in addition we have to make sure that A_2 is infinite. This can be done for instance by simultaneously meeting requirements of the form $A_2 \neq P_e$ which ensure $A_2 \notin P$ and thus that A_2 is infinite. Since we handle this type of requirements for the set A_1 and since there is no problem in merging two lists of requirements, in the following we will ignore the task of making A_2 infinite.)

The fact that A_1 meets requirement R^1_e can be expressed as follows. Let

$C^1_e = \{X\uparrow s: \exists\sigma(|\sigma| < s \;\&\; X(\sigma) \neq P_e(\sigma))\}$.

Then A_1 meets R^1_e iff $A_1\uparrow s \varepsilon C^1_e$ for some s. Similarly, A_i meets R^i_e, i = 2,3, iff the premise of R^i_e is false or $A_i\uparrow s\varepsilon C^i_e$ for some s, where

$C^2_e = \{X\uparrow s: \exists\sigma(|\sigma| < s \;\&\; X(\sigma) = 0 \;\&\; P_e(\sigma) = 1)\}$

and

$C^3_e = \{X\uparrow s: \exists\sigma,\tau(|\sigma|,|\tau| < s \;\&\; f_e(\sigma) = \tau \;\&\; X(\sigma) \neq X(\tau))\}$.

So, by determining an initial segment of A_i in an appropriate way, we can guarantee that A_i meets the requirement R^i_e. Moreover, assuming that the premise of R^i_e is correct, there are infinitely many stages s such that for given $A_i\uparrow s$ there is a 1-step extension $A_i\uparrow s+1$ of $A_i\uparrow s$ with $A_i\uparrow s+1\varepsilon C^i_e$ (Intuitively speaking: either the premise of R^i_e fails, whence R^i_e is met trivially, or in the course of the construction of A_i there are infinitely many chances to ensure R^i_e by appropiately extending the so far enumerated part of A_i by length 1). For R^1_e this is obvious, since, for any s, any $A\uparrow s$ and any string σ of length s, we obtain an extension $A\uparrow s+1 \varepsilon C^1_e$ of $A\uparrow s$ by choosing $A\uparrow s+1$ so that $A(\sigma) \neq P_e(\sigma)$. For R^2_e we consider such s where, for some σ of length s, $P_e(\sigma) = 1$ and choose $A\uparrow s+1$ with $A\uparrow s+1(\sigma) = 0$. By premise of R^2_e, infinitely many such stages s exist. Finally, for R_e^3 consider stages s such that there are strings σ and τ with $\sigma \neq \tau, |\sigma| \leq |\tau| = s$ and $f_e(\sigma) = \tau$ or $f_e(\tau) = \sigma$ (Note that by premise of R_e^3 infinitely many such stages s must exist). For given $A\upharpoonright s$ we then choose an extension $A\upharpoonright s+1$ such that $A\upharpoonright s+1(\sigma) \neq A\upharpoonright s+1(\tau)$ (In contrast to the extensions for R_e^1 and R_e^2, here the extension $A\upharpoonright s+1$ in general depends on the given initial segment $A\upharpoonright s$; namely in the cases where $|\sigma| < s$ and thus $A\upharpoonright s+1(\sigma)$ is determined by $A\upharpoonright s$).

We can conclude that A_i meets R_e^i $(i = 1,2,3)$ if

$$(3.1)\ \overset{\infty}{\exists} s \exists X\upharpoonright s+1\ (X\upharpoonright s+1 \text{ extends } A_i\upharpoonright s \text{ and } X\upharpoonright s+1 \varepsilon C_e^i) \Rightarrow \exists s (A_i\upharpoonright s \varepsilon C_e^i).$$

This fact is (implicitly) used in the usual construction of the sets A_i: At stage s+1 of the construction we choose $e \leq s$ minimal (if there is any) such that R_e^i is not yet met at stage s (i.e. $\nexists t \leq s(A_i\upharpoonright t\varepsilon C_e^i)$) and R_e^i can be ensured at stage s+1 (i.e. there is some $X\upharpoonright s+1$ extending $A_i\upharpoonright s$ such that $X\upharpoonright s+1\varepsilon C_e^i$). Then we let $A_i\upharpoonright s+1 = X\upharpoonright s+1$ for such an extension thus meeting R_e^i. So, for given e and for s_e such that

$$\forall e' < e(\exists t(A_i\upharpoonright t\varepsilon C_{e'}^i) \Rightarrow \exists t < s_e(A_i\upharpoonright t\varepsilon C_{e'}^i)),$$

at any stage $s > s_e$ R_e^i will have highest priority for being met in the above described way. Hence, if the premise of (3.1) is correct, then, for some s, $A_i\upharpoonright s\varepsilon C_e^i$. So (3.1) is satisfied for each e eventually thus implying that A_i has the desired property.

The fact that a property which can be enforced by diagonalization can be ensured by an infinite list of conditions of the form (3.1) is not typical for diagonalizations over P but it is true for diagonalizations over any complexity class. What is typical for diagonalizations over P is the fact that the classes C_e^i in (3.1) are of low complexity, namely, for appropriate encodings, $C_e^i \varepsilon P$. We can make this more precise using the following observation: Sets A_i as above can be constructed within any given infinite recursive set B. In particular we can construct *tally* sets A_i with the above properties. Since for tally A we interpret initial segments $A\upharpoonright s$ of A as strings of length s (see §2), in case of tally sets A_i the sets C_e^1, C_e^2 and C_e^3 can be written as

$$C_e^1 = \{\sigma : \exists n < |\sigma| (\sigma(n) \neq P_e(0^n))\}$$

$$C_e^2 = \{\sigma : \exists n < |\sigma| (\sigma(n) = 0 \ \&\ P_e(0^n) = 1)\}$$

$$C_e^3 = \{\sigma : \exists m,n < |\sigma| (f_e(0^m) = 0^n \ \&\ \sigma(m) \neq \sigma(n))\}$$

and (3.1) changes to

$$(3.1')\ \overset{\infty}{\exists} s \exists j \leq 1\ (A_i\upharpoonright s * \langle j\rangle \varepsilon C_e^i) \Rightarrow \exists s (A_i\upharpoonright s \varepsilon C_e^i).$$

Now one can easily check that $C_e^1, C_e^2, C_e^3 \varepsilon P$.

The above analysis of diagonalizations over P and PF leads us to the following definition.

3.1. Definition. A property $\mathcal{Q}$ can be enforced by a *p-standard diagonalization* if there is a sequence $\{C_e : e \in \mathbb{N}\}$ of polynomial time computable sets such that for any tally set A the following holds: If, for every $e \in \mathbb{N}$,

(3.2) $\overset{\infty}{\exists} s \exists i \leq 1 (A \upharpoonright s * \langle i \rangle \in C_e) \Rightarrow \exists s (A \upharpoonright s \in C_e)$

then A has property $\mathcal{Q}$.

The above given arguments show that being in P, p-immunity and non-p-m-autoreducibility can be enforced by p-standard diagonalizations. Some more examples of such properties will be given in §5. Note that by merging lists $\{C_e^1 : e \in \mathbb{N}\}$ and $\{C_e^2 : e \in \mathbb{N}\}$ to one list $\{C_e : e \in \mathbb{N}\}$ with $C_{2e} = C_e^1$ and $C_{2e+1} = C_e^2$, with two properties $\mathcal{Q}_1$ and $\mathcal{Q}_2$ also their conjunction $\mathcal{Q}_1$ & $\mathcal{Q}_2$ can be enforced by p-standard diagonalization (We have implicitly used this fact in the proof that p-immunity can be enforced by p-standard diagonalization).

In the next section we will show that there are recursive tally sets having *all* properties which can be enforced by p-standard diagonalizations. So in particular for any property $\mathcal{Q}$ which can be enforced by a p-standard diagonalization there is a recursive (tally) set having this property.

4. P-GENERIC SETS.

We now introduce the central notion of this paper.

4.1. Definition. A tally set A is *p-generic* if for every polynomial time computable set C

(4.1) $\overset{\infty}{\exists} s \exists i \leq 1 (A \upharpoonright s * \langle i \rangle \in C) \Rightarrow \exists s (A \upharpoonright s \in C)$.

If $A \upharpoonright s \in C$ then we say A *hits* C. The name p-genericity stems from a similarity between Definition 4.1 and the definition of a generic set for forcing notions in set theory.

P-genericity is the strongest property that can be ensured by p-standard diagonalization.

4.2. Proposition.

(i) P-genericity can be enforced by p-standard diagonalization.

(ii) If A is p-generic and $\mathcal{Q}$ can be enforced by p-standard diagonalization then A has property $\mathcal{Q}$.

Proof. (i) Choose $\{C_e : e \in \mathbb{N}\}$ to be the enumeration $\{P_e : e \in \mathbb{N}\}$ of P. (ii) Any set $\{C_e : e \in \mathbb{N}\}$ of polynomial time computable sets is contained in $\{P_e : e \in \mathbb{N}\}$.

Note that in particular no p-generic set can be in P, since - as mentioned in the preceding section - the property of being not in P can be enforced by a p-standard diagonalization.

We now show that p-generic sets actually exist.

4.3. Theorem. There is a recursive p-generic set.

Proof. We effectively construct a p-generic set A in stages. To make A p-generic it suffices to meet the requirements

$$R_e: \quad \exists^{\infty} s \, \exists i \leq 1 (A\upharpoonright s * \langle i \rangle \in P_e) \Rightarrow \exists s (A\upharpoonright s \in P_e) \quad (e \in \mathbb{N}).$$

At stage s+1 of the construction below we determine the value of $A(0^s)$. So, by the end of stage s, $A\upharpoonright s$ will be defined and can be used in the description of stage s+1.

We say R_e is *satisfied at (the end of) stage* s if, for some $t \leq s$, $A\upharpoonright t \in P_e$. Note that once R_e is satisfied at some stage it is satisfied at all later stages and R_e is met. Requirement R_e *requires attention at stage* s+1 if it is not satisfied at stage s and $A\upharpoonright s * \langle i \rangle \in P_e$ for some $i \leq 1$. If R_e requires attention at stage s+1 then at stage s+1 we can ensure that $A\upharpoonright s+1 \in P_e$ (and thus that R_e is satisfied) by choosing the appropriate value for $A(0^s)$. It might happen that at some stages more than one requirement requires attention. In this case we give the requirement with least index among the requirements requiring attention *highest priority* and ignore the other ones.

We now give the construction of A.

Stage 0. Do nothing.

Stage s+1. If no requirement R_e, $e \leq s$, requires attention then let $A(0^s) = 0$. Otherwise choose e and i minimal (in this order) such that R_e requires attention and $A\upharpoonright s * \langle i \rangle \in P_e$. Set $A(0^s) = i$ and say R_e is *active*.

This completes the construction.

Obviously the construction is effective and $A\upharpoonright s$ is defined by the end of stage s. So A is recursive. That the requirements R_e are met and thus that A is p-generic follows from the following claim.

Claim. For every e, R_e requires attention only finitely often and is met.

The claim is proved by induction on e. Fix e and, by inductive hypothesis, assume the claim correct for $e' < e$. Then we can choose s_0 such that no requirement $R_{e'}$, $e' < e$, requires attention after stage s_0. Now if R_e requires attention at some stage $s_1 > s_0$ then R_e becomes active at stage s_1 and - as pointed out above - is satisfied at all later stages. So R_e does not require attention after stage s_1.

To see that R_e ist met, w.l.o.g. assume that $\overset{\infty}{\exists} s \exists i \leq 1 (A\upharpoonright s * \langle i\rangle \in P_e)$. We have to show that R_e is satisfied at some stage and thus A hits P_e. But if this were not the case then R_e would require attention at infinitely many stages, a contradiction.

This completes the proof of the theorem.

5. PROPERTIES OF P-GENERIC SETS.

In this section we summarize some properties of p-generic sets. We first point out that p-genericity is invariant under finite variations and that the complement of a p-generic set relative to $\{0\}^*$ is p-generic too.

5.1. Theorem. Let A be p-generic. Then

(i) $\{0\}^* - A$ is p-generic

(ii) for any $B \subseteq \{0\}^*$ such that $B \overset{*}{=} A$, B is p-generic.

By (4.1), a p-generic set A hits any set $C \in \mathcal{P}$ if, for infinitely many initial segments $A\upharpoonright s$ of A, there are extensions $A\upharpoonright s * \langle i\rangle (i \leq 1)$ by length 1 which belong to C. As the following theorem shows this property of p-generic sets can be strengthened in two directions. First, A will still hit C if there infinitely often are extensions by any constant (finite) length in C; secondly, A will hit C not just once but infinitely often. Roughly speaking, the former shows that p-generic sets also have all properties enforcable by finitely iterated p-standard diagonalizations. So, by Proposition 4.2 (i), such iterated diagonalizations are not more powerful than simple p-standard diagonalizations.

5.2. Theorem. Let A be p-generic. Then for all $C \in \mathcal{P}$

$$(5.1)\quad \exists n \geq 1 \overset{\infty}{\exists} s \exists \sigma (|\sigma| \leq n \ \& \ A\upharpoonright s * \sigma \in C) \Rightarrow \overset{\infty}{\exists} s (A\upharpoonright s \in C).$$

Proof of Theorem 5.2. We prove by induction on n that for all $C \in \mathcal{P}$

$$(5.2)\quad \overset{\infty}{\exists} s \exists \sigma (|\sigma| = n \ \& \ A\upharpoonright s * \sigma \in C) \Rightarrow \overset{\infty}{\exists} s (A\upharpoonright s \in C)$$

holds.

n = 1. Fix $C \in \mathcal{P}$ and assume that the premise of (5.2) holds. Let

$$C_m = \{\sigma : |\sigma| \geq m \ \& \ \sigma \in C\} \quad (m \in \mathbb{N}).$$

Then $C_m \in \mathcal{P}$ and $\overset{\infty}{\exists} s \exists i \leq 1 (A\upharpoonright s * \langle i\rangle \in C_m)$. So, by p-genericity of A, A hits each C_m and thus A hits C infinitely often.

$n \to n + 1$. Fix C and assume

$$(5.3)\quad \overset{\infty}{\exists} s \exists \sigma (|\sigma| = n + 1 \ \& \ A\upharpoonright s * \sigma \in C).$$

To show that A hits C infinitely often, let

$$C' = \{\sigma : \exists i \leq 1 (\sigma * \langle i\rangle \in C)\}$$

Then $C' \varepsilon P$ and, by (5.3),

$$\overset{\infty}{\exists} s \, \exists \sigma (|\sigma| = n \,\&\, A{\uparrow}s * \sigma \varepsilon C')$$

So, by inductive hypothesis,

$$\overset{\infty}{\exists} s (A{\uparrow}s \varepsilon C'), \text{ i.e. } \overset{\infty}{\exists} s \, \exists i \leq 1 (A{\uparrow}s * \langle i \rangle \varepsilon C)$$

It follows, again by inductive hypothesis, that A hits C infinitely often.

We now turn to some examples of properties studied in the literature which can be enforced by p-standard diagonalizations. A set A is *p-selective* if there is a polynomial time computable function $f: \Sigma^* \times \Sigma^* \to \Sigma^*$ such that $\forall \sigma, \tau \varepsilon \Sigma^* \, (f(\sigma,\tau) \varepsilon \{\sigma,\tau\}$ and $(A \cap \{\sigma,\tau\} \neq \emptyset \Rightarrow f(\sigma,\tau) \varepsilon A))$ (cf. Selman [8]).

A is *p-m-mitotic* if

$$A =^p_m A \cap B =^p_m A \cap \overline{B}$$

for some $B \varepsilon P$; otherwise A is *non-p-m-mitotic* (cf. Ambos-Spies [1]).

5.3. Theorem. Let A be p-generic. Then

(i) A is p-immune

(ii) A is not p-selective

(iii) A is non-p-m-mitotic

(iv) A is non-p-m-autoreducible.

The following structural theorem on p-generic sets implies many properties of those sets.

5.4. Theorem. Let A be p-generic. Then, for any subset B of A, $A =^p_m B$ iff $A \overset{*}{=} B$.

Note that parts (i) and (iii) of Theorem 5.3 follow from Theorem 5.4. A further consequence of the theorem is that infinite p-splittings of a p-generic set yield p-m-incomparable sets.

5.5. Corollary. Let A be p-generic and B be a polynomial time computable set such that $A \cap B$ and $A \cap \overline{B}$ are infinite. Then $A \cap B$ and $A \cap \overline{B}$ have incomparable p-m-degrees.

Proof. By Theorem 5.4. and the fact that for $B \varepsilon P$ and any A,

$$\deg^p_m A = \deg^p_m (A \cap B) \cup \deg^p_m (A \cap \overline{B}).$$

P-generic sets can be used to distinguish various polynomial time reducibility notions as p-1-reducibility, p-m-reducibility and variants of p-truthtable reducibilities. (The definitions not given here can be found in Ladner et al. [6].)

5.6. Theorem. Let A be p-generic. Then

(i) $A \oplus A \not\leq^p_1 A$

(ii) $\overline{A} \not\leq^p_m A$

(iii) $C_n = \{0^k \mid \{0^{k \cdot n}, \ldots, 0^{k \cdot n+n-1}\} \cap A \neq \emptyset\} \not\leq^p_{(n-1)\text{-tt}} A, \; n \geq 2$

5.7. Corollary. (Ladner et al. [6])

$\leq^P_{tt} \not\Rightarrow \leq^P_{btt} \not\Rightarrow \leq^P_{(n+1)-tt} \not\Rightarrow \leq^P_{n-tt} \not\Rightarrow \leq^P_m \not\Rightarrow \leq^P_1 \quad (n \geq 1).$

6. ON THE COMPLEXITY OF P-GENERIC SETS.

The construction of a p-generic set in the proof of Theorem 4.3 can easily be modified to produce an exponential time computable p-generic set. On the other hand we can obtain arbitrarily complex p-generic sets; i.e. for any recursive set B there is a p-generic set A such that $A \not\leq^P_T B$. To construct such an A we just have to add the requirements

$\hat{R}_e : A \neq M_e^B$

to the construction in 4.3. These additional requirements, handled in the usual way, do not seriously interfere with the previous requirements.

We do not know whether - assuming $P \neq NP$ - p-generic sets exist in NP. We can show, however, that this question cannot be answered by a proof which relativizes. The notion of p-genericity is relativized in the usual way.

6.1. Definition. For any B, a tally set A is *p^B-generic* if, for every $C \in P^B$, (4.1) holds.

6.2. Theorem. There are recursive sets A and B such that
(i) $P^A \neq NP^A$ and there is a set in NP^A which is p^A-generic.
(ii) $P^B \neq NP^B$ and no NP^B-set is p^B-generic.

Theorem 6.2 provides a new approach to oracle dependence results. To show that the existence of sets with a certain property Q inside NP is oracle dependent, it suffices to show, that Q can be enforced by a p-standard diagonalization and that this fact relativizes. For instance, by relativizing Theorem 5.3, we obtain the following corollary.

6.3. Corollary. There are recursive sets A and C, such that $C \in NP^A$ and
(i) C is p^A-immune
(ii) C is not p^A-selective
(iii) C is non-p^A-m-mitotic
(iv) C is non-p^A-m-autoreducible.

7. LIMITS OF P-STANDARD DIAGONALIZATIONS AND STRONGLY P-GENERIC SETS.

Our notion of p-standard diagonalization covers the common diagonalizations over polynomial time computable sets and functions. In particular it subsumes diagonalizations over polynomial time bounded *many-one* reductions. It doesn't cover, however, diagonalizations over polynomial time bounded *Turing* reductions. The latter type of diagonalizations requires us to consider extensions of the set under construction of polynomial length not just ones of length 1 (or of constant length, cf. Theorem 5.2), as in the case of p-standard diagonalizations.

To give an example for this limitation on p-standard diagonalizations, we look at the analogue of p-m autoreducibility for p-Turing reducibility introduced in [1]. Call a set A *p-T-autoreducible* if, for some n, $\forall\sigma(A(\sigma) = M_n^{A-\{\sigma\}}(\sigma))$. Then neither p-T-autoreducibility nor the complementary property can be enforced by p-standard diagonalization.

7.1. Theorem. There are recursive p-generic sets A and B such that A is p-T-autoreducible but B is not.

We can extend our diagonalization notion, however, to cover diagonalizations over p-Turing reductions too.

7.2. Definition. (i) A property Q can be enforced by *generalized p-standard diagonalization* if there is a sequence $\{C_e : e\in\mathbb{N}\}$ of polynomial time computable sets such that for any tally set A the following holds: If, for every $e\in\mathbb{N}$

(7.1) $\exists$ polynomial p $\overset{\infty}{\exists} s \exists\sigma(|\sigma| \leq p(s)$ & $A\upharpoonright s * \sigma\in C_e) \Rightarrow \exists s(A\upharpoonright s\in C_e)$.

then A has property Q.

(ii) A tally set A is *strongly p-generic* if for every $C\in P$

(7.2) $\exists$ polynomial p $\overset{\infty}{\exists} s \exists\sigma(|\sigma| \leq p(s)$ & $A\upharpoonright s * \sigma\in C) \to \exists s(A\upharpoonright s\in C)$.

Like Proposition 4.2, strong p-genericity is the strongest property enforcable by a generalized p-standard diagonalization.

7.3. Theorem. The property of not being p-T-autoreducible can be enforced by a generalized p-standard diagonalization.

For more examples of properties involving p-T-reducibility which can be enforced by generalized p-standard diagonalizations we refer the reader to [2].

We conclude with the result that strongly p-generic sets exist.

7.4. Theorem. There is a recursive strongly p-generic set.

The proof of Theorem 7.4 is more involved than that for Theorem 4.3. So our construction only yields a strongly p-generic set computable in double exponential time.

Acknowledgements. We like to thank C.Jockusch, Jr., and J.Mohrherr for a conversation with the first author which was stimulating for this research.

REFERENCES.

[1] Ambos-Spies,K., P-mitotic sets, in: E.Börger, G.Hasenjaeger and D.Rödding, Eds., Logic and machines: Decision problems and complexity, SLNCS (to appear in 1984). Preprint: Techn. Report Nr. 167 (1983) Universität Dortmund.

[2] Ambos-Spies,K., Fleischhack,H., and Huwig,H., Diagonalizations over polynomial time computable sets, submitted for publication. Preprint: Techn. Report Nr. 177 (1984) Universität Dortmund.

[3] Benett,C.H. and J.Gill, Relative to a random oracle A, $P^A \neq NP^A \neq CO\text{-}NP^A$ with probability 1, SIAM Comp. 10 (1981) 96-113.

[4] Homer,S. and W.Maass, Oracle dependent properties of the lattice of NP-sets, TCS 24(1983) 279-289

[5] Jockusch, C., Notes on genericity for r.e. sets, handwritten notes.

[6] Ladner,R.E., Lynch,N.A., and Selman, A.L., A comparison of polynomial time reducibilities, TCS 1 (1975) 103-123.

[7] Maass, W., Recursively enumerable generic sets, J.Symb.Logic 47 (1982) 809-823.

[8] Selman,A.L., P-selective sets, tally languages, and the behaviour of polynomial time reducibilities on NP, Math. Systems Theory 13 (1979) 55-65.

FUNCTIONAL DEPENDENCIES AND DISJUNCTIVE EXISTENCE CONSTRAINTS IN DATABASE RELATIONS WITH NULL VALUES

Paolo Atzeni (*) and Nicola M. Morfuni (**)

(*) IASI-CNR. Viale Manzoni 30. 00185 Roma Italy.
(**) Dipartimento di Informatica e Sistemistica. Università di Roma
Via Buonarroti 12. 00185 Roma Italy.

1. INTRODUCTION

There is a general agreement in the database literature on the need for representing partial information in relations in order to increase their capacity and flexibility in capturing the semantics of the real world.

Much work has already been done on the subject (see, Zaniolo [1981] or Maier [1983] for a review): special values, called *null values* (or, simply, *nulls*) have been introduced and studied from various points of view. Unfortunately the results are not yet completely satisfactory: various interpretations have been proposed for nulls and some interesting properties have been shown for each, but no complete theory has yet been formulated for any of them.

In order to be actually useful, the nulls should have natural semantics and allow a generalization of the relational theory which preserves most of the important results in a straightforward manner. According to similar considerations, Zaniolo [1981,1982] has recently proposed a deeper study of the most primitive interpretation of nulls: the *no-information* interpretation, under which a null associated with an attribute in a tuple means that no information is available about that attribute for that tuple. This type of null is the most general, since it can be used to model every kind of missing or incomplete information, and its semantics is certainly simple and well understood. On the other hand, it does not allow any representation of knowledge at intermediate degrees between the no-information and the complete specification; but this price is largely compensated by the benefits gained.

The aim of this paper is the study, in this framework, of two meaningful classes of integrity constraints, functional dependencies and disjunctive existence constraints.

Integrity constraints play a crucial role in the design theory of relational databases and therefore their properties have been deeply investigated with regard to database relations without null values. In such a framework, *functional dependencies* (FDs) are the most natural and, as a consequence, studied class of integrity constraints. Recently, various authors (Vassiliou [1980], Lien [1982], Imielinski and Lipski [1983]) have considered FDs with regard to relations with null values (abbreviated NFDs). Only the treatment in Lien [1982] is suitable of application to null values under the no-information interpretation and we will therefore adopt it.

Disjunctive existence constraints (DECs) are a means to control the presence of null values in relations, as useful in modelling some real world situations. For example, as suggested even in Codd [1970], where the relational model was first proposed and the possibility of using null values briefly examined, null values should not be allowed in the primary key of any relation. Moreover, there may exist conceptual relationships between sets of attributes, relating the presence or absence of null values for some attributes to their presence or absence for some other attributes. Various ways of formalizing this concept have been proposed in the literature (Sciore [1980], Maier [1980], Goldstein [1981]). Among them, the DECs form a very general class, which include the *existence constraints* (EC, Maier [1980]) and was shown in Goldstein [1981] to be almost equivalent to that of *objects* (Sciore [1980]).

Sound and complete systems of inference rules for the derivation of NFDs, ECs and DECs have been proposed, respectively in Lien [1982], Maier [1980] and Goldstein [1981]. In this paper we study the inference rules for the joint class of NFDs and DECs, which, to the best of our knowledge, has never been addressed. The main result is that there can be no complete, finite set of rules for the class of NFDs and DECs, while such a set does exist for a larger class of constraints, which contains also a weaker version of functional dependency, called fictitious functional dependency. The analogous (but independent) result is then derived for the joint class of NFDs and ECs, which is contained in the above class.

2. BASIC CONCEPTS

Due to space limitations, we omit a review of terminology, introducing only the specific concepts and following, as long as possible, the notations of Ullman [1982] and Maier [1983].

Allowing the presence of nulls, a *tuple* over a set of attributes X is a mapping t which associates with each attribute A $\in$ X either a value of the domain of A or the null value $\emptyset$. A tuple t is *total on* A (or A-*total*) if t.A is not null and *total on* X (X-*total*) if it is total on each attribute A $\in$ X. If a tuple is total on all the attributes and so null-free it is said *total*.

2.1. *Functional Dependencies and Null Values*

In the classical theory, a *functional dependency* (FD) is a statement f: X $\longrightarrow$ Y, where X,Y are sets of attributes. A null-free relation r over a scheme R(U) (with XY $\subseteq$ U) satisfies f (we say also that f holds in r) if for each pair of tuples $t_1,t_2 \in r$ such that $t_1.X=t_2.X$ then $t_1.Y=t_2.Y$.

According to Lien [1982], a *functional dependency with nulls* (NFD) X $\longrightarrow$ Y holds in a relation r over a scheme R(U) (with XY $\subseteq$ U) if for each pair of X-total tuples $t_1,t_2 \in r$, such that $t_1.X=t_2.X$ then $t_1.Y = t_2.Y$.

For null-free relations the definition of NFD reduces to that of FD and so it is a correct generalization of the concept. Moreover, it is coherent with the no-information interpretation. In fact, tuples with nulls in attributes in X cannot cause a violation of a dependency X $\longrightarrow$ Y: the nulls mean that no-information is available about those attributes. On the other hand, two X-total tuples, t_1,t_2 such that $t_1.X= t_2.X$ and t_2 is A-total while t_1 is not, violate a dependency X $\longrightarrow$ Y with A $\in$ Y: the first tuple indicates that no-information is available about the value for A associated with $t_1.X$, while the second indicates that the value for A associated with $t_2.X=t_1.X$ does exist, and this violates the natural definition of functional dependency that if the values for X are the same for two tuples, both tuples must contain the same information for the attributes in Y.

Useful concepts in dependency theory are those of implication and inference rule. Given a set of constraints that hold in a relation it is often possible to deduce that other constraints also hold in that relation. A constraint i is *implied* by a set of constraints I on a relation scheme R(U) if it holds in all the relations that satisfy all the constraints in I. The set of all the constraints implied by I is called the *closure* of I and indicated with I^+. Two sets of constraints are *equivalent* if their closures are identical. An *inference rule* is a rule that allows the derivation of a constraint from some other constraints. The basic requirement for each inference rule is to be *sound*, that is to derive from I only constraints that are in I^+. Moreover, it is important to have sets of inference rules that are *complete*, i.e., that allow the derivation of all the constraints in I^+.

It is well known (Armstrong [1974], Beeri, Fagin, Howard [1977]) that the following is a sound and complete set of inference rules for FDs:

F_1 (reflexivity) If $Y \subseteq X$, then $X \longrightarrow Y$ holds
F_2 (augmentation) If $X \longrightarrow Y$ holds, then $XZ \longrightarrow YZ$ also holds
F_3 (transitivity) If $X \longrightarrow Y$ and $Y \longrightarrow Z$ hold, then $X \longrightarrow Z$ also holds.

Moreover, the two following rules are sound

F_4 (union) If $X \longrightarrow Y$ and $X \longrightarrow Z$ hold, then $X \longrightarrow YZ$ also holds
F_5 (decomposition) If $X \longrightarrow YZ$ holds, then $X \longrightarrow Y$ also holds.

It is immediate to prove that reflexivity, augmentation, union and decomposition are sound rules for NFDs also, while transitivity is not, as shown by the counterexample relation in fig. 1, which satisfies both $A \longrightarrow B$ and $B \longrightarrow C$ but does not satisfy $A \longrightarrow C$.

r

A	B	C
a_1	∅	c_1
a_1	∅	c_2

Fig. 1.

It is evident from the example that the unsoundness of the rule is caused by the presence of nulls in the attribute(s) Y (B in the example) which implement the transitivity.

Lien [1982] proved that F_1, F_2, F_4, F_5 form a sound and complete set of inference rules for NFDs.

2.2. *Disjunctive Existence Constraints*

A *Disjunctive existence constraint* (DEC, Maier [1980]) is a statement $d: X \vdash S$, where X is a set of attributes and $S = \{Y_1, Y_2, \ldots, Y_n\}$ is a set of sets of attributes. $X \vdash \{Y_1, Y_2, \ldots, Y_n\}$ holds in a relation r over a scheme R(U) (with $XY_1Y_2 \ldots Y_n \subseteq U$) if for each X-total tuple $t \in r$, there is an $i \in \{1, 2, \ldots, n\}$ such that t is Y_i-total.

Goldstein [1981] showed that there is a sound and complete set of inference rules for DECs. We present a slightly modified version of it.

D_1 If $Y \subseteq X$, then $X \vdash \{Y\}$ holds;

D_2 If $X \vdash \{Y_1, Y_2, \ldots, Y_n\}$ holds, then, for any Z, $X \vdash \{Y_1, Y_2, \ldots, Y_n, Z\}$ also holds;

D_3 If $X \vdash \{Y_1, Y_2, \ldots, Y_m\}$ and $X \vdash \{Z_1, Z_2, \ldots, Z_n\}$ hold, then $X \vdash \{Y_1Z_1, \ldots, Y_1Z_n, \ldots, Y_mZ_1, \ldots, Y_mZ_n\}$ also holds;

D_4 If $X \vdash \{Y_1, Y_2, \ldots, Y_m\}$ and, for some i, $Y_i \vdash \{Z_1, Z_2, \ldots, Z_n\}$ hold, then $X \vdash \{Y_1, \ldots, Y_{i-1}, Z_1, \ldots, Z_n, Y_{i+1}, \ldots, Y_m\}$ also holds.

Given a set D of DECs over a scheme R(U) and a set of attributes $X \subseteq U$, let D^+ be the closure of D and call D_X the set of DECs in D^+ whose left hand side is X. The *closure* of a set of attributes X with respect to D, indicated with X_D, is a set of subsets of U such that:

1. $\{X \vdash X_D\}$ and D_X are equivalent;
2. there is no other $\{X \vdash S\}$ equivalent to D_X such that S contains less subsets of U than X_D.

It is proved in Goldstein [1981] that the closure X_D of X is unique.

2.3. *Existence Constraints*

A DEC $X \vdash S$ such that S contains a single set of attributes Y is called *existence constraint* (EC, Maier [1980]) and it is indicated with $X \vdash Y$. Obviously, it holds in a relation r over a scheme R(U) (with $XY \subseteq U$) if each X-total tuple $t \in R$ is also Y-total.

The study of inference rules for ECs leads to an interesting result (Maier [1980]): the rules obtained from the rules for FDs, substituting the symbol $\longrightarrow$ of FD with the symbol $\vdash$ of EC:

E_1 (reflexivity) If $Y \subseteq X$, then $X \vdash Y$ holds

E_2 (augmentation) If $X \vdash Y$ holds, then $XZ \vdash YZ$ also holds

E_3 (transitivity) If $X \vdash Y$ and $Y \vdash Z$ hold, then $X \vdash Z$ also holds

form a sound a complete set of inference rules for the derivation of ECs. This result has the important consequence that most of the theory developed for functional dependencies (such as closure and membership algorithms) can be extended to existence constraints with no further effort. A set of rules equivalent to E_1, E_2, E_3 can be obtained reducing the rules D_1, D_3, D_4 to ECs.

3. INTERACTION BETWEEN NFD'S AND DEC'S

As we said in the introduction, the goal of this paper is the study of the joint class of constraints containing both NFDs and DECs.

Analogously to what happens for other joint classes of constraints (e.g. FDs and MVDs, Beeri, Fagin and Howard [1977]), the rules for the two classes (F_1, F_2, F_4, F_5, D_1, D_2, D_3, D_4) are obviously sound also for the joint class. The following theorem guarantees that they are complete with respect to DECs, since, given any set I of NFDs and DECs, they allow the derivation of all the DECs in I^+: so we can say that NFDs do not influence DECs.

THEOREM 1. Let D and F be respectively a set of DECs and a set of NFDs and $I = D \cup F$. The DECs in I^+ are exactly those in D^+.

PROOF. It is easy to show that for any set D of DECs and any DEC do not implied by D there is a counterexample relation r (i.e. a relation satisfying all the DECs in D and not satisfying d) composed by a single tuple. But, since all one-tuple relations satisfy all the NFDs, r is a counterexample relation also for the joint class. □

The same result does not hold with respect to NFDs, as shown by the following example. Given the set of constraints

$$I = \{X \longrightarrow Y,\ Y \longrightarrow A,\ X \vdash\!\!- \{Y\}\}$$

it is impossible to derive, by means of the aforementioned rules, the NFD $X \longrightarrow A$; on the other hand, given any relation r satisfying the constraints in I, for any pair of X-total tuples $t_1, t_2 \in r$ such that $t_1.X = t_2.X$ we have that, for the DEC $X \vdash\!\!- \{Y\}$ (which is actually an EC), they are also Y-total and, for the NFD $X \longrightarrow Y$, $t_1.Y = t_2.Y$; then, for the NFD $Y \longrightarrow A$, $t_1.A = t_2.A$ and so r satisfies $X \longrightarrow A$. This means that $X \longrightarrow A$ is implied by I. Let us analyze the example. We have something that resembles the property of transitivity. In section 2.1 we have show that the transitivity rule is not sound for NFDs, because of the possible presence of null values in the middle term. In this case we have the DEC $X \vdash\!\!- \{Y\}$ which guarantees that, when a tuple is X-total (and this is the only case in which it can cause a violation of the NFD $X \longrightarrow A$) it is also Y-total, i.e. null free in the middle term. Analogously it could be proved that the set of constraints

$$I = \{X \longrightarrow Y_1 \ldots Y_p,\ Y_1 \longrightarrow A, \ldots, Y_p \longrightarrow A,\ X \vdash\!\!- \{Y_1, \ldots, Y_p\}\}$$

implies the NFD $X \longrightarrow A$. Here, we have various possible middle terms for the transitivity, at least one of which is guaranteed to be null free.

Formalizing the concept, we could prove the correctness of the rule

If $X \longrightarrow Y_1 \ldots Y_p$, $Y_1 \longrightarrow A, \ldots, Y_p \longrightarrow A$, $X \vdash \{Y_1, \ldots, Y_p\}$ hold,
then $X \longrightarrow A$ also holds

Unfortunately, it does not form, together with the other rules, a complete system. Again, given the set of constraints

$$I = \{X \longrightarrow Y_1 \ldots Y_p,\ Y_1 \longrightarrow A, \ldots, Y_p \longrightarrow A, A \vdash \{Y_1, \ldots, Y_p\}\}$$

it is still impossible to derive the NFD $X \longrightarrow A$, which instead could be easily proved to be implied by I. In this case, it is the DEC $A \vdash \{Y_1, \ldots, Y_p\}$ that guarantees the absence of null values on one of the possible middle terms Y_i. We could easily generalize the two examples and merge them in the following rule

If $X \longrightarrow Y_1 \ldots Y_p, Y_1 \longrightarrow A, \ldots, Y_p \longrightarrow A$, $XA \vdash \{Y_1, \ldots, Y_p\}$ hold,
then $X \longrightarrow A$ also holds

Again, the system is not yet complete: given the set of constraints

$$I = \{X \longrightarrow VWY,\ V \longrightarrow A,\ Y \longrightarrow Z,\ WZ \longrightarrow A,\ XA \vdash \{XYWZ, VX\}\}$$

the NFD $X \longrightarrow A$, though non-derivable by means of the rules, is implied by I, as it can be easily proved by contradiction.

The examples suggest that an NFD $X \longrightarrow A$ is implied by a set of constraints I if it is derivable from them by means of the classical rules for FDs (reflexivity, augmentation, transitivity) with respect to a set of attributes that must be null free in XA-total tuples, since for each pair of tuples violating $X \longrightarrow A$, at least one must be XA-total. Moreover, since a DEC $XA \vdash \{Y_1, \ldots, Y_p\}$ guarantees only that one of the sets $Y_1, \ldots, Y_p$ is null free in XA-total tuples, it results that $X \longrightarrow A$ is implied from I if it is derivable by means of the classical rules on each of the sets Y_i. In order to formalize this concept we introduce a new type of constraint, similar to NFD, but for the fact that it refers to tuples that are total on given sets of attributes, as suggested by the examples.

DEFINITION 1. A *fictitious functional dependency* (FFD) is a statement $X \overset{Z}{\rightarrowtail} Y$ (with $X \subseteq Z$). It holds in a relation r over a scheme R(U) (with $YZ \subseteq U$) if for each $t_1, t_2 \in r$, if t_1 is Z-total and $t_1.X = t_2.X$ then $t_1.Y = t_2.Y$. □

EXAMPLE 1. Given the relation scheme R(ABCD), the relations r_1, r_2 in fig. 2 satisfy the FFD $A \overset{AB}{\rightarrowtail} C$ (which is meaningful because $A \subseteq AB$), while the relation r_3 does not.

r_1

A	B	C	D
a_1	b_1	$\emptyset$	d_1
a_1	b_2	$\emptyset$	d_2
a_2	b_1	c_2	d_1
a_2	b_1	c_2	d_2

r_2

A	B	C	D
a_1	$\emptyset$	c_1	d_1
a_1	$\emptyset$	c_2	d_2
a_2	b_1	c_1	d_1

r_3

A	B	C	D
a_1	b_1	c_1	d_1
a_1	$\emptyset$	c_2	d_1

Fig. 2.

The satisfaction of $A \rangle\!\xrightarrow{AB} C$ in r_1 is equivalent to the satisfaction of the NFD $A \longrightarrow C$ since all the tuples are AB-total. $A \rangle\!\xrightarrow{AB} C$ holds in r_2, because the only AB-total tuple is the last one and no other tuple agrees with it on the attribute A. In r_3, instead, the FFD is not satisfied, since the first tuple is AB-total and agrees with the second one on the attribute A, while they disagree on the attribute C.□

The following theorem, whose easy proof is omitted, shows that the FFDs satisfy the requirements informally suggested by the examples, since sound rules for them can be obtained from the classical rules for FDs by means of straightforward technical modifications.

THEOREM 2. The inference rules for FFDs

FF_1 (reflexivity) If $Y \subseteq X \subseteq Z$, then $X \rangle\!\xrightarrow{Z} Y$ holds

FF_2 (augmentation) If $X \rangle\!\xrightarrow{Z} Y$ holds and $W \subseteq Z$, then $XW \rangle\!\xrightarrow{Z} YW$ also holds

FF_3 (transitivity) If $X \rangle\!\xrightarrow{W} Y$ and $Y \rangle\!\xrightarrow{W} Z$ hold, then $X \rangle\!\xrightarrow{W} Z$ also holds

are sound. □

Now we introduce the rules which allow the derivation of FFDs from NFDs and viceversa, in presence of DECs.

First of all, it is immediate from the definition that each FFD $X \rangle\!\xrightarrow{Z} Y$ is a strictly weaker constraint than the NFD $X \longrightarrow Y$. So the following rule for the joint class of NFDs,FFDs,DECs is sound:

J_1 If $X \longrightarrow Y$ holds and $X \subseteq Z$, then $X \rangle\!\xrightarrow{Z} Y$ also holds

The following theorem introduces and proves the soundness of the rule that allows the derivation of new NFDs, according to what suggested by the examples.

THEOREM 3. The rule

J_2 If $XA \vdash \{Y_1,\ldots,Y_p\}$ and for each i, $X \rangle\!\xrightarrow{Y_i} A$ hold,

then $X \longrightarrow A$ also holds

is sound.

PROOF. We proceed by contradiction. Suppose that there exist a relation r satisfying $X \vdash \{Y_1,\ldots,Y_p\}$ and, for each i, $X \overset{Y_i}{\rangle\!\!\longrightarrow} A$ and not satisfying $X \longrightarrow A$. Then, there must be two X-total tuples $t_1, t_2 \in r$ such that $t_1.X = t_2.X$ and $t_1.A \neq t_2.A$. Thus, at least one of them is XA-total and so, for the DEC $XA \vdash \{Y_1,\ldots,Y_p\}$, there is an i such that it is Y_i-total; but this means that r does not satisfy $X \overset{Y_i}{\rangle\!\!\longrightarrow} A$, against the hypothesis.□

The new rules can handle the examples given at the beginning of this section. Let us consider again the more general of them, which subsumes the others:

$$I = \{X \longrightarrow VWY,\ V \longrightarrow A,\ Y \longrightarrow Z,\ WZ \longrightarrow A,\ XA \vdash \{XYWZ, VX\}\}$$

We can derive (for J_1 and the decomposition rule, which, as well as the union rule, holds for FFDs too) $X \overset{XYWZ}{\rangle\!\!\longrightarrow} YW$, $Y \overset{XYWZ}{\rangle\!\!\longrightarrow} Z$, $WZ \overset{XYWZ}{\rangle\!\!\longrightarrow} A$, $V \overset{VX}{\rangle\!\!\longrightarrow} A$ and $X \overset{VX}{\rangle\!\!\longrightarrow} V$. Then (for FF_2 and FF_3) we have $X \overset{XYWZ}{\rangle\!\!\longrightarrow} A$ and $X \overset{VX}{\rangle\!\!\longrightarrow} A$ and, finally, (for J_2) $X \longrightarrow A$.

We can now state and prove the main theorem.

THEOREM 4. The rules F_1, F_2, F_4, F_5, D_1, D_2, D_3, D_4, $FF_1, FF_2, FF_3, J_1, J_2$ form a sound and complete system for the derivation of NFDs and DECs.

PROOF. The completeness of the rules for the derivation of DECs from NFDs and DECs has already been proven in theorem 1. With regard to the derivation of NFDs we proceed showing that for each NFD f non-derivable from a given set I of NFDs and DECs by means of the rules there is a counterexample relation r satisfying all the constraints in I and not satisfying f.

Let $I = D \cup F$, where D is a set of DECs and F a set of NFDs. If $f: X \longrightarrow Y$ is an NFD that cannot be derived from I by means of the rules, then there must be an attribute $B \in Y$ such that $X \longrightarrow B$ cannot be derived (otherwise for the union rule $X \longrightarrow Y$ would be derivable). Now let $(XB)_D = \{Z_1, Z_2, \ldots, Z_p\}$ be the closure of XB with respect to D. Since $X \longrightarrow B$ cannot be derived, there must exist an $i \in \{1,2,\ldots,p\}$, such that $X \overset{Z_i}{\rangle\!\!\longrightarrow} B$ is not derivable (otherwise, for J_2, $X \longrightarrow B$ would be derivable). Then, let

$$X_{FF} = \{A \mid A \in Z_i \text{ and } X \overset{Z_i}{\rangle\!\!\longrightarrow} A \text{ is derivable}\}$$

and r be the two tuple relation in fig. 3 (note that $X \subseteq X_{FF} \subseteq Z_i$).

X_{FF}	$Z_i - X_{FF}$	$U - Z_i$
1 1 ... 1	1 1 ... 1	∅ ∅ ... ∅
1 1 ... 1	2 2 ... 2	∅ ∅ ... ∅

Fig. 3.

1. r satisfies all the DECs in D.
   Let $d: V \vdash \{W_1, W_2, \ldots, W_m\} \in D$. If $V \not\subseteq Z_i$, then d is satisfied because the tuples are not V-total. Otherwise, (for D_1) $Z_i \vdash \{V\}$ and (for D_4) $Z_i \vdash \{W_1, W_2, \ldots, W_m\}$ are derivable; on the other hand (Goldstein [1981]) the closure of Z_i is exactly $\{Z_i\}$ and this implies (Goldstein [1981]) that, for each j, $W_j \subseteq Z_i$; so, for each j, both tuples are W_j-total.
2. r satisfies all the NFDs in F.
   Let $f: V \longrightarrow W \in F$. If $V \not\subseteq X_{FF}$, f is trivially satisfied. If $V \subseteq X_{FF}$, $X \rangle\!\xrightarrow{Zi} V$ is derivable. We proceed showing that for each $A \in W$, $V \longrightarrow A$ is satisfied (and, for the union rule, this guarantees that $V \longrightarrow W$ is satisfied). If $A \notin Z_i$, $V \longrightarrow A$ is satisfied. If $A \in Z_i$, then (for J_1) from $V \longrightarrow A$ and $V \subseteq X_{FF} \subseteq Z_i$, $V \rangle\!\xrightarrow{Zi} A$ is derivable and (for FF_3) $X \rangle\!\xrightarrow{Zi} A$ is derivable and so $A \in X_{FF}$ and then $V \longrightarrow A$ is satisfied.
3. r does not satisfy $X \longrightarrow B$.
   Since Z_i is an element of the closure of XB with respect to D, for the properties of the closure (Goldstein [1981]) $B \in Z_i$; on the other hand, for the definition of X_{FF}, $B \notin X_{FF}$. So, $B \in Z_i - X_{FF}$ and the two tuples of r agree on X and disagree on B. □

The following theorem shows the analogous result for the derivation of NFDs and ECs. Its proof, similar to that of theorem 4, is omitted. It refers to a rule which is the specialization of J_2 to ECs, as follows:

J_2' If $XA \vdash Y$ and $X \rangle\!\xrightarrow{Y} A$ hold, then $X \longrightarrow A$ also holds

THEOREM 5. The rules F_1, F_2, F_4, F_5, E_1, E_2, E_3, FF_1, FF_2, FF_3, J_1, J_2' form a sound and complete system for the derivation of NFDs and ECs. □

Theorem 4 and 5 prove the completeness of the rules for the derivation of NFDs,ECs,DECs from NFDs,ECs,DECs, while we have said little (theorem 2) about the derivation of FFDs and the derivation from sets of constraints containing also FFDs. This is due to the fact that FFDs are not natural constraints (this is the reason for the word "fictitious") and so there could be little interest in their specific treatment. Actually, we introduced them only as auxiliary constraints useful for the derivation of NFDs. However, a complete axiomatization for them exists, but because of space limitations we omit it.

The importance of FFDs is stressed by the following theorem, which shows that there can be no finite system for the derivation of NFDs and DECs.

THEOREM 6. There can be no finite, complete set of inference rules for the class of constraints containing only NFDs and DECs.

PROOF. The proof proceeds by contradiction. If there were a finite set of rules, there would be an integer n equal to the maximum number of premises in the rules.
Let us consider a set of n+1 constraints

$$I = \{A_0 \longrightarrow A_1, \ldots, A_{n-1} \longrightarrow A_n, A_o A_n \vdash \{A_1 \ldots A_{n-1}\}\}$$

By means of FFDs we could see that I implies the NFD $A_0 \longrightarrow A_n$. On the other hand, no NFD-DEC rule could use (for hypothesis) all the n+1 constraints as premises. If we considered only subsets of I with $m \leq n$ constraints, we could only derive (as it can be easily checked using the FFDs) NFDs that are derivable by means of the rules F_1, F_2, F_4, F_5, none of which subsumes two or more constraints in I, and so they cannot be used by a rule with $m \leq n$ premises to derive $A_0 \longrightarrow A_n$. □

The proof of theorem 6 refers to a DEC which is actually an EC, so it can be used to prove the following theorem which states the analogous result for NFDs and ECs.

THEOREM 7. There can be no finite, complete set of inference rules for the class of constraints containing only NFDs and ECs. □

4. CONCLUDING REMARKS

We have shown that there can be no finite, complete set of inference rules for the joint class of NFDs and DECs, while it does exist for a strictly larger class, including another type of constraint, the FFD. So we got a situation analogous to that of embedded multivalued dependencies (which do not have a complete axiomatization, Sagiv and Walecka [1982] and Parker and Parsaye-Ghomi [1980]) and template dependencies (which include embedded multivalued dependencies and have a complete axiomatization, Sadri and Ullman [1980]).

ACKNOWLEDGEMENTS

The authors would like to thank Francois Banchilon, Rick Hull, Marina Moscarini and Stott Parker for helpful discussions. In particular,

Rick Hull gave suggestions for theorem 6 and its proof.

REFERENCES

1. W.W. ARMSTRONG: "Dependency Structures of Data Base Relationships". *Proc. 1974 IFIP Congress*, North-Holland Pub. Co. Amsterdam, 1974, pp. 580-583.

2. C. BEERI, R. FAGIN, J.H. HOWARD: "A Complete Axiomatization for Functional and Multivalued Dependencies". *Proc. of ACM SIGMOD Int'l Conf. on Management of Data*, Toronto, Canada, 1977, pp.47-61.

3. E.F. CODD: "A Relational Model of Data for Large Shared Data Banks". *Comm. ACM* 13(6), 1970, pp. 377-387.

4. B.S. GOLDSTEIN: "Constraints on Null Values in Relational Databases". *Proc. 7th Int'l Conf. on Very Large Data Bases*, Cannes, France, 1981, pp. 101-110.

5. T. IMIELINSKI, W. LIPSKI: "Incomplete Information and Dependencies in Relational Databases". *Proc. of ACM-SIGMOD Int'l Conf. on Management of Data*, San Jose, CA, 1983, pp. 178-184.

6. Y.E. LIEN: "On the Equivalence of Database Models". *J. ACM* 29(2), 1982, pp. 333-362.

7. D. MAIER: "Discarding the Universal Instance Assumption: Preliminary Results". Technical Report 80-008 Dept. of Comp. Sc. SUNY at Stonybrook, NY, March 1980. Presented at the XP1 Workshop, Stonybrook, NY, June 1980.

8. D. MAIER: *The Theory of Relational Databases*, Computer Science Press, Rockville, MD, 1983.

9. D.S. PARKER, K. PARSAYE-GHOMI: "Inferences Involving Embedded Multivalued Dependencies and Transitive Dependencies". *Proc. of ACM-SIGMOD Int'l Conf. on Management of Data*, Los Angeles, CA, 1980, pp. 52-57.

10. F. SADRI, J.D. ULLMAN: "Template Dependencies: A Large Class of Dependencies in Relational Databases and Its Complete Axiomatization". *J. ACM* 29(2), 1982, pp. 363-372.

11. Y. SAGIV, S.F. WALECKA: "Subset Dependencies and a Completeness Result for a Subclass of Embedded Multivalued Dependencies". *J. ACM* 29(1), 1982, pp. 103-117.

12. E. SCIORE: "The Universal Instance and Database Design". Technical Report #271, Dept. of EECS, Princeton University, Princeton, NJ, 1980.

13. J.D. ULLMAN: *Principles of Database Systems*, 2nd ed., Computer Science Press, Potomac, MD, 1982.

14. Y. VASSILIOU: "Functional Dependencies and Incomplete Information". *Proc. 6th Int'l Conf. on Very Large Data Bases*, Montreal, Canada, 1980, pp. 260-269.

15. C. ZANIOLO: "Database Relations with Null Values". Unpublished Manuscript 1981. An extended abstract appeared in *Proc. ACM Symposium on Principles of Database Systems*, Los Angeles, CA, 1982, pp. 27-33.

THE ALGEBRA OF RECURSIVELY DEFINED PROCESSES AND THE ALGEBRA OF REGULAR PROCESSES

J.A. Bergstra and J.W. Klop

Centrum voor Wiskunde en Informatica, Kruislaan 413, AMSTERDAM

ABSTRACT. We introduce recursively defined processes and regular processes, both in presence and absence of communication. It is shown that both classes are process algebras. As an example of recursively defined processes, Bag and Stack are discussed in detail. It is shown that Bag cannot be recursively defined without merge. We introduce fixed point algebras which have useful applications in several proofs.

INTRODUCTION. ACP, Algebra of Communicating Processes, was introduced in Bergstra & Klop [3]. It combines a purely algebraic formulation of a part of Milner's CCS [9] with an algebraic presentation of the denotational semantics of processes as given by de Bakker & Zucker [1,2]; moreover it includes two laws on communication of atomic actions which are also present in Hennessy [6]. The ingredients of ACP are the following:

- a finite set A of so-called atomic actions a,b,c,... including a constant δ for deadlock (or failure). With $\underline{A}$ we denote $A - \{\delta\}$, the proper actions.
- a mapping $.|. : A \times A \to A$, called the communication function. If $a|b = c$ then c is the action that results from simultaneously executing a and b. Processes will cooperate by sharing actions rather than sharing data.
- a subset H of A (usually H contains the actions which must communicate with other actions in order to be executable). The elements of H are called subatomic actions.
- a signature of operations $\cdot, +, \|, \lfloor\!\lfloor, |, \delta, \partial_H$. (For $x \cdot y$ we will often write xy.)

The axioms of ACP are displayed in Table 1 on the next page.

These axioms reflect in an algebraic way that + represents choice, $\cdot$ represents sequential composition and $\|$ the merge operator.

The operations $\lfloor\!\lfloor$ (left merge) and $|$ (communication merge) are auxiliary ones. Our primary interest remains for $+, \cdot, \|$. The process $x \lfloor\!\lfloor y$ is like $x \| y$, but takes its first step from x, and $x|y$ is like $x\|y$ but requires the first action to be a communication (between a first step of x and a first step of y).

1. PRELIMINARIES

1.1. Models of ACP. The axioms of ACP allow for a large variety of models ('process algebras'). In [3,5] we investigated the 'standard' model A^∞ for ACP which is used throughout this paper.

We will quickly describe the construction of the standard model A^∞. First one constructs A_ω, the initial model of ACP seen as an equational specification over the signature with a constant for each atom. The process algebra A_ω contains only finite processes and hence cannot solve fixed point (or recursion) equations, such as $X = aX + b$. One way of completing A_ω is as follows.

Let A_ω mod n (for short, A_n) be for $n \geqslant 1$, the homomorphic image of A_ω obtained by identifying two processes p,q in A_ω if their 'trees' coincide up to depth n. (More precisely, if their projections $(p)_n, (q)_n$ coincide. Here $(a)_n = a$, $(ax)_{n+1} = a(x)_n$, $(ax)_1 = a$, $(x+y)_n = (x)_n + (y)_n$.) The A_n are also process algebras with operations $+^n$ etc. defined as $(x +^n y) = (x+y)_n$ etc.

$x + y = y + x$	A1
$x + (y + z) = (x + y) + z$	A2
$x + x = x$	A3
$(x + y).z = x.z + y.z$	A4
$(x.y).z = x.(y.z)$	A5
$x + \delta = x$	A6
$\delta.x = \delta$	A7
$a \mid b = b \mid a$	C1
$(a \mid b) \mid c = a \mid (b \mid c)$	C2
$\delta \mid a = \delta$	C3
$x \parallel y = x \mathbin{\|\!\!\lfloor} y + y \mathbin{\|\!\!\lfloor} x + x \mid y$	CM1
$a \mathbin{\|\!\!\lfloor} x = a.x$	CM2
$(ax) \mathbin{\|\!\!\lfloor} y = a(x \parallel y)$	CM3
$(x + y) \mathbin{\|\!\!\lfloor} z = x \mathbin{\|\!\!\lfloor} z + y \mathbin{\|\!\!\lfloor} z$	CM4
$(ax) \mid b = (a \mid b).x$	CM5
$a \mid (bx) = (a \mid b).x$	CM6
$(ax) \mid (by) = (a \mid b).(x \parallel y)$	CM7
$(x + y) \mid z = x \mid z + y \mid z$	CM8
$x \mid (y + z) = x \mid y + x \mid z$	CM9
$\partial_H(a) = a$ if $a \notin H$	D1
$\partial_H(a) = \delta$ if $a \in H$	D2
$\partial_H(x + y) = \partial_H(x) + \partial_H(y)$	D3
$\partial_H(x.y) = \partial_H(x).\partial_H(y)$	D4

Table 1.

Now A^{∞} is defined as the projective limit of the finite process algebras A_n, $n \geq 1$. That means that the elements of A^{∞} are the projective sequences $(p_1, p_2, \ldots, p_n, \ldots)$ where $p_n \in A_n$ and such that $(p_{n+1})_n = p_n$; the operations are defined coordinate-wise.

All process algebras introduced in this paper will be subalgebras of A^{∞}.

Another way of completing the algebra A_{ω} of finite processes is as in De Bakker & Zucker [1,2] as a metrical completion. Furthermore one obtains a large collection of process algebras starting from process graphs (as in the sequel) and dividing out some notion of bisimulation. Such 'graph models' will not be considered in this paper; see [5].

1.2. Restricted signatures. It is useful to consider a smaller set of operations on processes, for instance: only + and $\cdot$. Then one may forget δ and consider structures

$$\underline{A}_{\omega}(+,\cdot),\ \underline{A}_n(+,\cdot),\ \underline{A}^{\infty}(+,\cdot)$$

where $\underline{A} = A - \{\delta\}$. Furthermore, under the assumption that $a \mid b = \delta$ for all $a, b \in A$, we may add $\parallel$ and $\mathbin{\|\!\!\lfloor}$ to the signature of these algebras, thus obtaining

$$\underline{A}_{\omega}(+,\cdot,\parallel,\mathbin{\|\!\!\lfloor}),\ \underline{A}_n(+,\cdot,\parallel,\mathbin{\|\!\!\lfloor}) \text{ and } \underline{A}^{\infty}(+,\cdot,\parallel,\mathbin{\|\!\!\lfloor}).$$

Of course these structures can be constructed immediately without any reference to communication. Let PA be the following axiom system (see Table 2). Then $\underline{A}_{\omega}(+,\cdot,\parallel,\mathbin{\|\!\!\lfloor})$ is just the initial algebra of PA.

$x + y = y + x$	A1
$x + (y + z) = (x + y) + z$	A2
$x + x = x$	A3
$(x + y).z = x.z + y.z$	A4
$(x.y).z = x.(y.z)$	A5
$x \| y = x ⌊⌊ y + y ⌊⌊ x$	M1
$a ⌊⌊ x = a.x$	M2
$ax ⌊⌊ y = a(x \| y)$	M3
$(x + y) ⌊⌊ z = x ⌊⌊ z + y ⌊⌊ z$	M4

Table 2.

1.3. Linear terms and guarded terms. Let $X_1,\ldots,X_n$ be variables ranging over processes. Given a (restricted) signature of operators from $+, \cdot, \|, ⌊⌊, |, \partial_H, \delta$ two kinds of terms containing variables $X_1,\ldots,X_n$ are of particular importance:

(i) Linear terms. These are inductively defined as follows:

- atoms a, δ and variables X_i are linear terms,
- if T_1 and T_2 are linear terms then so are $T_1 + T_2$ and aT_1 (for $a \in A$).

An equation $T_1 = T_2$ is called linear if T_1, T_2 are linear.

(ii) Guarded terms. The unguarded terms are inductively defined as follows:

- X_i is unguarded,
- if T is unguarded then so are $T + T'$, $T \cdot T'$, $\partial_H(T)$, $T \| T'$, $T ⌊⌊ T'$, $T|T'$ (for every T').

A term T is guarded if it is not unguarded.

1.4. Process graphs. A process graph g for an action alphabet A is a rooted directed multigraph with edges labeled by elements of A. Here g may be infinite and may contain cycles. Process graphs (or transition diagrams) constitute a very useful tool for the description of processes. In this section we will consider finite process graphs, possibly containing cycles.

Let g be a finite process graph over A. We show how to find a semantics of g in A^∞. To each node s of g with a positive outdegree, attach a process name X_s. Then the following system of guarded linear equations arises:

$$X_s = \sum_{(a,t) \in U} a \cdot X_t + \sum_{a \in V} a \qquad (E_X)$$

where $U = \{(a,t) \mid g: s \xrightarrow{a} t$ & t has positive outdegree$\}$, $V = \{a \mid \exists t\ g: s \xrightarrow{a} t$ & t has outdegree 0$\}$. This system E_X has a unique solution in A^∞ and with s_0 the root of g, we define: $[\![g]\!] = p_{s_0}$, where $\langle p_s \rangle$ solves E_X.

1.5. Operations on process graphs. We assume that $.|.$ is defined as a communication function: $A \times A \to A$. Now let g,h be two process graphs for A. We define new process graphs as follows:

- $g+h$ results by glueing together the roots of g and h, provided these roots are acyclic, i.e. not lying on a cycle. (Otherwise g,h must be unwinded to make the roots acyclic; for a more precise account see [5].)
- $g \cdot h$ results by glueing together the root of h and all endpoints of g,
- $\partial_H(g)$ results by replacing all labels $a \in H$ by δ in g,
- $g \| h$ is the cartesian product of the node sets $\{s,s',..\}$ and $\{t,t',..\}$ of g resp. h provided with labeled edges as follows:
  - (i) $(s,t) \xrightarrow{a} (s',t)$ if in g we have $s \xrightarrow{a} s'$
  - (ii) $(s,t) \xrightarrow{a} (s,t')$ if in h we have $t \xrightarrow{a} t'$
  - (iii) $(s,t) \xrightarrow{a} (s',t')$ if for some $b,c \in A$ we have $b|c = a$ and $s \xrightarrow{b} s'$ in g, $t \xrightarrow{c} t'$ in h.
- $g \mathbin{\lfloor\!\lfloor} h$ is defined like $g\|h$, but leaving out all transitions of types (ii) and (iii) if s is the root of g,
- $g|h$ is defined like $g\|h$ but leaving out all transitions of types (i) and (ii) if s resp. t is the root of g resp. h.

Of course we have $[\![g+h]\!] = [\![g]\!]+[\![h]\!]$ etc. More precisely: $[\![\ ]\!]$ as in 1.4 is a homomorphism from the collection of finite process graphs (with acyclic roots) with operations as just described, to the process algebra A^∞.

2. REGULAR PROCESSES

2.1. The algebra of regular processes. For $p \in A^\infty$ the collection Sub(p) of subprocesses of p is defined by:

$p \in \mathrm{Sub}(p)$

$ax \in \mathrm{Sub}(p) \Rightarrow x \in \mathrm{Sub}(p)$, provided $a \neq \delta$

$ax+y \in \mathrm{Sub}(p) \Rightarrow x \in \mathrm{Sub}(p)$, provided $a \neq \delta$.

We define $p \in A^\infty$ to be regular if Sub(p) is finite, and denote with $r(A^\infty)$ the collection of regular processes in A^∞. Now, noting that the operations in 1.5 on process graphs preserve finiteness, we have immediately the following facts:

THEOREM 2.1.1. (i) *If p is regular then there is a finite process graph g with* $[\![g]\!] = p$, *and conversely.*

(ii) *The class of regular processes is closed under the operations* $+, \cdot, \|, \mathbin{\lfloor\!\lfloor}, |, \partial_H$. *Hence* $r(A^\infty)$ *is a subalgebra of* A^∞.

(iii) $r(A^\infty)$ *contains exactly the solutions of finite systems of guarded linear equations.* □

2.2. CSP program algebras. In this subsection we illustrate the use of the algebras $r(A^\infty)$ by giving an interpretation of simplified CSP programs in such algebras.

Let Σ be an algebraic signature and let X be a set of variables. A CSP component program S is defined by:

$$S ::= b \mid b \,\&\, x{:=}t \mid b \,\&\, C!t \mid b \,\&\, C?x \mid S_1;S_2 \mid S_1 \Box S_2 \mid \underline{\text{while}}\ b\ \underline{\text{do}}\ S\ \underline{\text{od}}.$$

Here b is a boolean (quantifier free) expression. The action b is a guard, which can only be passed when it evaluates to true; b & p can only be executed if b is true. It is usual to abbreviate true & p to p. All variables x must occur in X. Further, C is an element of a set of channel names.

A CSP program P is a construct of the form $[S_1 \| \ldots \| S_k]$ with the S_i CSP-component programs.

Remark. Originally the CSP syntax indicates restrictions: the S_i must work with different variables, the channels are used to interconnect specific pairs of components. (See Hoare [7,8].) However, from our point of view these restrictions are just guidelines on how to obtain a properly modularised system (semantically their meaning is not so clear).

Let a CSP program $P = [S_1 \| \ldots \| S_n]$ be given. We will evaluate an intermediate semantics for it by embedding it in a process algebra. First we fix a set of atomic actions; these are:

(i) $b_1, \neg b_1, b_1 \wedge b_2$ if b_1, b_2 occur in P,

(ii) b & x:=t if x and t occur in P, for all b from (i)

(iii) b & C!t if C!t occurs in P, for all b from (i)

(iv) b & C?x if C?x occurs in P, for all b from (i).

Let us call this alphabet of actions A_{CSP-P}. If we delete all actions of the form b & C!t or b & C?x we obtain A_P. So A_P contains the proper actions that evaluation of P can involve, while A_{CSP-P} contains the subatomic actions as well. H contains the actions of the form b & C!t and b & C?x.

Next we fix a communication function. All communications lead to δ, except the following ones: $b_1 \,\&\, C!t \mid b_2 \,\&\, C?x \;=\; (b_1 \wedge b_2) \,\&\, x{:=}t$.

We will first find an image $[\![P]\!]$ of P in A^{∞}_{CSP-P}. This is done using the notation of μ-calculus. We use an inductive definition for subprograms of the component programs first:

$$[\![b]\!] = b$$

$$[\![b \,\&\, x{:=}t]\!] = b \,\&\, x{:=}t$$

$$[\![b \,\&\, C!t]\!] = b \,\&\, C!t$$

$$[\![b \,\&\, C?x]\!] = b \,\&\, C?x$$

$$[\![S_1;S_2]\!] = [\![S_1]\!] \cdot [\![S_2]\!]$$

$$[\![S_1 \Box S_2]\!] = [\![S_1]\!] + [\![S_2]\!]$$

$$[\![\underline{\text{while}}\ b\ \underline{\text{do}}\ S\ \underline{\text{od}}]\!] = \mu x(b \cdot [\![S]\!] \cdot x + \neg b).$$

Here $\mu x(b \cdot [\![S]\!] \cdot x + \neg b)$ is the unique solution of the equation $X = b \cdot [\![S]\!] \cdot X + \neg b$. It is easily seen that the solution $\underline{X}$ is regular whenever $[\![S]\!]$ is regular.

Inductively one finds that $[\![S]\!]$ is regular for each component program S. Finally for the program P we obtain: $[\![P]\!] = [\![\ [S_1 \| \ldots \| S_n]\ ]\!] = \partial_H([\![S_1]\!] \| \ldots \| [\![S_n]\!])$.
We can now draw two interesting conclusions:

(i) $[\![P]\!]$ is regular;

(ii) $[\![P]\!]$ can just as well be (recursively) defined in $\underline{A}_P^{\infty}(+,\cdot)$ (so without any mention of communication).

Proof. (i) $[\![S_i]\!]$ is regular because it is defined using linear recursion equations only. Consequently the $[\![S_i]\!]$ are in $r(A^{\infty}_{CSP-P})$ and so is $[\![P]\!]$ because $r(A^{\infty}_{CSP-P})$ is a subalgebra of A^{∞}_{CSP-P}.
(ii) follows from (i) and Theorem 2.1.1(iii).

Remark. In general one must expect that a recursive definition of $[\![P]\!]$ not involving merge will be substantially more complex than the given one with merge.

3. RECURSIVELY DEFINED PROCESSES

3.1. The algebra of recursively defined processes. Let $X = \{X_1,\ldots,X_n\}$ be a set of process names (variables). We will consider terms over X composed from atoms $a \in A$ and the operators $+, \cdot, \|, \lfloor\!\lfloor, |, \partial_H$. A system E_X of guarded fixed point equations for X is a set of n equations $X_i = T_i(X_1,\ldots,X_n)$, $i = 1,\ldots,n$, with $T_i(X_1,\ldots,X_n)$ a guarded term.

THEOREM 3.1.1. *Each system E_X of guarded fixed point equations has a unique solution in $(A^{\infty})^n$.*

PROOF. See De Bakker & Zucker [1,2]; essentially E_X is seen as an operator $(A^{\infty})^n \rightarrow (A^{\infty})^n$ which under suitable metrics is a contraction and has exactly one fixed point, by Banach's fixed point theorem. □

Definition. $p \in A^{\infty}$ is called recursively definable if there exists a system E_X of guarded fixed point equations over X with solution $(p,q_1,\ldots,q_{n-1})$. With $R(A^{\infty})$ (not to be confused with $r(A^{\infty})$) we denote the subalgebra of recursively defined processes. This is indeed a process algebra:

PROPOSITION 3.1.2. *The recursively defined processes constitute a subalgebra of A^{∞}.*

PROOF. Let $E_X = \{X_i = T_i(X) \mid i = 1,\ldots,n\}$ and $E_Y = \{Y_j = S_j(Y) \mid j = 1,\ldots,m\}$. Let $E_Z = E_X \cup E_Y \cup \{Z = T_1(X) \| S_1(Y)\}$. Now if E_X defines p and E_Y defines q, then E_Z defines $p\|q$. Likewise for the other operations. □

Remark. For algebras with restricted signatures the above construction of a subalgebra of recursively defined processes is equally valid. Of course, the equations will then use the restricted signatures only. This leads to algebras like

$$R(\underline{A}^{\infty}(+,\cdot)) \text{ and } R(\underline{A}^{\infty}(+,\cdot,\|,\lfloor\!\lfloor)).$$

3.2. Recursive definitions and finitely generated process algebras. Let $p_1,\ldots,p_n$ be processes in A^∞. Then $A_\omega(p_1,\ldots,p_n)$ will denote the subalgebra of A^∞ generated by $p_1,\ldots,p_n$.

Let $X_1,\ldots,X_n$ be a set of new names for processes, and let $\underline{X}_1,\ldots,\underline{X}_n$ be processes in A^∞. Then with $A_\omega(\underline{X}_1,\ldots,\underline{X}_n)$ we denote an algebra as above but with the names $X_1,\ldots,X_n$ added to the signature.

We define $A_\omega(\underline{X}_1,\ldots,\underline{X}_n)$ to be a fixed point algebra if the $\underline{X}_i$ are the solutions in A^∞ of some system E_X of guarded fixed point equations where $X = \{X_1,\ldots,X_n\}$.

Remark. Let us denote with $A_\omega[X_1,\ldots,X_n]$ the free ACP algebra generated over new names $X_1,\ldots,X_n$. For each set of interpretations $\underline{X}_1,\ldots,\underline{X}_n$ there is a homomorphism $\phi\colon A_\omega[X_1,\ldots,X_n] \to A_\omega(\underline{X}_1,\ldots,\underline{X}_n)$. Now suppose that E_X is a system of guarded fixed point equations for $X = \{X_1,\ldots,X_n\}$. Then

$$A_\omega[X_1,\ldots,X_n]/E_X$$

is the algebra obtained by dividing out the congruence generated by E_X. On the other hand, let $\underline{X}_1,\ldots,\underline{X}_n$ be the unique solutions of E_X in A^∞. There is again a homomorphism

$$\phi\colon A_\omega[X_1,\ldots,X_n]/E_X \to A_\omega(\underline{X}_1,\ldots,\underline{X}_n).$$

Both algebras $A_\omega[X_1,\ldots,X_n]/E_X$ and $A_\omega(\underline{X}_1,\ldots,\underline{X}_n)$ may be vastly different however. Being an initial algebra of a finite specification, $A_\omega[X_1,\ldots,X_n]/E_X$ is semicomputable. It can easily be proved that $A_\omega(\underline{X}_1,\ldots,\underline{X}_n)$ is in general cosemicomputable. One can also give an example (see [4]) where $A_\omega(\underline{X}_1,\ldots,\underline{X}_n)$ is not computable (has an undecidable word problem).

THEOREM 3.2.1. *Let* $\underline{X}_1,\ldots,\underline{X}_n$ *be solutions of the system of guarded fixed point equations* E_X. *Then the fixed point algebra* $A_\omega(\underline{X}_1,\ldots,\underline{X}_n)$ *is closed under taking subprocesses.*

PROOF. Let $p \in A_\omega(\underline{X}_1,\ldots,\underline{X}_n)$. Then for some term T we have $p = T(\underline{X}_1,\ldots,\underline{X}_n)$; after substitutions corresponding to $X_i = T_i(X_1,\ldots,X_n)$ we may assume that T is guarded. Using the axioms of ACP one can rewrite $T(X_1,\ldots,X_n)$ into the form $\Sigma a_i \cdot R_i(X_1,\ldots,X_n) + \Sigma b_i$. Consequently all immediate subprocesses of p, i.e. the $R_i(\underline{X}_1,\ldots,\underline{X}_n)$, are in $A_\omega(\underline{X}_1,\ldots,\underline{X}_n)$ as well. □

This theorem gives a useful criterion for recursive definability (to be used in Section 4):

COROLLARY 3.2.2. (i) *Let* $p \in R(\underline{A}^\infty(+,\cdot,\|,\lfloor\!\lfloor))$. *Then* Sub(p) *is finitely generated using* $+,\cdot,\|,\lfloor\!\lfloor, a \in A$.

(ii) *Likewise for the restricted signature of* $+,\cdot, a \in A$. □

3.3. Finitely branching processes.

Definition. Let $p \in A^\infty$. (i) Then G_p is the canonical process graph of p, defined as follows. The set of nodes of G_p is $\mathrm{Sub}(p) \cup \{o\}$. Here o is a termination node. The root of G_p is p. The (labeled and directed) edges of G_p are given by:

(1) if $a \in \mathrm{Sub}(p)$ then $a \xrightarrow{a} o$ is an edge,

(2) if $ax \in \mathrm{Sub}(p)$ then $ax \xrightarrow{a} x$ is an edge,

(3) if $a + y \in \mathrm{Sub}(p)$ then $a + y \xrightarrow{a} o$ is an edge,

(4) if $ax + y \in \mathrm{Sub}(p)$ then $ax + y \xrightarrow{a} x$ is an edge.

(If p has only infinite branches, the termination node o can be discarded.)

(ii) Let $p \xrightarrow{a_0} p_1 \xrightarrow{a_1} \ldots$ be a maximal path in G_p (i.e. infinite or terminating in o). Then $a_0a_1\ldots$ is a trace of p.

(iii) p is perpetual if all its traces are infinite.

(iv) $\|p\|$, the breadth of p, is the outdegree of the root of G_p. Here $\|p\| \in \mathbb{N}$, or $\|p\|$ is infinite.

(v) p is finitely branching if for all $q \in Sub(p)$, $\|q\|$ is finite.

(vi) p is uniformly finitely branching if $\exists n \in \mathbb{N}\ \forall q \in Sub(p)\ \|q\| < n$.

The proof of the following proposition is routine and omitted.

PROPOSITION. *The uniformly finitely branching processes constitute a subalgebra of* A^∞. □

The next theorem gives further criteria for recursive definability of processes.

THEOREM 3.3.1. (i) *Recursively defined processes are finitely branching.*
(ii) *Moreover, processes recursively defined using only* $+,\cdot$ *are uniformly finitely branching.*
(iii) *There exists a process* $p \in R(\underline{A}^\infty(+,\cdot,\|,\lfloor\!\lfloor))$ *which is not uniformly finitely branching.*

PROOF. (i),(ii): straightforward. (iii): Consider the solution $\underline{X}$ of $X = a + b(Xc \| Xd)$. It is proved in [4] that $\underline{X}$ is not uniformly finitely branching. □

THEOREM 3.3.2. *Let* E_X *be a system of guarded fixed point equations over* $+,\cdot,A,X$. *Suppose the solutions* $\underline{X}$ *are perpetual. Then they are regular.*

PROOF. Since the $\underline{X}_i$ in $\underline{X} = \{\underline{X}_1,\ldots,\underline{X}_m\}$ are perpetual, we have $\underline{X}_i \cdot p = \underline{X}_i$ for every $p \in A^\infty$. Therefore every product $X_i \cdot t$ in E_X may be replaced by X_i without altering the solution vector $\underline{X}$. This leads to a system E'_X where only prefix multiplication is used, or in other words, containing only linear equations (see 1.3). Hence the solutions $\underline{X}$ of E'_X are regular, by Theorem 2.1.1(i). □

COROLLARY 3.3.3. *Let* p *be a finitely branching and perpetual process. Let* Sub(p) *be generated using* $+,\cdot$ *by a finite subset* $X \subseteq Sub(p)$. *Then* p *is regular.*

PROOF. Say $X = \{q_1,\ldots,q_m\}$. Since p is finitely branching, and hence also the q_i are finitely branching, we can find guarded expressions (using $+,\cdot$ only) $T(X_1,\ldots,X_n)$ and $T_i(X_1,\ldots,X_{m_i})$ such that

$$\begin{cases} p = T(p_1,\ldots,p_n) \\ q_i = T_i(q_{i1},\ldots,q_{im_i}),\ i = 1,\ldots,m. \end{cases}$$

Here the p_k $(k = 1,\ldots,n)$ and q_{ij} $(i = 1,\ldots,m;\ j = 1,\ldots,m_i)$ are by definition in Sub(p); therefore the p_k and q_{ij} can be expressed in $q_1,\ldots,q_m$. So there are guarded $+,\cdot$-terms T' and T'_i such that

$$\begin{cases} p = T'(q_1,\ldots,q_m) \\ q_i = T'_i(q_1,\ldots,q_m),\ i = 1,\ldots,m. \end{cases}$$

Since p is perpetual, every subprocess of p is perpetual; in particular the q_i

$(i=1,\ldots,m)$. By the preceding theorem p and the q_i are now regular. □

Remark. The condition 'finitely branching' is necessary in this Corollary, as the following example shows. Consider

$$p = \sum_{i=1} a^i b^\omega,$$

or more precisely, p is the projective sequence $(p_1, p_2, \ldots, p_n, \ldots)$ with

$$p_n = \sum_{i=1}^{n} a^i b^{n-i}.$$

Then the canonical transition diagram G_p is as in Figure 1. Now p is perpetual and

$$Sub(p) = \{p\} \cup \{a^n b^\omega \mid n \geq 0\},$$

so Sub(p) is generated by its finite subset $\{p, b^\omega\}$; yet p is not regular.

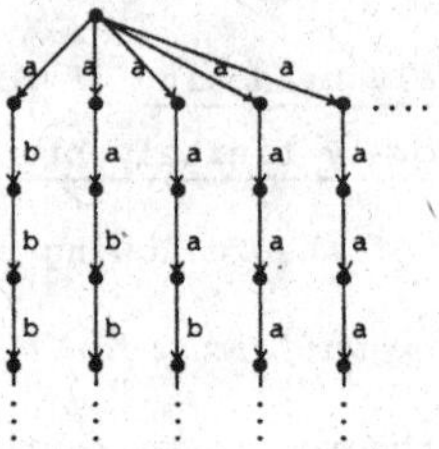

Figure 1.

3.4. Recursive definitions for Bag, Counter and Stack. Let D be a finite set of data values. Let $A = D \cup \underline{D}$, where $\underline{D} = \{\underline{d} \mid d \in D\}$. Let us first consider a bag B over D; its actions are:

d: add d to the bag

$\underline{d}$: take d from the bag.

The initial state of B is empty. Thus the behaviour of B is some process in A^∞.

Similarly the stack S is represented by a process in A^∞.

A counter C is a process in $\{0,p,s\}^\infty$ where the actions 0,p,s have the following meaning:

0: assert that C has value 0

p: add one to the counter

s: subtract one from the counter (if possible).

Now the following recursive definitions of B,C and S can be given (see Table 3):

$B = \sum_{d \in D} d \cdot (\underline{d} \parallel B)$
$\begin{cases} S = \sum_{d \in D} d \cdot T_d \cdot S \\ T_d = \underline{d} + \sum_{b \in D} b \cdot T_b \cdot T_d \quad \text{for all } d \in D \end{cases}$
$\begin{cases} C = (0 + s \cdot H) \cdot C \\ H = p + s \cdot H \cdot H \end{cases}$

Table 3.

For a discussion of the equation for Bag B in Table 3, see [5]. The recursive definition of Stack S is equivalent to one of Hoare [8]. The equations for Counter C are similar to those for S when D = {s} and p stands for $\underline{s}$. It only has the extra option for testing on value 0. In the following section some further information on these recursive definitions will be given.

4. TECHNICAL ASPECTS OF DIFFERENT RECURSIVE DEFINITION MECHANISMS

In this final section we will provide some information about particular recursive definition mechanisms. Namely: systems of equations (over +,•) have greater expressive power than single recursion equations (Theorem 4.1); adding $\|$ to +,• yields more expressive power (Theorem 4.2); adding communication yields more expressive power.

<u>THEOREM 4.1</u>. C *(Counter) and* S *(Stack) as in Table 3 cannot be defined by means of a single equation over* $A^\infty(+,\cdot)$.

<u>PROOF</u>. Immediately, by Theorem 3.3.2 and the fact that C and S are clearly not regular.□

<u>THEOREM 4.2</u>. B *(Bag) cannot be recursively defined over* $A^\infty(+,\cdot)$ *(provided its domain of values contains at least two elements).*

<u>PROOF</u>. First let us note that the proviso in the statement of the theorem is necessary: If the domain of values D = {a} then B as in Table 3 is recursively defined by $B = a(\underline{a}\|B)$. Now it is not hard to see that an equivalent definition for B can be given without $\|$:

$$\begin{cases} B = aCB \\ C = \underline{a} + aCC. \end{cases}$$

(This can be seen by constructing the process graph. Or: note that the behaviour of Bag with singleton value domain is identical to that of a Stack over the same domain, and use the recursive definition for S in Table 3.)

Let D be the domain of values and suppose D = {a,b}. (The case $D = \{a_1,\ldots,a_n\}$, $n \geq 2$, follows easily.) Then Bag B over {a,b} is defined by

$$B = a(\underline{a} \| B) + b(\underline{b} \| B).$$

(Some alternative and equivalent definitions are: $B = a(\underline{a}\|B) \| b(\underline{b}\|B)$, or $B = (a\underline{a} + b\underline{b}) \lfloor\!\lfloor B$, or $B = (a\underline{a}\|b\underline{b}) \lfloor\!\lfloor B$, or $B = \{X\|Y,\ X = a(\underline{a}\|X),\ Y = b(\underline{b}\|Y)\}$, or the system of recursion equations $\{B = X_1\|Y_1,\ X_1 = aX_2X_1,\ X_2 = \underline{a} + aX_2X_2,\ Y_1 = bY_2Y_1,\ Y_2 = \underline{b} + bY_2Y_2\}$. The last system is of interest since it shows - after the present theorem is proved - that the algebra $R(A^\infty(+,\cdot))$ is not closed under $\|$.)

We will show that B cannot recursively be defined over +,•, i.e. $B \notin R(A^\infty(+,\cdot))$. We start with some observations about B. Its canonical process graph is as in Figure 2(a):

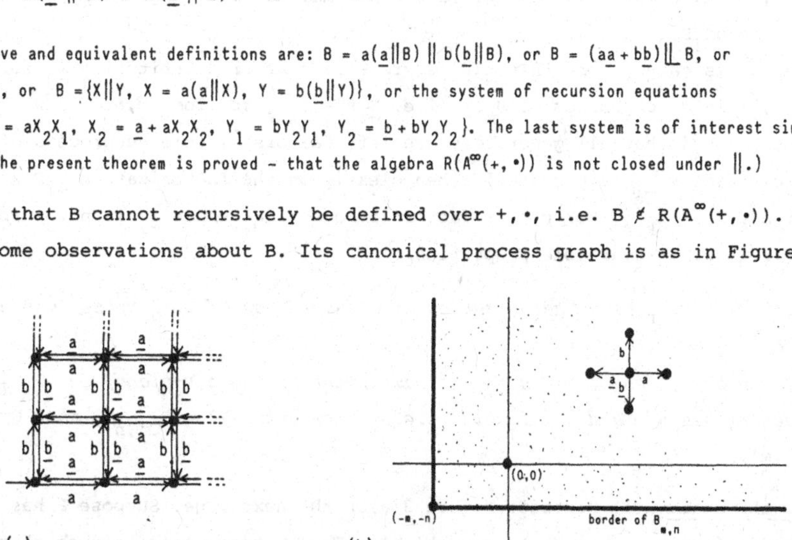

<u>Figure 2</u> (a) (b)

The subprocesses of B are the $B_{m,n}$ $(m,n \geq 0)$ where $B = B_{0,0}$; the $B_{m,n}$ satisfy for all $m,n \geq 0$:

$$B_{m,n} = aB_{m+1,n} + \underline{a}B_{m-1,n} + bB_{m,n+1} + \underline{b}B_{m,n-1}$$

with the understanding that summands in which a negative subscript appears, must vanish. (E.g.: $B_{1,0} = aB_{2,0} + \underline{a}B_{0,0} + bB_{1,1}$.) Graphically we display the $B_{m,n}$ in the "a-b-plane" as in Figure 2(b) on the preceding page. Here the root of the displayed subprocess $B_{m,n}$ is at (0,0) and all traces of $B_{m,n}$ stay confined in the indicated quadrant.

(The subprocesses $B_{m,n}$ are by Theorem 3.2.1 generated by $B,a,b,\underline{a},\underline{b}$ via $+,\cdot,\|,\lfloor\!\lfloor$; indeed it is easy to compute that $B_{m,n} = a^m \| b^n \| B$.)

Now suppose for a proof by contradiction that $B \in R(A^{\infty}(+,\cdot))$. Then, by Corollary 3.2.2, the collection of subprocesses $B_{m,n}$ $(m,n \geq 0)$ is finitely generated using $+,\cdot$ only by say $\underline{X}_1,\ldots,\underline{X}_k$. Let the $B_{m,n}$ therefore be given by

$$B_{m,n} = T_{m,n}(\underline{X})$$

where $T_{m,n}(X)$ are terms involving only $+,\cdot,a,\underline{a},b,\underline{b},X$. (Here $X = (X_1,\ldots,X_k)$ contains the variables of the system of recursive definitions yielding solutions $\underline{X}$ and used to define B.)

We may assume that every occurrence of X_i in $T_{m,n}$ is immediately preceded by some $u \in A = \{a,\underline{a},b,\underline{b}\}$. If not, we expand the corresponding $\underline{X}_i$ as

$$\underline{X}_i = a\underline{X}_{i1} + \underline{a}\,\underline{X}_{i2} + b\underline{X}_{i3} + \underline{b}\,\underline{X}_{i4}$$

(some summands possibly vanishing) and replace $\underline{X}_i$ by its subprocesses $\underline{X}_{i1},\ldots,\underline{X}_{i4}$ in the set of generators $\underline{X}$.

Further, we may take $T_{m,n}$ to be in normal form w.r.t. rewritings $(x+y)z \to xz+yz$. Now consider an occurrence of X_i in $T_{m,n}$. Then X_i is contained in a subterm of the form uX_iP, $u \in A$, P maybe vanishing. Take P maximal so, i.e. uX_iP is not a proper subterm of some uX_iPQ.

Then it is easy to see that $\underline{X}_i\underline{P}$ (where $\underline{P}$ is P after substituting $\underline{X}_j$ for X_j, $j = 1,\ldots,k$) is a subprocess of $B_{m,n}$, i.e. $\underline{X}_i\underline{P} = B_{k,\ell}$ for some k,ℓ.

Thus we find that all generators are left-factors of some subprocess of B. If such a left-factor $\underline{X}_i$ is perpetual, then clearly in the factorization $\underline{X}_i\underline{P} = B_{k,\ell}$ we have already $\underline{X}_i = B_{k,\ell}$. For proper factorizations (i.e. where $\underline{X}_i$ is not perpetual) we have the following remarkable properties:

<u>CLAIM</u>. *Let* $PQ = B_{m,n}$ *be a factorization of a subprocess of* B. *Suppose* P *is not perpetual. Then:*

(i) all finite traces of P *end in the same point of the* a,b-*plane;*

(ii) P *determines* n,m *and* Q *uniquely (i.e. if moreover* $PQ' = B_{m',n'}$, *then* $Q = Q'$ *and* $n,m = n',m'$*).*

<u>Proof of the claim</u>. (i) Consider Figure 3(a) on the next page. Suppose P has traces σ,σ' ending in different points (k,ℓ) and (k',ℓ'). Then Q has a trace ρ such that $\sigma\rho$ leads

to the border of $B_{m,n}$. However, then the trace $\sigma'\rho$ exceeds this border, contradicting the assumption $PQ = B_{m,n}$.

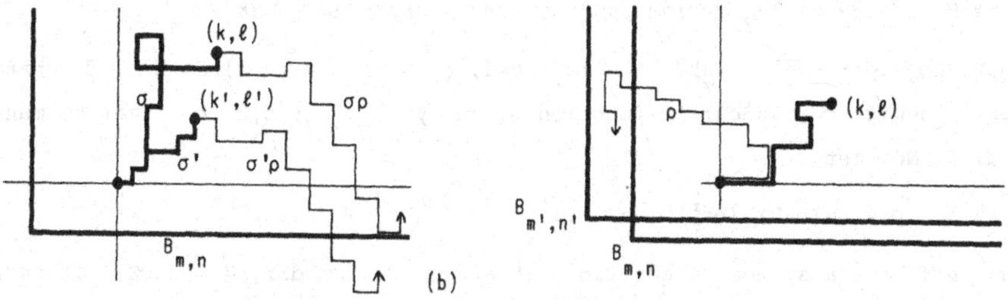

Figure 3 (a) (b)

(ii) To see that $B_{m,n}$ is uniquely determined, consider Figure 3(b) above and let $PQ' = B_{m',n'}$. Say that P's finite traces terminate in (k,ℓ). Now consider a trace ρ in P which avoids this 'exit point'. (Here the argument breaks down for the case of a singleton value domain $D = \{a\}$.) Since (k,ℓ) is P's only exit point (by (i)), ρ is confined to stay in P as long as it avoids (k,ℓ). But then a trace ρ as in Figure 3(b) which enters the symmetrical difference of the areas occupied in the a,b-plane by $B_{m,n}$ and $B_{m',n'}$ leads to an immediate contradiction.

The unicity of Q is proved by similar arguments. (Note that Q is itself a subprocess of B.)

This ends the proof of the Claim. A corollary of the Claim is that in the equations $B_{m,n} = T_{m,n}(\underline{X})$ every $\underline{X_i P}$ (as defined above) can be replaced by B_{k_i,ℓ_i} depending on i alone. Therefore the set of generators can be taken to consist of a finite subset of the collection of $B_{m,n}$, say $\{B_{k_i,\ell_i} \mid i = 1,\ldots,p\}$.

However, by Corollary 3.3.3, B must then be regular, an evident contradiction. Hence B cannot be recursively defined with + and • alone. □

We conclude this paper with the observation that communication yields strictly more expressive power. As a preparation we need another criterion for recursive definability:

THEOREM 4.3. *Let* $\underline{X}$ *be recursively defined over* $A^{\infty}(+,\cdot,\|,\lfloor\!\lfloor)$ *and suppose* $\underline{X}$ *is not finite* ($\underline{X} \notin A_{\omega}$). *Then* $\underline{X}$ *has an infinite regular (i.e. eventually periodic) trace.* □

The proof requires a syntactical analysis for which we refer to [4]. The intuition of the proof can be hinted at by the following example; here we write for variables X_i, X_j in a system $E_X = \{X_i = T_i(X) \mid i = 1,\ldots,n\}$:

$X_i \overset{w}{\dashrightarrow} X_j$ if X_j occurs in $T_i(X)$ and the 'path' w 'leads to' this occurrence of X_j.

Example. Let E_X be $\{X_1 = a(X_2 \lfloor\!\lfloor X_3) + a,\ X_2 = bc(X_3 \| X_3),\ X_3 = aaX_1X_3\}$, then

$$X_1 \overset{a}{\dashrightarrow} X_2 \overset{bc}{\dashrightarrow} X_3 \overset{aa}{\dashrightarrow} X_1,$$

hence $\underline{X}_1$ contains a trace $(abcaa)^{\omega}$.

THEOREM 4.4. *There is a process* $p \in \{a,b\}^{\infty}$ *which cannot be recursively defined in* $\{a,b\}^{\infty}(+,\cdot,\|,⌊\!⌊)$ *but which can be recursively defined in* $\{a,b,c,d,\delta\}^{\infty}(+,\cdot,\|,⌊\!⌊,|,\partial_H)$ *where* H *and the communication function are appropriately chosen.*

PROOF. Consider the alphabet $A = \{a,b,c,d,\delta\}$, with $H = \{c,d\}$ as set of subatomic actions and with communication function given by: $c|c = a$; $d|d = b$; other communications equal δ. Now let

$$p = ba(ba^2)^2(ba^3)^2(ba^4)^2\ldots$$

and consider the system of equations $\{X = cXc + d,\ Y = dXY,\ Z = dXcZ\}$. It turns out that $p = \partial_H(d\,c\,Y\|Z)$. To prove this, consider the processes

$$p_n = \partial_H(dc^nY\|Z)$$

for $n \geq 1$. Now we claim that for all $n \geq 1$: $p_n = ba^nba^{n+1}p_{n+1}$, which immediately yields the result. Proof of the claim:

$$p_n = \partial_H(dc^nY\|Z) = \partial_H(dc^nY\|dXcZ) = ba^n\partial_H(Y\|Xc^ncZ) =$$

$$ba^n\partial_H(dXY\|(cXc+d)c^{n+1}Z) = ba^nb\partial_H(XY\|c^{n+1}Z) =$$

$$ba^nba^{n+1}\partial_H(Xc^{n+1}Y\|Z) = ba^nba^{n+1}\partial_H(dc^{n+1}Y\|Z) =$$

$$ba^nba^{n+1}p_{n+1}.$$

The fact that p cannot be recursively defined without communication is an immediate consequence of Theorem 4.3. □

REFERENCES

[1] DE BAKKER, J.W. & J.I. ZUCKER, Denotational semantics of concurrency, Proc. 14th ACM Symp. on Theory of Computing, p.153-158 (1982).

[2] DE BAKKER, J.W. & J.I. ZUCKER, Processes and the denotational semantics of concurrency, Information and Control, Vol.54, No.1/2, p.70-120, 1982.

[3] BERGSTRA, J.A. & J.W. KLOP, Process algebra for communication and mutual exclusion, Report IW 218/83, Mathematisch Centrum, Amsterdam 1983.

[4] BERGSTRA, J.A. & J.W. KLOP, The algebra of recursively defined processes and the algebra of regular processes, Report IW 235/83, Mathematisch Centrum, Amsterdam 1983.

[5] BERGSTRA, J.A. & J.W. KLOP, Algebra of Communicating Processes, in: Proceedings of the CWI Symposium Mathematics and Computer Science (eds. J.W. de Bakker, M. Hazewinkel and J.K. Lenstra), CWI Monograph Series, North-Holland. To appear.

[6] HENNESSY, M., A term model for synchronous processes, Information and Control, Vol.51, No.1(1981), p.58-75.

[7] HOARE, C.A.R., Communicating Sequential Processes, C.ACM 21 (1978), 666-677.

[8] HOARE, C.A.R., A Model for Communicating Sequential Processes, in: "On the Construction of Programs" (ed. R.M. McKeag and A.M. McNaghton), Cambridge University Press, 1980 (p.229-243).

[9] MILNER, R., A Calculus for Communicating Systems, Springer LNCS 92, 1980.

ALGEBRAIC SPECIFICATION OF EXCEPTION HANDLING AND ERROR RECOVERY

BY MEANS OF DECLARATIONS AND EQUATIONS

MICHEL BIDOIT (*)

(*) CNRS, ERA 452 "AL KHOWARIZMI"
Laboratoire de recherche en Informatique
Bat. 490 Universite de PARIS-SUD
91405 - ORSAY CEDEX FRANCE

ABSTRACT: In this paper, we first discuss the various algebraic approaches to exception handling specification. We show that none of them is completely satisfactory, and we explain why the algebraic specification of exception handling (error introduction, error propagation and error recovery) must not be made using only equations, but also "declarations". We present an approach allowing all forms of error handling, and at the same time keeping specifications well-structured and easily understandable.

I - INTRODUCTION

Most of the time errors or exceptions are first considered at the last step of implementation. For instance, error messages and diagnostics in a compiler are often considered as if they were implementation-dependant and they are not specified in the language's formal definition nor in the language manual. The same situation also holds for telephone switching systems. In these systems, error messages sent to the operator are treated at the last minute; indeed when a telephone switching system is put into service, many error messages that were only useful for development purposes are deleted, and the others, supposed to be relevant, are kept in the final system. This practice is somewhat contradictory in view of the fact that in telephone switching systems, permanent service is a very strong requirement. Moreover, specifying error handling and error recovery policy too late, that is after specification of the normal behaviour of the system is completed, often results in expensive modifications of earlier design decisions.

The development process and the overall quality of programs would certainly be significantly improved if errors and exceptions were systematically dealt with. In [GOG 77], Goguen suggests some basic principles that seem to us sufficiently important to be recalled here:

(1) Think about errors from the beginning, from the preliminary design stage on.

(2) Include all exceptional state behavior, especially error messages, directly in the specifications.

(3) As much information as is helpful about what went "wrong" (or exceptional) should be provided, as a basis for debugging (or further processing in an exceptional state).

The reason why these requirements are not respected in practice may be that very few methodological and linguistic tools are available to specify, develop and transform programs with exception handling. This situation is especially bad at the specification level where a new formalism is necessary in order to be able to specify error cases and error recovery.

Since the work of Liskov, Zilles and Guttag [LZ 75, GUT 75], algebraic data types have been considered as a major tool for writing hierarchical, modular and implementation-independant specifications. Unfortunately, since 1976 this formalism has been shown to be incompatible with the use of operations that return error messages for some values of their arguments. In the example below we briefly sketch out where the problem lies.

Example 1: Assume that one of the equations of the data type presentation is "variable-erasing", i.e. looks like "F(...x...y...) = H(...x...)" (e.g., POP(PUSH e s) = s, or TOP(PUSH e s) = e, or TIMES(0 x) = 0, etc...). Assume now that some operation G is undefined (or must return an error message) for some specific values vi of its arguments, and that the codomain of G is the type of the erased variable (e.g., TOP with TOP(EMPTY), or POP with POP(EMPTY), or PRED with PRED(0), etc...). A lot of troubles may arise depending on the choices made by the designer:

-1- If the designer says nothing about G(vi) (e.g. TOP(EMPTY), PRED(0)), the data type will not be sufficiently complete (and, indeed, the error message not specified at all).

-2- If the designer introduces some equation like "G(vi) = UNDEF" or "G(vi) = ERROR", with some extra constant UNDEF or ERROR, the situation does not look better: what is F(...UNDEF...) ? The most obvious idea is that errors should propagate, i.e. one adds equations like F(...UNDEF...) = UNDEF. This results in a considerable amount of new equations to be added; moreover, such error propagation leads to inconsistencies. In fact with the above erasing equation, every correct term can be shown to be equivalent to UNDEF: F(...x...G(vi)...) is equivalent to H(...x...) on the one hand, and to F(...x...UNDEF...) i.e. UNDEF on the other. Thus H(...x...) is equivalent to UNDEF.

The situation described in the above example is well-known, and several attempts have been made in order to remedy at it. These attemps can be characterized as follows:

-1- In some works, the algebraic approach is given up in favour of an algorithmic approach or an operational approach [LOE 81, EHR 81]. The problem described in the above example disappears if operation properties are specified by means of algorithms: an error will correspond to some special case of halting, and no inconsistencies arise, since there is no explicit equivalence between terms. Unfortunately, these approaches lead to very complicated proofs, since one has to prove the equivalence of two algorithms in order to prove the equivalence of two expressions. Similar remarks hold with the operational approach where properties of operations are specified by means of rewrite rules.

-2- Other works rely on the partial algebra approach. In this approach, no new objects are introduced; therefore there is no insufficient completeness, nor error propagation. But this approach needs an entirely new formalism [BW 82], and it does not really solve the error handling specification problem, since errors are simply avoided.

-3- In the other works, errors values are explicitly introduced: one error value for each sort in [ADJ 76], a partition of the carriers into okay values and erroneous values in [GOG 77], and distinct sorts for okay values and erroneous values in [GOG 78]. Therefore all these approaches must face the error propagation problem. In [ADJ 76] the propagation is explicitly described by means of equations. Unfortunately this approach leads to unlegible specifications in which normal cases and erroneous cases are mixed together: such an approach is incompatible with modular, structured specifications. However, this approach has demonstrated that abstract data types with errors are equationally specifiable. In [GOG 77], the propagation (meta) rule is not expressed by equations, but is encoded into the models: the algebras taken into consideration are called "error-algebras". In [BG 83] it is shown that the formalism described in [GOG 77] is not correct, since every ground term can be shown to be equivalent to one error value. Moreover, since all operations must be strict ones, error recovery is not possible in the error-algebra framework. In [GOG 78], Goguen suggests considering error propagation as a special case of coercion and overloading; unfortunately, the examples described in this paper are not consistent with the formalism [BG 83], nor is error recovery possible.

-4- More recently, three new approaches have been proposed. In [PLA 82], Plaisted describe a rigorous treatment of the error-algebras of Goguen; however, this formalism is not powerful enough for our purposes, since strict functions do not allow error recovery. In [EHR 83], another treatment of error-algebras is proposed; this one allows all forms of error handling, but is made possible only because there is no (implicit) error propagation. Thus, error propagation must be specified case by case, which seems practicable only if there is just one error value for each sort. In the other cases, the criticisms that we have made about the classical equational approach of [ADJ 76] remain true, even if this formalism allows error recovery. In [BGP 83], a new formalism, derived from the work described in [GOG 78], is described: correct values and erroneous values are split into different, disjoint sorts. Thus an operator which may produce some errors has two or more possible sorts as codomains. For instance, the arity of the (multi-target) operator pop will be stated as follow:

"pop : Stack --> Stack U Stack-err."

The underlying notion of algebra has to be re-examined, and a precise meaning has to be provided for the axioms. The multi-target algebras framework allow all forms of error handling, but the situation remains quite complicated, since the error propagation rule makes no sense in this framework; thus "error propagation" must be specified case by case. Note also that the use of coercion and overloading leads to complicated signatures, and that some (problematic) features of the partial algebras approach appear in the multi-target algebras: due to the classical rules on the composition of the operations, some terms may be undefined: for instance, "pop(underflow)" is not a term since underflow is of type Stack-err and the domain of pop is Stack.

In this paper we describe a new formalism where all forms of error handling are possible. Our formalism is very close to the one introduced in [EHR 83], but we show how an implicit error propagation rule may be encoded into the models without losing the possibility of error recovery. Thus all the equations necessary to specify error propagation may be avoided, and the specifications remain well-structured and easily understandable. We shall also use "repartition functions" similar to those introduced in [BGP 83].

II - SPECIFYING EXCEPTION HANDLING AND ERROR RECOVERY BY MEANS OF DECLARATIONS

In this section we explain why exception cases and error recovery cases should not be specified by means of equations, but rather by means of "declarations".

Remember that in the error-algebras framework described in [GOG 77], equations are divided into ok-equations and error-equations. The validity of an ok-equation is defined as follow:

> "An ok-equation M = N is valid in an error-algebra A if and only if, for every assignment a of the variables of M and N into elements of A, if BOTH a(M) and a(N) denote ok-values of A, then a(M) and a(N) must be equal"

while the validity of an error-equation is defined by:

> "An error-equation M = N is valid in an error-algebra A if and only if, for every assignment a of the variables of M and N into elements of A, if ONE of a(M) or a(N) denotes an error-value of A, then a(M) and a(N) must be equal (hence both must denote error-values of A)."

Thus ok-equations are used just to identify ok-elements, while error-equations are used to identify error-elements as well as to force some elements to be erroneous ones.

Assume that we want to define the validity of "recovery-equations" by analogy with the validity of error-equations; this would lead to the following definition:

for every assignment a of the variables of M and N into elements of A, if ONE of a(M) or a(N) denotes an ok-value of A, then a(M) and a(N) must be equal (hence both must denote ok-values of A).

This definition seems to work very well with a recovery-equation like "push(x, underflow) = empty". Unfortunately, the previous definition will lead to recover "push(error-element, underflow)", which seems undesirable! However, unwanted recovery will not occur if one uses recovery-equations both members of which have the same variables (e.g. "push(x, underflow) = push(x, empty)"). But things will go awry if one uses recovery-equations like "push(x, underflow) = push(top(push(x, underflow)), empty).

Our claim is that neither error cases nor recovery cases should be specified by means of equations, but rather by means of "declarations". Thus some terms will be declared to be erroneous, others will be declared to be ok. Ok-equations and error-equations will be used to identify ok-values and error-values respectively, no more. This will lead to more structured specifications, since the specification of the error policy (error introduction and error recovery) will be made apart from the equations. Moreover, our framework will implement the following natural propagation rule: "errors propagate unless their recovery is specified". In order to allow a careful recovery policy and the use of non-strict functions, we shall use three distinct kinds of variables (to distinguish between two kinds of variables was already suggested in [EHR 83]): ordinary variables may range over the whole carrier set, ok-variables may only range over the ok-part of the corresponding carrier set, error-variables may only range over the error part of the corresponding carrier set. As a syntactical convenience, ok-variables will always be suffixed by "+", while error-variables will always be suffixed by "-" (e.g. x+, y-, etc.).

The necessary theoretical material is described beginning in Section IV. In the next section we illustrate how an algebraic specification of a stack, including exception handling and error recovery, can fit into our framework.

III - THE STACK WITH EXCEPTION HANDLING AND ERROR RECOVERY

Before giving the specification of the stack, we must make precise what kind of stack we have in mind. In our stack, we shall have an infinite number of error elements, with two specific values: underflow, which will be obtained (as the result) when popping the empty stack; and crash, which will be obtained when popping underflow. Stack terms obtained from the "crash" stack are definitively erroneous. Underflow is an erroneous stack, but one can recover from this state by pushing an okay element onto it. In all cases pushing an erroneous element onto a stack leads to the crash stack.

Here is our stack specification:

SPECIF STACK

```
SORTS Stack, Element
OPERATIONS
empty     :                 --> Stack
underflow :                 --> Stack
crash     :                 --> Stack
push      : Element Stack --> Stack
pop       : Stack         --> Stack
top       : Stack         --> Element
EXCEPTION CASES
e1:       underflow
e2:       crash
e3:       pop(empty)
e4:       top(empty)
RECOVERY CASES
r1:       push(x+, underflow)
OK-EQUATIONS
ok1:      pop(push(x,p)) = p
ok2:      top(push(x,p)) = x
ok3:      push(x, underflow) = push(x, empty)
ERROR-EQUATIONS
err1:     pop(empty) = underflow
err2:     pop(underflow) = crash
err3:     push(x-, p) = crash
END STACK
```

In this example, note that nothing more is required than "top(empty) is an exception case"; however, if one wants to identify top(empty) with an erroneous element, say "bottom", an error-equation "top(empty) = bottom" may be added. Furthermore, if one wants to identify all erroneous values of sort Element with "bottom", this can be achieved by adding the following error-equation: "x = bottom".

In the same manner, the equation ok3 is not absolutely necessary; however, in our case we do not want to just specify that pushing an okay element onto the underflow stack is a recovery case, but also that the stack obtained is equal to pushing the same element onto the empty stack.

One explication is also needed for the error-equation err3: note that we have not (explicitly) specified that push(x-, p) is an error term; this is simply a consequence of the natural error propagation rule, since x- denotes an error element.

IV - E,R-ALGEBRAS

In this section we show how the results of [ADJ 78] carry over to our notion of algebra. Our carrier sets are split into okay values and error values, and we use three kinds of variables: ordinary variables, ok-variables x+, and error-variables y-. In the following, "generalized variable" will mean a variable of any kind.

DEFINITION 1: "E,R-signature"
An E,R-signature is a triple < Sigma, Exc, Rec > where:
- Sigma is a signature, i.e. a set of sorts S and a set of operation names with their arity.
- Exc and Rec are two sets of terms (built from the signature Sigma and generalized variables). Exc is the set of Exceptions declarations and Rec is the set of Recovery declarations.

REMARK: E,R-signature means signature with Exception and Recovery cases. Note that we do not need to distinguish between ok-operations and error-operations [GOG 77], nor between safe and unsafe operations [EHR 83]. Indeed most of the operations may produce both okay and error values (except constant operations), and such a distinction would therefore not be very relevant.

In the definition below, a "safe assignment" means an assignment of the variables into elements of the carrier sets such that ok-values are assigned to ok-variables and error-values are assigned to error-variables. The concept of "safe assignment" is an especially important one, since it allows one to recover error values carefully. For instance, in the Stack example described in Section III, the declaration "push(x+, empty)" in Rec will lead to recover "push(ell, empty)" (where ell is supposed to be an okay element), but not "push(bottom, empty)".

DEFINITION 2: "E,R-algebra"
Given some E,R-signature < Sigma, Exc, Rec >, an E,R-algebra A (w.r.t. this E,R-signature) is a Sigma-algebra such that:
(i) Each carrier As (s in S) is defined as the disjoint union of two sets As-ok and As-err (the ok-values of type s and the error-values of type s).
(ii) For each term t in Exc and each "safe assignment" sa of the variables of t into elements of A, sa(t) must denote an error-value of A.
(iii) For each term t in Rec and each "safe assignment" sa of the variables of t into elements of A, sa(t) must denote an ok-value of A.
(iv) For every operation name F: s1x...xsn --> s and for every a1,...,an in As1,...,Asn respectively, the following holds:

if one of the ai is an error-value (i.e. ai is in Asi-err),

and if there does not exist a term t in Rec and a "safe assignment" sa such that sa(t) denotes F(a1,...,an)

then F(a1,...,an) is an error-value, i.e. is in As-err.

REMARKS:
(i) expresses the fact that the carrier sets are split into ok-values and error-values.
(ii) ensures that cases declared exceptional in Exc are effectively exceptional values in all models (this condition is similar to "error operators always create

error elements" in [GOG 77]).
(iii) is the symmetric condition for recovery cases.
(iv) embodies the idea that errors propagate unless some recovery has been specified.

Note that some E,R-signatures may not have any corresponding E,R-algebra; this may happen if the exception and recovery cases are "contradictory". Such signatures will be called E,R-inconsistent, and we shall give later sufficient conditions for a signature to be E,R-consistent (intuitively, a signature will be E,R-consistent if no term of Exc is unifiable with a term of Rec).

DEFINITION 3: "E,R-consistent"
An E,R-signature is E,R-consistent if and only if there exists at least one E,R-algebra with respect to this signature.

In the following, signatures will always be assumed to be E,R-consistent.

V - REPARTITION FUNCTIONS, E,R-MORPHISMS AND THE E,R-INITIAL MODEL

In this section, we define the repartition functions associated with an E,R-signature. A similar concept has been previously introduced in [BGP 83]; it will be used to characterize the various possible partitions of the (ground) term algebra in a simple manner. Repartition functions will also be a key concept in the study of the validity problem and the study of all the models specified by a given E,R-presentation.

DEFINITION 4: "Repartition functions"
An E,R-repartition function REP is a (total) mapping of the Sigma ground terms into (OK, ERR) such that:
for each term t = Ft1...tn
(i) If t is a REP-safe-instance of some term T in Exc, then REP(t) = ERR.
(ii) If t is a REP-safe-instance of some term T in Rec, then REP(t) = OK.
(iii) If none of the two above cases applies and if one of the subterms t1,...,tn (say tj) is such that REP(tj) = ERR, then REP(t) = ERR.
When none of these three cases applies, REP(t) may be arbitrarily chosen.

REMARK: In the above definition, a REP-safe-instance of T is defined (by analogy with Section IV) as an assignment of the variables of T into ground terms such that, if x+ is an ok-variable, it will be assigned to a term u such that REP(u) = OK, and if y- is an error-variable, it will be assigned to a term v such that REP(v) = ERR. This definition is well-founded on the size of terms. Unfortunately, the first two conditions may be contradictory, even if the signature is assumed to be E,R-consistent (take a constant operator a, two unary functions f and g, Exc = f(g(x)), Rec = f(x+): this signature is consistent, but (i) and (ii) above may be contradic-

Therefore we add the following non-contradiction restriction in order for Definition 4 to make sense:

NON-CONTRADICTION CONDITION: An E,R-signature will be said "non-contradictory" if and only if, for each T in Exc and T′ in Rec, T and T′ are not unifiable. This condition is always assumed to hold in the following.

For lack of space we can not delve more deeply into this point here; however, the definition of "unifiable" must be conveniently refined in order to take into account the three kinds of variables (e.g. push(x+, underflow) and push(y-, p) should not be declared unifiable). The usual meaning of "unifiable" would lead to a bit too strong non-contradiction condition.

An ordering can be defined over the repartition functions as follows:

DEFINITION 5: "The repartition functions ordering"
Let REP1 and REP2 be two repartition functions. REP1 << REP2 if and only if, for each (ground) term t, we have: REP1(t) = ERR ==> REP2(t) = ERR.

Now the main result over repartition functions can be stated:

PROPOSITION 1: "The complete lattice of repartition functions"
With the above ordering, the repartition functions form a complete lattice; the maximum REP1vREP2 of two repartition functions REP1 and REP2 is defined by:

REP1(t) = ERR or REP2(t) = ERR <==> REP1vREP2(t) = ERR

while their minimum REP1^REP2 is defined by:

REP1(t) = ERR and REP2(t) = ERR <==> REP1^REP2(t) = ERR.

The minimum repartition function is the function REPinit defined by:
For each term t = Ft1...tn not specified by one of the three cases enumerated in Definition 4, we choose: REPinit(t) = OK.
The maximum repartition function is the function REPterm defined by:
For each term t = Ft1...tn not specified by one of the three cases enumerated in Definition 4, we choose: REPterm(t) = ERR.

Proof: by induction over ground terms and a case analysis over the values of the repartition functions.

Repartition functions are related to (ground) term E,R-algebras by the following lemma:

LEMMA 1: "The ground term E,R-algebras"
Let GT denote the usual ground term algebra. To each repartition function REP is associated an E,R algebra GT-REP defined by:
for each ground term t, if REP(t) = OK then t is in GT-REP-ok, else t is in GT-REP-err.

REMARK: As a direct consequence of the previous lemma, we note that if the non-contradiction condition holds, then the signature is E,R-consistent.

DEFINITION 6: "E,R-morphisms"
Given some E,R-signature and two E,R-algebras A and B (w.r.t. this signature), an E,R-morphism h: A --> B is a family of mappings hs: As --> Bs such that:
- h is an algebra morphism in the usual sense and
- For each s in S, hs(As-err) is a subset of Bs-err (i.e. errors are preserved).

If h is an isomorphism then we have hs(As-ok) = Bs-ok and hs(As-err) = Bs-er for each sort s.

THEOREM 1: "The initial E,R-algebra"
E,R-algebras (w.r.t. some E,R-signature) and E,R-morphisms form a category. This category has an initial algebra, GT-REPinit.

Proof: follows directly from Proposition 1 and Lemma 1.

VI - E,R-PRESENTATIONS AND THE VALIDITY PROBLEM

DEFINITION 7: "E,R-presentation"
An E,R-presentation is an quintuple < Sigma, Exc, Rec, ok-E, err-E > such that:
- < Sigma, Exc, Rec > is an E,R-signature.
- ok-E and err-E are two sets of Sigma-equations. The equations of ok-E are called "ok-equations", while the equations of err-E are called "error-equations".

REMARK: Note that this definition is different from the definitions given in [GOG 77] or in [PLA 82]. Since we have not distinguished between ok-operations and error-operations, no restrictive conditions over ok-equations nor error-equations are necessary in our framework. Furthermore, the same equation may appear both in ok-E and err-E. However, equations of ok-E have a different meaning than equations of err-E:

DEFINITION 8: "E,R-validity"
Let A be an E,R-algebra.
- A |= e where e: M = N is an ok-equation if and only if, for every safe assignment sa of the variables of M and N into elements of A, if BOTH sa(M) and sa(N) denote ok-values of A, then sa(M) and sa(N) must be equal.

- A |= e where e: M = N is an error-equation if and only if, for every safe assignment sa of the variables of M and N into elements of A, if BOTH sa(M) and sa(N) denote error-values of A, then sa(M) and sa(N) must be equal.

This definition allows one to define the models of an E,R-presentation P: these models are the E,R-algebras that satisfy the ok-equations and the error-equations of P. These models, together with all E,R-morphisms, form a category. Unfortunately, this category may not have an initial object, as can be shown by similar examples to those described in [PLA 82].

In the following example we show how a strict "if-then-else", as well as a non strict one, can be specified.

EXAMPLE:

(1) A strict "if-then-else" operation may be specified as follows:

ok-E: if TRUE then x else y = x

if FALSE then x else y = y

No exception declaration is necessary, since we have an implicit error propagation rule.

(2) A non-strict "if-then-else" operation may be specified as follows:

Rec: if TRUE then x+ else y

if FALSE then x else y+

ok-E: if TRUE then x else y = x

if FALSE then x else y = y

VII - CHARACTERIZATION OF THE MODELS BY MEANS OF CONGRUENCES

In this section, we assume given an E,R-presentation P, and the non-contradiction condition is assumed to hold.

GT denotes the ground term algebra associated to this presentation (note that GT is a term algebra, NOT a term E,R-algebra). Two congruences =ok= and =err= are defined in a canonical way over GT: =ok= (resp. =err=) is the smallest congruence (in the classical sense) generated by the ok-equations (resp. the error-equations).

DEFINITION 9: "P-compatibility"

A repartition function REP and a congruence == over GT are said to be P-compatible if and only if the following three conditions hold, for every tuple (t, t') of ground terms:

(i) [REP (t) = REP (t') = OK and t =ok= t'] ==> t == t'.

(ii) [REP (t) = REP (t') = ERR and t =err= t'] ==> t == t'.

(iii) [t == t'] ==> REP (t) = REP (t').

REMARK: Note that the fact that == is assumed to be a congruence (in the classical sense) over GT is especially important; this fact, together with condition (iii), will ensure that some terms are effectively erroneous ones. For instance, these two conditions will ensure that pred(0 + 0) is erroneous, if REP(pred(0)) = ERR:

* 0 + 0 is okay, so is 0 and they verify 0 + 0 =ok= 0, hence 0 + 0 == 0
* since == is a congruence, we must have pred(0 + 0) == pred(0)
* but since REP(pred(0)) = ERR, (iii) implies REP(pred(0 + 0)) = ERR.

Thus, the previous definition will often be used in the following way:

" if REP(t) = ERR and t == t' then REP(t') = ERR "

Note that some repartition functions may not have any corresponding compatible congruence. Such repartition functions will be called P-inconsistent. The two following theorems relate the P-compatibility condition with the E,R-algebras satisfying P.

THEOREM 2: "The REP-initial E,R-algebra satisfying P"
Given an E,R-presentation P and a P-consistent repartition function REP, there exists a smallest congruence P-compatible with REP, say =i=. GT-REP/=i= is initial in the class of all the E,R-algebras A satisfying P and such that REP(t) = OK if and only if t denotes an ok-value in A.

THEOREM 3: "Characterization of the finitely generated P-models"
Given an E,R-presentation P and a model M of P (i.e. an E,R-algebra M satisfying P), there exists only one tuple (REP, ==) such that:
(i) REP is a repartition function.
(ii) == is a congruence over M.
(iii) REP and == are P-compatible.
(iv) REP(t) = OK if and only if t denotes an ok-value in M.
(v) t == t' if and only if t and t' denote the same value in M.

Conversely, to each tuple (REP, ==) P-compatible is associated a model M of P defined by:
(i) M = GT/==.
(ii) M-ok is the set of congruence classes [t] with REP(t) = OK.

VIII - FURTHER DEVELOPMENTS AND CONCLUSION

An operational semantics of a subclass of our E,R-presentations may be defined. This operational semantics will be defined by means of inside-outside hierarchical rewritings for ground terms, and by means of contextual rewritings for terms with generalized variables. This operational semantics will be well-defined if the two set of equations can be viewed as two sets of rewrite rules and if these two sets have the finite Church-Rosser property (including the exception cases and the recovery cases for the computation of critical pairs). In this case the operational semantics coincides with the algebraic semantics. If the rewriting systems have not the Church-Rosser property, some extension of the Knuth-Bendix completion procedure can be defined in order to find rewritings systems equivalent to the algebraic semantics.

Our formalism may be extended in order to allow a larger class of declarations and axioms. Our results extend without problems if one allows "positive conditional declarations" and "positive conditional equations", that is, declarations of the form:
" [E1 & ... & En & D1 & ... & Dm] ==> D "

and axioms of the form :

" [E1 & ... & En & D1 & ... & Dm] ==> E "

where Ei denotes an ok-equation or an error-equation, and Dj denotes an exception declaration or a recovery declaration (the type of equation and declaration must be added to each elementary equation or declaration).

Thus the formalism described in this paper seems to be very promising, as it allows one to specify all forms of error handling, and at the same time keeps specifications well-structured and easily understandable. Moreover, our formalism can be seen as an attempt to provide a precise and formal semantics to the fairly simple looking approach described by Guttag in [GUT 78].

ACKNOWLEDGMENTS

The work reported here was partially supported by D.A.I.I. Contract Number 82.35.033 and the C.N.R.S. (Greco de Programmation). Special thanks are due to Professor Marie-Claude Gaudel for her patient encouragement and many helpful suggestions and discussions. I also thank Professor Gerard Guiho for his comments on previous versions of this paper.

REFERENCES

[ADJ 76] Goguen J., Thatcher J. Wagner E., "An Initial Algebra approach to the specification, correctness, and implementation of abstract data types" in Current Trends in Programming Methodology, Vol.4, Yeh Ed. Prentice Hall, 1978 (also IBM Report RC 6487, October 1976).

[BG 83] Bidoit M., Gaudel M.C., "Etudes des methodes de specification des cas d'exceptions dans les types abstraits algebriques", Report L.R.I, Orsay, 1983.

[BGP 83] Boisson F., Guiho G., Pavot D., "Algebres a Operateurs Multicibles" Report LRI 132, Orsay, June 1983.

[BW 82] Broy M., Wirsing M., "Partial Abstract Data Types" Acta Informatica, Vol.18-1, Nov 1982.

[EHR 81] Engels G., Pletat V., Ehrich H. "Handling Err}iors and Exceptions in the Algebraic Specification of Data Types" Osnabruecker Schriften zur Mathematik, July 1981.

[EHR 83] Gogolla M., Drosten K., Lipeck U., Ehrich H., "Algebraic and operational semantics of specifications allowing exceptions and errors" Proc. 6th GI-Conference on Theoretical Computer Science, LNCS 145, 1983, Springer-Verlag.

[GOG 77] Goguen J.A., "Abstract errors for abstract data types" in Formal Description of Programming Concepts E.J. NEUHOLD Ed., North Holland, New York 1977.

[GOG 78] Goguen J.A., "Exception and Error Sorts, Coercion and Overloading Operators" S.R.I. Research Report, 1978.

[GUT 75] Guttag J.V., "The Specification and Application to Programming" Ph.D. Thesis, University of Toronto, 1975.

[GUT 78] Guttag J.V., "Notes on Type Abstraction (Version 2)" I.E.E.E. Transactions on Software Engineering, 1979.

[LOE 81] Loeckx J., "Algorithmic Specifications of Abstract Data Types" ICALP 1981.

[LZ 75] Liskov B., Zilles S., "Specifications techniques for Data Abstractions" I.E.E.E. Transactions on Software Engineering, Vol. SE-1 N 1, March 1975.

[PLA 82] Plaisted D. "An initial algebra semantics for error presentations" Unpublished Draft, 1982

Building the Minimal DFA for the Set of all Subwords of a Word On-line in Linear Time.

by

A. Blumer, J. Blumer, A. Ehrenfeucht*,
D. Haussler and R. McConnell

Department of Mathematics and Computer Science
University of Denver
Denver, Colorado 80208

*Department of Computer Science
University of Colorado at Boulder
Boulder, Colorado 80302

All correspondence to D. Haussler.

Authors A. Blumer and D. Haussler gratefully acknowledge the support of NSF grant IST-8317918 and Author A. Ehrenfeucht the support of NSF grant MCS-8305245.

Abstract

Let a partial deterministic finite automaton be a DFA in which each state need not have a transition edge for each letter of the alphabet. We demonstrate that the minimal partial DFA for the set of all subwords of a given word w, $|w| > 2$, has at most $2|w| - 2$ states and $3|w| - 4$ transition edges, independently of the alphabet size. We give an algorithm to build this minimal partial DFA from the input w on-line in linear time.

Introduction

In the classic string matching problem for text, we are given a text w and a pattern string x and we want to know if x appears in w, i.e. if x is a subword of w. Standard approaches to this problem involve various methods for preprocessing x so that the text w can be rapidly searched ([Aho 75], [Boy 77], [Knu 77]). Since each search still takes time proportional to the length of w, this method is inappropriate when many different patterns are examined against a fixed text, e.g. for repeated lookups in any fixed textual database. In this case, it is desirable to preprocess the text itself, building an auxiliary data structure which allows one to determine if x is a subword of w in time proportional to the length of x, not w. Data structures with this property (known as "suffix trees" or "compact position trees", earlier as "PATRICIA trees") have been developed ([Maj 80], [McC 76], [Wei 73], [Mor 68]) and used in a wide variety of pattern matching applications, in addition to the classic string matching problem given above ([Maj 80], [Apo 83], [Rod 81]).

Clearly, a deterministic finite automaton (DFA) which recognizes the set of all subwords of w would serve as an auxiliary index for w in the above sense. This automaton can also be partial, in the sense that each state need not have a transition on each letter. We demonstrate the feasibility of this approach by showing that the minimal partial DFA for the set of all subwords of w has less than $2|w|$ states and $3|w|$ transition edges, and can be built on-line in linear time. The space occupied by this automaton is comparable to that of the compact position tree, and the construction algorithm has the advantage of being on-line in the sense that it builds the automaton with one left to right scan of the text, producing the correct minimal DFA for each prefix of the text as it proceeds (see [Maj 80] for a discussion of the advantages of an on-line algorithm).

The development of these results can be given as follows. (Some of these results were announced in [Blu 83]). We begin in Section 1 by demonstrating the existence of a deterministic finite automaton which recognizes the set of all subwords of w with at most $2|w|$ states for $|w| > 1$ (Lemma 1). A partial DFA which still accepts all subwords of w can be derived from this automaton by omitting the non-accepting state and all transition edges leading into it. This partial DFA has less than $3|w|$ transition edges, independently of the size of the alphabet on which the text is defined (Lemma 2). Since all states in this partial DFA are accepting, it is essentially a directed acyclic graph with unlabelled nodes, and edges labelled by letters of the alphabet. We call it the Directed Acyclic Word Graph (DAWG) for w. An algorithm to build the DAWG is given in [Blu 83], and extended to finite sets of words in [Blu 84]. Seiferas and Chen ([Sei 83]) have independently developed a similar algorithm for a modified version of the DAWG. They point out that portions of this data structure were incorporated as an auxiliary structure in Weiner's construction algorithm for the compact position tree ([Wei 73]), but with the following twist: the subwords indexed are a subset of those of the *reverse* of the word w. Other close relatives of the DAWG appear in [Pra 73] and [Sli 80].

We use Lemmas 1 and 2 to derive exact upper bounds of $2|w| - 2$ states and $3|w| - 4$ transition edges for the minimal partial DFA recognizing the subwords of w (Theorem 1). A series of strings which achieve these upper bounds is also given. Examination of the differences between the DAWG and the minimal partial automaton (Lemma 3 and Theorem 2) shows that it is not difficult to modify the DAWG construction algorithm given in [Blu 83] so that it constructs the minimal automaton. We present this algorithm in Section 2. Stages of construction for this algorithm, as compared to those for the DAWG algorithm, are illustrated in Figure 1. The final product is compared to that for the suffix tree construction in Figure 2.

Notation

Throughout this paper Σ denotes an arbitrary nonempty finite alphabet and Σ^* denotes the set of all strings over Σ. The empty word is denoted by λ. For any $w \in \Sigma^*$, $|w|$ denotes the length of w. If $w = xyz$ for words $x, y, z \in \Sigma^*$, then y is a *subword* of w, x is a *prefix* of w, and z is a *suffix* of w. In addition to the standard notation for finite automata, we use the word *partial DFA* (for the alphabet Σ) to denote a deterministic finite automaton in which each state need not have a transition for every letter of Σ. The *minimal* partial DFA for a given language is the partial DFA that recognizes the language and has the smallest number of states (uniqueness follows from

Nerode's theorem [Rab 59]).

Section 1. The Minimal Automaton

We begin with a brief look at some aspects of the subword structure of a fixed, arbitrary word w. In particular, for each subword y of w, we will be interested in the set of positions in w immediately following occurrences of y.

Definition. Let $w = a_1 \cdots a_n$, $a_1, \ldots, a_n \in \Sigma$, be a word in Σ^*. For any nonempty y in Σ^*, the *end-set* of y in w is given by $endpos_w(y) = \{j : y = a_i \cdots a_j\}$ for some i and j, $1 \le i \le j \le n$. $endpos_w(\lambda) = \{0, 1, 2, \ldots, n\}$. We shall say that x and y in Σ^* are equivalent (on w) if $endpos_w(x) = endpos_w(y)$. This relation is denoted by $x \equiv^{D_w} y$. For any word x, the equivalence class of x with respect to $\equiv^{D_w}$ is denoted $[x]_{\equiv^{D_w}}$. The equivalence class of all words x such that $endpos_w(x) = \phi$, i.e. all words which are not subwords of w, is called the ***degenerate*** class. All other classes are ***nondegenerate***. ▪

For any w, $\equiv^{D_w}$ is clearly a right invariant equivalence relation. Thus, the equivalence relation $\equiv^{D_w}$ leads us directly to the definition of a finite automaton for the set of all subwords of w, using the well-known machinery developed by A. Nerode (see [Rab 59]).

Definition. For any word w, A_w is the deterministic finite automaton with alphabet Σ and states corresponding to equivalence classes under $\equiv^{D_w}$ such that

1. The start state of A_w is $[\lambda]_{\equiv^{D_w}}$
2. For any state $[x]_{\equiv^{D_w}}$ and any letter $a \in \Sigma$, there is a transition edge for $[x]_{\equiv^{D_w}}$ to $[xa]_{\equiv^{D_w}}$ on letter a.
3. All nondegenerate equivalence classes correspond to accepting states and the degenerate class corresponds to the only non-accepting state. ▪

Lemma 1. For any $w \in \Sigma^*$, A_w recognizes the set of all subwords of w. In addition, A_w has at most max $(2|w|, |w| + 2)$ states.

Proof. That A_w recognizes the set of all subwords of w follows from Nerode's theorem ([Rab 59]). For the size bound, we treat the case where $w = a^n$, $n \ge 0$, separately. In this case, there are $|w| + 1$ distinct nondegenerate equivalence classes induced by $\equiv^{D_w}$ and hence $|w| + 2$ classes in total, giving $|w| + 2$ states. When w does not have this special form (i.e. when there are at least two distinct letters in w), we note that for any $x, y \in \Sigma^*$, if $endpos_w(x) \cap endpos_w(y)$ is not empty, then x is a suffix of y or vice versa, hence $endpos_w(x) \subseteq endpos_w(y)$ or vice versa. It follows that the containment relation on $\{endpos_w(x) : x$ is a subword of $w\}$ forms a tree. Since this tree has at most $|w|$ leaves and each internal node has degree at least two, it has at most $2|w| - 1$ nodes. Thus counting the degenerate class, there are at most $2|w|$ equivalence classes induced by $\equiv^{D_w}$, giving at most $2|w|$ states in A_w. ▪

The use of the tree to bound the number of states in the above proof is similar to the technique used in [Wei 73] to bound the number of nodes in the compact position tree. In fact this tree of containment for the end-sets of w is isomorphic to the compact position tree for the reverse of the word w, when w has a unique beginning symbol (see [Sei 83]).

The number of transition edges in A_w will be the product of the number of states in A_w and the size of the alphabet Σ. However, most of these edges lead to the non-accepting state (corresponding to the degenerate class), from which there is no exit. We will get a better bound on the number of edges by considering the equivalent partial DFA.

Definition. Let D_w be the automaton derived from A_w by deleting the one non-accepting state of A_w and all transitions leading to this state. Following [Blu 83], D_w is called the Directed Acyclic Word Graph (DAWG) for w. The *source* of D_w is the the start state and the *sink* of D_w is the state corresponding to $[w]_{\equiv_{D_w}}$. ▪

From the definition of D_w, it is clear that it is in fact a directed acyclic graph with edges labeled from Σ, with one source and one sink (see Figure 1). It is not necessary to distinguish between accepting and non-accepting states, because all states are accepting. Further, every state of D_w lies on a path from the source of D_w to the sink of D_w and given $|w| \geq 1$, the sequence of labels on each distinct path from the source of D_w to the sink of D_w forms a distinct nonempty suffix of w.

These properties can be used to establish the following.

Lemma 2. Let N be the number of states in D_w and E be the number of edges in D_w, where w is nonempty. Then $E \leq N + |w| - 2$.

Proof. Since every state of D_w is reachable from the source of D_w by a directed path, we can find a directed spanning tree of D_w, rooted at the source. This will have $N-1$ edges. With each edge of D_w which is not in the spanning tree, we can associate a unique path in D_w from the source to the sink. Since each of these paths forms a unique nonempty suffix of w, there are at most $|w|$ such paths. In fact, since at least one of the suffixes of w must correspond to a path in the spanning tree, there are at most $|w| - 1$ such paths. Hence $E \leq (N-1)+(|w|-1) = N+|w|-2$. ▪

Since D_w has one less state than A_w, Lemmas 1 and 2 can be combined to give overall bounds for D_w of $2|w| - 1$ states and $3|w| - 3$ edges, when $|w| > 1$, i.e. when $2|w|$ dominates $|w| + 2$.

We now turn our attention to the relationship between D_w and the minimal partial DFA that recognizes the set of subwords of w, which we will denote M_w.

In some cases, M_w can be considerably smaller than D_w. For example, if $w = ab^n$, $a, b \in \Sigma$ and $n \geq 1$, then D_w achieves the upper bound of $2|w| - 1$ states (with $2|w| - 1$ edges), while M_w has only $|w| + 1$ states (and only $|w| + 1$ edges). On the other hand, if $w = ab^nc$, $a, b, c \in \Sigma$ and $n \geq 1$, then $D_w = M_w$, and D_w has $2|w| - 2$ states and $3|w| - 4$ edges. The following theorem shows that this is the worst case.

Theorem 1. For any $w \in \Sigma^*$, $|w| > 2$, M_w has at most $2|w| - 2$ states and $3|w| - 4$ edges, and at least $|w|+1$ states and $|w|$ edges.

Proof For the upper bound, we show that when $|w| > 2$, D_w has $2|w| - 1$ states only when $w = ab^n$ for some $a, b \in \Sigma$. As mentioned above, M_w is small in this case. It follows from Lemma 1 that for all other w of length greater than 2, D_w has at most $2|w| - 2$ states and hence at most $3|w| - 4$ edges by Lemma 2. Hence M_w is bounded in this manner as well.

Our basic claim is verified by examining the tree of containment for the sets in $\{endpos_w(x) : x \text{ is a subword of } w\}$, as in the proof of Lemma 1. For D_w to have $2|w| - 1$ states, this must be a binary tree with $|w|$ leaves, one for each of the end-sets $\{1\}$, $\{2\}$, ..., $\{|w|\}$. This can only occur when the first letter of w is unique, because otherwise there is no subword x of w such that $endpos_w(x) = \{1\}$. If the first letter is unique, no end-set contains $\{1\}$ except $endpos_w(\lambda)$, which is the root of the tree. Since the tree is binary, the root of the tree has degree 2, which implies that there is an end-set $\{2,3,...,|w|\}$, i.e. that all of the remaining letters are identical.

The lower bound follows from the fact that M_w accepts a finite language and so must be acyclic. Thus there must be at least a state for each letter in w and a start state, yielding a total of at least $|w|+1$ states. Similarly, there must be an edge for each letter in w. The string a^n is a case where this bound is tight. ▪

We now turn our attention to the question of determining precisely how the DAWG D_w differs from the minimal partial DFA. Examples are given in Figure 1.

Definition. Let $\equiv^{M_w}$ denote the canonical right invariant equivalence relation on the set of all subwords of w, i.e. $x \equiv^{M_w} y$ if and only if for all $z \in \Sigma^*$, xz is a subword of w if and only if yz is a subword of w. For any word x, $[x]_{\equiv^{M_w}}$ is the equivalence class of x with respect to $\equiv^{M_w}$. ▪

By Nerode's theorem ([Rab 59]), M_w has one state corresponding to each equivalence class determined by $\equiv^{M_w}$, with the exception of the degenerate class (which is the same as the degenerate class of $\equiv^{D_w}$). Further, since the equivalence classes determined by $\equiv^{D_w}$ are right-invariant, each equivalence class $[x]_{\equiv^{M_w}}$ (i.e. each state in M_w) is the union of one or more equivalence classes determined by $\equiv^{D_w}$ (i.e. the identification of one or more states in D_w). An equivalence class $[x]_{\equiv^{D_w}}$ which does not contain the longest member of $[x]_{\equiv^{M_w}}$ is called a ***redundant class***.

We now give precise bounds on the discrepancy between the size of D_w and the size of M_w.

Definition. The *tail* of a nonempty word w, denoted $tail(w)$, is the longest suffix of w which occurs elsewhere as a substring of w. ▪

Note that when the last letter of w is unique, $tail(w) = \lambda$.

Definition. Let $w = w_1 x w_2$, with $w_1, w_2, x \in \Sigma^*$, $x \neq \lambda$. This occurrence of x in w is the ***first occurrence of x in a new left context*** if x occurs at least twice in $w_1 x$ and there exists $a \in \Sigma$ such that every occurrence of x in $w_1 x$ is preceded by a except the last one. $stem(w)$ is the shortest nonempty prefix of $tail(w)$ which occurs (as a prefix of $tail(w)$) for the first time in a new left context. If no such prefix exists, then $stem(w)$ is undefined. ▪

Examples. If $w = abcbc$ then $tail(w) = bc$ and $stem(w) = b$. If $w = aba$ or abc or $abcdbcbc$ then $stem(w)$ is undefined.

Lemma 3. $[x]_{\equiv^{D_w}}$ is a redundant class, where x is the longest word in $[x]_{\equiv^{D_w}}$, if and only if $stem(w)$ is defined and x is a prefix of $tail(w)$ such that $|x| \geq |stem(w)|$.

Proof *If part:* Let $stem(w)$ be defined and let x be a prefix of $tail(w)$ such that $|x| \geq |stem(w)|$. Clearly x occurs as a prefix of $tail(w)$ for the first time in a new left context. Assume that every prior occurrence of x is preceded by the letter a. Since x is not always preceded by a, ax is not in $[x]_{\equiv_{D_w}}$, and hence x is the longest word in $[x]_{\equiv_{D_w}}$. Let $w = w_1 x w_2$, where $tail(w) = xw_2$. Assume that there exists a $z \in \Sigma^*$ such that xz is a subword of w but axz is not. Consider the leftmost occurrence of xz in w. Let $w = u_1 xz u_2$ for this occurrence. If $|u_1| < |w_1|$ then u_1 must end in a, contradicting our assumption. However if $|u_1| \geq |w_1|$ then xzu_2 is a suffix of $tail(w)$, and thus this cannot be the leftmost occurrence of xz. This contradiction implies that xz is a subword of w if and only if axz is a subword of w, hence $x \equiv^{M_w} ax$. It follows that $[x]_{\equiv_{D_w}}$ is redundant.

Only if part: Let y be the longest word in $[x]_{\equiv_{M_w}}$. Since $[x]_{\equiv_{D_w}}$ is redundant, $|y| > |x|$. Since $x \equiv^{M_w} y$, for any $z \in \Sigma^*$, xz is a subword of w if and only if yz is a subword of w. It follows that the leftmost occurrence of y in w ends in the same position as the leftmost occurrence of x in w. Hence x is a proper suffix of y, i.e. $y = ux$ for some nonempty string u. Let a be the last letter of u. There must be an occurrence of x in w which is not preceded by a, otherwise $x \equiv^{D_w} ax$, contradicting the fact that x is the longest word in $[x]_{\equiv_{D_w}}$. Consider the leftmost occurrence of x in w which is not preceded by a. Let $w = w_1 x w_2$ for this occurrence. Let b be the last letter of w_1. Since xw_2 is a subword of w and $x \equiv^{M_w} y$, yw_2 is a subword of w. Hence axw_2 is a subword of w. It follows that xw_2 occurs at least twice in w. However, since this was the leftmost occurrence of x which was not preceded by a, it cannot be the case that bxw_2 occurs more than once in w. Thus $xw_2 = tail(w)$ and hence x is a prefix of $tail(w)$. Further, since this was the first occurrence of x not preceded by a, x is appearing for the first time in a new left context, and so $stem(w)$ is defined and $|x| \geq |stem(w)|$. ∎

It follows that every redundant state in D_w can be uniquely associated with a nonempty prefix of $tail(w)$, as described above. Thus we have

Theorem 2. Let M be the number of states in M_w and N be the number of states in D_w. If $stem(w)$ is undefined then $M = N$. Otherwise $M = N - (|tail(w)| - |stem(w)| + 1)$. ∎

We also obtain

Corollary 1. If the last letter of w is unique, or if $tail(w)$ does not occur for the first time in a new left context, then $D_w = M_w$.

Proof. In both cases $stem(w)$ is undefined. ∎

It is observed in [Sei 83] that $D_w = M_w$ when the last letter of w is unique.

The following technical lemma is also useful.

Lemma 4. For any $w \in \Sigma^*$ and $a \in \Sigma$, if $tail(wa) \neq tail(w)a$ then (i) if $[x]_{\equiv_{D_w}}$ is redundant then $[x]_{\equiv_{D_{wa}}}$ is not redundant and (ii) if $stem(wa)$ is defined then $stem(wa) = tail(wa)$.

The proof uses techniques similar to those used in Lemma 3, and is omitted.

Section 2. The construction algorithm

We have previously given an algorithm to build D_w on-line in linear time ([Blu 83], [Blu 84]). Given a correct DAWG for a word w, and a new letter a, the algorithm constructs the DAWG for wa by adding states which correspond to the new equivalence classes that are created when a is appended to w. At each such iteration, a new state is added for $[wa]_{\equiv_{D_{wa}}}$, which is the class all subwords of wa which are not subwords of w. At most one additional new state is added during this iteration. This new state is formed by "splitting" the equivalence class which includes *tail*(wa), when *tail*(wa) appears for the first time in a new left context.

We partition the outgoing edges associated with each state into two types, called ***primary*** edges and ***secondary*** edges. An edge leading to a state is ***primary*** if it is on the longest path from the source to that state; otherwise, it is ***secondary***. The primary or secondary designation allows the algorithm to determine whether an equivalence class should be split or not. In addition, each state $[x]_{\equiv_{D_w}}$ is augmented with a ***suffix pointer*** [McC 76], which is a pointer to the state representing the equivalence class of the longest proper suffix of the shortest member of $[x]_{\equiv_{D_w}}$. The suffix pointers allow new states and edges to be installed in the DAWG without extended searches.

Lemmas 3 and 4 indicate a way to modify the algorithm for constructing D_w into one which builds M_w, again on-line in linear time. Essentially, all we need do is avoid the addition of redundant states by splitting states too soon. This requires a little bookkeeping in order to save the information needed to create the new states when they cease to be redundant. This is illustrated in Figure 1. The linear time bound on this algorithm is analogous to the one on the algorithm for building D_w given in [Blu 84]. It should be pointed out that while the total processing time of this algorithm is linear in the length of w, the processing time for each letter of w is not bounded by any constant. Thus we use an amortized complexity analysis as in [McC 76] to achieve the desired time bound.

We now give a description of the algorithm to build M_w, which is given below as three procedures, ***buildma***, ***update***, and ***split***. ***Buildma*** is the main procedure, which takes as input a word w, builds M_w by processing w on-line letter by letter, and returns the start state of M_w. After each letter is processed, M_w is correct for the prefix of w up to this point. With each new letter, ***buildma*** modifies the current M_w by calling the procedure ***update***, giving ***update*** the letter to be processed and the current sink state ($[w]_{\equiv_{M_w}}$). ***Update*** takes this information and in step 1 (see below) creates a new state, the new sink for the updated M_w, and installs the appropriate edges to this new state. ***Update*** also determines whether any equivalence class represented by an already existing state becomes redundant, and if so, records this fact by incrementing the global counter ***splits*** and recording information pertinent to the redundant class in the global queues ***children*** and ***oldsuffix***. This is done in step 3c, where a secondary outgoing edge indicates that the longest member of ***suffixstate*** is ***stem***(w), and a non-zero value of splits indicates that we are past ***stem***(w) and so ***suffixstate*** must be redundant (see Lemma 3). If ***tail***(w) does not begin at the same place as ***tail***(wa), the redundant classes cease to be redundant (Lemma 4), and in step 3d, ***update*** calls the third procedure ***split*** to split them into new classes one by one, using the information that was stored in *children* and *oldsuffix*. *Split* creates a new state and adjusts the edges leading to that state. It then returns the new state it creates, which is used in performing the next split. Finally, in step 5, *update* returns the new sink state it creates.

Detailed descriptions of these procedures are given below. Note also that the variables *source*, *children*, *parent*, *oldsuffix*, and *splits* are global to all three procedures.

buildma (*w*)

1. Initialize the global queues *children* and *oldsuffix* to be empty, and set the variable *splits* to 0.
2. Create a state named *source* and let *currentsink* be *source*.
3. For each letter *a* of *w* do:
   Let *currentsink* be *update* (*currentsink*, *a*).
4. Return *source*.

update (*currentsink*, *a*)

1. Create a state named *newsink* and a primary edge labeled *a* from *currentsink* to *newsink*.
2. Let *currentstate* be *currentsink* and let *suffixstate* be undefined.
3. While *currentstate* isn't *source* and *suffixstate* is undefined do:
   a. Let *currentstate* be the state pointed to by the suffix pointer of *currentstate*.
   b. If *currentstate* has a primary outgoing edge labeled *a* and *splits* is 0, then let *suffixstate* be the state that this edge leads to.
   c. Else, if *currentstate* has a secondary outgoing edge labeled *a* or a primary outgoing edge labeled *a* with *splits* a nonzero value then:
      1. Let *suffixstate* be the state reached from *currentstate* by the edge labeled *a*.
      2. Increment the value of *splits* to reflect that another split is pending.
      3. If *splits* is 1, let *parent* be *currentstate*.
      4. Add *suffixstate* to the end of the queue *children* and add the state *newsink* to the end of the queue *oldsuffix*.
   d. Else,
      1. For $i = 1$ to *splits*, remove *topchild* and *topsuffix* from the front of the queues *children* and *oldsuffix* respectively and let *parent* be *split*(*parent*, *topchild*, *topsuffix*).
      2. If the "for" loop above was executed, let *currentstate* be *parent* and set *splits* = 0.
      3. Create a secondary edge from *currentstate* to *newsink* labeled *a*.
4. If *suffixstate* is still undefined, let *suffixstate* be *source*.
5. Set the suffix pointer of *newsink* to point to *suffixstate* and return *newsink*.

split (*parentstate*, *childstate*, *oldsuffixstate*)

1. Create a state called *newchildstate*.
2. Make the secondary edge from *parentstate* to *childstate* into a primary edge from *parentstate* to *newchildstate* (with the same label).
3. For every primary and secondary outgoing edge of *childstate*, create a secondary outgoing edge of *newchildstate* with the same label and leading to the same state.
4. Set the suffix pointer of *newchildstate* equal to that of *childstate*.
5. Set the suffix pointer of *oldsuffixstate* to point to *newchildstate*.
6. Set the suffix pointer of *childstate* to point to *newchildstate*.
7. Let *currentstate* be *parentstate*.
8. While *currentstate* isn't *source* do:
    a. Let *currentstate* be the state pointed to by the suffix pointer of *currentstate*.
    b. If *currentstate* has a secondary edge to *childstate*, make it a secondary edge to *newchildstate* (with the same label).
    c. Else, break out of the while loop.
9. Return *newchildstate*.

Acknowledgement

We would like to thank Hermann Maurer for his comments on [Blu 83], which led us to look at minimal automata and to thank Joel Seiferas for pointing out his recent work in this area, and for sending us this work and several related papers.

References

[Aho 75] Aho, Alfred V. and Margaret J. Corasick; "Efficient string matching: an aid to bibliographic research," *CACM*, v. 18, no. 6, June 1975, 333-340.

[Apo 83] Apostolico, A. and F. P. Preparata; "Optimal off-line detection of repetitions in a string," *Theoretical Computer Science*, v. 22, 1983, 297-315.

[Blu 83] Blumer, A., J. Blumer, A. Ehrenfeucht, D. Haussler, R. McConnell; "Linear Size Finite Automata for the Set of all Subwords of a Word: An Outline of Results," *Bul. Euro. Asso. Theor. Comp. Sci.*, 21, (1983), 12-20.

[Blu 84] Blumer, A., J. Blumer, A. Ehrenfeucht, D. Haussler, R. McConnell; "Building a Complete Inverted File for a Set of Text Files in Linear Time," *Proc. 16th ACM Symp. Theo. Comp.*, May 1984, to appear.

[Boy 77] Boyer, R.S. and J.S.Moore; "A fast string searching algorithm," *CACM*, v. 20, no. 10, Oct. 1977, 762-772.

[Knu 77] Knuth, Donald E., James H. Morris, and Vaughan R. Pratt; "Fast pattern matching in strings," *SIAM J. Comput.*, v. 6, no. 2, June 1977, 323-350.

[Maj 80] Majster, M. E. and Angelika Reiser; "Efficient on-line construction and correction of position trees," *SIAM J. Comput.*, v. 9, no. 4, Nov. 1980, 785-807.

[McC 76] McCreight, Edward M.; "A space-economical suffix tree construction algorithm," *JACM*, v. 23, no. 2, April 1976, 262-272.

[Mor 68] Morrison, Donald R.; "PATRICIA - Practical Algorithm To Retrieve Information Coded In Alphanumeric," *JACM*, v. 15, no. 4, October 1968, 514-534.

[Pra 73] Pratt, V. R., "Improvements and applications for the Weiner repetition finder," unpublished manuscript, May 1973 (revised Oct. 1973, March 1975).

[Rab 59] Rabin, M. O. and D. Scott; "Finite automata and their decision problems," *IBM J. Res. Dev.* (3) 1959, 114-125.

[Rod 81] Rodeh, Michael, Vaughan R. Pratt, and Shimon Even; "Linear algorithm for data compression via string matching," *JACM*, v. 28, no. 1, Jan. 1981, 16-24.

[Sei 83] Seiferas, J. and M.T.Chen; "Efficient and elegant subword-tree construction," *Univ. of Rochester 1983-84 C.S. and C.E. Research Review*, 10-14.

[Sli 80] Slisenko, A. O., "Detection of periodicities and string matching in real time," (English translation) *J. Sov. Math.*, 22 (3) (1983) 1316-1387. (originally published 1980).

[Wei 73] Weiner, P.; "Linear pattern matching algorithms," *IEEE 14th Annual Symposium on Switching and Automata Theory*, 1973, 1-11.

Figure 1

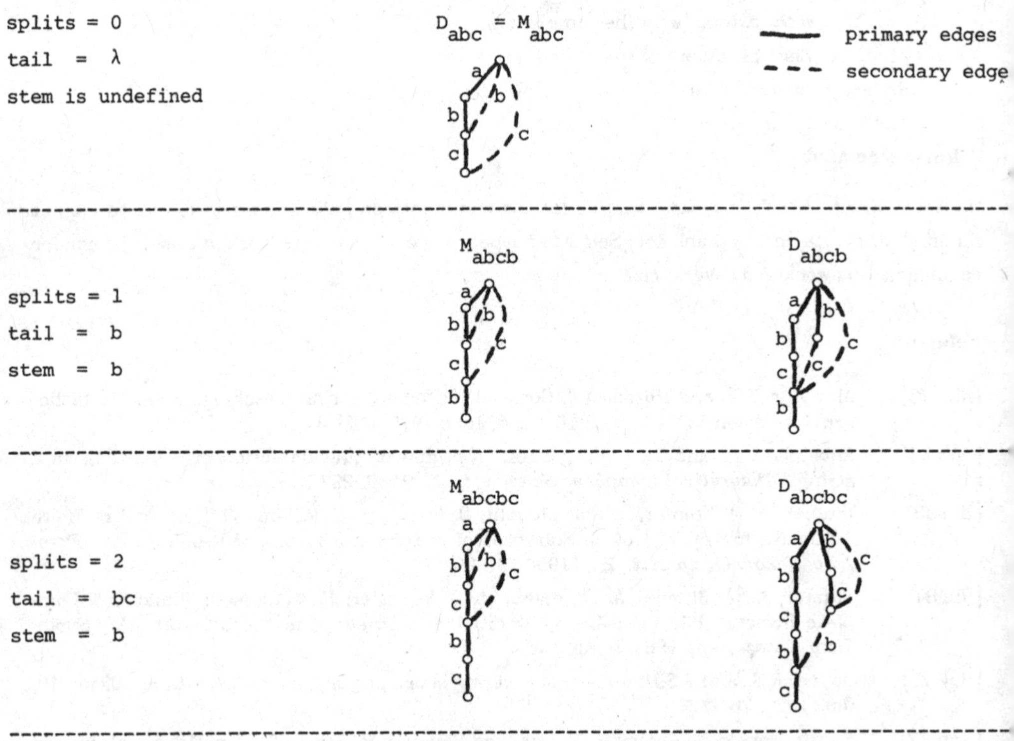

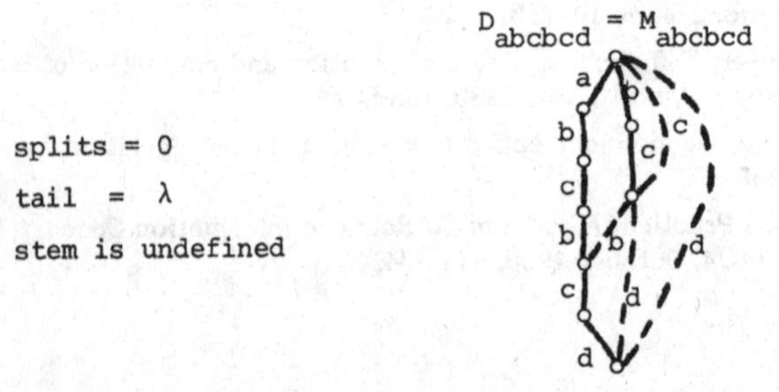

Figure 2

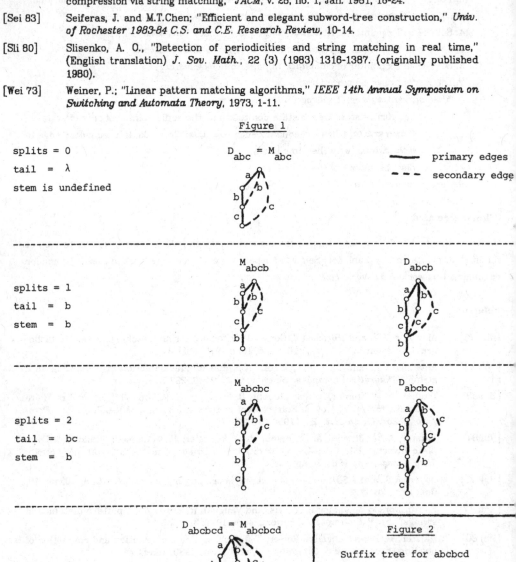

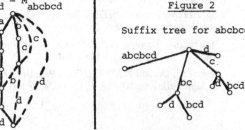

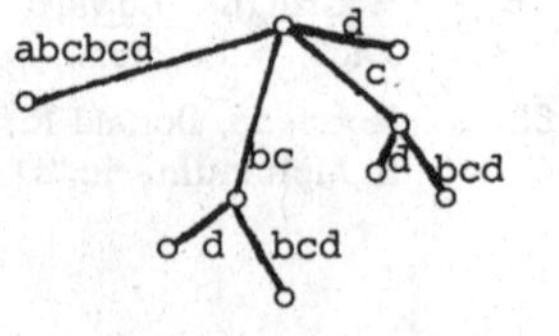

THE COMPLEXITY AND DECIDABILITY OF SEPARATION™ (1)

Bernard Chazelle(2), *Thomas Ottmann*(3),
Eljas Soisalon-Soininen(4), *and Derick Wood*(5)

ABSTRACT

We study the difficulty of solving instances of a new family of sliding block puzzles called **SEPARATION™**. Each puzzle in the family consists of an arrangement in the plane of n rectilinear wooden blocks, $n > 0$. The aim is to discover a sequence of rectilinear moves which when carried out will separate each piece to infinity. If there is such a sequence of moves we say the puzzle or arrangement is *separable* and if each piece is moved only once we say it is *one-separable*. Furthermore if it is one-separable with all moves being in the same direction we say it is *iso-separable*.

We prove:

(1) There is an $O(n \log n)$ time algorithm to decide whether or not a puzzle is iso-separable, where the blocks have a total of n edges.

(2) There is an $O(n \log^2 n)$ time algorithm to decide whether or not a puzzle is one-separable.

(3) It is decidable whether or not a puzzle is separable.

(4) Deciding separability is NP-hard.

(5) There are puzzles which require time exponential in the number of edges to separate them.

1. INTRODUCTION

The Simba puzzle consists of 10 rectangular wooden blocks arranged in a tray one of whose side has a gap. The purpose of the puzzle is to re-arrange the blocks by sliding them north, south, east, or west so that the largest block can escape through the gap. In [GY] the translation problem for rectangles is studied. The aim is to translate the original figure to some new position by moving each rectangle once and only once. Moreover as in Simba the rectangles are not allowed to slide over each other, so it is useful to think of the rectangles as rectangular wooden blocks.

In this paper we consider rectilinear wooden blocks rather than rectangular ones, we restrict movements to be only in the northerly, southerly, easterly and westerly directions as in Simba, we allow, in general, each block to be moved many times, and we concentrate on separating the blocks rather than translating the arrangement, configuration, or puzzle. In Simba the separation of one specific block is the purpose of the puzzle, while in [GY] the translation of a figure yields a sequence of moves, which enable the rectangles to be separated from each other, in the given order. This intuitive notion of separation can be expressed more precisely as moving each block independently to infinity without sliding over any other block. This is the definition of a family of puzzles called **SEPARATION™**.

In Section 2 we consider **SEPARATION™** in which each piece is only allowed to move once, that is iso- and one-separability. In Section 3 we investigate the decidability status of **SEPARATION™** when each piece is allowed a finite, but unbounded, number of moves. We show, assuming for simplicity the initial arrangement is *loose* in a way which is made more precise later, that separability is decidable (this result can be generalized). In Section 4 we demonstrate that decidability is NP-hard and that there are separable puzzles which require exponential time to

---

(1) The work of the first author was supported in part by the Office of Naval Research and the Defense Advanced Research Projects Agency under Contract N00014-83-K-0146 and ARPA Order No. 4786 and under a National Science Foundation Grant No. MCS-8303925, that of the third by a grant from the Alexander von Humboldt Foundation, and that of the fourth by a Natural Sciences and Engineering Research Council of Canada Grant No. A-5692.

(2) Computer Science Department, Brown University, Box 1910, Providence, R.I. 02912, U.S.A.

(3) Institut für Angewandte Informatik und Formale Beschreibungsverfahren, Universität Karlsruhe, Postfach 6380, D-7500 Karlsruhe, W. Germany.

(4) Department of Computer Science, University of Helsinki, Tukholmankatu 2, SF-00250 Helsinki 25, Finland.

(5) Data Structuring Group, Department of Computer Science, University of Waterloo, Waterloo, Ontario N2L 3G1, Canada.

separate them. Finally we close with a discussion of some further problems and results in Section 5.

The original motivation for the problems discussed here was the generalization of the results of [GY] to rectilinear polygons, and an interest in moving rectilinear objects through rectilinear passages, see [HJW], [LPW], [OSC], [R], and [SS1-3]. **SEPARATION™** can also be viewed as the opposite of two-dimensional bin packing, see [BCR], or compaction, see [SLW]; we thought, in fact, of calling it BIN UNPACKING!

2. ISO- AND ONE-SEPARABILITY OF SEPARATION™

In this section we sketch the proof of the following theorems.

Theorem 2.1 *Given a puzzle consisting of* p *pieces with a total of* n *edges, one-separability can be determined in* $O(n \log^2 n)$ *time and* $O(n \log n)$ *space.*

In *one-separability* each piece is only allowed to move once, but it may move in any one of the four directions. To approach an efficient solution to this version of the puzzle we first consider a special case in which the pieces must move in the same direction, that is *iso-separability.*

Theorem 2.2 *Given a puzzle consisting of* p *pieces with a total of* n *edges, iso-separability can be determined in* $O(n \log n)$ *time and* $O(n)$ *space.*

Without loss of generality assume that easterly movement is only allowed. Then an arrangement such as Figure 2.1 is not easterly-separable, although it is iso-separable, while that of Figure 2.2 is not even separable.

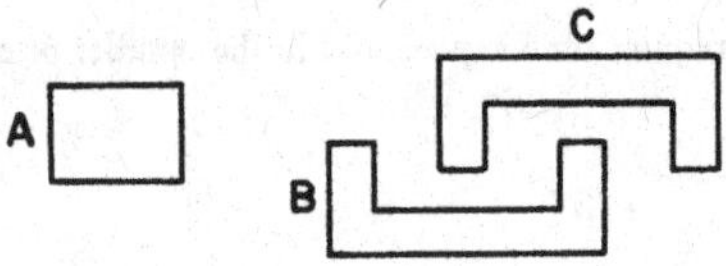

Figure 2.1

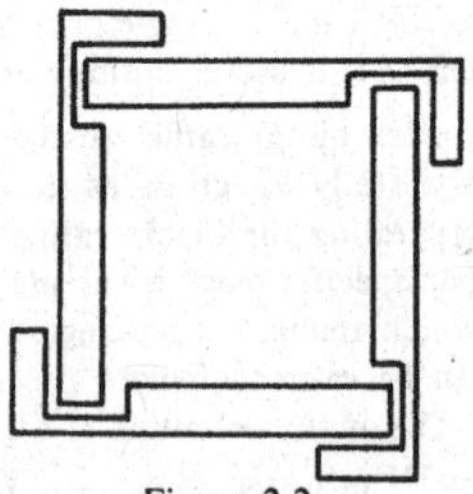

Figure 2.2

Returning to Figure 2.1 a viewer in the far east when looking over the puzzle can see that a leading edge of B (outlined in bold-face) is trapped between a leading and trailing edge of C, whereas when it is viewed from the south, see Figure 2.3, the leading edges of B and C are free. We say that B *traps* C, and is *trapped by* C, with respect to the east-west direction. Similarly A, in Figure 2.1, which is trapped neither by B nor C, is *blocked* by B and C. In other words A cannot be moved east until both B and C have been so moved. We say a piece is *free* if it is neither trapped nor blocked with respect to the given direction. Note that the relation traps is symmetric, whereas blocks is not. The relation traps is captured by:

A piece A traps a piece B, in a given puzzle with respect to the east-west direction, if and only if the *EW*-convex hulls of A and B have a non-empty intersection.

We say a piece is *EW-convex* if its intersection with a straight line, in the east-west direction, is either empty or a line segment. The *EW-convex hull* of a piece is the smallest *EW*-convex piece containing the given piece, see Figure 2.4 for an example. Note that the *EW*-convex hull does not affect the leading and trailing edges (or portions thereof). These simple observations are the key to the decidability of iso- and one-separability. An efficient

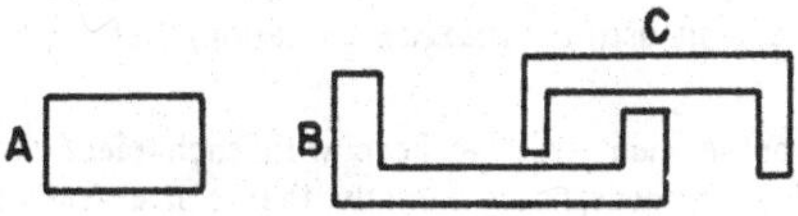

Figure 2.3

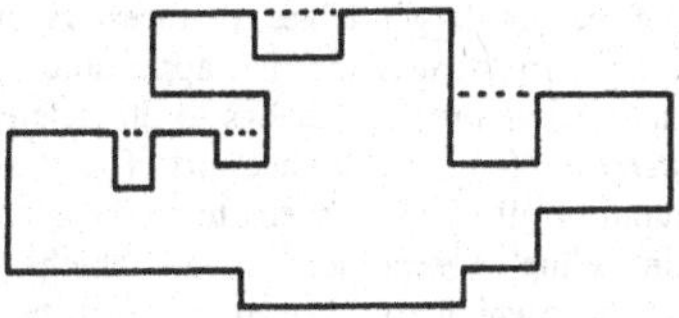

Figure 2.4

algorithm is based on the segment tree, see [BW]. Without more ado we give a high-level algorithm.

Algorithm *EASTERLY-SEPARABILITY*;

Step 1: Replace each piece with its *EW*-convex hull.

Step 2: Sort the leading and trailing edges of the pieces in ascending order according to their x-projection.

Step 3: Construct a skeletal segment tree based on the y-fragments determined by the y-projections of the leading and trailing edges.

Step 4: Insert the leading and trailing edges into the segment tree in x-sorted order.

Step 5: Attempt to peel the segment tree.

end *EASTERLY-SEPARABILITY*.

Step 4 ensures that each nodelist (of the edges which cover or mark a node) is sorted from east-to-west. Therefore, in Step 5, a necessary condition for the separation of a piece is that all appearances of its leading and trailing edges are in the first and possibly, second positions of its associated nodelists. This is because two leading edges of different pieces having the same x-projection must have disjoint y-projections (since they cannot overlap).

In order to begin to peel the segment tree (Step 5) we have to find a piece which is free, that is none of its edges are trapped or blocked. For this purpose we add further information to each node of the segment tree. Let $cover(u)$ denote the set of edges which mark or cover the node u. This is usually implemented as a doubly-linked list called the nodelist. Now let $easternmost(u)$ denote the set of first appearances in $cover(v)$, for all proper descendants v of u [†]. We say an edge of a piece is *blocked* if it lies to the west of the edge of some piece and their y-projections overlap, otherwise it is *free*. As pointed out above, an edge e which appears in the first position in its nodelist is a candidate for freedom. It might not be free because either there is a larger or smaller blocking edge to its east. If the blocking edge is larger it will appear in the cover set of some proper ancestor of the nodes covered by e, while if it is smaller it will appear in the cover set of some proper descendant. Let e appear in $cover(u)$ for some node u. Then the first case can be determined by examining the cover sets of the root-to-u path. A larger blocking edge will appear in the first position of one of these nodelists. The second case involves the use of $easternmost(u)$, since a smaller blocking edge must appear in it, since it too must appear first in some nodelist of a descendant of u. Indeed e is blocked by a smaller edge if and only if the most easterly of the edges in

---

[†] Actually since a leading and trailing edge of the same piece may both cover the same node this should really be the set of first, and possibly second, appearances.

easternmost(u) is to the east of e. This uses the *maxeast* operation, that is the *easternmost* sets can be organized as priority queues.

Now to prepare for peeling the segment tree we keep with each piece not only the number of its nodelist appearances, but also the number of free appearances. Initially, that is after Step 4, no appearances are free, hence a traversal of the tree is made and for each node u, the first appearance in *cover*(u) e, say, is tested for freedom. This involves examining $O(\log n)$ nodes. Since the *easternmost* sets are also constructed during Step 4, this traversal requires $O(n \log^2 n)$ time. If, after the traversal, no piece has its free count equal to its appearance count, then no piece can be separated from the others in an easterly direction. However if there is a free piece, each of its appearances is deleted and the *cover* and *easternmost* sets updated at all affected nodes. Removing an edge e from *cover*(u) for some node u is straightforward, as is its removal from *easternmost*(v) for all proper ancestors v of u. It is more difficult, however, to update freedom information for the remaining pieces. The edge e may block either smaller edges at descendants of u, or larger edges at ancestors of u. The latter situation is the more straightforward one - simply re-consider the freedom of the first appearances in *cover*(v) for all ancestors v of u. Indeed unless the edge furthest east in *easternmost*(v) belongs to the deleted piece, freedom cannot be affected. In the former situation the edges in *easternmost*(v), for all ancestors of u and u itself are the only ones which may be affected. It appears that the freedom of all of them needs to re-considered. To avoid this we modify the definition of *easternmost*(u) by not including appearances in it which are already blocked below u, thus *easternmost*$(root)$ is the set of appearances which are blocked, at worst, by *cover*$(root)$. Let λu and ρu denote the left and right child of node u, and for a node u, define left and right sets L and R, respectively, by:

$$L = \begin{cases} maxeast(cover(\lambda u)), & \text{if } cover(u) \neq \emptyset \text{ and } maxeast(cover(\lambda u)) \\ & \text{is east of } maxeast(easternmost(\lambda u)) \text{,and} \\ easternmost(\lambda u), & \text{otherwise}. \end{cases}$$

R is defined similarly. Now let:

$$easternmost(u) \text{ be } L \cup R .$$

Recall that an edge e at a node u only *directly* blocks appearances of edges at nodes below it if they appear in *easternmost*(u). Now *easternmost*(u) after removal of e requires no further updating. Therefore consider *easternmost*(πu), that is the parent of u. We need to add to *easternmost*(πu) those appearances from *easternmost*(u) which were blocked by e but are no longer blocked at u. These appearances can be found by a range query of *easternmost*(u) using the x-coordinates of e and $e' = maxeast(cover(u) - \{e\})$. Note that if this query has a non-empty result then e' is blocked from below and otherwise e' is the only new addition to *easternmost*(πu). Now consider $\pi\pi u$, the newly added appearances in *easternmost*(πu) must be divided into those which should be added to *easternmost*$(\pi\pi u)$, and those which are blocked at πu. But this is similar to the previous reduction. The newly-freed appearances are those added to *easternmost*$(root)$ which are to the east of *maxeast*(*cover*$(root)$).

Observe that an appearance can be added to at most $O(\log n)$ *easternmost* sets and each addition requires $O(\log n)$ time. Thus each appearance contributes at most $O(\log^2 n)$ time during updating.

Fortuitiously this modified *easternmost* set is sufficient for the earlier stages of the algorithm, hence there are no major changes to be considered.

Now Theorem 2.1 follows because deletion and insertion of an edge can affect $O(\log n)$ nodes and, thus, require the updating of $O(\log n)$ priority queues each of size $O(n)$. Although we have only discussed the deletion of an appearance when it is in the first position of a nodelist, it is straightforward to modify this to deal with an appearance at any position (the segment tree has a dictionary of appearances for each edge, providing access, in constant time, to each appearance). We keep four segment trees, one for each direction, at any stage we check if there is a piece having all its edges free with respect to one of the directions. If there is we delete its edges from all four trees, and repeat the process until there are either no free pieces or no pieces at all.

Clearly we can apply Theorem 2.1 to solve the iso-separability problem as well, but we can improve the solution by way of:

Theorem 2.3 *A puzzle is easterly-separable if and only if the EW-convex hulls of its pieces are disjoint.*

Proof: Straightforward. □

Clearly a puzzle is easterly-separable if and only if it is westerly-separable. Now it can be determined in $O(n \log n)$ time and $O(n)$ space whether or not two pieces intersect, by way of a simple extension to the algorithm in [E] for rectangle intersections. Thus Theorem 2.2 follows.

3. THE DECIDABILITY OF SEPARATION™

In this section we sketch the proof that separability is decidable - as one should expect. First observe that the number of moves can be independent of the size of the puzzle. Consider the puzzle consisting of four pieces in Figure 3.1. The only way that A and B can be separated is by moving the two U-shaped pieces out of A. The two U-shaped pieces can only be moved alternately *a distance dependent on the narrowness of the* U *s.* This distance can be made smaller than any $\varepsilon > 0$, hence the total number of moves to achieve separation is independent of the number of edges.

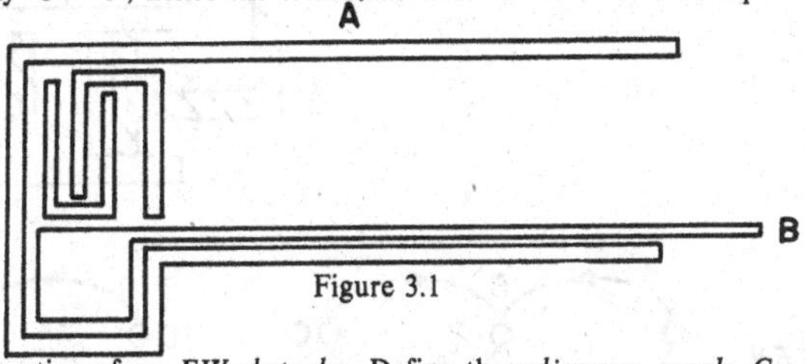

Figure 3.1

We now introduce the notion of an *EW-obstacle.* Define the *adjacency graph* G_{EW} of a puzzle as follows. The pieces in the puzzle are the nodes of G_{EW}, and the directed edges of G_{EW} are determined by:

For all pieces p and q in the puzzle, there is an edge (p,q) in G_{EW}, if and only if p and q have a common segment e that is they abutt, and p is to the west, locally, of e and q is to the east, locally, of e.

Now any (directed) cycle in G_{EW} is called an *EW-obstacle.* Clearly *NS-obstacles* can be defined similarly from the corresponding graph G_{NS}. Figure 3.2(a) illustrates an EW-obstacle and G_{EW} while Figure 3.2(b) gives a similar situation which is not an EW-obstacle. Informally an EW-obstacle represents a cluster of pieces none of which can be moved in the EW-direction *at all.* Moreover there is no hope that they can be moved in the EW-direction unless some movement in the NS-direction is first made. Clearly an EW-obstacle which is also a NS-obstacle, called an *obstacle,* can never be moved. In Figure 3.3 $\{A,B\}$ and $\{D,E\}$ are obstacles.

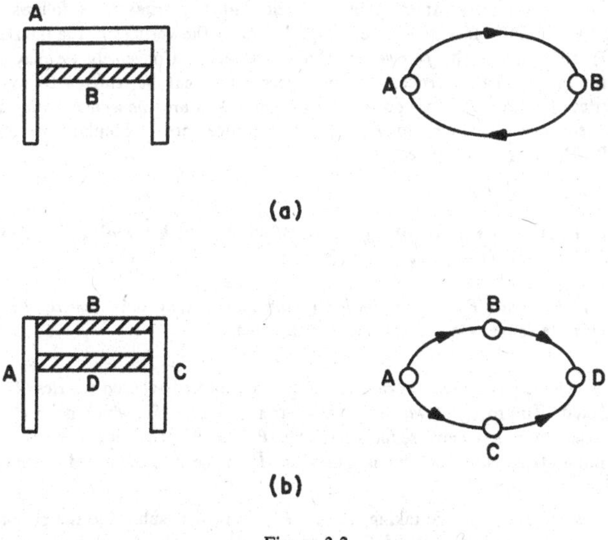

Figure 3.2

For the sake of simplicity, we introduce the notion of *loose* puzzle.

Definition A puzzle is *loose* if it has neither EW- nor NS-obstacles.

To show that separability is decidable for loose puzzles we make a number of preliminary observations.

First, observe that a puzzle is separable if and only if it can be transformed by a sequence of moves into a

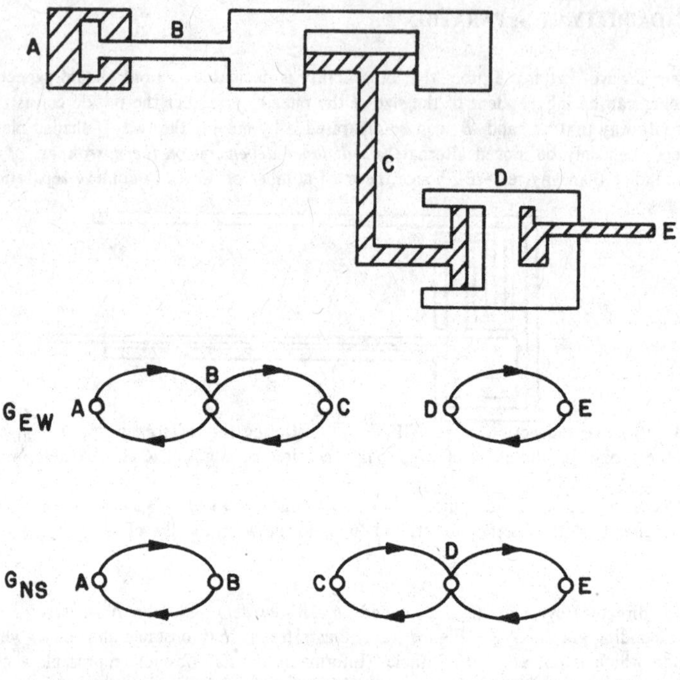

Figure 3.3

puzzle in which all pieces are no closer than some distance d in the EW- or NS-direction, where d is greater than the maximum height and length of the pieces.

Second it is useful to form an abstraction of a puzzle called a *scheme*, as follows. A scheme is a pair (L_{EW}, L_{NS}) of lists giving the EW and NS order, respectively, of the vertices in the puzzle, where each vertex is specified as a pair (i,j) to designate the j-th vertex of the i-th piece. Conversely we may say that a scheme is a pair (L_{EW}, L_{NS}) of permutations of the vertices of some pieces, which can be *realized* by some puzzle formed from them. We say two puzzles P_1 and P_2 formed from the same pieces are *connected* if they have the same scheme and there exists a move sequence taking P_1 to P_2 (and, hence, vice versa). Similarly we say that a set of puzzles P is *connected* if all P_1, P_2 in P are connected.

We first prove:

Lemma 3.1 *Let* (L_{EW}, L_{NS}) *be a scheme for a given set of pieces, which is realized by a loose puzzle. Then* P, *the set of all puzzles which realize* (L_{EW}, L_{NS}), *is connected.*

Proof Sketch: We say P_1 *and* P_2 *are x-similar (y-similar)* if they both realize the same scheme and all corresponding vertices have the same x-coordinates (y-coordinates).

(A) To show that P is connected we demonstrate that for two arbitrarily-chosen puzzles P_1 and P_2 in P, P_1 and P_2 are connected. To prove this we show that there is a puzzle P, which is in P, is x-similar to P, is y-similar to P_2, and there is a move sequence taking P_1 to P. Showing there is a move sequence taking P to P_2 is a similar step. Note that P is indeed in P, since if it contained overlapping pieces this would contradict the orders L_{EW} and L_{NS}.

(B) To show that there is a move sequence taking P_1 to P, we further subdivide the problem. Let H be a horizontal line below both P_1 and P. We define a new puzzle Q which lies above H, has at least one piece of Q abutting H, has been allowed to "drop" as far as possible without crossing H, and is x-similar to both P_1 and P. Thinking of the pieces having weight and of them dropping under gravity is what is meant here.

If we show that Q can be obtained from P_1, then, clearly, P can be obtained from Q.

(C) To show that there is a move sequence taking P_1 to Q we carry out the following algorithm.

For each piece $p_1,...,p_k$ in turn:

Move p_i downwards as far as possible, without crossing H. This destroys edges of the kind (p_i,q) and possibly creates a new edge of the form (q,p_i). Moreover it preserves x-similarity. If p_i reaches H then it is *frozen* at H, and is never moved again. Moreover freezing propagates - if p_i abutts a frozen p_j then p_i is also frozen.

The above process is iterated until a frozen puzzle is obtained, which is Q. We claim it is both unique and independent of P_1, in the sense that any puzzle R in P x-similar to P_1 would give rise to Q. We must also show that the process converges and is finite. We omit the details of this proof, simply remarking that it can be shown that each non-frozen piece can be moved in at most k iterations of the process. Finiteness follows, essentially, by observing that each piece, when it is moved, is moved at least distance δ, where δ is the minimum non-zero y-distance between successive (with respect to L_{NS}) vertices in P_1. Uniqueness is straightforward. □

Theorem 3.2 *Let P_1 be a loose puzzle. Then it is decidable whether or not P_1 is separable.*

Proof Sketch:

(A) Let P_2 be an ordered horizontal placement of the pieces in P_1 such that there is a north-south line which can be drawn between any two pieces p_i and p_j, with p_i wholly to its west and p_j wholly to its east or vice versa. Then P_1 is separable if and only if there is a move sequence taking P_1 to P_2.

(B) Let (L^i_{EW}, L^i_{NS}) be the scheme of P_i, $i = 1,2$. Now let G be a graph whose nodes are (realizable) schemes of the set of pieces of P_1. For all (realizable) schemes S_1 and S_2, there is an edge (S_1, S_2) if and only if there is a puzzle P realizing both S_1 and S_2. This is possible only if P contains two co-linear edges. Such a P represents the point of change between two schemes. During a move sequence taking P_1 to P_2 (if it exists) there will be time instants when such points of change are crossed, while at all other instants the current scheme is unchanged. Thus P_1 can be transformed into P_2 if and only there is a path in G from a scheme of P_1 to a scheme of P_2, that is separability has been reduced to reachability in a graph. Since reachability is easily determined, separability is decidable if and only if G can be constructed. G can be constructed if it is decidable whether or not a given scheme is realizable. But this corresponds to determining whether or not the linear system of equalities and inequalities $L(S)$ of a given scheme S has a solution. The equalities are given by the interdistances between vertices of each piece, whereas the inequalities are given by the lists (L_{EW}, L_{NS}) of S. The simplex method can be used to solve $L(S)$, hence separability is decidable. □

Using fairly similar techniques, it is possible to extend this result to the case where the puzzle is not loose. We must omit the proof because of space limitations.

4. COMPLEXITY OF SEPARATION™

We sketch the proofs of two results in this section, namely **SEPARATION™** is shown to be NP-hard by reducing the partition problem to it and that there are separable puzzles which require exponential time.

For the first proof sketch note that we only consider the predicate: *can the given instance of* **SEPARATION™** *be separated?* The *partition problem* is: given n weighted objects partition them into two equally-weighted subsets. The reduction is illustrated in Figure 4.1.

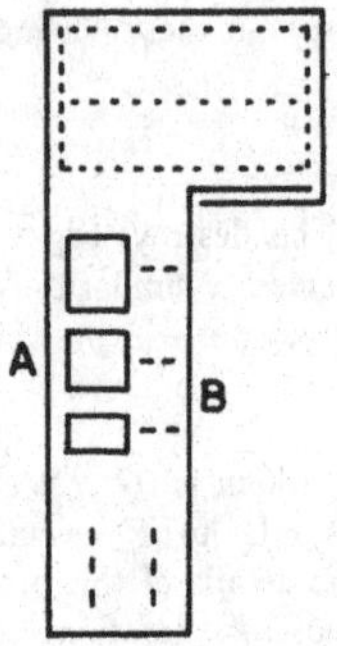

Figure 4.1

The puzzle is so tightly defined that none of the P_i can be separated unless B is moved west as far as A, when B can be moved by sliding it south. However this is possible if and only if the set of P_is can be partitioned and placed above B. Observe that there is enough working space to the west of B to manipulate the P_is. Thus we have:

Theorem 4.1 **SEPARATION™** *is NP-hard.*

In Section 2 we demonstrated that there are separable puzzles which require a number of moves independent of the size of the puzzle. However the moves required to separate the puzzle are self-evident. We close this section with one further example which is separable, but non-trivially, see Figure 4.2.

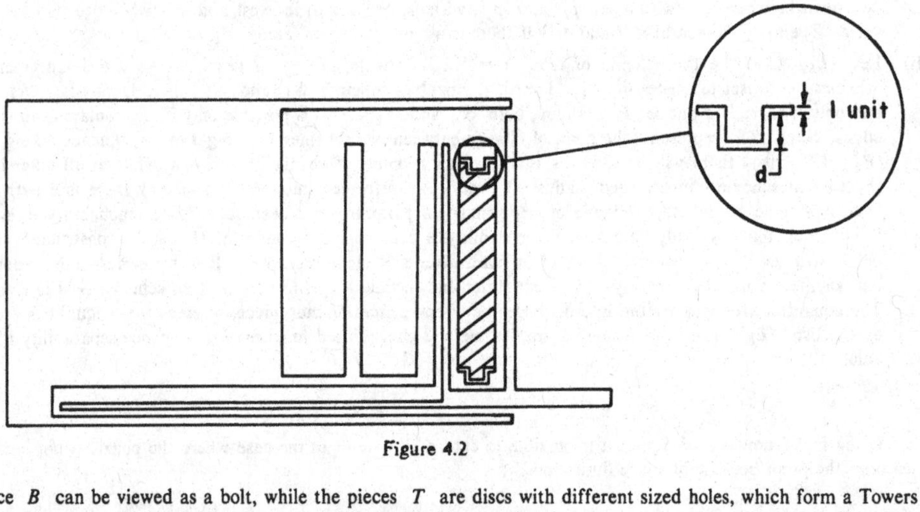

Figure 4.2

The piece B can be viewed as a bolt, while the pieces T are discs with different sized holes, which form a Towers of Hanoi. Note that the thickness of m discs, if arranged in sorted order, is $m+d$ units, where each disc has a thickness of 1 unit and its hole is d units deep. In unsorted order they form a tower which is md units high.

Now to release the bolt B all discs in T need to be moved. They can only be moved into the two wells and the connecting passage, but because of the considerable difference in height between sorted and unsorted order, this forces the discs to be moved almost according to the standard Towers of Hanoi sequence, especially when $d = m$. Without belabouring the details we have:

Theorem 4.2 *The puzzle illustrated in Figure 4.2 requires an exponential number of moves to separate it.*

5. DISCUSSION

We have introduced, **SEPARATION™**, a new family of sliding block puzzles and investigated some aspects of its complexity and decidability. Clearly much remains to be done. For example in Simba, one designated piece must be separated first, clearly this requirement and variants of it can be placed in our general framework. Again how efficiently can two-separability be decided? And, in general, given a k, how efficiently can k-separability be determined?

REFERENCES

[BCR] Baker, B.S., Coffman Jr., E.G., and Rivest, R.L., Orthogonal Packings in Two Dimensions, *SIAM Journal on Computing 9* (1980), 846-855.

[BW] Bentley, J.L., and Wood, D., An Optimal Worst-Case Algorithm for Reporting Intersections of Rectangles, *IEEE Transactions on Computers, C-29* (1980), 571-577.

[E] Edelsbrunner, H., A Time- and Space-Optimal Solution for the Planar All Intersecting Rectangles Problem. Tech. Rep., University of Graz, IIG Rep. 50, April 1980.

[GY] Guibas, L.J., and Yao, F.F., On Translating a Set of Rectangles, *Proceedings of the Tenth Annual ACM-SIGACT Symposium on Theory of Computing* (1980), 154-160.

[HJW] Hopcroft, J.E., Joseph, D.A., and Whitesides, S.H., On the Movement of Robot Arms in 2-Dimensional Bounded Regions, *Proceedings of the 23rd Annual Symposium on Foundations of Computer Science*, (1982), 280-289.

[LPW] Lozano-Perez, T., and Wesley, M., An Algorithm for Planning Collision-Free Paths among Polyhedral Obstacles, *Communications of the ACM 22* (1979), 560-570.

[OSC] O'Dúnlaing, C., Sharir, M., and Yap, C.K., Retraction: A New Approach to Motion Planning, *Proceedings of the Fifteenth Annual ACM Symposium on Theory of Computing* (1983), 207-220.

[R] Reif, J., Complexity of the Mover's Problem and Generalizations, *Proceeding of the 20th Annual Symposium on Foundations of Computer Science* (1979), 421-427.

[SLW] Schlag, M., Liao, Y.Z., and Wong, C.K., An Algorithm for Optimal Two-Dimensional Compaction Layouts, IBM Research Center, Yorktown, Research Report RC 9739, 1982.

[SS1] Schwartz, J.T., and Sharir, M., On the Piano Mover's Problem: I. The Special Case of a Rigid Polygonal Body Moving amidst Polygonal Barriers, *Communications on Pure and Applied Mathematics* (1983), to appear.

[SS2] Schwartz, J.T., and Sharir, M., On the Piano Mover's Problem: II. General Techniques for Computing Topological Properties of Real Alagebraic Manifolds, *Advances in Applied Mathematics* (1983), to appear.

[SS3] Schwartz, J.T., and Sharir, M., On the Piano Mover's Problem: III. Coordinating the Motion of Several Independent Bodies: The Special Case of Circular Bodies Moving amidst Polygonal Barriers, New York University Courant Institute Computer Science Technical Report, 1983.

CONCURRENT TRANSMISSIONS IN BROADCAST NETWORKS

Charles J. Colbourn
Department of Computational Science
University of Saskatchewan
Saskatoon, Saskatchewan, S7N 0W0
CANADA

Andrzej Proskurowski
Department of Computing Science
Royal Institute of Technology
Stockholm 70
SWEDEN

on leave from
Department of Computer and Information Science
University of Oregon
Eugene, Oregon, 97403
U.S.A.

Abstract

A linear time algorithm for determining the maximal number of collision-free transmissions in an arbitrary series-parallel network is developed. The method operates by a recursive contraction of the network to a single edge; during this contraction process, information is retained concerning each of the subnetworks which has been eliminated. This efficient solution contrasts with the known NP-completeness of the problem for general networks.

1. Preliminaries

Broadcast networks in general, and packet radio networks in particular, consist of a set of sites which communicate on a common frequency. Typically, the strength of the signal is such that one site can only transmit to a small subset of the other sites. Such networks operate asynchronously; when a site has a message to transmit, it simply broadcasts it to every site within range. When a site is in range of two senders which are transmitting concurrently, a *collision* occurs, and neither message is received correctly at this site. Similarly, a site engaged in transmitting a message cannot successfully receive a message from another site concurrently. For most satellite networks, in which every site can transmit directly (via the satellite) to all other sites, this constrains the network to have at most one concurrent successful transmission; a well-known example is the ALOHA network [1]. In the general case in which sites can receive from a small subset of the other sites, it is possible that many concurrent transmissions can be successful. A set of sites which can successfully transmit concurrently (each message arriving successfully at at least one site) is termed a *sending set*.

The problem of determining the maximum size of a sending set can be rephrased in a graph-theoretic setting, as follows [7]. Each site is represented by a vertex; an edge connects two vertices when one site is in range of the other. Our model is an undirected graph, since we assume that each site is equipped with a transmitter of equal power. Farley and Shacham [7] model a sending set an an "open-irredundant" set of vertices. In a graph G = (V,E), this is a set of OIR of vertices having the property that every vertex v of OIR has at least one neighbour p(v) in V - OIR which is adjacent to no vertex of OIR except v. This vertex p(v) is termed the *private neighbour* of v; if all vertices in OIR were to transmit simultaneously, there may be some collisions, but all |OIR| messages will be delivered successfully since the message from v will arrive without collision at p(v), for every vertex in OIR.

These observations transform the broadcast network problem into a graph theoretic one. Nevertheless, this transformation does not enable us to find an efficient solution. In fact, Even, Goldreich and Tong [3] have shown that deciding whether a graph has an open-irredundant set of size at least k is NP-complete. This severely limits any hope of finding efficient methods to produce maximum sending sets; one might still hope to find efficient techniques for handling special classes of networks. Initial research along these lines has appeared in [6], where a linear algorithm for finding maximum sending sets in trees is described.

In this paper, we develop a linear time algorithm for finding maximum sending sets in a special class of graphs called partial 2-trees. A *2-tree* can be defined recursively as follows:

1. The single edge {x,y} is a 2-tree.
2. If G is a 2-tree and {x,y} is an edge of G, another 2-tree is produced by adding a new vertex z along with the two edges {x,z} and {y,z}.

A *partial 2-tree* is simply a partial subgraph of a 2-tree. The class of 2-trees has many alternative characterizations [9], and has been studied as the class of "minimum isolated failure immune" networks [4, 5,10]. Many algorithmic questions in graph theory have been studied on 2-trees; the definitional property of 2-trees which facilitates the development of efficient algorithms is that the removal of some edges together with their endvertices disconnects the 2-tree. Moreover, such minimal separators correspond precisely to "interior" edges.

Partial 2-trees have also been widely studied in networks research, since partial 2-trees include the series-parallel networks. Two-terminal series-parallel networks form a sub-class of the series-parallel networks studied by Duffin [2]. Duffin establishes that series-parallel networks are precisely those connected graphs with no subgraph homeomorphic to the complete 4-vertex graph. Partial 2-trees are exactly the class of graphs with no subgraph homeomorphic to the 4-vertex complete graph; hence, we can effectively solve network problems on series-parallel graphs by translating the problem into the domain of 2-trees. In fact, the elegant recursive structure of 2-trees has been exploited to efficiently solve many network problems on series-parallel graphs, such as Steiner tree [10] and network reliability [8,11].

In [10], an algorithm is given which recognizes partial 2-trees in linear time, and computes a set of *virtual edges* whose addition would produce a 2-tree. This preprocessing can be used to transform problems on partial 2-trees (series-parallel networks) into problems on 2-trees. This enables us to exploit the recursive structure of 2-trees (and consequently, the separator structure) in developing an efficient solution technique. We adopt this approach in presenting our algorithm.

2. Sending sets in 2-trees

Given an arbitrary series-parallel network, we first locate a set of virtual edges whose addition transforms the network into a 2-tree [10]; each edge in the resulting 2-tree is tagged "real" or "virtual". Our strategy in finding a maximal sending set in the network is to arrive at a *labelling*, a consistent classification of each vertex of the network as being in one of five categories:

1. IY - in the sending set, has a private neighbour selected
2. IN - in the sending set, but needs a private neighbour
3. OY - out of the sending set, is a private neighbour

4. ON - out of the sending set, is not a private neighbour, but is not adjacent to any vertex in the sending set
5. OC - out of the sending set, is not a private neighbour, and is covered by a vertex in the sending set.

The algorithm proceeds by systematically reducing the 2-tree to a single edge as follows. At every step, a vertex of degree 2, say z, is chosen for deletion. The neighbours of z, x and y, are mutually adjacent. Our technique will be to summarize information about the triangle {x,y,z} (and, possibly, subgraphs separated from the rest of the network by the edges {x,z} and {y,z}) and associate it with the edge {x,y}, allowing us to then delete the vertex z.

More precisely, at a general step in the reduction, each edge {x,y} corresponds to a subgraph S which has been reduced onto this edge. Each edge (x,y) has twenty-five statistics, some of them unfeasible, associated with it; these give the size of a maximum sending set in S, in each of the twenty-five cases corresponding to the various choices of labelling for x and y (five choices for x times five choices for y). For example, the OC-IN measure for (x,y) is the size of a maximum sending set in S under the assumption that x is labelled OC and y is in labelling IN .

We first describe the initialization of these measures. At the outset, the subgraph S reduced onto an edge {x,y} is simply the edge {x,y}. We identify two cases. If {x,y} is a real edge, we set the twenty-five measures as follows:

x/y	IY	IN	OY	ON	OC
IY	N	N	1	N	N
IN	N	0	N	N	0
OY	1	N	N	N	N
ON	N	N	N	0	N
OC	N	0	N	N	N

Three values appear in the table. The entry "N" signifies that this combination is impossible - for example, it is impossible for x to have a private neighbour (thus far) unless y is that private neighbour. The entry "0" signifies that, although no contradiction is inherent, it is also the case that no sender already has their private neighbour. Finally, the entry "1" signifies that 1 sender has a private neighbour. For implementation purposes, one can select N to be a large negative number. A similar table presents the initial values for a virtual edge:

x/y	IY	IN	OY	ON	OC
IY	N	N	N	N	N
IN	N	0	N	0	N
OY	N	N	N	N	N
ON	N	0	N	0	N
OC	N	N	N	N	N

Having carried out this initialization, the algorithm proceeds with the following general step. Identify a vertez z of degree 2 and locate the only neighbours x and y of z. Now retrieve the statistics associated with the three edges {x,y}, {x,z}, and {y,z}. We update the set of statistics associated with the edge {x,y} and then delete the vertex z. The three sets of statistics encode information about subgraphs which have been previously reduced onto these three edges. Two of these subgraphs intersect at x, two at y, and two at z. In order to produce information about the subgraph which is the union of these three, we must combine only those statistics in which vertices x, y, and z are used in a consistent manner. For example, we cannot combine statistics for subgraphs intersecting at x if x is assumed to be "in" in one subgraph and "out" in the other. In fact, one can verify that the only consistent usages, together with the resulting labelling of the vertex, are:

1. IY and IN gives IY
2. IN and IN gives IN
3. OY and ON gives OY
4. OC and ON gives OC
5. OC and OC gives OC
6. ON and ON gives ON

All other combinations are inconsistent; it is essential to note here that an IY-IY combination is inconsistent since it would assign *two* private neighbours to a node. The update operation proceeds by trying each of the 125 possible labellings of x, y, and z, enumerating each consistent way of obtaining these, and summing the corresponding entries from the three tables of statistics. The results are entered into one of the twenty-five entries in the table for {x,y}, according to the labelling of x and y. When more than one result is produced for the same entry, the maximum of the values is selected. Having recomputed all entries in the table for {x,y}, the vertex z is deleted.

This process is repeated until the graph remaining is just a single edge. At this time, the size of the maximum sending set is the largest entry in the table for the last edge. A sending set of this size can be retrieved if a local labelling for x, y, and z is recorded together with each corresponding entry for {x,y}.

3. Timing and Correctness

We first establish timing, and then correctness, for the algorithm described in section 2.

Theorem 3.1: The algorithm in section 2 completes its task in time which is linear in the size of the input network.
Proof:

Completion to a 2-tree is done in linear time [10]. Initialization of the tables for each edge requires time which is linear in the number of edges. Next observe that n-2 reduction steps are performed for an n-vertex input network; hence, it suffices if each update requires constant time. Identifying a vertex of degree 2 can be done in constant time, by maintaining a list of degree 2 vertices throughout; the only candidates for addition to the list are the neighbours of a deleted vertex z. Using an adjacency list, one can locate the neighbours of the degree 2 vertex; in total, one sees each edge at most twice throughout the computation and hence this requires constant time on average. Next one must update the tables. The number of computations required here, although large, is a constant number of arithmetic and comparison operations. Finally, extracting the end result is a simple maximum operation of a constant number of terms.

Theorem 3.2: The algorithm in section 2 determines the maximum size of a sending set in the input graph.
Proof:

One must ensure that in initialization and recomputation, two conditions hold. The first is that the selections made are consistent; that is, that the labelling assigned to each vertex is consistent with the labellings of its neighbours. The second is that every pair of a sender with its private neighbour is counted exactly once. Once these two conditions are established, the correctness of the result follows from the exhaustiveness of the examination of consistent selections and the selection of the maximum size at each step.

In initialization, one can verify that consistent selections are allowed, and all inconsistent selections are deemed impossible. In verifying the consistency of the reduction rules, one must verify that every consistent possibility is allowed. Combining "in" with "out" vertices is inconsistent, and hence we must consider, in addition to those called consistent, the possibilities IY-IY, OY-OY, and OY-OC. The first says that a vertex has two private neighbours; since each pair would be counted once, the size of the sending set would account two for the single combined vertex, and hence this is inconsistent. The OY-OY case states that a vertex is a private neighbour of two different senders, which contradicts the definition. Finally, the OY-OC case says that a private neighbour of one sender is covered by another sender; again, this contradicts the definition. The remaining cases are all consistent.

In order to check that the number produced is correct, it is important to ascertain what is being counted at each step. The entries in a table are counting the actual number of vertices which have been assigned IY, or equivalently the number which have been assigned OY. Note that inconsistencies arise unless each IY vertex has exactly one OY neighbour and vice versa. Furthermore, in combining vertices both IY and OY vertices are produced from exactly one IY and OY vertex, respectively.

4. Directed Networks

Currently, the graph-theoretical model employed uses an undirected graph, because all senders are assumed to have transmitters of the same strength. This will often not be the case, particularly in mobile radio networks, in which stationary despatchers have more powerful transmitters than the mobile units. In order to allow different strengths for transmitters, we need only modify the graph-theoretic model to represent the network as a directed graph, in the obvious manner.

The size of maximum sending sets in this directed graph model are not necessarily related to the size of maximum sending sets in the underlying undirected graph; this can be seen, for instance, by noting that a tournament, or oriented complete graph, with 2n vertices can have a maximum sending set of size n.

Nonetheless, our algorithm can be easily modified to find maximum sending sets in directed networks whose underlying graph is a partial 2-tree. The algorithm in section 2 requires only one minor change in the initialization phase. We must initialize the 25 measures for a directed edge. When there is an edge from x to y and not from y to x, we initialize the measure on the edge (x,y) as follows:

x/y	IY	IN	OY	ON	OC
IY	N	N	1	N	N
IN	N	0	N	N	0
OY	N	N	N	N	N
ON	N	0	N	0	N
OC	N	N	N	N	N

5. Future Research

Although this algorithm operates in linear time, it employs substantially more book-keeping that the linear time solution for trees. It seems reasonable to expect that some of the techniques used in simplifying that solution could profitably be employed here, although the asymptotic performance will remain unchanged. Perhaps of more interest from an applications standpoint is to consider the problem of sending sets in mobile radio networks. In this case, the graph is dynamically changing, but the changes are local; thus, changes in the sending set may also remain localized, enabling the development of an incremental algorithm to solve the problem.

Acknowledgements

David Kirkpatrick suggested the extension to directed networks. We would also like to acknowledge the National Science Foundation's support of the Second West Coast Conference on Computing in Graph Theory, during which this research was initiated. Research of the first author is supported by NSERC Canada under grant number A5047.

References

[1] N. Abramson, "The ALOHA System - Another Alternative for Computer Communications", Proc. AFIPS FJCC 37 (1970).

[2] R.J. Duffin, "Topology of series-parallel networks", J. Math. Anal. Appl. 10 (1965) 303-318.

[3] S. Even, O. Goldreich and P. Tong, "On the NP-completeness of certain network testing problems", TR 230, Computer Science Department, Technion, Haifa, Israel.

[4] A.M. Farley, "Networks immune to isolated failures", Networks 11 (1981) 255-268.

[5] A.M. Farley and A. Proskurowski, "Networks immune to isolated line failures", Networks 12 (1982) 393-403.

[6] A.M. Farley and A. Proskurowski, "On computing the open irredundance number of a tree", Proceedings of the Second West Coast Conference on Computing in Graph Theory, Eugene OR, 1983, proceedings to appear, also Technical Report UO-CIS-TR-83-/4, Dept. of Computer and Information Science, University of Oregon, 1983.

[7] A.M. Farley and N. Shacham, "Senders in Broadcast Networks: Open Irredundancy in Graphs", Congressus Numerantium 38 (1983) 47-57.

[8] E.M. Neufeld and C.J. Colbourn, "The most reliable series-parallel networks", Networks, to appear.

[9] D.J. Rose, "On simple characterizations of k-trees", Discrete Math. 7 (1974) 317-322.

[10] J.A. Wald and C.J. Colbourn, "Steiner trees, partial 2-trees, and minimum IFI networks", Networks 13 (1983) 159-167.

[11] J.A. Wald and C.J. Colbourn, "Steiner trees in probabilistic networks", Microelectronics and Reliability 23 (1983) 837-840.

LINEAR SEARCHING FOR A SQUARE IN A WORD.

---oOo---

Max CROCHEMORE
Laboratoire d'Informatique
Université de Haute-Normandie
BP 67
76130 MONT-SAINT-AIGNAN

Abstract.- Searching a square in a word may be implemented in time proportional to the length of the word on a randomm access machine provided the alphabet is fixed.

Domain Algebras

Peter Dybjer

Programming Methodology Group
Department of Computer Sciences
Chalmers Technical University
S-412 96 Gothenburg, Sweden

Abstract: This paper proposes a way of relating domain-theoretic and algebraic interpretations of data types. It is different from Smyth, Plotkin, and Lehmann's *T*-algebra approach, and in particular the notion of homomorphism between higher-order algebras is not restricted in the same way, so that the usual initiality theorems of algebraic semantics, including one for inequational varieties, hold. *Domain algebras* are defined in terms of concepts from elementary category theory using Lambek's connection between cartesian closed categories and the typed λ-calculus. To this end axioms and inference rules for a theory of *domain categories* are given. Models of these are the standard categories of domains, such as Scott's information systems and Berry and Curien's sequential algorithms on concrete data structures. The set of axioms and inference rules are discussed and compared to the PP_λ-logic of the LCF-system.

1. Introduction

The task of this paper is to investigate the relationship between the algebraic and the denotational/domain-theoretic approach to programming language semantics and program proving. Both approaches have contributed to our understanding of these two topics in various ways. The algebraic approach has for example given a nice treatment of some topics of practical importance - such as structural induction, compiler correctness (Burstall and Landin (1969), Morris (1973), Thatcher, Wagner and Wright (1981)), modular specification (Burstall and Goguen (1977), Mosses (1982)), and the definition of quotient types - which the theory of domains alone does not deal with. The algebraic approach has however mostly used a notion of first-order, many-sorted, discrete (i.e. carriers are sets) algebra following ADJ (1978). This notion is insufficient for some computing applications, since it does not allow higher-order types and operators, and since it does not give a satisfactory semantics of non-terminating computations.

The question of how to unify the two approaches was partially answered by ADJ (1977) Courcelle and Nivat (1976), and others who introduced first-order continuous algebras. Initial algebra theorems similar to those for first-order discrete algebras were proved see e.g. ADJ (1976), (1977), Bloom (1976), Courcelle and Nivat (1976), Meseguer (1977) and Milner (1979).

Another partial answer was given by Smyth and Plotkin (1982) and Lehmann and Smyth (1981). Their notion of *T*-algebra includes continuous and higher-order algebras as special cases. They also made the connection between initial anarchic algebras and least solutions of domain equations very clear. But unfortunately, their notion of higher-order homomorphism is too restrictive to give the algebraic preliminaries which are needed for the treatment of the topics enumerated above.

A somewhat different connection between algebraic specifications and domain equations as explored by Ehrich and Lipeck (1983) who considered "algebraic domain equations" hich are essentially of the form $X = T(X)$, where T is a first-order parameterized data ype.

A third partial answer was imported from categorical logic: Obtułowicz (1977) and erry (1979) and (1981b) interpreted some languages in cartesian closed categories using ambek's (1972) connection between typed λ-calculi and cartesian closed categories; arsaye-Ghomi (1982) defined a notion of discrete higher-order algebra also based on artesian closed categories and proved the initial algebra theorems. He did not conider ordered algebras however, and Poigne (1983) cast doubt on his claim of having a eneral method for constructing extensional models.

In this paper we wish to define a notion of *domain algebra* which (i) allows higherrder operators, (ii) has partially ordered sets as carriers, (iii) allows fixed point ormation, (iv) has a satisfactory notion of homomorphism. Both the *T*-algebra and the artesian closed category approach are possible starting points. In section 2 we shall riefly explain what happens if the *T*-algebra approach is pursued. In section 3 and 4 e introduce the notions of domain category and domain algebra, which are based on rder-enriched cartesian closed categories. (Such categories have earlier been used by erry (1979), (1981b) for interpretations of Plotkin's (1976) language PCF. Ordernriched categories were first used in computing science by Wand (1977).)

On a proof-theoretic level we provide a link between algebraic/equational-style and CF-style theorem proving. Moreover, we have as models the standard cartesian closed ategories of domains, but also (initial) syntactic term models, and quotients of these.

In the final section we discuss the proposed notions and suggest possible modificaions.

. T-algebras

myth and Plotkin (1982) and Lehmann and Smyth (1981) defined a notion of *T*-algebra as ollows:

If T is an endofunctor on a category $\underline{C}$, then a *T-algebra* is a $\underline{C}$-arrow $f \in TA \to A$ for ome $\underline{C}$-object A. A *T-homomorphism* between two *T*-algebras $f \in TA \to A$ and $g \in TB \to B$ is a -arrow $h \in A \to B$, such that

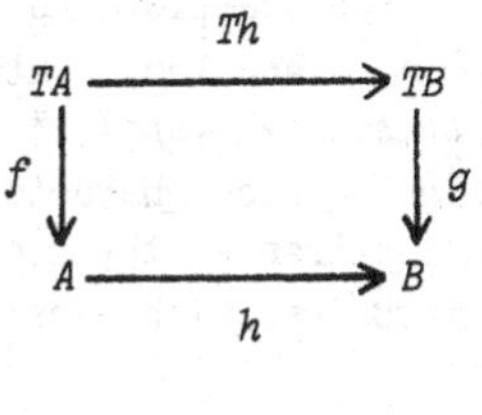

ommutes.

By choosing $\underline{\underline{C}}$ to be $\underline{\underline{Set}}$ or $\underline{\underline{CPO}}$ (or more generally, $\underline{\underline{Set}}^n$ or $\underline{\underline{CPO}}^n$, if there are n sorts) discrete or continuous algebras are obtained respectively. First-order algebras correspond to polynomial T-functors, for example for lists of natural numbers $T(X) = 1+N \times X$. In order to define higher-order algebras a definition of an exponentiation (or function space) functor $\Rightarrow$ is needed. But the usual definition of exponentiation, see e.g. Plotkin (1980), does not work, since it is contravariant in its first argument, and the definition of T-homomorphisms only applies to covariant functors.

Smyth, Plotkin and Lehmann solved this problem by considering the subcategory (of $\underline{\underline{CPO}}$) $\underline{\underline{CPO}}^E$ of cpos and embeddings. An embedding is a continuous function $e \in A \to B$ to which we can associate a (unique right adjoint continuous function) projection $p = e^R \in B \to A$, such that $e\ p \leq id_A$ and $p\ e = id_B$. On $\underline{\underline{CPO}}^E$ a covariant exponentiation $\Rightarrow^E$ can be defined from the contravariant $\Rightarrow$ on $\underline{\underline{CPO}}$ by letting $A \Rightarrow^E A' = A \Rightarrow A'$ on objects, and if $f \in A \to B$ and $f' \in A' \to B'$ then $f \Rightarrow^E f' = f^R \Rightarrow f' \in A \Rightarrow A' \to B \Rightarrow B'$.

For each T on $(\underline{\underline{CPO}}^E)$, constructed from a higher-order signature in this manner, there is an initial T-algebra $\alpha \in TA \to A$ for some object A, and some isomorphism α. Moreover, A is a least solution of the domain equation $X \cong TX$.

But this notion of a higher-order homomorphism as an embedding is too restrictive for investigations of topics such as implementations, compiler correctness and the equational specification of quotient types. For example, only trivial quotients are defined by embeddings. Alternatively, we could choose the category $\underline{\underline{CPO}}^P$ of cpos and projections (or some other category with morphisms which have adjoints) and do the same trick, but this is also unsatisfactory for similar reasons. For example, in Dybjer (1983) a quotient type (the free continuous monoid) which is not defined by a projection is given. There are other possibilities for solving the problem, but all seems to fail and one feels inclined to agree with a statement in Lehmann and Smyth (1981): "*It seems that functional data types are not definable equationally*".

We shall see in the following section that this is no longer true when we choose a quite different notion of domain algebra which is based on order-enriched cartesian closed categories.

3. Domain Categories

In the presentation of domain algebras we will use notation and concepts from elementary category theory - why? Category-theoretic ideas are now often used in discussions both of domain theory, see Scott (1982), and algebraic specification theory. They provide abstract characterizations of product and function spaces, for example. As Lambek (1974) showed, there is a direct connection between cartesian closed categories and typed λ-calculi, in fact "categorical combinators" (*id*,*fst*,*snd*,<>,Λ,*apply*,* below) provide a variable-free alternative to λ-notation. We also get a nice characterization of higher-order signatures in terms of graphs and of domain algebras in terms of diagrams in *domain categories* (order-enriched cartesian closed categories, with least elements of hom-posets, and closed under fixed points).

First, we give axioms and inference rules for a theory of domain categories, following the style of presentation used by Martin-Löf (1979). Models of these axioms are categories such as the cpos (and continuous functions), Plotkin (1980); the strongly lgebraic cpos, Smyth (1982); the information systems, Scott (1982); the effectively given domains, Smyth (1978); the concrete data structures (and sequential algorithms), Berry and Curien (1982).

In section 4 higher-order signatures and higher-order algebras are defined, and the usual initial algebra theorems are stated. For full proofs of these theorems we refer to Dybjer (1983).

There are five kinds of judgments in the theory of domain categories:

i. A object

ii. $A = B$ (assumes A object and B object)

iii. $f \in A \to B$ (assumes A object and B object)

iv. $f = g \in A \to B$ (assumes $f \in A \to B$ and $g \in A \to B$)

v. $f \leq g \in A \to B$ (assumes $f \in A \to B$ and $g \in A \to B$)

We remark that the judgment that a is an element (or a constant term) of the type A ($a \in A$) will be represented by $a \in 1 \to A$, and that functions of several arguments (or terms with several free variables) $A_1, \ldots, A_n$ will be represented by morphisms with source $A_1 \times \ldots \times A_n$. For detailed explanations of the connection between typed λ-calculus and cartesian closed categories, see Lambek (1980), Scott (1980), Poigne (1983) and Dybjer (1983). Also note that the language is polymorphic, since all terms are given together with their types it is not necessary to have subscripts (just as in Martin-Löf (1979)).

General Rules

$$A = A$$

$$\frac{A = B}{B = A}$$

$$\frac{A = B \quad B = C}{A = C}$$

$$\frac{f \in A \to B \quad A = A' \quad B = B'}{f \in A' \to B'}$$

$$\frac{f \leq f' \in A \to B \quad A = A' \quad B = B'}{f \leq f' \in A' \to B'}$$

$$f \leq f \in A \to B$$

$$\frac{f \leq f' \in A \to B \quad f' \leq f'' \in A \to B}{f \leq f'' \in A \to B}$$

$$\frac{f \leq f' \in A \to B \quad f' \leq f \in A \to B}{f = f' \in A \to B}$$

(the last rule is valid both ways)

Rules for Composition and Identity

$$\frac{f\ \varepsilon\ A \to B \qquad g\ \varepsilon\ B \to C}{g\ f\ \varepsilon\ A \to C}$$

$$\frac{f < f'\ \varepsilon\ A \to B \qquad g < g'\ \varepsilon\ B \to C}{g\ f < g'\ f'\ \varepsilon\ A \to C}$$

$$\frac{f\ \varepsilon\ A \to B \qquad g\ \varepsilon\ B \to C \qquad h\ \varepsilon\ C \to D}{(h\ g)\ f = h\ (g\ f)\ \varepsilon\ A \to D}$$

$$id\ \varepsilon\ A \to A$$

$$\frac{f\ \varepsilon\ A \to B}{f\ id = f\ \varepsilon\ A \to B \qquad id\ f = f\ \varepsilon\ A \to B}$$

Rules for Terminal Object

$$1 \text{ object}$$

$$* = \bot\ \varepsilon\ A \to 1$$

$$\frac{f\ \varepsilon\ A \to 1}{f = \bot\ \varepsilon\ A \to 1}$$

Rules for Binary Products

$$\frac{A \text{ object} \qquad B \text{ object}}{A \times B \text{ object}}$$

$$\frac{f\ \varepsilon\ A \to B \qquad g\ \varepsilon\ A \to C}{\langle f, g\rangle\ \varepsilon\ A \to B \times C}$$

$$\frac{f < f'\ \varepsilon\ A \to B \qquad g < g'\ \varepsilon\ A \to C}{\langle f, g\rangle < \langle f', g'\rangle\ \varepsilon\ A \to B \times C}$$

$$fst\ \varepsilon\ A \times B \to A \qquad snd\ \varepsilon\ A \times B \to B$$

$$\frac{f\ \varepsilon\ A \to B \qquad g\ \varepsilon\ A \to C}{fst\ \langle f, g\rangle = f\ \varepsilon\ A \to B \qquad snd\ \langle f, g\rangle = g\ \varepsilon\ A \to C}$$

$$\frac{h\ \varepsilon\ A \to B \times C}{\langle fst\ h, snd\ h\rangle = h\ \varepsilon\ A \to B \times C}$$

Rules for Exponentiation

$$\frac{A \text{ object} \qquad B \text{ object}}{A \Rightarrow B \text{ object}}$$

$$\frac{f\ \varepsilon\ A \times B \to C}{\Lambda(f)\ \varepsilon\ A \to B \Rightarrow C}$$

$$\frac{f < f'\ \varepsilon\ A \times B \to C}{\Lambda(f) < \Lambda(f')\ \varepsilon\ A \to B \Rightarrow C}$$

$$apply \in (A \Rightarrow B) \times A \to B$$

$$\frac{f \in A \times B \to C}{apply \, \langle \Lambda(f) \, fst, snd \rangle = f \in A \times B \to C}$$

$$\frac{g \in A \to B \Rightarrow C}{\Lambda(apply \, \langle g \, fst, snd \rangle) = g \in A \to B \Rightarrow C}$$

ules for Bottom

$$\bot \in A \to B$$

$$\frac{f \in A \to B}{\bot \leq f \in A \to B}$$

$$\frac{f \in A \to B}{\bot f = \bot \in A \to C}$$

ules for Prefixed Points

$$\frac{f \in A \to A}{fix\,(f) \in 1 \to A}$$

$$\frac{f \in A \to A}{f \, fix\,(f) \leq fix\,(f) \in 1 \to A}$$

$$\frac{f \in A \to A \quad a \in 1 \to A \quad f\,a \leq a \in 1 \to A}{fix\,(f) \leq a \in 1 \to A}$$

From these rules follow e.g.

$$\langle \bot, \bot \rangle = \bot \in A \to B \times C$$

$$\Lambda(\bot) = \bot \in A \to B \Rightarrow C$$

$$\frac{f \in A \to A}{f \, fix\,(f) = fix\,(f) \in 1 \to A}$$

$$\frac{f \leq f' \in A \to A}{fix\,(f) \leq fix\,(f') \in 1 \to A}$$

A map F from a domain category $\underline{\underline{C}}$ to a domain category $\underline{\underline{D}}$ is a *domain functor* if it reserves all the "distinguished data", see Lambek and Scott (1980), of domain ategories, i.e. objects, morphisms, source, target, =, composition, *id* (the data which rdinary functors preserve) and $\leq$, $\bot$, *fix*, *1*, *, ×, ⟨⟩, *fst*, *snd*, =>, Λ, *apply*.

.. Domain Algebras

n papers on algebraic semantics (first-order) signatures are usually defined by a pair $S, \Sigma\rangle$ where S is a set of sorts and Σ is an S^*S-indexed set of operators. For example, he lists of natural numbers are defined by $S = \{NAT, LIST\}$, $\Sigma_{NAT} = \{0\}$, $\Sigma_{NATNAT} =$ $suc\}$, $\Sigma_{LIST} = \{nil\}$, $\Sigma_{NATLISTLIST} = \{cons\}$. For the purpose of illustration the following figure would be used, see e.g. ADJ (1978):

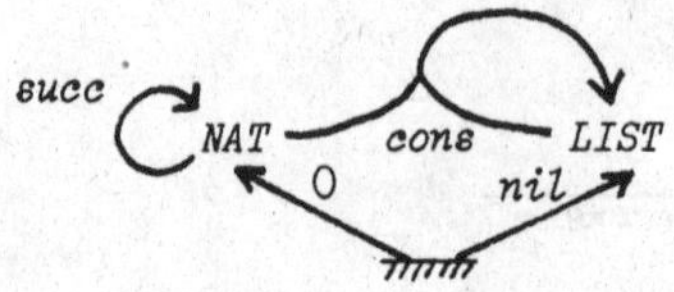

This is not a graph, but becomes one if we add nodes $NAT \times LIST$ and 1:

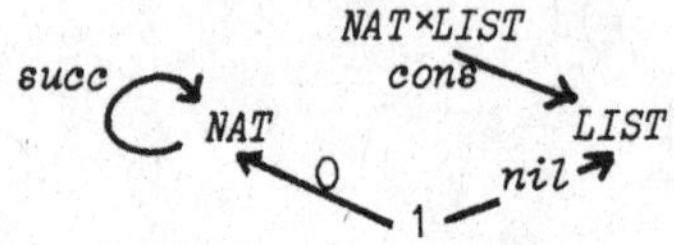

Using this idea *higher-order signatures* are defined as graphs whose nodes are called *sorts*, whose edges are called *operators*, and whose sort set is subject to the following rules:

$$1 \text{ sort}$$

$$\frac{a \text{ sort} \quad b \text{ sort}}{a \times b \text{ sort}}$$

$$\frac{a \text{ sort} \quad b \text{ sort}}{a \Rightarrow b \text{ sort}}$$

Similarly, algebras on a signature $\langle S, \Sigma \rangle$ are usually defined as a pair $\langle A_S, A_\Sigma \rangle$, where A_S is an S-indexed family of sets and A_Σ is an $S^* S$-indexed family of operations (of appropriate types).

Viewing signatures as graphs (with 1 and ×), and recalling the definition of a categorical diagram on a graph, we see that such ordinary many-sorted first-order algebras could be defined as diagrams in $\underline{\underline{Set}}$ which preserve products, (generalizing the above notation we could require $A_{a \times b} = A_a \times A_b$), and terminals ($A_1 = \{\emptyset\}$).

Similarly, *domain algebras* are defined as diagrams on higher-order signatures in domain categories, which preserve 1, ×, and $\Rightarrow$. I.e. let Σ be a higher-order signature and let J: $\Sigma \to \underline{\underline{C}}$ be a diagram (on Σ in the domain category $\underline{\underline{C}}$). Then J is a domain algebra provided it obeys the following rules:

$$\frac{a \text{ sort}}{J(a) \textit{ object}}$$

$$J(1) = 1$$

$$\frac{a \text{ sort} \quad b \text{ sort}}{J(a \times b) = J(a) \times J(b)}$$

$$\frac{a \text{ sort} \quad b \text{ sort}}{J(a \Rightarrow b) = J(a) \Rightarrow J(b)}$$

A *domain homomorphism* between two domain algebras J: $\Sigma \to \underline{\underline{C}}$ and J': $\Sigma \to \underline{\underline{C}}'$ is a domain functor H: $\underline{\underline{C}} \to \underline{\underline{C}}'$, such that

$$\frac{a \text{ sort } (\mathit{in}\ \Sigma)}{H(J(a)) = J'(a)}$$

$$\frac{\sigma \in a \to b\ (\mathit{in}\ \Sigma)}{H(J(\sigma)) = J'(\sigma) \in J'(a) \to J'(b)}$$

We could also introduce signature morphisms and homomorphisms between algebras on different signatures).

The domain algebras and domain homomorphisms on a higher-order signature Σ form a category, and in the same way as usual we can construct its initial object. Let $\underline{\underline{D}}_\Sigma$ be the (syntactic) domain category of terms over Σ (each term is generated from Σ by a finite number of applications of the rules for domain categories (of the first and third kind), i.e. Σ is closed up under 1, ×, =>, *, *fst*, *snd*, <>, Λ, *apply*, , and *fix*) under the partial order relation generated by a finite number of applications of the rules for domain categories (of the fourth and fifth kind). Then the syntactic domain algebra $I\colon \Sigma \to \underline{\underline{D}}_\Sigma$ is defined by $I(a) = a$ if a is a sort in Σ, and $I(\sigma) = \sigma \in a \to b$ if $\sigma \in a \to b$ is an operator in Σ.

We have the following:

Theorem: $I\colon \Sigma \to \underline{\underline{D}}_\Sigma$ is an initial object in the category of domain algebras and domain homomorphisms on Σ.

(Note that the unique homomorphism from $I\colon \Sigma \to \underline{\underline{D}}_\Sigma$ to a (perhaps concrete) domain category is an order-theoretic analogue of an algebra in Lawvere's sense, i.e. a functor from a free algebraic theory to $\underline{\underline{Set}}$.)

A Σ-*inequality* is a pair of morphisms in $\underline{\underline{D}}_\Sigma$ with the same source and the same target. Note that inequalities with free variables here are represented as pairs of terms without free variables, cf the remark in the previous section.) The Σ-inequality $f \leq f' \in A \to B$ is *satisfied* by the domain algebra $J\colon \Sigma \to \underline{\underline{C}}$ iff $J^\#(f) \leq J^\#(f') \in J(A) \to J(B)$, where $J^\#\colon \underline{\underline{D}}_\Sigma \to \underline{\underline{C}}$ is the unique domain homomorphism from I to J.

A domain algebra on a signature Σ (a Σ-algebra) which satisfies a set of inequalities INQ is called a Σ,INQ-algebra. The Σ,INQ-algebras and Σ-homomorphisms form a category whose initial object (as usual) can be constructed proof-theoretically or be defined model-theoretically.

In order to do this we need to introduce the concept of a *quotient category*, see MacLane (1971). Here we give a different, but equivalent, definition, which we claim to be more natural:

Let $\underline{\underline{C}}$ be a category and R be a family of relations on the hom-sets of $\underline{\underline{C}}$. If R obeys the rules for equality of morphisms in categories (replace = by R in the general rules and the rules for composition and identity in section 2) then R is called a *category congruence*. We denote the *quotient category* of $\underline{\underline{C}}$ w.r.t R by $\underline{\underline{C}}/R$, i.e. the category which has the same objects as $\underline{\underline{C}}$ and R-equivalence classes of morphisms of $\underline{\underline{C}}$ as morphisms.

Similarly, if $\underline{C}$ is a domain category and R obeys all rules for $\leq$ in domain categories (together with R^{*} for =, where $fR^{*}g$ iff fRg and gRf), then R is a *domain category order-congruence*. Then the order-enriched category $\underline{C}/R$, which has the same objects as $\underline{C}$ and R^{*}-equivalence classes of morphisms under the R-ordering as morphisms, is a domain category.

Let $Q: \Sigma \to \underline{\underline{D}}_{\Sigma}/\leq_{INQ}$ be defined by $Q(a) = a$ if a is a sort in Σ and $Q(\sigma) = [\sigma]_{\leq^{*}_{INQ}} \in a \to b$ if $\sigma \in a \to b$ is an operator in Σ, where $\leq_{INQ}$ is the *proof-theoretic* family of relations defined by $f \leq_{INQ} f' \in A \to B$ iff $INQ \vdash f \leq f' \in A \to B$ (i.e. $f \leq f' \in A \to B$ can be proved from the assumptions in INQ using the rules in section 2; hence $\leq_{INQ}$ clearly is a domain category order-congruence).

Theorem: $Q: \Sigma \to \underline{\underline{D}}_{\Sigma}/\leq_{INQ}$ is an initial Σ, INQ-algebra.

Moreover, a *model-theoretic* family of relations M_{INQ} on the hom-sets of $\underline{\underline{D}}_{\Sigma}$ is defined by $f\ M_{INQ}\ f' \in A \to B$ iff all Σ, INQ-algebras satisfy $f \leq f' \in A \to B$. We have

Theorem: $f\ M_{INQ}\ f' \in A \to B$ iff $f \leq_{INQ} f' \in A \to B$.

This theorem says that the logic of inequalities given in section 2 is complete for domain categories (in our presentation this result becomes trivial - still it corresponds precisely to the completeness of first-order many-sorted equational logic of Benabou (1968) and Goguen and Meseguer (1981), and of first-order many-sorted inequational logic of Bloom (1976)).

5. Discussion

How is the choice of rules for domain categories justified, and how do these rules relate to the PPλ-logic of the LCF-system of Milner, Morris, and Newey (1975)?

We have had two governing principles: (i) The set of rules should axiomatize the standard categories of domains, and not contain rules which only hold in some particular category. (ii) The rules should be nicely "algebraic" and admit construction of initial models in a similar way to the first-order discrete case.

As a consequence we have decided to abandon PPλ's (i) extensionality rule

$$\frac{\forall x. f(x) \leq g(x)}{f \leq g}$$

and (ii) rule of Scott-induction for admissible predicates, and replace them with the weaker rules of (i) the monotonicity of Λ which implies a variant of the ξ-rule

$$\frac{f \leq g}{\lambda x. f \leq \lambda x. g}$$

and (ii) the leastness of *fix*.

PPλ's rules are satisfied by $\underline{\underline{CPO}}$, but of course this axiomatization is incomplete (cf Streicher's (1983) result on definability in effectively given domains).

We shall discuss the following aspects of our definitions: (i) completeness and alge-raicity of the hom-posets; (ii) extensionality; (iii) cartesian closure; (iv) power of he theory of domain categories.

(i) We have chosen to accept CPO and Guessarian's (1982) category of posets closed nder algebraic directed sets (also cf the rational algebraic theories of ADJ (1976)) as roper domain categories. However, in particular in the light of Scott (1981) and 1982) many would argue that it is an (the?) essential aspects of a domain that it is ompletely determined by its finite parts. The alternative approach which suggests tself, but which we have not pursued, is to axiomatize only the finite elements (mor-hisms) and as a second step construct some completion. From this point the restriction hat only quotients specified by inequalities between finite morphisms should be con-idered becomes natural (cf the powerdomain constructions).

(ii) There is an interesting category of domains which is not extensional: Berry and urien's (1982) sequential algorithms on concrete data structures. We refer to erry (1981a) for arguments against demanding extensionality for categories of domains.

(iii) The categorical axioms for product and function spaces are "abstract" charac-erizations and thus cartesian closure provides a criterion for whether a particular ategory of domains is closed under the "right" notions of product and function space. his view has been common in recent domain theory, and as a consequence e.g. the ategory of ω-algebraic cpos and continuous functions, which is not cartesian closed, as been rejected as a proper category of domains for denotational semantics, see Plot-in (1980) and Smyth (1982).

What about coproducts then? We cannot add rules for categorical coproducts to the ules for domain categories without creating an inconsistent system. This is not a ajor problem in the algebraic/equational approach, where operators on abstract data ypes are interpreted as morphisms of quotient categories. In denotational semantics ne instead uses a "synthetic" approach, see Lehmann and Smyth (1981), where operators re interpreted as elements of reflexive domains. Here the use of sums of domains is ssential, but these sums cannot be categorical coproducts in any category of (cartesian losed) domains. For example, PPλ axiomatizes a separated sum with injections and the perations *outl*, *outr*, *isl*, *isr*, see Milner, Morris and Newey (1975).

This situation is not entirely satisfactory. Recently, in the domain theory nterpretation of his intuitionistic type theory, Martin-Löf interprets +, $\times$, and $\rightarrow$ not s categorical sum, product, and exponentiation, but as sligthly modified constructions in the category of information systems of Scott (1982)), see notes from his talk and rom the discussion on domain theory and type theory in Karlsson and Petersson (1983). n particular, the axioms establishing the uniqueness of the mediating morphisms, (e.g., or products, $\langle fst\ h, snd\ h\rangle = h$) do not hold. This is necessary to get a correspondence etween the denotational semantics and the lazy operational semantics of the programs of ype theory, which require, e.g. $\langle\bot,\bot\rangle \neq \bot$. We could thus modify our rules for domain ategories so that they axiomatize Martin-Löf's proposed "almost cartesian closure", nstead of the standard notion of cartesian closure.

(iv) The axioms and inference rules for domain categories form a logic of inequalities whose power is inbetween many-sorted equational logic and PPλ. With the additional power obtained by doing structural induction in the initial models some interesting proofs can be done. An example is the compiler correctness proof in Dybjer (1983) which is substantially simpler than the corresponding proof in PPλ by Cohn (1978) who uses Scott-induction in an essential way. However, it seems that a calculus of inequalities is not always sufficient for reasoning about programs, and at least a fragment of predicate calculus is needed. PPλ suggests how to do such an extension, but there are some problems, such as the formulation of the admissibility criterion for predicates to be used in Scott-induction, and the absence of a general structural induction principle for reflexive domains.

6. Acknowledgments

I wish to thank Rod Burstall, Per Martin-Löf, Gordon Plotkin, Axel Poigne, Mike Smyth, Tomas Streicher, and Andrzej Tarlecki for discussions and criticism. I also wish to thank the members of the Programming Methodology Group in Gothenburg for support and for contributing to a stimulating environment.

7. References

ADJ (= Goguen, J.A., Thatcher, J.W., Wagner, E.G., Wright, J.B.) (1976), "Rational Algebraic Theories and Fixed-Point Solutions", Proceedings 17th IEEE Symposium on Foundations of Computer Science, Houston, Texas, pp 147-158

ADJ (= Goguen, J.A., Thatcher, J.W., Wagner, E.G., Wright, J.B.) (1977), "Initial Algebra Semantics and Continuous Algebras", JACM 24, 1, pp 68-95

ADJ (= Goguen, J.A., Thatcher, J.W., Wagner, E.G.) (1978), "An Initial Algebra Approach to the Specification, Correctness and Implementation of Abstract Data Types", in "Current Trends in Programming Methodology", R.Yeh ed., Prentice-Hall

Benabou, J. (1968), "Structures algebraic dans les categories", Cahiers de topologie et geometrie differentiell 10, pp 1-24

Berry, G. (1979), "Modèles complètement adèquats et stables des lambda-calculs typès", Thèse de doctorat d'etat ès sciences mathematiques, l'universitè Paris VII

Berry, G. (1981a), "On the Definition of Lambda Calculus Models", Proceedings International Colloquium on Formalization of Programming Concepts, Lecture Notes in Computer Science 107 (Springer Verlag, Berlin), pp 218-230

Berry, G. (1981b), "Some Syntactic and Categorical Constructions of Lambda-Calculus Models", Rapport INRIA 80

Berry, G. and Curien, P.L. (1982), "Sequential Algorithms on Concrete Data Structures" Theoretical Computer Science 20, pp 265-321

Bloom, S.L. (1976), "Varieties of Ordered Algebras", Journal of Computer and System Sciences 13, pp 200-212

Burstall, R.M. and Goguen, J.A. (1977), "Putting Theories Together to Make Specifications", Proceedings of the 5th IJCAI, pp 1045-1058

Burstall, R.M. and Landin, P.J. (1969), "Programs and their Proofs: An Algebraic Approach", Machine Intelligence 4, Edinburgh University Press, pp 17-44 ohn, A.J. (1978), "High Level Proofs in LCF", Report CSR-35-78, Department of Computer Science, University of Edinburgh

ourcelle, B. and Nivat, M. (1976) "Algebraic Families of Interpretations", Proceedings of the 17th FOCS, Houston

ybjer, P. (1983), "Category-Theoretic Logics and Algebras of Programs", Ph.D.thesis, CTH

hrich, H.D. and Lipeck, U. (1983), "Algebraic Domain Equations", Theoretical Computer Science 27, pp 167-196

oguen, J.A. and Meseguer,J. (1981), "Completeness of Many-Sorted Equational Logic", SIGPLAN Notices 16, pp 24-32

uessarian, I. (1982) "Survey on some Classes of Interpretations and some of their applications", Laboratoire Informatique Theorique et Programmation, 82-46, Univ. Paris VII

arlsson, K. and Petersson, K., (eds) (1983), "Workshop on Semantics of Programming Languages", CTH

ambek, J. (1972), "Deductive Systems and Categories III", Proceedings Dalhousie Conference on Toposes, Algebraic Geometry and Logic, Lecture Notes in Mathematics 274, Springer-Verlag, pp 57-82

ambek, J. (1980), "From Lambda-Calculus to Cartesian Closed Categories", in To H.B. Curry: Essays on Combinatory Logic, Lambda Calculus and Formalism, J.P. Seldin and J.R. Hindley (eds.), pp 376-402

ambek, J. and Scott, P.J. (1980), "Intuitionist Type Theory and the Free Topos", Journal of Pure and Applied Algebra 19, pp 215-257

ehmann, D.J. and Smyth, M.B. (1981), "Algebraic Specification of Data Types: A Synthetic Approach", Mathematical Systems Theory 14, pp 97-139

acLane, S. (1971), "Categories for the Working Mathematician", Springer-Verlag, Berlin

artin-Löf, P. (1979), "Constructive Mathematics and Computer Programming", 6th International Congress for Logic, Methodology and Philosophy of Science, Hannover

eseguer, J. (1977) "On Order-Complete Universal Algebra and Enriched Functorial Semantics", Proceedings of FCT, Lecture Notes in Computer Science 56 (Springer-Verlag, Berlin)

ilner, R. (1979), "Flow Graphs and Flow Algebras", JACM 26, pp 794-818

ilner, R., Morris, L., Newey, M. (1975), "A Logic for Computable Functions with Reflexive and Polymorphic Types", Proc. Conference on Proving and Improving Programs, Arc-et-Senans

orris, F.L. (1973), "Advice on Structuring Compilers and Proving them Correct", Proceedings, ACM Symposium on Principles of Programming Languages, Boston, pp 144-152

osses, P.D. (1982), "Abstract Semantic Algebras!", DAIMI Report PB-145, Computer Science Department, Aarhus University

btułowicz, A. (1977), "Functorial Semantics of the λ-$\beta\eta$-calculus" in Proceedings of FCT, Lecture Notes in Computer Science 56 (Springer-Verlag, Berlin)

arsaye-Ghomi, K. (1982), "Higher Order Abstract Data Types", Ph.D. thesis, Department of Computer Science, UCLA

lotkin, G.D. (1976), "LCF Considered as a Programming Language", Theoretical Computer Science 5, pp 223-256

lotkin, G.D. (1980), "Domains", Edinburgh CS Dept, lecture notes.

Poigne, A. (1983), "On Semantic Algebras Higher Order Structures", Forschungsbericht 156, Abt. Informatik, Universitat Dortmund

Scott, D.S. (1980), "Relating Theories of the Lambda-Calculus", in To H.B. Curry: Essays on Combinatory Logic, Lambda Calculus and Formalism, J.P. Seldin and J.R. Hindley (eds), pp 404-450

Scott, D.S. (1981), "Lectures on a Mathematical Theory of Computation", Technical Monograph PRG-19, Oxford University Computing Laboratory

Scott, D.S. (1982), "Domains for Denotational Semantics", Proceedings 9th International Colloquium on Automata, Languages and Programming, Aarhus, Springer-Verlag Lecture Notes in Computer Science, pp 577-613

Smyth, M.B. (1978), "Effectively Given Domains", Theoretical Computer Science 5

Smyth, M.B. (1982), "The Largest Cartesian Closed Category of Domains", Report CSR 108-82, Computer Science Department, University of Edinburgh

Smyth, M.B. and Plotkin, G.D. (1982), "The Category Theoretic Solution of Recursive Domain Equations", SIAM Journal on Computing 11

Streicher, T. (1983), "Definability in Scott Domains", in Proc. Workshop on Semantics of Programming Languages, CTH

Thatcher, J.W., Wagner, E.G., Wright, J.B. (1981), "More on Advice on Structuring Compilers and Proving them Correct", Theoretical Computer Science 15, pp 223-249

Wand, M. (1977), "Fixed-Point Constructions in Order-Enriched Categories", Technical Report 23, Computer Science Department, Indiana University, Bloomington

PRINCIPALITY RESULTS ABOUT SOME MATRIX LANGUAGES FAMILIES

Didier FERMENT,
L.I.T.P. 248, 2 Place Jussieu,
75251 PARIS Cedex 05, France

Extend abstract :

We investigate the family of matrix languages (studied by A. Salomaa) and the family of matrix languages of index less than K (studied by J. Beauquier and G. Paun), for each $K \geq 1$. We solve an open problem : all these families are principal rational cones. Moreover, we establish a relation between their respective generators.

INTRODUCTION

In formal language theory, the basic hierarchy of language families has been obtained by imposing restrictions on the form of rewriting rules. A natural generalization is to restrict the process of generation of a grammar, that is, to restrict also the manner the productions are used : in such a grammar, a control device lets through acceptable derivations only (S. Greibach, 77, A. Salomaa, 73). For instance, Salomaa has studied contrext-free matrix languages generated by context-free matrix grammars. In such grammars, rules are not used independently from each other but only some specified sequences of rules (the matrices) are allowed. The generative capacity of matrix grammars is more important thant the capacity of context-free grammars. In this framework, Paun (77, 79, 80, 81, 83) and Beauquier (79) have studied the effect of the finite index restriction : an upper bound of the number of nonterminal occurrences appearing at each step of a derivation is fixed. The family of matrix languages and, for each $K \geq 1$, the family of matrix languages of index less than K are known to be rational cones (Salomaa, 73 and Paun, 83). By means of the construct of Chomsky-Schützenberger, we establish the principality of all these cones. Moreover, we exhibit a strong relation between their respective generators.

SECTION 1 : Definitions, notations and results about matrix languages

We assume the reader to be familiar with the basis of formal language theory (see Berstel 79) and particularly with the basis of matrix language theory (see Salomaa 73).

Let V be an alphabet ; the free monoid generated by V is denoted V^* and its unit (the empty word) by ε. Let U be a subset of V and let W be a word. Then $/W/_U$ denotes the number of occurrences of letters of U in W. $/W/$ denotes the lenght of W.

An context-free grammar is a 4-tuple, $G = \langle V_T, V_N, S, P\rangle$ where V_T is the set of terminal letters, V_N is the set of variables, $V_N \cap V_T = \emptyset$, S is the axiom, and P is the set of rewriting rules : $P \subseteq V_N \times (V_N \cup V_T)^*$. We note : $V_G = V_N \cup V_T$.

An context-free matrix grammar or M-Grammar is a pair (G,M) where G is an context-free grammar and M a finite set of matrix. A matrix is a finite sequence of rules : $m = [r_1, r_2, \ldots, r_n]$ with $n \geq 1$ and $\forall i \in [1,n]$, $r_i \in P$. A derivation of such a grammar consists of a sequence of matrix derivations, where the derivation of a matrix m is the sequence of applications of its rules : r_1, then $r_2, \ldots$, then r_n. (see Salomaa, 73).

The matrix language generated by (G,M) is denoted $L(G,M)$, and the family of matrix languages Malg.

Example 1 :

Let us consider the context-free grammar

$G = \langle\{a,b,c\}, \{S,X,Y\}, S, P\rangle$

with the following set of rules :

$P = \{S \to XY,\ X \to aXb,\ Y \to cY,\ X \to \varepsilon,\ Y \to \varepsilon\}$,

and the set of matrices :

$M = \{[S \to XY],$

$[X \to aXb,\ Y \to cY],$

$[X \to \varepsilon, Y \to \varepsilon]\}$.

It is easy to see that

$L(G,M) = \{a^n b^n c^n / n \geq 0\}$.

An context-free controled grammar or C-grammar is a pair (G,C) where C is a context-free grammar and C is a rational language on the alphabet P (the set of rewriting rules). C is the control set (see Salomaa, 73). (G,C) generates the controled language $L(G,C)$ defined as it follows :

$L(G,C) = \{W/W \in V_T^*$ and there exists a derivation $S \xrightarrow[G]{*} W$ such that the sequence of derived rules is a word of the control set $C\}$.

Let $A = \langle P, Q, Q^+, q^-, \delta\rangle$ be a finite automaton, then (G,A) also defines a C-grammar and A is the control automaton. The family of controled languages is denoted Calg.

Example 2 :

Let us consider the context-free grammar G of the example 1. We note :

r_1 the rule $(S \to XY)$,

r_2 the rule $(X \to aXb)$,

r_3 the rule $(Y \to Yc)$,

r_4 the rule $(X \to \varepsilon)$,

r_5 the rule $(Y \to \varepsilon)$,

and we consider the control set C defined by the following rational expression :

$$r_1.(r_2.r_3)^*.\ r_4.r_5$$

it is easy to see that

$$L(G,M) = \{a^n b^n c^n / n \geq 0\}.$$

Let now (G,C) be a C-grammar as above.

For a derivation

$$d : S = w_o \xrightarrow{r_1} w_1 \xrightarrow{r_2} w_2 \longrightarrow \dots \xrightarrow{r_n} w_n,$$

we define its index,

$$ind_{(G,C)}(d) = \max \{|w_i|_{V_N} / \forall\ i \in [o,n]\}.$$

For a word $w \in V_T^*$, we set :

$$ind_{(G,C)}(w) = \min \{ind_{(G,C)}(d)/d \text{ is a derivation of } w \text{ in } (G,C)\},$$

and $ind(G,C) = \max \{ind_{(G,C)}(w)/w \in L(G,C)\}$.

The index of a C-language L is

$$ind(L) = \min \{ind(G,C) / L = L(G,C)\}.$$

For each $K \geq 1$, we denote Clif(K) the family of controled languages of index less than K, and Clif the family of C-languages of finite index.

In the same way we define a "matrix index". So, we introduce $ind_{(G,M)}(d)$, $ind_{(G,M)}(w)$, ind(G,M) and for a M-language L, ind(L). The corresponding families are Mlif and Mlif(K), for each $K \geq 1$.

Remark 1 : This definition of matrix index seems to be different from the definition of Paun which computes the index of a derivation only from the words obtained before and after the application of each matrix. But there exists an algorithm which, for each M-grammar of index K in the sens of Paun, builds a M-grammar of index K in our sens, generating the same language.

Example 3 :

Let us consider the matrix grammar (G',M') with

$G' = \langle\{a,b,c\}, \{S,A,B,C\},S,P'\rangle$,

$P' = \{S \to ABC,\ A \to aA, B \to bB,\ c \to cC,\ A \to \varepsilon,\ B \to \varepsilon,\ C \to \varepsilon\}$,

$M' = \{[S \to A\ B\ C]$,

$[A \to aA,\ B \to bB,\ C \to cC]$,

$[A \to \varepsilon,\ B \to \varepsilon,\ C \to \varepsilon]\}$.

The index of the derivation

$S \to ABC \to aAbBcC \to abc$ is 3.

The index of the word abc relative to the matrix grammar (G',M') is 3.

The index of the matrix grammar (G',M') is 3.

Therefore, the index of the language $\{a^n b^n c^n / n \geq 0\}$ is less than 3.

As the matrix grammar (G,M) of the example 1 generates the language $\{a^n b^n c^n / n \geq 0\}$ and is of index 2, the "matrix index" of this language is less than 2.

By examples 1 and 2, we have :

$\{a^n b^n c^n / n \geq 0\} \in \text{Mlif}(2)$,

$\{a^n b^n c^n / n \geq 0\} \in \text{Clif}(2)$.

We recall some results of Beauquier (79) and Paun (77,79,80,81,83) about matrix languages of finite index :

- a lemma on the existence of iteratives n-tuples,
- a transfert theorem of iterative n-tuples,
- the property that, for any integer K, Mlif(K) is a rational cone and $\text{Mlif}(K) \not\subseteq \text{Mlif}(K+1)$,
- the property that Mlif is a non-principal full -AFL closed by substitution and $D_2'^{*} \notin \text{Mlif}$.

SECTION 2 : Preliminaries

First, we establish that, under fixed finite index, matrix grammars and controled grammars generate the same family of languages.

Proposition 1 : $\forall K \geq 1$, Clif(K) = Mlif(K)

□ 1) Consider the M-grammar (G,M) with $M = \{m_i / i \in [1,\mu]\}$ and $m_i = [r_1^{(i)}, r_2^{(i)}, \ldots, r_{ni}^{(i)}]$. According to Salomaa (73), we can choose the control set :

$C = (\bigcup_{1 \leq i \leq \mu} r_1^{(i)} . r_2^{(i)} \ldots r_{ni}^{(i)})^{*}$, and we obtain L(G,M) = L(G,C).

Moreover, we have ind(G,M) = ind(G,C).

2) Let (G,A) be a C-grammar with $A = \langle P,Q,Q^{+},q^{-},\delta\rangle$. We construct an equivalent M-grammar (G',M') according to the following idea : the behaviour of the control automaton can be simulated during the derivation if the state is encoded into a variable. We set :

$V'_N = V_N \cup \overline{V_T} \cup \{\bar{\varepsilon}\} \cup (V_N \cup V_T \cup \{\varepsilon\}) \times Q,$

where $\overline{V_T} = \{\bar{a}/a \in V_T\}$, and

$G' = \langle V_T, V'_N, (S,q^-), P' \rangle.$

The set of rules P' and the matrices of M are defined as it follows :

$\forall\, v, v' \in V_N,\ \forall\, x,x' \in V_T \cup \{\varepsilon\},\ \forall\, q,q' \in Q,\ \forall\, w_1,w_2 \in V_G^*,$

a) $[(v,q) \to w_1(v',q')w_2] \in M$ if and only if $r = (v \to w_1 v' w_2)$ and $r \in P$ and $\delta(q,r) = q'$,

b) $[(v,q) \to w_1(x',q')w_2] \in M$ iff $w_1 x' w_2 \in V_T^*$ and $r = (v \to w_1 x' w_2)$ and $r \in P$ and $\delta(q,r) = q'$,

c) $[(v,q) \to v, v' \to (v',q)] \in M,$

d) $[(x,q) \to \bar{x},\ v' \to (v',q)] \in M,$

e) $[\bar{x} \to x] \in M,$

f) $[(x,q) \to x] \in M$ iff $q \in Q^+$.

It is easy to verify $L(G',M') = L(G,C)$ and $ind(G,C) = ind(G',M')$. □

Remark 2 : The construction of the proof b defines and establishes a normal form for matrix grammars.

Now, we establish a normal form for the rules of a M-grammar.

Definition 1 : A M-grammar (G,M) or a C-grammar (G,C) is in quadratic form if and only if

$P \subseteq V_N \times (\{\varepsilon\} \cup V_N \cup V_T \cup V_T.V_N \cup V_N.V_T \cup V_N.V_N).$

Proposition 2 : For each M-language L, there exists a M-grammar (G,M) in quadratic form such that $L = L(G,M)$ and $ind(G,M) = ind(L)$.

The proof uses the classical construction of a grammar in quadratic form for context-free languages (see Berstel, 79).

Definition 2 : A M-grammar is in Normal Matrix Form iff each matrix of M is of one of these types : $[v \to \varepsilon]$, $[v \to a]$, $[v \to v']$, $[v \to av']$, $[v \to v'a]$, $[v \to v'v'']$, $[v \to v',\ v'' \to v''']$ and $v' \neq v''$, where v,v',v'',v''' are variables and a is a terminal letter.

Proposition 3 : For each matrix language L, there exists a M-grammar (G,M) in N.M.F. such that $L = L(G,M)$ and $ind(G,M) = ind(L)$.

□ We modify the proposition 1 ; we substitute the matrices,

$[(v,q) \to \overline{(v,q)},\ v \to (v,q)],$

$[\overline{(v,q)} \to v,\ (v,q) \to (v,q)],$

where $\overline{(v,q)}$ and (v,q) are news variables, to the matrix $[(v,q) \to v, v \to (v,q)]$. This new and the proposition 2 gives the proof.□

Now, we define the part of index less than K of a language L relatively to its grammar G ;

$<L>_G^{\leq K} = \{w/w \in L$ and $\exists\, d = (S \xrightarrow[G]{*} w) : ind_G(d) \leq K\}$. And we prove :

Proposition 4 : For each $K \geq 1$ and for each M-grammar (G,M),

$(<L(G,M)>_{(G,M)}^{\leq K}) \in Mlif(K)$.

The same result is obtained with controled grammars.

□ The proof is based onto the following idea : if A is the control automaton of the C-grammar (G,A), then it is associated to an automaton which computes the number of occurences of variables :

$A_K = <P, [0,K], \{0\}, 1, \delta_K>$,

$\forall\, r = (g \to d) \in P$ and $\forall\, m \in [0,K]$,

if $m - /g/_{V_N} + /d/_{V_N} \leq K$ then $\delta_K(m,r) = m - /g/_{V_N} + /d/_{V_N}$

We obtain : $<L(G,A)>_{(G,A)}^{\leq K} = L(G, A \times A_K)$. □

SECTION 3 : Principality of the cones Calg and Clif(K)

In order to obtain these results, the proof is in three steps :

1 - We perform the Chomsky-Schützenberger construction : $\forall$(G,M) in N.M.F., there exist an integer n, a morphism ψ, a local rational language K such that $L(G) = \psi(D_n'^{*} \cap K)$.

2 - To the Chomsky-Schützenberger construction, we add the encoding of each matrix and we obtain : for any (G,M) in N.M.F., there exist n, ψ, K such that : $L(G,M) = \psi(Dc(n) \cap K)$, where $DC(n)$ is a "controled Dyck language" (in a sense that we shall define).

3 - The n parenthesies of the language $DC(n)$ are encoded by the five parenthesies of the generator F_5 : for any integer n, there exists a non-erasing morphism φ such that

$DC(n) = \varphi^{-1}(F_5)$.

First, with the Chomsky-Schützenberger construction, we prove :

Proposition 5 : For each matrix grammar (G,M) in normal matrix form, there exist an integer n, a language denoted $DC(n)$, an alphabetic morphism ψ, a local rational language K such that :

$L(G,M) = \psi(DC(n) \cap K)$.

□ We assume the reader to be familiar with the Chomsky-Schützenberger construction (see chapter II, Berstel, 79).

Consider the M-grammar (G,M) in N.M.F. where $V_N = \{v_1, v_2, \ldots, v_\gamma\}$ and $V_T = \{y_1, y_2, \ldots, y_{\mu-1}\}$. We note y_μ the empty word ε.

We define the parenthesies which encode the rules :

$Xn = \{a_{ij}/i \in [1,\gamma],\ j \in [1,\mu]\} \cup \{b_{ijk}/i,\ j \in [1,\gamma],\ k \in [1, 2\mu - 1]\}$
$\cup \{c_{ijk},\ d_{ijk}/i,j,k \in [1,\gamma]\}$; therefore $n = 2\gamma^3 + \gamma^2(2\mu-1) + \gamma\mu$;

$\overline{X}n = \{\overline{x} / x \in Xn\}$ and $Zn = Xn \cup \overline{Xn}$.

The proof is in three steps.

Step 1 : The matrix grammar (G_z, M_z), where the terminal alphabet is Zn, is defined as it follows :

z.1) $[V_i \to a_{ij}.\overline{a_{ij}}] \in M_z$ iff $[v_i \to y_j] \in M$,

z.2) $[v_i \to b_{ijk} v_j \overline{b_{ijk}}] \in M_z$ iff

either $k \in [1, \mu-1]$ and $[v_i \to y_k v_j] \in M$,

or $k \in [\mu+1, 2\mu-1]$ and $[v_i \to v_j y_{k-\mu}] \in M$,

or $k = \mu$ and $[v_i \to v_j] \in M$,

z.3) $[v_i \to c_{ijk} d_{ijk} v_j \overline{d_{ijk}}\ v_k \overline{c_{ijk}}] \in M_z$

iff $[v_i \to v_j v_k] \in M$,

Z.4) $[v_{i1} \to b_{i1j1\mu} v_{j1} \overline{b_{i1j1\mu}},\ v_{iZ} \to b_{i2j2\mu} v_{j2} \overline{b_{i2j2\mu}}] \in M_z$ iff

$[v_{i1} \to v_{j1},\ v_{i2} \to v_{j2}] \in M$ (i.e. $v_{j1} \neq v_{i2}$).

The alphabetic morphism ψ' from Z_n^* into V_T^* :

$\forall x \in Zn$, $\psi'(x)$ = if $x = a_{ij}$ then y_j,

if $x = b_{ijk}$ and $k \in [1,\mu-1]$ then y_k

if $x = b_{ijk}$ and $k \in [\mu+1, 2\mu-1]$ then $y_{k-\mu}$,

else ε,

gives the following results :

$$L(G,M) = \psi(L(G_z, M_z)) \quad (1),$$

$$ind(G,M) = ind(G_z, M_z) \quad (2).$$

Step 2 : Now, we introduce a "controled language of parenthesies" defined by its matrix grammar (G_1, M_1). The grammar G_1 generates the "well-formed" words over the n pairs of parenthesies. The control of derivations is realized by the set of matrix M_1 :

1.1) $[S \to \varepsilon] \in M_1$,

1.2) $[S \to SS] \in M_1$,

1.3) $[S \to a_{ij} S \overline{a_{ij}}] \in M_1$ iff $[v_i \to v_j] \in M$,

1.4) $[S \to b_{ijk}\ S\ \overline{b_{ijk}}] \in M_1$ iff

either $k \in [1, \mu-1]$ and $[v_i \to y_k v_j] \in M$,

or $k \in [\mu+1, 2\mu-1]$ and $[v_i \to v_j y_{k-\mu}] \in M$,

or $k = \mu$ and $[v_i \to v_j] \in M$,

1.5) $[S \to c_{ijk} S \overline{c_{ijk}}] \in M_1$ iff $[v_i \to v_j v_k] \in M$,

1.6) $[S \to d_{ijk} S \overline{d_{ijk}}] \in M_1$ iff $[v_i \to v_j v_k] \in M$,

1.7) $[S \to b_{i1j1\mu} T \overline{b_{i1j1\mu}},\ S \to b_{i2j2\mu} S \overline{b_{i2j2\mu}},\ T \to S] \in M_1$ iff

$[v_{i1} \to v_{j1}, v_{i2} \to v_{j2} \in M$.

We can remark that the variable T is necessary, for forbiding the direct derivation :

$$S \to b_{i1j1\mu}\, b_{i2j2\mu}\, S\, \overline{b_{i2j2\mu}}\, \overline{b_{i1j1\mu}} \;;$$

This realizes the condition $v_{j1} \neq v_{i2}$.

<u>The local rational language</u> K' defined in the Chomsky-Schützenberger construction, selects only the "good" consecutions of parenthesies.

By means of the following associations between the matrices of the two M-grammars (G_z,M_z) and (G_1,M_1) :

the matrix (z.1) with the matrices (1.3) and (1.1),

the matrix (z.2) with the matrix (1.4),

the matrix (z.3) with the matrices (1.5),(1.2),(1.6),

the matrix (z.4) with the matrix (1.7),

we prove these two results :

- $L(G_z,M_z) = L(G_1,M_1) \cap K'$ (3),
- the index for some word is the same in each of the M-grammars (G_z,M_z) and (G_1,M_1). (4)

<u>Step 3</u> : We set $N = \max(N1,N2)$ where

$N1 = \mathrm{card}\{m/m \in M_1$ and is of the type $[S \to xS\bar{x}]\}$

$N2 = \mathrm{card}\{m/m \in M_1$ and its lenght is $3\}$.

And we define <u>the controled Dyck language DC(n)</u> by its grammar $\underline{(G_2,M_2)}$.

The grammar G_2 generates the "well-formed" words over the 3N pairs of parenthesies of the alphabet Z_{3N}. The matrices of M_2 are : $[S \to \varepsilon]$, $[S \to SS]$, and, for each $i \in [1,N]$, $[S \to x_i\, S\, \overline{x_i}]$ and $[S \to x_{i+N}\, T\, \overline{x_{i+N}}, S \to x_{i+2N}\, S\, \overline{x_{i+2N}}, T \to S]$. We remark that the matrix grammar (G_2,M_2) is greater than this of (G_1,M_1). In fact, we prove that there exists an alphabetic morphism $h : Z_{3N}^{*} \to Z_n^{*}$ such that :

$$L(G_1,M_1) = h(L(G_2,M_2)) \qquad (5),$$

$$\forall w_1 \in L(G_1,M_1),\ \forall w_2 \in L(G_2,M_2), \text{ if } w_1 = h(w_2) \text{ then } \mathrm{ind}_{(G_1,M_1)}(w_1) = \mathrm{ind}_{(G_2,M_2)}(w_2). \qquad (6)$$

Since $\psi = \psi' \circ h$ is an alphabetic morphism and $K = h^{-1}(K')$ is a local rational language, (1), (3) and (5) yields :

$$L(G,M) = \psi(DC(n) \cap K).$$

This ends the proof of the proposition 5. □

From (2), (4), (6), we obtain an other consequence :

$$\forall w \in L(G,M),\ \forall (w_2 \in L(G_2,M_2), \text{ if } w \in \psi(w_2) \text{ then } \mathrm{ind}_{(G,M)}(w) = \mathrm{ind}_{(G_2,M_2)}(w_2) \qquad (7)$$

From proposition 5 and (7), we obtain :

Corollary 1 : For each matrix grammar (G,M) in normal matrix form and of finite index K, there exist an integer N, an alphabetic morphism ψ and a local rational language K such that :

$$L(G,M) = \psi(<DC(n)>^{\leq K}_{(G_2,M_2)} \cap K).$$

In the next step of the proof, we encode the 3N pairs of parenthesies of the matrix language DC(n) by the five pairs of the controled language F5 : the relation between the indices of parenthesies : x_{i+N}, x_{i+2N}, generated by the matrix $[S \to x_{i+N}\, T\, \overline{x_{i+N}},\ S \to x_{i+2N} S\, \overline{x_{i+2N}},\ T \to S]$ authorizes the encoding of the parenthesies, as we shall check it in the proof. This explains the choice of the form of the controled Dyck language.

The language F5 is generated by the C-grammar (G_5, C_5) where $G_5 = <Z_5, \{S\}, S, P_5>$ and $P_5 = \{S \xrightarrow{r_o} \varepsilon,\ S \xrightarrow{r_6} SS\} \cup \{\forall\, i \in [1,5],\ S \xrightarrow{r_i} x_i\, S\, \overline{x_i}\}$, and the control set C_5 is described by the following rational expression :

$$(r_o + r_4.(r_1)^+.r_5 + r_4.r_4.(r_2.r_3)^+.r_5.r_5 + r_6)^*.$$

Proposition 6 : For each integer $n \geq 1$, there exists a non-erasing morphism φ from Z_{3N}^* into Z_5^* such that : $\varphi^{-1}(F5) = DC(n)$.

□ First, we define the non-erasing morphism φ

$\forall\, i \in [1,N]$, $\varphi(x_i) = x_4(x_1)^i x_5$, $\varphi(\overline{x_i}) = \overline{x_5}(\overline{x_1})^i\overline{x_4}$,

$\varphi(x_{i+N}) = x_4(x_2)^i x_5$, $\varphi(\overline{x_{i+N}}) = \overline{x_5}(\overline{x_2})^i\overline{x_4}$,

$\varphi(x_{i+2N}) = x_4(x_3)^i x_5$, $\varphi(\overline{x_{i+2N}}) = \overline{x_5}(\overline{x_3})^i\overline{x_4}$.

The principal idea of this proof is that :

(I.1) the derivation $S \xrightarrow{r_4(r_1)^i r_5} x_4(x_1)^i x_5\, S\, \overline{x_5}(\overline{x_1})^i\overline{x_4}$ simulates the matrix $[S \to x_i\, S\, \overline{x_i}.]$,

(I.2) the two derivations :

$S \to x_4(x_2)^i x_5\, S\, \overline{x_5}\,(\overline{x_2})^i\overline{x_4}$,

$S \to x_4(x_3)^i x_5\, S\, \overline{x_5}\,(\overline{x_3})^i\overline{x_4}$.

obtained by the control word $r_4.r_4.(r_2.r_3)^i.r_5.r_5$ simulates the matrix $[S \to x_{i+N}\, T\, \overline{x_{i+N}},\ S \to x_{i+2N}\, S\, \overline{x_{i+2N}},\ T \to S]$.

In order to state the inclusion $\varphi^{-1}(F5) \subseteq DC(n)$, we prove, for each terminal derivation $S \overset{*}{\to} w_5$ of (G_5, C_5) such that $w_5 \in \varphi(Z_{3N}{}^*)$, that there exists a terminal derivation $S \overset{*}{\to} w_2$ of (G_2, M_2) such that $\varphi(w_2) = w_5$.

Let $S \xrightarrow[(G_5,C_5)]{*} w_5$ be a derivation such that $w_5 \in \varphi(Z_{3N}{}^*)$. With the use of technical properties of the biprefix code $\varphi(Z_{3N})$, we prove that the control word $r_4.(r_1)^i_4. r_5$ generates only a derivation : $S \to x_4(x_1)^i x_5\ S\ \overline{x_5}(\overline{x_1})^i\overline{x_4}$; and the control word $r_4.r_4.(r_2.r_3)^i.r_5.r_5$ generates only, and in the same time, the two derivations : $S \to x_4(x_2)^i x_5\ S\ \overline{x_5}(\overline{x_2})^i\overline{x_4}$ and $S \to x_4(x_3)^i x_5\ S\ \overline{x_5}(\overline{x_3})^i\overline{x_4}$. Then, we can use the associations (I.1) and (I.2) to construct the derivation $S \xrightarrow[(G_2,M_2)]{*} w_2$ related to the derivation $S \xrightarrow[(G_5,C_5)]{*} w_5$.

The other inclusion is easily verified by means of (I.1) and (I.2). This ends the proof. □

About the proof of proposition 6, we remark :

$\forall\ w_2 \in DC(n)$, $\forall\ w_5 \in F5$, if $\varphi(w_2) = w_5$

then $ind_{(G_2,M_2)}(w_2) = ind_{(G_5,C_5)}(w_5)$.

By proposition 6 and (8), we have the following consequence :

<u>Corollary 2</u> : For each integers $n \geq 1$ and $K \geq 1$, there exists a non-erasing morphism φ such that :

$$\varphi^{-1}(\langle F5\rangle^{\leq K}_{(G_5,C_5)}) = \langle DC(n)\rangle^{\leq K}_{(G_2,M_2)}.$$

From the propositions 3, 5 and 6, on one hand, and from the propositions 3, 4 and corollaries 1, 2, on the other hand, we conclude :

<u>Proposition 7</u> : For each matrix language L, there exist an alphabetic morphism ψ and a non-erasing morphism φ, and a local rational language K such that

$$L = \psi(\varphi^{-1}(F5) \cap K).$$

<u>Corollary 3</u> : The family Malg is a principal rational cone of generator F5.

We note F5(K) the language $\langle F5\rangle^{\leq K}_{(G_5,C_5)}$.

<u>Proposition 8</u> : For each integer $K \geq 1$, for each matrix language L of index K, there exist two morphisms ψ and φ, and a local rational language K such that :

$$L = \psi(\varphi^{-1}(F5(K)) \cap K).$$

<u>Corollary 4</u> : For each integer $K \geq 1$, the family Mlif(K) is a principal rational cone of generator F5(K).

The relation between the generators of different families of matrix languages is trivial : the generator of the family of matrix languages of index less than K is the part of index no greater than K of the generator of the family of matrix languages.

At last by Beauquier's arguments (79), we know that the matrix language F5 is in Malg\(Alg ∩ Mlif).

Though the matrix grammars have a generative capacity more important than the context-free grammars, the family of matrix languages satisfies many properties which are verified by the context-free family. This fact justifies the different investigations about the family of matrix languages.

Acknowledgments

The author is deeply grateful to professor Joffroy Beauquier for all of his help in developing this paper.

References

BEAUQUIER J. (79) : Deux familles de langages incomparables, Information and Control 43, 101-122.

BERSTEL J. (79) : Transductions and Context-Free languages, B.G. Teubner, Stuttgart.

GREIBACH S.A. (77) : Control Sets on Context-Free Grammar Forms, J. Computer Systems Sci. 15, 35-98.

PAUN G. (77) : On the index of grammars and languages, Inf. and Control 35, 259-266.

PAUN G. (79) : On the family of finite index matrix languages, J.C.S.S. 18, 267-280.

PAUN G. (80) : O ierarchie infinita de limbaje matriceale, St. Cerc. Math., Bucaresti, 32, 267-280.

PAUN G. (81) : Gramatici Matriciale, Editura Stiintifica si Enciclopeca, Bucuresti.

PAUN G. (83) : Some Context-free like properties of finite index matrix languages, Bull. Math. Soc. Sci. Math. R.S. Roumanie, 27, 83-87.

SALOMAA A. (73) : Formal Languages, Academic Press, New York and London.

ORIENTED EQUATIONAL CLAUSES AS A PROGRAMMING LANGUAGE

L. Fribourg

Laboratoires de Marcoussis - C.G.E.
91460 Marcoussis - France

ABSTRACT

In the Prolog language, Horn clauses of first-order logic are regarded as programs, and the resolution procedure is used as an interpreter.
In this paper, we present the formalism of Horn oriented equational clauses (Horn clauses with a rewrite rule as the head part, and a list of equations as the body part). We show that such a formalism can be interpreted as a logic language with built-in equality, and that a procedure, based on clausal superposition, can be used as an interpreter.
We define, the operational,model-theoretic and fixpoint semantics of the language, and prove their equivalence.
Then we point out the advantages of such a programming language :

- embodying Prolog ,
- mixing functional and relational features ,
- handling the equality relation

Lastly, we present experiments performed with an implemented interpreter.

1. Introduction

Van Emden and Kowalski have shown that sentences of Predicate Logic can be regarded as programs [EK]. This provides a theoretical model of the language Prolog [CCK,Co]. The language Prolog is based on Horn clause resolution . Our concern in this paper is to cover up two missing points of standard Prolog :

- the handling of functions ,
- the handling of the equality relation .

To reach such goals, several theoretical models were proposed [BDL][HD] and recently an extension of Prolog by inclusion of assertions about equality has been implemented [Ko].
In this paper, we propose an alternative approach which basically consists in performing the computations through the rule of clausal superposition. Clausal superposition indeed allows at once the replacement of an equal by an equal and the derivation of resolvents [Fr1] .
The statements handled by clausal superposition are Horn oriented equational clauses (Horn clauses with a rewrite rule as the head part , and a list of equations as the body part). The computation procedure hereafter presented combines some aspects of the resolution procedure [Ro] (as used in Prolog) with some aspects of the rewrite system completion (used for refutation and computation purposes in [HDe,De]).
The theoretical model of our programming language made of equational clauses is given in the framework of Predicate Logic with Equality. In keeping with [EK], we define the operational, model-theoretic and fixpoint semantics and we prove their equivalence.
We then point out the advantages of the language :

- handling the equality relation ,
- embodying Prolog programs ,
- mixing functional and relational features .

2. Equational logic programs

2.1. Equational clauses

definition 2.1.1

An *equational clause* is a first-order logic (with equality) formula of the form $L_1=R_1,\ldots,L_p=R_p$ <- $M_1=N_1,\ldots,M_q=N_q$,
where each L_i,R_i,M_j,N_j ($1\leq i\leq p, 1\leq j\leq q$) is a term.

definition 2.1.2

An *equational goal clause* is an equational clause of the form <- $M_1=N_1,\ldots,M_q=N_q$

definition 2.1.3

An *equational definite clause* is an equational clause of the form :
$L=R$ <- $M_1=N_1,\ldots,M_q=N_q$.

An equational definite clause C is implicitly *oriented* from left to right : the leftmost equation L=R must be viewed as the rewrite rule $L\rightarrow R$
In the following, we assume that an *orientation rule* Δ is given, i.e. a function which maps any couple of terms <M,N> either into the equation M=N or into N=M .

definition 2.1.4

An *equational logic program* is a finite set of equational definite clauses.

definition 2.1.5

An *equational Horn clause* is a clause which is either an equational definite clause or an equational goal clause.

Equational Horn clauses constitute the statements of our programming language. In the following, the computational use of equational Horn clauses will be referred to as the *equational logic* programming ; it will be compared to the *classical logic* programming with standard Horn clauses.

2.2. Operational semantics of equational logic programs

In equational logic programming, computation is not performed with resolution, but with *clausal superposition* and *reflecting*. Clausal superposition, as defined in [Fr1], is an oriented form of the rule of paramodulation [RW], whereas reflecting is a form of resolution against the axiom X=X.

definition 2.2.1

A *trivial* equation is an equation of the form T=T ,where T is a term.

definition 2.2.2

Let G be the goal <- $M_1=N_1,\ldots,M_q=N_q$. The *trivial deletion* rule consists in removing from G all the equations $M_i=N_i$ ($1\leq i\leq q$), such that :

- $M_i=N_i$ is trivial ,
- $M_j=N_j$ is trivial , for all $1\leq j\leq i$.

definition 2.2.3

Let G be the goal <- $M_1=N_1,\ldots,M_q=N_q$,
and let C be the definite clause $L=R$ <- $L_1=R_1,\ldots,L_r=R_r$.
Then G' is a *goal-superposant* from C on G at occurrence t ,using the most general unifier σ ,if either:

- M_1 has a subterm T_1 at occurrence t_1 unifiable with L, by m.g.u. σ $(T_1\sigma = L\sigma)$
- G' is the goal obtained by trivial deletion from
  <- $(M_1[t_1\leftarrow R]=N_1,L_1=R_1,\ldots,L_r=R_r,M_2=N_2,\ldots,M_q=N_q)\sigma$

or :

- N_1 has a subterm U_1 at occurrence u_1 unifiable with L, by m.g.u. σ $(U_1\sigma = L\sigma)$
- G' is the goal obtained by trivial deletion from
  $<- (M_1=N_1[u_1\leftarrow R], L_1=R_1,\ldots,L_r=R_r, M_2=N_2,\ldots,M_q=N_q)\sigma$.

If the subterm T_1 (resp. U_1) is non-variable, the goal G' is said to be a *strict* goal-superposant of C on G

example :

C : rational(X,Y)=rational(Z,W) <- X×W=Z×Y
G : <- rational(2,3)×Y=rational(X,6)×4
G' : <- rational(Z,W)×Y=rational(X,6)×4 , 2×W=Z×3

definition 2.2.4

Let C : $L=R$ <- $L_1=R_1,\ldots,L_r=R_r$ and C': $L'=R'$ <- $L'_1=R'_1,\ldots,L'_s=R'_s$ be two definite clauses .

C'' is a ***definite-superposant*** of C on C' ,at occurrence t', using the m.g.u σ, if :
- L' has a subterm T' at occurrence t' unifiable with L $(T'\sigma = L\sigma)$
- C'' is the definite clause :
  $P=Q <- (L_1=R_1,\ldots,L_r=R_r,L'_1=R'_1,\ldots,L'_s=R'_s)\sigma$,
  where P=Q is the equation obtained by Δ-orienting the critical pair
  $<L'\sigma[t'\leftarrow R],R'\sigma>$.

If the subterm T' is non variable, then C'' is said to be a *strict* definite-superposant of C on C' .

example :

C : rational(X,1)=X <-
C' : rational(X,Y)=rational(Z,W) <- X×W=Z×Y
C'' : rational(Z,W)=X <- X×W=Z×1

definition 2.2.5

Let G be the goal <- $M_1=N_1,\ldots,M_q=N_q$.

G' is a ***reflectant*** of G using the m.g.u. σ, if :
- $M_1\sigma = N_1\sigma$
- G' is the goal obtained by trivial deletion from <- $(M_2=N_2,\ldots,M_q=N_q)\sigma$

Reflecting is the inference rule by which G yields G'

example :

G : <- rational(Z,W)×Y=rational(X,6)×4 , 2×W=Z×3
G' : <- 2×6=X×3

definition 2.2.6

Let Q be an equational logic program, and G,G' two equational goals.

A ***linear RS-derivation*** of G' from Q ∪ {G},denoted $Q \cup \{G\} \vdash_{RS} G'$, is a finite sequence $G_0,G_1,\ldots,G_n$ of goals such that :

1) G_0 is G ,and G_n is G'
2) for all i , $1 \le i \le n$, G_i is either :
   (a) a reflectant of G_{i-1} , or
   (b) a (goal) superposant of a clause of Q on G_{i-1} .

A ***linear RS-refutation*** of Q ∪ {G} is a linear RS-derivation of the empty clause from Q ∪ {G} .

definition 2.2.7

Let P be a (equational logic) program .

An ***extension*** Q of P is a program defined by a finite list $C_1,\ldots,C_m$ of definite clauses such that ,for all i ,$1 \le i \le m$, C_i is either :

(a) a member of P , or

(b) a (definite) superposant of C_j and C_k , for $j,k<i$.

definition 2.2.8 :

Let P be a program , and G,G' two goals.

An *RS-derivation* of G' from P ∪ {G} ,is a linear RS-derivation of G' obtained from {G} and some extension Q of P.

An *RS-refutation* of P ∪ {G} is an RS-derivation of the empty clause from P ∪ {G}.

In equational logic programming, the computation rules are thus (clausal) superposition and reflecting. These computation rules, unlike the classical resolution rule, can produce new definite clauses ,i.e. new statements of the program .
An equational logic program P can thus be seen as a dynamic object. It can possibly be extended without termination. Nevertheless, any computation consists in a linear derivation from a *finite* extension of P with the initial goal statement.

Another difference with classical logic programs is that the procedure invocation does not proceed by matching with the whole leftmost atom but only with the left-hand side of this atom. Therefore, the left-hand side (and no longer the whole atom) must be interpreted as the procedure name, the remaining part of the clause standing for the procedure body.
Thus equational logic languages have strong ***functional*** features, whereas standard Prolog is purely ***relational***.

3. Model-theoretic semantics

The reader is assumed to be familiar with the interpretation , model and logical consequence notions. These notions classically extend to first order logic with equality (see [RW]). The definitions given hereunder are slightly simpler because the only predicate involved is equality.

definition 3.1

Given a set Q of equational clauses,the set of ***axioms of equality*** for Q is the set defined as :

$$EA(Q) = \{ X=X \leftarrow \} \cup \{ X=Y \leftarrow Y=X \} \cup \{ X=Z \leftarrow X=Y, Y=Z \}$$
$$\cup \{ F(X_1,X_2,\ldots,X_k)=F(Y_1,X_2,\ldots,X_k) \leftarrow X_1=Y_1 ,$$

for all k-ary function symbol F occurring in Q and each argument of F } ,

where $X,Y,Z,X_1,X_2,\ldots,X_k,Y_1$ denote variables .

definition 3.2

Let Q be a set of clauses, and let L and R be two terms.

The equation L=R is an ***E-logical consequence*** of Q (denoted $Q \models_E L=R$) iff it is a logical consequence of Q ∪ EA(Q) (i.e. $Q \cup EA(Q) \models L=R$) .

Let P be an equational logic program .
The ***Herbrand universe*** of P is the set of all ground terms composed of the constant and function symbols appearing in P (in the case that P has no constants, add some constant, say ***a***, to P).
The ***Herbrand base*** B(P) of P is the set of all ground equations M=N, where M and N belong to the Herbrand universe U(P) of P.
A ***Herbrand interpretation*** I of P is any subset of the Herbrand base of P.
In the following, the symbol $=_I$ denotes the congruence modulo I.
Let us now introduce the notion of Herbrand E-model.

definition 3.3

Let I be a Herbrand interpretation and let C be the equational clause :

$L_1=R_1,\dots,L_p=R_p \leftarrow M_1=N_1,\dots,M_q=N_q$

C is *E-true* in I iff for every ground substitution η :

$L_i\eta =_I R_i\eta$,for some i ($1\le i\le p$), or $\sim (M_j\eta =_I N_j\eta)$,for some j ($1\le j\le q$).

C is *E-false* in I iff it is not E-true.

definition 3.4

Let I be a Herbrand interpretation and Q a set of equational clauses..

I is a ***Herbrand E-model*** of Q iff each clause in Q is E-true in I.

Remark

Beware that our notion of Herbrand E-model is distinct from the one of R-interpretation defined in [RW] (an R-interpretation of Q is an E-model of Q, but the converse is false in general).

PROPOSITION 3.1

Let Q be a set of equational clauses. Q has a Herbrand E-model iff Q $\cup$ EA(Q) has a Herbrand model.

We now transpose the classical notion of the least Herbrand model of a logic program.

definition 3.5

Let I and J be two interpretations of a set Q of equational clauses.

The *E-intersection* of I and J (denoted I Ω J) is the subset of the equations M=N of I such that M $=_J$ N .

The definition of the operator Ω is not symmetric . However the congruences defined by I Ω J and J Ω I coincide (M $=_{I \Omega J}$ N iff M $=_I$ N and M $=_J$ N)

The definition of Ω naturally extends to a countable (ordered) set of interpretations.

PROPOSITION 3.2

Let Q be a set of equational Horn clauses ,and let L be a non empty set of Herbrand E-models for Q.

Then Ω L is a Herbrand E-model of Q .

The proof is exactly the same as the one given at §5 in [EK] , except that the membership relation of an atom A to an interpretation I is replaced by the congruence relation of the sides of an equation A modulo I .

definition 3.6

A Herbrand E-model I of Q is a ***least*** Herbrand E-model of Q if ,for any Herbrand E-model J of Q, $=_I \subseteq =_J$.

The congruences of all the least Herbrand E-models coincide, and define the so-called ***least model congruence*** .

Let P be an equational logic program.

Let **EM(P)** be the non empty set (supposed ordered) of all Herbrand E-models of P.

By proposition 3.2 , the intersection Ω **EM(P)** of all the Herbrand E-models of P is a Herbrand E-model, and clearly is a least Herbrand E-model of P.

The following proposition gives a characterization of the least model congruence .

PROPOSITION 3.3

Let L=R be a member of the Herbrand base B(P) of P .

$L =_{\Omega\, EM(P)} R$ iff $P \models_E L=R$

Proof: $P \models_E L=R$

iff $P \cup EA(P) \models L=R$

iff $P \cup EA(P) \cup \{<\!-\ L=R\}$ has no model

iff $P \cup EA(P) \cup \{<\!-\ L=R\}$ has no Herbrand model (by Skolem-Lowenheim theorem)

iff $P \cup \{<\!-\ L=R\}$ has no Herbrand E-model (by proposition 3.1)

iff $(<\!-\ L=R)$ E-false in all the Herbrand E-models of P

iff $L =_I R$,for any Herbrand E-model I of P

iff $L =_{\cap EM(P)} R$.

4. Fixpoint semantics

Let P be an equational logic program and B(P) the Herbrand base of P . Given a Herbrand interpretation I, the symbol $\rightarrow_I$ denotes the reduction relation by I , considered as a set of rewrite rules ; $\overset{*}{\rightarrow}_I$ denotes the reflexive-transitive closure of $\rightarrow_I$ (see [HO]).

In keeping with [EK], we associate with the program P a mapping S_P of Herbrand interpretations, as follows :

definition 4.1

For any Herbrand interpretation I, DS, GS_P, S_P are the transformations which respectively map I to :

- $DS(I) = \{ L=R \in B(P) /$ L=R is a Δ-oriented critical pair of two members of I $\}$
- $GS_P(I) = \{ L=R \in B(P) / (L=R <\!-\ M_1=N_1,\dots,M_q=N_q)$ is a ground instance of a clause in P, and for any i ($1 \le i \le q$), there exists a term K_i such that $M_i \overset{*}{\rightarrow}_I K_i$ and $N_i \overset{*}{\rightarrow}_I K_i \}$
- $S_P(I) = DS(I) \cup GS_P(I)$.

Remarks

DS(I) can be seen as the set of all the (definite) superposants of I, viewed as a set of definite clauses.

$GS_P(I)$ is obtained from I by applying sequences of (goal) superposition.

DS, GS_P and S_P are monotonic (for the order of set inclusion $\subseteq$)

As usual ,for any mapping T , we define the mappings $T^n(I)$ by :

$T^0(I) = I$, $T^{n+1}(I) = T(T^n(I))$

definition 4.2

An interpretation I is an ***E-fixpoint*** of S_P (or I is E-closed under S_P) iff the congruences $=_I$ and $=_{S_P(I)}$ are identical .

Remark

Since $I \subseteq S_P(I)$, I is an E-fixpoint iff $=_{S_P(I)} \subseteq =_I$.

definition 4.3

An E-fixpoint I of S_P is a ***least*** E-fixpoint of S_P if , for any E-fixpoint J of S_P , $=_I \subseteq =_J$.

The congruences of all the least E-fixpoints coincide, and define the so-called ***least fixpoint congruence*** .

5. Fixpoint and Model-theoretic semantics

Let us show the equivalence between fixpoint and model-theoretic semantics.

LEMMA 5.1 :

Let M and N be terms of the universe of Herbrand and I an interpretation .

$M =_I N$ iff $M \xrightarrow{*}_{DS^n(I)} K$ and $N \xrightarrow{*}_{DS^n(I)} K$, for some term K and some integer n.

The proof is a direct transposition of the proof of theorem 4.1 of [Fr1] (completeness of A-paramodulation) in the ground unit case .
The result holds, independently of the chosen orientation rule Δ .

THEOREM 5.1

Let P be an equational program and I be an interpretation of P.

Then I is an E-model of P iff $=_{S_P(I)} \subseteq =_I$

Proof :

(=>) Let us suppose that I is an E-model of P . Let L=R be an equation of $S_P(I)$. By definition, there exist either :

- some ground instance of a clause in P , $L=R \leftarrow M_1=N_1,\dots,M_q=N_q$ with ,for every i ($1 \le i \le q$), a term K_i such that $M_i \xrightarrow{*}_I K_i$ and $N_i \xrightarrow{*}_I K_i$, or
- two equations of I which superpose themselves into L=R.

In the first case, $M_i =_I N_i$, for $1 \le i \le q$. Since I is an E-model of P, we have : $L =_I R$. In the second case, we have also : $L =_I R$.
So in both cases if $L=R \in S_P(I)$, then $L =_I R$. Therefore, $=_{S_P(I)} \subseteq =_I$.

(<=) Let us suppose that I is not an E-model of P, and let us show that $=_{S_P(I)} \not\subseteq =_I$.
Since I is not an E-model, I E-falsifies a ground instance of a clause in P of the form L=R $\leftarrow M_1=N_1,\dots,M_q=N_q$.
So, we have : (1) $\sim(L =_I R)$ and (2) $M_i =_I N_i$,for $1 \le i \le q$
From (2) and lemma 5.1 : $M_i \xrightarrow{*}_{DS^{ni}(I)} K_i$, and $N_i \xrightarrow{*}_{DS^{ni}(I)} K_i$, for some integer ni and for some term K_i ($1 \le i \le q$) .
So ,by monotonicity, $M_i \xrightarrow{*}_{S_P^{ni}(I)} K_i$ and $N_i \xrightarrow{*}_{S_P^{ni}(I)} K_i$, for $1 \le i \le q$.
Therefore : $L=R \in GS_P(S_P^{\ n}(I))$, for $n = \max \{ni\}_{1 \le i \le q}$.
Hence : (2') $L=R \in S_P^{\ n+1}(I)$
Clearly, from (1) and (2'), it follows : $=_{S_P(I)} \not\subseteq =_I$, q.e.d.

Theorem 5.1 states that I is an E-model of P iff I is an E-fixpoint of S_P .
Let us now compare the least model congruence of P with the least fixpoint congruence of S_P .
Let **EC(P)** be the set of all the Herbrand interpretations E-closed under S_P. From theorem 5.1 , it easily follows that :

- the congruences modulo $\cap$ **EC(P)** and modulo $\cap$ **EM(P)** are identical .
- $\cap$ **EC(P)** is E-closed under S_P .

Thus, the least model congruence and the least fixpoint congruence coincide. Hence, the *model-theoretic* and the *fixpoint* semantics coincide.

The following proposition gives a characterization of the least E-fixpoint congruence.

PROPOSITION 5.1

Let P be a program , M and N two terms of the Herbrand universe U(P). Let W abbreviate $\cup_{m=0}^{\infty} S_P{}^m(\phi)$.
Then $M =_{\Omega\, EC(P)} N$ iff $M =_W N$.

The proof is similar to the proof given at §8 in [EK] , but makes use of the congruence relation and superposition rule instead of the membership relation and hyperresolution rule .

6. Operational and Model-theoretic Semantics

Let us state the equivalence between the operational and model-theoretic semantics. The underlying result of this equivalence is the completeness of RS-deduction for first-order logic with equality. As in paramodulation (see [RW]), the completeness proof requests the inclusion of the set of functional reflexive units.

definition 6.1

For a given set Q of clauses , the set of the ***functional reflexive units*** is the set defined as :

$Q^f = \{ F(X_1,...,X_k)=F(X_1,...,X_k)$<- , for all k-ary function symbol F occurring in Q $\}$.

THEOREM 6.1

Let P be an equational logic program, and M,N two terms of U(P).
Then $M =_{\Omega\, EM(P)} N$ iff $P \cup P^f \cup \{$<- M=N$\}$ has an RS-refutation.

The proof cannot be given by lack of place (the whole proof is in [Fr2]).

The theorem 6.1 states that the *success set* of $P \cup P^f$ (i.e. the set of ground equations M=N of B(P) such that $P \cup P^f \cup \{$<- M=N$\}$ has an RS-refutation) coincide with the *least model congruence* of P. Thus, the operational and model-theoretic semantics coincide, modulo the inclusion of the functional reflexive units in P.

By analogy with paramodulation, we conjecture that the theorem 6.1 still holds when the set P^f of functional reflexive units is removed and when superposition is restricted to strict superposition.

When some functions are associative and/or commutative, the completeness theorem 6.1 is still valid if associative/commutative unification is used instead of ordinary unification, even though the corresponding axioms of associativity/commutativity are not added (see [Pl,Sl], for completeness proofs of such extensions). The building-in of associativity-commutativity into RS computations through AC-unification is thus justified (see [Fa], for AC-unification algorithms).

7. Formal features of equational logic programming

7.1. A mixed functional-relational language embodying Prolog

Equational logic naturally has functional features (see §2.2) However, it can also behave as a relational language as well as Prolog .
Through the formalism of equational clauses indeed, we have until now dealt with formulas involving no predicate but equality. Yet it is easy to handle a general

predicate of the form R(T,U,V), simply by translating it into the equation R(T,U,V)=true , where 'true' denotes a new constant symbol .
An attractive feature of this coding is that (goal) superposition with such equations simulates the resolution rule [Fr1]. For instance, the superposition of R(T,U,V)=true<- on <- R(T,U,V)=true gives the goal <-true=true , which becomes the empty clause after trivial deletion.
Through this coding, any Prolog program P can be straightforwardly translated into an equational one P'. Given P' and an initial goal G', the RS-derivation procedure computes nothing else than the resolvents of P' against the goal statements, and thus behaves exactly as a Prolog interpreter.
The relational program P' can indeed be refined by replacing predicates by functions. The example given in appendix illustrates this flexibility ; moreover, it illustrates that the input-output reversing property of Prolog is maintained in equational logic programs.

7.2. A Prolog-like language with built-in equality

Equational Horn clauses constitute a very convenient way to integrate the equality relation in a Prolog-like language. The handling of equations allows the replacement of an equal by an equal. Furthermore, the leftmost equations are actually oriented, and the replacements are only applied from left to right. This discards useless paramodulants, and enables the language to efficiently handle the sensitive property of substitutivity.
The examples given in [Ko] have been successfully implemented. As an illustration, we give a small program which allows to decide if a number (integer or rational) is equal to a list member :

rational(X,Y)=rational(Z,W) <- X×W=Z×Y
rational(X,1)=X <-
member(X,X.Y)=true <-
member(X,Y.Z)=true <- member(X,Z)=true

For the following input : <- member(rational(4,X) , (2.(3.((Y.Z).(rational(2,7).NIL))))) , the computed answers are $\{X \leftarrow 2\}$ and $\{X \leftarrow 14\}$.
Note that the computation succeeds, in spite of the permutativity of the head equation rational(X,Y)=rational(Z,W).

8. Implementation

A prototype implementation, based on the theorem-proving program SEC [Fr1], has been realized. SEC is an extension of the Knuth-Bendix algorithm implemented at INRIA within the FORMEL system. Unlike most Prolog interpreters, the search plan of SEC is complete (smallest components strategy). Relatively to the RS-derivation procedure described above, SEC presents two main differences :

- SEC computes the strict superposants only, and makes no use of the functional reflexive units.
- SEC normalizes the reducible terms, with the rewrite system made of the unit definite clauses .

An interpreter, called SLOG (LOGic with Superposition), is under development at Laboratoires de Marcoussis.

9. Conclusion

We have presented in this paper a programming language based on Horn equational clauses .
This formalism allows the handling of equality and the combination of both relational and functional approaches .
We have defined operational semantics by describing the computations performed with an interpreter of the language. The major inference rule used by the interpreter, is the operation of clausal superposition which is a powerful inference rule for first-order logic with equality.
Model-theoretic and fixpoint semantics have also been defined and have been shown equivalent to the operational ones.
First experimental results confirm that the interpreter behaves as a standard Prolog interpreter for classical Horn clauses, and,in addition, efficiently handles statements about equality .

ACKNOWLEDGEMENT
I would like to thank Laurent Kott who first suggested the computational use of equational clauses, and Herve Gallaire for helpful discussions and support.

REFERENCES

[BDL]Bellia,M.,Degano,P. & Levi,G.,A functional plus predicate logic programming language,Proc. Logic Programming Workshop (Jul. 1980),334-347.
[CCK]Colmerauer,A.,Van Caneghem,M. & Kanoui,H.,PROLOG II, manuels de reference, d'utilisation et d'exemples,GIA:Groupe d'Intelligence Artificielle, Marseille,1982.
[Co] Colmerauer,A.,Prolog in 10 figures,Proc. IJCAI,Karslruhe,1983,487-499.
[De] Dershowitz,N., Computing with rewrite systems, Report No ATR-83 (8478)-1, The Aerospace Corporation,El Segundo,California,1983.
[EK] van Emden M.H. & Kowalski R.A.,The Semantics of Predicate Logic as a Programming Language,JACM 23,4 (Oct. 1976),733-742.
[Fa] Fages,F.,Associative-Commutative Unification,Proc. CADE-7,Napa,1984.
[Fr1]Fribourg,L.,A Superposition Oriented Theorem Prover,Technical Report 83/11,L.I.T.P (to appear in TCS,short version in Proc. IJCAI-83,923-925).
[Fr2]Fribourg,L.,Oriented equational clauses as a programming language, Technical Report 83/51,L.I.T.P,Paris,1983.
[HD] Hoffman,C.M. & O'Donnell,M.J.,Programming with equations, ACM trans on programming languages and systems 4,1 (Jan. 1982),83-112.
[HDe]Hsiang,J. & Dershowitz,N.,Rewrite methods for clausal and non-clausal theorem proving,Proc. 10th ICALP,Barcelona,1983.
[HO] Huet G. & Oppen D.C.,Equations and Rewrite Rules: A Survey, Formal language theory: perspectives and open problems,ed. Ronald V. Book,Academic Press, New-York,1980,349-405.
[Ko] Kornfeld,W.,Equality for Prolog,Proc. IJCAI,Karlsruhe,1983,514-519.
[Pl] Plotkin, G.,Building in equational theories, Machine Intelligence 7,B Meltzer and D.Michie,Eds,Halsted Press, New-York,1973,73-90.
[Ro] Robinson,J.A.,A machine-oriented logic based on the resolution principle, J.ACM 12,1 (Jan. 1965),23-41.
[RW] Robinson,G.A. & Wos L.,Paramodulation and theorem proving in first order theories with equality, Machine Intelligence 4, Meltzer & Michie,Eds,American Elsevier, New-York,1969,135-150.
[Sl] Slagle,J.R., Automated Theorem-Proving for Theories with Simplifiers, Commutativity and Associativity, J.ACM 21:4 (Oct 1974),622-642.

APPENDIX

A computational experiment with SEC

The following Prolog program P1, borrowed to [Co], computes the sum of two integers, using the successor relation :

```
C1 : +(1,X,Y) <- succ(X,Y)
C2 : +(U,Y,W) <- succ(X,U),+(X,Y,Z),succ(Z,W)
C3 : succ(1,2) <-
C4 : succ(2,3) <-
     ...
C10: succ(8,9) <-
```

Three successive goals are computed :

```
G1 : <- +(4,3,X)        answer : {X←7}
G2 : <- +(4,X,7)        answer : {X←3}
G3 : <- +(X,Y,5)        answers : {X←1,Y←4}, {X←2,Y←3}, {X←3,Y←2}, {X←4,Y←1} .
```

Computation with such a relational program is clearly highly expensive. Computation of G3 leads for instance to 8! calls of C2, the body literal +(X,Y,Z) being involved before Z has been evaluated to 4 through the computation of succ (Z,5).
In return, the translation of the classical clauses C1,...,C10 into equational clauses gives a very natural program P2 :

```
EC1 : +(1,X)=succ(X) <-
EC2 : +(succ(X),Y)=succ(+(X,Y)) <-
EC3 : 2=succ(1) <-
EC4 : 3=succ(2) <-
      ...
EC10: 9=succ(8) <-
```

- the goal G1 has now the following form :
  <- +(4,3)=X ,
  which is evaluated to ,
  <- succ(succ(succ(succ(succ(succ(1))))))=X ,
  and gives by reflecting the answer :
  {X←succ(succ(succ(succ(succ(succ(1))))))}

- the goal G2 has now the form :
  <- +(4,X)=7 ,
  which is evaluated to :
  <- succ(succ(succ(succ(X))))=succ(succ(succ(succ(succ(succ(1)))))) ,
  and gives by reflecting the answer :
  {X←succ(succ(1))}

- the goal G3 has now the form :
  <- +(X,Y)=5 ,
  which is evaluated to :
  <- +(X,Y)=succ(succ(succ(succ(1)))) .

By superposition with EC1 and reflecting ,we get the first answer :
{X←1, Y←succ(succ(succ(1)))} .
On the other hand, by superposition of G3 with EC2, we have :
<- succ(+(X',Y))=succ(succ(succ(succ(1)))), with X bound to succ(X')
Then,through superposition with EC1 and reflecting,we get the second answer :
{X'←1, Y←succ(succ(1))} ,so {X←succ(1), Y←succ(succ(1))} .
The process going on, we find the two last answers :
{X←succ(succ(1)), Y←succ(1)} and {X←succ(succ(succ(1))), Y←1}
The computation of the successful answers is thus straightforward .
Unfortunately, the computation does not end,for ,by superposition with EC2 , we generate the infinite following sequence of clauses :
<- succ(succ(succ(...(succ(+(X,Y)))...))))=succ(succ(succ(succ(1))))
which clearly has no answer .

For the above inputs, the most suitable program (combining the straightforward computation mode of P2 and the termination of P1) is the program P2' obtained from P2 by substituting EC1,EC2 by :

EC1' : +(1,X,succ(X))=true <-
EC2' : +(succ(X),Y,succ(Z))=true <- +(X,Y,Z)=true

However, the program P2' is generally less powerful than the pure functional program P2, because the ability of evaluating the function +(X,Y) is lost . The resolution with P2'of the inequation +(X,Y)≤5 for instance would be much more clumsy than with P2 . Nevertheless, the program P2' illustrates the flexibility of the language of equational clauses as a mixed functional-relational language.

At last, let us notice that, if the clauses EC3,...,EC10 had been oriented the other way, similar computations would have been performed, but with an *extended* program. For instance, from a clause EC3' : succ(1)=2 <- , one would have derived (by normalized superposition with EC2) the definite clause : +(2,Y)=succ(succ(Y)) <- .

RELATIONAL ALGEBRA OPERATIONS AND SIZES OF RELATIONS

Danièle GARDY and Claude PUECH

Laboratoire de Recherche en Informatique, Bat 490, Université de Paris-Sud, 91405 Orsay Cédex, France.

1. INTRODUCTION.

As Relational Data Base Systems are now commercially available, the importance of the so-called *Query Optimization* is more and more evident. Some important work has already been devoted to the subject: [2, 3, 4, 10, 11, 13, 15, 16, 17, 18, 20, 21] , but most of it is based on heuristics and empirical observations.

As many authors pointed out, the size of the relations involved is one of the most important parameters; many queries can be decomposed in several ways into more elementary operations, and the overall performance of the query is highly dependent on the sizes of the intermediate relations produced by these intermediate operations; for example, as is well known, selection and projection operators should be applied as soon as possible as they provide a result whose cardinality is smaller than the one of their operands.

In this paper, we study the general problem of estimating the size of relations obtained as results of the basic relational algebra operators as a function of the size of their operands. Some related work can be found in [5, 6, 7, 8, 9, 16]

The originality of the proposed method (use of generating functions for describing relations) lies in its "generality": we propose to associate to every relation scheme and its possible dependencies † a generating function, and (as far as possible) to every relational algebra operator an operator acting on the generating functions associated on the operands; moreover, we try to give a systematic method for associating relations and generating functions ††.

This approach can be useful in two different ways:

(i) we could apply the machinery in an automatic way to produce the generating functions; then, deal with them by using some formal system in order to produce the distribution of the sizes of the results.

† see [12] or [19] for definitions of relational data base theory.

†† in the sequel, for the sake of simplicity, we use "relation" instead of "relation scheme and its possible dependencies"

(ii) we can try to find classes of relations for which the generating functions have simple forms (usually they factorize) so as to be able to pull the calculations to the end and obtain closed formulae for the distribution of the sizes of results, its mean, variance ...

In the present paper, we develop point (ii). It is worth noting that although, for simplicity, we present the results either for "free" relations (no functional dependency) or for relations with a single functional dependency, some (but not all) more general cases can be solved as well with the same techniques.

The plan of the paper is the following: in Section 2, we give our probabilistic model(s) of relations, and show how to associate generating functions to relations; in Section 3, we deal with projections (the results obtained in this section can be useful in other domains as well: in *Data Analysis* projections of the initial multidimensional data on well chosen subspaces are used to obtain accurate "summaries" of the data; visually meaningful projections in two or three dimensions are also used in *Graphics* outputs); in Section 4, we deal with binary relational operators (intersection, union, difference) whose definition doesn't give any particular role to any particular attribute (as a consequence, the results are valid under any kind of hypothesis on the dependencies); in Section 5, we study equijoins and semijoins, whose importance in query optimization is well known; the last section gives directions for future research.

As regards the probabilistic hypotheses, let us mention that our hypotheses are, for finite domains, quite general; although the expressions obtained are more complicated in the "general" case (probability p_i for attribute X to have value i) the derivations are not very different from those for the uniform case; as was pointed out several times (see, for example[14]) skewed distributions of attribute values often arise in practice.

2. DESCRIPTION OF RELATIONS BY MEANS OF GENERATING FUNCTIONS.

We first give our probabilistic hypotheses on relations: in the sequel, we suppose that:

(i) distinct attributes of a record (tuple) are independent;

(ii) the probability of a relation is proportional to the probabilities of its records.

In other words, if R is a relation with $R[A_1, A_2, \cdots, A_n]$ as scheme, the probability of R is evaluated as:

$$p(R) = k \prod_{l \text{ tuple of } R} p(l) = k \prod_{l \text{ tuple of } R} \prod_{a_i \in l} p(a_i)$$

where the a_i are the components of tuple l, and k is a "normalization" constant which makes P a probability.

Let us mention that our method can be applied easily with a slightly different hypothesis (iii), instead of (ii):

(iii) the probability of relation R is evaluated as:

$$p(R) = k \prod_{l \text{ tuple of } R} p(l) \prod_{l \text{ not tuple of } R} (1-p(l))$$

$$= k' \prod_{l \text{ tuple of } R} \frac{p(l)}{(1-p(l))}$$

which could be more appropriate in some circumstances.

The description of relations by means of generating functions is made by using the following elementary lemmas: lemma 1 is a simple rewriting of the definition of a relation but, as it doesn't make any assumption on the relation, it can be used under all circumstances by an "automatic analyzer"; lemma 2 describes *free* relations (i.e. without any functional dependency); lemma 3 describes relations with a single functional dependency and lemma 4 is useful for the study of binary operators on relations.

Lemma 1: *The formal polynomial*

$$P(\xi) = k \sum_{[R]} \prod_{t \in R} p(t)\xi_t \quad \text{where} \quad k = \frac{1}{\sum_{[R]} \prod_{t \in R} p(t)}$$

describes all relations with given scheme $[R]$, *in the following sense: the coefficient of* $\xi_{t_1}\xi_{t_2} \cdots \xi_{t_l}$ *in* P *is equal to the probability of the relation whose records are* $t_1, t_2, \cdots, t_l$.

Lemma 2: *The formal polynomial*

$$P(\xi) = k \prod_{t \in D} (1+p(t)\xi_t) \quad \text{where} \quad k = \frac{1}{\prod_{t \in D} (1+p(t))}$$

describes all the possible free relations on D, *the domain of tuples.*

Lemma 2': *The formal polynomial*

$$P(\xi,\eta) = k \prod_{t_X \in D_X} \prod_{t_Y \in D_Y} (1+p(t_X)p(t_Y)\xi_{t_X}\eta_{t_Y})$$

where $k = \dfrac{1}{\prod_{t_X \in D_X} \prod_{t_Y \in D_Y} (1+p(t_X)p(t_Y))}$ *describes all possible free relations* $R(X,Y)$ *on* $D = D_X \times D_Y$, *in the following sense: the coefficient of* $\xi_{t'_1}\eta_{t''_1}\xi_{t'_2}\eta_{t''_2} \cdots \xi_{t'_n}\eta_{t''_n}$ *in* $P(\xi,\eta)$ *is equal to the probability of the relation whose records are:* $t'_1t''_1, t'_2t''_2, \cdots, t'_nt''_n$.

Lemma 3: *The formal polynomial*

$$P(\xi,\eta) = k \prod_{t_X \in D_X} (1+p(t_X)\xi_{t_X} \sum_{t_Y \in D_Y} p(t_Y)\eta_{t_Y}) \quad where \quad k = \frac{1}{\prod_{t_X \in D_X} (1+p(t_X))}$$

describes all relations $R[X,Y]$ with functional dependency $X \to Y$.

Remark: Due to the functional dependency $X \to Y$ which is translated into the expression $\xi_{t_X}\sum p(t_Y)\eta_{t_Y}$, all the ξ_{t_X} are different in one monomial, which is not the case in Lemma 2'.

Lemma 4: *Let $P(\xi,\eta)$ be the formal polynomial associated to relation scheme $R[X,Y]$, and $Q(\xi',\zeta)$ the formal polynomial associated to relation scheme $S[X,Z]$; then, the formal polynomial:*

$$\Pi(\xi,\xi',\eta,\zeta) = P(\xi,\eta)Q(\xi',\zeta)$$

describes all couples of relations with these relation schemes.

Remark: In the lemmas X,Y,Z denote either an attribute or a set of attributes.

Notation: In the sequel we use the following notation:

$$\varphi(R_1{:}x_1, \cdots, R_i{:}x_i / S_1{:}y_1, \cdots, S_j{:}y_j) = \sum p_{r_1, \cdots, r_i; s_1, \cdots, s_j} x_1^{r_1} \cdots x_i^{r_i} y_1^{s_1} \cdots y_j^{s_j}$$

where the sum is taken over all $r_1, \cdots, r_i; s_1, \cdots, s_j$, and $p_{r_1, \cdots, r_i; s_1, \cdots, s_j}$ is the probability for relation R_1 to have size r_1, ... , for relation R_i to have size r_i, conditionned by: $|S_1| = s_1$, ... , $|S_j| = s_j$ ($|S_i|$ is the size of relation S_i).
As a consequence:

$$\varphi(R_1{:}x_1, \cdots, R_i{:}x_i / S_1{:}y_1, \cdots, S_j{:}y_j) = \frac{\varphi(R_1{:}x_1, \cdots, R_i{:}x_i, S_1{:}y_1, \cdots, S_j{:}y_j)}{\varphi(S_1{:}y_1, \cdots, S_j{:}y_j)}$$

3. PROJECTIONS.

We consider here relations $R[X,Y]$ with two (sets of) attributes X and Y, and study the size of the projection of R on the (set of) attribute(s) Y, denoted by $\Pi_Y(R)$.

The main result of this section is the following theorem:

Theorem 1: *The generating function of the sizes of R and its projection $\Pi_Y(R)$: $\varphi(R{:}x, \Pi_Y(R){:}y)$ is obtained from $P(\xi,\eta)$ (cf lemma 2' and lemma 3) by the following transform:*
- replace each ξ_{t_X} ($t_X \in D_X$) by x;

- then, for each $t_Y \in D_Y$, replace $\eta_{t_Y}^{\alpha}$ by 1 if $\alpha = 0$, y otherwise ($\alpha \geq 1$).

We give here a few consequences of theorem 1. As usual, means and variances are obtained by differentiation of the generating functions.

Corollary 1: *The probability, for a free relation $R[X,Y]$ of size l to have a projection $\Pi_Y(R)$ of size r is equal to †:*

$$\frac{[x^l\alpha^r]\prod_{i=1}^{d_X}[1-\alpha+\alpha\prod_{j=1}^{d_Y}(1+p_i\bar{p}_j x)]}{[x^l]\prod_{i=1}^{d_X}\prod_{j=1}^{d_Y}(1+p_i\bar{p}_j x)]}$$

(where the p_i and $\bar{p}_j$ are the respective probabilities of components t_X and t_Y of tuples t). This probability can also be expressed as:

$$\sum_{k=0}^{r}(-1)^{r-k}\binom{d_X-k}{r-k}\frac{[x^l]\sum_{1\leq i_1<\cdots<i_k\leq d_X}\prod_{m=1}^{k}\prod_{j=1}^{d_Y}(1+p_{i_m}\bar{p}_j x)]}{[x^l]\prod_{i=1}^{d_X}\prod_{j=1}^{d_Y}(1+p_i\bar{p}_j x)]}$$

As for the uniform case (same probability for every attribute value),

Corollary 2: *Under the uniform hypothesis, the probability for a free relation $R[X,Y]$ of size l to have a projection $\Pi_Y(R)$ of size r is equal to:*

$$\frac{\binom{d_X}{r}}{\binom{d_X d_Y}{l}}\sum_{k=0}^{r}(-1)^{r-k}\binom{r}{k}\binom{kd_Y}{l}$$

The mean of the distribution of the sizes of projections is equal to:

$$d_X[1-\frac{\binom{d_X d_Y-d_Y}{l}}{\binom{d_X d_Y}{l}}]$$

and its variance:

$$d_X^2[\frac{\binom{d_X d_Y-2d_Y}{l}}{\binom{d_X d_Y}{l}}-\frac{\binom{d_X d_Y-d_Y}{l}^2}{\binom{d_X d_Y}{l}^2}]+d_X[\frac{\binom{d_X d_Y-d_X}{l}}{\binom{d_X d_Y}{l}}-\frac{\binom{d_X d_Y-2d_Y}{l}}{\binom{d_X d_Y}{l}}]$$

† we denote by $[x^l]f(x)$ the coefficient of x^l in the Taylor expansion of f

For relations with a single functional dependency, we can prove results such as:

Corollary 3: *The probability, for a relation $R[X,Y]$ with a single functional dependency $X \to Y$, of size l, to have a projection on Y of size r is given by the expression:*

$$\sum_{k=1}^{r} (-1)^{r-k} \binom{d_Y-k}{r-k} \sum_{1 \le i_1 < \cdots < i_k \le d_Y} (\bar{p}_{i_1} + \cdots + \bar{p}_{i_k})^l$$

Corollary 4: *Let $R[X,Y]$ be a relation with a single functional dependency, r its size. Under the uniform hypothesis, the distribution of the size of $\Pi_Y(R)$ has mean:*

$$d_Y(1-(1-\frac{1}{d_Y})^r)$$

and variance:

$$d_Y^2((1-\frac{2}{d_Y})^r-(1-\frac{1}{d_Y})^{2r}) + d_Y((1-\frac{1}{d_Y})^r-(1-\frac{2}{d_Y})^r)$$

Corollary 5: *Let $R[X,Y]$ be a relation with a single functional dependency, r its size. Under the non-uniform hypothesis , the distribution of the size of $\Pi_Y(R)$ has mean:*

$$\sum_{t_Y \in D_Y} [1-(1-p(t_Y))^r]$$

and variance:

$$\sum_{t_Y \in D_Y} (1-p(t_Y))^r - [\sum_{t_Y \in D_Y} (1-p(t_Y))^r]^2 + \sum_{t_Y \in D_Y, t'_Y \in D_Y, t_Y \ne t'_Y} [1-p(t_Y)-p(t'_Y)]^r$$

4. INTERSECTIONS, UNIONS, DIFFERENCES, SELECTIONS.

We suppose in this section that R and S are two relations with the same relation scheme over a domain D of size d. Using lemma 4 to obtain a formal description of the couple (R,S), we can prove:

Theorem 2: *Let Λ be one of the following binary operators on relations: intersection ($\cap$), union ($\cup$), symetric difference (∇), complement (-). The generating function*

$$\varphi(R{:}x, S{:}y, \Lambda(R,S){:}z)$$

is obtained from the generating function $f(t_1,\ldots,t_d,t'_1,\ldots,t'_d)$ *by substituting, for each* i $(1 \le i \le d)$, *a monomial* $x^\alpha y^\beta z^\gamma$ *to* $t_i^k t'^l_i$, *according to the rules given by Table 1.*

	$R \cap S$	$R \cup S$	$R \nabla S$	R-S	
$t_i^0 t'^0_i$	1	1	1	1	
$t_i^1 t'^0_i$	xz	x	xz	xz	
$t_i^0 t'^1_i$	yz	y	yz	y	
$t_i^1 t'^1_i$	xyz	xyz	xy	xy	

Table 1: Substitutions.

From this theorem several corollaries can be obtained for the distributions (and means and variances) of sizes of resulting relations.

If needed (for example, for the study of the composition of operations) a similar theorem could be obtained giving the formal polynomial associated to the relation $\Lambda(R,S)$. Here we need only the generating functions for the sizes of $\Lambda(R,S)$.

As for the case of selections, it can be reduced to an intersection problem.

5. EQUIJOINS AND SEMIJOINS.

Let $R[X,Y]$ and $S[X,Z]$ be two distinct relation schemes, $\lambda(R,S)$ be the equijoin of R and S on attribute X, and $\mu(R,S)$ the semijoin of R and S, i.e. the projection on the attributes X and Y of $\lambda(R,S)$ (or the equijoin of R and $\Pi_X(S)$ on attribute X).

The basic transforms on generating functions associated to equijoins and semijoins are described in theorem 3.

Theorem 3: *The generating functions relative to equijoin size:*

$$\varphi(R{:}x, S{:}y, \lambda(R,S){:}z)$$

and semijoin size:

$$\varphi(R{:}x, S{:}y, \mu(R,S){:}z)$$

are obtained from the formal polynomial $\Pi(\xi,\xi',\eta,\zeta)$ *associated to the couple* $R \times S$ *(cf Lemma 4) by the following transforms:*

- *first, for each* t_Y *of* D_Y, *and each* t_Z *of* D_Z, *replace* η_{t_Y} *by* x *and* ζ_{t_Z} *by* y;
- *then, for each* t_X *of* D_X, *replace* $(\xi_{t_X})^k (\xi'_{t_X})^l$:
  - *by* z^{kl}, *in the case of equijoins,*

- *by* x^k *if* $l>0$, 1 *otherwise, in the case of semijoins.*

Under the uniform hypothesis, the generating function for semijoin size can be expressed as a sum according to the following corollary:

Corollary 6: *Under the uniform hypothesis, the generating function for the size of the semijoin* $\mu(R,S)$ *of* $R[X,Y]$ *and* $S[X,Z]$ *is given by:*

$$\varphi(R:x,S:y,\mu(R,S):z) = \sum_{0 \le m \le l \le d_X} (-1)^{m+l} \binom{d_X}{l} \binom{l}{m} f_l(x,y) g_m(z)$$

where $f_l(x,y)$ *is obtained from the formal polynomial* $f_R((x_i),(y_j))$ *describing relation* R *by substituting* y *to each* y_j, x *to* l *of the* x_i, 1 *to the other* x_i; $g_m(z)$ *is obtained from the formal polynomial* $g_S((x'_i),(z_k))$ *describing relation* S *by substituting* z *to each* z_k, 1 *to* m *of the* x'_i, 0 *to the other* x'_i.

Corollary 6 makes no assumption on the relation schemes for R and S. The only hypothesis is the uniform distribution of attribute values in their domains which guarantees that f_R and g_S are symetric functions of the x_i and x'_i respectively.

If we suppose, moreover, that R and S are either free relations or relations with a single functional dependency, we can obtain explicit formulae for the generating function of the semijoin size.

Corollary 7: *Let* $R[X,Y]$ *and* $S[X,Z]$ *be either free relations or relations with a single functional dependency. Under the uniform hypothesis, the generating function*

$$\varphi(R:x,S:y,\mu(R,S):z)$$

for the semi-join is given by table 2 (where $X \dagger Y$ *means there is no functional dependency between* X *and* Y*).*

For the mean and variance of the distribution, we can prove:

Corollary 8: *Let* $R[X,Y]$ *and* $S[X,Z]$ *be either free relations or relations with a single functional dependency. Let* r *denote the size of* R, s *the size of* S, *and:*

$$\alpha = \frac{\binom{d_X d_Z - d_Z}{s}}{\binom{d_X d_Z}{s}} \qquad \alpha_1 = \left(1 - \frac{1}{d_X}\right)^s$$

$$\beta = \frac{\binom{d_X d_Z - 2d_Z}{s}}{\binom{d_X d_Z}{s}} \qquad \beta_1 = \left(1 - \frac{2}{d_X}\right)^s$$

R	S	φ
$X \dagger Y$	$X \dagger Z$	$[(1+y)^{d_Y}+(1+xy)^{d_Y}[(1+z)^{d_Z}-1]]^{d_X}$
$X \dagger Y$	$X \to Z$	$[(1+y)^{d_Y}+d_Z z(1+xy)^{d_Y}]^{d_X}$
$X \dagger Y$	$Z \to X$	$\sum_{k=0}^{d_X}\binom{d_X}{k}(1+kz)^{d_Z}(1+xy)^{kd_Y}[(1+y)^{d_Y}-(1+xy)^{d_Y}]^{d_X}$
$X \to Y$	$X \dagger Z$	$[1+d_Y y+(1+d_Y xy)[(1+z)^{d_Z}-1]]^{d_X}$
$X \to Y$	$X \to Z$	$[1+d_Y y+d_Z z(1+d_Y xy)]^{d_X}$
$X \to Y$	$Z \to X$	$\sum_{k=0}^{d_X}\binom{d_X}{k}(1+kz)^{d_Z}(1+d_Y xy)^k[d_Y y(1-x)]^{d_X-k}$
$Y \to X$	$X \dagger Z$	$\sum_{k=0}^{d_X}\binom{d_X}{k}[(1+z)^{d_Z}-1]^k(1+d_X y+ky(x-1))]^{d_Y}$
$Y \to X$	$X \to Z$	$\sum_{k=0}^{d_X}\binom{d_X}{k}d_Z z^k[1+d_X y+ky(x-1))]^{d_Y}$
$Y \to X$	$Z \to X$	$\sum_{0 \le k \le l \le d_X}(-1)^{k+l}\binom{d_X}{l}\binom{l}{k}(1+kz)^{d_Z}[1+d_X y+ly(x-1))]^{d_Y}$

Table 2: Generating function for semijoin size.

Under the uniform hypothesis, the mean value of the size of the semijoin $\mu(R,S)$ (which does not depend on the relation scheme for S) is given by Table 3, and the variance of the distribution of semijoin sizes is given by Table 4.

$X \dagger Y$	$X \to Y$	$Y \to X$
$r(1-\alpha)$	$\frac{rs}{d_X}$	$r(1-\alpha_1)$

Table 3: Mean size of semijoin.

Note that when the domains are large the variance is approximately equal to $\frac{rs}{d_X}$, except in the case $X \dagger Y$, $X \dagger Z$ for which the approximate value is: $\frac{rs}{d_X d_Y}$

In the uniform case, the distribution of equijoin sizes, its mean and variance, can also be expressed by closed formulae.

Corollary 9: *Let $R[X,Y]$ and $S[X,Z]$ be either free relations or relations with a single functional dependency. Under the uniform hypothesis, the generating function for the size of the equijoin:*

$$\varphi(R{:}x, S{:}y, \lambda(R,S){:}z)$$

is given by Table 5 (which has to be completed by symmetry).

R	S	Variance
$X^\dagger Y$	$X^\dagger Z$	$r\alpha\dfrac{(d_X-1)d_Y+r(d_Y-1)}{d_X d_Y-1}-r^2\alpha^2+r(r-1)\dfrac{d_X(d_Y-1)}{d_X d_Y-1}\beta$
$X^\dagger Y$	$X \to Z$	$\dfrac{rs}{d_X}(1-\dfrac{s}{d_X})\dfrac{d_X d_Y-r}{d_X d_Y-1}$
$X^\dagger Y$	$Z \to X$	$r\alpha_1\dfrac{(d_X-1)d_Y+r(d_Y-1)}{d_X d_Y-1}-r^2\alpha_1^2+r(r-1)\dfrac{d_X(d_Y-1)}{d_X d_Y-1}\beta_1$
$X \to Y$	$X^\dagger Z$	$r\alpha+r(r-1)\beta-r^2\alpha^2$
$X \to Y$	$X \to Z$	$\dfrac{rs}{d_X-1}(1-\dfrac{r}{d_X})(1-\dfrac{s}{d_X})$
$X \to Y$	$Z \to X$	$r\alpha_1+r(r-1)\beta_1-r^2\alpha_1^2$
$Y \to X$	$X^\dagger Z$	$r(1+\dfrac{r-1}{d_X})\alpha-r^2\alpha^2+r(r-1)(1-\dfrac{1}{d_X})\beta$
$Y \to X$	$X \to Z$	$\dfrac{rs}{d_X}(1-\dfrac{1}{d_X})$
$Y \to X$	$Z \to X$	$r(1+\dfrac{r-1}{d_X})\alpha_1-r^2\alpha_1^2+r(r-1)(1-\dfrac{1}{d_X})\beta_1$

Table 4: Variance of the distribution of semijoin size.

R	S	φ
$X^\dagger Z$	$X^\dagger Y$	$[\sum_{k=0}^{d_Y}\binom{d_Y}{k}y^k(1+x^k z)^{d_Z}]^{d_X}$
$X \to Z$	$X^\dagger Y$	$[(1+y)^{d_Y}+d_Z z(1+xy)^{d_Y}]^{d_X}$
$X \to Z$	$X \to Y$	$(1+d_Y y+d_Z z+d_Y d_Z xyz)^{d_X}$
$Z \to X$	$X^\dagger Y$	$\sum_{k=0}^{d_X d_Y} y^k \sum_{0 \le u_i \le d_Y; u_1+\cdots+u_{d_X}=k}\binom{d_Y}{u_1}\cdots\binom{d_Y}{u_{d_X}}[1+z\sum_{i=1}^{d_X}x^{u_i}]^{d_Z}$
$Z \to X$	$X \to Y$	$\sum_{k=0}^{d_X}\binom{d_X}{k}(d_Y y)^k[1+d_X z+kz(x-1)]^{d_Z}$
$Z \to X$	$Y \to X$	$\sum_{k=0}^{d_Y}\binom{d_Y}{k}\sum_{0 \le u_i; u_1+\cdots+u_{d_X}=k}\binom{k}{u_1 \cdots u_{d_X}}[1+z\sum_{i=1}^{d_X}x^{u_i}]^{d_Z}$

Table 5: Generating function for equijoin size.

Corollary 10: *Let $R[X,Y]$ and $S[X,Z]$ be either free relations or relations with a single functional dependency. Under the uniform hypothesis, the distribution of equijoin size has mean:*

$$\frac{rs}{d_X}$$

Its variance is given in Table 6 (which is symmetric).

R	S	Variance
$X^{\dagger}Z$	$X^{\dagger}Y$	$\frac{rs}{d_X}\times\frac{d_X-1}{d_X}\times\frac{d_Xd_Y-r}{d_Xd_Y-1}\times\frac{d_Xd_Z-s}{d_Xd_Z-1}$
$X^{\dagger}Z$	$X\to Y$	$\frac{rs}{d_X}\times\frac{d_Xd_Z-s}{d_Xd_Z-1}\times\frac{d_X-r}{d_X}$
$X^{\dagger}Z$	$Y\to X$	$\frac{rs}{d_X}\times\frac{d_X-1}{d_X}\times\frac{d_Xd_Z-s}{d_Xd_Z-1}$
$X\to Z$	$X^{\dagger}Y$	$\frac{rs}{d_X}\times\frac{d_Xd_Y-r}{d_Xd_Y-1}\times\frac{d_X-s}{d}$
$X\to Z$	$X\to Y$	$\frac{rs}{d_X-1}\times\frac{d_X-r}{d_X}\times\frac{d_X-s}{d_X}$
$X\to Z$	$Y\to X$	$\frac{rs}{d_X}\times\frac{d_X-s}{d_X}$
$Z\to X$	$X^{\dagger}Y$	$\frac{rs}{d_X}\times\frac{d_X-1}{d_X}\times\frac{d_Xd_Y-r}{d_Xd_Y-1}$
$Z\to X$	$X\to Y$	$\frac{rs}{d_X}\times\frac{d_X-r}{d_X}$
$Z\to X$	$Y\to X$	$\frac{rs}{d_X}\times\frac{d_X-1}{d_X}$

Table 6: Variance for equijoin size.

Although the results become much more intricate, similar results can be obtained in the non uniform case. For example:

Corollary 11: *Let $R[X,Y]$ and $S[X,Z]$ be two relations with functional dependencies $X\to Y$ and $X\to Z$.*
Under the non-uniform assumption:

$$\varphi[R{:}x, S{:}y, \lambda(R,S){:}z] = \prod_{t_X\in D_X}\left(1+p(t_X)(y+z)+p(t_X)^2xyz\right)$$

6. DIRECTIONS FOR FUTURE RESEARCH

We have now tools for obtaining the distribution of the sizes of results of relational algebra operations in several well understood cases. We intend to pursue our work in the following directions:

i) evaluate, using our results, the overall performance of basic relational queries, taking into account several possible implementations of the relations (hash tables ...) and the "physical" cost of retrieval.

ii) study the effect of "cascades" of operations on the sizes of relations;

iii) study the influence of the size of the domain (the approach can also be used to study infinite domains);

iv) try to deal with more complex dependencies (several dependencies, multivalued dependencies ...);

iv) test the usefulness of our approach for implementing an automatic "size_of_result" analyzer, a first step towards a "query optimizer"...

Let us also mention that some of our results seem useful for analyzing the size of compacted files obtained, for example, by the method described in [1]

References

1. F. Bancilhon, Ph. Richard, and M. Scholl, *On line processing of compacted relations*, Proc. VLDB 82, Mexico 1982.
2. M.W. Blasgen and K.P. Eswaran, "On the Evaluation of Queries in Relational Data Base Systems," RJ1745 (April 1976). IBM Research Report, IBM Research Center, San Jose
3. S. Christodoulakis, *Estimating Block Transfers and Join Sizes*, Proc. SIGMOD 83, San Jose, Cal. 1983.
4. W.W. Chu and P. Hurley, "Optimal query processing for distributed database systems," *IEEE Transactions on Computers* **C-31**(9)(1982).
5. R. Demolombe, *Estimation of the number of tuples satisfying a query expressed in Predicate Calculus language* , Proc. VLDB 80 1980.
6. R. Demolombe, "How to improve performance of relational DBMS," pp. 229-233 in *Proc. IFIP 83*, ed. Mason R.E.A.,Elsevier Science Publishers (1983).
7. D. Gardy, *Evaluation de résultats d'opérations de l'algèbre relationnelle*, Thèse de Troisième Cycle, Université de Paris-Sud, Orsay 1983.
8. E. Gelenbe and D. Gardy, "On the sizes of projections, I," *Information Processing Letters* **14**(1)(1982).
9. E. Gelenbe and D. Gardy, *The size of Projections of Relations Satisfying a Functional Dependency*, Proc. VLDB 82, Mexico 1982.
10. L.R. Gotlieb, *Computing joins of relations*, Proc. SIGMOD 78 1978.
11. A.R. Hevner and S.B. Yao , "Query processing in distributed data base systems," *IEEE Transactions On Software Engineering*, (1979).
12. D. Maier, *The Theory of Relational Databases*, Computer Science Press (1983).

13. T.H. Merrett and Ekow Otoo, *Distributions models of relations*, Proc. VLDB 79, Rio de Janeiro 1979.

14. A.Y. Montgomery, Y.J. D'Souza, and S.B. Lee , "The cost of relational algebraic operations on skewed data: estimates and experiments," pp. 235-241 in *Proc. IFIP 83*, ed. Mason R.E.A.,Elsevier Science Publishers (1983).

15. Ph. Richard, *Evaluation of the size of a query expressed in relational algebra*, Proc. SIGMOD 81 1981.

16. A.S. Rosenthal, "Note on the expected size of a join," *SIGMOD Record* 11(4) pp. 19-25 (1981).

17. P. Griffiths Selinger, M.M. Astrahan , M.M. Chamberlin , R.A. Lorie, and T.G. Price, *Access path selection in a relational Database System*, Proc. ACM SIGMOD 1979.

18. J.M. Smith and P.Y.T. Chang, "Optimizing the performance of a relational algebra Database interface," *CACM* 18(10)(1975).

19. J.D. Ullmann, *Principles of data base systems*, Computer Science Press (1980).

20. S.B. Yao, "An attribute based model for data base access cost analysis," *ACM TODS*, (1977).

21. S.B. Yao, "Optimization of Query Evaluation Algorithms," *ACM TODS* 4(2) pp. 133-155 (1979).

SOME RESULTS ABOUT FINITE AND INFINITE

BEHAVIOURS OF A PUSHDOWN AUTOMATON

Danièle GIRAULT-BEAUQUIER
Université Paris VII
UER de Mathématiques
2, Place Jussieu - 75251 PARIS CEDEX 05 FRANCE

ABSTRACT :

We are interested in infinitary languages recognized by a pushdown automaton. We, then, give theorems of characterization of such closed, central, normal or perfect languages (considering a number of hypothesis of continuity in computations of the automaton, for last three classes). Besides, it is proved that, given the same hypothesis, the largest central (respectively normal, perfect, language included in an algebraic infinitary language, remains algebraic.

INTRODUCTION :

A general theory of infinitary languages appeared in the last few years. (5, 3, 2, 6). One of the main motivations for such a research is a practical one. An infinitary language is a suitable model to describe the set of behaviours of a given process, which, at any time can perform given number of actions. A process can be stopped after a finite time or work for ever, a behaviour of a given process is, therefore, a finite or infinite sequence of actions, i.e. a finite or infinite word written on the alphabet of actions.

Closed processes play an important part in practice, so it is necessary to have a criterion to recognize them. Besides, when faced with the problem of synchronization of processes, the need to avoid deadlocks appears and so to test if a process is deadlock-free, or if not, to obtain the largest possible deadlock-free process contained in the process. So we naturally introduce the notions of infinitary central language (every word of the language extends into an infinite word of the language : so, it appears that a central language is deadlock-free), the dual notion of infinitary normal language (for every infinite word of the language, every left factor of this word extends into a finite word of the language), to end, that of a perfect language, i.e. normal and central.

In practice, most processes can be done by automata, in particular by finite automata or pushdown automa. These problems of closedness,centrality,normality and perfection were first studied by M. Nivat (6) within the scope of infinitary rational languages, i.e. recognized by finite automata : a characterization of closed rational infinitary languages (respectively central, normal) is obtained. Besides, it is proved that the largest central language L^c (respectively normal L^N, perfect L^P) contained in a rational infinitary language is computable and rational.

We consider in this paper, the case of infinitary languages recognized by pushdown automata (i.e. infinitary algebraic languages), and we mean to get similar results.

Thus, we obtain a characterization of closed infinitary algebraic languages. Unfortunately, the largest central (respectively normal, perfect) language included in a given infinitary algebraic language is generally not algebraic. Hence the idea if looking for sufficient conditions to ensure this algebraic character. These conditions relate to successful computations of the automaton, and warrant extensions of them exist.

It is then proved that if a language L is recognized by a f.i. continuous automaton (respectively i.f. continuous, bi-continuous), then L^c is computable and algebraic (respectively L^N, L^P is computable and algebraic). Given the same hypothesis, theorems of characterization of central, normal, perfect languages are provided.

I. REDUCED PUSHDOWN AUTOMATA

We first need to give a result concerning a canonical form of pda's which recognize infinitary languages.

Let Σ be a finite alphabet.

An infinitary language L is a subset of $\Sigma^\infty = \Sigma^* \cup \Sigma^\omega$.

We denote by L_{fin} the set $L \cap \Sigma^*$, and L_{inf} the set $L \cap \Sigma^\omega$.

We recall (2) that the infinitary language recognized by a pda

$$A = (K,\Sigma,\Gamma,\delta,q_o,Z_o,K_{fin},K_{inf}) \text{ is :}$$

$L^\infty(A) = L^*(A) \cup L^\omega(A)$, where

$L^*(A) = \{u \in \Sigma^*/(q_o,Z_o) \xrightarrow{u} (q,\gamma) \text{ and } q \in K_{fin}\}$, and

$L^\omega(A) = \{u \in \Sigma^\omega/(q_o,Z_o) \xrightarrow{u}\!\!> K_{inf}\Gamma^* (*)\}$.

(*) $(q_o,Z_o) \xrightarrow{u}\!\!> K_{inf}\Gamma^*$ means that there exists a computation of A reading u, which passes infinitely many times in K_{inf}. For a fixed Σ, <u>$Alg(\Sigma^\infty)$</u> is the family of infinitary languages L such that $L = L^\infty(A)$ for some A.

<u>Definition</u>

Let $A = (K,\Sigma,\Gamma,\delta,q_o,Z_o,K_{fin},K_{inf})$ be a pda, and let q and q' be two states of A.

- We say that <u>q is accessible from</u> q_o iff $(q_o,Z_o) \xrightarrow{*} (q,\gamma)$.

And we define <u>$Acc(q_o)$</u> $= \{q \in K/q$ is accessible from $q_o\}$

- We say that <u>q is coaccessible</u> from q' iff :

for every $\gamma \in \Gamma^*$ such that $(q_o,Z_o) \xrightarrow{*} (q,\gamma)$, then $(q,\gamma) \xrightarrow{*} (q',\gamma')$.
Let $K' \subset K$: we define $Coacc(K') = \{q \in K / \exists\, q' \in K'\ q$ is coaccessible from $q'\}$

- q is said to <u>be alive with respect to K'</u> iff for every γ such that $(q_o,Z_o) \xrightarrow{*} (q,\gamma)$, there exists an infinite word u such that $(q,\gamma) \xrightarrow{u}\!\!> K' x \Gamma^+$
We define <u>Viv(K')</u> $= \{q \in K/q$ is alive with respect to $K'\}$.

Finally K' is said to be <u>alive</u> iff every $q \in K'$ is alive with respect to K'.

<u>Definition</u>

A pda $A = (K,\Sigma,\Gamma,\delta,q_o,Z_o,K_{fin},K_{inf})$ is said to be reduced iff :

i) $K = Acc(q_o)$

ii) $K = Coacc(K_{fin} \cup K_{inf})$

iii) K_{inf} is alive.

<u>Theorem</u>

For every pda A, there exists a reduced pda A_r which recognizes the same infinitary language.

<u>Scheme of the proof</u>

It is based upon few results concerning stack's words :

<u>Lemma I.1</u> :

For every $q \in K$, the set $\{\gamma \in \Gamma^* / (q_o,Z_o) \xrightarrow{*} (q,\gamma)$ is rational.

<u>Lemma I.2</u> :

For every $q \in K$ and $K' \subset K$, the set $\{\gamma \in \Gamma^* / (q_o,Z_o) \xrightarrow{\omega}\!\!> K' x \Gamma^+\}$ is rational.

<u>Lemma I.3</u> :

For every $q \in K$ and $K' \subset K$, the set $\{\gamma \in \Gamma^* / (q,\gamma) \xrightarrow{*} (q',\gamma')$ and $q' \in K'\}$ is rational.

On the other hand, we obtain :

<u>Lemma I.4</u> :

Let $A = (K,\Sigma,\Gamma,\delta,q_o,Z_o)$ be a pda and let $R \subset \Gamma^*$ be a rational language recognized by the finite automaton $B = (K',\Gamma,\delta',p'_o,K'_+)$ such that $p'_o \mid\!\frac{Z_o}{B}\ p_o$. Then there exists a canonical pda A_R such that :

for every computation $(q_o,Z_o) \longrightarrow (q_1,\gamma_1) \to \ldots \to (q_n,\gamma_n)$ of A, there exists a computation $((q_o,p_o),Z'_o) \longrightarrow ((q_1,p_1),\gamma'_1) \to \ldots \to ((q_n,p_n),\gamma'_n)$ of A_R

such that $p_i \in K'_+$ iff $\gamma_i \in R$, and conversely.

Remarks :

1) This pda A_R is obtained by encoding the rational set R in states of the pda, and by replacing letters Z of Γ by triples (p,z,p'), where p is the state of the finite automaton $\mathcal{B}$ before reading Z, and p' is the state after reading Z.

2) The lemma still holds for a finite number of rational languages $R_1,R_2,\ldots,R_n$. It suffices to consider the cartesian product of the associated finite automata.

We are now able to prove the theorem

$$\text{Let : } C = \{(q,\gamma)/(q_o,Z_o) \xrightarrow{*} (q,\gamma) \xrightarrow{*} (q',\gamma') \text{ and } q' \in K_{fin} \cup Viv(K_{inf})\}$$

$$D = \{(q_o,Z_o)\} \cap C$$

$$C_{inf} = C \cap K_{inf} x \Gamma^* \cap Viv(K_{inf}) x \Gamma^+$$

$$C_{fin} = C \cap K_{fin} x \Gamma^*$$

We have, in some way, reduced the set of configurations of the pda. So, L_{fin} is the set of finite words u for which there exists a computation of A, reading u, such that every configuration belongs to C and the final configuration belongs to C_{fin}.

On the other hand, L_{inf} is the set of infinite words u for which there exists a computation of A, reading u, such that every configuration belongs to C and configurations belong to C_{inf} infinitely many times. It is, then easy to prove, using lemma I.1, I.2, I.3, that :

$$C = \bigcup_{q \in K} \{q\} \times R_q$$

$$C_{fin} = \bigcup_{q \in K_{fin}} \{q\} \times S_q \quad \text{and} \quad C_{inf} = \bigcup_{q \in K_{inf}} \{q\} \times T_q$$

where for any q, R_q, S_q, T_q are rational sets : we shall note them : $R_1,R_2,\ldots,R_n$. So, owing to lemma I.4, we are in position to build a pda $A_{R_1,\ldots,R_n}$ and to conveniently choose $K_1 \subset K x K'$ and $K_2 \subset K x K'$ such that :

$$L^\infty(A) = L^\infty(A_{R_1,\ldots,R_n}, K_1,K_2)$$

At last, $(A_{R_1,\ldots,R_n}, K_1,K_2)$ is easily checked to be reduced

II. CLOSEDNESS

We give here a characterization of closed algebraic infinitary languages.

First, some notations and results are recalled : (3,1)

Σ^∞ is provided with usual metric space structure.

We define for $u \in \Sigma^\infty$ $FG(u) = \{v \in \Sigma^*/v$ is a left factor of $u\}$

for $L \subset \Sigma^\infty$ $FG(L) = \bigcup_{u \in L} FG(u)$

The <u>adherence</u> of an infinitary language L is :

$$\underline{Adh(L)} = \{u \in \Sigma^\omega / \ FG(u) \subset FG(L)\}$$

We recall that L is closed (for topology induced by metric structure) iff $L_{inf} = Adh(L)$.

The main result is the following :

<u>Theorem</u> :

Let $L \in Alg(\Sigma^\infty)$. L is closed iff there exists a quasi-real time pda A(4) such that $L^\infty(A) = L$, and $K = K_{inf}$.

<u>Proof</u> :

i) Let $L \in Alg(\Sigma^\infty)$, and L be closed.

There exists a quasi-real time pda A s.t. $L^\infty(A) = L$.

It suffices to observe that if A is quasi-real time, so is the reduced associated pda A_r. If $A_r = (K,\Sigma,\Gamma,\delta,q_o,K_{fin},K_{inf})$, let $A' = (K,\Sigma,\Gamma,\delta,q_o,Z_oK_{fin},K)$.

Therefore, $L^\infty(A') = L^\infty(A_r)$, since L is closed.

ii) Conversely, suppose $L = L^\infty(A)$ and A is a quasi-real time pda s.t. $K_{inf} = K$.

Let $u \in Adh(L)$. Thus, for every $n \in N^+$, the set of computations of A reading $u(1)\ u(2)..u(n)$ is finite and not empty. We apply Koenig's lemma. Whence there exists a computation of A reading u and $u \in L_{inf}$ since $K = K_{inf}$.

<u>III. CENTRALITY, NORMALITY, PERFECTION</u>

<u>A) Centrality</u>

<u>Definition</u>

Let $L \subset \Sigma^\infty$. L is said to be central iff $L_{fin} \subset FG(L_{inf})$.

Since union of any number of central languages is central, the largest central language contained in L does exist, we denote it by L^c. Clearly, one has :

$$L^c = (L_{fin} \cap FG(L_{inf})) \cup L_{inf}$$

Unfortunately L^c is generally not algebraic, as proved in this example : $L = \{a^nb^n/n \in a^+\}.c^+.d^+ \cup a^+\{b^nc^n/n \in a^+\}\ d^\omega$.

Whence $L^c_{fin} = \{a^nb^nc^n/n \in N^+\}d^+$. And $L^c_{fin} \notin Alg(\Sigma^*)$.

<u>Definition</u>

A pda $A = (K,\Sigma,\Gamma,\delta,q_o,Z_o,K_{fin},K_{inf})$ is said to be <u>f.i. continuous</u> iff for $u \in L^*(A)$ and $v \in L^\omega(A)$ such that $u \in FG(v)$, every successful computation of u

extends in a successful one of v.

L is said f.i. continuous iff there exists a f.i. continuous pda A s.t. $L = L^{\infty}(A)$. This hypothesis yields few results :

Theorem III.A.1

Let L be a f.i. continuous language. Then L^c is algebraic.

Sketch of the proof :

It suffices to observe that :

$$L^c_{fin} = L_{fin} \cap FG(L_{inf}) = \{u \in \Sigma^* / (q_o, Z_o) \xrightarrow{u} (q,\gamma) \text{ and } \exists\, v \in \Sigma^{\omega}\ (q,\gamma) \xrightarrow{v}\!\!>> K_{inf}.\Gamma^+\}$$

So, using Lemma I.1 and I.4, L^c_{fin} is algebraic.

Theorem III.A.2

Let L be a f.i. continuous language. L is central iff there exists a reduced pda $A = (K,\Sigma,\Gamma,\delta,q_o,Z_o,K_{fin},K_{inf})$ such that $K = Viv(K_{inf})$.

Proof

i) If $K = Viv(K_{inf})$, it is quite obvious that L is central.

ii) Conversely, let L be a central f.i. continuous language. There exists a f.i. continuous pda A s. t. $L = L^{\infty}(A)$. Moreover the associated reduced pda A_r remains f.i. continuous. So, it is easy to prove that the set K_r of states of A_r is alive with respect to $K_{r\ inf}$.

B) Normality

Definition :

Let $L \subset \Sigma^{\infty}$. L is said to be normal iff $FG(L_{inf}) \subset FG(L_{fin})$.

Since union of any number of normal languages is normal, the largest normal language contained in L does exist. We denote it by L^N.

Obviously, one has :

$$L^N = L_{fin} \cup (L_{inf} \cap Adh(L_{fin}))$$

The situation is the same as for L^c : generally, L^N is not algebraic. For example ; $L = \{a^n b^n / n \in N^+\}\ c^+ d^+ \cup a^+ \{b^n c^n / n \in N^+\} d^{\omega}$.

$$L^N_{inf} = \{a^n b^n c^n / n \in N^+\} d^{\omega}$$

Clearly, L^N_{inf} is not algebraic.

Definition :

A pda $A = (K,\Sigma,\Gamma,\delta,q_o,Z_o,K_{fin},K_{inf})$ is said to be i.f. continuous iff for $u \in \Sigma^*$, $w \in L^*(A)$, $v \in L^{\omega}(A)$ such that $u \in FG(w) \cap FG(v)$, for every successful computation c of A, reading v, every beginning of c, reading u, extends in a successful computation of w.

L is said i.f. continuous iff there exists a i.f. continuous pda which recognizes it.

i.f. continuity yields the following :

Theorem III.B.1

Let L be a i.f. continuous language. Then L^N is algebraic.

Scheme of the proof :

It suffices to observe that :

$$L^N_{inf} = L_{inf} \cap Adh(L_{fin})$$

Whence, an infinite word $u \in L^N_{inf}$ iff there is a computation of u :

$(q_o,Z_o) \to (q_1,\gamma_1) \to \ldots \to (q_n,\gamma_n) \to \ldots$ s.t. for infinitely many $n, q_n \in K_{inf}$ and $(q_n,\gamma_n) \xrightarrow{*} K_{fin} \times \Gamma^*$.

So, using lemma I.3 and I.4, we prove that L^N is algebraic.

Theorem III.B.2

Let L be a i.f. continuous language. Thus, L is normal iff there exists a pda $A = (K,\Sigma,\Gamma,\delta,q_o,Z_o,K_{fin},K_{inf})$ such that $L = L^\infty(A)$ and $K = Coacc(K_{fin})$.

Proof :

i) if A satisfies $K = Coacc(K_{fin})$, clearly, $L^\infty(A)$ is normal.

ii) conversely, suppose L to be recognized by a i.f. continuous pda A, then A_r is i.f. continuous, too. So $L = L^\infty(A_r)$ and necessarily, $K = Coacc(K_{fin})$.

C) Perfection

Perfection is conjonction of normality and centrality.

Definition

A language $L \subset \Sigma^\infty$ is perfect iff it is normal and central.

Of course, the largest perfect language L^P contained in a given language L is generally not algebraic. Whence the necessity to introduce notion of bi-continuity for a pda.

Definition

A pda is said to be bi-continuous iff it is both f.i and i.f. continuous.

A language is bi-continuous iff it is recognized by a bi-continuous pda. (Note that if a language is both f.i. and i.f. continuous, it is not necessarily bi-continuous).

So, we obtain, for bi-continuous languages a characterization of perfect ones, and a computation of the largest perfect language contained in a given language.

Theorem III.C.1

Let L be a bi-continuous language. Then L^P is algebraic.

Sketch of the proof :

The proof is in three steps :

i) First, we define for a finitary language L, the limit of L, denoted by Elim(L) :

$$\mathrm{Elim}(L) = \{u \in \Sigma^\omega / \ |FG(u) \cap L| = \omega\}$$

We claim that L^P is the language below :

$$L = L_{fin} \cap FG(L_{inf} \cap \mathrm{Adh}M) \cup ((\mathrm{Adh}M) \cap L_{inf}) \text{ where } M = L_{inf} \cap \mathrm{Elim}(L_{fin})$$

In order

ii) to prove that L^P_{inf} is algebraic it suffices to observe that :

a) $u \in L^P_{inf}$ iff there is a computation $(q_i,\gamma_i)_{i\in N}$ of A reading u such that

1) $|\{i \in N / q_i \in K_{inf}\}| = \omega$ and for every i :

2) there is a computation of an infinite word, which begins in (q_i,γ_i) configuration, and passes infinitely often through states in K_{fin}

b) applying lemma I.2 and I.4, we obtain that L^P_{inf} is algebraic.

iii) one can finally observe that $u \in L^P_{fin}$ iff there exists a computation of A, $(q_i,\gamma_i)_{i\leq N}$, reading u such that $q_N \in K_{fin}$, and 2) holds for integer N. So, using lemma I.2 and I.4, we can build a pda which recognizes L_{fin}.

Theorem III.C.2

Let L be a bi-continuous language. L is perfect iff there exists a pda A such that $L = L^\infty(A)$ and $K = \mathrm{Coacc}(K_{fin}) = \mathrm{Viv}(K_{inf})$.

Proof :

This property is an obvious consequence of theorems III.A.2 and III.B.2

REFERENCES

(1) A. Arnold and M. Nivat, Comportements de processus, Colloque AFCET, Les Mathématiques de l'Informatique, Paris (1982), p. 35-68.

(2) R. Cohen and A. Gold, Theory of ω-languages, Jour. Comp. Syst. Sci. Vol. 15 (1977), p. 169-184.

(3) S. Eilenberg, Automata, languages and machines, Vol. A, Academic Press (1974).

(4) M.A. Harrison, Introduction to formal language theory, Addison Wesley (1969).

(5) R. McNaughton, Testing and generating infinite sequences by a finite automaton, Inf. and Control, Vol. 9 (1966), p. 521-530.

(6) M. Nivat, Behaviours of synchronized systems of processes, Cours de D.E.A. 1981-82, L.I.T.P., Paris VII.

ON THE RELATIONSHIP OF CCS AND PETRI NETS

Ursula Goltz
Lehrstuhl für Informatik II
RWTH Aachen
Büchel 29-31
D-5100 Aachen
West-Germany

Alan Mycroft
Institutionen för
Informationsbehandling
Chalmers Tekniska Högskola
S-412 96 Göteborg
Sweden

Abstract   We give a partial order semantics to (pure) CCS via a translation into Petri nets and prove that the interleaved behaviour of the resulting nets is equivalent to Milner's semantics. We show that a large class of CCS programs can be represented by finite nets and that this is impossible for the whole CCS.

1. Introduction

Milner introduced CCS (calculus of communicating systems) /Mi/ as a method for describing and analysing systems of communicating processes. Essential in this approach is the concept of synchronised communication. Petri net theory /Br,Re1/ is a more general model to descibe concurrent systems with more varied synchronisation mechanisms. The aim of this work is to give a translation of CCS into net theory, which can be seen as giving a net semantics to CCS denotationally. As CCS imposes more structure on the representation of systems, one might consider it as a higher-level language than Petri nets. However, we will attempt to justify our approach with the following arguments.

An important notion in net theory is the notion of concurrency. There is no linear timescale when we describe systems such that events in the system would occur in some total order. Rather, we want to know which events are causally dependent on each other such that one event has to have occurred before the other is possible. On the other hand, there may be events which may occur independently. Such events are considered as being concurrent with one another.

For CCS, the semantics is given by derivation rules or in terms of synchronisation trees. In both approaches the parallel occurrence of two actions like in $b_1|b_2$ where $b_1 \Leftarrow \alpha.NIL$ and $b_2 \Leftarrow \beta.NIL$ is modelled by all possible interleavings. The corresponding synchronisation tree would be

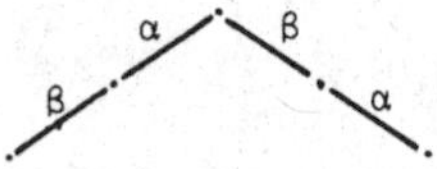

(by using the expansion theorem /Mi/). However, the expression $b_3 \Leftarrow \alpha.\beta.NIL + \beta.\alpha.NIL$ has exactly the same semantics. As "+" represents a non-deterministic choice, one might say that concurrency is here described by non-determinism. This is discussed in /Mi/ and is motivated by introducing the notion of a sequential observer.

In our approach, we will translate $b_1|b_2$ to

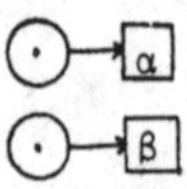

and b_3 to

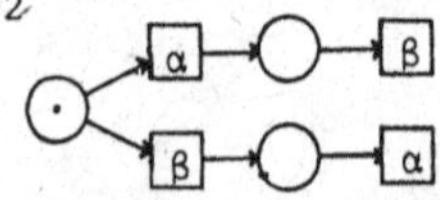

We see that the non-determinism in b_3 is represented as a branched place whereas we would consider $b_1|b_2$ as a concurrent deterministic system.

We claim that for certain investigations it might be interesting to distinguish concurrency and non-determinism clearly, for instance when discussing fairness problems. It turns out that there are several ways of introducing non-determinism into CCS-programs. First, we have the explicit non-determinism introduced by "+". But furthermor we shall see that, even if the parallel execution is not modelled by non-deterministic

terleaving, the "|"-operator can still introduce non-deterministic choices. For
ample consider

$\alpha.NIL|\bar{\alpha}.NIL$ and $\alpha.\beta.NIL|\bar{\alpha}.NIL|\alpha.\gamma.NIL\setminus\alpha$

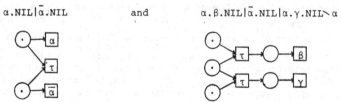

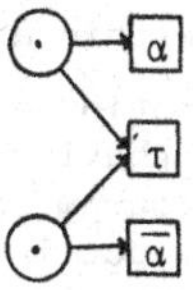

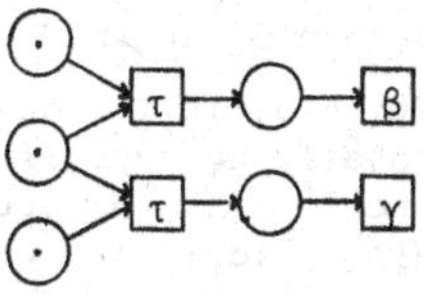

is is also discussed in /Ab/.

our translation we actually give a new semantics to CCS since we are able to stinguish for example the programs $b_1|b_2$ shown above, which are not distinguished the normal semantics. We can also sequentialise all observable actions in the haviour of the net by building the sequential observer into the net, similarly to /Wi2/.

other reason for translating CCS into Petri nets is the fact that there are several thods of analysing nets which might be used then to investigate properties of CCS-ograms. Conversely, we hope to find, by giving this translation, an interesting bclass of Petri nets with nice structural properties.

ere have already been other attempts to investigate the relationship between CCS and t theory. Milner himself started the comparison in /Mi/ by considering an example. nskel /Wi1/ later gave an alternative semantics to CCS in terms of event structures. this approach, concurrency is less directly represented than in our net translation. later defined a category of nets in /Wi2/ which exhibits as co-products and products r "+"- and "|"-operators on occurrence nets. Unfortunately his definition of "+" does t respect CCS semantics on folding and so seemingly cannot be used to derive finite t representations of CCS programs. A subset of CCS is related to 'superposed automata' ts in /Ci1,Ci2/. /Ab/ gives a semantics to a subset of CCS in terms of communication aces. The idea of non-interleaved semantics is of course not restricted to CCS. The proach of /Wi1/ works for different kinds of concurrent languages. In /Re2/, a non-terleaved semantics is given for CSP and applied to fairness.

is paper is organised as follows. In section 2 and 3 we give the basic notions of CCS d Petri nets, respectively. Then we give a translation method of CCS into possibly finite occurrence nets in section 4 and show that the translation corresponds to CCS mantics. In section 5, we give a method for translating a large class of CCS programs to finite marked nets. All proofs are omitted because lack of space. They can be und in the full version of the paper /GM1/.

CCS

is section describes the (pure) CCS as defined by Milner /Mi/. We start by assuming e existence of a set Λ of actions where Λ has a partition $(\Delta,\bar{\Delta})$ with bijection $\bar{\cdot}: \Delta\to\bar{\Delta}$ ich is also used for the inverse mapping. α,β,λ will be used to range over Λ. In dition we will use an infinite set $\Omega=\{\omega_1,\bar{\omega}_1,\omega_2,\bar{\omega}_2,\ldots\}$ of invisible actions whose rpose is to preserve the uniqueness of actions restricted by $B\setminus\alpha$ (see section 5). e symbol τ will be used to indicate an unobservable action or an internal communic-ion. μ and υ will be used to range over $\Lambda\cup\Omega\cup\{\tau\}$.

CCS term or behaviour (ranged over by B) is given by the syntax below where b ranges er a set of behaviour names. A CCS program (ranged over by P) is of the form

$$b_1 \Leftarrow B_1 \quad \ldots \quad b_n \Leftarrow B_n \ \underline{\text{in}}\ B_0 .$$

ere the B_i may only contain behaviour names in the set $\{b_1,\ldots,b_n\}$. A term is given by

$$B \ ::= \ NIL \mid \alpha.B \mid \tau.B \mid B+B' \mid B|B' \mid B\{\theta\} \mid B\setminus\alpha \mid b$$

ere θ (a substitution) is a bijection on Λ which respects $\bar{\cdot}$. The set of all CCS programs is written CCS. CCS-Term is the set of all CCS terms.

A program P will be further assumed to follow Milner's restriction of well-guardedness: there should be no chain $b_{k_1}...b_{k_n}$ with $k_1=k_n$ such that each B_{k_i} contains an unguarded occurrence of $b_{k_{i+1}}$. An occurrence of b in B is guarded if it occurs within a term $\nu.B'$. For the purposes of section 5, it is convenient to introduce the notion of P being totally-guarded: P is totally guarded if every occurrence of any behaviour name b within any B_i occurs within a term $\nu.b$. A fortiori a totally-guarded program is well-guarded. However a converse also holds: any well-guarded program can be put into totally-guarded form by appropriately textually expanding and refolding behaviour definitions. Such a transformation preserves all derivation rules (proof omitted).

3. Net theoretic notions

3.1 Definition

(i) $N=(S,T;F,\ell)$ is called a net iff
  (a) S and T are disjoint sets (places and transitions, respectively), $\ell : T \to L$ is a map from T to some set L of labels,
  (b) $F \subseteq (S\times T) \cup (T\times S)$, F is called the flow relation,
  (c) $\forall t\in T \;\; \exists s\in S$ with sFt.

  N is called finite iff $S\cup T$ is finite.

(ii) For $x\in S\cup T$ $\;{}^{\bullet}x := \{y \mid yFx\}$ is called the preset of x, $x^{\bullet} := \{y \mid xFy\}$ is called the postset of x.

  For $X\subseteq S\cup T$, let ${}^{\bullet}X := \bigcup_{x\in X} {}^{\bullet}x$ and $X^{\bullet} := \bigcup_{x\in X} x^{\bullet}$.

(iii) Let ${}^{\circ}N := \{ x\in S\cup T \mid {}^{\bullet}x = \emptyset \}$.

(iv) For $X\subseteq S\cup T$, let $N\restriction X := (S\cap X, T\cap X; F\cap X^2, \ell\restriction(T\cap X))$.

Graphically we represent places and transitions as circles and boxes, respectively. The flow relation is indicated by arcs between the corresponding circles and boxes. Transitions will be inscribed by their labels. Given a net $N=(S,T;F,\ell)$, we will denote the components of N by S_N, T_N, F_N and ℓ_N. We denote $S\cup T$ by N if no confusion is possible. Note that we allow the empty net, which will be denoted by $\emptyset$.

We will represent (possibly infinite) behaviours with occurrence nets - a subclass of acyclic nets with places which can only be forwardly branched. They were introduced by /NPW,Wi2/. Many definitions in this section come from /Wi2/.

3.2 Definition We say a net N is cycle-free iff $\forall x\in N \; \neg(xF_N^+x)$ (where F_N^+ denotes the transitive closure of F_N). In such cases we define

(i) $x<_N y$ iff xF_N^+y, the index N is omitted when obvious from context,
  $x \;\underline{li}\; y$ iff $x\leq y$ or $y\leq x$,

(ii) $x\#_N y$ iff $\exists t,t'\in T_N$, $t\neq t'$, ${}^{\bullet}t\cap{}^{\bullet}t'\neq\emptyset$, $t\leq x$, $t'\leq y$
  (x and y are in conflict),

(iii) $x \;\underline{co}\; y$ iff $x=y \vee \neg(x \;\underline{li}\; y \vee x\#y)$,
  $X\subseteq S_N$ is called a slice iff $\forall x,y\in X \;\; x \;\underline{co}\; y$ and $\forall x\in N\setminus X, \exists y\in X, \neg(x \;\underline{co}\; y)$

3.3 Definition A net N is called an occurrence net iff

(i) N is cycle-free, $|{}^{\circ}N|<\omega$, $\forall t\in T_N \; |t^{\bullet}|<\omega$,

(ii) $\forall s\in S_N$, $|{}^{\bullet}s|\leq 1$,

(iii) $\#_N$ is irreflexive.

<u>3.4 Definition</u> Let N be an occurrence net.

(i) For $x \in N$, $X \subseteq N$, $\downarrow x := \{y \in N \mid y \leq x\}$, $\downarrow X := \bigcup_{x \in X} \downarrow x$, $\uparrow x := \{y \in N \mid x \leq y\}$, $\uparrow X := \bigcup_{x \in X} \uparrow x$.

(ii) N is <u>founded</u> iff $\forall x \in N$, $\downarrow x$ is finite.

(iii) $\mathrm{depth}_N : N \to \mathbb{N}$ is defined by

(a) for $s \in {}^{\circ}N$, $\mathrm{depth}_N(s) = 1$,

(b) for $t \in T_N$, $\mathrm{depth}_N(t) = \max\{\mathrm{depth}_N(s) \mid s \in {}^{\bullet}t\}$,

(c) for $s \in S_N \setminus {}^{\circ}N$, $\mathrm{depth}_N(s) = \mathrm{depth}_N(t) + 1$ for the unique $t \in {}^{\bullet}s$.

<u>3.5 Definition</u> Let N_1, N_2 be occurrence nets.

N_1 is an <u>(initial) subnet</u> of N_2 ($N_1 \leq N_2$) if $N_1 = N_2 \restriction X$ for some X and $N_1 = \emptyset$ or

(i) ${}^{\circ}N_1 = {}^{\circ}N_2$,

(ii) $\forall x \in N_2, y \in N_1 : x \leq_{N_2} y \Rightarrow x \in N_1$ (N_1 is left closed in N_2),

(iii) $\forall t \in N_1 : t^{\bullet} \subseteq N_1$ or $t^{\bullet} \cap N_1 = \emptyset$ (where $t^{\bullet}$ refers to N_2) and

(iv) $\forall s \in N_1$, $t \in s^{\bullet}$: $\mathrm{depth}_{N_2}(t) = \mathrm{depth}_{N_2}(s) \Rightarrow t \in N_1$ ($s^{\bullet}$ refers to N_2).

<u>3.6 Lemma</u> Let N , N' be occurrence nets.

(i) $N \leq N' \Rightarrow \forall x \in N$, $\mathrm{depth}_N(x) = \mathrm{depth}_{N'}(x)$.

(ii) Let $X_i := \{x \in N \mid \mathrm{depth}(x) \leq i\}$, $i \in \mathbb{N}$. $i \leq j \Rightarrow N \restriction X_i \leq N \restriction X_j$.

We will use the notion of initial subnet to define a subclass of occurrence nets.

<u>3.7 Lemma</u> Let $N_1 \leq N_2 \leq \ldots$ be an ω-chain of finite occurrence nets, let $N := \bigcup_{i \in \omega} N_i$.
($\bigcup_{i \in \omega} N_i$ denotes componentwise union of nets) .

(i) N is an occurrence net, in particular ${}^{\circ}N$ is finite and $t^{\bullet}$ is finite for all $t \in T_N$.

(ii) $\forall n$ $\{x \in N \mid \mathrm{depth}(x) = n\}$ is finite.

Such limit nets $\bigcup N_i$ give a subclass of occurrence nets with only finite non-determinism and parallelism. (Note however they may still have infinitely branched places - see example 3 in section 4.2). Moreover they are founded and give least upper bounds of their defining chains.

Since we are not interested in the actual names of elements, we will not distinguish between isomorphic nets. Furthermore, we do not want to distinguish between nets which only differ with respect to places with equal pre- and postsets. This is required for the correctness of the theorem in section 4.3.

<u>3.8 Definition</u> Let N , N' be occurrence nets.

(i) N is <u>isomorphic</u> to N' ($N \equiv N'$) iff there exists a bijection $\beta : N \to N'$ with $s \in S_N \Leftrightarrow \beta(s) \in S_{N'}$, $x F_N y \Leftrightarrow \beta(x) F_{N'} \beta(y)$ and $\ell_N = \ell_{N'} \circ \beta$.

(ii) $\mathrm{Normal}(N) := N''$ where $S_{N''} := (S_N \setminus \{s \in S_N \mid s^{\bullet} = \emptyset\})/R$ with
$R = \{(s_1, s_2) \mid s_1, s_2 \in S_N, s_1^{\bullet} = s_2^{\bullet}$ and ${}^{\bullet}s_1 = {}^{\bullet}s_2\}$,
$T_{N''} := T_N/\mathrm{id}$, $[x] F_{N''} [y]$ iff $x F_N y$, $\ell_{N''}([t]) := \ell_N(t)$.

(iii) N is <u>equivalent</u> to N' $(N \cong N')$ iff $\text{Normal}(N) \equiv \text{Normal}(N')$.

Define $[N] := \{N' \mid N' \cong N\}$.

3.9 Definition

(i) $\underline{Occ} = \{[\bigcup_{i \in \omega} N_i] \mid N_1 \leq N_2 \leq \ldots$ is a chain of finite occurrence nets$\}$

(ii) Let $[N_1], [N_2] \in \underline{Occ}$. $[N_1] \leq [N_2]$ iff $\exists N_1' \in [N_1], N_2' \in [N_2]$ with $N_1' \leq N_2'$.

(iii) $\emptyset$ will denote $[\emptyset] = \{\emptyset, \bigcirc, \bigcirc\bigcirc, \bigcirc\bigcirc\bigcirc, \ldots\}$.

3.10 Proposition $(\underline{Occ}, \leq)$ is a cpo with least element $\emptyset$. The least upper bound of a chain $[N_1] \leq [N_2] \leq \ldots$ is given by $[\bigcup_{i \in \omega} N_i']$, using any chain $N_1' \leq N_2' \leq \ldots$ with $\forall i, N_i' \in [N_i]$.

(It can be shown this least upper bound is independent of the chosen representatives, but this depends crucially on our definition of initial subnet.)

In section 4, we will recursively define operations on <u>Occ</u> which correspond to the CCS operators and thereby translate CCS programs into <u>Occ</u>. The representation of CCS programs as finite nets is considered in section 5. For this we use the notion of place/transition-nets with arc-weights /GS/.

3.11 Definition

(N,M) is called a <u>marked net</u> iff

(i) $N = (S,T;F,\ell)$, where S and T are disjoint sets and $F : (S \times T) \cup (T \times S) \to \mathbb{N}$, $\ell : T \to L$ where L is a set of labels.

(ii) $M : S \to \mathbb{N}$ (M gives a token count for each place and is called a <u>marking</u> of N).

We use here an extended flow relation representing arc weights and assume unlimited capacities of places. The behaviour of such nets is given by the usual firing rule: A transition $t \in T$ is M-enabled iff $\forall s \in S, M(s) \geq F(s,t)$. It may then fire yielding a successor marking M' with $M'(s) = M(s) - F(s,t) + F(t,s)$ for all $s \in S$.

The behaviour of marked nets may be described in terms of occurrence nets using the notion of unfolding /NPW,Wi2,GM2/. We generalise a definition of /GM2/ to marked nets.

3.12 Definition

Let (N,M) be a marked net, K an occurrence net and $f: K \to N$ a function which satisfies

(i) $f(S_K) \subseteq S_N$, $f(T_K) \subseteq T_N$, $\ell_N \circ f = \ell_K$ (f is sort- and label-preserving),

(ii) $\forall s \in S_N$, $M(s) = |f^{-1}(s) \cap {}^{\circ}K|$ (the initial slice represents the initial marking)

(iii) $\forall t \in T_K$, $s \in S_N$, $F_N(s,f(t)) = |f^{-1}(s) \cap {}^{\bullet}t|$ $\wedge$ $F_N(f(t),s) = |f^{-1}(s) \cap t^{\bullet}|$ (f respects the environment of transitions),

(iv) $\forall$ finite slices X of K, $t \in T_N$,

$|f^{-1}(t) \cap \{t' \in T_K : {}^{\bullet}t \subseteq X\}| = \max\{n \in \mathbb{N}: \forall s \in S_N, |f^{-1}(s) \cap X| \geq n \cdot F_N(s,t)\}$.

(exactly the enabled transitions of N are represented in K).

Then K is called an <u>unfolding</u> of (N,M) and is unique up to isomorphism. This enables us to write $\mathcal{U}(N,M)$ for K.

Unfolding will relate our finite net representations to the occurrence net translation.

<u>Example:</u>

(N,M)

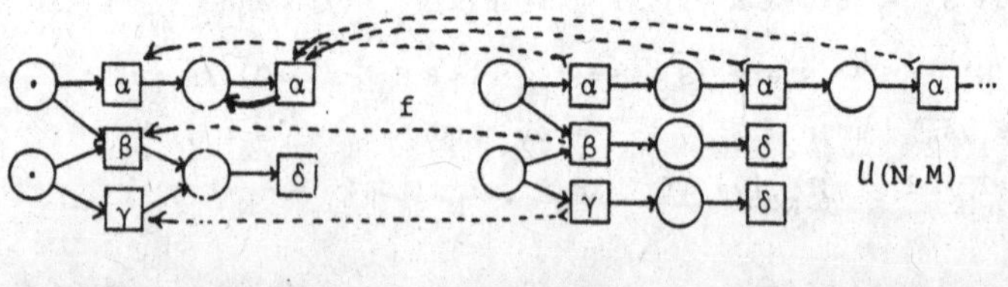

. Translation of CCS into occurrence nets

e now turn to the problem of expressing CCS behaviours in terms of occurrence nets. ection 4.1 introduces operations on occurrence nets which correspond to CCS operators. he following section shows how to translate a CCS program into an occurrence net descr- bing its behaviour for a non-interleaving semantics. Section 4.3 proves that this gives (strongly) equivalent behaviour if we impose an interleaving semantics.

.1 Operations on Occ for the CCS operators

e will define operations corresponding to CCS operators on <u>Occ</u>, the equivalence classes f occurrence nets representable as least upper bounds of chains of finite occurrence ets (see section 3). They are defined by operations on representatives but are indep- ndent of the chosen representatives. The net label set L is to be $\Lambda \cup \{\tau\}$. In /Wi2/ he given operators for "+" and "|" are obtained by categorical constructions /Winskel, ersonal communication/.

1) Let $[N_1], [N_2] \in$ <u>Occ</u> (w.l.o.g. we assume N_1 and N_2 are disjoint representatives). Then the <u>disjoint union of $[N_1]$ and $[N_2]$</u> is defined $[N_1] \uplus [N_2] := [N_1 \uplus N_2]$, where $N \uplus N' := (S_N \cup S_{N'}, T_N \cup T_{N'}; F_N \cup F_{N'}, \ell_N \cup \ell_{N'})$.

2) Let $[N], [N'] \in$ <u>Occ</u> (disjoint from each other and $N \times N'$). Then the <u>non-deterministic combination of [N] and [N']</u> is $[N] + [N'] := [N + N']$ with $N + N' := N'$ if $N=\emptyset$, $N + N' := N$ if $N'=\emptyset$, $N + N' := (S,T;F,\ell)$ otherwise, where
$S := (S_N \setminus {}^{\circ}N) \cup (S_{N'} \setminus {}^{\circ}N') \cup {}^{\circ}N \times {}^{\circ}N'$; $T := T_N \cup T_{N'}$; $\ell := \ell_N \cup \ell_{N'}$;
$F := ((F_N \cup F_{N'}) \cap (S \times T)^2) \cup \{((s,s'),t) \mid s \in {}^{\circ}N,\ s' \in {}^{\circ}N',\ t \in s^{\bullet} \cup s'^{\bullet}\}$;

3) Let $\nu \in \Lambda \cup \{\tau\}$, $[N] \in$ <u>Occ</u> . Then $\nu.[N] := [N']$, where $S_{N'} := S_N \uplus \{s_o\}$, $T_{N'} := T_N \uplus \{t_o\}$, $F_{N'} := F_N \cup \{t_o\} \times {}^{\circ}N \cup \{(s_o,t_o)\}$, $\ell_{N'} := \ell_N \cup \{(t_o,\nu)\}$.

4) If $\theta : \Lambda \cup \{\tau\} \rightarrow \Lambda \cup \{\tau\}$ and $[N] \in$ <u>Occ</u> then $[N]\{\theta\} := [(S_N, T_N; F_N, \theta \circ \ell_N)]$.

5) Let $A \subseteq \Lambda \cup \{\tau\}$, $[N] \in$ <u>Occ</u> . Then $[N] \setminus A := [N \upharpoonright X]$ where $X := (S_N \cup T_N) \setminus \uparrow\{t \in T_N \mid \ell_N(t) \in A \cup \bar{A}\}$. For $\alpha \in \Lambda \cup \{\tau\}$, $[N] \setminus \alpha$ abbreviates $[N] \setminus \{\alpha\}$.

learly the results of all operations are again elements of <u>Occ</u>. If we ignore ommunication possibilities (still specified by port names) the disjoint union (1) orresponds to the intuitive effect of the "|"-operator, the two nets are executed ndependently of each other. The other operations correspond directly to CCS operations, s indicated by symbol overloading. The idea of restriction is to delete communication ossibilities (transitions) and their subsequent behaviours. The "+"-operator of CCS orresponds to the non-deterministic choice between two components. In terms of nets represents the introduction of conflicts between all pairs of initial transitions the two nets involved.

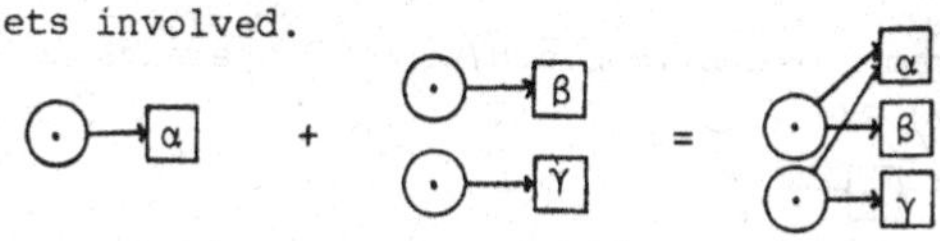

o define communication on nets, we first introduce an operation which describes the fect of two single transitions in a net communicating with one another.

) Let $[N] \in$ <u>Occ</u>, $t_1,t_2 \in N$. For i=1,2 let $N_i = N \upharpoonright \uparrow(t_i^{\bullet})$, (the "net behind t_i"). Now, let $N_i' = (S_i',T_i',F_i',\ell_i') \equiv N_i$ for i=1,2 and such that N,N_1',N_2' are disjoint.

Then $\underline{\text{Comm}}_{(t_1,t_2)}(N) := N'$ where

$S_{N'} := S_N \cup S'_1 \cup S'_2$; $T_{N'} := T_N \cup T'_1 \cup T'_2 \cup \{t_o\}$ where t_o is disjoint from N, N'_1, N'_2

$F_{N'} := F_N \cup F'_1 \cup F'_2 \cup ({}^\bullet t_1 \cup {}^\bullet t_2) \times \{t_o\} \cup \{t_0\} \times ({}^\circ N'_1 \cup {}^\circ N'_2)$; $\ell_{N'} := \ell_N \cup \ell'_1 \cup \ell'_2 \cup \{(t_o,\tau)\}$.

(N' is actually an arbitrary representative of an isomorphism class. Our uses of Comm will be such that this arbitrariness is harmless.)

The effect of this operation corresponds to the intuition of CCS communication. The partners may choose to synchronise or they may proceed autonomously. In each case, we wish to represent all further possibilities of behaviour. Hence after the communication everything that was possible after the autonomous actions can happen as well.

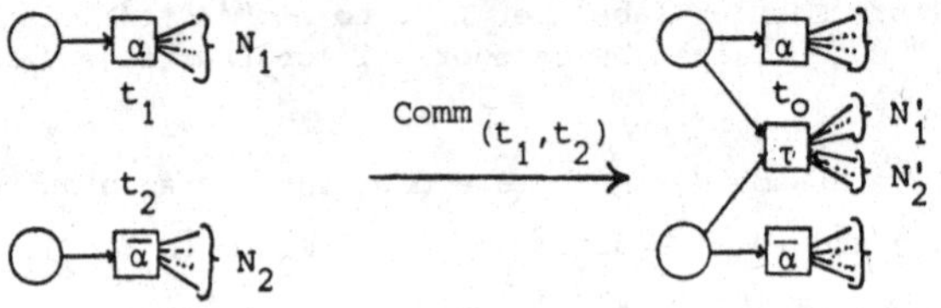

We now use this operation to define a "|"-operator for elements of $\underline{\text{Occ}}$ which puts its two operands in parallel and introduces all new possibilities for communication.

(7) (i) Let N, N' be disjoint finite occurrence nets. We define $N|N'$ inductively by:

Let $N_1 := N \cup N'$. Now assume $N_i = (S,T,F,\ell)$ is defined.

Let $C_i := \{(t,t')_j \mid 1 \le j \le n\}$ be the finite set of unordered pairs $(t,t') \in T^2$ with

(a) $\text{depth}(t) = i$, $\text{depth}(t') \le i$ (b) $\ell(t) = \overline{\ell(t')}$

(c) $\exists s \in {}^\circ N, \exists s' \in {}^\circ N', s \le_{N_i} t \wedge s' \le_{N_i} t'$ (d) $t\ \underline{\text{co}}\ t'$ in N_i.

Then $N_{i+1} := \underline{\text{Comm}}_{(t,t')_n} \circ \dots \circ \underline{\text{Comm}}_{(t,t')_1}(N_i)$.

Now $N|N' := \bigcup_{i \in \omega} N_i$.

(ii) Let $[N_1],[N_2] \in \underline{\text{Occ}}$. Then, for i=1,2, there exist chains $N_{i1} \le N_{i2} \le \dots$ with N_{ij} finite, $N_{1j} \cap N_{2j} = \emptyset$ for all j and $[N_i] = \bigcup_{j \in \omega} [N_{ij}]$.

Then $[N_1] | [N_2] := \bigcup_{j \in \omega} [N_{1j} | N_{2j}]$.

Due to the monotonicity of "|" on finite nets (see later) $N_{1j}|N_{2j}$ yields a cha

Note that this definition of $N|N'$ only introduces communications between N and N'. It does not introduce possible communications within N or N' since these will have already been inserted by our inductive translation process (see section 4.2). In section 5.1 we will use a monadic $\underline{\text{Comm}}$ operation on nets which introduces all possible communications in one step.

As an example, consider the CCS program $b \Leftarrow \alpha.b$ $\underline{\text{in}}$ $b|\overline{\alpha}.\text{NIL}$. The operands to the "|"-operator are the nets N and N' given by

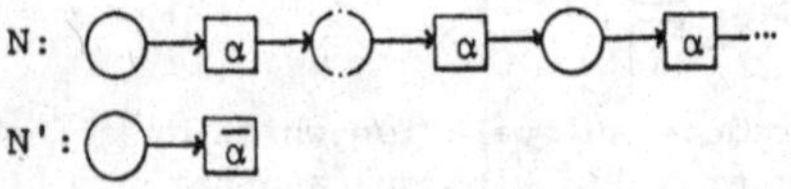

$N | N'$ is shown in section 4.2, example 3.

This definition of a communication operator on occurrence nets is not restricted to CCS. By changing condition (i) (c) accordingly, it may be generalised to introduce synchronisations described by the synchronisation algebras of /Wi1/.

roposition "+" and "|" are commutative and associative operations on Occ and both have ave identity $\emptyset$.

e conclude this section be showing that the operations on nets we have defined are ontinuous with respect to the $\leq$ ordering on Occ. This, together with the existence f a least element, is sufficient to ensure the well-definedness of recursive definitions equired by the translation process.

roposition The operations $\alpha.[N]$, $[N]+[N']$, $[N]|[N']$, $[N]\setminus A$, $[N]\{\theta\}$ are continuous in N] and [N'].

.2 The translation definition

his section gives the translation of CCS programs into members of Occ. It is given by mapping $\mathcal{O}$: CCS → Occ which can be understood either as a translation scheme or as an lternative semantic definition of CCS with net theory as the meta-language. To do this e require the notion of environment (ranged over by ρ) Env := BId → Occ where BId is he set of CCS behaviour identifiers. Environments give the net associated with the ossibly recursive behaviour name b. We define an auxiliary semantic function

$$\mathcal{E}: \text{CCS-Term} \rightarrow \text{Env} \rightarrow \text{Occ}$$

$$\mathcal{E}[\![\text{NIL}]\!]\rho = \emptyset$$

$$\mathcal{E}[\![\nu.B]\!]\rho = \nu.\mathcal{E}[\![B]\!]\rho$$

$$\mathcal{E}[\![B+B']\!]\rho = \mathcal{E}[\![B]\!]\rho + \mathcal{E}[\![B']\!]\rho$$

$$\mathcal{E}[\![B|B']\!]\rho = \mathcal{E}[\![B]\!]\rho \mid \mathcal{E}[\![B']\!]\rho$$

$$\mathcal{E}[\![B\{\theta\}]\!]\rho = (\mathcal{E}[\![B]\!]\rho)\{\theta\}$$

$$\mathcal{E}[\![B\setminus\alpha]\!]\rho = (\mathcal{E}[\![B]\!]\rho)\setminus\alpha$$

$$\mathcal{E}[\![b]\!]\rho = \rho(b)$$

nd then define

$$\mathcal{O}: \text{CCS} \rightarrow \text{Occ}$$

$$\mathcal{O}[\![b_1 \Leftarrow B_1 \ldots b_n \Leftarrow B_n \ \underline{\text{in}}\ B_o]\!] = \mathcal{E}[\![B_o]\!]\rho_o$$

$$\underline{\text{where}}\quad \rho_o = \underline{\text{fix}}(\lambda\rho.\lambda b_i.\mathcal{E}[\![B_i]\!]\rho)$$

r, less formally, $\underline{\text{whererec}}\ \ \rho_o(b_i) = \mathcal{E}[\![B_i]\!]\rho_o$.

xamples:

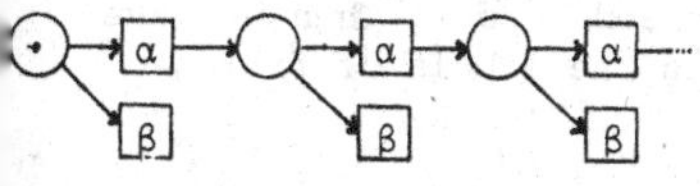

1: b ⇐ α.b + β.NIL in b

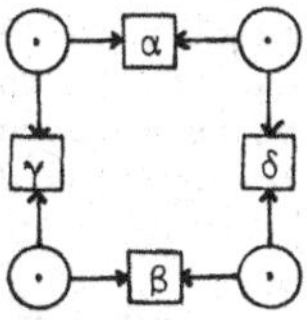

2: b ⇐ α.NIL | β.NIL in b+(γ.NIL | δ.NIL)

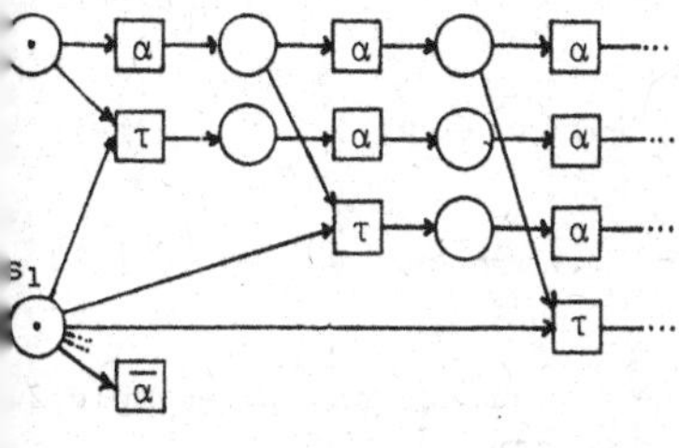

3: b ⇐ α.b in b | $\overline{\alpha}$.NIL

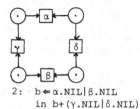

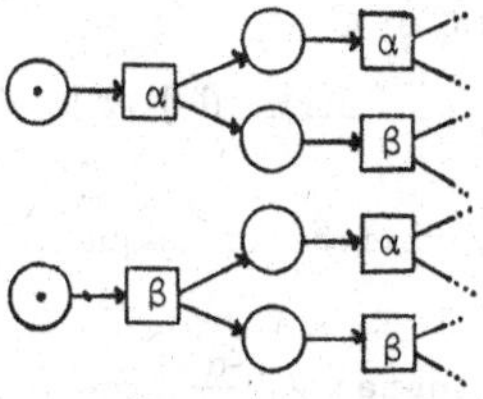

4: b ⇐ α.b | β.b in b

Examples 1 and 2 show how the non-determinism introduced by "+" is represented as branched places. The second one shows how "+" on nets works for a more complicated example. Considering example 3, we see how the implicit non-determinism in CCS, introduced by communication possibilities, is also represented by branched places. Example 4 shows a behaviour which we consider as concurrent but deterministic. Furthermore it exhibits the generation of unbounded parallelism in CCS. (We emphasise the initial places of the nets by marking them with tokens.)

The possible computations of a CCS program may be represented by certain left closed subnets of its occurrence net translation. These subnets contain only unbranched places, as non-deterministic choices are resolved during computations. For example two possible computations of example 3 are shown below.

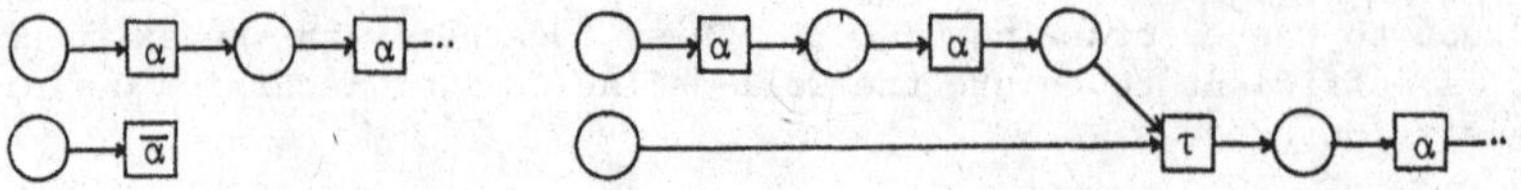

Deterministic systems may be characterised by having exactly one (maximal) computation (e.g. example 4, the occurrence net translation represents the only possible computation). This notion of computation is for example useful for considering fairness. In /GM2/, the relationship between <u>unfoldings</u> of marked nets yielding occurrence nets and their <u>processes</u> (computations of marked nets, based on place-unbranched nets) is investigated. It turns out that this relationship corresponds to that of linear time and branching time semantics /Ba/.

4.3 Semantic equivalence of CCS programs and their translations

In this section, we justify the translation given in the previous section by showing that the sequentialised behaviour of the resulting occurrence nets corresponds exactly to the operational semantics of CCS programs. /Mi/ defines the semantics of CCS in terms of a derivation relation $B \xrightarrow{\nu} B'$ on CCS terms. These have an implicit dependence on the environment of definitions, $D = (b_1 \Leftarrow B_1 \ldots b_n \Leftarrow B_n)$. For our purposes we need to make this dependence explicit and define a derivation relation on CCS programs $P = (D\ \underline{\text{in}}\ B)$, $P' = (D'\ \underline{\text{in}}\ B')$ by

$$P \xrightarrow{\nu} P' \quad \text{iff} \quad B \xrightarrow{\nu} B' \quad \text{and} \quad D = D'$$

where "=" is textual equality on definitions.

We now introduce a derivation relation for occurrence nets which describes their behaviour.

<u>Definition</u> Let N be an occurrence net, $G \subseteq ({}^{\circ}N)^{\bullet}$, $G \neq \emptyset$, with $\forall t_1, t_2 \in G : t_1\ \underline{co}\ t_2$

Then $N \xrightarrow{G} N'$ iff $N' = N \restriction X$ where $X = (S_N \cup T_N) \setminus \{x \in N \mid \exists y \in G \text{ with } x \leq y \text{ or } x \# y\}$.

For $t \in T_N$, we abbreviate $N \xrightarrow{\{t\}} N'$ by $N \xrightarrow{t} N'$.

Clearly such derivations describe the firing of a set of concurrent transitions G . The future behaviour of the net after such a step is reprsented by the resulting occurrence net. If we restrict ourselves to one-elementary steps, that is $|G| = 1$, then such derivation sequences correspond exactly to the usual firing rule (putting tokens on the initial places of the occurrence net). This imposes an interleaving semantics on the net by forcing the transitions to occur in some order. Then we have a direct equivalence of CCS and net semantics by considering the labels of firing transitions.

<u>Definition</u> Let $[N] \in \underline{Occ}$. $[N] \xrightarrow{\nu} [N']$ iff $\exists N'' \in [N'], \exists t$ with $N \xrightarrow{t} N''$ and $\ell_N(t) = \nu$

<u>Theorem</u> Let $P, P' \in \underline{CCS}$, $[N] \in \underline{Occ}$,

(i) $P \xrightarrow{\nu} P' \Rightarrow \mathcal{O}[\![P]\!] \xrightarrow{\nu} \mathcal{O}[\![P']\!]$

(ii) $\mathcal{O}[\![P]\!] \xrightarrow{\nu} [N] \Rightarrow \exists P'' \in \underline{CCS}$ with $\mathcal{O}[\![P'']\!] = [N]$ and $P \xrightarrow{\nu} P''$.

<u>Corollary</u> Hence, for any $P \in \underline{CCS}$, derivation sequences $\xrightarrow{\nu_1} \ldots \xrightarrow{\nu_n}$ of P and $\mathcal{O}[\![P]\!]$ correspond.

<u>Remark:</u> The derivation relation instance $\xrightarrow{\alpha}$ reduces the occurrence net in example 2 into the net 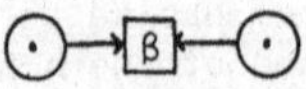 rather than the 'expected' 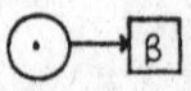 for $NIL \mid \beta.NIL$.

This explains why we defined Occ based on the equivalence relation $\cong$.

5. Folding, or finite net representations

So far we have concerned ourselves with giving a net semantics for CCS in terms of occurrence nets. However, it would be more useful to have a representation of CCS programs as finite marked nets whose behaviours (unfoldings) correspond to such occurrence nets. Let us turn again to the examples of section 4.2. The net corresponding to the simple program in example 3 has a complicated structure (e.g. place s_1 is infinitely branching) and is difficult to draw or understand. We could remark that this net is complicated because the implicit non-determinism in CCS is complicated but this is avoiding the issue. Moreover the nets 1,3,4 can indeed be represented by the simpler marked nets below.

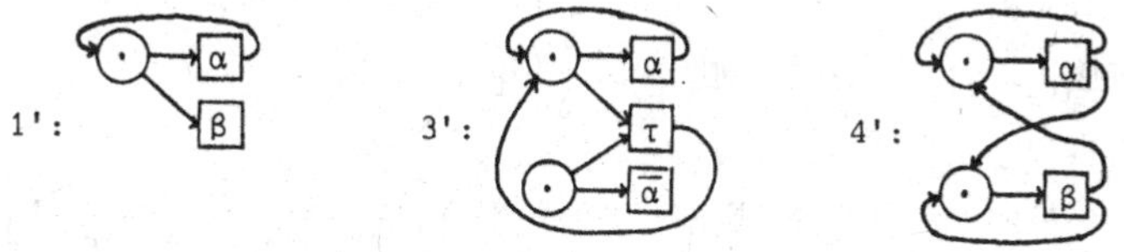

The unfoldings of these nets are precisely the occurrence nets of section 4.2. So, the problem is to determine a finite marked net representation of a CCS program. A more general problem is to fold a given (labelled) occurrence net into a finite net, thereby inverting the unfolding operation. Unfortunately, these problems are insoluble in general since CCS (and hence its occurrence net behaviours) is Turing powerful, whereas finite marked nets are not. As a specific example consider a counter (this solves /Mi, ex 4.2/) given by:

$$c \Leftarrow \iota.(c\{\beta/\alpha\} \mid \beta.c)\setminus\beta + \delta.\bar{\alpha}.NIL$$
$$z \Leftarrow \iota.(c\{\beta/\alpha\} \mid \beta.z)\setminus\beta + \zeta.z$$
$$\text{in} \quad z.$$

This counter has actions ι (increment, always possible), δ (decrement, possible iff count > 0) and ζ (zero test, possible iff count = 0). Such a behaviour cannot be represented as a finite marked net (N,M) since this would require an infinity of markings M_i, $i<\omega$, representing counter states. Moreover, we need $M_i \not\leq M_j$ $\forall i \neq j$ where $\leq$ is pointwise ordering on markings (because $M \leq M'$ means than (N,M') has all the behaviour possibilities of (N,M)). This is impossible since $\mathbb{N}^n$ has nc infinite set of pairwise incomparable vectors.

This power of CCS arises from the fact that recursive use of the $B\setminus\alpha$ operator creates a new 'private' action (relabelled with $B\{\theta\}$) which can be used to store information. We will now show that a subset of CCS (powerful enough for many applications) can be represented by finite nets in a precise sense. For this it is useful to first characterise the translation in an alternative manner.

5.1 Alternative characterisation of $\mathcal{O}[\![P]\!]$

This section develops an alternative 'two-pass' version $\mathcal{O}'$ of the translation function $\mathcal{O}$ defined in section 4.2. We can think of the translation generated by $\mathcal{O}'$ as an occurrence net in which communication possibilities are merely indicated by appearances of complementary labels. This is similar to the way CCS programs specify communication possibilities and results in more manageable nets.

To do this we introduce new semantic functions $\mathcal{O}'$ and $\mathcal{E}'$ with functionalities and definitions as for $\mathcal{O}$ and $\mathcal{E}$ in section 4.2 but with the label set L now $\Lambda \cup \Omega \cup \{\tau\}$ and with the following replacements: (the full version formalises them)

$$\mathcal{E}'[\![B \mid B']\!]\rho = \mathcal{E}'[\![B]\!]\rho \uplus \mathcal{E}'[\![B']\!]\rho$$

$$\mathcal{E}'[\![B\setminus\alpha]\!]\rho = (\mathcal{E}'[\![B]\!]\rho)\{\omega/\alpha\} \quad \text{where } \omega \in \Omega \text{ is a 'new' label name.}$$

The desire to introduce communication after translation by $\mathcal{O}'$ means that we have to use the label names in Ω to retain the identities of the restricted labels $\setminus\alpha$.

We now introduce a monadic form, Comm(N), of the "|"-operator on Occ from section 4. This has the effect of implementing the communication left implicit in $\mathcal{O}'[\![P]\!]$, and is defined in terms of $\underline{\text{Comm}}_{(t_1,t_2)}$ from section 4.1.

Definition

(i) Let N be a finite occurrence net. We define Comm(N) inductively by:

Let $N_1 := N$. Now assume $N_i := (S,T;F,\ell)$ is defined

Let $C_i := \{(t,t')_j \mid 1 \leq j \leq n\}$ be the finite set of unordered pairs $(t,t') \in T^2$ with

(a) $\text{depth}(t) = i$, $\text{depth}(t') \leq i$; (b) $\ell(t) = \overline{\ell(t')}$

(c) t $\underline{co}$ t' in N_i

Then $N_{i+1} := \underline{\text{Comm}}_{(t,t')_n} \circ \ldots \circ \underline{\text{Comm}}_{(t,t')_1}(N_i)$.

Now $\underline{\text{Comm}}(N) := \bigcup_{i \in \omega} N_i$.

(ii) Let $[N] \in \underline{\text{Occ}}$. Then there exist $N_1 \leq N_2 \leq \ldots$ with N_j finite and $[N] = \bigcup_{j \in \omega} [N_j]$.

Now $\underline{\text{Comm}}([N]) := \bigcup_{j \in \omega} [\underline{\text{Comm}}(N_j)]$.

We now show that $\mathcal{O}$ and $\mathcal{O}'$ are closely related in the sense that we obtain $\mathcal{O}'$ from $\mathcal{O}$ by introducing the possible communications (and forgetting the ω-transitions).

Proposition $\underline{\text{Comm}}(\mathcal{O}'[\![P]\!]) \setminus \Omega = \mathcal{O}[\![P]\!]$.

5.2 Translation to finite nets

This section uses the (apparently) more regular structure of $\mathcal{O}'[\![P]\!]$ to derive finite marked nets by quotienting. A direct construction is also possible, but we prefer the two stage construction. For the reasons of section 5 we will disallow the $B\{\theta\}$ and $B\setminus\alpha$ forms of CCS term for the rest of this section. (Actually, provided θ only acts on finitely many action names, we can easily incorporate the former too.)

Another restriction we will make, although this time it entails no loss of expressibilit is to only consider totally-guarded CCS programs (see section 2). Consider the program $P = b \Leftarrow \alpha.b$ in $b + \beta.\text{NIL}$. This gives an occurrence net as shown below together with its smallest folding and an incorrect folding.

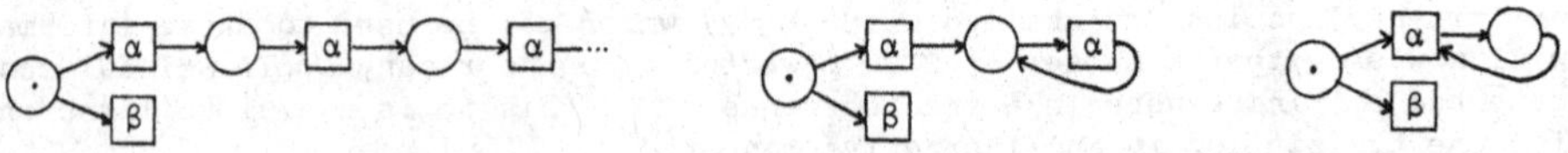

The point to notice is that the correct folding has two α transitions whereas the program only has one explicitly indicated. However, the totally-guarded version of P, $b \Leftarrow \alpha.b$ in $\alpha.b + \beta.\text{NIL}$, has two textual occurrences of α which we can use in the folding process.

The intuition behind the generation of finite nets is that we translate the terms B_i in the program $b_1 \Leftarrow B_1 \ldots b_n \Leftarrow B_n$ in B_o by translating them separately in an environment where each b_j is bound to NIL. The n+1 resulting nets are cross-connected by introducing an arc from the transition preceeding each reference to b_j (these are unique by total-guardedness) to each of the initial places of the translation of B_j.

Formally, we change the definition of $\mathcal{O}'$ so that each place or transition introduced by the translation is additionally labelled with a textual position (these represent loci of control") within the CCS program being translated.

efinition For $P \in \underline{CCS}$, $N[\![P]\!]$ is the normal form representative (well defined up o isomorphism) of $\mathcal{O}'[\![P]\!]$, labelled additionally with textual positions as described bove.

t is necessary to use normal form representatives to ensure that the net is regular nough to fold.

efinition For $P \in \underline{CCS}$, let $N = N[\![P]\!]$. We define $M[\![P]\!]$ to be the quotient marked et $N/R := ((S,T;F,\ell),M)$ defined by

$$S := S_N/R;\quad T := T_N/R;\quad \ell[x] := \ell_N(x);$$

$$F([x],[y]) := 1 \text{ if } \exists x' \in [x],\ y' \in [y] \text{ such that } x'F_N y' ,$$
$$:= 0 \text{ otherwise}$$

$$M([x]) := 1 \text{ if } \exists x' \in [x] \text{ such that } {}^{\bullet}x' = \emptyset ,$$
$$:= 0 \text{ otherwise}$$

here xRy iff x and y have the same position label in N nd [ ] indicate equivalence classes of R .

e now show that the finite marked net $M[\![P]\!]$ we obtain has exactly the same dynamic ehaviour as $\mathcal{O}'[\![P]\!]$. (Recall $[N[\![P]\!]] = \mathcal{O}'[\![P]\!]$.)

roposition $M[\![P]\!]$ is finite and $U(M[\![P]\!]) = N[\![P]\!]$.

ext, we define a communication operation, MComm, on folded marked nets.

efinition Let (N,M) be a marked net. Let C be the set of all unordered pairs $(t,t') \in T_N \times T_N$ with $\ell_N(t) = \overline{\ell_N(t')}$.

Then let $\underline{MComm}(N,M) := (N',M)$ where $S_{N'} := S_N$, $T_{N'} := T_N \uplus C$, $\ell_{N'} := \ell_N \cup C\times\{\tau\}$,

for $(t,t') \in C$, $s \in S_N$, $F_{N'}(s,(t,t')) = F_N(s,t) + F_N(s,t')$,

$F_{N'}((t,t'),s) = F_N(t,s) + F_N(t',s)$,

for all $x,y \in N$, $F_{N'}(x,y) = F_N(x,y)$.

ence MComm introduces, for every pair of transitions t,t' with complementary labels, n additional transition labelled τ . Its pre- and postsets correspond to ${}^{\bullet}t \cup {}^{\bullet}t'$ nd $t^{\bullet} \cup t'^{\bullet}$ (taking the sums of the respective arc-weights). Note that this definition oes "no copying" of the "nets behind t and t' ".

xample: (showing also how arc-weights are introduced)

et $P = (b \Leftarrow \alpha.b + \bar{\alpha}.b \ \underline{in}\ \beta.b \mid \gamma.b)$

$M[\![P]\!]$

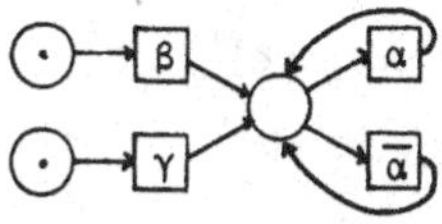

$\underline{MComm}(M[\![P]\!])$

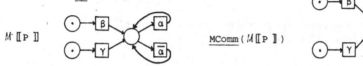

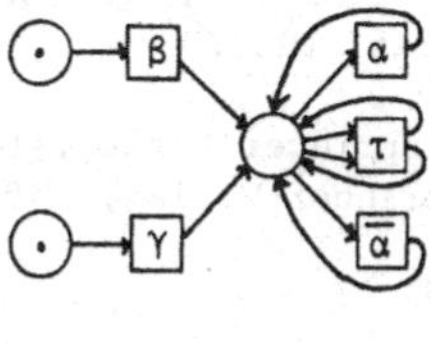

e are now able to relate our finite net translation to $\mathcal{O}$ of section 4.2 which gave possibly infinite) occurrence nets, by showing that they are related by the notion of nfolding from section 3.

roposition For $P \in \underline{CCS}$, totally-guarded and not containing $B\{\theta\}$ or $B\setminus\alpha$,

(i) $U(\underline{MComm}(M[\![P]\!])) = \underline{Comm}(U(M[\![P]\!])) \in \mathcal{O}[\![P]\!]$,

(ii) $\underline{MComm}(M[\![P]\!])$ is finite.

hus $\mathrm{MComm}(M[\![P]\!])$ is a finite marked net whose (sequentialised) behaviour is that of P.

Conclusions

A natural continuation of the work is to extend it to value-passing CCS using the notion of individual (or distinct) tokens /GS/. Further, an interesting problem is to characterise exactly the subset of CCS which is expressible as finite marked nets. This is related to the problem of determining those occurrence nets which may be folded into finite marked nets thereby partially inverting the unfolding process.

Acknowledgements

We are grateful to our institutions for enabling us to work together. Several people have contributed to this work with discussion and helpful criticism. In particular we would like to thank Mogens Nielsen, Wolfgang Reisig, Glynn Winskel and the ICALP referees for their valuable suggestions.

References

/Ab/ Abramsky, S. Eliminating local non-determinism: a new semantics for CCS. Report 290, Computer systems laboratory, Queen Mary College, London, 1981.

/Ba/ de Bakker, et al. Linear time and branching time semantics for recursion with merge. LNCS 154: Proceedings 10th ICALP, Barcelona, 1983.

/Br/ Brauer, W. (ed) Net theory and applications. LNCS 84: Proceedings of the advanced course on net theory and applications, Hamburg, 1980.

/Ci1/ de Cindio, et al. Superposed automata nets. IF 52: Selected papers from the 1st and 2nd european workshop on applications and theory of Petri nets, 1982.

/Ci2/ de Cindio, et al. Milner's CCS and Petri nets. IF 66: Selected papers from the 3rd european workshop of applications and theory of Petri nets, 1983.

/GM1/ Goltz, U., Mycroft, A. On the relationship of CCS and Petri nets. Research report, Inst. för informationsbehandling, Chalmers TH, Göteborg, 1984.

/GM2/ Goltz, U., Mycroft, A. Net behaviour representations and equivalence notions. Submitted to 4th european workshop on applications and theory of Petri nets, 1984.

/GS/ Genrich, H.J., Stankiewicz-Wiechno, E. A dictionary of some basic notions of net theory. In /Br/.

/Mi/ Milner, R. A calculus of communicating systems. LNCS 92, 1980.

/NPW/ Nielsen, M., Plotkin, G.D., Winskel, G. Petri nets, event structures and domains. Theoretical Computer Science 13(1) 1981.

/Re1/ Reisig, W. Petrinetze - eine einführung. Springer-Verlag, 1982. (To appear in english.)

/Re2/ Reisig, W. Partial order semantics versus interleaving semantics for CSP-like languages and its impact on fairness. LNCS: Proceedings 11th ICALP, Antwerp, 1984 (This volume.)

/Wi1/ Winskel, G. Event structure semantics for CCS and related languages. DAIMI report PB-159, Århus University. Shorter version in LNCS 140: Proceedings 9th ICALP, 1982.

/Wi2/ Winskel, G. A new definition of morphism on Petri nets. LNCS: Proceedings 1st symposium on theoretical aspects of computer science, Paris, 1984.

[LNCS = Springer-Verlag, lecture notes in computer science]
[IF = Springer-Verlag, informatik fachberichte]

COMMUNICATING FINITE STATE MACHINES WITH PRIORITY CHANNELS

M. G. Gouda and L. E. Rosier

Department of Computer Sciences
University of Texas at Austin

Abstract

Consider a network of two communicating finite state machines which exchange messages over two one-directional, unbounded channels, and assume that each machine receives the messages from its input channel based on some fixed (partial) priority relation. We address the problem of whether the communication of such a network is deadlock-free and bounded. We show that the problem is undecidable if the two machines exchange two types of messages. The problem is also undecidable if the two machines exchange three types of messages, and one of the channels is known to be bounded. However, if the two machines exchange two (or less) types of messages, and one channel is known to be bounded, then the problem becomes decidable. The problem is also decidable if one machine sends one type of message and the second machine sends two (or less) types of messages; the problem becomes undecidable if the second machine sends three types of messages. The problem is also decidable if the message priority relation is empty. We also address the problem of whether there is a message priority relation such that the priority network behaves like a FIFO network. We show that the problem is undecidable in general, and present some special cases for which the problem becomes decidable.

1. Introduction

Networks of communicating finite state machines have proven extremely useful in the modeling [4], analysis [1,2,22], and synthesis [13,24] of communication protocols and distributed systems. However, most previous work (c.f. [1-4,13,17,22-24]) has focused on FIFO networks, i.e. networks where each machine receives the messages from its input channel based on the well known First-In-First-Out discipline. In this paper, we consider instead priority networks where messages are received based on a fixed, partial-ordered priority relation. There are two practical reasons to consider this class of networks:

i. In a number of existing communication protocols and distributed systems, messages are actually received based on a fixed priority relation rather than a FIFO discipline. (For example, INTERRUPT messages have a higher priority over sequenced messages in the packet layer of X.25 [20].) It is more appropriate to model and analyze such systems using priority networks than FIFO networks.

ii. In many cases, it is possible to select some fixed priority relation such that the resulting priority network behaves like a FIFO network. (See Section 7.)

In this paper, we consider a network of two communicating finite state machines that exchange messages over two unbounded, one-directional channels. Each machine has a finite number of states (called nodes) and state transitions (called edges). Each state transition of a machine is accompanied by either sending one message to the output channel of the machine or receiving one message from the input channel of the machine. (Formal definitions are presented later.)

An example of a priority network is shown in Figure 1. It consists of two machines, machine M is called the requestor and machine N is called the responder. The requestor continuously sends a request message and receives a reply message. There are two types of requests, "regular" and "urgent"(denoted g_1 and g_2 respectively in Figure 1), and two types of replies, "regular" and "urgent" (denoted g'_1 and g'_2 respectively in Figure 1). After the requestor sends a g_1 message, it waits to receive a g'_1 message; however it can also send a g_2 message in which case it must first

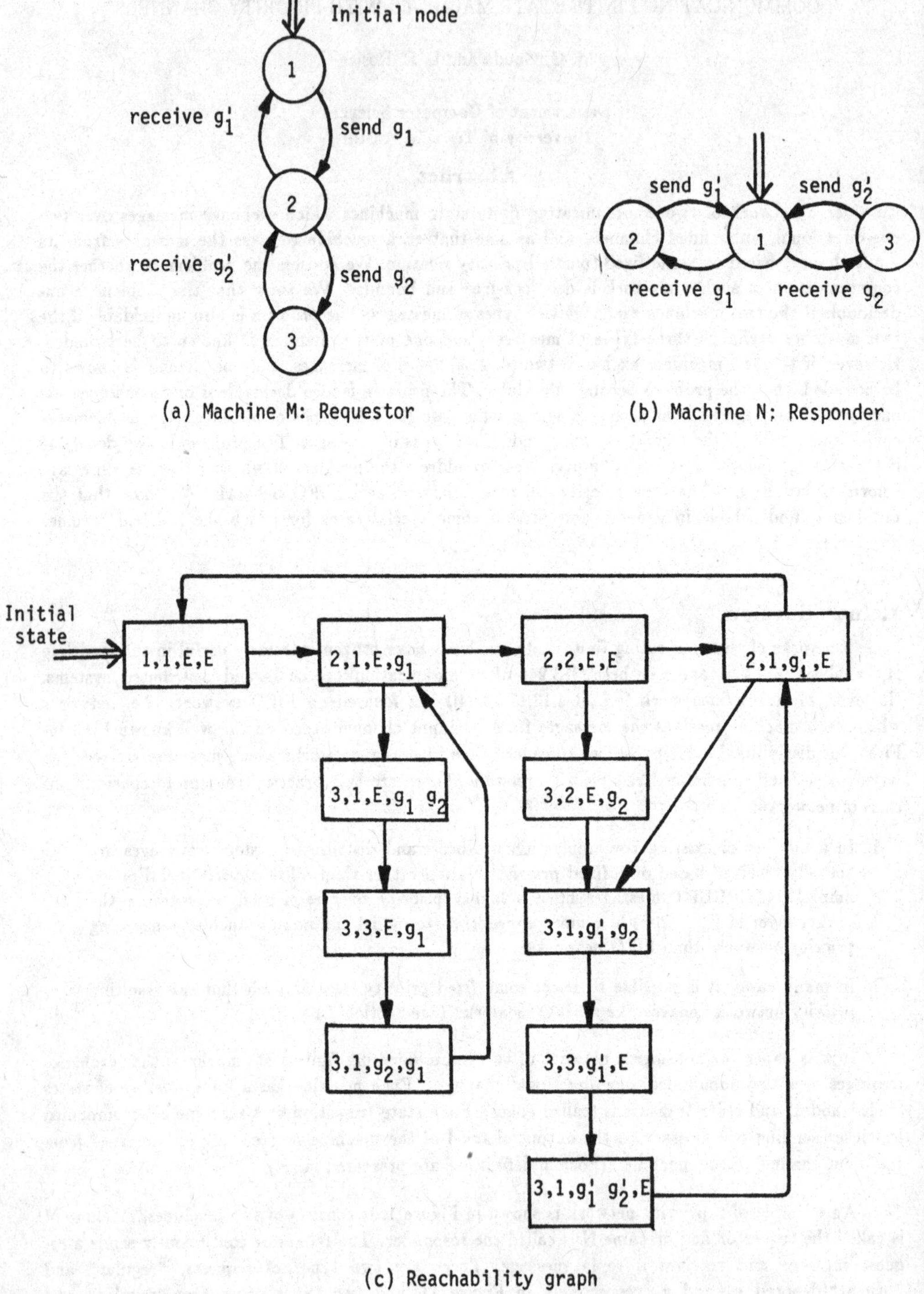

(a) Machine M: Requestor

(b) Machine N: Responder

(c) Reachability graph

Figure 1 A priority network example

receive the corresponding g'_2 message before receiving the g'_1 message. This implies that g_2 and g'_2 have higher priorities than g_1 and g'_1 respectively. Figure 1c shows the "state reachability graph" of the network. Each node in this graph corresponds to one reachable state of the network, and is labelled by a four-tuple: The first (second) component refers to a node in machine M (N), and the third (fourth) component refers to the contents of the input channel of machine M(N), where E denotes the empty channel. Notice that the only next state after $[3,1,E,g_1g_2]$ is $[3,3,E,g_1]$, and not $[3,2,E,g_2]$; this is because g_2 has a higher priority than g_1.

This model is equivalent, in computational power, to certain classes of extended Petri nets, in particular those with coloured or priority tokens [6,15]. However, the model presented here is more concise (since the channels and their contents are not modeled explicitly), and so is more convenient to use in modeling communication protocols and distributed systems.

Our results focus on the problem of whether the communication of a priority network is deadlock-free (i.e. the network can never reach a state after which no further progress is possible), and/or bounded (i.e. the number of reachable states is finite). We provide decidability/undecidablility results for these problems with respect to restricted classes of priority networks. We consider restrictions on the number of allowed message types and the size of the priority relation. We also examine the case where one of the two channels is known to be bounded. The results presented here define sharp boundaries between the decidable and undecidable cases. They also depart considerably from similar results in the literature concerning FIFO networks[2,17].

Most of the proofs have been omitted in this shortened paper. An interested reader can find these proofs and some examples in [5]. The paper is organized as follows. In Section 2, the model of priority networks is presented formally. In Section 3, we show that the problem of detecting deadlocks and unboundedness is undecidable even if the machines exchange only two types of messages. We also consider the case where one of the two channels is known to be bounded, and show that three types of messages can make the problem undecidable in this case. (This problem is decidable in the case of FIFO networks[2].) Then in Section 4, we show that the same problem becomes decidable if only two types of messages are allowed. In Section 5, we consider the case of one of the two machines sending one type of message. We show that the problem is undecidable if the other machine sends three or more types of messages, and is decidable if the other machine sends two or less types of messages. (Both problems are decidable in the case of FIFO networks[17].) However, the latter result can be generalized to the case of three or more messages, if only two message types are mentioned in the priority relation. In Section 6, we examine the simplification (or reduction) of the message priority relation. In particular, we argue that if the message priority is reduced, and if the network after the reduction is deadlock-free and bounded, then the network before the reduction is also deadlock-free and bounded. Moreover, if the priority is reduced to the limit (i.e. all messages are received on a random basis), then the problems of detecting deadlocks and/or unboundedness are reduced to the reachability and unboundedness problems of vector addition systems [10-12,18], and so are decidable. In Section 7, we discuss how to select the message priority relation such that the priority network behaves like a FIFO network.

2. Priority Networks

A *message system* is an ordered pair $(G,\prec)$, where G is a finite, nonempty set of *messages*, and $\prec$ is a partial order over G called the *message priority relation*. If two distinct messages g_1 and g_2 in G are such that (g_1,g_2) is in $\prec$, denoted by $g_1 \prec g_2$, then g_2 is said to have a *higher priority* than g_1. The number $|G|$ of the messages in set G of a message system is called the *size* of the message system.

A *communicating machine* M over a message system $(G,\prec)$ is a finite directed labelled graph with two types of edges namely *sending* and *receiving edges*. A sending (receiving) edge is labelled send(g) (receive(g)) for some message g in G. One of the nodes in M is identified as the *initial node*, and each node in M is reachable by a directed path from the initial node. For convenience, we assume that each node in M has at least one outgoing edge; outgoing edges of the same node have distinct labels. If the outgoing edges of a node are all sending (all receiving), then the node is called a *sending* (*receiving*) *node*; otherwise it is called a *mixed node*.

Let M and N be two communicating machines over the same message system $(G,\prec)$; the pair (M,N) is called a *priority network* of M and N.

A *state* of network (M,N) is a four-tuple [v,w,x,y], where v is a node in M, w is a node in N, and x and y are two multisets of messages in G. Informally, a state [v,w,x,y] of network (M,N) means that the execution of the two machines M and N has reached nodes v and w (respectively), while the input channels of M and N contain the multisets x and y (respectively) of messages.

The *initial state* of a priority network (M,N) is $[v_0,w_0,E,E]$, where v_0 is the initial node of M, w_0 is the initial node of N, and E is the empty multiset.

Let s=[v,w,x,y] be a state of a priority network (M,N), and let e be an outgoing edge of node v or w. A state s' of (M,N) is said to *follow* s *over* e iff one of the following four conditions are satisfied:

i. e is a sending edge, labelled send(g), from v to v' in M, and s'=[v',w,x,y'] where y' is obtained by adding exactly one g to y.

ii. e is a sending edge, labelled send(g), from w to w' in N, and s'=[v,w',x',y] where x' is obtained by adding exactly one g to x.

iii. e is a receiving edge, labelled receive(g), from v to v' in M, and x contains at least one g, and s'=[v',w,x',y] where x' is obtained by removing exactly one g from x, and if v has an outgoing edge labelled receive(g'), where $g \prec g'$, then x contains no g'.

iv. e is a receiving edge, labelled receive(g), from w to w' in N,and y contains at least one g, and s'=[v,w',x,y'] where y' is obtained by removing exactly one g from y, and if w has an outgoing edge labelled receive(g'), where $g \prec g'$, then y contains no g'.

The last parts of conditions iii and iv mean that messages are received in accordance with their priorities; the highest priority available message is received first. (Unrelated messages can be received in any order.)

Let s and s' be two states of a priority network (M,N); state s' is said to *follow* s iff there exists an edge e in M or N such that s' follows s over e.

Let s and s' be two states of network (M,N); state s' is *reachable from* s iff either s=s' or there exist states $s_1, s_2, \ldots, s_r$ such that $s=s_1$, $s'=s_r$, and for i=1,...,r-1, s_{i+1} follows s_i.

A state of network (M,N) is *reachable* iff it is reachable from the initial state of (M,N).

A reachable state s=[v,w,x,y] of a priority network (M,N) is called a *deadlock state* iff the following three conditions are satisfied:

i. Both v and w are receiving nodes.

ii. Either x=E (the empty multiset) or for any message g in x, there is no outgoing edge, from node v, labelled receive(g).

iii. Either y=E or for any message g in y, there is no outgoing edge, from node w, labelled receive(g).

If no reachable state of network (M,N) is a deadlock state, then the communication of (M,N) is said to be *deadlock-free*.

Let (M,N) be a priority network over (G,$\prec$). The input channel of machine M (N) is said to be *bounded* by some positive integer K iff for any reachable state [v,w,x,y] of (M,N), $|x|$ ($|y|$) $\leq$ K, where $|x|$ is the number of messages in the multiset x. The communication of a network is *bounded* by K iff each of its two channels is bounded by K. If there is no such K, then the communication of (M,N) is *unbounded*.

Given a priority network of two communicating machines, it is often required to establish that its communication is both deadlock-free and bounded. Unfortunately, the problem of whether the communication of such a network is both deadlock-free and bounded is undecidable in general as is shown in the next section.

3. Undecidable Results

In the next two sections, we consider the problem of detecting deadlocks and unboundedness for three classes of priority networks:

1. The message system is of size less than or equal two.
2. The message system is of size less than or equal two, and one of the two channels is known to be bounded.
3. The message system is of size greater than or equal three, and one of the two channels is known to be bounded.

In this section, we show that the problem is undecidable for classes 1 and 3, and in Section 4, we show that the problem is decidable for class 2. These results are interesting since they depart from the corresponding results for similar classes of FIFO networks. More specifically, the problem is decidable for classes 2 and 3 of FIFO networks, but remains undecidable for class 1 of FIFO networks [2].

Theorem 1: It is undecidable whether the communication of a class 1 priority network is both deadlock-free and bounded.

Proof: We show that any 2-counter machine T [14] (to be defined later), with no input, can be simulated by a priority network (M,N) over a message system (G,$\prec$) such that the following three conditions are satisfied:

i. $G=\{g_0,g_1\}$, and $\prec=\{g_0 \prec g_1\}$.

ii. The communication of (M,N) is deadlock-free.

iii. The communication of (M,N) is bounded by K iff the values of the two counters of T never exceed K.

Assume that there is an algorithm A to decide whether the communication of any such network is deadlock-free and bounded; then this algorithm can decide whether any 2-counter machine T halts as follows. First, construct from T a priority network which satisfies the above three conditions. Second, apply algorithm A to this network. If the answer is "yes", then (from conditions ii and iii above) T has a finite number of reachable configurations and its halting can be decided by exploring all the reachable configurations. If the answer is "no", then (from ii and iii above) T does not halt. Since it is undecidable whether any 2-counter machine halts [14], algorithm A cannot exist. It remains now to describe how to simulate any 2-counter machine by a priority network which satisfies the above three conditions; but first we define briefly 2-counter machines.

A 2-counter machine [7,14] is an offline deterministic Turing machine whose two storage tapes are semi-infinite, and whose tape alphabet contains only two symbols Z and B. The first (left-most) cells in both tapes are marked with Z symbols; all other tape cells are marked with B (for blank) symbols. Initially, each tape head scans the first cell of its tape. A nonnegative integer "i" can be stored at a tape by moving the tape head i cells to the right. Each move of the machine increments (decrements) , by one, each of the two stored numbers by moving the respective tape head one cell to the right (left). Each move of the machine depends on whether each of the two stored integers is currently greater than or equal zero. This is checked by examining the symbol in the currently scanned cell in each tape: A Z symbol indicates that the integer is zero, whereas a B symbol indicates that it is greater than zero.

Let T be a 2-counter machine; T can be simulated by a priority network (M,N) over $(G,\prec)$, where $G=\{g_0,g_1\}$ and $\prec=\{g_0\prec g_1\}$. Machine M simulates the finite control of T while N acts as an "echoer" that transmits the contents of its input channel to its output channel. At some instants, the number of g_1 messages in the network equals $2^{i}*3^{j}$ where i and j are the two integers currently stored in the counters of T. The g_0 messages are used for synchronization between M and N.

The simulation uses well known techniques from [14]. Each move of T is simulated by eight successive stages of moves executed by the two machines. Machine N executes stages 1,3,5, and 7, while machine M is waiting to receive a g_0 message. Machine M executes stages 2,4,6, and 8, while machine N is waiting to receive a g_0 message. Next, we describe these stages in more detail. (The four stages executed by N are identical; we describe only one of them namely stage 1.)

Stage 1: First M receives a g_0 message; it then receives all the g_1 messages from its input channel, and for each one, it sends one g_1 message. (N can determine that it has received the last g_1 by expecting to receive either g_0 or g_1. Since $g_0\prec g_1$, then the last of the g_1 messages has already been received when N receives g_0. This same "trick" is used in all other stages.) Finally, N sends two g_0 messages, then awaits a g_0 message via its input channel which is currently empty.

Stage 2: First M receives a g_0 message; it then receives all the g_1 messages from its input channel, and for each one, it sends one g_1 message. After this M "determines" and "remembers" whether the number of received g_1 messages in this stage is divisible by 2. Finally, M sends two g_0 messages, then awaits a g_0 message. The next stage for M is stage 4.

Stage 4: Similar to stage 2 except that M determines and remembers whether the number of g_1 messages received in this stage is divisible by 3.

Stage 6: First, M receives a g_0 message. Now, M has determined the counter contents of T and is ready to simulate the T move. If T increments (decrements) the first counter, then M sends two (one) g_1 messages for each one (two) g_1 message it receives from its input channel. This has the effect of multiplying (dividing) by 2 the number of g_1 messages in the network. Finally, M sends two g_0 messages, then awaits a g_0 message.

Stage 8: Similar to stage 6 except that the number of g_1 messages in the network is multiplied or divided by 3 depending on the move of T being simulated.

The above simulation proceeds until T reaches a halting state in which case M starts to behave like N as an "echoer", i.e. M starts to transmit the contents of its input channel to its output channel executing stages similar to stage 1. It is straightforward to show that this network satisfies the above three conditions.[]

Theorem 2: It is undecidable whether the communication of a class 3 priority network is both deadlock-free and bounded. The result holds even if the message system is of size three and the message priority relation has two elements.

Proof: As in the proof of Theorem 1, we show that any 2-counter machine T can be simulated by a priority network (M,N) over $(G,\prec)$ such that the following three conditions are satisfied:

i. $G=\{g_0,g_1,g_2\}$, $\prec=\{g_0\prec g_1,\ g_0\prec g_2\}$, and the input channel of one machine, say M, is known to be bounded.

ii. The communication of (M,N) is deadlock-free.

iii. The communication of (M,N) is bounded by 2K+6 iff the values of the two counters of T never exceed K.

Machine M simulates the finite control of T while N acts as a "source" for the new messages to be added to the input channel of M. The number of g_1 (g_2) messages in the input channel of M corresponds to the integer stored in the first (second) counter of T. The g_0 messages are used for synchronization between M and N. Each move of T is simulated by the following five steps:

i. M waits to receive either g_0 or g_1. If it receives g_0, it recognizes that the value of the first counter is zero. If it receives g_1, it recognizes that the value of the first counter is greater than zero and waits until it receives g_0.

ii. Similar to step i except that message g_2 is waited for instead of g_1.

iii. M sends a g_0 message to N.

iv. On receiving g_0, N sends back six messages, two of type g_0, two of type g_1, and two of type g_2.

v. M receives zero or two messages of each of the two types g_1 and g_2 so that it increments or decrements the value of each counter according to the simulated move of T.

The above simulation proceeds until T reaches a halting state in which case M starts to preserve the contents of its input channel fixed. So in each move M sends one message g_0 to N, then receives all the six messages sent by N. It is straightforward to show that this network satisfies the above three conditions.▯

The proofs of Theorems 1 and 2 show that the property of freedom of deadlocks and boundedness is undecidable. The same proofs also show that boundedness (by itself) is undecidable. To show that freedom of deadlocks (by itself) is undecidable, the proofs of Theorems 1 and 2 need to be modified slightly. The simulation of the 2-counter machine T proceeds as discussed before until T halts, in which case M enters a special node that has a self-loop labelled receive(g) for each message g in G. In other words, T halts iff (M,N) can reach a deadlock. This proves that freedom of deadlocks (by itself) is undecidable.

4. A Decidable Case: $|G|=2$ And One Channel Is Bounded

In this section, we show that detecting deadlocks and/or unboundedness for class 2 priority networks is decidable. For the sake of discussion in this section, let (M,N) be a class 2 priority network over $(G,\prec)$ where $G=\{g_1,g_2\}$ and $\prec=\{g_1\prec g_2\}$, and assume that the input channel of one machine, say M, is bounded by the positive integer K.

Theorem 3: It is decidable whether the communication of any class 2 priority network is both deadlock-free and bounded.□

From the proof of Theorem 3, boundedness (by itself) is decidable for class 2 priority networks. The following theorem shows that freedom of deadlocks (by itself) is also decidable for the same class.

Theorem 4: It is decidable whether the communication of any class 2 priority network is deadlock-free.□

Theorems 3 and 4 can be proven by showing that any class 2 priority network can be simulated using a 1-counter machine. In these proofs, we have assumed that the bound of the bounded channel in any class 2 priority network is known. Suppose, however, that this is not the case. In this case, the bound can be obtained by an unbounded search (by Theorem 1 this is the best we can hope for) using the simulation procedure in the proof of Theorem 4. In this procedure, if the bounded channel is not bounded by some assumed value K, then the simulating 1-counter machine can reach a state where the bounded channel has K+1 messages.

5. The Case of One Machine Sending One Type of Message

Consider a priority network (M,N) over (G,$\prec$), where one machine, say N, sends one type of message, i.e. there is a message g in G such that each sending edge in N is labelled send(g). The other machine M is assumed to send any number of message types from G. Let s_M denote the number of distinct message types sent by M. The decidability of the problem of whether the communication of any such network is both deadlock-free and bounded depends on the value of s_M:

i. If $s_M=1$, then the problem can be reduced [3,23] to the problem of "whether the reachability set of any vector addition system is finite?" which is decidable [11,12,18]. (See the next section.)

ii. If $s_M=2$, then the problem is decidable as discussed in this section.

iii. If s_M is greater than or equal 3, then the problem becomes undecidable. This can be shown using an identical proof to that of Theorem 2.

(These results for priority networks are different from the corresponding results for FIFO networks. The problem for FIFO network is always decidable, and in fact Nondeterministic Logspace Complete, regardless of the value of s_M [17].)

Theorem 5: Let (M,N) be a priority network over (G,$\prec$), and assume that M sends two types of messages g_1 and g_2, where $g_1 \prec g_2$, and that N sends one type of message. The communication of (M,N) is unbounded iff one of the following two conditions is satisfied:

A. There are two reachable states s=[v,w,x,y] and s'=[v,w,x',y'] such that the following three conditions hold:
 i. s' is reachable from s.
 ii. If state s' is reached from s via a state s"=[v",w",x",y"], then $|y"_2|>0$, where $|y"_2|$ is the number of g_2 messages in y".
 iii. Either($|x| \leq |x'|$ and $|y_1| \leq |y'_1|$ and $|y_2| < |y'_2|$),
 or ($|x| \leq |x'|$ and $|y_1| < |y'_1|$ and $|y_2| \leq |y'_2|$),
 or ($|x| < |x'|$ and $|y_1| \leq |y'_1|$ and $|y_2| \leq |y'_2|$),
 where
 $|x|$ is the number of messages in x,
 $|y_i|$ (i=1,2) is the number of g_i messages in y, and
 $|y'_i|$ (i=1,2) is the number of g_i messages in y'.

B. There are two reachable states $s=[v,w,x,y]$ and $s'=[v,w,x',y']$ such that the following three conditions hold:
  i. s' is reachable from s.
  ii. $|y_2|=|y'_2|=0$.
  iii. Either($|x|\leq|x'|$ and $|y_1|<|y'_1|$),
  or ($|x|<|x'|$ and $|y_1|\leq|y'_1|$).

Based on this theorem, it is straightforward to construct an algorithm to decide boundedness for any priority network where one machine sends one type of message and the other machine sends two types of messages. Two comments concerning this algorithm are in order:

i. The algorithm is guaranteed to terminate. This is because (from the proof of Theorem 5) every infinite path whose nodes are labelled with distinct states in tree T must reach, after a finite number of nodes, two nodes whose state labels satisfy condition A or B.

ii. The algorithm can decide boundedness; hence it can be used to decide both boundedness and freedom of deadlocks. This completes the proof for the following theorem.

Theorem 6: It is decidable whether the communication of a priority network, where one machine sends one type of message and the other machine sends two types of messages, is both deadlock-free and bounded.▯

Theorems 5 and 6 can be generalized in a straightforward fashion to the class of priority networks where one machine sends one type of message, the other machine sends an arbitrary number of message types, and the message priority relation is a singleton set. They can also be generalized to class 3 priority networks where the priority relation is a singleton set. Note that the class 3 priority network constructed in the proof of Theorem 2 is such that one machine sends one type of message and the message priority relation has two elements. Hence, this is the best that can be done.

6. Priority Reduction and the Decidability of the Random Reception Discipline

Let $(G,\prec_1)$ and $(G,\prec_2)$ be two message systems with the same set of messages. $(G,\prec_2)$ is called a *priority reduction* of $(G,\prec_1)$ iff $\prec_2$ is a subset of $\prec_1$, i.e. for any two messages g_1 and g_2 in G, if $g_1\prec_2 g_2$, then $g_1\prec_1 g_2$.

In Theorem 7 below, we show that if the priorities of a message system for some network is reduced, and if the resulting communication (after the priority reduction) is shown to be deadlock-free and bounded, then the original communication (before the reduction) is also deadlock-free and bounded.

Theorem 7: Let R_1 denote a priority network (M,N) over $(G,\prec_1)$, and R_2 denote a priority network (M,N) over $(G,\prec_2)$. Assume that $(G,\prec_2)$ is a priority reduction of $(G,\prec_1)$. If the communication of R_2 is deadlock-free and bounded, then the communication of R_1 is deadlock-free and bounded.▯

Theorem 7 is useful iff priority reduction can lead to simpler proofs for freedom of deadlocks and boundedness. From the discussion at the end of Section 5, if the priority relation is reduced to a single element, then the problem becomes decidable for priority networks where one machine sends only one type of message and for class 3 priority networks. Also, the next theorem states that if the priorities are reduced to the limit (i.e. all sent messages are of equal priorities, and so are received on a random basis), then the problem of whether the communication is both deadlock-free and bounded becomes decidable.

Theorem 8: (The Random Reception Theorem) It is decidable whether the the communication of any priority network, with empty message priority relation, is deadlock-free and/or bounded.[]

It is straightforward to show that Theorem 8 can be generalized to the case of a priority network with r communicating machines (r greater than or equal 2) provided that the message priority relation is empty.

7. Achieving the FIFO Discipline Using Priorities

From Theorem 1 (or 2), priority networks can simulate any 2-counter machine; therefore they can simulate any FIFO network. In this section, we discuss the following special type of simulation. Given two communicating machines M and N whose message labels are taken from a finite set G of messages, is there a message priority relation $\prec$ such that the priority network (M,N) over (G,$\prec$) "behaves like a FIFO network". But before we define how a priority network behaves like a FIFO network, we first need to add more structure to the concept of a state of a priority network.

As defined in Section 2, a state of a priority network is a four-tuple [v,w,x,y], where both x and y are multisets of messages. We adopt the following convention:

i. Both x and y are represented as strings of messages.

ii. When a machine M (N) sends a message g, then g is concatenated to the right hand side of y (x) yielding y.g (x.g), where "." is the string concatenation operator.

iii. When a machine M (N) receives a message g, then the left-most occurrence of g in x (y) is removed.

From i and ii, if a message g is to the left of a message g' in x or y, then g must have been sent "before" g'. This implies that the left-most message in x (y) is the current "oldest" message in x (y). From iii, whenever a machine M or N receives a message g, it must receive the oldest available copy of this message. Notice that this convention does not violate the state reachability of a priority network; it merely indicates for any reachable state [v,w,x,y], the order in which the messages in x and y have been sent.

A priority network (M,N) over (G,$\prec$) is said to *behave like a FIFO network* iff the following four conditions are satisfied for any reachable state [v,w,x,y] of the network:

i. If x=g.x' and v has an outgoing edge labelled receive(g), then v has no outgoing edge labelled receive(g') for any other message g' in x'.

ii. If y=g.y' and w has no outgoing edge labelled receive(g), then w has no outgoing edge labeled receive(g') for any other message g' in y'.

iii. If x=g.x' and v has an outgoing edge labelled receive(g), then g'$\prec$g for any other message g' in x' where v has an outgoing edge labelled receive(g').

iv. If y=g.y' and w has an outgoing edge labelled receive(g), then g'$\prec$g for any other message g' in y' where w has an outgoing edge labelled receive(g').

The question "Given M,N, and G, is there a $\prec$ such that (M,N) over (G,$\prec$) behaves like a FIFO network?" may have a positive or negative answer depending on the given M,N, and G. Unfortunately, this question is undecidable in general. A proof of this can be outlined as follows. Simulate any 2-counter machine T using a priority network (M,N) over (G,$\prec$) that behaves like a FIFO network until T reaches a halting state in which case M and N start to execute two machines whose priority network does not, for any $\prec$, behave like a FIFO network. Thus T halts iff there is no $\prec$ such that (M,N) over (G,$\prec$) behaves like a FIFO network. See [5] for more details. It remains now to describe a priority network which simulates T while behaving like a FIFO network. One such network is as follows. One machine M simulates the finite control of T while the other machine N acts as an echoer which sends back each message it receives from M. The contents of the two counters of T are usually stored in the in input channel of M as: $g_1g_1...g_1g_0g_2g_2...g_2g_0$, where the number of occurrences of g_1 (g_2) represents the contents of the first (second) counter, and each occurrence of g_0 acts as a separator between the g_1 messages and the g_2 messages. For M to simulate one move of T, it must make two complete passes on the contents of the input channel:

i. In the first pass, M receives all the messages from its input channel, one by one, and sends them without change to its output channel. (The objective of this pass is for M to decide whether the value of each counter is zero or greater than zero.) Since the echoer N returns these messages to the input channel of M, and in order to avoid mixing the returned messages with the original messages, N must change each g_1 message to a g_3 message and each g_2 message to a g_4 message; the g_0 messages remain the same.

ii. In the second pass, M receives all the messages from its input channel, one by one, and sends them, after performing the appropriate action of T, to its output channel. N returns the messages to the input channel of M after changing each g_3 to g_1, and each g_4 to g_2; the g_0 messages remain the same.

It is straightforward to show that each receiving node in M or N has exactly two outgoing edges and that one of these edges is labelled receive(g_0). Therefore by selecting the message priority relation $\prec=\{ g_0\prec g_1, g_0\prec g_2, g_0\prec g_3, g_0\prec g_4 \}$, the priority network (M,N) over (G,$\prec$) behaves like a FIFO nework. This completes the proof of the following theorem.

Theorem 9: It is undecidable whether, for any two communicating machines M and N whose message labels are taken from a set G, there exists a message priority relation $\prec$ such that (M,N) over (G,$\prec$) behaves like a FIFO network.□

There are special cases for which the above problem becomes decidable. For instance, if the communication between M and N, assuming a FIFO discipline, is bounded (i.e. the number of distinct reachable states is finite), then the problem can be decided by exploring all reachable states. This can be applied to machines M and N in Figure 6, whose communication, assuming a FIFO discipline, is bounded. The result is the message priority relation $\prec=\{ g_1\prec g_2, g_1\prec g_3, g_1\prec g_4 \}$ that makes the priority network behave like a FIFO network.

The above decidability algorithm operates on the reachable state space of the network; hence it yields exponential complexity. In some cases the decidability algorithm needs only to operate on the directed graphs of the two machines yielding polynomial complexity. One such a case is where the two communicating machines are "compatible" as defined next.

Two communicating machines M and N are called *compatible* iff the directed graphs of M and N are isomorphic as follows:

i. For every sending (receiving) node in one machine, there is a receiving (sending) node in the other machine.

ii. Neither machine has any mixed nodes.

iii. For every sending (receiving) edge labelled send(g) (receive(g)) in one machine, there is a receiving (sending) edge labelled receive(g) (send(g)) in the other machine.

If a priority network (M,N) of two compatible machines behaves like a FIFO network, then its communication is guaranteed to be deadlock-free [4]. Moreover, if each directed cycle in M or N has at least one sending and one receiving edge, then the communication is also bounded [4]. The next theorem states that it is decidable whether a priority network of compatible machines behaves like a FIFO network. The decidability algorithm (in the theorem's proof) operates on the directed graphs of the two machines yielding polynomial complexity.

Theorem 10: It is decidable whether for any two compatible machines M and N whose message labels are taken from a set G, there exists a message priority relation $\prec$ such that (M,N) over (G,$\prec$) behaves like a FIFO network.▯

8. References

1. Bochmann, G., Finite State Description of Communication Protocols, *Computer* Networks, Vol. 2, 1978, pp.361-371.

2. Brand, D. and Zafiropulo, P., On Communicating Finite-State Machines, *J. ACM*, Vol. 30, No. 2, April 1983, pp. 323-342.

3. Cunha, P. and Maibaum, T., A Synchronization Calculus for Message-Oriented Programming, *Proc. 2nd International Conf. on Distributed Computing Systems*, April 1981, pp. 433-445.

4. Gouda, M., Manning, E. and Yu, Y., On the Progress of Communication between Two Finite State Machines, University of Texas, Department of Computer Sciences, Tech. Rep. No. 200, May 1982, revised August 1983.

5. Gouda, M. and Rosier, L., Priority Networks for Communicating Finite State Machines, Technical Report TR 83-10, Dept. of Computer Sciences, Univ. of Texas at Austin, August 1983. Submitted for publication.

6. Hack, M., Decidability Questions for Petri Nets, Ph.D. dissertation, Department of Electrical Engineering, MIT, 1975.

7. Hopcroft, J. and Ullman, J., "Introduction to Automata Theory, Languages, and Computation", Addison-Wesley, Reading, Mass., 1979.

8. Ibarra, O., Reversal-Bounded Multicounter Machines and their Decision Problems, *J. ACM*, Vol. 25, No. 1, 1978, pp. 116-133.

9. Ibarra, O. and Rosier, L., On Restricted One-Counter Machines, *Math. Systems Theory*, Vol. 14, 1981, pp. 241-245.

10. Karp, R. and Miller, R., Parallel Program Schemata, *J. of Computer and System Sciences*, Vol. 3, No.2, 1969, pp.147-195.

11. Kosaraju, S., Decidability of Reachability in Vector Addition Systems, *Proc. of the 14th Annual ACM Symp. on the Theory of Computing*, 1982, pp. 267-281.

12. Mayr, E., An Algorithm for the General Petri Net Reachability Problem, *Proc. of the 13th Annual ACM Symp. on the Theory of Computing*, 1981, pp. 238-246.

13. Merlin, P. and Bochmann, G., On the Construction of Communication Protocols and Module Specification, Pub. 352, Dept. dinformatique de recherche op' erationnelle, Universit'e de Montreal, January 1980.

14. Minsky, M., "Computation: Finite and Infinite Machines", Prentice Hall, Englewood Cliffs, NJ, 1967.

15. Peterson, J., "Petri Net Theory and the Modeling of Systems", Prentice Hall, Englewood Cliffs, NJ, 1981.

16. Rackoff, C., The Covering and Boundedness Problems for Vector Addition Systems, *Theor. Comput. Sci.*, Vol. 6, 1978, pp. 223-231.

17. Rosier, L. and Gouda, M., On Deciding Progress for a Class of Communication Protocols, in *Proc. of the Eighteenth Annual Conference on Information Sciences and Systems*, Princeton Univ., 1984.

18. Sacerdote, G. and Tenney, R., The Decidability of the Reachability Problem for Vector Addition Systems, *Proc. of the 9th Annual ACM Symp. on Theory of Computing*, 1977, pp. 61-76.

19. Savitch, W., Relationships between Nondeterministic and Deterministic Tape Complexities, *J. of Computer and System Sciences*, Vol. 4, No. 2, 1970, pp. 177-192.

20. Tannenbaum, A., "Computer Networks", Prentice Hall, Englewood Cliffs, NJ, 1981.

21. Valiant, L. and Paterson, M., Deterministic One-Counter Automata, *J. of Computer and System Sciences*, Vol. 10, 1975, pp. 340-350.

22. Yu, Y. and Gouda, M., Deadlock Detection for a Class of Communicating Finite State Machines, *IEEE Trans. on Comm.*, Vol. COM-30, No. 12, December 1982, pp. 2514-2518.

23. Yu. Y. and Gouda, M., Unboundedness Detection for a Class of Communicating Finite State Machines, to appear in *Information Processing Letters*.

24. Zafiropulo, P., et. al., Towards Analyzing and Synthesizing Protocols, *IEEE Trans. on Comm.*, Vol. COM-28, No. 4, April 1980, pp. 651-661.

A MODAL CHARACTERIZATION OF OBSERVATIONAL CONGRUENCE ON FINITE TERMS OF CCS

S. Graf and J. Sifakis
IMAG - Génie Informatique
BP 68, 38402 ST Martin-d'Hères Cédex, France

ABSTRACT : We propose a translation method of finite terms of CCS into formulas of a modal language representing their class of observational congruence. For this purpose, we define a modal language and a function associating with any finite term of CCS a formula of the language, satisfied by the term. Furthermore, this function is such that two terms are congruent if and only if the corresponding formulas are equivalent. The translation method consists in associating with operations on terms (action,+) operations on the corresponding formulas.

This work is a first step towards the definition of a modal language with modalities expressing both possibility and inevitability and which is compatible with observational congruence.

I. INTRODUCTION

When a logic L is used to express program specifications it naturally induces an equivalence relation $\sim^L$ on programs : two programs PROG1 and PROG2 are equivalent if they cannot be distinguished by any formula of L, i.e. PROG1$\sim^L$PROG2 iff for any formula F of L PROG1 $\models$F and PROG2 $\models$F are equivalent.

Using a logic L as a program specification tool sets the problem of its compatibility with respect to some equivalence relation $\simeq$ derived from the operational semantics of the description language. Such a relation defines a concept of operational equivalence which is supposed to be the most suitable and satisfactory in practice for the comparison of programs Then, a minimal requirement for the adequacy of L as a specification tool is that $\simeq\subseteq\sim^L$,i.e. if two programs are operationally equivalent then they have the same (equivalent) specifications. The non-validity of this condition implies that there exists a formula F of L and two operationally equivalent programs, the one satisfying F and the other not ; thus, using F to express a property, does not allow to characterize the most general class of behaviours corresponding to this property. If in addition, L is to be used as a verification tool then it is also necessary that $\sim^L\subseteq\simeq$ i.e. if two programs cannot be distinguished by formulas of L then they are equivalent. Consequently, the adequacy of L as both a specification and a verification tool, implies that the relations $\simeq$ and

$\sim^L$ agree.

The problem of the definition of logics compatible with some operational equivalence relation has been stated in [HM], [BR], [St] where simple modal languages have been proposed to characterize observational equivalence or congruence of CCS. This paper is a first step to the definition of a modal logic compatible with observational congruence of CCS by following a different approach.

We consider a very general modal language L(A) for which labelled trees (CCS-terms) on a vocabulary A constitute a class of models and try to define a sub-language L_0 such that $\sim^{L_0}$ coincides with observational congruence in CCS. A function $|\,|$ is defined, associating with any finite term t of CCS a formula $|t|$ of L(A) such that $|t|$ is satisfied by all the terms and only the terms congruent to t, i.e. $t \models |t|$ and for t_1, t_2 arbitrary finite terms, $t_1 \approx t_2$ iff $|t_1| \equiv |t_2|$, where $\approx$ is the observational congruence. Obviously, L_0 corresponds to the sub-language of L(A) generated by the elements of the image of $|\,|$. This approach has been adopted to (hopefully) avoid limitations of the works mentioned above, concerning the definition of modalities expressing inevitability and the modal characterization of classes of infinite behaviours. However, these two problems are not discussed in this paper.

For the definition of L(A) we have been inspired from [Ko] where a very general modal language with least fixpoint operator has been introduced. In part III we first give a modal characterization of strong equivalence of CCS to get the reader familiar with the principle of translation of terms into formulas. Then, we give a translation method of finite CCS terms into formulas representing their class of observational congruence. This method consists in associating with operations on terms (action,+) operations on the corresponding formulas. Finally, we discuss about the use of these results for the definition of a sufficiently powerful language compatible with observational congruence.

II. DEFINITION OF THE MODAL LANGUAGE

We introduce as in [Ko] the modal language L(A) as the sublanguage of the closed formulas of L'(A), defined on the logical constants true, false, a set of constants A and a set of variables X as follows,

- true, false $\in$ L'(A),
- $A \cup X \subseteq$ L'(A),
- $f, f' \in$ L'(A) implies $\neg f, f \vee f' \in$ L'(A)
- $f \in$ L'(A) implies $\langle f \rangle \in$ L'(A),
- $x \in X$ and x is free in $f \in$ L'(A) implies $\mu x.f(x) \in$ L'(A).

Semantics : The class of models of L(A) is the class of the labelled trees on A, T(A). A labelled tree t is defined as $t = (Q_t, q_0, \{\overset{a}{\rightarrow}\}_{a\in A})$ where,

- Q_t is a set of states, the nodes of t,
- $q_0 \in Q_t$ is the initial state, the root of t,
- $\{\overset{a}{\rightarrow}\}_{a\in A}$ is a set of transition relations, $\overset{a}{\rightarrow} \subseteq Q_t \times Q_t$;
  as t is a tree we have $\nexists q\in Q_t\ \nexists a\in A\ q\overset{a}{\rightarrow}q_0$ and $\forall q\in Q_t,\ q\neq q_0$, q has exactly one predecessor.

We define in the usual manner a satisfaction relation

$\models \subseteq (\bigcup_{t\in T(A)} (t\times Q_t))\times L(A)$.

For a formula $f\in L(A)$ we write,

- $t,q \models f$ iff $(t,q,f)\in \models$,
- $t \models f$ iff $t,q_0 \models f$ where q_0 is the root of t,
- $\models f$ iff $t\models f\ \forall\ t\in T(A)$.

For $t\in T(A)$, $q\in Q_t$, $f,f'\in L(A)$, $g\in L'(A)$ and $a\in A$,

- $t,q \models$ true,
- $t,q \models \neg f$ iff $t,q \not\models f$,
- $t,q \models f\vee f'$ iff $t,q \models f$ or $t,q \models f'$,
- $t,q \models a$ iff $\exists q'\in Q_t\ q'\overset{a}{\rightarrow}q$,
- $t,q \models \langle f\rangle$ iff $\exists q'\in Q_t\ \exists a\in A\ (q\overset{a}{\rightarrow}q'$ and $t,q' \models f)$,
- $t,q \models \mu x.g(x)$ iff $\forall f\in L(A)\ (\models g(f)\supset f$ implies $t,q \models f)$.

The notations false, $\wedge$, $\supset$, $\equiv$ are used in the standard manner.

We use the abbreviation $[f] := \neg\langle\neg f\rangle$ i.e.

- $t,q \models [f]$ iff $\forall q'\in Q_t\ \forall a\in A\ (q\overset{a}{\rightarrow}q'$ implies $t,q' \models f)$.

Notice that each state $q\in Q_t$ in $t=(Q_t,q_0,\{\overset{a}{\rightarrow}\}_{a\in A})$ defines a subtree t_q of t, with root q and set of states the set of the states reachable from q in t. Thus, the transition relations $\overset{a}{\rightarrow}$ can be considered as relations on T(A) and one can write $t_q\overset{a}{\rightarrow}t_{q'}$, instead of $q\overset{a}{\rightarrow}q'$. In the sequel we consider the class $L\langle A\rangle$ of the formulas where any element of A is written within the scope of one of the operators $\langle\ \rangle$ or [ ]. For such formulas f we have $t,q \models f$ iff $t_q \models f$ i.e. f is true at a state q of a tree t iff f is true for the subtree t_q of t. So, we consider only the satisfaction relation $\models \in T(A)\times L\langle A\rangle$.
The following properties are used.

Properties 1

For $t\in T(A)$ and f, f_i, $i\in J$, elements of $L\langle A\rangle$,

a) $t\models \langle a\wedge f\rangle$ iff $\exists t'\in T(A)(t\overset{a}{\rightarrow}t'$ and $t'\models f)$,

b) $t \models [\bigvee_{i \in J} a_i \wedge f_i]$ iff $\forall t' \in T(\tilde{A})(t \xrightarrow{a} t'$ implies $\exists i \in J(a = a_i$ and $t' \models f_i))$,

c) $\models <f \vee f'> \equiv <f> \vee <f'>$,

d) $\models <f \wedge f'> \supset <f> \wedge <f'>$.

Other properties of L(A) can be found in [Ko] where a complete axiomatization is given for a similar logic.

In the sequel we often simply write f instead of $\models f$.

III. MODAL CHARACTERIZATION

III.1 Strong Equivalence

In order to get the reader familiar with our approach, we give a modal characterization of strong equivalence of CCS in terms of formulas of the language described in II.

Definition 1

a) Consider the set of the terms P(A) built from a constant Nil, a set of unary operators A and a binary operator +, recursively defined by,

- $Nil \in P(A)$,
- $ap \in P(A)$ for $p \in P(A)$ and $a \in A$,
- $p+p' \in P(A)$ for $p, p' \in P(A)$.

b) For $a \in A$ the relation $\xrightarrow{a} \subseteq P(A) \times P(A)$ is defined as the smallest relation satisfying,

- $ap \xrightarrow{a} p$,
- $p_1 \xrightarrow{a} p'$ implies $p_1+p_2 \xrightarrow{a} p'$,
- $p_2 \xrightarrow{a} p'$ implies $p_1+p_2 \xrightarrow{a} p'$.

So, with a term p can be associated a labelled tree $t_p = (Q_p, p, \{\xrightarrow{a}\}_{a \in A}) \in T(A)$ where Q_p is a set of subterms of p and $\xrightarrow{a}$ is the relation defined above. In the sequel we identify a term $p \in P(A)$ with the tree t_p representing it. So, if f is any formula of L<A'> where A' is isomorphic to A, then we can write $p \models f$ instead of $t_p \models f$. As there is no risk of confusion, we shall not distinguish between a unary operator a and the corresponding constant of the modal language.

Properties 2

a) $Nil \models [false]$,

b) $p \models f$ implies $ap \models <a \wedge f> \wedge [a \wedge f]$,

c) $p \models <a \wedge f>$ implies $p+p' \models <a \wedge f>$ and $p'+p \models <a \wedge f>$,

d) $p_1 \models [f_1]$ and $p_2 \models [f_2]$ implies $p_1+p_2 \models [f_1 \vee f_2]$,

e) $p+Nil \models f$ iff $p \models f$,

f) $p+p' \models [f]$ iff $p \models [f]$ and $p' \models [f]$.

In the sequel we often omit conjuction operators in order to simplify formulas.

Definition 2 (strong equivalence)

Let $\sim$ be the greatest relation on $P(A)$ such that for $p_1, p_2 \in P(A)$,

$$p_1 \sim p_2 \text{ iff } \forall a \in A\ (p_1 \overset{a}{\to} p_1' \text{ implies } \exists p_2' (p_2 \overset{a}{\to} p_2' \text{ and } p_1' \sim p_2')) \text{and}$$
$$\forall a \in A\ (p_2 \overset{a}{\to} p_2' \text{ implies } \exists p_1' (p_1 \overset{a}{\to} p_1' \text{ and } p_1' \sim p_2')).$$

It has been shown that $\sim$ is a congruence [Mi] and it can be characterized by the axioms,

(A1) $(p_1+p_2) + p_3 = p_1 + (p_2+p_3)$,

(A2) $p_1+p_2 = p_2+p_1$,

(A3) $p+p = p$,

(A4) $p+Nil = p$.

Definition 3

Consider the function $|\,| \in P(A) \to L\langle A\rangle$ recursively defined by,

- $|Nil| = false$
- $|ap| = \langle a \wedge |p|\rangle \wedge [a \wedge |p|]$
- $$|p+p'| = \begin{cases} \bigwedge_{i\in I} \langle a_i \wedge |p_i|\rangle \bigwedge_{i\in J} \langle b_i \wedge |p_i'|\rangle \wedge [\bigvee_{i\in I} a_i \wedge |p_i| \vee \bigvee_{i\in J} b_i \wedge |p_i'|] \\ \qquad \text{if } |p| = \bigwedge_{i\in I} \langle a_i \wedge |p_i|\rangle \wedge [\bigvee_{i\in I} a_i \wedge |p_i|] \text{ and} \\ \qquad\quad |p'| = \bigwedge_{i\in J} \langle b_i \wedge |p_i'|\rangle \wedge [\bigvee_{i\in J} b_i \wedge |p_i'|] \\ |p| \text{ if } |p'| = [false] \\ |p'| \text{ if } |p| = [false] \end{cases}$$

It can easily be shown that $|\,|$ is a function associating with any term p a formula $|p|$ of the general form,

$$|p| = \begin{cases} [false] \\ \bigwedge_{i\in I} \langle a_i \wedge |p_i|\rangle [\bigvee_{i\in I} a_i \wedge |p_i|] \end{cases}$$ where I is a finite set of indices.

Example 1 : Computation of $|p|$ for $p=aNil+c(aNil+bNil)$

$|aNil| = \langle a[false]\rangle[a[false]]$

$|bNil| = \langle b[false]\rangle[b[false]]$

$|aNil+bNil| = \langle a[false]\rangle\langle b[false]\rangle[a[false] \vee b[false]]$

$|c(aNil+bNil)| = \langle c|aNil+bNil|\rangle[c|aNil+bNil|]$

$|aNil+c(aNil+bNil)| = \langle a[false]\rangle\langle c|aNil+bNil|\rangle[c|aNil+bNil| \vee a[false]]$.

The following theorem shows that the formula $|p|$ corresponding to a term p characterizes the equivalence class of p.

Theorem 1

For any pair of terms p, p' of $P(A)$, $p' \models |p|$ iff $p' \sim p$.

Proof

Proving this theorem amounts to proving the following three propositions,

(P1) $p \models |p|$,

(P2) $p' \models |p|$ implies $p' \sim p$,

(P3) $p' \sim p$ implies $|p'| \equiv |p|$.

(P1) By induction on the structure of the terms of P(A).

- $Nil \models [false]$ by property 2a).
- $p \models |p|$ implies $ap \models \langle a|p|\rangle[a|p|]$ by property 2b),
  implies $ap \models |ap|$ by definition 3.
- $p \models |p|$ implies $p+Nil \models |p|$ by property 2e),
  implies $p+Nil \models |p+Nil|$ by definition 3.
- $p \models |p|$ where $|p| = \bigwedge_{i\in I}\langle a_i|p_i|\rangle[\bigvee_{i\in I} a_i|p_i|]$ and
  $p' \models |p'|$ where $|p'| = \bigwedge_{i\in J}\langle b_i\ |p'_i|\rangle[\bigvee_{i\in J} b_i|p'_i|]$ implies
  $p+p' \models \bigwedge_{i\in I}\langle a_i|p_i|\rangle \bigwedge_{i\in J}\langle b_i|p'_i|\rangle[\bigvee_{i\in I} a_i|p_i| \vee \bigvee_{i\in J} b_i|p'_i|]$ by properties 2c) and 2d) which implies $p+p' \models |p+p'|$ by definition 3.

(P2) The proof is done by induction on the structure of the formulas $|p|$.

- $p \models [false]$ implies $\nexists p' \in P(A)\ \nexists a \in A\ p \xrightarrow{a} p'$,
  implies $p \sim Nil$.
- Consider a formula $|p|$ such that $\forall p' \in P(A)\ p' \models |p|$ implies $p' \sim p$.
  Then, for any term $p_1 \in P(A)$,
  $p_1 \models |ap|$ implies $p_1 \models \langle a|p|\rangle[a|p|]$ by definition 3,
  implies $\exists p_2 (p_1 \xrightarrow{a} p_2$ and $p_2 \models |p|)$ and
  $\forall p_2\ \forall b\ (p_1 \xrightarrow{b} p_2$ implies $b=a$ and $p_2 \models |p|)$,
  implies $\exists p_2 (p_1 \xrightarrow{a} p_2$ and $p_2 \sim p)$ and
  $\forall p_2\ \forall b\ (p_1 \xrightarrow{b} p_2$ implies $b=a$ and $p_2 \sim p)$,
  implies $p_1 \sim ap$ by definition 2;
- A similar proof can be done for $|p_1+p_2|$.

(P3) It is easy to verify that || preserves the axioms (A1)-(A4), that is for any instance of an axiom of the form $p=p'$ we have $|p| \equiv |p'|$. As (A1)-(A4) is a complete axiomatization of $\sim$, we obtain the result □.

III.2 Observational Congruence

In the rest of the paper we give results characterizing the observational congruence $\approx$ of CCS. In this case the set of the terms on an alphabet A containing a special symbol τ is considered ; τ represents a hidden or unobservable action. As in the previous section we define a function $|\ | \in P(A) \to L\langle A\rangle$ associating with a term p a formula $|p|$ satisfied by all the terms observationally congruent to p. We recall below the definition and some important properties of $\approx$ given in [Mi], [HM].

Definition 4

a) For $s=s_0\ldots s_n$ a sequence of A^*, write
$p\overset{s}{\to}p'$ iff $\exists\, p_1\ldots p_n \in P(A)\ p\overset{s_0}{\to}p_1\ldots p_n\overset{s_n}{\to}p'$.

b) For s a sequence of $(A-\{\tau\})^*$, write

$$p\overset{s}{\Rightarrow}p' \text{ iff } \begin{cases} p\xrightarrow{\tau^* s_0 \tau^* \ldots s_n \tau^*} p' & \text{if } s=s_0\ldots s_n \\ p\overset{\tau^*}{\to} p' & \text{if } s=\varepsilon, \text{ the empty word of } A^* \end{cases}$$

c) The observational equivalence $\sim\, = \bigcap_{k=0}^{\infty} \sim^k$, where

- $p\sim^0 p'$ for any p, $p'\in P(A)$,
- $p\sim^{k+1}p'$ if $\forall s\in(A-\{\tau\})^*[(p\overset{s}{\Rightarrow}p_1$ implies $\exists\, p_1'(p'\overset{s}{\Rightarrow}p_1'$ and $p_1\sim^k p_1'))$ and $(p'\overset{s}{\Rightarrow}p_1'$ implies $\exists\, p_1(p\overset{s}{\Rightarrow}p_1$ and $p_1\sim^k p_1'))]$.

It has been shown that $\sim$ is an equivalence relation. Denote by $\simeq$ the greatest congruence on P(A) such that $\simeq\subseteq\sim$. The following is a complete axiomatization of $\simeq$ on the finite terms of CCS[HM] :

(A1)-(A4) as defined in III.1,
(A5) $a\tau p=ap$,
(A6) $\tau p+p=\tau p$,
(A7) $a(p_1+\tau p_2)+ap_2=a(p_1+\tau p_2)$.

Properties 3 [HM]

a) $\tau(p_1+p_2)+p_1=\tau(p_1+p_2)$.
b) $p\sim p'$ iff $p\simeq p'$ or $p\simeq\tau p'$ or $\tau p\simeq p'$.

III.2.1 Translation of a term into its characteristic formula

The following definitions are used to introduce the function $|\,|$ translating terms into their characteristic formulas.

Definition 5

For the class of the formulas $f=\bigwedge_{i\in I}\langle a_i\wedge f_i\rangle\wedge[\bigvee_{i\in K}a_i\wedge f_i]$ such that the f_i's belong to L<A> and $\not\models f\equiv$false, define $\hat{f}$ as the formula $\hat{f}:=\bigvee_{i\in K}a_i\wedge f_i$.

Proposition 1

$\hat{}$ is a partial function from L<A> into L(A).

Proof : Given in [GS] □.

Corollary 1

For two formulas of L<A>, $f_1=\bigwedge_{i\in I_1}\langle a_i\wedge f_i\rangle[\bigvee_{i\in K_1}a_i\wedge f_i]$ and $f_2=\bigwedge_{i\in I_2}\langle b_i\wedge f_i'\rangle[\bigvee_{i\in K_2}b_i\wedge f_i']$ such that $\not\models f_1\equiv$false,
$f_1\equiv f_2$ implies $\bigwedge_{I_1}\langle a_i f_i\rangle\equiv\bigwedge_{I_2}\langle b_i f_i'\rangle$ and $[\bigvee_{K_1}a_i f_i]\equiv[\bigvee_{K_2}b_i f_i']$.
Notice that if for some $p\in P(A)$ $p\models f$ then $\hat{f}$ is such that $p'\models[\hat{f}]$ implies

$p+p' \models f$. That is, $[\hat{f}]$ characterizes a class of terms such that their addition to p preserves satisfaction of f.

Definition 6

Let f be a formula such that $\hat{f}$ is defined. Denote by E(f) the formula,

$$E(f) := \mu x.(f \vee \langle \tau \wedge x \rangle \wedge [\tau \wedge x \vee \hat{f}]).$$

Proposition 2

$$E(f) \equiv \lim_{k \to \infty} X_k \text{ where } X_0 = f \text{ and } X_{k+1} = X_k \vee \langle \tau \wedge X_k \rangle \wedge [\tau \wedge X_k \vee \hat{f}].$$

Proof : As the trees representing the terms of P(A) are of finite degree, the functional $\lambda x.\langle \tau x \rangle [\tau x \vee \hat{f}]$ is continuous. The result is obtained by application of the Knaster-Tarski theorem.□

The interest of defining E(f) will become evident later when it will be proved that if f represents a congruence class of a term p then E(f) represents the union of the congruence classes of p and of τp. For example, if p=aNil+bNil then the following tree representing a term congruent to τ(aNil+bNil) satisfies E(f).

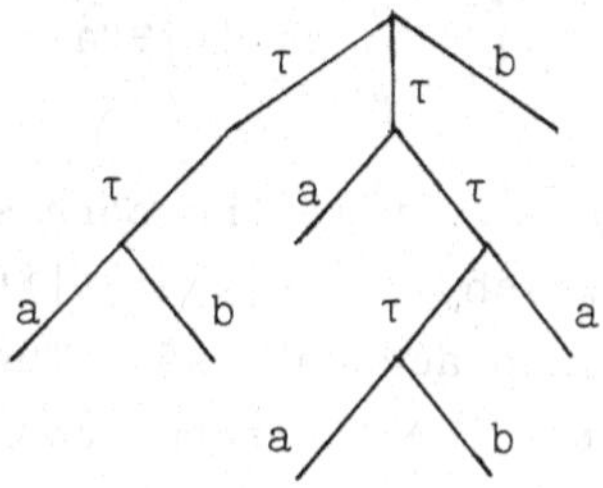

We define a function $|\,| \in P(A) \to L\langle A \rangle$ such that for any pair of terms p,p' of P(A), $p' \models |p|$ iff $p' \approx p$.

Notice that for such a function $|\,|$ the following three propositions hold :

A. $\forall p \in P(A)$ $p \models |p|$ (satisfaction),

B. $\forall p,p' \in P(A)$ $|p| \equiv |p'|$ implies $p \approx p'$ (soundness),

C. $\forall p,p' \in P(A)$ $p \approx p'$ implies $|p| \equiv |p'|$ (completeness).

The definition is given inductively by the following four rules. A subset STRICT is also defined in order to make easier the expression of the rules. STRICT is the set obtained by the rules given below and represents the set of formulas corresponding to terms p which are not congruent to some term of the form $\tau p'$.

Rule 1 : - $|Nil| = [false]$;

- $[false] \in$ STRICT.

Notice that Nil $\models$ [false] by property 2a).

Rule 2 :

$$-\ |\tau p| = \begin{cases} \tau^{\circ}|p| \text{ if } |p| \in \text{STRICT} \\ |p| \text{ otherwise} \end{cases}$$

where $\tau^{\circ}|p| = \langle \tau \wedge E|p| \rangle \wedge [\tau \wedge E|p| \vee |\hat{p}|]$;

$-\ |\tau p| \notin$ STRICT.

The reader is invited to compare this rule with the corresponding rule in the case of strong equivalence which is $|\tau p| = \langle \tau \wedge |p| \rangle [\tau \wedge |p|]$. In rule 2 we have replaced $|p|$ by $E|p|$ in order to take into account (A5). The formula $|\hat{p}|$ has been added to preserve satisfaction for terms congruent to p by property 3a) (take $p=p_1+p_2$).

Rule 3 : For $a \in A-\{\tau\}$

$$-\ |ap| = \begin{cases} a^{\circ}|p'| \text{ if there exists } p' \text{ such that } |p| \equiv \tau^{\circ}|p'| \\ a^{\circ}|p| \text{ otherwise} \end{cases}$$

where $a^{\circ}|p| = \langle a \wedge E|p| \rangle \wedge [a \wedge E|p| \vee |\hat{p}|[a/\tau]]$ and

$$|\hat{p}|[a/\tau] = \begin{cases} \bigvee_{i \in I'} a \wedge f_i \text{ whenever } |\hat{p}| \equiv \bigvee_{i \in I} a_i \wedge f_i \text{ and} \\ \qquad I' = \{i \in I \mid a_i = \tau\} \neq \phi \\ \text{false if } |\hat{p}| \equiv \text{false or } I' = \phi \end{cases}$$

$-\ |ap| \in$ STRICT.

It is interesting to compare this rule with the corresponding rule in the case of strong equivalence, which is $|ap| = \langle a \wedge |p| \rangle [a \wedge |p|]$. In rule 3, $|p|$ is replaced by $E|p|$ to take into account (A5). The formula $|\hat{p}|[a/\tau]$ has been added to preserve satisfaction for terms congruent to ap by application of (A7). In fact, for $p=p_1+\tau p_2$ one gets $ap \simeq ap+ap_2$. The formula added caracterizes all terms ap_2 such that $ap \simeq ap+ap_2$ by (A7). Finally, notice that in the case $|p| \equiv \tau^{\circ}|p'|$, using $|p'|$ instead of $|p|$ is necessary in order to preserve (A5).

Rule 4 :

$$-|p_1+p_2| = \begin{cases} |p_1| \text{ if } |p_2| \equiv [\text{false}] \\ |p_2| \text{ if } |p_1| \equiv [\text{false}] \\ |p_1| \oplus |p_2| \text{ otherwise} \end{cases}$$

where for $|p_1| = \bigwedge_{i \in I_1} \langle a_i \wedge E|p_i| \rangle [\bigvee_{i \in I_1} \widehat{a_i^{\circ}|p_i|}]$,

$|p_2| = \bigwedge_{i \in I_2} \langle b_i \wedge E|p'_i| \rangle [\bigvee_{i \in I_2} \widehat{b_i^{\circ}|p'_i|}]$,

$|p_1| \oplus |p_2| = \bigwedge_{i \in I'_1} \langle a_i \wedge E|p_i| \rangle \bigwedge_{i \in I'_2} \langle b_i \wedge E|p'_i| \rangle [|\hat{p}_1| \vee |\hat{p}_2|]$.

The sets of indices I'_1 and I'_2 are defined by

$I'_1 = \{i \in I_1 \mid \nexists j \in I_2 \ c(a_i p_i, b_j p'_j)\}$, $I'_2 = \{j \in I_2 \mid \nexists i \in I_1 \ c(b_j p'_j, a_i p_i)\}$,

where c is the predicate

$c(ap, bp')$ iff $[\widehat{a^{\circ}|p|}] \supset [\widehat{b^{\circ}|p|}]$ and not $[\widehat{a^{\circ}|p|}] \equiv [\widehat{b^{\circ}|p|}]$;

$-|p_1| \oplus |p_2| \notin$ STRICT iff $|p_1| \oplus |p_2| \equiv \tau^{\circ}|p|$ for some $|p|$.

It will be shown that $|p| = \bigwedge_{i \in I} \langle a_i \wedge E|p_i| \rangle [\bigvee_{i \in I} \widehat{a_i^{\circ}|p_i|}]$ is the most general form of the formulas of the image of $||$ for $p = \sum_{i \in I} a_i p_i$. A comparison between this rule and the corresponding rule in the case of strong equivalence shows that the same principle is applied with the difference that a factor may be "eliminated" to take into account (A6) and (A7). The predicate c(ap,bp') has been defined so that it is true whenever $ap+bp' \approx bp'$ by these axioms but not $ap \approx bp'$.

Example 2 : Computation of $|p|$ for $p = aNil + \tau(aNil+bNil)$:

$|aNil| = \langle aE[false]\rangle[aE[false]]$

$|bNil| = \langle bE[false]\rangle[bE[false]]$

$|aNil+bNil| = \langle aE[false]\rangle\langle bE[false]\rangle[aE[false] \vee bE[false]]$

$|\tau(aNil+bNil) = \langle\tau E|aNil+bNil|\rangle[\tau E|aNil+bNil| \vee aE[false] \vee bE[false]]$

$|aNil+\tau(aNil+bNil)| = \langle\tau E|aNil+bNil|\rangle[\tau E|aNil+bNil| \vee aE[false] \vee bE[false]]$.

The absence of the factor $\langle aE[false]\rangle$ in the result is due to the fact that $c(aNil,\tau(aNil+bNil))$ is satisfied i.e.

$$[aE[false]] \supset [|\widehat{\tau(aNil+bNil)}|] \text{ but not } [aE[false]] \equiv [|\widehat{\tau(aNil+bNil)}|].$$

Proposition 3

$||$ is a function from P(A) into $L\langle A\rangle$.

Proof : Given in [GS].

Lemma 1 :

For any term of P(A), $|p| \notin$ STRICT iff $\exists p'\ |p| \equiv \tau^\circ|p'|$.

Proof : By the fact that $\tau^\circ|p'| \notin$ STRICT and by application of the rules 1 and 3 it is not possible to obtain a formula $|p| \equiv \tau^\circ|p'|$ for some p'□

Theorem 2 (satisfaction)

$\forall p \in P(A)\ p \models |p|$.

Proof : By induction on the structure of P(A), given in [GS].□

III.2.2 Soundness of the translation method

The soundness of the translation method will be deduced from a series of lemmas given below which have all the same hypothesis, the induction hypothesis used in the proof of proposition 4.

Let F be a set of formulas of the image of $||$ such that,

(1) $\forall |p| \in F$, $\forall p' \in P(A)$ $|p'|$ subformula of $|p|$ implies $|p'| \in F$.

(2) $\forall |p| \in F$, $\forall p' \in P(A)$ $p' \models |p|$ implies $p' \approx p$.

The following lemmas give properties of F and have been proved in [GS].

Lemma 2

$\forall |p| \in F$, $\forall p' \in P(A)$ $p' \models [|\hat{p}|]$ implies $p+p' \approx p$.

Lemma 3

$\forall |p| \in F$, $\forall p' \in P(A)$ $p' \models E|p|$ implies $p' \approx p$ or $p' \approx \tau p$.

Lemma 4

$\forall |p| \in F$, $\forall p' \in P(A)$ $p' \models \tau^{\circ}|p|$ implies $p' \approx \tau p$.

Lemma 5

$\forall |p| \in F$, $\forall p' \in P(A)$ $p' \models a^{\circ}|p|$ implies $p' \approx ap$.

Lemma 6

$\forall |p_1|, |p_2| \in F$, $[|\hat{p}_1|] \equiv [|\hat{p}_2|]$ implies $p_1 \approx p_2$.

Lemma 7

For $|p_1|, |p_2| \in F$, $p \in P(A)$ $p \models |p_1| \oplus |p_2|$ implies $p \approx p_1 + p_2$.

Proposition 4

$\forall p, p' \in P(A)$ $p' \models |p|$ implies $p' \approx p$.

Proof : By induction on the structure of the formulas.

1) $p' \models [\text{false}]$ implies $p' \approx Nil$.

2) Let F be a set of formulas of the image of $|\,|$ such that
- $\forall |p| \in F$, $\forall p' \in P(A)$ $|p'|$ subformula of $|p|$ implies $|p'| \in F$.
- $\forall |p| \in F$, $\forall p' \in P(A)$ $p' \models |p|$ implies $p' \approx p$.

By lemmas 4, 5 and 7 the operations on formulas preserve this property.□

Now the soundness theorem follows as in III.1.

Theorem 3 (soundness)

$\forall p, p' \in P(A)$ $|p'| \equiv |p|$ implies $p' \approx p$.

Proof : $|p'| \equiv |p|$ implies $p' \models |p|$ by theorem 2 which implies $p' \approx p$ by proposition 4.□

III.2.3 Completeness of the translation method

As (A1)-(A7) is a complete axiomatization of the observational congruence we can proceed as in the proof of (P3) in theorem 1.

Lemma 8

(A1) $|(p_1+p_2)+p_3| \equiv |p_1+(p_2+p_3)|$,
(A2) $|p_1+p_2| \equiv |p_2+p_1|$,
(A3) $|p+p| \equiv |p|$,
(A4) $|p+Nil| \equiv |p|$.

Proof : The proof of (A2), (A3) and (A4) is trivial. So it remains to prove (A1) i.e. $(|p_1| \oplus |p_2|) \oplus |p_3| \equiv |p_1| \oplus (|p_2| \oplus |p_3|)$. If some p_i is such that $|p_i| \equiv [\mathrm{false}]$ then the result follows by (A4). Otherwise, each $|p_i|$ is of the general form $|p_i| = \bigwedge_j < a_{ij} E |p_{ij}| > [|\hat{p}_i|]$. If some term of the form $<aE|p|>$ of $|p_1|$ is eliminated in $|p_1| \oplus |p_2|$ then it is eliminated in $|p_1| \oplus (|p_2| \oplus |p_3|)$ because the relation defined by the predicate $c(ap,bp') = ([\widehat{|ap|}] \supset [\widehat{|bp'|}]) \wedge \neg([\widehat{|ap|}] \equiv [\widehat{|bp'|}])$ is transitive and antisymmetrical.□

Lemma 9

(A5) $|a\tau p| \equiv |ap|$.

Proof : If $|p| \notin$ STRICT then $|p| \equiv \tau^\circ |p'|$ for some $|p'| \in$ STRICT. This implies $|\tau p| \equiv \tau^\circ |p'|$, which implies $|a\tau p| \equiv a^\circ |p'|$ and $|ap| \equiv a^\circ |p'|$.
If $|p| \in$ STRICT then $|\tau p| = \tau^\circ |p|$ which implies $|a\tau p| = a^\circ |p|$ and $|ap| = a^\circ |p|$.
Thus $|a\tau p| \equiv |ap|$.□

Lemma 10

(A6) $|\tau p + p| \equiv |\tau p|$.

Lemma 11

(A7) $|a(p_1 + \tau p_2) + ap_2| \equiv |a(p_1 + \tau p_2)|$.

Proofs of lemmas 10 and 11 are given in [GS].

By using lemmas 8, 9, 10, 11 and reasoning as in proof of theorem 1 (P3) we get,

Theorem 4 (completeness)

$\forall p, p' \in P(A)$ $p \approx p'$ implies $|p| \equiv |p'|$.

Theorem 5 (characterization)

The function $|\,|$ characterizes observational congruence i.e. for any pair p, p' of terms of P(A), $p' \models |p|$ iff $p' \approx p$.

Proof : By theorems 2 and 4 and proposition 4.□

IV. DISCUSSION

This work has been motivated by the search for a sufficiently powerful modal language compatible with observational congruence in CCS. By following an approach different from that one of [BR] [HM] [St] we obtained a characterization of congruence classes on finite terms. A similar characterization has been obtained for the class of recursively defined controllable CCS processes i.e. processes p for which there exists some p' observationally equivalent to p and p' has no τ-transition [Gr]. These results brought us to study a language L_0 for the specification of controllable CCS processes which contains that one proposed in [HM]. L_0 is a certain subset of the set of formulas built from the constants

[true] and [false] by using logical operators and two independant modal operators $\textcircled{\lambda}$ and $\langle\!\langle\lambda\rangle\!\rangle$ for $\lambda\in A$. Their meaning is given by,

$$\langle\!\langle\tau\rangle\!\rangle F = \mu y.(F\vee<\tau\wedge y>)$$
$$\langle\!\langle a\rangle\!\rangle F = <a\wedge \langle\!\langle\tau\rangle\!\rangle F>$$
$$\textcircled{\tau}\ F = \mu y.(F\vee<\tau\wedge y>\wedge[\tau\wedge y\vee\hat{F}])$$
$$\textcircled{a}\ F = <a\wedge\ \textcircled{\tau}\ F>\wedge[a\wedge\ \textcircled{\tau}\ F\vee\hat{F}[a/\tau]]$$

where F is a formula and $\hat{F}$ is such that $\forall p\in P(A)\ p\models[\hat{F}]$ iff $\exists p'\ p+p'\models F$ i.e $\hat{}$ is an extension of the function defined in III.2.1.

Notice that $\textcircled{\tau}$ F and $\textcircled{a}$ F are generalizations of E(F) and a°F. The formula $\textcircled{\tau}$ F characterizes all the terms which either satisfy F or their only possible derivations are τ-derivations until some state is reached for which F or $\hat{F}$ is true. In a similar manner $\textcircled{a}$ F characterizes all the terms for which the only possible derivations are of the form $a\tau^*$ until some state is reached satisfying F or $\hat{F}$. Thus the modality $\textcircled{\lambda}$ expresses eventuality or inevitability. On the other hand the formulas $\langle\!\langle\tau\rangle\!\rangle$ F and $\langle\!\langle a\rangle\!\rangle$ F express the fact that it is possible to satisfy F by executing a sequence of τ^* or a sequence of $a\tau^*$ respectively. Obviously, $\langle\!\langle a\rangle\!\rangle$ in [HM] is equivalent to $\langle\!\langle\tau\rangle\!\rangle\langle\!\langle a\rangle\!\rangle$ in L_0. This language has been partially studied in [Gr], and it will be presented in a forthcoming paper.

REFERENCES

[BR] Brookes S.D. and Rounds W.C. Behavioural equivalence relations induced by programming logics. Proceedings 10th ICALP, 83, LNCS Vol.15

[Gr] Graf S. Logiques du temps arborescent pour la spécification et la preuve de programmes. Thèse 3ème Cycle, IMAG, Grenoble, February, 84

[GS] Graf S. and Sifakis J. A modal characterization of observational congruence on finite terms of CCS. R.R. n° 402, IMAG, November 83

[HM] Hennessy M. and Milner R. On observing nondeterminism and concurrency. Proceedings 7th ICALP, 80. LNCS Vol. 85

[Ko] Kozen D. Results on the propositional μ-calculus. Proceedings 9th ICALP, 82. LNCS Vol. 140

[Mi] Milner R. A calculus of communicating systems. LNCS Vol. 92

[St] Stirling C. A proof theoretic characterization of observational equivalence. University of Edinburgh, Internal Report CSR-132-83.

COMMUNICATION COMPLEXITY

Juraj Hromkovič
Department of Theoretical Cybernetics
Komensky University
842 15 Bratislava
Czechoslovakia

Abstract. We shall consider the communication complexity introduced by Papadimitriou and Sipser [4]. The hierarchy of this communication complexity is proved for both deterministic and nondeterministic models. The communication complexity hierarchy for k-way communication is also established.

INTRODUCTION AND DEFINITIONS.

The communication complexity considered in this paper was introduced by Papadimitriou and Sipser [4]. This new complexity measure provides a direct lower bound for minimum bisection width [6] of any chip recognizing a language L and, therefore, for the area-delay squared product of the chip. This connection can be found in most work on VLSI lower bounds [1,2,3,8,9].

Now, let us define the communication complexity in the same way as in [4]. A protocol on inputs of the length 2n is a pair $D_n = (\Pi, \Phi)$, where Π is a partition of $\{1,2,\dots,2n\}$ into two sets S_I and S_{II} of equal size, and Φ is a function from $\{0,1\}^n \times \{0,1,\$\}^*$ to $\{0,1\}^* \cup \{\text{accept}, \text{reject}\}$. For a given string c in $\{0,1,\$\}^*$, the function Φ has the property (called the prefix-freeness property) that for no two y, y' in $\{0,1\}^n$ is the case that $\Phi(y,c)$ is a proper prefix of $\Phi(y',c)$.

The computation of D_n on an input x in $\{0,1\}^{2n}$ is the string $c = c_1\$c_2\$\dots\$c_k\$c_{k+1}$, where $k \geq 0$, $c_1,\dots,c_k \in \{0,1\}^*$, $c_{k+1} \in \{\text{accept},\text{reject}\}$, such that for each integer j, $0 \leq j \leq k$, we have

1. if j is even, then $c_{j+1} = \Phi(x_I, c_1\$c_2\$\dots\$c_j)$, where x_I is the input x restricted to the set S_I and
2. if j is odd, then $c_{j+1} = \Phi(x_{II}, c_1\$c_2\$\dots\$c_j)$, where x_{II} is the input x restricted to the set S_{II}.

Let $L \subseteq \{0,1\}^*$ be a language and $\Delta = \langle D_n \rangle$ be a sequence of deterministic protocols. We say Δ recognizes L if, for each n and each x in $\{0,1\}^{2n}$, the computation of D_n on input x is finite, and ends with accept iff $x \in L$. Let f be a function from naturals to naturals. We say that L is recognizable within communication f, $L \in COMM(f)$, if there is a sequence of protocols $\Delta = \langle D_n \rangle$ such that for all n and each $x \in \{0,1\}^{2n}$ the computation of D_n on x is of the length at most f(n).

Clearly, this model of communication is deterministic but nondeterminism can be introduced naturally by allowing Φ in our definition of a "distributed algorithm" to be a relation, as opposed to a function. The prefix-freeness property generalizes to: for $x, x' \in \{0,1\}^n$ if $(x,c,w), (x',c,w) \in \Phi$ then w is not a proper prefix of w'. The resulting object is called a nondeterministic protocol. We say a sequence of such protocols $\Delta = \langle D_n \rangle$ recognizes a language L if, for all n and all inputs x in $\{0,1\}^{2n}$, there exists a computation of D_n which ends in accept iff $x \in L$. The communication complexity is defined as the length of the shortest such computation on each input in L, maximized over all inputs of length 2n. The family of languages recognizable by nondeterministic protocols in communication f is denoted NCOMM(f).

Obviously, communication n is always enough for recognizing any language. Papadimitriou and Sipser [4] proved for the deterministic model that there are languages which cannot be recognized with the communication complexity less than n and that for any function $f(n) \leq \log_2 n$ there are languages recognizable within communication f(n) but not within communication f(n)-1. It was also proved in [4] that $NCOMM(f(n)) \subseteq COMM(2^{f(n)})$ and that there is a language in $NCOMM(1+\log_2 n)$ which requires linear communication in the deterministic case.

We shall show in this paper that for any function $0 \leq f(n) \leq n$ and any real constant $0 < c < 1$, there is a large number of languages recognizable within communication f(n) but not with communication cf(n). This result is shown for deterministic model, in nondeterministic case it is established for $c < 1/2$. It then follows that for arbitrary constant $c : 0 < c < 1/2$ there are languages which do not belong to NCOMM(cn).

Let C and D be families of languages. We define $C \wedge D = \{L \mid L \in C$ and $L \in D\}$ and denote by $\mathcal{L}_n$ the family of languages which are subsets of the set $\{0,1\}^{2n}$. To prove the results introduced we shall look for bounds for the number of languages in $COMM(f(n)) \wedge \mathcal{L}_n$ $(NCOMM(f(n)) \wedge \mathcal{L}_n)$, denoted by $cap(COMM(f(n)) \wedge \mathcal{L}_n)$.

Furthermore, we shall study k-way communication complexity introduced by Papadimitriou and Sipser [4] as follows. Let $c = c_1\$c_2 \ldots c_k\$c_{k+1}$ be a computation of a protocol D_n. We say that c has k rounds. D_n is a k-way protocol if all of its computation have at most k rounds.

$COMM_k(f)$ ($NCOMM_k(f)$) is the family of all languages that can be recognized by sequences of k-way (nondeterministic) protocols within the communication f. Results analogous to those for general model of the communication complexity are established for the k-way communication complexity too. For one-way communication complexity it is shown that there is a large number of languages recognized within communication complexity f(n) but not within communication complexity f(n)-1.

For arbitrary functions f and g defined on naturals we define $f \sim g$ iff $\lim_{n\to\infty} f(n)/g(n) = 1$. We shall show that

$$\log_2(\mathrm{cap}(COMM_1(f(n)) \wedge \mathcal{L}_n)) \sim 2^{n+f(n)} \quad \text{and that}$$
$$\log_2(\log_2(\mathrm{cap}(COMM(f(n)) \wedge \mathcal{L}_n))) \sim n+f(n).$$

This paper consists of 4 Sections. In Section 1 we prove some results for one-way communication complexity. The hierarchy of deterministic communication complexity is established in Section 2. In Section 3 we introduce a special model of communication complexity to show an interesting property of the general model of the communication complexity considered. We shall conclude this paper with Section 4, where the hierarchy of nondeterministic communication complexity is established.

1. ONE-WAY COMMUNICATION COMPLEXITY.

In this Section we shall study the hierarchy of one-way communication complexity for both deterministic and nondeterministic models. At first we shall bound the number of languages in $COMM_1(f(n)) \wedge \mathcal{L}_n$.

<u>Lemma 1.</u> Let f be a function from naturals to naturals, such that $0 \leq f(n) \leq n$. Then

$$\mathrm{cap}(COMM_1(f(n)) \wedge \mathcal{L}_n) \geq 2^{2^{n+f(n)}} .$$

<u>Proof</u>. Let us consider a language $L \subseteq \{0,1\}^{2n}$. Let j be an integer in $\{1,2,\ldots,2n\}$ such that there exists two words $x = x_1 \ldots x_{j-1} 1 x_{j+1} \ldots x_{2n}$ and $y = x_1 \ldots x_{j-1} 0 x_{j+1} \ldots x_{2n}$, with x_i in $\{0,1\}$ for $i = 1,2,\ldots,2n$, such that one of the words x, y belongs to L and the other word does not belong to L. Then the number j is called a <u>determining position.</u> The number of all languages in $\mathcal{L}_n$ with at most n+f(n) determining positions is at least $2^{2^{n+f(n)}}$,

since we can construct such languages in the following way. We divide 2^{2n} words of the length 2n into such $2^{n+f(n)}$ classes so that each class involves $2^{n-f(n)}$ words with fixed symbols on determining positions. Clearly, we can construct the languages by allocating accept or reject to the classes considered. This can be done in exactly

$$2^{2^{n+f(n)}} \text{ different ways.}$$

Now, we shall show that each language $L \subseteq \{0,1\}^{2n}$ with at most n+f(n) determining positions can be recognized by some protocol $D_n = (\pi, \Phi)$. The partition π is such that S_I contains f(n) determining positions and S_{II} contains n determining positions. Using the function Φ the computer I sends the contents of f(n) determining positions in S_I to the computer II. It is easy to see that the computer II having access to all of the n+f(n) determinig positions can decide about the acceptance or rejection.

<u>Lemma 2.</u> Let f be a function from naturals to naturals such that $0 \leq f(n) \leq n$. Then

$$\text{cap}(\text{COMM}_1(f(n)) \wedge \mathcal{L}_n) \leq 2^{2n}(2^{f(n)}+2)^{2^n} \cdot 2^{2^{n+f(n)}} .$$

<u>Proof.</u> We shall prove this assertion by bounding the number of all protocols with f communication bound according to all different ways how protocols can split the input words into classes which can be accepted or rejected. Clearly, the number of all partitions π is exactly

$$\binom{2n}{n} < 2^{2n}.$$

Let us consider the protocols with fixed partition now. Clearly, considering the prefix-freeness property, the number of all communications which computer I sends to computer II is at most $2^{f(n)}$. It means that I divides its 2^n inputs into $2^{f(n)}+2$ classes (some classes can be empty when I sends the smaller number of communications or does not use the possibility to accept or to reject), what can be done in at most

$$(2^{f(n)}+2)^{2^n} \text{ different ways.}$$

Then computer II decides about acceptance for at most $2^{n+f(n)}$ classes of the input words (each of the $2^{f(n)}$ classes determined by communications is combined with each of inputs of II). This can be done by at most $2^{2^{n+f(n)}}$ different ways.

Using the bounds obtained in Lemmas 1 and 2 we can formulate the main result of this Section.

Theorem 1. Let $0 \leq f(n) \leq n$ be a function from naturals to naturals such that $\lim_{n\to\infty} f(n) = \infty$. Then

$$\log_2(\mathrm{cap}(\mathrm{COMM}_1(f(n)) \wedge \mathcal{L}_n)) \sim 2^{n+f(n)}.$$

Clearly, considering Theorem 1 we have the expected result that, for one-way communication complexity, using f(n) +1 communication complexity we can recognize substantially more languages than using communication complexity f(n). We formulate this result in the following theorem.

Theorem 2. Let $0 \leq f(n) \leq n-1$ be a function from naturals to naturals such that $\lim_{n\to\infty} f(n) = \infty$. Then

$$\lim_{n\to\infty} \mathrm{cap}(\mathrm{COMM}_1(f(n)) \wedge \mathcal{L}_n)/\mathrm{cap}(\mathrm{COMM}_1(f(n)+1) \wedge \mathcal{L}_n) = 0,$$

i.e. $\mathrm{COMM}_1(f(n)) \subsetneq \mathrm{COMM}_1(f(n)+1)$.

Continuing in a similar manner as before we can prove the following hierarchy results for nondeterministic one-way communication complexity.

Lemma 3. Let $0 \leq f(n) \leq n$ be a function from naturals to naturals. Then

$$\mathrm{cap}(\mathrm{NCOMM}_1(f(n)) \wedge \mathcal{L}_n) \leq 2^{2n} \; 2^{(f(n)+2)\cdot(2^{n+f(n)}+2^{n+1})}.$$

Using Lemmas 1 and 3 we obtain the following theorem.

Theorem 3. Let $0 < c < 1$ be a real number and $0 \leq f(n) \leq n$ be a function from naturals to naturals such that $\lim_{n\to\infty} f(n) = \infty$. Then

$$\lim_{n\to\infty} \mathrm{cap}(\mathrm{NCOMM}_1(cf(n)) \wedge \mathcal{L}_n)/\mathrm{cap}(\mathrm{COMM}_1(f(n)) \wedge \mathcal{L}_n) = 0.$$

i.e. $\mathrm{COMM}_1(f(n)) - \mathrm{NCOMM}_1(cf(n)) = \emptyset$.

Finishing this Section we formulate the hierarchy result which is a consequence of Theorem 3.

Corollary 1. Let $0 < c < 1$ be an arbitrary real number and let f : $0 \leq f(n) \leq n$ be a function from naturals to naturals such that $\lim_{n\to\infty} f(n) = \infty$. Then

$$\mathrm{NCOMM}_1(cf(n)) \subsetneq \mathrm{NCOMM}_1(f(n)).$$

2. DETERMINISTIC COMMUNICATION COMPLEXITY.

In this Section we shall prove a hierarchy for deterministic communication complexity and for k-way communication complexity. These results are based on the calculation of an upper bound for the number of languages in $COMM(f(n)) \wedge \mathcal{L}_n$ given in the following lemma.

Lemma 4. Let $0 \leq f(n) \leq n$ be a function from naturals to naturals. Then

$$cap(COMM(f(n)) \wedge \mathcal{L}_n) \leq 2^{2n} \cdot f(n) \cdot 2^{(f(n))^2} \; 2^{(f(n)+1)f(n) \cdot 2^{n+f(n)+1}} .$$

Proof. We shall prove this assertion bounding the number of all different protocols (according to all different ways a protocal can divide the inputs words into classes for which it decides about the acceptance) $D_n = (\Pi, \Phi)$.

Clearly, the number of all partitions Π is exactly $\binom{2n}{n} < 2^{2n}$. Let us consider the protocols with fixed partition now. Let $k \leq f(n)$ be the maximal number of rounds of a protocol and, for $i = 1,2,\ldots,k$, c_i be the maximal number of different communications which a computer sends to the other computer in the i-th step of D_n. Since $1 \leq c_i \leq 2^{f(n)}$ the number of all possibilities how to choose k and $c_1,\ldots,c_k$ is at most $f(n) 2^{(f(n))^2}$.

Now, we shall consider the protocols with fixed partition Π and fixed $k, c_1, \ldots, c_k$. Clearly, we can assume that $c_1 \cdot c_2 \cdot \ldots \cdot c_k \leq 2^{f(n)}$. So the number of different communications which I can send to II in the first step is c_1, what follows the protocol can divide the inputs of computer I into at most c_1+2 classes. Obviously, the number of all possibilities how 2^n elements can be divided into c_1+2 disjoint sets is

$$(c_1+2)^{2^n} .$$

In the second step a protocol can divide, for each communication (the number of communications is at most c_1) the 2^n inputs of computer II into c_1+2 disjoint classes, what can be made at most by

$$(c_2+2)^{2^n \cdot c_1}$$

different ways. Thus, we have at most $c_1 \cdot c_2$ communications and a pair of classes for each communication. The first class of each pair contains some inputs of I, the second class contains some inputs of II. In the third step the protocol can divide for each of the $c_1 \cdot c_2$ communications the first class of each communication into at most c_3+2 disjoint subclasses. Let the number of elements in the first classes be $a_1, a_2 \dots$ $\dots a_j$, where $j = c_1 \cdot c_2$. Obviously

$$\sum_{i=1}^{j} a_i = 2^n \cdot c_2 .$$

Then we can bound the number of ways the protocol can perform the third step by

$$\prod_{i=1}^{j} (c_3+2)^{a_i} = (c_3+2)^{2^n \cdot c_2} .$$

Using the same reasoning as in the third step of the protocol we can bound the number of all possibilities for the j-th step of the protocol communication by

$$\prod_{i=1}^{c_1 \cdot \dots \cdot c_{j-1}} (c_j+2)^{a_i} = (c_j+2)^{2^n \cdot c_2 \cdot c_4 \cdot \dots \cdot c_{j-1}} \leq (c_j+2)^{2^{n+f(n)}} \quad \text{for } j \text{ odd}$$

, and by

$$\prod_{i=1}^{c_1 \cdot \dots \cdot c_{j-1}} (c_j+2)^{a_i} = (c_j+2)^{2^n \cdot c_1 \cdot c_3 \cdot \dots \cdot c_{j-1}} \leq (c_j+2)^{2^{n+f(n)}} \quad \text{for } j$$

even (obviously, a_i have the same maening for the j-th step as in the third step of protocol).

In such a way we obtain the upper bound of the number of all possibilities how a protocol can make all its k communication steps

$$\prod_{d=1}^{k} (c_d+2)^{2^{n+f(n)}} \leq \prod_{d=1}^{k} (2^{f(n)}+1)^{2^{n+f(n)}} \leq 2^{f(n) \cdot (f(n)+1) 2^{n+f(n)}} .$$

Now, the protocol have to do already only the last step in which it can give "accept" or "reject" for at most $2^{n+f(n)}$ different arguments, what can be done in at most

$$2^{2^{n+f(n)}}$$

different ways. A simple calculation now proves the validity of our lemma.

Using the result of Lemma 4 we can formulate the main result of this Section. We omit the proof which is analogous to the proof of Theorem 3.

<u>Theorem 4.</u> Let $0 \leq f(n) \leq n$ be a function from naturals to naturals such that $\lim_{n \to \infty} f(n) = \infty$ and let c be a real number such that $0 < c < 1$. Then

$$\lim_{n\to\infty} \operatorname{cap}(\mathrm{COMM}(cf(n)) \wedge \mathcal{L}_n)/\operatorname{cap}(\mathrm{COMM}_1(f(n)) \wedge \mathcal{L}_n) = 0 ,$$

i.e. $\mathrm{COMM}_1(f(n)) - \mathrm{COMM}(cf(n)) \neq \emptyset$.

We conclude this Section with a theorem concerning the hierarchy results which are consequences of Theorem 4.

Theorem 5. Let $0 < c < 1$ be a real number and k be a natural number. Let $0 \leq f(n) \leq n$ be a function from naturals to naturals such that $\lim_{n\to\infty} f(n) = \infty$. Then

$$\mathrm{COMM}(cf(n)) \subseteq\neq \mathrm{COMM}(f(n))$$
$$\mathrm{COMM}_k(cf(n)) \subseteq\neq \mathrm{COMM}_k(f(n)) .$$

3. COUNTERBALANCED COMMUNICATION COMPLEXITY.

In this Section we shall define and study a special type of the protocols to show an interesting property of communication complexity. We shall show that the power of one-way communication complexity model is substantially greater than the power of the model of communication complexity in which we require that both computers must send some amount of information to the other computer. First, we give a definition of this model of communication complexity.

Let $0 < c < 1/2$ be a real number. Let D_n be a protocol which works within communication f. Then we say that the protocol is c-counterbalanced iff the number of all different communications which I can send to II is at least $2^{cf(n)}$ and the number of all different communications which II can send to I is at least $2^{cf(n)}$. The subclass of COMM(f(n)) recognized by c-counterbalanced protocols will be denoted by $\mathrm{COMM}^c(f(n))$.

Lemma 5. Let $0 < c < 1/2$ be a real number and $d = 1-c$. Let $0 \leq f(n) \leq n$ be a function from integers to integers. Then

$$\operatorname{cap}(\mathrm{COMM}^c(f(n)) \wedge \mathcal{L}_n) \leq 2^{2n} \cdot f(n) 2^{(f(n))^2} 2^{f(n)(1+f(n)) 2^{n+df(n)+1}} .$$

Proof. Realizing that the numbers of different communications, which a computer send to the other computer in the j-th step of D_n, c_j have to be such that $c_1 \cdot c_3 \cdots c_h \leq df(n)$ and $c_2 \cdot c_4 \cdots c_m \leq df(n)$ (where $h = k$, $m = k-1$ if k is odd and $m = k$, $h = k-1$ if k is even) we can prove this assertion in the same way as Lemma 4.

Obviously, in the similar way as Lemma 2 the following result can be proved.

Lemma 6. Let $0 < c < 1/2$ be a real number and $d = 1-c$. Let $0 \leq f(n) < n$ be a function from naturals to naturals. Then

$$cap(COMM^c(f(n)) \wedge \mathcal{L}_n) \geq 2^{2^{n+df(n)}} .$$

Now, using the introduced Lemmas, we can formulate two theorems which shows that one-way communication complexity is "better" than c-counterbalanced communication complexity and that , for $a > b$, b-counterbalanced communication complexity is "better" than a-counterbalanced communication complexity.

Theorem 6. Let $0 < c < 1/2$ be a real number and $d = 1-c$. Let $0 \leq f(n) \leq n$ be a function from naturals to naturals such that $\lim_{n\to\infty} f(n) = \infty$ and let $\varepsilon > 0$ be a real number. Then

$$\lim_{n\to\infty} cap(COMM^c(f(n)) \wedge \mathcal{L}_n)/cap(COMM_1((d+\varepsilon)f(n)) \wedge \mathcal{L}_n) = 0 ,$$

i.e. $COMM_1((d+\varepsilon)f(n)) - COMM^c(f(n)) \neq 0$.

Theorem 7. Let $0 < b < a < 1/2$ be arbitrary reals and let $0 \leq f(n) \leq n$ be a function from naturals to naturals such that $\lim_{n\to\infty} f(n) = \infty$. Then

$$\lim_{n\to\infty} cap(COMM^a(f(n)) \wedge \mathcal{L}_n)/cap(COMM^b(f(n)) \wedge \mathcal{L}_n) = 0,$$

i.e. $COMM^a(f(n)) \not\subseteq COMM^b(f(n))$.

Concluding this Section we will still formulate a consequence of the introduced theorems.

Corollary 2. Let $0 < c < 1/2$ be a real number. Then the most languages does not belong to $COMM^c(n)$.

4. NONDETERMINISTIC COMMUNICATION COMPLEXITY.

In this Section we shall obtain hierarchy results for nondeterministic communication complexity using very similar way as proving the hierarchy result of deterministic communication complexity.

Lemma 7. Let $0 \leq f(n) \leq n-1$ be a function from naturals to naturals. Then

$$cap(NCOMM(f(n)) \wedge \mathcal{L}_n) \leq 2^{2n} f(n) 2^{(f(n))^2} 2^{f(n) 2^{n+2f(n)+1}} .$$

Proof. We shall prove this assertion bounding the number of all different (in the sense as in Lemma 4) nondeterministic protocols $D_n = (\Pi, \Phi)$. Clearly, the number of all Π is exactly $\binom{2n}{n} \leq 2^{2n}$.

Let us consider the protocols with fixed partition Π now. Let $k \leq f(n)$ be the maximal number of rounds of a protocol and, for $i = 1,\ldots,k$, c_i be the number of all different i-th communications. Since $1 \leq c_i \leq 2^{f(n)}$, the number of all possibilities how to choose k and $c_1,\ldots,c_k$ is at most

$$2^{(f(n))^2} \cdot f(n) .$$

Now, we shall consider nondeterministic protocols with fixed partition Π and fixed k, $c_1, \ldots, c_k$. Clearly, in the first step the nondeterministic protocol divides 2^n inputs of I in at most c_1+2 classes which (as opposed deterministic case) have not to be disjoint. We can bound the number of all possibilities, how 2^n elements can be divided in arbitrary c_2+2 sets, by

$$\left(2^{(c_1+2)}\right)^{2^n} = 2^{2^n (c_1+2)} .$$

In the second step nondeterministic protocol can divide, for each communication (the number of all communications is at most c_1), the 2^n inputs of II in c_2+2 classes, what can be made at most by

$$\left(2^{(c_2+2)2^n}\right)^{c_1} = 2^{2^n \cdot c_1 \cdot (c_2+2)}$$

different methods.

It is easy to see that in the j-th step nondeterministic protocol can divide each subclass of inputs of I or II, corresponding with a communication (the number of all communications is at most $c_1 \cdot \ldots \cdot c_{j-1}$), in at most c_j+2 subclasses what can be made at most by

$$\left(2^{(c_j+2)2^n}\right)^{c_1 \cdot c_2 \cdot \ldots \cdot c_{j-1}} = 2^{2^n \cdot c_1 \cdot c_2 \cdot \ldots \cdot c_{j-1} (c_j+2)} \leq 2^{2^{n+2f(n)}}$$

different ways.

In such a way we obtain the upper bound of the number of all possibilities how a nondeterministic protocol can make all its k communication steps:

$$\prod_{d=1}^{k} 2^{2^{n+2f(n)}} \leq 2^{f(n)\,2^{n+2f(n)}} .$$

Now, nondeterministic protocol have to do already only the last step in which it can give "accept" or "reject" , for at most $2^{n+f(n)}$ different arguments, what can be made by at most

$$2^{2^{n+f(n)}}$$

different methods. Using a simple arrangement we can already obtain the result of Lemma 7.

Considering the assertion of Lemma 7 we can formulate the main result of this Section. We omit the proof because it can be made in the same way as the proof of Theorem 3.

Theorem 8. Let $0 \leq f(n) \leq n$ be a function from naturals to naturals such that $\lim_{n\to\infty} f(n) = \infty$ and let $0 < c < 1/2$ be a real number. Then

$$\lim_{n\to\infty} \mathrm{cap}(\mathrm{NCOMM}(cf(n)) \wedge \mathfrak{L}_n)/\mathrm{cap}(\mathrm{COMM}_1(f(n)) \wedge \mathfrak{L}_n) = 0 ,$$

i.e. $\mathrm{COMM}_1(f(n)) - \mathrm{NCOMM}(cf(n)) \neq \emptyset$.

Now, we are formulating the hierarchy results for nondeterministic communication complexity which are simple consequences of Theorem 7.

Theorem 9. Let $0 < c < 1/2$ be a real number and k be a natural number. Let $0 \leq f(n) \leq n$ be a function from naturals to naturals such that $\lim_{n\to\infty} f(n) = \infty$. Then $\mathrm{NCOMM}(cf(n)) \neq\subseteq \mathrm{NCOMM}(f(n))$

$$\mathrm{NCOMM}_k(cf(n)) \neq\subseteq \mathrm{NCOMM}_k(f(n)) .$$

Corollary 3. Let $0 < c < 1/2$ be a real number. Then the most languages does not belong to $\mathrm{NCOMM}(cn)$.

Finishing this paper we shall still formulate a theorem which shows an interesting result concerning deterministic communication complexity.

Theorem 10. Let $0 \leq f(n) \leq n$ be a function from naturals to naturals. Then

$$\log_2(\log_2(\mathrm{cap}(\mathrm{COMM}(f(n)) \wedge \mathfrak{L}_n))) \sim n+f(n) .$$

Proof. Obviously, using Lemma 1 we have

$$g(n) = \log_2(\log_2(\mathrm{cap}(\mathrm{COMM}(f(n)) \wedge \mathfrak{L}_n))) \geq n+f(n) .$$

Considering Lemma 4 we obtain

$$g(n) \leq \log_2 2n + 4\log_2(f(n)+1) + \log_2(\log_2(f(n))) + n + f(n) + 1 =$$
$$= (n + f(n))(1+\delta(n)), \text{ where } \lim_{n\to\infty} \delta(n) = 0.$$

ACKNOWLEDGEMENTS.

I would like to thank Branislav Rovan for its comments concerning this work and Pavol Ďuriš for some interesting discusions. I am grateful to my teatcher of combinatorial analysis Eduard Toman by this occasion too.

This work was supported as a part of SPZV I - 5 - 7/7 grant.

REFERENCES.

[1] Abelson, Lower bounds on information transfer in distributed computations. Proc. of the 19-th Annual Symposium on Foundations of Computer Science, 1978.

[2] Lipton and Sedgewick, Lower bounds for VLSI. Proc. of the 13-th Symposium on Theory of Computing, 1981, 300-307.

[3] Melhorn and Schmidt, Las Vegas is better than determinism in VLSI and distributed computing. Proc. of the 14-th Annual Symposium on Theory of Computing, 1982, 330-337.

[4] Papadimitriou and Sipser, Communication Complexity. Proc. of the 23-th Annual Symposium on Foundations of Computer Science, 1982, 189-195.

[5] Savage, Area - time tradeoffs for matrix multiplication and related problems in VLSI models. Proc. of the Allerton Conference, 1979 .

[6] Thompson, Area-time complexity of VLSI. Proc. of the 11-th Annual Symposium on Theory of Computing, 1979, 81-88.

[7] Vuillemin, A combinatorial limit on the computational power of VLSI circuits. Proc. of the 11-th Annual Symposium on Foundations of Computer Science, 1980, 294-300.

[8] Yao, Some complexity questions related to distributive computing. Proc. of the 11-th Annual Symposium on Theory of Computing, 1979, 209-311.

[9] Yao, The entropic limitations on VLSI computations. Proc. of the 13-th Annual Symposium on Theory of Computing, 1981, 308-311.

SPACE AND TIME EFFICIENT SIMULATIONS AND CHARACTERIZATIONS OF SOME RESTRICTED CLASSES OF PDAS[1]

Oscar H. Ibarra,[2]
Sam M. Kim,[3]
Louis E. Rosier[4]

Abstract

In this paper we present some space/time efficient Turing machine algorithms for recognizing some subclasses of DCFL's. In particular, we show that the finite minimal stacking and "simple" strict restricted (a subclass of strict restricted) deterministic pushdown automata (FMS-DPDA's, SSR-DPDA's, respectively) can be simulated by offline Turing machines simultaneously in space S(n) and time $n^2/S(n)$ for any tape function S(n) satisfying $\log n \leq S(n) \leq n$ which is constructable in $n^2/S(n)$ time. Related techniques can be used to give interesting characterizations of 2-head 2-way finite automata, both deterministic and nondeterministic. In particular we show that a 2-head 2-way deterministic finite automataton is equivalent to a simple type of 2-way deterministic checking stack automaton. This is in contrast to a result which shows that 2-way nondeterministic checking stack automata are equivalent to nondeterministic linear bounded automata. We also show that a language L is accepted by a 2k-head two-way nondetermistic finite automaton if and only if it is accepted by a k-head two-way nondeterministic pushdown automaton which makes at most one reversal on its stack.

1. Introduction

The study of context-free (CF) languages is an important topic in computer science. Recently, there has been a lot of work finding time and/or space efficient algorithms for recognizing CF languages. It was shown in [14] that an arbitrary CF language can be recognized in $O(\log^2 n)$ space. The algorithm, however, requires $O(n^{\log n})$ time. For the deterministic case an algorithm that runs simultaneously in $O(\log^2 n)$ space and $O(n^2/\log^2 n)$ time is known[1,24]. This result generalizes to an algorithm that runs in S(n) space and $n^2/S(n)$ time for any constructable function S(n), satisfying $\log^2 n \leq S(n) \leq n$. Whether or not the $\log^2 n$ can be reduced is still open.

At present it is not known whether O(log n) space is sufficient to recognize an arbitrary CF language. This seems unlikely, however, as results in [19,20] show that an affirmative answer would imply the equivalence of deterministic and nondeterministic linear bounded automata. It is reasonable to expect, however, that large subclasses of the CF languages are recognizable in O(log n) space, perhaps even all deterministic CF languages (DCFL's). Many subclasses recognizable in O(log n) space have been shown recently[12,13,15]. Among these are the bracket-languages of [17] and the parenthesis languages of [16]. Also in [12] it was shown that both finite minimal stacking and strict restricted deterministic pushdown automata could be simulated in O(log n) space. Such machines can recognize deterministic finite turn languages, Dyck languages, standard languages, structured context-free languages and left most Szilard languages of phase structured grammars (see [12]).

In this paper, we present some space/time efficient Turing machine algorithms for recognizing some subclasses of DCFL's. In particular, we show that the finite minimal stacking and "simple" strict restricted (a subclass of strict restricted) deterministic pushdown automata (FMS-DPDA's, SSR-DPDA's, respectively) can be simulated by offline Turing machines simultaneously in space S(n) and time $n^2/S(n)$ for any tape function S(n) satisfying $\log n \leq S(n) \leq n$ which is constructable in $n^2/S(n)$ time. The O(log n) space algorithms, presented in [12], for finite minimal stacking and strict restricted DPDA's require $O(n^2)$ and $O(n^3)$ time, respectively. For "simple" strict restricted DPDA's the time in [12] could be reduced to $O(n^2)$ in a straightforward manner. For the case of finite minimal stacking machines we show that one work tape is sufficient when S(n) is between log n and n/log n. We note that while the SSR-DPDA's are more restricted than the strict restricted DPDA's of [12], each language shown to be recognizable (in [12]) by the strict restricted machines is also recognizable by the "simple" ones. At this time we are unable to generalize this result to the strict restricted case.

Related techniques can be used to give interesting characterizations of 2-head 2-way finite automata, both deterministic and nondeterministic. In particular we show that a 2-head 2-way deterministic finite automaton is equivalent to a simple type of 2-way deterministic checking stack automaton. This is in contrast to a result, in [10], which shows that 2-way nondeterministic checking stack automata are equivalent to nondeterministic linear bounded automata (see also [7]). We also show that a language L is accepted by a 2k-head two-way nondeterministic finite automaton if and only if it is accepted by a k-head two-way nondeterministic pushdown automaton which makes at most one reversal on its stack.

---

[1]This research was supported in part by NSF Grants MCS 81-02853 and MCS 83-04756.

[2]Department of Computer Science, University of Minnesota, Minneapolis MN 55455.
[3]Department of Mathematical Sciences, Rensselaer Polytechnic Institute, Troy, NY 12181.
[4]Department of Computer Sciences, University of Texas, Austin, TX 78712.

2. Preliminaries

We assume the reader is familiar with the definitions of Turing machines (TM's), deterministic pushdown automata (DPDA's) and finite automata (FA's). Basically, we employ the definitions and notation of DPDA's given in [12] (and [23]). The reader should consult these sources, if they are unfamiliar. A DPDA M is a 7 tuple $M=<Q,\Sigma,\Gamma,\delta,q_0,Z_0,F>$, where

Q is a (finite) set of states,
Σ is the (finite) input alphabet,
Γ is the (finite) pushdown alphabet,
q_0 is the initial state,
Z_0 (in Γ) is the bottom-of-stack marker
$F \subseteq Q \times \Gamma$ is the set of accepting modes, and
δ is the transition function.

In addition to the usual restrictions placed on δ, in order to insure that the DPDA M has at most one next move defined at each step and is therefore deterministic (see [12,23]), each DPDA is assumed to be defined according to a normal form which requires the following restrictions:

(1) If $\delta(q, \epsilon, Z) = (q', \alpha)$, then $|\alpha| = 0$.
(2) If $\delta(q, a, Z) = (q', \alpha)$, where $a \neq \epsilon$, then $|\alpha| \leq 2$.
(3) If $|\alpha|=2$, then Z is not changed.

We remark that both classes of DPDA's, i.e. FMS-DPDA's and SSR-DPDA's, can be put into this normal form in such a manner that the resulting machines remain in the same subclass. See [10,12,23] for the technique involved.

The checking stack automata (CSA's) are similar to PDA's, but once a symbol is written on the stack it cannot be erased. A CSA's stack head may, however, enter the stack, but once this has been done the CSA loses the capability to write additional symbols on the stack.

A "simple" 2-way checking stack automaton (S-CSA) is a CSA with an additional restriction that once the input head turns (makes a reversal), the machine loses the ability to write on the stack (as it does when the stack head enters the stack). It can be shown that S-CSA's are equivalent to CSA's and that they accept exactly the context sensitive languages[10]. It is open whether deterministic CSA's (DCSA) and S-DCSA's (deterministic S-CSA's) are equivalent. We assume that all S-DCSA's we are going to study in this paper are normalized as follows:

(1) There is no ϵ-mode writing, i.e. the input head moves for each write operation.
(2) The stack grows by 1 for each stacking operation.

Given a S-DCSA it can be normalized using similar techniques as those that were used with the DPDA's.

A k-head 2-way finite automaton is a single tape finite state automaton with k read heads. On each move the machine can simultaneously read the k input cells (scanned by the k heads), change its internal state and move each head one cell in either direction. Such machines cannot, however, detect the coincidence of heads. A k-head two-way pushdown automata is defined similarly, except that it also has the use of an auxiliary pushdown store. Precise definitions for these two classes of automata can be found in [21,22].

3. A space and time efficient simulation of FMS-DPDA's

Following Igarashi [12], let $C \xrightarrow{w} C'$ be a derivation, i.e. the sequence of configurations (of the DPDA), beginning with C, in which the DPDA reads input w, and ends up in configuration C'. Let $|C|$ denote the stack height of configuration C. C_i is said to be a stacking configuration in the derivation if and only if it is not followed by any configuration with stack height less than or equal to $|C_i|$ in the derivation. Let C_0 be the initial configuration. Suppose the machine takes t moves to get from a configuration C_0 to C' while reading w (i.e. $C_0 \xrightarrow{w} C'$). Then C_i is a minimal stacking configuration in the derivation (from C_0 to C') at time t if and only if one of the following two conditions are met.

(1) C_i is the first stacking configuration in the derivation.
(2) There is a configuration of height $> |C_i|$ between C_i and the stacking configuration immediately preceding it in the derivation.

Notice that during the computation C_i may be a minimal stacking configuration at some time t and may or may not be at a later time t'. It is a dynamic property that changes as a computation proceeds. In Figure 1, for example, points 0, 1 and 2 correspond to minimal stacking configurations at time t_1 while points 0, 3 and 4 represent the minimal stacking configurations at time t_2.

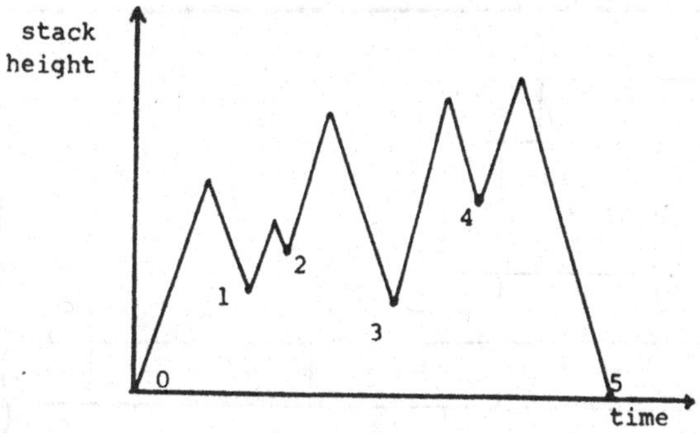

Figure 1. **Minimal Stacking Configurations**

Now we are ready to show the following:

Theorem 1. A FMS-DPDA can be simulated by an offline TM with a single worktape in $O(S(n))$ space and $O(n^2/S(n))$ time for any function $S(n)$, where $\log n \leq S(n) \leq n/\log n$ and $S(n)$ is tape constructable by an off line single tape TM in $n^2/S(n)$ time.

Proof. Let M be a k-minimal stacking DPDA. Then we will construct an offline single tape TM M' that will simulate M. The idea is to divide the stack of M into $O(n/S(n))$ blocks each of size $S(n)$. At any instant, M' will have at most the two topmost blocks of stack symbols represented on the simulation block (SB) of the worktape. It will be used as a "mini-stack" during the simulation. Along with the simulation block SB, the worktape is organized into multitracks which will contain other information such as the input head position, the block number and the current minimal stacking information which is required for the simulation.

We let a stacking configuration of M be denoted by a 5-triple (A,Q,I,B,S) where A is a stack symbol, Q a state, I the input head position, B the block number and S is the offset of the position of the stack symbol into the block. Now we are ready to present the organization of the worktape for M' in detail as shown in Figure 2. We use following notation:

IP: current input position
BN: current block number
MB: pairs of input head positions and the states each corresponding to a minimal stacking point within the current blocks. Each pair is stored on a separate track. There are k tracks for this. These tracks will behave like a pushdown stack.
MG: Like MB, MG has k tracks. Each track contains a minimal stacking configuration (A, Q, I, B, S) not associated with the current block. These tracks also function as a LIFO structure.
SB: This track is used for the stack blocks. The cells in SB can be thought of as being indexed 1 through $2*S(n)$. There are boundary markers at SB(1), SB(S(n)) and SB(2*S(n)). There is a subtrack for the markers to indicate minimal stacking points in the blocks.
SC: This track is used for scratch (work) space.

M' will simulate a move of M using its input head to read the input and the SB as the stack (or more precisely as a window into the stack). After each move of the simulation, if the stack height of M changes (thus the SB position representing the top of the stack changes), then M' will move all the information requiring $O(\log n)$ bits on the other tracks, a position in the same direction, and then update the input head position, IP. This insures that this information is always "close" to the worktape head, and hence the updating the counter on each step of the simulation does not take too long ($O(\log n)$ time to be exact). The fact that M is k-minimal stacking will allow M' to regenerate the other blocks, when they are needed, using at most $O(\log n)$ additional space. The operation of M' will be divided into $O(n/S(n))$ phases. At the beginning of a phase the top block of $S(n)$ stack symbols will be represented on the lower half of SB and the remaining upper half of it is used for growth of the

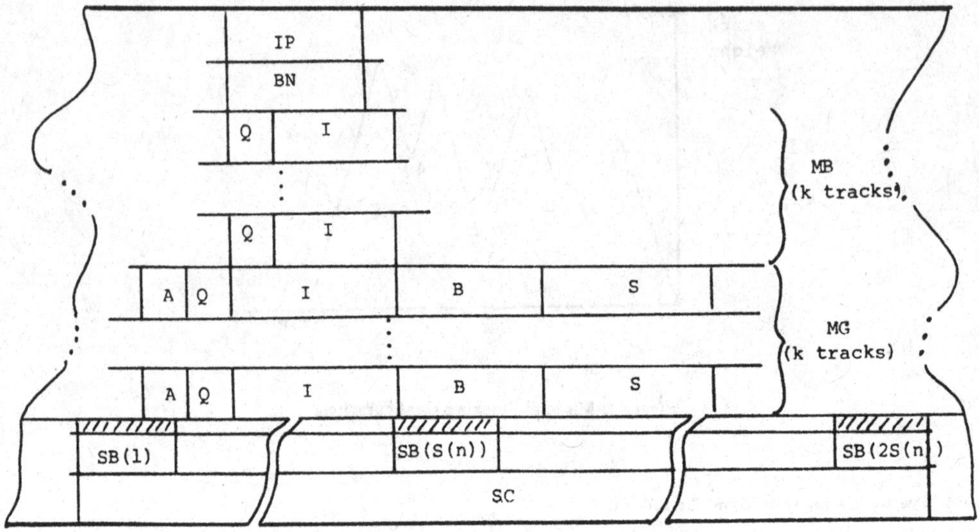

Figure 2. The Worktape of M'

stack. Thus M' can simulate at least S(n) moves before the simulation requires a stack symbol from another block of the stack. A phase ends when the next required stack position is not available on the blocks currently on the SB. At this time some informational bookkeeping and block restoration must follow before the next phase of the simulation takes place. In each phase the new minimal stacking configurations, if any, are recorded by keeping the pair of states and the input head positions, and by marking the minimal stacking points on the (SB) block. If a phase ends with the SB full, then the minimal stacking information from the SB blocks is moved to the dedicated tract which keeps the current minimal stacking information, to be used for the block reconstruction. Then the SB is erased. If a phase ends with the SB empty, there is no additional information to be saved. In either case, the block contents for the next phase of the simulation is then restored on the lower half of SB using the minimal stacking information.

Figure 3 illustrate how the next block (block 2) is reconstructed, when the phase with block 3 ends at time t with the SB empty. M' searches the current minimal stacking information (contained in the MG, which at this time represents points 0, 1, 2, 4, 6 and 7 of Figure 3(a)), and writes the stack symbol from each of the minimal stacking points which occurs in block 2 (points 4, 6 and 7) on their corresponding positions in the SB and marks them (see Figure 3(c)). Starting with the minimal stacking point of the height of the current block, if any, or with the next lower one otherwise (2 in this case), M is simulated until the stack height reaches the current block (h_2). Then M', using SB as the stack, continues the simulation until it meets the next minimal stacking point (point 4 of Figure 3(c)), where upon it will use the information corresponding to that minimal stacking point, to resume the simulation from that time. This process is repeated until M' finally meets the block boundary, (the center mark of SB). Notice that the sequence of moves made from one of the minimal stacking points to another consists only of pushing or rewriting moves. Now that the complete contents of the topmost block are available on the SB we are ready for the next simulation phase.

Now we present the algorithm for the simulation:

begin
(//MG, MB and BN are globals. Assume the work head is on SB top unless otherwise specified. q,π and Z are the current state, the input symbol at position IP and the stack top symbol of M, respectively. push S(A) means push A onto the top of stack S. $w^{(1)}$ is the topmost symbol of w in the stack.//)
(1) IP←0; BN←0; q←q_0; SB(1)←Z_0; Z←Z_0;
(2) push MG(Z_0,q_0,0,0,0); (//This is the first minimal stacking configuration//)
repeat

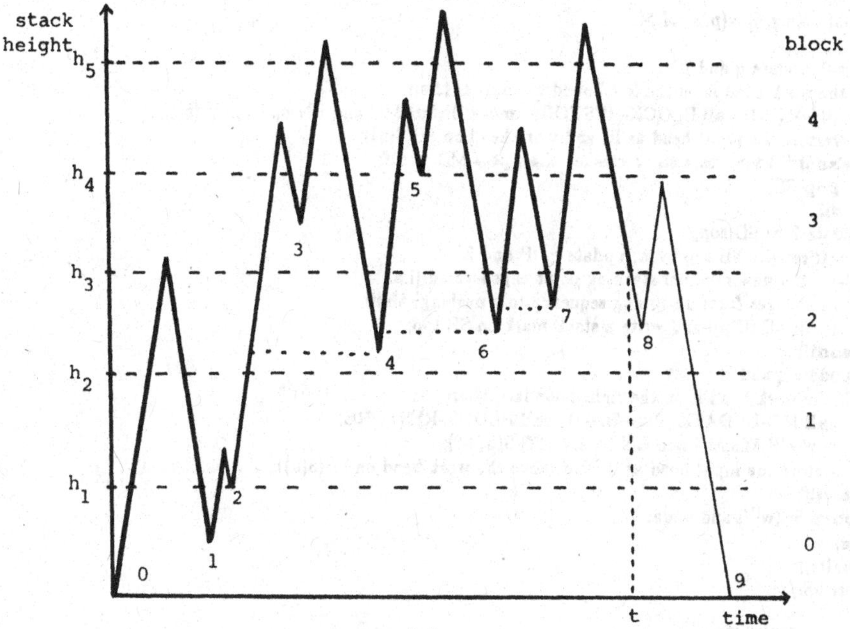

(a)

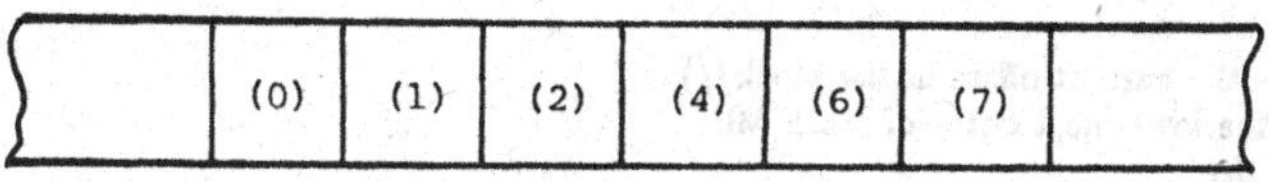

(b)

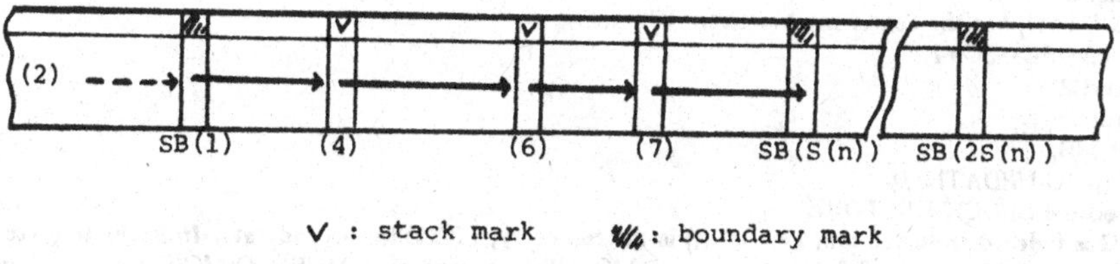

(c)

Figure 3. **Block restoration:**
(a) Time-space profile,
(b) Minimal stacking information at time t (contained in MG),
(c) The restoration for block 2.

```
(3) simulate δ(q,π,Z)=(p,w) of M;
case
  (4) |w|=0: update q and IP;
      if the work head is on the left boundary marker then
          BN←BN-1; call BLOCK-RESTORE; move IP,MB,MG and BN up to SB(S(n));
          restore the input head as IP and work head on SB(S(n));
        else if SB top has a stack marker then pop MB endif;
          pop SB;
      endif;
      update Z as SB top;
  (5) |w|=1: rewrite SB top by w; update q, IP and Z;
  (6) |w|=2: if a new minimal stacking point is generated (i.e.,
          M changes from a popping sequence to a pushing) then
          push MB(IP,q) and write a stack mark on SB top;
        endif;
        update q and IP;
        if the work head is on the right boundary then
          call MG-UPDATE; BN←BN+1; call BLOCK-RESTORE;
          move IP,MB,MG and BN back to SB(S(n)+1);
          restore the input head as IP and move the work head on SB(S(n));
        endif;
       push SB(w^(1)) and update Z;
 endcase;
until(M halts);
end(//algorithm//)
```

Procedure MG-UPDATE
(//Cell SB(S(n)) has the center marker. MB is indexed from the top, i.e., MB(1) is the top entry, MB(2) the second entry from the top, etc. Each of the information I and Q in i-th entry of MB will be named as I(MB(i))and Q(MB(i)).//)

```
begin
 SC←1;    (// SC is the current offset in the block//)
 find the index j of the lowermost entry of stack MB;
 for i=1 to 2*S(n) do
   begin
     if SB(i) has a stack marker then
       push MG(SB(i),Q(MB(j)),I(MB(j)), BN,SC); j←j-1;
     endif;
     if SB(SC) has the center marker then SC←1;
       else SC←SC+1;
     endif;
   end;
 clear MB;
end (//MG-UPDATE//)
```

Procedure BLOCK-RESTORE
(//MG is indexed from the top, i.e., MG(l) is the top entry, MG(2) the second entry from the top, etc. Each of the information A, Q, I, B, and S in i-th entry of MG will be named as A(MG(i)), Q(MG(i)), etc. q',π' and Z' are the current state, current input symbol (possibly null) and top stack symbol of M respectively.//)

```
begin
 (1) Search MG from top to bottom until the first i-th entry is found
     such that either one of the following two conditions is met.
     (a) B(MG(i))< BN
     (b) B(MG(i))= BN and S(MG(i))=1

 (2) position the input head as I(MG(i));
   SC←B(MG(i)); q'←Q(MG(i)); Z'←A(MG(i)); SB(S(MG(i)))←Z';
   if (a) then
     while SC<BN do
       repeat
         simulate δ(q',π',Z')=(p,w) of M; update q' and Z';
         if |w|=1 then rewrite SB top by Z'
           else(//|w|=2//)
             if the work head does not read the center mark
                then push SB(Z')
```

```
        endif;
      endif;
    until(work head reads the center marker)
    erase SB and write Z' on SB(1); SC←SC+1;
    position the work head on SB(1);
  endwhile
endif

(3) for j=i-1 down to 1 do
    begin
      SB(S(MG(j)))←(A(MG(j)), marker) (//marker contains 'v'//)
      Push MB(I(MG(j)), Q(MG(j))); erase MG(j);
    end;

(4) move the work head on SB(1); SBFULL←false;
    repeat
      repeat
        simulate δ(q',π,Z')=(p,w) of M; update q' and Z';
        if |w|=1 then rewrite SB top by Z';
          else(//|w|=2//)
            if the work head is on the center mark then SBFULL←true;
            move the worktape head one step to the right;
            if the cell does not have a stack mark then write Z';
            endif;
        endif
      until (SBFULL or the work head reads a stack mark);
      if a stack mark is read then
        Z'←current SB symbol which is marked; i←i-1; q'←Q(MB(i));
        position the input head as I(MB(i));
      endif
    until (SBFULL);
end (//BLOCK-RESTORE//)
```

For the execution time of the main program, steps (1) and (2) run in constant time. The global time needed for step (3) and step (5) is no more than O(nlog n). It is easily seen that the time needed for MG-UPDATE is O(S(n)log S(n)). The time analysis of BLOCK-RESTORE can be observed from the following:

(i) Block (1) needs O(log n) time,
(ii) Block (2) needs O(n) time,
(iii) Block (3) (the marking of the block) needs O(S(n)log S(n)) time, and
(iv) Block (4) (the actual restoration for the block) needs O(S(n)) time.

Since those subroutines are called at most O(n/S(n)) times, steps (4) and (6) of the main routine need at most $O(n/S(n)*(n + S(n)\log S(n))) = O(n^2/S(n)+n\log S(n))$ steps. So the overall time is $O(n^2/S(n)+n\log n)$, i.e. $O(n^2/S(n))$ if $S(n)\leq n/\log n$ and O(nlog n) otherwise. □

It seems difficult to achieve the same time bound $O(n^2/S(n))$ when the space is in the range $n/\log n<S(n)\leq n$ with only one worktape. The bottleneck seems to be the global time of O(nlog S(n)) needed to count the displacement on the block and O(nlog n) to update the stacking points MB and the input position counter IP. With a multitape TM, however, we can achieve the time $O(n^2/S(n))$ for the whole range. For the upper range we can simply use the algorithm for general DPDA's by Braumuhl and Verbeck[1].

4. Simple Strict Restricted DPDA's

In this section we introduce the simple strict restricted DPDA's (SSR-DPDA's) and show that they can be simulated by an offline TM simultaneously in S(n) space and $O(n^2/S(n))$ time for any "nice" function, $\log n \leq S(n)\leq n$.

Definition. A DPDA $M=\langle Q,\Sigma,\Gamma,\delta,q_0,Z_0,F\rangle$ is called simple strict restricted if both of the following conditions are met:

(1) If $\delta(q,\epsilon,A)$ is defined, then for all $B\in\Gamma$ and $a\in\Sigma$, $\delta(q,a,B)$ is not defined.

(2) If $\delta(q,\pi,A) = (q', \alpha)$ and $\delta(q,\pi,B) = (q'', \gamma)$, then either
(i) $\alpha^{(1)}=\gamma^{(1)}$ and $|\alpha| = |\gamma|$ and $q'=q''$
or (ii) q' or $q'' \in D$

where A and B are arbitrary elements of Γ, q an arbitrary state, $\pi \in \Sigma \cup \{\epsilon\}$, D is a set of dead states from which nothing may be accepted, and $\alpha^{(1)}$ is the topmost symbol of the string α in the stack. The reader should note the difference between this definition and that of the strict restricted DPDA defined in [12]. The languages presented in [12] as examples of languages accepted by SR-DPDA's (Dyck languages, Standard languages, structured context-free languages[12,19] and leftmost Szilard languages of phase structured grammars[13]), are also accepted by SSR-DPDA's. The constructions are straightforward. An example can be found in [12].

We are now ready to show the following:

Theorem 2. A SSR-DPDA M can be simulated by an offline singletape TM M', in O(S(n)) space and $0(n^2/S(n))$ time, for any function S(n) where $\log n \leq S(n) \leq n$, whenever S(n) is tape constructable by an offline singletape TM in $0(n^2/S(n))$ time.

Proof. Again, as in Theorem 1, we divide the stack into O(n/S(n)) blocks each of size S(n). The simulation used in Theorem 1 was such that the moves of a given block were those moves which directly followed the moves of the previous phase in the computation. Thus any given block of the stack may be presented in the mini-stack during different phases of the simulation. However in this simulation, we simulate all the moves which occur within a given block of the stack in a single phase. Thus, if we let Figure 4 represent a computation, then all moves which M takes with the stack top in block i are simulated in the same phase. To do this we assume that if a dead state is entered then it is not entered until the stack top is in the block currently being processed. The simulation therefore involves looking for the move where M enters a dead state.

Let a partial configuration (P-C) of M be a 4-triple (q,w,i,h) where q is the state of M, w an input, i the input head position and h the stack height. From the two restrictions SSR-DPDA M has, it can be seen that M', given a valid P-C from a computation of M, can trace the exact sequence of the P-C's up to any possible partial configuration in 0(log n) space and 0(n) time. Furthermore, M' can compute the exact symbol M will write in that configuration at any height.

For the simulation on block i, M' starts with the initial P-C $(q_0,w,0,0)$ and traces the P-C's until block i is entered. Then M' will initiate the actual simulation on the block using a worktape as a mini-stack. If M' crosses the left or the right boundary of the block, it quits the actual simulation phase and traces the partial configuration until M's stack enters the block again. A block simulation phase will be completed when there is no more input. Then the simulation for the next higher block is initiated. The simulation continues until M rejects or M' sees a block simulation phase where no configuration occurs within that block.

For an efficient simulation the worktape of M' is organized as in Figure 5, where SB is the mini-stack of size S(n), H the current block height, which is the stack height of SB(1), and C_1 and C_2 are counters for downward

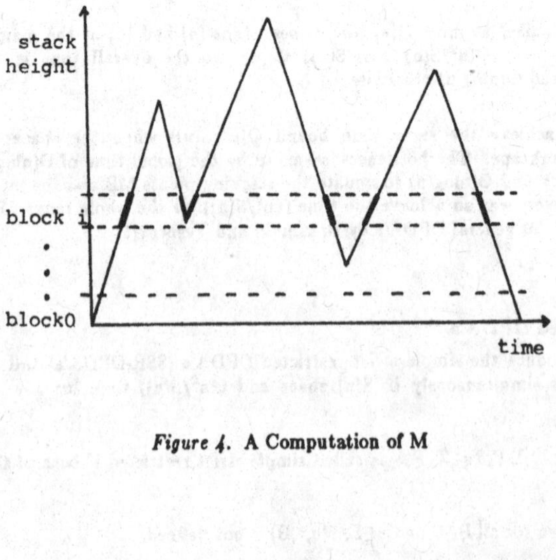

Figure 4. A Computation of M

displacement and upward displacement from SB, respectively.

Using techniques presented in [4], the manipulation of counters C_1 and C_2 can be accomplished in $O(n)$ time for each phase. Since there are $O(n/S(n))$ phases, the overall time is $O(n^2/S(n))$. We leave the formal details to the reader. □

5. A Characterization of 2-head 2-way Deterministic Finite Automata

In this section, we show the equivalence of 2-head 2-way DFA's and the simple deterministic checking stack automata (S-DCSA). First we introduce an interesting lemma which will be needed for the next theorem. This lemma is actually a simplified version of a similar theorem on GSM's given in [9].

Lemma 1. Given a DFA M, one can construct a 1-head 2-way DFA M', such that for every input and every reachable configuration (input head position and state) of M on that input, M' will, when:

(1) its head is scanning the corresponding location of the same input, and
(2) it is given the state of M

halt in a configuration which:

(1) yields the state of M for the configuration immediately preceding the one given, and
(2) has the tape head scanning the position scanned by the previous configuration of M.

Proof. The basic idea is to construct the set of possible previous states of q, say $(q_1,q_2,\ldots,q_k)$. Then the subsets of possible predecessors of each of these states (i.e., $Q_{11},Q_{21},\ldots,Q_{k1}$) are constructed. Each set is then replaced by the sets of predecessors for the entire set (i.e., $Q_{12},Q_{22},\ldots Q_{k2}$). The process is iterated using the tape head to read the input tape (during the process it is moving backward), until either only one such subset, say Q_{rm}, $1 \leq r \leq k$, is nonempty or the left endmarker is reached (assume the start state of M is in Q_{rj} in this case). Then the predecessor state of q is q_r. Now M' moves forward one step, picks two states each from any state subset available, simulates M forward until the next states are equal (i.e. q) and then backs up one step. For more details, see [9]. □

We are now ready to show the following:

Theoerem 3. 2-head 2-way DFA's are equivalent, in computational power, to simple deterministic checking stack automata (S-DCSA's).

Proof. It is straight forward to see that a 2-head 2-way DFA can be simulated by a S-DCSA. Thus, we need only to show the converse.

Let M be a S-DCSA. We assume M is normalized (as described in section 2). We construct a 2-head 2-way DFA M' that will simulate M. To simulate a step of M, M' needs the state, the input and the stack symbol of M's present configuration. For the simulation, M' will keep the state and top stack symbol of M in its control. One of

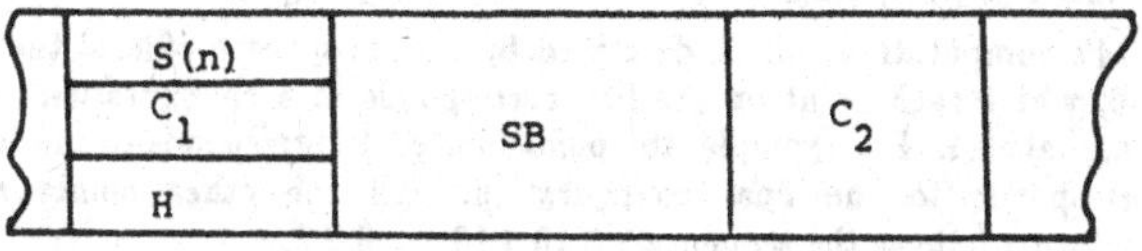

Figure 5. The Worktape of M'

its heads, say H1, will simulate the input head of M. The other head (H2) will be used to simulate the stack. The position of H2 will correspond to the position of M's input head when the stack symbol in the control was the topmost symbol. Now we need to show how a move of M can be simulated. If the next move of M is an upward stroke, then H2 is moved to the right and the control is changed to reflect the new topmost stack symbol and M's new state. (Also the position of H1 may change.) If the next move of M is a downward stroke, then M' needs H2 to backup one position. The state and the stack symbol generated by the previous stacking move of M must be ascertained. Notice that, since M is a S-DCSA, there is 1-1 correspondence between a_l and Z_l, $(1 \leq i \leq l)$ from the input $a_1a_2...a_m$ and stack contents $Z_1Z_2....Z_m$ respectively for some $1 \leq m \leq n$. If we assume each state of M keeps the stack symbol generated in that state (or the topmost stack symbol if M is no longer stacking), we can retrieve the stack symbol from the state. Now the problem is, given a stacking state and the corresponding input, to compute the next stacking state for the following two cases:

(i) the stack head moves to the right (an upstroke), and
(ii) the stack head moves to the left (a downstroke).

Case (i) was discussed earlier and presents no problem since the information obtained at the location H2 and the information in the finite state control allow the new stack location, its contents and the new stacking state to be calculated. Case (ii) requires that, given an input position and its state, we be able to compute (with only the head H2) the previous state (which also recovers the desired stack symbol). This can be done using the idea from lemma 1. □

6. A Characterization of Nondeterministic Multihead Finite Automata

Let k-2PDA (k-2FA) denote a nondeterministic k-head two-way pushdown automata (finite automata). In this section, we shall prove the following theorem a corollary of which gives a simple characterization of k-2FA's:

Theorem 4. Let $k \geq 1$.
(i) If L is accepted by a k-2PDA which makes at most r pushdown reversals (r, a positive integer), then L can be accepted by a $2k\lfloor \log_2(r+1) \rfloor$-2FA.
(ii) If L is accepted by a 2k-2FA, then L can be accepted by a k-2PDA which makes at most 1 pushdown reversal.

Theorem 4 (ii) has been shown in [22]. Our proof of Theorem 4 (ii) is similar to that in [22] although somewhat simpler.

Corollary 1. Let $k \geq 1$. L is accepted by a 2k-2FA if and only if it is accepted by a k-2PDA which makes at most one pushdown reversal.

Proof. Let M' be a k-2DPDA which is r-reversal bounded (i.e., on every input, M' makes at most r pushdown reversals or alternations between increasing and decreasing the length of the pushdown store). A configuration of M', on an input w, is a triple (q,w,i,α) which represents that M' is in state q with the stack contents α and the input head is scanning the i-th symbol of w. Clearly, by adding "dummy" pushdown symbols, we can convert M' to an equivalent k-2PDA M which has the following properties:

(1) On every move, M pops or pushes exactly one symbol,
(2) M's initial configuration is $(q_0,w,0,z_0)$, and
(3) M's accepting configuration is $(f, w, 0, Z_0)$ where f is the only accepting state.

On a given input, M's computation can be described by a time-space profile of the stack (see [8]) such as the one shown in Figure 6, where each point on the line corresponds to a configuration. In the figure, only the configurations of interest are labeled. For example, the point labeled 1 corresponds to the initial configuration and the point labeled 2 corresponds to the final configuration. All the other points represent intermediate configurations. The computation follows the sequence 1,3,10,4,16,.....,9,6,2.

Let $\alpha \underset{\dagger x\$}{\longrightarrow} \beta$ denote that M, on the input †x$, takes a direct transition from the configuration α to the configuration β, and let $\alpha \underset{\dagger x\$}{\longrightarrow} \beta$ represent its transitive and reflexive closure. By $(\alpha_1,\beta_1) \underset{\dagger x\$}{\longrightarrow} (\alpha_2,\beta_2)$, we mean $\alpha_1 \underset{\dagger x\$}{\longrightarrow} \alpha_2$, $\alpha_2 \underset{\dagger x\$}{\longrightarrow} \beta_2$ and $\beta_2 \underset{\dagger x\$}{\longrightarrow} \beta_1$. If $\alpha_2 = \beta_2$, we call the pair (α_2,β_2) a terminal. In the figure (10,10), (16,16), (14,14),..etc., are terminals. They will lead to no pair of configurations.

Now we describe a nondeterministic procedure ALPHA which traverses the profile along the space line (from the bottom to the top in Figure 6), starting from the pair of initial and accepting configurations. The procedure uses a pushdown store, which keeps pairs of configurations which have not yet been processed. A similar algorithm was described in [8].

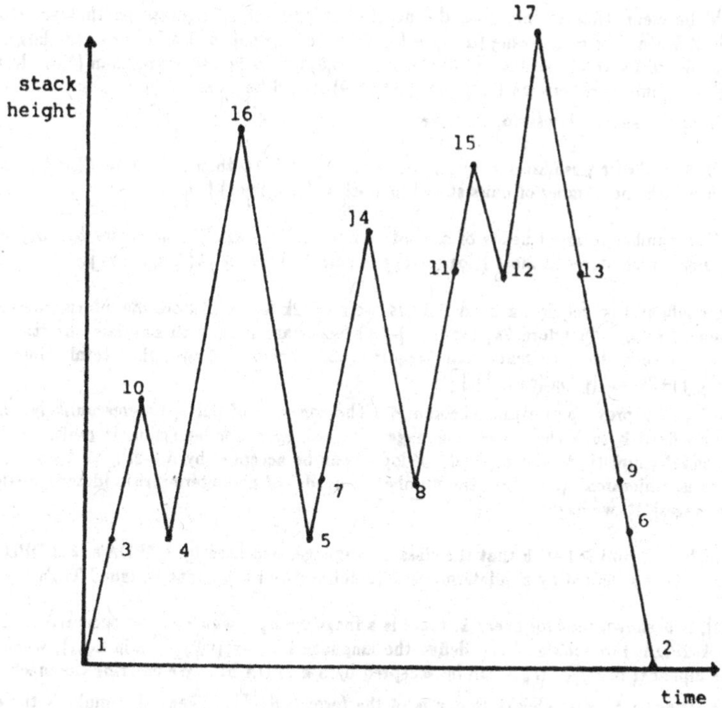

Figure 6. **Profile of a computation**

Procedure ALPHA (†x$)
(//The procedure guesses a profile for the input †x$ and processes it. There is one pushdown stack S which is initially empty. push S(y) pushes y on top of the stack S while pop S(y) pops S and returns the top element in y//)

```
begin
  (α,β)←(initial configuration, accepting configuration)
  repeat
   case
     (1) α=β: (//(α, β) is a terminal//)
        if the stack S empty then output ('ACCEPT'); halt
          else pop S((α,β))
        endif
     (2) α≠β: Nondeterministically do (i) or (ii):
        (i) guess a pair (α1,β1);
            if (α,β) --†x$--> (α1,β1) then
               (α,β)←(α1,β1);
            else output ('reject'); halt;
            endif
        (ii) Guess pairs (α,γ) and (γ,β) and do
  (a) or (b):
                   (a) push S((α,γ)); (α,β)←(γ,β);
                   (b) push S((γ,β)); (α,β)←(α,γ);
        endcase
     forever
end (ALPHA)
```

It should be clear, that to minimize the number of pairs of configurations, that are stored in the stack, ALPHA, when it has a choice of storing (α, γ) or (γ, β), stores the pair which "covers" the larger number of reversals. For example, in Figure 4, between (3,5) and (5,6), (3,5) covers less reversals than (5,6). In this case, ALPHA should push (5,6). Similarly, between (7,8) and (8,9), (8,9) should be stored.

Formalizing the above discussion, we have:

Lemma 1. If M makes r pushdown reversals on input †x$ ($r \geq 1$), then procedure ALPHA can accept †x$ in a computation in which the number of pairs stored in stack is $\lfloor \log_2(r+1) \rfloor -1$.

Lemma 2. The number of input heads of a nondeterministic two-way FA necessary to carry out the procedures ALPHA on inputs which stores at most $\lfloor \log_2(r+1) \rfloor -1$ pairs in stack is $2k\lfloor \log_2(r+1) \rfloor$.

Proof. Each configuration requires k heads. Thus, we need 2k heads to store the information contained in a pair of configurations (α, β). Therefore $2k\lfloor \log_2(r+1)-1 \rfloor)$ heads are needed to simulate the stack of the procedure ALPHA. To process the current pair requires 2k heads. Thus the total number of heads is $2k(\lfloor \log_2(r+1)-1 \rfloor)+2k=2k(\lfloor \log_2(r+1) \rfloor)$. □

Lemma 1 and 2 prove part (i) of Theorem 4. The converse of part (i) seems unlikely. In fact, we believe that there is no fixed k such that every language accepted by a nondeterministic multihead 2-way FA (i.e., a language of nondeterministic tape complexity of log n) can be accepted by a k-2PDA. Using translations and the fact that there is a hierarchy (based on the number of heads) of nondeterministic (deterministic) multihead two-way PDA languages[11], we have:

Theorem 5. There is no $k \geq 1$ such that the class of languages accepted by k-2PDA's (k-2 DPDA's) is identical to the class of languages accepted by nondeterministic (deterministic) log n-tape bounded TM's.

Proof. In [11], it is shown that for every k, there is a language L_{k+1} which can be accepted by a (k+1) - 2PDA M, but not by a k-2PDA. For such an L_{k+1}, define the language $L'_{k+1}=\{(x\#)^{|x|} \mid x \text{ in } L_{k+1}\}$, where # is a new symbol not in the alphabet of L_{k+1}. L'_{k+1} can be accepted by a k-2PDA M'. We describe the machine M' briefly.

Given a string y, M' first checks that y is of the form $(x\#)^{|x|}$. Then, M' simulates the computation of M such that all k heads of M' are in the i-th block of $(x\#)^{|x|}$ if an only if the k+1st head of M is in the i-th position of the input x. The k heads are in their proper locations in the i-th block. Determining the symbol under the k+1st head and updating its position is easily carried out by M' using the pushdown store. Thus, L'_{k+1} can be accepted by a k-2PDA. If k-2PDA languages are the same as nondeterministic log n-tape bounded languages, then L'_{k+1} can be accepted by a log n-tape bounded TM Z'. We can now construct from Z', another log n-tape bounded TM Z accepting L_{k+1}. It follows that L_{k+1} can also be accepted by a k-2PDA which is impossible by [11]. The deterministic case is handled similarly. □

A special case of Theorem 5, when k=1 and the device is deterministic, has been shown in [5] by a different argument. The deterministic version of Theorem 5 has also been observed in [22].

Theorem 4 part (ii) is the converse of part (i) for the case when r=1. This result was shown in [22]. For completeness, we give a proof which is similar to that in [22] although somewhat simpler.

Let M be a 2k-2FA. Assume that M accepts if and only if all its heads are on the right end marker and the state is f (which we assume to be a halting state). We construct a k-2PDA M' accepting the same language of M. M' operates as follows:

The k heads of M' simulate the first k heads of M. The current symbols scanned by the last k heads of M are recorded as a k-tuple in the finite control of M'. Initially, the k-tuple recorded is (c, c, ..., c). M' computes like M. In addition, if head i, $k+1 \leq i \leq 2k$, is moved in direction $d_i \neq 0$, M' guesses a symbol, say b, which is going to be scanned next by the head i and stores the information as (b,i,d_i) in the stack. Then the k-tuple $(a_1, \ldots, a_i, \ldots, a_k)$ is updated to $(a_1, \ldots, b, \ldots, a_k)$. The process is continued until M' enters the accepting state f with its k heads on $ and the recorded k-tuple is ($, $,..., $). M' then uses the k-heads to check that the sequence of symbols, guessed to carry out the simulation of the last k heads of M, is consistent with the input. The simulation is, of course, done in reverse, until all k heads are on the left end marker and the stack contains Z_0. M' accepts the input when this happens. □

References

1) Braunmuhl, B. and Verbeek, R., A recognition algorithm for deterministic CFLs optimal in time and space, *Proc. 21st IEEE-FOCS*, pp. 411-420 (1980).

2) Cook, S., An observation on time-storage tradeoff, *JCSS*, Vol. 9, pp. 308-316 (1974).

3) Cook, S., Deterministic CFL's are accepted simultaneously in polynomial time and log squared space, *Proc. 11th ACM Symp. on Theory of Comp.*, pp. 338-345 (1979).

4) Fischer, P., Meyer, A. and Rosenberg, A., Counter machines and counter languages, *MST*, Vol. 2, No. 3, pp. 265-283 (1968).

5) Galil, Z., Two-way deterministic pushdown automaton languages and some open problems in the theory of computing, *MST*, Vol. 10, pp. 211-228 (1977).

6) Ginsburg, S. and Harrison, M., Bracketed context-free languages, *JCSS*, Vol. 1, pp. 1-23 (1967).

7) Greibach, S., Checking automata and one-way stack languages, *JCSS*, Vol. 3, pp. 196-217 (1969).

8) Gurari, E. and Ibarra, O., Path systems: constructions, solutions and applications, *SIAM J. Comput.*, Vol. 9, No. 2, pp. 348-374 (1980).

9) Hopcraft, J. and Ullman, J., Unified theory of automata, The Bell System Technical J., Vol. 46, No. 8, pp. 1793-1829 (1967).

10) Ibarra, O., Characterizations of some tape and time complexity classes of Turing Machines in terms of multihead and auxiliary stack automata, *JCSS*, Vol. 5, No.2, pp. 88-117 (1971).

11) Ibarra, O., On two-way multihead automata, *JCSS*, Vol. 7, pp. 28-36 (1973).

12) Igarashi, Y., Tape bounds for some subclasses of deterministic context-free languages, *Information and Control*, Vol. 37, pp. 321-333 (1978).

13) Igarashi, Y., The tape complexity of some classes of Szilard languages, *SIAM J. Comput.*, Vol. 6, No. 3, pp. 461-466 (1977).

14) Lewis, P., Hartmanis, J., and Stearns, R., Memory bounds for the recognition of context-free and context-sensitive languages, *IEEE Conf. Record on Switching Circuit Theory and Logic Design*, pp. 191-202 (1965).

15) Lipton, R. and Zalcstein, Y., Word problems solvable in logspace, *Computer Science Department, Yale University, Tech. Report #6* (1976).

16) Lynch, N., Logspace recognition and translation of parenthesis languages, *JACM*, Vol. 24, No. 4, pp. 583-590 (1977).

17) Mehlhorn, K., Bracket-languages are recognizable in logarithmic space, *Information Processing Letters*, Vol. 5, No. 6, pp. 168-170 (1976).

18) Moriya, E., Associate languages and derivational complexity of formal grammars and languages, *Information and Control*, Vol. 22, pp. 139-162 (1973).

19) Richie, R. and Springsteel, F., Language recognition by marking automata, *Information and Control*, Vol. 20, pp. 313-330 (1972).

20) Sudborough, I., A note on tape-bounded complexity classes and linear context-free languages, *JACM*, Vol. 22, No. 4, pp. 499-500 (1975).

21) Sudborough, I., On tape-bounded complexity classes and multihead finite automata, *JCSS*, 10, pp. 338-345 (1979).

22) Sudborough, I., On deterministic context-free languages, multihead automata, and the power of an auxiliary pushdown store, *8th Annual ACM Symp. on Theory of Computing*, pp. 141-148 (1976).

23) Valiant, L., Decision problems for families of deterministic pushdown automata, *Ph.D. thesis, University of Warwick, U.K.* (1973).

24) Verbeek, R., Time-space trade-offs for general recursion, *Proc. 22nd IEEE-FOCS*, pp. 228-234 (1981).

A COMPLETE AXIOM SYSTEM FOR ALGEBRA OF CLOSED-REGULAR EXPRESSION

Hiroyuki IZUMI*†
Yasuyoshi INAGAKI*
and
Namio HONDA**
*Faculty of Engineering, Nagoya University,
Furo-cho, Chikusa-ku, Nagoya 464 JAPAN
**Faculty of Engineering, Toyohashi University of Technology, Toyohashi, Aichi Prefecture 440 JAPAN
†Presently, belonging to Fujitsu Laboratory,
Kawasaki 211 JAPAN

1. Introduction

The concept of closed languages was introduced by Boasson and Nivat [1]. The authors have also introduced the concept of closed regular set in their paper [2], which is a natural extension of regular set so that it may contain infinite strings. They have proved that the set equation $X = BX + C$ ($\varepsilon \notin B$) on closed regular sets has the unique solution $X = B^{\infty}C$ and the class of closed regular sets is the smallest class which contains finite sets of finite strings and is closed under operations $\cdot$(concatenation), + (union) and ∞ (∞-closure).

Based on these results, this paper introduces closed regular expressions and proposes a complete axiom system for closed regular expressions. If the object is restricted to regular sets of finite strings then our axiom system coincides with Salomaa's axiom system of regular expressions [3].

2. Definitions and Notations

Let Σ be an alphabet. Σ^* and Σ^{ω} denote the set of all finite sequences of symbols from Σ and that of all ω-sequences of symbols from Σ, respectively. Σ^{∞} stands for the union of Σ^* and Σ^{ω}, i.e., $\Sigma^{\infty} = \Sigma^* + \Sigma^{\omega}$. We use the symbols ε and ϕ to denote the null string and the empty set, respectively. We call a subset of Σ^{∞} a <u>∞-language</u>.

The <u>concatenation</u> $(\cdot)$ on Σ^{∞} is defined by: for any X and Y in Σ^{∞},

$$X \cdot Y = \begin{cases} a_1 a_2 \ldots a_n \, b_1 b_2 b_3 \ldots \text{ if } X = a_1 a_2 \ldots a_n \in \Sigma^* \\ \qquad\qquad\qquad\qquad \text{and } Y = b_1 b_2 \ldots \text{ in } \Sigma^\infty \\ X \text{ if } X \in \Sigma^\omega \end{cases}$$

That is, the concatenation on Σ^∞ is defined similarly to the case on Σ^* besides if X is a ω-sequence then $X \cdot Y = X$ for any Y in Σ^∞.

We define the operations $\cdot$, $*$, ω, and ∞ on ∞-languages as follows: We denote the set of the nonnegative integers by N. Let A and B be ∞-languages.

$A \cdot B = \{ x \cdot Z \in \Sigma^\infty \mid x \in A \cap \Sigma^* \text{ and } Z \in B \} + A \cap \Sigma^\omega$

$A^* = \{ \varepsilon \} + A + A^2 + \ldots + A^n + \ldots = \cup_{i \in N} A^i$,

where $A^0 = \{ \varepsilon \}$ and $A^{i+1} = A^i . A$ for any $i \in N$.

$A^\omega = \{ X \in \Sigma^\omega \mid X = x_0 \, x_1 \, x_2 \ldots x_i \ldots, \; \forall i \in N, \, x_i \in [A \cap \Sigma^* - \{ \varepsilon \}] \} + (A \cap \Sigma^*)^* \cdot (A \cap \Sigma^\omega)$

$A^\infty = A^* + A^\omega$

The following proposition 1 contains the identities wich will be used in the sequel. The proofs for them are found in the references [1] and [4].

Proposition 1 For any $A, B, C, \subset \Sigma^\infty$,

(1) $AB = (A \cap \Sigma^*)B + (A \cap \Sigma^\omega)$

(2) $A\{ \varepsilon \} = A = \{ \varepsilon \}A$

(3) $A\phi = A \cap \Sigma^\omega$

(4) $\phi A = \phi$

(5) $(AB)C = A(BC)$

(6) $A(B + C) = AB + AC$

(7) $(A + B)C = AC + BC$

(8) $A^* = \{ \varepsilon \} + AA^* = (\{ \varepsilon \} + A)^*$

(9) $A^\omega = AA^\omega = (A - \{ \varepsilon \})^\omega = A^\omega B = A^\omega \phi$

(10) $A^\infty = \{ \varepsilon \} + AA^\infty = (\{ \varepsilon \} + A)^\omega$

(11) $A^\infty \phi = A^\omega$

(12) $A^\omega + A^*B = A^\infty B$

(13) $\phi^* = \phi^\infty = \{ \varepsilon \}$

(14) $\phi^\omega = \phi$

(15) IF $A \subset \Sigma^\omega$, $A^\omega = A$ and $A^\infty = A^* = \{ \varepsilon \} + A$

3. Closed Regular Expression

For any $X = a_0 \, a_1 \ldots a_i \ldots \in \Sigma^\infty$ and any $i \in N$, we define

$X/i = a_0 \, a_1 \ldots a_i$.

For any $A \subset \Sigma^\infty$, fg A and adh A are defined as follows [1]:

$\text{fg } A = \{ x \in \Sigma^* \mid Z \in \Sigma^\infty, \, xZ \in A \}$

$$\text{adh } A = \{ X \in \Sigma^{\omega} \mid \forall i \in N, X/i \in \text{fg } A \}$$

A ∞-language $A \subset \Sigma^{\infty}$ is called a closed language (cl-language) if adh $A \subset A$.[1] An ω-language $A \subset \Sigma^{\omega}$ is called an ω-regular set if A can be represented as $A = \bigcup_{j=1}^{m} B_j C_j$ for some integer m, where B_j and C_j are regular sets for j = 1, 2, ..., m. Further, a ∞-language $A \subset \Sigma^{\infty}$ is called a ∞-regular set if A can be represented as the union of some regular sets and ω-regular sets. If a ∞-language A is a cl-language and a ∞-regular set, then we call it a closed regular set (cl-regular set).

The authors have proved in the paper [2] that the family of cl-regular sets is the smallest family containing finite sets of finite symbol sequences which is closed under the operations • (concatenation), + (union) and ∞-operation. This fact suggests the following definition:

Definition 1 Let Σ be an alphbet. A closed regular expression (cl-regular expression) on Σ is any finite string of symbols from the set

$$\Sigma \cup \{ +, \cdot, \infty, (,), \phi \}$$

that may be formed according to the following rules:

(1) ϕ is a cl-regular expression.

(2) For any $a \in \Sigma$, a is a cl-regular expression.

(3) If α and β are cl-regular expressions, then $(\alpha \cdot \beta)$, $(\alpha + \beta)$, and (α^{∞})

are cl-regular expressions.

The parentheses and the symbol • are generally omitted when it will not cause confusion. If cl-regular expressions α and β are identical as strings on $\Sigma \cup \{ +, \cdot, \infty, (,), \phi \}$, we will write $\alpha \equiv \beta$.

A cl-regular expression describes a cl-regular set according to our usual interpretation of the set operation. That is,

Definition 2 Let us denote the cl-regular set which a cl-regular expression α describes by $|\alpha|$. Then,

(1) $|\phi| = \phi$ (the empty set)

(2) $|a| = \{ a \}$ for any $a \in \Sigma$

(3) For any cl-regular expressions α and β,

$$|(\alpha \cdot \beta)| = |\alpha| \cdot |\beta|$$
$$|(\alpha + \beta)| = |\alpha| + |\beta|$$
$$|(\alpha^{\infty})| = |\alpha|^{\infty}$$

We can easily prove that $|\phi^{\infty}| = \{\varepsilon\}$ and $|\alpha^{\infty}\phi| = |\alpha|^{\omega}$ by using the identities (11) and (13) given in Proposition 1. So, we will use the expressions ε and α^{ω} as the abbreviations of ϕ^{∞} and $\alpha^{\infty}\phi$, respectively. If the cl-regular expressions α and β describe the same cl-regular set, then α and β are said to be equivalent and written as $\alpha = \beta$.

4. Solution of the set equation X = BX + C

Let X be the set variable over ∞-languages on Σ. Assume that B and C are cl-regular sets and the $\varepsilon \notin B$. Then the cl-regular solution of the equation $X = BX + C$ are given as follows: If $C = \phi$ and $B \cap \Sigma^{\omega} = \phi$ then the cl-regular solution is

$$X = \phi \text{ or } X = B^{\infty}C \ (= B^{\omega}).$$

Otherwise, the cl-regular solution is uniquely determined as

$$X = B^{\infty}C.$$

This result has been proved by the authors [2].

Remark Park [4] has discussed the equation $X = BX + C$ on Σ^{∞} and has given the maximal fix-point solution $X = B^{\omega} + B^*C$. But he has also shown an example such that $\cap_{i=1}^{\infty} F^{i}(\Sigma^{\infty}) \neq B^{\omega} + B^*C$, where $F(X) = BX + C$.

5. An algebra of cl-regular expressions

We propose an axiom system to characterize equalities of cl-regular expressions. For this purpose, we need some concepts concerning cl-regular expressions. They are empty word property, empty word expression, empty set property and finite word property. Intuitively, a cl-regular expression α has the empty word property if $|\alpha|$ contains the empty word ε. Particularly, if $|\alpha| = \{\varepsilon\}$ then α is an empty word expression. If $|\alpha| = \phi$ then α has the empty set property. If $|\alpha|$ is a set of finite words then α has the finite word property. Formal definitions are given in the following.

Definition 3 A cl-regular expression is said to have the empty word property (e.w.p.) if the following condition holds:

(1) If $\alpha \equiv (\beta^{\infty})$ for some cl-regular expression β, then α has e.w.p.

(2) If $\alpha \equiv (\beta + \gamma)$ for some β and γ, then α has e.w.p. if β or γ has e.w.p.

(3) If $\alpha \equiv (\beta\gamma)$ for some β and γ, then α has e.w.p. if both of β and γ have e.w.p.

Property 1 For any cl-regular expression α, α has the e.w.p. if and only if $\varepsilon \in |\alpha|$.

Definition 4 A cl-regular expression α is said to be an empty word expression (e.w.e.) if the following condition holds:

(1) If $\alpha \equiv (\phi^{\infty})$ then α is e.w.e.

(2) If $\alpha \equiv (\beta^{\infty})$ and β is e.w.e., then α is e.w.e.

(3) If $\alpha \equiv (\beta + \gamma)$ and both β and γ are e.w.e. then α is e.w.e.

(4) If $\alpha \equiv (\beta\gamma)$ and both β and γ are e.w.e. then α is e.w.e.

Property 2 For any cl-regular expression α, α is an e.w.e. if and only if $|\alpha| = \{ \varepsilon \}$.

Definition 5 The empty set property (e.s.p.) and the finite word property (f.w.p.) of a cl-regular expression are defined as follows:

(1) If $\alpha \equiv \phi$ then α has e.s.p.

(2) If $\alpha \equiv \phi$, $\alpha \equiv a$ (for some $a \in \Sigma$) or α is e.w.e. then α has f.w.p.

(3) If $\alpha \equiv (\beta + \gamma)$ and both β and γ have e.s.p. [or f.w.p.] then α has e.s.p. [or f.w.p.]

(4) If $\alpha \equiv (\beta\gamma)$ and β has e.s.p. then α has e.s.p.

(5) If $\alpha \equiv (\beta\gamma)$ and β has f.w.p. and γ has e.s.p. then α has e.s.p.

(6) If $\alpha \equiv (\beta\gamma)$ and both β and γ have f.w.p. then α has f.w.p.

(7) If $\alpha \equiv (\beta^{\infty})$ and if β has e.s.p. or β is e.w.e. then α has e.w.p.

Property 3 For any cl-regular expression α,

(1) α has e.s.p. if and only if $|\alpha| = \phi$.

(2) α has f.w.p. if and only if $|\alpha| \cap \Sigma^{\omega} = \phi$.

Now we give an axiom system $\mathcal{S}$ for cl-regular expressions as follows. The axiom system $\mathcal{S}$ consists of the following twelve axioms (1) to (12) and two inference rules RI and RII.

Axiom For any cl-regular expressions α, β, and γ,

(1) $\alpha + (\beta + \gamma) = (\alpha + \beta) + \gamma$

(2) $\alpha(\beta\gamma) = (\alpha\beta)\gamma$

(3) $\alpha + \beta = \beta + \alpha$

(4) $\alpha(\beta + \gamma) = \alpha\beta + \alpha\gamma$

(5) $(\alpha + \beta)\gamma = \alpha\gamma + \beta\gamma$

(6) $\alpha + \alpha = \alpha$

(7) $\alpha + \phi = \alpha$

(8) $\phi\alpha = \phi$

(9) $\alpha\phi = \phi$ if α has f.w.p.

(10) $\alpha\phi^{\infty} = \alpha$

(11) $\alpha^{\infty} = \phi^{\infty} + \alpha\alpha^{\infty}$

(12) $\alpha^{\infty} = (\phi^{\infty} + \alpha)^{\infty}$

Inference Rules

RI. (Substitution) Let X_1 be a cl-regular expression and X_2 be the cl-regular expression obtained by replacing a sub-expression Y_1 of X_1 with a cl-regular expression Y_2. Then, from $X_1 = Z$ and $Y_1 = Y_2$ we can deduce $X_2 = Z$ as well as $X_2 = X_1$. That is,

$$\frac{X_1 = Z,\ Y_1 = Y_2}{X_2 = Z} \quad \text{and} \quad \frac{Y_1 = Y_2}{X_2 = X_1}$$

RII. Assume that Y has not e.w.p. Except for the case that X has e.s.p. but Y has not e.s.p., we can deduce $X = Y^{\infty}Z$ from the equation $X = YX + Z$. That is,

$$\frac{X = YX + Z}{X = Y^{\infty}Z}$$

Remark The inference rule RII can not apply to the equation $X = YX + Z$ if X has e.s.p. but Y has not e.s.p. This is because if we allow it then we would deduce the equation $\phi = a^{\infty}\phi = a^{\omega}$ from the equation $\phi = a\phi + \phi$. In fact, as we have described in the section 4, if $B \cap \Sigma^{\omega} = \phi$ then the equation $X = BX + \phi$ has the solutions $X = \phi$ and $X = B^{\omega}$. But, from $\phi = a\phi + \phi$ we should deduce $\phi = \phi$ but not $\phi = a^{\omega}$.

We will write $\vdash_{\mathcal{S}} \alpha = \beta$ or simple $\vdash \alpha = \beta$ if the equation $\alpha = \beta$ can be deduced in our axiom system.

Proposition 2 For any cl-regular expressions X, Y, Z, X_1, X_2, Y_1 and Y_2, we have

(1) $\vdash X = X$.

(2) If $\vdash X = Y$ then $\vdash Y = X$.

(3) If $\vdash X = Y$ and $\vdash Y = Z$ then $\vdash X = Z$.

(4) If $\vdash X_1 = X_2$ and $\vdash Y_1 = Y_2$ then
$\vdash X_1 + Y_1 = X_2 + Y_2$,
$\vdash X_1Y_1 = X_2Y_2$, and
$\vdash X_1^{\infty} = Y_2^{\infty}$.

6. Soundness and Completeness of the Axiom System $\mathcal{S}$

By using the result described in the section 4, we can prove the soundness and completeness of our axiom system $\mathcal{S}$ for cl-regular expressions.

Theorem 1 The axiom system $\mathcal{S}$ is sound. That is, if $\vdash_{\mathcal{S}} X = Y$ then $|X| = |Y|$.

(Proof) For any equalities $X = Y$ given as axioms (1) to (8), we can prove $|X| = |Y|$ by using identies of proposition 1.

For the axiom (9), note that $|\alpha| \subset \Sigma^*$ by property 3 since α has f.w.p. and that for any $A \subset \Sigma^*$ $A\phi = \phi$. Thus, $|(\alpha\phi)| = |\alpha| \cdot |\phi| = |\alpha| \cdot \phi = \phi = |\phi|$. That is, $|\alpha\phi| = |\phi|$.

From $|\phi^{\infty}| = \{\varepsilon\}$ and (2) of proposition 1, we have $|\alpha\phi^{\infty}| = |\alpha| \cdot |\phi|^{\infty} = |\alpha|\{\varepsilon\} = |\alpha|$. Thus, the soundness of axiom (10) is proved.

By using the fact $|\phi^{\infty}| = \{\varepsilon\}$ and (11) of proposition 1, we can prove the soundness of axioms (11) and (12) in a similar way to the case of axiom (10).

Next, assume that by using the inference rule RI we deduce an equality $\alpha' = \beta'$ from $\alpha = \beta$ such that $|\alpha| = |\beta|$. It is clear by the definition of RI that $|\alpha'| = |\beta'|$.

Finally, we prove the soundess of the equality obtianed by applying the inference rule RII.

Assume that an equality $\alpha = \beta\alpha + \gamma$ holds. Then, by definition 2, we have

$$|\alpha| = |\beta| \cdot |\alpha| + |\gamma| \qquad \text{(a)}$$

Since β has not e.w.p., $|\beta|$ does not contain ε, i.e., $\varepsilon \notin |\beta|$. If α has not e.s.p. then since $|\alpha| \neq \phi$ the results described in section 4 asserts that $|\alpha| = |\beta|^{\infty}|\gamma| = |\beta^{\infty}\gamma|$. If α has e.s.p. then since $|\alpha| = \phi$ we have $|\gamma| = \phi$ from (a). On the other hand, in this case, from the assumption of RII, β must have e.s.p., too. This means $|\beta| = \phi$. Thus, we have

$$|\alpha| = \phi = \phi^{\infty}\phi = |\beta|^{\infty}|\gamma| = |\beta^{\infty}\gamma|$$

This completes the proof.

Theorem 2 The axiom system $\mathcal{S}$ is complete. That is, if $|X| = |Y|$ then $\vdash_{\mathcal{S}} X = Y$.

The proof of this theorem is similar to that of the completeness of Salomaa's axiom system [3] and omitted here.

7. Examples

Some examples of the equality deduced by the axiom system $\mathcal{S}$ are given in this section. Let us consider the following two equations:

(1) For any cl-regular expression X,

$$X^{\omega} = XX^{\omega}$$

(2) For any positive integer m, if X is a cl-regular expression which has not e.w.p., then

$$X^{\omega} = (X^{m})^{\omega}$$

We can easily convince the validity of these two equalities. In fact, as Theorem 2 says, we can deduce them by the axiom system $\mathcal{S}$. That is, $\vdash_{\mathcal{S}} X^{\omega} = XX^{\omega}$ and $\vdash_{\mathcal{S}} X^{\omega} = (X^{m})^{\omega}$. The proof schemes are shown by Figs.1 and 2, respectively.

Note that we can apply the rule RII at the final step in Fig. 2. Assume X^{∞} has e.s.p.. Then, X^{∞} has f.w.p.. This means that X has e.s.p. because X has not e.w.p. by the assumption. Thus, X has e.s.p., too. This means the condition for RII is satisfied.

[Axiom (7)]

$$X + \phi = X$$

[Axiom (8)] ———— [(2) of Proposition 2]

$$\phi X = \phi \qquad X = X + \phi$$

———— [RI]

$$X = X + \phi X$$

[(1) of Proposition 2] ———— [Axiom 3]

$$X = X \qquad X = \phi X + X$$

———— [RI] ———— [RII]

$$X^{\infty} = \phi^{\infty} + XX^{\infty},\ \phi = \phi \qquad X = \phi^{\infty} X$$

———— [(4) of Proposition 2] ———— [(2) of Proposition 2]

$$X^{\infty}\phi = (\phi^{\infty} + XX^{\infty})\phi \qquad \phi^{\infty} X = X$$

———— [Axiom (5)] ———— [RI]

$$X^{\infty}\phi = \phi^{\infty}\phi + (XX^{\infty})\phi \qquad \phi^{\infty}\phi = \phi$$

———— [RI]

$$X^{\infty}\phi = \phi + (XX^{\infty})\phi$$

———— [Axiom (3) and (7)]

$$X^{\infty}\phi = (XX^{\infty})\phi$$

———— [Axiom (2)]

$$X^{\infty}\phi = X(X^{\infty}\phi)$$

Fig. 1 Deduction of $X^{\infty}\phi = X(X^{\infty}\phi)$, that is, $X^{\omega} = XX^{\omega}$.

[(1) of Proposition 2] [the result of Fig. 1]

$$\frac{X = X \qquad X^{\infty}\phi = X(X^{\infty}\phi)}{X(X^{\infty}\phi) = XX(X^{\infty}\phi)}\,[(4)\ \text{of Proposition 2}]$$

$$\frac{X(X^{\infty}\phi) = XX(X^{\infty}\phi) \qquad X^{\infty}\phi = X(X^{\infty}\phi)}{X^{\infty}\phi = XX(X^{\infty}\phi)}\,[\text{RI}]$$

$X^{\infty}\phi = XX(X^{\infty}\phi)$ ---------- $X^{\omega} = X^2 X^{\omega}$

[(1) of Proposition 2]

$$\frac{XX = XX \qquad X^{\infty}\phi = X(X^{\infty}\phi)}{XX(X^{\infty}\phi) = XXX(X^{\infty}\phi)}\,[(4)\ \text{of Proposition 2}]$$

$$\frac{XX(X^{\infty}\phi) = XXX(X^{\infty}\phi) \qquad X^{\infty}\phi = XX(X^{\infty}\phi)}{X^{\infty}\phi = XXX(X^{\infty}\phi)}\,[\text{RI}]$$

$X^{\infty}\phi = XXX(X^{\infty}\phi)$

similar steps proceed

$X^{\infty}\phi = X^{m}(X^{\infty}\phi)$

[Axiom (7)]

$$\frac{\alpha + \phi = \alpha}{X^{m}(X^{\infty}\phi) + \phi = X^{m}(X^{\infty}\phi)}\,[\text{RI}]$$

$$\frac{X^{m}(X^{\infty}\phi) + \phi = X^{m}(X^{\infty}\phi) \qquad X^{\infty}\phi = X^{m}(X^{\infty}\phi)}{X^{\infty}\phi = X^{m}(X^{\infty}\phi) + \phi}\,[\text{RI}]$$

$$\frac{X^{\infty}\phi = X^{m}(X^{\infty}\phi) + \phi}{X^{\infty}\phi = (X^{m})^{\infty}\phi}\,[\text{RI}]$$

Fig. 2 Deduction of $X^{\omega} = (X^{m})^{\omega}$, that is, $X^{\infty}\phi = (X^{m})^{\infty}\phi$.

8. Conclusion

In this paper we have introduced the concept of cl-regular expression, proposed the axiom system $\mathcal{S}$ for cl-regular expressions, and proved the soundness and completeness of the system $\mathcal{S}$. The system $\mathcal{S}$ will be a base for algebraic studies on cl-regular sets. On the other hand, the system $\mathcal{S}$ coincides with the Salomm's axiom system if we restrict the objects to the regular sets of finite strings. In this sense, our axiom system is a natural extension of Salomaa's axiom system to allow cl-regular set including infinite strings.

The referee kindly informed the authors that an axiom system for ω-regular expressions has earlier been introduced by K. Wagner [6]. But the use of closed regular expressions in this paper leads to our axiom system $\mathcal{S}$, a more elegant and natural one than the use of ω-regular expressions.

Acknowledgement

The authors would like to express their thanks to Dr. Teruo Fukumura, Professor of Nagoya University, for his encouragement to conduct this work. They also thank their colleagues for their helpful discussions.

References

[1] Boasson, L. and Nivat, M., "Adherences of languages", JCSS, vol. 20, pp.285-309 (1980)

[2] Izumi, H., Inagaki, Y. and Honda, N., "Right Linear Equations on Set Containing Infinite Sequences", The Transactions of the Institute of Electronics and Communication Engineers of Japan, Section D, vol. J66-D, no. 8, pp.993-999 (Aug., 1983)

[3] Salomaa, A., "Two complete axiom systems for the algebra of regular events", JACM, vol. 13, pp.138-169, (1966)

[4] Park, D., "Concurrency and automata on infinite sequences", Lecture Notes in Computer Sciences, no. 104, pp.167-183, Springer-Verlag (1981)

[5] Izumi, H., Inagaki, Y., and Honda, N., "An algebra of Closed Regular Expression and A Complete Axiom System", Report of Techical Group, TGAL83-1, IECE, Japan (March, 1983)

[6] Wagner, K., "Eine Axiomatisierung der Theorie der regularen Folgenmengen", EIK 12, 7, pp.337-354 (1976)

THE COMPLEXITY OF FINDING MINIMUM-LENGTH GENERATOR SEQUENCES
(EXTENDED ABSTRACT)

Mark Jerrum
Department of Computer Science
University of Edinburgh
Edinburgh, Scotland.

INTRODUCTION

A permutation group is most commonly specified by listing a set of permutations which together generate the group. The computational utility of this method of specifying permutation groups rests on the observation that every group can be generated by a rather small set of permutations. Indeed, it can be shown that every permutation group on n letters has a generator set of cardinality at most n−1 [10]. Perhaps the most fundamental problem in the computational study of permutation groups is that of PERMUTATION GROUP MEMBERSHIP: given a group G specified as a set of generators, and a permutation π, determine whether π is a member of G. By providing a complexity analysis of an algorithm of Sims [14], Furst et al. [5] were able to show that PERMUTATION GROUP MEMBERSHIP is in P (the class of predicates computable by polynomial time bounded deterministic Turing machines).

Although an efficient algorithm exists for verifying that a permutation is a member of a given group, the problem of exhibiting a succinct expression for the permutation in terms of the generators of the group appears to be computationally more demanding. In order to explain this phenomenon, Even and Goldreich [4] introduced a quantified version of the membership problem for permutation groups. The MINIMUM GENERATOR SEQUENCE problem is the following: given a set of generators $(\pi_1, \ldots, \pi_k)$ of a permutation group G, a target permutation $\tau \in G$ and an integer B, determine whether there is some sequence of the generators (π_i), of length not greater than B, whose composition is the permutation τ. In the context of Rubik's Cube puzzle ([1], p. 760) the MINIMUM GENERATOR SEQUENCE problem is that of whether a given final configuration can be reached from a given initial configuration by a sequence of at most B elementary moves. (The elementary moves correspond, of course, to the generators of the permutation group.) No computationally feasible solution to this problem is known, even for the case of the standard 3×3×3 cube. In contrast to this, the problem of determining whether the final configuration is reachable from the initial configuration by an <u>arbitrary length</u> sequence of elementary moves is just a special case of PERMUTATION GROUP MEMBERSHIP, and hence is soluble in polynomial time. The reachability question can thus be resolved for a generalised n×n×n Rubik's Cube, even when n is substantial.

The intractability of the quantified version of the problem is explained by Even and

Goldreich [4], who demonstrate that MINIMUM GENERATOR SEQUENCE is NP-hard ([9], p. 324). As a practical demonstration of the intractability of a problem, an NP-hardness result is perfectly adequate; from a theoretical viewpoint it is more satisfying to pin-point the complexity of the problem by showing it to be complete for some class. In the full version of this paper [11] it is shown that MINIMUM GENERATOR SEQUENCE is complete for PSPACE with respect to log-space reducibility. This result suggests that the problem is not in NP, for that would imply NP=PSPACE, a conclusion that most would consider unlikely. Furthermore it is shown there that the problem remains PSPACE-complete even when severe restrictions are placed on allowed instances. An interesting feature of the MINIMUM GENERATOR SEQUENCE problem is that it does not fall under the headings of "two-person games" or "formal languages" which cover the great majority of known PSPACE-complete problems.

In order to gain insight into the finer structure of the MINIMUM GENERATOR SEQUENCE problem, Driscoll and Furst [3] consider instances of the problem for which approximate solutions can be computed efficiently. That investigation is continued here, although the results obtained are of a rather different flavour. Several "standard" generator sets for the symmetric and alternating groups are considered, and it is shown that for these particular cases, an exact solution can be computed in polynomial time. Of particular interest is the case where the generator set consists of the "cyclicly-adjacent transpositions". Thus it is shown that, from an initial arrangement of distinct objects on a circle, one can compute quickly the number of interchanges of adjacent objects required to realise any other arrangement. Surprisingly, this problem appears substantially more difficult to solve than the related one (for which a solution has been known for some time) in which the objects are arranged on a line segment.

NOTATION

If X is a set, then the symmetric group on X, denoted by Sym(X), is the set of all bijections from X to itself (permutations) with function composition as the group operation. A permutation group on X is any subgroup of Sym(X); the degree of such a group is just the cardinality of X. The alternating group on X, denoted by Alt(X) is the subgroup of Sym(X) containing precisely the even permutations of Sym(X) ([7], p. 59). Conventionally, we shall denote permutations by Greek letters; in particular the identity of a permutation group will always be denoted by ι. Composition of permutations is denoted by juxtaposition; when a sequence of permutations occur together, the compositions are to be performed in order from left to right.

In this paper, we do not study permutation groups in isolation, but rather their relation to specified sets of generators. If K is any subset of Sym(X) then the group generated by K, denoted by ⟨K⟩, is the smallest subgroup of Sym(X) which contains K. The order of a permutation group G, denoted by |G| is the number of permutations contained in G, while the order of a permutation, π, is the order of the group generated by π, that is $|\langle\pi\rangle|$.

Let $K \subseteq Sym(X)$ and $\tau \in \langle K\rangle$. Define $L(\tau, K)$ to be the minimum length of a sequence of permutations from K whose composition is τ. The MINIMUM GENERATOR SEQUENCE problem may then be expressed as follows:

Input: τ, K and an integer B.
Output: True if and only if $L(\tau, K) \leq B$.

It is reasonable to define $L(\tau, K)$ to be infinity if $\tau \notin \langle K\rangle$.

Finally, if i and j are integers with $i \leq j$, then $[i, j]$ will denote the set of integers which are not less than i and not greater than j. If x is an integer, and m a positive integer, then (x mod m) will signify the unique element of $[0, m-1]$ which is congruent to x, modulo m.

NEGATIVE RESULTS

As we have remarked, Even and Goldreich were able to demonstrate that MGS is NP-hard. Indeed, if we insist that the integer B of the problem instance is specified in unary notation, the problem is easily seen to be in NP, and hence NP-complete. (Nondeterministically generate all sequences of generators of length not greater than B, checking in polynomial time for each sequence whether its composition is τ.) A different situation obtains if, as is conventional, the integer B is specified in binary notation. It is easy to verify, by constructing suitable examples, that $L(\tau, K)$ may be exponential in the degree of the permutations involved; thus the obvious nondeterministic algorithm for MGS is no longer polynomial time bounded. As a result, in the formulation where B is specified in binary notation, membership of MGS in NP is not immediate. In fact, in the light of the following theorem, membership of MGS in NP is rather unlikely.

Theorem 1: MINIMUM GENERATOR SEQUENCE is complete for PSPACE with respect to log-space reducibility.

Proof: (Outline) We firstly show that MGS is a member of PSPACE. Suppose K is a set of generators, and τ a target permutation, all of the same degree. The following algorithm, for determining whether $L(\tau, K) \leq B$ for any integer B, can be implemented on a linear space bounded nondeterministic Turing machine:

```
σ:=ι;   (identity permutation)
for i:=1 to B do begin
    nondeterministically select π∈K;
    σ:=σπ;
    if σ=τ then accept
end
```

It follows from a theorem of Savitch [13] that MGS is in DSPACE(n^2), and hence in PSPACE.

The PSPACE-hardness of MGS is established by means of a generic tranformation ([6], p. 39). A detailed account of the construction employed can be found in see [11]; here, only a simplified sketch is provided in order to give the flavour of the proof. Let M be a single tape deterministic Turing machine with space bound p, where p is a polynomial , $p(n) \geq n$. Let $w \in \Sigma^n$ be any word over the input alphabet, Σ, of M and set $m=p(n)$. We may assume that, before accepting any input, M scans the leftmost m squares of its tape, overwriting those squares with the blank symbol, b, and leaving the head over the first tape square. This assumption, which ensures that M has a unique accept configuration, is made without loss of generality; since p is fully space-constructible ([9], p. 297) any machine which does not satisfy the assumption can be modified to one which does, and which operates within the same space bound.

We shall construct an instance of MGS for which true is returned if and only if M accepts w. Let $T = \{0, 1, \ldots, m-1\}$ be an indexing of the tape squares of M, Q be the set of states of M, Γ be the tape alphabet of M, and let $\Delta = T \times \Gamma \cup Q$ (the union here is disjoint). In the problem instance we construct, all permutations are members of $\mathrm{Sym}(\Delta \times X) = \mathrm{Sym}(T \times \Gamma \times X \cup Q \times X)$, where X is some set whose cardinality is "sufficiently large" (though still bounded by a polynomial in n). We shall, in fact, restrict our attention to permutations π which satisfy the following two conditions:

1. π respects the partition $\mathcal{B} = \{\{d\} \times X : d \in \Delta\}$ of the underlying set $\Delta \times X$, i.e. for any $d \in \Delta$ the image $\{d\} \times X$ under π is of the form $\{d'\} \times X$ for some $d' \in \Delta$.

2. π respects the partition $\mathcal{B}' = \{\{i\} \times \Gamma \times X : i \in T\}$ of $T \times \Gamma \times X$. Moreover the induced action of π on the blocks of $\mathcal{B}'$ is cyclic, i.e. of the form

   $$\{i\} \times \Gamma \times X \longmapsto \{(i-h) \bmod m\} \times \Gamma \times X$$

   for some $h \in \mathbb{Z}$.

Forget temporarily the role of X and consider the induced action of permutations of the blocks of $\mathcal{B}$. Suppose the permutation π satisfies the above conditions. Let $q_0 \in Q$ be the initial state of M, and let $\{q\} \times X$ $(q \in Q)$ be the image of $\{q_0\} \times X$ under π. Let $b \in \Gamma$ be the distiguished blank symbol of M, and for each $i \in T$ let $\{((i-h) \bmod m, s_i)\} \times X$ $(s_i \in \Gamma)$ be the image of $\{(i, b)\} \times X$ under π. We provide an interpretation of π in terms of a configuration of the Turing machine M: namely π corresponds to M being in state q, with tape contents $s_0 s_1 \ldots s_{m-1}$, and with the head positioned over the square h. The reason for condition (2) above is now clear: it represents the constraint that all tape squares must be translated by equal amounts.

We now introduce some specific elements of G together with their interpretations in terms of the machine M. Firstly, define the permutation λ by

$$\lambda: \quad (i,s,x) \longmapsto ((i+1) \bmod m, s, x), \qquad (i,s,x) \in T \times \Gamma \times X.$$

From now on, permutations are assumed to stabilise pointwise all elements in their domain which are not mentioned specifcally; thus the restriction of λ to $Q \times X$ is taken to be the identity. To interpret λ, note that if the permutation π is viewed as specifying a configuration of the machine M, as suggested above, then $\pi\lambda$ corresponds to the configuration obtained from π by shifting the head left by one tape square. A right shift of the head may be encoded as a permutation ρ in a similar way. Next, for each $s \in \Gamma$ define τ_s by

$$\tau_s: \quad \left.\begin{array}{l} (0,b,x) \longmapsto (0,s,x) \\ (0,s,x) \longmapsto (0,b,x) \end{array}\right\} \quad x \in X$$

If in the interpretation of π as a configuration of M the tape square under the head contains a blank, then in the interpretation of $\pi\tau_s$ the square under the head contains the symbol s (and vice versa). Thus the effect of τ_s is to change the symbol under the head from a blank to s, and vice versa. (No interpretation is offered if the symbol under the head is neither b nor s.) Similarly, for each $q \in Q$ we may define a permutation τ_q whose interpretation is a change of state of M from q_0 to q, and vice versa.

Using sequences of the above permutations, one can mirror the operation of the machine M. Composition with the permutation λ and ρ may be used to simulate left and right shifting of the tape head. The permutations $\{\tau_s: s \in \Gamma\}$ may be used to change the symbol on the tape square under the head from s to s': compose first with τ_s to erase the old symbol and then $\tau_{s'}$ to write in the new one. The permutations $\{\tau_q: q \in Q\}$ can be used to change the state from q to q': first compose with τ_q then with $\tau_{q'}$. Note that all the symbol changes are effected by first erasing and then rewriting, while all state transitions are via temporary excursions to q_0; this will be seen later to be a technical convenience.

For the purposes of the reduction, we must arrange that sequences of permutations cannot simulate improper transitions of the machine M. To ensure this we introduce a group action within blocks of $\mathcal{B}$. The nature of the action within blocks is not considered here, but the effect of the action is to allow certain permutations to be introduced which can effectively check the the current configuration of the machine M. Thus, for each state $q \in Q$ there is a permutation σ_q which can confirm if the current state of the machine M is q. Informally, permutations are classified as "admissible" or "inadmissible". If π is an admissible permutation corresponding to machine M being in state q, then $\pi\sigma_q$ is an admissible permutation corresponding to M being in the same state. If, however, π is an admissible permutation corresponding to M being in some state other than q, then $\pi\sigma_q$ is an inadmissible permutation. The inadmissible permutations are suitably "scrambled" so that once an inadmissible permutation has been created, it is very expensive to convert it into an admissible permutation by composition with the generators of the problem instance. Since the target permutation is chosen to be admissible, the creation of an admissible permutation at any point of the simulation is a fatal error.

The generator set, K, of the instance of MGS corresponding to the pair (M, w) contains one permutation for each possible transition of the machine M. A typical member of K is of the form

$$\sigma_s \tau_s \tau_{s'} \sigma_q \tau_q \tau_{q'} \lambda$$

and encodes the transition of M from state q with symbol s under the head, to state q' with s overwritten by s' and the head left shifted by one position. The various constituent permutations in the above product are to be interpreted as follows:

- σ_s: Confirm current symbol under head is s
- τ_s: erase s (overwrite with b)
- $\tau_{s'}$: write s' onto tape square under head
- σ_q: confirm current state is q
- τ_q: change state from q to q_0
- $\tau_{q'}$: immediately reset state to q'
- λ: shift head one place to the left.

Let the integer bound B of the problem instance be $m|\Sigma|^m|Q|$; note that the length of the binary representation of B is bounded by a polynomial in n. If M accepts w then it must do so within B steps, since B is the total number of possible configurations of M. Suppose that π_{init} and π_{acc} are permutations corresponding to the initial configuration, with $w \in \Sigma^n$ on the tape, and the unique accept configuration respectively. (The accept configuration is unique because the machine M erases its tape prior to accepting.) We would like to claim that π_{acc} can be obtained from π_{init} by successive composition with at most B generators from K if and only if M accepts w. Equivalently,

$$\text{M accepts w} \iff L(\pi_{init}^{-1}\pi_{acc}, K) \leq B.$$

The obstacle to be faced is that the correspondence between permutations and configurations of M is not 1-1; thus π_{init} and π_{acc} are not uniquely defined. Details of how this technical issue is resolved can be found in [11]

The next two theorems suggest that MGS remains computationally intractable, even when the form of problem instances is severely restricted. Let MGS WITH GENERATORS OF ORDER TWO be the problem derived from MGS by imposing the constraint that every permutation in the generator set of the problem instance be of order 2 (i.e. self-inverse), and let TWO GENERATOR MGS be the problem obtained by restricting the generator set of the problem instance to be of cardinality 2.

Theorem 2: MGS WITH GENERATORS OF ORDER TWO is complete for

PSPACE with respect to log-space reducibility.

Proof: Reduction from MGS. (See [11].)

Theorem 3: TWO GENERATOR MGS is complete for PSPACE with respect to log-space reducibility.

Proof: Reduction from MGS WITH GENERATORS OF ORDER TWO. (See [11].)

We shall demonstrate, in the next section, that MGS is soluble in deterministic polynomial time if the generator set has only one element. Theorem 3 therefore represents the best possible restriction on generator set size.

POSITIVE RESULTS

Further insights into the complexity of MINIMUM GENERATOR SEQUENCE can gained by investigating restrictions or variations of the problem which are computationally tractable. One result of this kind is due to Driscoll and Furst [3]. They demonstrate that if a generator set K consists only of cycles of bounded degree, then any member of the group ⟨K⟩ can be expressed as a sequence of $O(n^2)$ generators; moreover such a sequence can be found in polynomial time. In this section we investigate versions of MGS which are so restricted that exact solutions can be computed in polynomial time. Firstly, we establish the promised (unsurprising) result, which shows that theorem 3 is the best possible.

Theorem 4: Let π, τ be elements of Sym[0, n−1]. Then $L(\tau, \{\pi\})$ is computable in time polynomial in n.

Proof: For each i, $0 \leq i < n$, let a_i be the smallest non-negative integer such that $i\pi^{a_i} = i\tau$, and let m_i be the length of the cycle in π containing i. Then $L(\tau, \{\pi\})$ is a solution for x in the system of congruences

$$x \equiv a_i \pmod{m_i}, \qquad 0 \leq i < n;$$

it is, moreover, the smallest non-negative solution to this system. (If the system has no solution, then $L(\tau, \{\pi\}) = \infty$). Note that both a_i and m_i, $0 \leq i < n$, are efficiently computable. The system of congruences may be checked for consistency, and a minimum non-negative solution found, by using the Chinese remainder technique ([8], p. 94).

Another way of obtaining computationally tractable subproblems is to fix the generator set, rather than having it as part of the problem instance. There are a number of "natural" systems of generators for the symmetric and alternating groups which are obvious candidates for this fixed generator set. Perhaps the simplest example is provided by the set of all transpositions on a set X; it is well known that this is a generator set for the symmetric group on X. The following result was known to Cayley [2]:

> Theorem 5: Let K_t be the set of all transpositions on $[0,n-1]$, that is, all permutations of the form (i,j) for $0\leq i<j<n$. If $\pi\in\mathrm{Sym}[0,n-1]$ then $L(\pi,K_t) = n-c(\pi)$, where $c(\pi)$ is the number of disjoint cycles (including those of length 1) which compose π.

There is a straightforward proof of the above, which proceeds by considering how the cycle structure of a permutation is affected when the permutation is composed with a transposition. A similar style of proof also suffices for the following theorem. (Recall that the set of all 3-cycles on $[0,n-1]$ is a generator set for the alternating group, $\mathrm{Alt}[0,n-1]$.)

> Theorem 6: Let K_{3c} be the set of all 3-cycles on $[0,n-1]$, that is, all permutations of the form (i,j,k) with i, j and k distinct. If $\pi\in\mathrm{Alt}[0,n-1]$ then $L(\pi,K_{3c}) = (n - c_{odd}(\pi))/2$, where $c_{odd}(\pi)$ is the number of odd length cycles (including those of length 1) in the factorisation of π into disjoint cycles.

Results concerning adjacent transpositions may be obtained using the notion of <u>inversion</u> of a permutation ([12], p. 11). If $\pi\in\mathrm{Sym}[0,n-1]$, define $I(\pi)$, the <u>inversion number</u> of π, by $I(\pi) = |\{(i,j) : 0\leq i<j<n,\ i\pi>j\pi\}|$.

> Theorem 7: Let K_{at} be the set of all adjacent transpositions on $[0,n-1]$, that is, all permutations of the form $(i-1,i)$ for $0<i<n$. Then $L(\pi,K_{at}) = I(\pi)$.

The proof of the above theorem is straightforward; it is perhaps surprising therefore that the case of cyclicly-adjacent transpositions is significantly more troublesome. The set, K_{cat}, of <u>cyclicly-adjacent transpositions</u> is obtained, from the set K_{at} of adjacent transpositions considered above, by adding the single permutation which transposes 0 and n-1. The additional symmetry possessed by the new generator set might suggest that it would be easier to deal with than the set of adjacent transpositions from which it was derived. The problem of determining the shortest expression of a given permutation in terms of cyclicly-adjacent transpositions can in fact be solved in deterministic polynomial time; however, showing this to be so requires significantly more effort than one might expect a priori.

Let $(\pi_i\in K_{cat}: 1\leq i\leq \ell)$ be a sequence, of length ℓ, of generators chosen from K_{cat}. Let $(\sigma_i: 0\leq i\leq \ell)$ be the partial products of this sequence; that is, $\sigma_0=\iota$, and $\sigma_i=\pi_1\ldots\pi_i$ for $1\leq i\leq \ell$. Define the function ϕ: $\mathbb{Z}\to\{-1,0,1\}$ by

$$\phi(i)\begin{cases} = -1 & \text{if } i\equiv-1 \pmod n\\ = +1 & \text{if } i\equiv+1 \pmod n\\ = 0 & \text{otherwise.}\end{cases}$$

Define the <u>displacement vector</u>, $\underline{d}(\pi_1\ldots\pi_\ell)\in\mathbb{Z}^n$, of the sequence $\pi_1\ldots\pi_\ell$ to be the vector whose i^{th} component is

$$d_i(\pi_1 \ldots \pi_\ell) = \sum_{j=1}^{\ell} \phi(i\sigma_j - i\sigma_{j-1}).$$

Note that, denoting the product $\pi_1 \ldots \pi_\ell$ by π, we have

$$d_i(\pi_1 \ldots \pi_\ell) = i\pi - i \qquad (\text{mod } n)$$

and $$\sum_{i=0}^{n-1} d_i(\pi_1 \ldots \pi_\ell) = 0.$$

The next theorem allows the search for minimum-length generator sequences to be restricted to permutation sequences with given displacement vector.

Theorem 8: Let π be a member of Sym[0, n-1], and let $\underline{x} = (x_0, \ldots, x_{n-1})$ be a solution to the integer programme

$$\text{Minimise} \sum_{i=0}^{n-1} |x_i| \quad \text{over } \underline{x} \in \mathbb{Z}^n$$

$$\text{subject to} \sum_{i=0}^{n-1} x_i = 0 \text{ and } x_i = i\pi - i \qquad (\text{mod } n). \qquad (1)$$

Then $\exists$ a minimum-length generator sequence $\pi_1 \ldots \pi_\ell$ for π with $\underline{d}(\pi_1 \ldots \pi_\ell) = \underline{x}$

Although we cannot define inversion number directly for permutations, we can do so for displacement vectors. If $\underline{x} \in \mathbb{Z}^n$, define the inversion number, $I(\underline{x})$, of $\underline{x}$ by

$$I(\underline{x}) = \left| \{ (i,j) : 0 \leq i < j \leq n-1, \ (i+d_i > j+d_j) \vee (i+d_i+n < j+d_j) \} \right|.$$

Intuitively, $I(\underline{x})$ counts the number the number of pairs (i,j) which must be interchanged in order to achieve the required displacement vector $\underline{x}$. The significance of inversion number to the current problem is explained by the following theorem.

Theorem 9: Let $\pi \in \text{Sym}[0, n-1]$ and let $\underline{x}$ be a solution to the integer programme (1). Then $L(\pi, K_{cat}) = I(\underline{x})$

The computation of $L(\pi, K_{cat})$ is thus reduced to the solution of the integer programme (1). Fortunately, an optimal solution to the latter can be found quite straightforwardly. We start with the (feasible) solution $x_i = i\pi - i$ and make a series of improvements to the solution until optimality is achieved. The algorithm given in figure 1 bé used for the purpose.

Although this section has concentrated on finding fast (polynomial time) algorithms for computing the function $L(\pi, K)$, it is a short step from there to actually deriving an minimum-length expression for π in terms of the generators K. One might, for example, use the following informally-described algorithm (which runs in polynomial time if the subroutine for computing the function L does):

1. Using the procedure for computing the function L, find a permutation $\sigma \in K$ which satisfies $L(\sigma^{-1}\pi, K) = L(\pi, K) - 1$.

2. Choose σ as the first permutation in the required sequence; the remainder of the sequence may be obtained by applying (1) recursively to $\sigma^{-1}\pi$.

Usually, however, more efficient methods than the above naive one are available.

```
for i:=0 to n-1 do x_i := iπ-i;
(Compute feasible solution.)
repeat
    Choose i to minimise x_i;
    Choose j to maximise x_j;
    if x_j-x_i ≤ n then exit
    else begin
        x_i := x_i+n;
        x_j := x_j-n
        (feasibility of the solution is preserved by the above)
    end
end (repeat)
(x is an optimal solution to the linear programme (1).)
```

Figure 1: Solving the integer programme.

CONJECTURE

Let MGS FOR TRANSITIVE GROUPS be the restricted version of MGS obtained by insisting that the generator set of the problem instance generate a transitive group. (The completeness results presented here rest on constructions in which the generator sets do not generate transitive groups; thus the proofs cannot be carried across to the new variant.) By slightly modifying a proof in Even and Goldreich's paper [4], it is not difficult to show that MGS FOR TRANSITIVE GROUPS is NP-hard. Now, it has been conjectured that there exists a polynomial f, such that if K is any set of permutations generating a transitive group of degree n, and π is any member of that group, then $L(\pi, K) \leq f(n)$. Informally, no matter how perversely a set of generators is chosen, they will always efficiently generate the group. If this were the case, then MGS FOR TRANSITIVE GROUPS would clearly be in NP and hence NP-complete. Thus, while MGS FOR TRANSITIVE GROUPS is itself computationally intractable, it may well be "easier" that the general problem.

REFERENCES

1. Berlekamp, E.R., Conway, J.H. and Guy, R.K. "Winning Ways, Vol. 2 – Games in Particular". Academic Press, 1982.

2. Cayley, A. Note on the Theory of Permutations. Philosophical Magazine 34 (1849), pp. 527-529.

3. Driscoll, J.R. and Furst, M.L. On the Diameter of Permutation Groups. Proc. 15th ACM Symposium on Theory of Computing, 1983, pp. 152-160.

4. Even, S. and Goldreich, O. The Minimum-length Generator Sequence Problem is NP-hard. J. Algorithms 2 (1981), pp. 311-313.

5. Furst, M., Hopcroft, J. and Luks, E. Polynomial-time Algorithms for Permutation Groups. Proc. 21st IEEE Symposium on Foundations of Computer Science, IEEE, 1981, pp. 36-41.

6. Garey, M.R. and Johnson, D.S. "Computers and Intractability – A Guide to the Theory of NP-Completeness". Freeman, San Francisco, 1979.

7. Hall, M. "The Theory of Groups". Macmillan, New York, 1959.

8. Hardy, G.H. and Wright, E.M. "An Introduction to the Theory of Numbers". Oxford, 1938.

9. Hopcroft, J.E. and Ullman, J.D. "Introduction to Automata Theory, Languages and Computation". Addison-Wesley, 1979.

10. Jerrum, M.R. A Compact Representation for Permutation Groups. Proc. 23rd IEEE Symposium on Foundations of Computer Science, 1982, pp. 126-133.

11. Jerrum, M.R. The Complexity of Finding Minimum-length Generator Sequences. Internal Report CSR-139-83, Department of Computer Science, University of Edinburgh, July, 1983. (Submitted to Theoretical Computer Science).

12. Knuth, D.E. The Art of Computer Programming. Volume 3: "Sorting and Searching". Addison-Wesley, 1973.

13. Savitch, W.J. Relationships between Nondeterministic and Deterministic Tape Complexities. J. Computer and Systems Sciences 4 (1970), pp. 177-192.

14. Sims, C.C. Computational Methods in the Study of Permutation Groups. In "Computational Problems in Abstract Algebra", Leech, J. (Ed.), Pergamon Press, 1970, pp. 169-183.

On probabilistic tape complexity and fast circuits for matrix inversion problems

(Extended Abstract)

Hermann Jung
Sektion Mathematik
Humboldt-Universität zu Berlin
DDR - 1086 Berlin
PSF 1297

1. Introduction: Some problems have been shown to be solvable by probabilistic algorithms which are more efficient than the known deterministic ones (4,7,13) or which are provably better than all corresponding deterministic algorithms solving these problems (6), respectively. Nevertheless, the general question of how much randomization may help to design highly efficient algorithms is one of the open key-problems in theoretical computer science.
In the first part of our paper we propose a complete problem for logn tape bounded probabilistic Turing machines, which interprets the nature of space bounded probabilistic computations as some kind of classical well-known iteration algorithms for solving systems of linear equations. In the second part, we give fast circuits for the inversion of matrices with small bandwidth. As a corollary we obtain new upper bounds for the tape used in the simulation of probabilistic tape bounded Turing machines by deterministic ones.

2. Definitions: Probabilistic time and tape complexity classes were introduced in detail by J.GILL (7).
We consider standard multitape Turing machine acceptors (8). A probabilistic Turing machine (PTM) is a Turing machine with distinguished states, called coin-tossing states. For each coin-tossing state, the finite control unit specifies two possible next states. The computation of a PTM is deterministic except that in coin-tossing states the machine tosses an unbiased coin to decide between the two possible next states.
Given a PTM M and an input x, $P_M(x)$ denotes the probability that M, with input x, enters an accepting state, and the language accepted by M is defined by

$$L(M) := \{x : P_M(x) > 1/2\}.$$

In previous papers (7,14) a PTM M was said to be working within space

S(n) (time T(n), resp.) if M, with input x of length n, did not use more than S(n) tape during all possible computations (time T(n), resp.). Here we are interested in lower-order tape complexity, where the full tape constructibility is too restrictive. Therefore we define:

A language L is said to be accepted

1) by a PTM within S(n) space ($L \in$ PrSPACE(S(n)))
   iff there is a PTM M with
   $L(M) = L = \{x : Pr(M \text{ accepts } x \text{ within } S(|x|) \text{ space}) > 1/2\}$
2) by a bounded error PTM within S(n) space ($L \in$ BPrSPACE(S(n)))
   iff there is a PTM M and an $\varepsilon > 0$ with
   $L(M) = L = \{x : Pr(M \text{ accepts } x \text{ within } S(|x|) \text{ space}) > 1/2 + \varepsilon\}$,

where $|x|$ denotes the length of x.

Remarks:

1. In case S(n) is fully tape-constructible, it makes no difference to the obvious probabilistic tape complexity classes defined in (7).
2. It is easy to see that BPrSPACE(S(n)) is closed under complementation (using methods of GILL (7)).
3. For $S(n) \in o(\log n)$ it is an open problem whether PrSPACE(S(n)) is closed under complementation, too (for S(n)=logn, this closure property was proved in (13,15)).
4. FREIVALDS (6) proved that $L = \{0^n 1^n : n > 0\}$ is in BPrSPACE(O(1)), which leads to the inclusion
   NSPACE(S(n)) $\subset$ BPrSPACE(S(n)), for $S(n) \in o(\log n)$.
5. In the same paper (6) it was proved that there is no gap-theorem for probabilistic tape complexity classes as there is for the deterministic and nondeterministic ones.

3. A complete problem for PrSpace(logn):

There are several complete problems for probabilistic polynomial time complexity classes, which are very similar to the corresponding NP-complete languages (7). On the other hand, it seems to be very sophisticated to construct complete problems for tape complexity classes also in this way. One reason for the numerous difficulties in finding such problems is the ability of an S(n)-tape bounded PTM to work much longer than the corresponding deterministic machines. We can bound the computation time of an S(n)-tape PTM only by $2^{2^{O(S(n)+\log n)}}$.

J.SIMON (14) and H.JUNG (9) used a $\log^2 n$-tape reduction for any language in PrSPACE(logn) to a matrix inversion problem in order to find nontrivial deterministic upper bounds for the probabilistic logn-tape complexity class. A.BORODIN, S.COOK and N.PIPPENGER (3) considered a logn-depth uniform circuit reduction to the inversion problem of matrices with formal power series as elements. For any of these problems it is unknown whether they can be solved by a probabilistic logn space bounded algorithm.

In this part of our paper, we want to show that probabilistic space bounded computations and deterministic matrix iteration processes are in some sense equivalent.

The matrix inversion problem under consideration is the following:

MATIN

input: nxn matrix $A = (a_{ij})$, where a_{ij} are n-bit rational numbers with the property

$$|a_{ii}| > \sum_{i \neq j} |a_{ij}| \quad , \quad \text{for all } 1 \leq i \leq n$$

problem: "$c_{1n} > 0$?", where $A^{-1} = C = (c_{ij})$.

Theorem 1: All languages belonging to PrSPACE(logn) can be reduced to MATIN by deterministic logn tape reductions, i.e. MATIN is PrSPACE(logn)-hard.

Proof (Sketch): We refine the method of J.SIMON (14) to make the reduction easier and to reduce PrSPACE(logn) to the defined special kind of a matrix inversion problem - the MATIN.

Let M be any logn-tape bounded PTM and w an input word of length n.

As a first step, we reduce the pair (M,w) to a matrix Q which describes a Markov process defined by the PTM M working on the input w. The set of all configurations of M (with logn tape) on the input w becomes the set of states $S = \{s_1, s_2, \ldots, s_m\}$ of the Markov process. We enumerate the states in such a way that s_1 represents the initial, s_{m-1} the rejecting and s_m the accepting configuration. Without loss of generality, we assume that M has only one accepting and one rejecting configuration, and that M stops with probability 1 in one of these two. This can be done by adding a probabilistic clock to M (see (7,13)).

Let Q be the mxm matrix with q_{ij} being the probability of an one-step transition (on M) from the configuration s_i to the configuration s_j, i.e. $q_{ij} \in \{0, 1/2, 1\}$.

It is obvious that for a given M, we can compute Q for any w within O(log|w|) space. We can easily see that

$$\text{M accepts w} \quad \text{iff} \quad \lim_k (e_1^T \cdot \sum_{v=0}^{k} Q^v \cdot e_m) > 1/2 \ ,$$

where e_1^T is the 1xm row matrix (1,0,...,0) and $e_m = (0, \ldots, 0, 1)^T$.

In the next step of our reduction algorithm, we construct the following mxm matrix $B = (b_{ij})$:

$$b_{ij} := \begin{cases} q_{ij} - 2^{-n^d} & , \text{ if } q_{ij} > 0 \\ 0 & , \text{ else} \end{cases}$$, where d is a constant (not depending on n) such that

$$\lim_k \left(e_1^T \cdot \sum_{v=0}^{k} Q^v \cdot e_m\right) > 1/2 \quad \text{iff} \quad e_1^T \cdot \sum_{v=0}^{\infty} B^v \cdot e_m > 1/2 .$$

This constant d can be easily found in the same way as the probabilistic clock was introduced and used in (7,13).

Finally, we construct the following mxm matrix $A = (a_{ij})$ with:

$$a_{ij} := \begin{cases} -b_{ij} & , \text{ if } j \neq m-1,\ i \neq j,\ (i,j) \neq (m-1,m) \\ b_{ij} & , \text{ if } j = m-1 \\ 1-b_{ij} & , \text{ if } i = j \\ 2^{-n^d} - 1 & , \text{ if } (i,j) = (m-1,m) \end{cases} ,$$

where d is the constant chosen above.

Remark that s_{m-1} and s_m represent stopping configurations and therefore the entries of the (m-1)-th and the m-th row of B are equal to zero.

Under the assumption that M stops with probability 1 in one of these configurations, it is easy to see that:

$$\lim_k \left(e_1^T \cdot \sum_{v=0}^{k} Q^v \cdot e_m\right) > 1/2 \quad \text{iff} \quad \lim_k \left(e_1^T \cdot \sum_{v=0}^{k} Q^v \cdot e_m\right) > \lim_k \left(e_1^T \cdot \sum_{v=0}^{k} Q^v \cdot e_{m-1}\right)$$

hence (by construction of B)

$$\text{M accepts w} \quad \text{iff} \quad e_1^T \cdot \sum_{v=0}^{\infty} B^v \cdot e_m > e_1^T \cdot \sum_{v=0}^{\infty} B^v \cdot e_{m-1}$$

and following the definition of A (note that $\sum_{v=0}^{\infty} B^v = (I-B)^{-1}$)

$$\text{M accepts w} \quad \text{iff} \quad e_1^T \cdot A^{-1} e_m > 0 ,$$

where e_{m-1} denotes the matrix $(0,\ldots,0,1,0)^T$.

It is obvious that we can perform all steps of our reduction within O(log|w|) space.

<u>Theorem 2</u>: MATIN is in PrSPACE(logn).

<u>Proof (Sketch)</u>: We have to define a probabilistic algorithm which decides whether a certain element of the inverse of a given matrix is greater than zero and which can be computed on a PTM within logn tape.

Without loss of generality, we suppose that the given nxn matrix A has the property that $\|A\| \leq 1$, where $\|A\|$ denotes the matrix norm $\max_{1\leq i\leq n} \sum_{j=1}^{n} |a_{ij}|$. Otherwise, we would consider the matrix $A' := \frac{A}{\|A\|}$.

At first we recall a well-known method of successive approximation of an inverse matrix. The iteration may be written in the form

$$X_{v+1} := (I-DA)X_v + D$$

which originates from the fixed point approach

$$I-AX+DX = DX$$

with the unique solution $X = A^{-1}$.

I denotes the nxn regular unit matrix and $D = (d_{ij})$ the following nxn diagonal matrix:

$$d_{ij} := \begin{cases} 0 \text{ , if } i \neq j \\ -1 \text{ , if } a_{ii} < 0 \\ +1 \text{ , if } a_{ii} > 0 \end{cases} .$$

Provided that we define $X_0 := I$, we get

$$X_{k+1} = (I-DA)^{k+1} + \sum_{v=0}^{k} (I-DA)^v \cdot D \quad .$$

Under the assumption: $\|A\| \leq 1$ and $|a_{ii}| > \sum_{i\neq j} |a_{ij}| \quad (1 \leq i \leq n)$

it is obvious that

$$\|I-DA\| < 1$$

and hence

X_k must vanish in the limit, i.e.

$$X_k \xrightarrow[k\to\infty]{} \left(\sum_{v=0}^{\infty} Q^v\right) \cdot D = A^{-1} \quad \text{, where } Q := (I-DA) \; .$$

We simulate this iteration by a Markov process with the set of states $S = \{s_1, \ldots, s_{n+1}, s_1', \ldots, s_{n+1}', \bar{s}\}$ and the following transition probabilities:

$$Pr(s_i \to s_j) := \begin{cases} q_{ij} & \text{, if } i,j \leq n \text{ and } q_{ij} > 0 \\ 1 - \sum_{j=1}^{n} |q_{nj}| & \text{, if } i = n \text{ , } j = n+1 \text{ and } d_{nn} > 0 \\ 1 & \text{, if } i = j = n+1 \\ 0 & \text{, else} \end{cases}$$

$$Pr(s_i' \to s_j') := Pr(s_i \to s_j)$$

$$Pr(s_i \to s_j') := \begin{cases} -q_{ij} & \text{, if } i,j \leq n \text{ and } q_{ij} < 0 \\ 1 - \sum_{j=1}^{n} |q_{nj}| & \text{, if } i = n \text{ , } j = n+1 \text{ and } d_{nn} < 0 \\ 0 & \text{, else} \end{cases}$$

$Pr(s_i' \longrightarrow s_j) := Pr(s_i \longrightarrow s_j')$,

and with $\bar{s}$ as a garbage collector:

$$Pr(\bar{s} \longrightarrow s_j) = Pr(\bar{s} \longrightarrow s_j') = 0 \ , \ \text{for } 1 \leq j \leq n+1$$

$$Pr(\bar{s} \longrightarrow \bar{s}) = 1$$

$$Pr(s_i \longrightarrow \bar{s}) = Pr(s_i' \longrightarrow \bar{s}) = \begin{cases} 1 - \sum_{j=1}^{n} |q_{ij}| \ , & \text{if } i \leq n-1 \\ 0 & , \text{else} \end{cases} .$$

According to this definition, the states $s_1, \ldots, s_n$ and $s_1', \ldots, s_n'$ represent the positive resp. negative values in our iteration process. It can be easily proved by induction over k that the following lemma is true:

Lemma 1: Let k be any positive integer, $P := Q^k$ and let $Pr(s_i \xrightarrow{k} s_j)$ denote the probability that the Markov process, starting from s_i, reaches s_j in exactly k steps. Than it holds:

$$p_{ij} = Pr(s_i \xrightarrow{k} s_j) - Pr(s_i \xrightarrow{k} s_j') \quad , \quad \text{for } 1 \leq i,j \leq n \ .$$

Using this lemma it is evident that

$$Pr(s_1 \xrightarrow{*} s_{n+1}) - Pr(s_1 \xrightarrow{*} s_{n+1}') > 0 \quad \text{iff} \quad c_{1n} > 0 \quad ,$$

where $C := A^{-1} = \sum_{v=0}^{\infty} Q^v \cdot D$ and $Pr(s_i \xrightarrow{*} s_{n+1})$ denotes the probability that the Markov process, starting from s_i, reaches s_{n+1} after a finite number of steps.

To finish the proof of Theorem 2 we have to simulate the described Markov process by a PTM working within O(logn) space.

This can be done in an obvious way.

From the Theorem 1 and 2 we derive a

Corollary 1: MATIN is logn-space complete for PrSPACE(logn) .

The above results show that the computational time of a logn-tape bounded PTM is closely related to the speed of convergence of the corresponding matrix iteration process. Obviously, we have only an exponential upper bound for the time needed by a PTM (7). Using the results of (1) we can improve this bound to be polynomial if we consider the matrix inversion problem for symmetric matrices.

On the other hand, from the theory of matrices in numerical analysis we know many more matrix inversion algorithms, converging better than the iteration algorithm used here. It would be of great interest to find an iteration algorithm solving MATIN with the properties:

(i) It converges in polynomial time

(ii) Each step can be performed by a logn-tape bounded PTM within polynomial time .

4. A new algorithm for the inversion of banded matrices:

For any function $b(n) \in O(n)$ let MATIN(b(n)) be the matrix inversion problem restricted to nxn matrices with bandwidth b(n) . UDEPTHSIZE(d(n),s(n)) denotes the class of languages acceptable by uniform circuits simultaneously within d(n) depth and s(n) size. For the exact definitions see (2,12).

The main result of this section is:

Theorem 3:

MATIN(b(n)) is in UDEPTHSIZE($\log n \cdot (\log b(n) + \log\log n)$, $n^{O(1)}$) .

Proof (Sketch):

Let A be an nxn matrix with bandwidth b(n), n-bit elements and $|a_{ii}| > \sum_{i \neq j} |a_{ij}|$ for $1 \leq i \leq n$.

During the fast parallel matrix inversion algorithm of CSANKY (5) we have to compute the n-th power A^n of A, hence we cannot derive any advantage from the property of A to have a small bandwidth. This is the reason why we must find a new fast parallel inversion algorithm for banded matrices.

To test whether the element c_{1n} of the inverse matrix $C = A^{-1}$ is greater than zero, we can solve the system of linear equations

(*) $A\,x = e_n$,

where e_n is the matrix $(0,\dots,0,1)^T$.

Without loss of generality, we assume that n is a multiple of b(n) and $k := n/b(n)$. A is subdivided into k^2 b(n)xb(n) submatrices A_{ij} with the property that $A_{ij} = 0$ for $|i-j| > 1$.

step 1: We extend the nxn-system (*) to an mxm system $A' \cdot x' = e_m$, introducing a set of n-b(n) fictious variables, where $m = 2n-b(n)$. $A' = (A'_{ij})$, where A'_{ij} are b(n)xb(n) matrices defined by:

$$A'_{ij} := \begin{cases} A_{\frac{i+1}{2},\frac{j+1}{2}} & \text{, if } i \text{ odd and } (\ i = j \text{ or } i = j+2\ ) \\ A_{\frac{i+1}{2},\frac{j+2}{2}} & \text{, if } i \text{ odd and } i = j-1 \\ I & \text{, if } i \text{ even and } i = j \\ -I & \text{, if } i \text{ even and } i = j-1 \\ 0 & \text{, else} \end{cases}$$

i.e. A' has the form as illustrated in Fig.1 .

It is easy to see that:

(i) $c_{1n} = c'_{1m}$, where $C' = (A')^{-1}$,

(ii) A can be reduced to A' simultaneously within logn depth and polynomial size.

$$A' = \left[\begin{array}{cc|cc|cc|c}
A_{11} & A_{12} & 0 & 0 & & & \\
0 & I & -I & 0 & & & 0 \\
\hline
A_{21} & 0 & A_{22} & A_{23} & 0 & 0 & \\
0 & 0 & 0 & I & -I & 0 & \\
\hline
 & & \cdot & \cdot & \cdot & \cdot & \\
 & & & \cdot & \cdot & \cdot & \cdot \\
 & & & & \cdot & \cdot & \cdot \\
 & 0 & & & 0 & I & -I \\
\hline
 & & & & A_{kk-1} & 0 & A_{kk}
\end{array}\right]$$

Fig.1

step 2: We add the following mxm matrix $\bar{A} = (\bar{a}_{ij})$, with

$$\bar{a}_{ij} := \begin{cases} 2^{-n^d} & \text{, if } \lfloor i/b(n) \rfloor \text{ is even or zero and } j = i+3b(n) \\ 0 & \text{, else} \end{cases}$$

where d is some constant such that

$$c'_{1m} > 0 \quad \text{iff} \quad \bar{c}_{1m} > 0 \quad \text{, with } \bar{C} := (A'+\bar{A})^{-1}.$$

Note that the existence of d immediately follows from the fact that we can bound the condition number of A' from below with 2^{-n^c}, for a certain constant c not depending on n.

step 3: Let B be the submatrix of $A'+\bar{A}$ such that

$$A'+\bar{A} = \left[\begin{array}{ccccc|c} & & B & & & B' \\ \hline 0 & \cdots & A_{kk-1} & & 0 & A_{kk} \end{array}\right] ,$$

where B' is an $(m-b(n)) \times b(n)$ matrix of the form $\begin{bmatrix} 0 \\ \vdots \\ 0 \\ A_{k-1k} \\ -I \end{bmatrix}$.

Hence B is an $(m-b(n)) \times (m-b(n))$ matrix with bandwidth $O(b(n))$ as illustrated in Fig.2:

$$B = \begin{bmatrix} B_{11} & B_{12} & & & & \\ B_{21} & B_{22} & B_{23} & & & \\ & B_{32} & B_{33} & B_{34} & & \\ & & & \cdot & & \\ & & & & \cdot & \\ & & & & B_{ll-1} & B_{ll} \end{bmatrix}$$

, where the B_{ij} are $2b(n) \times 2b(n)$ matrices, $l := k-1$ and

$$B_{i,i+1} = \begin{bmatrix} 0 & 2^{-n^d} I \\ -I & 0 \end{bmatrix}$$

is always regular.

Fig.2

We compute in parallel the inverse matrices $(B_{i,i+1})^{-1}$, for $1 \leq i \leq l-1$.

step 4: We transform the singular $(m-b(n))\times m$ system of linear equations with the coefficient matrix $(B\,B')$ into an equivalent $(m-b(n))\times m$ system with the coefficient matrix $(D\,D')$ of the form:

$$D = \begin{bmatrix} D_{11} & I & & & & \\ D_{21} & 0 & I & & \mathcal{O} & \\ \cdot & & & \cdot & & \\ \cdot & & & & \cdot & \\ \cdot & & & & & \cdot \\ D_{l-1,1} & & \mathcal{O} & & & I \\ D_{l1} & & & & & 0 \end{bmatrix}$$

Fig.3

where the D_{i1} are certain $2b(n)\times 2b(n)$ matrices and D' is an $(m-b(n))\times b(n)$ matrix.

This can be done within $\log l$ (i.e. $O(\log n)$) iterations. In each iteration step we have to compute in parallel the product and the sum of two $2b(n)\times 2b(n)$ matrices.

step 5: It remains to compute the inverse of the $m\times m$ matrix:

$$\left[\begin{array}{ccccc|c} & & D & & & D' \\ \hline 0 & \cdots & A_{k,k-1} & & 0 & A_{kk} \end{array}\right]$$

In fact, this demands the same depth and size as needed to inverse an $O(b(n))\times O(b(n))$ matrix.

Remark: To perform the steps 3,4 and 5 of our algorithm, we turn to the residuen arithmetic, i.e. we compute these steps in parallel for matrices over a finite field of characteristic p (in parallel for a polynomial number of primes $p \le n^c$). For further details, see (9).

We obtain the assumed bounds for depth and size because:

- turning to the residuen arithmetic takes $O(\log n)$ depth,
- the inversion of a $b(n)\times b(n)$ matrix over a finite field of characteristic p takes $O(\log b(n)\cdot(\log b(n) + \log\log p))$ depth (4),
- each iteration in step 4 costs $O(\log b(n) + \log\log p)$ depth,
- by using the nice algorithm of REIF (11) for computing the product of n n-bit integers within depth $O(\log n \log\log n)$, the algorithm of the Chinese remainder theorem can be computed within $O(\log n\cdot\log\log n)$ depth,
- all this can be done simultaneously within polynomial size,

which proves the theorem.

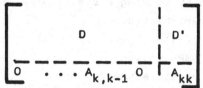

Using a result of BORODIN (2) and combining the reduction methods of MONIEN/SUDBOROUGH (10) with the technique used above we get as a corollary:

Corollary 2: $PrSPACE(S(n)) \subseteq DSPACE(logn \cdot (S(n) + loglogn))$,
for $S(n) \in O(logn)$.

Since FREIVALDS (6) proved that the language $L = \{0^n1^n : n \geq 1\}$ belongs to BPrSPACE(O(1)) we can conclude

Corallary 3:
$NSPACE(S(n)) \subset BPrSPACE(S(n)) \subseteq PrSPACE(S(n)) \subseteq DSPACE(S(n)\ logn)$,
for logn -constructible $S(n) \in o(logn) \cap \Omega(loglogn)$.

This extends the result of MONIEN/SUDBOROUGH (10) from the nondeterministic to the probabilistic case. Our algorithm seems to be applicable to a broader class of problems than the algorithm of (10), which solves only a special graph problem.
It remains to remark that we can improve the above results for bounded error PTMs with very small space bounds:

Theorem 4: $BPrSPACE(S(n)) \subseteq DSPACE(2^{O(S(n))} \cdot logn)$

The proof is straight foreward by solving a system of linear equations in an O(logn)-bit fixed point arithmetic.
Theorem 4 leads to

Corollary 4: $BPrSPACE(O(1)) \subseteq DSPACE(logn)$,
which is known to be the best possible upper bound.

References:

(1) R.Aleliunas, R.M.Karp, R.J.Lipton, L.Lovasz, Random walks, universal traversal sequences and the complexity of maze problems. 20th Annual Symposium on Foundations of Computer Science, 1979, 218-223

(2) A.Borodin, On relating time and space to size and depth. SIAM J.Computing 6 (1977), 733-744

(3) A.Borodin, S.Cook, N.Pippenger, Parallel computation for well-endowed rings and space-bounded probabilistic machines. TR #162/83, Dept. of Comp. Sci., University of Toronto, 1983

(4) A.Borodin, J.von zur Gathen, J.E.Hopcroft, Fast parallel matrix and gcd computations. Information and Control 52,3(1982), 241-256

(5) L.Csanky, Fast parallel matrix inversion algorithms. SIAM J.Computing 5 (1976), 618-623

(6) R.V.Freivals, Probabilistic two-way machines. 10th Symposium on Mathematical Foundations of Computer Science, 1981, LNCS 118, 33-45

(7) J.Gill, Computational complexity of probabilistic Turing machines. SIAM J.Computing 6 (1977), 675-695

(8) J.H.Hopcroft, J.D.Ullman, Formal languages and their relation to automata. Addison-Wesley, Reading MA, 1969

(9) H.Jung, Relationships between probabilistic and deterministic tape complexity. 10th Symposium on Mathematical Foundations of Computer Science, 1981, LNCS 118, 339-346

(10) B.Monien, I.H.Sudborough, On elimating nondeterminism from Turing machines which use less than logarithm worktape space. 6th Coll. on Automata, Languages and Programming, 1979, LNCS 71, 431-445

(11) J.H.Reif, Logarithmic depth circuits for algebraic functions. TR-35-82, Harvard Un., Aiken Comp. Lab., Cambridge MA, 1982

(12) W.L.Ruzzo, On uniform circuit complexity. Journal of Computer and System Sciences 22 (1981), 365-383

(13) W.L.Ruzzo, J.Simon, M.Tompa, Space-bounded hierarchies and probabilistic computations. 14th Annual ACM Symposium on Theory of Computing, 1982

(14) J.Simon, On the difference between one and many. 4th Coll. on Automata, Languages and Programming, 1977, LNCS 52, 480-491

(15) J.Simon, Space-bounded probabilistic Turing machine complexity classes are closed under complement. 13th Annual ACM Symposium on Theory of Computing, 1981, 158-167

ON THREE-ELEMENT CODES

Juhani Karhumäki
Department of Mathematics
University of Turku
Turku, Finland

ABSTRACT

We show that three-element codes have some special properties which do not hold even for four-element codes. Firstly, for each three-element code A, if u and v are words in $\text{pref}(xA^{\omega}) \cap \text{pref}(yA^{\omega})$, with $x,y \in A$, $x \neq y$, then one of them is a prefix of the other, i.e., among the words which can be covered in two different ways from left to right there exists a unique maximal (possibly infinite) element. Secondly, each three-element code has a bounded delay in at least one direction.

1. INTRODUCTION

Codes, or injective morphisms of free semigroups, are very natural and important objects in formal language theory. Hence, it is not surprising that a lot of research has been done, cf. [1], in studying their properties since the 1950s when the systematic study of codes was initiated by Schützenberger, cf. [8]. An interesting class of codes, especially from the point of view of an easy decoding, is the family of bounded delay codes, cf. [1], [2], [6] or [7].

The aim of this article is to show that three-element codes possess certain properties which are not true for codes in general, or even for four-element codes. Thus we are, in a sense, looking for characterization results of three-element codes. For binary codes, i.e., for two-element codes, such a result is known and easily obtainable: A binary set $A = \{\alpha,\beta\}$ is a code if and only if it is aperiodic, i.e., the primitive roots of α and β are different. In particular, each binary code has a bounded delay in both directions.

It is also well-known that a three-element code need not have a bounded delay in both directions. However, as a main result of this paper, we are able to prove that such a code has always a bounded delay in at least one direction.

This result is based on another special property of three-element codes established recently in [3] and discussed more in section 3 of this paper. This property is as follows: For each three-element code A there exists a unique maximal (possibly infinite) word ω_A such that it can be covered from left to right in two different ways, that is to say, there exists a unique maximal (possibly infinite) word in $\bigcup_{\substack{x,y \in A \\ x \neq y}} \mathrm{pref}(xA^\omega) \cap \mathrm{pref}(yA^\omega)$. Here, of course, the word maximal refers to the partial order "... is a prefix of ..." .

We also give examples showing that neither of the above mentioned properties of three-element codes does not hold for all four-element codes.

2. PRELIMINARIES

We assume that the reader is familiar with the basic notions of formal languages and codes, cf., e.g., [7] or [1]. To fix our terminology we, however, specify the following.

A free monoid generated by an alphabet Σ is denoted by Σ^* and its identity by 1 . Further we set $\Sigma^+ = \Sigma^* - \{1\}$. Elements of Σ^* are called words. The notations Σ^ω and ${}^\omega\Sigma$ are used for the sets of all infinite words, or ω-words, from left to right and from right to left, respectively. We call an ω-word w in Σ^ω (resp. in ${}^\omega\Sigma$) <u>periodic</u> if there exists a finite word p such that $w = p^\omega$ (resp. $w = {}^\omega p$) .

For a word x we denote by $|x|$ its length and by $\mathrm{pref}_k(x)$ (resp. $\mathrm{suf}_k(x)$) , for $k \geq 0$, its prefix (resp. suffix) of length k . If $|x| < k$ we set $\mathrm{pref}_k(x) = \mathrm{suf}_k(x) = x$. Let x and y be words. We write $x < y$ (resp. $y > x$) if x is a prefix (resp. suffix) of y. Further we use the notation $x \wedge_p y$ (resp. $x \wedge_s y$) for the <u>maximal common prefix</u> (resp. <u>suffix</u>) of the words x and y . Clearly, $\wedge_p$ and $\wedge_s$ are associative. The notation $y^{-1}x$ (resp. xy^{-1}) is used for the left (resp. right) quotient of x by y . It should be clear when and how the above notions can be extended to words in $\Sigma^* \cup \Sigma^\omega$ or in $\Sigma^* \cup {}^\omega\Sigma$.

For a language A , $\mathrm{pref}(A)$ (resp. $\mathrm{suf}(A)$) denotes the set of all prefixes (resp. suffixes) of words in A , and the ω-languages A^ω and ${}^\omega A$ are defined in a natural way.

A language $C = \{c_i \mid i \in I\} \subseteq \Sigma^*$ is a <u>code</u> if C is free with C as a base, or equivalently, if the morphism $h: I^* \to \Sigma^*$ defined by $h(i) = c_i$ is injective. Further we say that a code C has a <u>bounded</u>

delay p from left to right if the following holds: For any words u and v in C^* and for any elements α and β in C, if $\alpha u < \beta v$ and $|u| > p$, then necessarily $\alpha = \beta$. A code is said to have a bounded delay from left to right if it has a bounded delay p from left to right for some $p \geq 0$. The corresponding notions from right to left are defined analogously using suffixes.

Let A be a language and w a word or an ω-word. We say that A covers w from left to right if $w \in \text{pref}(A^\omega)$. Moreover, we say that A covers ambiguously w from left to right if there exist words α and β in A, with $\alpha \neq \beta$, such that $w \in \text{pref}(\alpha A^\omega) \cap \text{pref}(\beta A^\omega)$. Let *Amb*(A) denote the set of all (finite or infinite) words ambiguously covered by A from left to right. The corresponding notions from right to left are defined analogously.

3. THE STRUCTURE OF *AMB*(A)

In this section we recall and slightly reformulate the result of [3] characterizing the structure of *Amb*(A) in the case when A is a three-element code.

Let $A = \{\alpha,\beta,\gamma\} \subseteq \Sigma^*$ be a three-element code. Further let $h: I^* \to \Sigma^*$, where $I = \{1,2,3\}$, be the morphism defined by $h(1) = \alpha$, $h(2) = \beta$ and $h(3) = \gamma$. We say that A is from left to right reduced if $\text{card}(\text{pref}_1(A)) \geq 2$ and that it is from left to right strongly reduced if, moreover, one of the words of A is a prefix of another. Consequently, the code $\{\alpha,\beta,\gamma\}$ is from left to right strongly reduced if and only if one of the words α, β and γ is a prefix of another and the third starts with a different letter than the other two. Of course, the above notions from right to left are defined analogously.

We have the following simple but useful result, cf. [3].

LEMMA 1. Let $A = \{\alpha,\beta,\gamma\}$ be a code and $\rho = \alpha^\omega \wedge_p \beta^\omega \wedge_p \gamma^\omega$. Then $A' = \rho^{-1}A\rho$ is from left to right reduced and, moreover, if A has the unbounded delay from left to right , then A' is from left to right strongly reduced. □

Lemma 1 was an important tool when proving the main result of [3] which is as follows:

THEOREM 1. Let A be a three-element code. There exist words x and y such that $Amb(A) = \text{pref}(xy^\omega)$.

The message of Theorem 1 is that for any three-element code A ,

$Amb(A)$ contains the unique maximal element with respect to the partial order $<$. Let us denote this word by ω_A. Clearly, ω_A is finite if and only if A has a bounded delay.

Now a natural question arises: In how many ways can the unique maximal element of $Amb(A)$ be covered? Our next result gives the answer to this question in the case when ω_A is infinite.

<u>THEOREM 2.</u> Assume that ω_A is infinite. Then there exist exactly two words υ and $\bar{\upsilon}$ in I^ω such that $\omega_A = h(\upsilon) = h(\bar{\upsilon})$. Moreover, neither of the words υ and $\bar{\upsilon}$ is periodic.

<u>Proof.</u> Since ω_A is infinite, A must have the unbounded delay and hence, by Lemma 1, we may assume that A is from left to right strongly reduced. Let υ and $\bar{\upsilon}$ be words in I^ω such that $pref_1(\upsilon) \neq pref_1(\bar{\upsilon})$ and $\omega_A = h(\upsilon) = h(\bar{\upsilon})$.

We assume that there exists also a word υ' such that $h(\upsilon') = \omega_A$ and $\upsilon' \notin \{\upsilon,\bar{\upsilon}\}$. Clearly, either $\upsilon' \wedge_p \upsilon$ or $\upsilon' \wedge_p \bar{\upsilon}$ is finite and nonempty, say $\tau = \upsilon' \wedge_p \upsilon \neq 1$. Then $h(\tau^{-1}\upsilon) = h(\tau^{-1}\upsilon')$, with $pref_1(\tau^{-1}\upsilon) \neq pref_1(\tau^{-1}\upsilon')$. Therefore, Theorem 1 implies that $h(\tau^{-1}\upsilon) = \omega_A$ and, hence, $\omega_A = h(\tau^\omega)$.

Now, let $\bar{\upsilon} = \upsilon_0(\upsilon_1)^\omega$, where $|h(\upsilon_1)|$ is a multiple of $|h(\tau)|$, say $|h(\upsilon_1)| = i|h(\tau)|$. Then we have $h(\upsilon_0\upsilon_1\upsilon_1) = h(\tau^i\upsilon_0\upsilon_1)$, a contradiction since $pref_1(\tau) \neq pref_1(\upsilon_0)$. This argumentation proves also the second sentence of the theorem. □

It is worth emphasizing that Theorem 2 does not hold for finite prefixes of ω_A. Such words may have more than two covers. Indeed, let $A = \{ab,aba,babb\}$ and $w = ababab$. Then w is a prefix of $\omega_A = aba(bab)^\omega$ and, however, w has four different covers: $w = aba.bab = ab.aba.b = ab.ab.ab. = ab.ab.ab$. Even in the case when ω_A itself is finite it can have more than two covers, consider, e.g., the code $\{ab,aba,baabb\}$. Observe also that although υ and $\bar{\upsilon}$ are nonperiodic ω_A may be periodic. Indeed, for the code $A = \{ab,aba,baba\}$ we have $\omega_A = (ab)^\omega$.

We conclude this section with an example showing that the structure of $Amb(A)$ for a four-element code can be much more complicated than Theorem 1 allows. We extend the above mentioned three-element code $\{ab,aba,babb\}$ to the code

$$A' = \{ab,aba,babb,bbabba\} .$$

Then a straightforward consideration shows that, cf.also [3],

$$Amb(A') = \mathrm{pref}(aba(bbabba)^*(bab)^\omega \cup aba(bba)^\omega \cup abab(babbab)^*abb((abbabb)^*(babbab)^*)^\omega)$$

3. BOUNDED DELAY PROPERTIES

Let us start this section by considering a two-element code $B = \{\alpha,\beta\}$. It is straightforward to see, cf. [4], that $Amb(B) = \mathrm{pref}(\alpha\beta \wedge_p \beta\alpha)$. In particular, this means that B has a bounded delay from left to right and, hence, by symmetry also from right to left.

On the other hand, the ω-word ab^ω and the code $\{a,ab,bb\}$ shows that a three-element code need not have a bounded delay from left to right. However, as an application of Theorems 1 and 2, we are able to prove the following result.

THEOREM 3. Each three-element code has a bounded delay at least in one direction.

The proof of Theorem 3 goes via a sequence of four lemmas. From now on let $A = \{\alpha,\beta,\gamma\} \subseteq \Sigma^*$ be a three-element code having the unbounded delay in both directions. We assume that Σ is binary and define the morphism h as in the previous section. Further, in the spirit of Theorem 1 let ω_A and ${}_A\omega$ be the unique infinite words which can be covered from left to right and from right to left, respectively, in two different ways. We call A from left to right (resp. from right to left) periodic if ω_A (resp. ${}_A\omega$) is periodic.

We start the proof of Theorem 3 with the following lemma which, we believe, is interesting on its own, too.

LEMMA 2. Let $A = \{\alpha,\beta,\gamma\}$ be from left to right strongly reduced. Then for each words u and v in A^* the word $u \wedge_p v$ is in A^*.

Proof. We assume that $u \in \alpha A^*$ and $v \in \beta A^*$. Then, by Theorem 1, $u \wedge_p v < \omega_A$ and hence $u \wedge_p v \in \{u \wedge_p \omega_A, v \wedge_p \omega_A\}$. Therefore, it is enough to show that $u \wedge_p \omega_A \in A^*$. This is done by induction on $|u \wedge_p \omega_A|$.

If $u < \omega_A$ we are done. So let $u \not< \omega_A$. We illustrate our assumptions in Figure 1

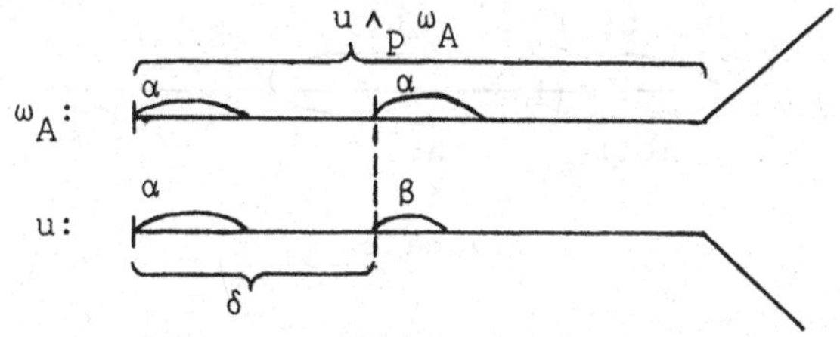

Figure 1

where δ is defined by

$$\delta = h(h^{-1}(u) \wedge_p 1h^{-1}(\alpha^{-1}\omega_A)) .$$

By Theorem 2, δ is unique. Further we set

$$\omega' = \delta^{-1}\omega_A \quad \text{and} \quad u' = \delta^{-1}u .$$

If $\delta = u \wedge_p \omega_A$ we are done. Consequently, let

$$|\delta| < |u \wedge_p \omega_A| \qquad .$$

so that ω' and u' are nonempty words such that $pref_1(u') = pref_1(\omega')$ and $pref_1(h^{-1}(u')) \neq pref_1(h^{-1}(\omega'))$. Hence we may assume that $\omega' \in \alpha A^\omega$ and $u' \in \beta A^*$. Therefore Theorem 1 yields $u' \wedge_p \omega' < \omega_A$ and hence $u' \wedge_p \omega' \in \{u' \wedge_p \omega_A , \omega' \wedge_p \omega_A\}$. Consequently, by induction hypothesis, $u' \wedge_p \omega' \in A^*$ and the lemma has been proved. □

Observe that in the proof of the previous lemma we did not use the fact that A has the unbounded delay.

As our second lemma we establish

LEMMA 3. If A is from right to left strongly reduced, then it is from left to right periodic.

Proof. By Theorem 2, there exist two infinite words, say $\upsilon = xy^\omega$ and $\bar{\upsilon} = \bar{x}\bar{y}^\omega$, with $pref_1(x) \neq pref_1(\bar{x})$, such that $h(\upsilon) = h(\bar{\upsilon}) = \omega_A$. Moreover, by the second sentence of this theorem neither $x \wedge_s y \notin \{x,y\}$ nor $\bar{x} \wedge_s \bar{y} \notin \{\bar{x},\bar{y}\}$. Consequently, we may, possibly modifying the words x, $\bar{x}$, y and $\bar{y}$, assume that all of them are nonempty and that they satisfy the following conditions: $|h(y)| = |h(\bar{y})|$, $pref_1(x) \neq pref_1(\bar{x})$, $suf_1(x) \neq suf_1(y)$ and $suf_1(\bar{x}) \neq suf_1(\bar{y})$. We illustrate our assumptions in Figure 2.

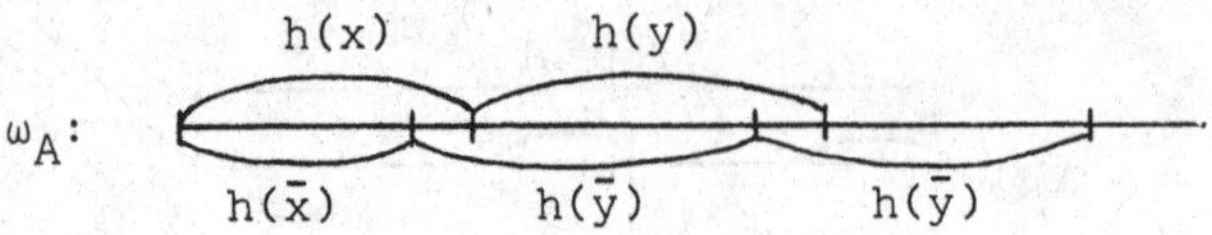

Figure 2

Clearly, $|h(x)| \neq |h(\bar{x})|$, say $|h(x)| > |h(\bar{x})|$. Now, since A is from right to left strongly reduced, we obtain, again by Theorem 1, that

$$_A\omega > h(\bar{x})^{-1}h(x) = h(\bar{x}\bar{y})^{-1}h(xy) .$$

Let $\tau = h(x) \wedge_s h(xy)$. Then, by Lemma 2, τ is in A^+. In particular, since A is a code, it follows that $|\tau| > |h(\bar{x})^{-1}h(x)|$. Therefore the maximal common suffix $\bar{\tau}$ of the words $h(\bar{x})$ and $h(\bar{x}\bar{y})$ is non-empty and hence, again by Lemma 2, in A^+. Consequently, we have $\tau h(y^\omega) = \bar{\tau}h(\bar{y}^\omega)$ with τ and $\bar{\tau}$ in A^+. So it follows from Theorem 2 and from the relations $suf_1(x) \neq suf_1(y)$, $suf_1(\bar{x}) \neq suf_1(\bar{y})$, $|\tau| \leq |h(x)|$ and $|\bar{\tau}| \leq |h(\bar{x})|$ that $\tau = h(x)$ and $\bar{\tau} = h(\bar{x})$. This means that $\omega_A = (h(x)h(y)(h(x))^{-1})$ proving the lemma. □

Now, we obtain easily our next lemma.

<u>LEMMA 4.</u> Each three-element code A having the unbounded delay in both directions is periodic in both directions.

<u>Proof.</u> Assume the contrary, say ω_A is not periodic. Then, by Lemma 3, A is not from right to left strongly reduced. Let, according to Lemma 1, μ be a word such that $A' = \mu A \mu^{-1}$ is from right to left strongly reduced. Clearly, also A' has the unbounded delay in both directions and $\omega_{A'} = \mu\omega_A$. Now, since ω_A is not periodic from left to right neither is $\omega_{A'}$ a contradiction to Lemma 3. □

As our last lemma we sharpen the previous result as follows.

<u>LEMMA 5.</u> For each three-element code A having the unbounded delay in both directions there exist words p_1 and p_2 such that $\omega_A = (p_1p_2)^\omega$ and $_A\omega = {}^\omega(p_2p_1)$.

<u>Proof.</u> By Lemma 4, there exist words p and $\bar{p}$ such that $\omega_A = p^\omega$ and $_A\omega = {}^\omega\bar{p}$. We assume, by symmetry, that $|p| \geq |\bar{p}|$ and that p is primitive. Further we may assume, cf. the proof of Lemma 4, that A is from right to left strongly reduced. Finally, as at the beginning of the

proof of Lemma 3, let x, $\bar{x}$, y and $\bar{y}$ be nonempty words such that $h(xy^{\omega}) = h(\bar{x}\bar{y}^{\omega}) = \omega_A$ and, moreover, $\mathrm{pref}_1(x) \neq \mathrm{pref}_1(\bar{x})$, $\mathrm{suf}_1(x) \neq \mathrm{suf}_1(y)$ and $\mathrm{suf}_1(\bar{x}) \neq \mathrm{suf}_1(\bar{y})$.

Let

(1) $$p = rst$$

be the factorization of p such that

$$h(x) \in p^*r \quad \text{and} \quad h(\bar{x}) \in p^*rs$$

(or symmetrically $h(x) \in p^*rs$ and $h(\bar{x}) \in p^*r$). Then the primitiveness of p yields

$$h(y) \in (str)^+ \quad \text{and} \quad h(\bar{y}) \in (trs)^+ .$$

In (1) r and t must be nonempty, otherwise A would not be a code, cf. the choice of x, $\bar{x}$, y and $\bar{y}$. We shall show that

(2) $$s = 1 .$$

We assume that $|h(x)| > |h(\bar{x})|$ (the other possibility is handled in the same manner) and illustrate our assumptions in Figure 3.

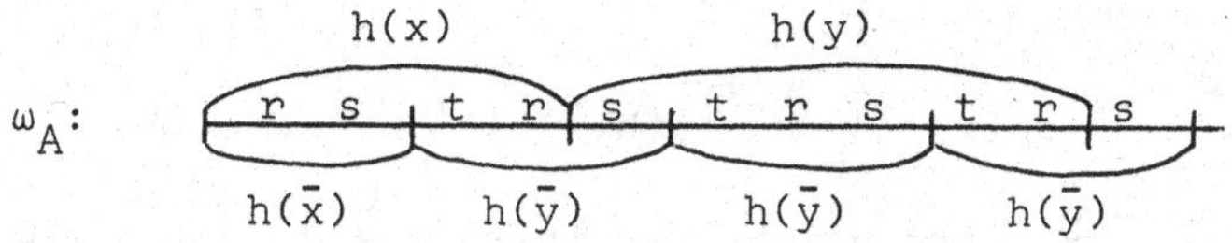

Figure 3

We define

$$\sigma = \max\{\, z \mid z \in \mathrm{suf}((rst)^*) \cap \mathrm{suf}(A^*)\} .$$

If σ is infinite, then (2) follows from the uniqueness of A^{ω} from the primitiveness of p and from the relations $\sigma h(xy) > \sigma h(x)$ and $\sigma h(\bar{x}\bar{y}) > \sigma h(\bar{x})$, where $\mathrm{suf}_1(x) \neq \mathrm{suf}_1(y)$, $\mathrm{suf}_1(\bar{x}) \neq \mathrm{suf}_1(\bar{y})$ and σ is in ${}^{\omega}A$. So we assume that σ is finite.

First we derive from the facts that A is from right to left strongly reduced and Σ is binary that σ is nonempty. The same argument shows that σ is neither in A^+. Now, let x' be a word such that $h(x') > \sigma$. Then, by Lemma 2, we obtain

$$\sigma h(x) = h(x'x) \wedge_s h({}^{\omega}y) \in A^+$$

and, symmetrically,

$$\sigma h(\bar{x}) = h(x'x) \wedge_s h({}^{\omega}\bar{y}) \in A^+ .$$

Therefore

$$\sigma h(x)h(y^{\omega}) = \sigma h(\bar{x})h(\bar{y}^{\omega}) \quad \text{with} \quad \sigma h(x) \quad \text{and} \quad \sigma h(\bar{x}) \quad \text{in} \quad A^* .$$

This is illustrated in Figure 4.

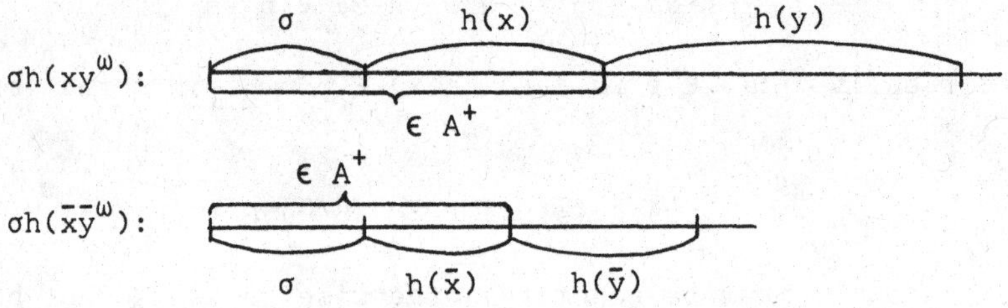

Figure 4

Let

$$x_1 = (h^{-1}(\sigma h(x)) \wedge_p h^{-1}(\sigma h(\bar{x})))^{-1} h^{-1}(\sigma h(x))$$

and

$$\bar{x}_1 = (h^{-1}(\sigma h(x)) \wedge_p h^{-1}(\sigma h(\bar{x})))^{-1} h^{-1}(\sigma h(\bar{x})) .$$

Clearly, x_1 and $\bar{x}_1$ are unique. Further $x \neq x_1$ and $\bar{x} \neq \bar{x}_1$, since σ is not in A^*, and both x_1 and $\bar{x}_1$ are nonempty since A is a code. Now we consider the relations $\text{pref}_1(x_1) \neq \text{pref}_1(\bar{x}_1)$ and $h(x_1y^{\omega}) = h(\bar{x}_1\bar{y}^{\omega})$ and apply the argumentation used at the end of the proof of Lemma 3. This yields that $|h(x_1)| > |h(x)|$ and, hence, by the primitiveness of p and by Theorem 1, we obtain

(3) $\qquad |\sigma| \geq |p| .$

By the definition of σ, we have $h({}^{\omega}y) > \sigma h(x)$ and $h({}^{\omega}\bar{y}) > \sigma h(\bar{x})$. Therefore both $\sigma h(x)$ and $\sigma h(\bar{x})$ are suffixes of ${}_{A}{}^{\omega}$ and, hence, the shorter one is a suffix of the other, i.e., $\sigma h(x) > \sigma h(\bar{x})$. This together with the relation $\sigma h(\bar{x}) < \sigma h(x)$, cf. Figure 4, yield

$$\sigma h(x) \in \text{suf}((h(\bar{x})^{-1}h(x))^+) .$$

On the other hand, by definition of σ, we have

$$\sigma h(x) \in \mathrm{suf}((str)^{+}) .$$

Consequently, the relation $|\sigma h(x)| \geq |str| + |h(\bar{x})^{-1}h(x)|$, implied by (3), guarantees that the primitive roots of the words str and $h(\bar{x})^{-1}h(x)$ are the same, cf., e.g., [5, p.10]. This contradicts with the primitiveness of p unless $s = 1$. So we have established (2).

From (2) and from the fact that $|h(x)| > |h(\bar{x})|$ we obtain $|h(x)| \geq |p|$. This together with (3) yield

$$|\sigma h(x)| \geq 2|p| .$$

We also have

$$^{\omega}\bar{p} = {}_{A}\omega > \sigma h(x)$$

and

$$^{\omega}\tilde{p} > \sigma h(x) ,$$

where $\tilde{p}$ is a conjugate of p. These three conditions together with our assumption $|p| \geq |\bar{p}|$ imply that $\bar{p}$ and $\tilde{p}$, and hence also $\bar{p}$ and p, are conjugates. In fact, $p = rt$ and $\bar{p} = tr$. □

Now, finally, we are ready for the

Proof of Theorem 3. Assume the contrary that a three-element code A has the unbounded delay in both directions. Then, by Lemma 5, there exist words p_1 and p_2 such that $\omega_A = (p_1p_2)^{\omega}$ and ${}_{A}\omega = {}^{\omega}(p_2p_1)$. Moreover, according to the proof of Lemma 5, there exists a word y such that $h(y) = (p_1p_2)^{i}$ for some $i \geq 1$. Hence, $h(y^{\omega}) = \omega_A$, a contradiction with the second sentence of Theorem 2. □

One essential point in the above proof was that if a three-element code A has the unbounded delay in both directions then both ω_A and ${}_{A}\omega$ are periodic (Lemma 4). It is interesting to note that, as we have already seen, one of these words may really be periodic.

As a result of Theorem 3 we can easily list all maximal three-element codes.

COROLLARY. All maximal three-element codes over $\{a,b\}$ are as follows: $\{aa,ab,b\}$, $\{a,ba,bb\}$, $\{aa,ba,b\}$ and $\{a,ab,bb\}$.

Proof. By a theorem of Schützenberger, cf. [1], any maximal code having a bounded delay is either a prefix or suffix code. □

We conclude this article with the following two remarks:

1) Theorem 3 does not hold for four-element codes. Indeed, the code {a,ab,bbab,bbbb} is a counterexample:

abbbbbbbb...   ...bbbbbbab

2) A three-element code may have an "α-shifted unbounded delay" in both directions. Now the code {aa,abb,bba} provides a counterexample:

...bbabbaabbabb...

ACKNOWLEDGEMENT. The author is grateful to Dr. T. Harju for useful discussions and to the Academy of Finland for the excellent working conditions.

REFERENCES

[1] Berstel,J. and Perrin,D., The Theory of Codes, (to appear).

[2] Colomb,S. and Gordon,B., Codes with bounded synchronization delay, Inform. and Control 8 (1965), 355-372.

[3] Karhumäki,J., A property of three-element codes, Proceedings of STACS84, Lecture Notes in Computer Science (Springer, 1984).

[4] Karhumäki,J., The Ehrenfeucht Conjecture: A compactness claim for finitely generated free monoids, Theoret. Comput. Sci. (to appear).

[5] Lothaire,M., Combinatorics on Words, Addison-Wesley, Reading, Mass (1983).

[6] De Luca,A., Perrin,D., Restivo,A. and Termini,S., Synchronization and simplification, Discrete Math. 27 (1979) 297-308.

[7] Salomaa,A., Jewels of Formal Language Theory, Computer Science Press, Rochville, Maryland (1981).

[8] Schützenberger,M.P., Une theorie algebraique du codage, Seminaire Dubreil-Pisot, annee 55-56, exp. n. 15 Inst. Henri Poincare, Paris (1956).

RECURSION DEPTH ANALYSIS FOR SPECIAL TREE TRAVERSAL ALGORITHMS

Peter Kirschenhofer, Helmut Prodinger
Institut für Algebra und Diskrete Mathematik
TU Vienna, A-1040 Vienna, Gußhausstraße 27-29, Austria

1. INTRODUCTION AND MAIN RESULTS

In this paper we are concerned with the analysis of special recursive algorithms for traversing the nodes of a planted plane tree (ordered tree; planar tree). Some by now classical results in this area are due to KNUTH [7], DE BRUIJN, KNUTH and RICE [1], FLAJOLET [2], FLAJOLET and ODLYZKO [3], FLAJOLET, RAOULT and VUILLEMIN [4], KEMP [6] and others and are summarized in the next few lines:

The most important tree structure in Computer Science are the binary trees. The inorder traversal (KNUTH [7]) is the following recursive principle:

Traverse the left subtree
Visit the root
Traverse the right subtree.

The most straightforward implementation uses an auxiliary stack to keep necessary nodes of the tree. The analysis of the expected time of the visit procedure is clearly linear in the size of the input tree. To evaluate recursion depth means to determine the average stack height as a function of the size of the tree. The recursion depth or height h of the binary tree is recursively determined as follows: If the family $\mathcal{B}$ of binary trees is given by the symbolic equation

$\mathcal{B} = \square +$ 

then $h(\square) = 0$ and $h($$) = 1 + \max\{h(t_1), h(t_2)\}$.

In [3] FLAJOLET and ODLYZKO determined the average value h_n of h in the family $\mathcal{B}_n$ of binary trees of size n to be

$$h_n \sim 2\sqrt{\pi n}.$$

The recursive visit procedure can be optimized in the case of binary trees by eliminating endrecursion: the resulting iterative algorithm keeps at each stage a list of right subtrees that still remain to be explored. The storage complexity of this optimized algorithm is easily seen to correspond exactly to the so-called left-sided height h^* defined by

$h^*(\square) = 0,\ h^*($$) = \max\{1+h^*(t_1), h^*(t_2)\}$.

Recalling that the rotation correspondence (KNUTH [7;2.3.2]) transforms a binary tree of n-1 internal (binary) nodes into a planted plane tree with n nodes, the average storage complexity of the optimized algorithm follows immediately by a result of DE BRUIJN, KNUTH and RICE [1] about the average height of planted plane trees:

$$h_n^* \sim \sqrt{\pi n},$$

where the index n again refers to the size of the trees.

It was already proposed in KNUTH's book to consider this kind of questions for other families of trees. Dealing with the family P of planted plane trees defined by

$$P = o + \underset{P}{\overset{\circ}{|}} + \underset{P\;P}{\overset{\circ}{\wedge}} + \underset{PPP}{\overset{\circ}{\wedge}} + \ldots$$

there are several meaningful analogues of the left-sided height of binary trees:

$$u(o) = 0;\; u\Big(\underset{t}{\overset{\circ}{|}}\Big) = u(t);\; u\Big(\underset{t_1\ldots t_r}{\overset{\circ}{\wedge}}\Big) = \max\{1+u(t_1),\ldots,1+u(t_{r-1}),u(t_r)\},\; r\geq 2$$

$$v(o) = 0;\; v\Big(\underset{t_1\ldots t_r}{\overset{\circ}{\wedge}}\Big) = \max\{r-i+v(t_i)\,|\,1\leq i\leq r\}$$

$$w(o) = 0;\; w\Big(\underset{t}{\overset{\circ}{|}}\Big) = 1 + w(t);\; w\Big(\underset{t_1\ldots t_r}{\overset{\circ}{\wedge}}\Big) = \max\{1+w(t_1),w(t_2),\ldots,w(t_r)\},\; r\geq 2$$

The "heights" u, w are better understood as follows. u counts the maximal number of edges not being a rightmost successor of a node in a chain connecting the root with a leaf. w counts the maximal number of edges which are leftmost successors of a node in a chain connecting the root with a leaf. For example we have for the tree t depicted below the values $u(t)=2$, $v(t)=4$, $w(t)=3$.

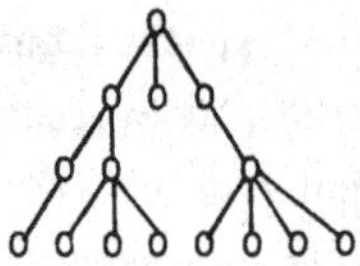

A short reflection tells us that u determines the recursion depth of the optimized tree traversal algorithm. (The non-optimized algorithm corresponds to the treatment of DE BRUIJN, KNUTH and RICE [1].)

The interpretation of v is a bit more complex: Recall that a binary tree can be used to represent arithmetic expressions; a simple strategy of the evaluation is "from right to left", i.e. to evaluate $\underset{t_1\quad t_2}{\overset{(op)}{\wedge}}$ we evaluate t_2, use one register to keep that value, evaluate t_1 and then perform "op". It is clear that the maximal number of registers during the evaluation of a binary tree is exactly h^*.

Planted plane trees are well suited to encode arithmetic expressions where k-ary operations may occur for any k. The same strategy as in the case of binary trees leads to v (evaluating $\underset{t_1\ldots t_r}{\overset{\circ}{\wedge}}$ from right to left during the consideration of t_i already r-i registers are used to keep intermediate values).

The interest in w originates from another source; however since this parameter fits well in the concept of asymmetric heights we have decided to include it into our discussion.

In any instance we are interested in the average value u_n, v_n, w_n of the "height" u, v, w of the trees in P_n, i.e. the trees of size n in P. Our main results are:

THEOREM. a) $u_n = \frac{1}{2}\sqrt{\pi n} - 1 + O(n^{-1/2})$

b) $v_n = \sqrt{\pi n} - \frac{5}{2} + O(n^{-1/2})$

c) $w_n = \frac{1}{2}\sqrt{\pi n} + O(n^{1/4+\varepsilon})$, for all $\varepsilon>0$.

These results are achieved by means of a detailed singularity analysis of corresponding generating functions in the following section.

2. PROOFS AND MINOR RESULTS

Let $P_h(z)$, $U_h(z)$, $V_h(z)$, $W_h(z)$ be the generating functions of trees in P with ordinary height or "height" u, v, w, respectively, $\leq h$ and $y(z)=(1-\sqrt{1-4z})/2$ the generating function of all trees in P. Then the generating functions of the sums of "heights" of trees of equal size are given by

$$\sum_{h\geq 0}(y-P_h),\ \sum_{h\geq 0}(y-U_h),\ \sum_{h\geq 0}(y-V_h) \text{ and } \sum_{h\geq 0}(y-W_h). \tag{1}$$

It is well known [1] that

$$P_0(z) = z;\ P_h(z) = z/(1-P_{h-1}(z)) \quad \text{and} \tag{2}$$

$$P_h(z) = \frac{u}{1+u}\cdot\frac{1-u^{h+1}}{1-u^{h+2}} \quad \text{where} \quad z = \frac{u}{(1+u)^2}\ . \tag{3}$$

LEMMA 1. $U_h(z) = P_{2h+1}(z)$.

Proof. We have $U_0(z) = \frac{z}{1-z}$ and because of

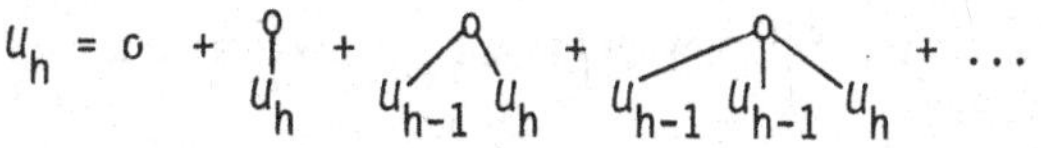

(with an obvious notation)

$$U_h(z) = z + \frac{zU_h(z)}{1-U_{h-1}(z)}\ , \text{ so that } \quad U_h = \frac{z}{1-\frac{z}{1-U_{h-1}}}\ ,$$

from which Lemma 1 follows immediately from (2) by induction.

An alternative proof can be given by defining the following map $\psi: U_h \to P_{2h+1}$ which turns out to be a bijection:

$\psi: U_0 \to P_1$ is defined by

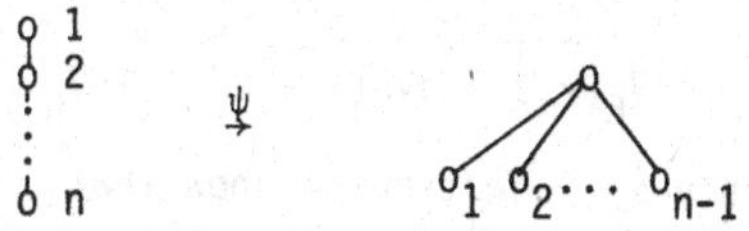

and, recursively, for $t\in U_h$ with subtrees $t_{rs}\in U_{h-1}$

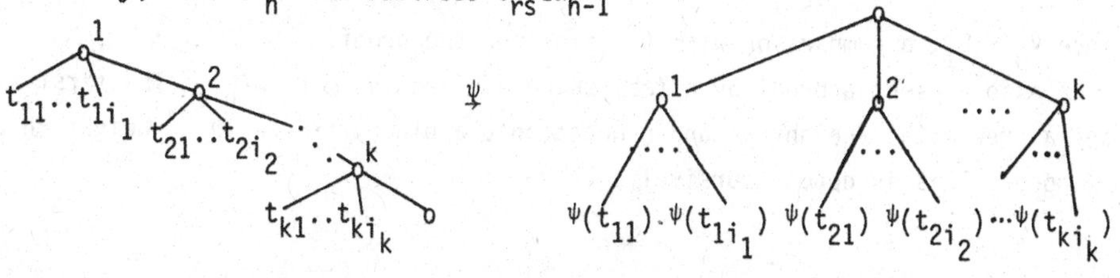

LEMMA 2. With $\mu(z) = 1-4z$ and some constants K_1, K_2 we have for $z \to 1/4$

$$\sum_{h\geq 0} (y-U_h) = K_1 - \frac{1}{8}\log\mu + \frac{1}{2}\mu^{1/2} + K_2\mu + \ldots$$

Proof.

$$\sum_{h\geq 0} (y-U_h) = \sum_{h\geq 0} (y-P_{2h+1}) = -\frac{u}{1+u} + \frac{1-u}{1+u} \sum_{h\geq 0} \frac{u^{2h+1}}{1-u^{2h+1}}$$

Now

$$\sum_{h\geq 0} \frac{u^{2h+1}}{1-u^{2h+1}} = \sum_{k\geq 1} d_1(k)u^k,$$

with $d(k) = d_1(k) + d_2(k)$, $d_2(2k) = d(k)$ where $d(k)$, $d_1(k)$, $d_2(k)$ denotes the number of all, odd or even divisors of k. So we have

$$\sum_{h\geq 0} (y-U_h) = -\frac{u}{1+u} + \frac{1-u}{1+u} \sum_{k\geq 0} d(k)u^k - \frac{1-u^2}{(1+u)^2} \sum_{k\geq 1} d(k)u^{2k}.$$

Now it is known [9] that

$$g(z) = \frac{1-u}{1+u} \sum_{k\geq 1} d(k)u^k = K_1' - \frac{1}{4}\log\mu + \frac{1}{4}\mu^{1/2} + K_2'\mu + \ldots \tag{4}$$

Since $u^2 = (\frac{z}{1-2z})^2 = 4\mu + O(\mu^2)$ it follows that

$$\frac{1-u^2}{(1+u)^2} \sum_{k\geq 1} d(k)u^{2k} = K_1'' - \frac{1}{8}\log\mu + \frac{1}{4}\mu^{1/2} + K_2''\mu + \ldots$$

Further $\frac{u}{1+u} = y(z) = (1-\mu^{1/2})/2$. Putting everything together the lemma follows. □

By a complex contour integration (compare [3]) the local expansion of Lemma 2 "translates" into the following asymptotic behaviour of the coefficients.

LEMMA 3. $\sum_{h\geq 0} (y-U_h) = \sum_{n\geq 0} z^n 4^n (\frac{1}{8n} - \frac{1}{4\sqrt{\pi}} \frac{1}{n^{3/2}} + O(\frac{1}{n^2}))$.

Dividing by $|P_n| = \frac{1}{n}\binom{2n-2}{n-1} = \frac{1}{4\sqrt{\pi}} 4^n n^{-3/2}(1 + O(\frac{1}{n}))$ we achieve part a) of our main theorem.

LEMMA 4. $V_h(z) = P_{h+1}(z)$.

Proof. In the same style as in Lemma 1 we find

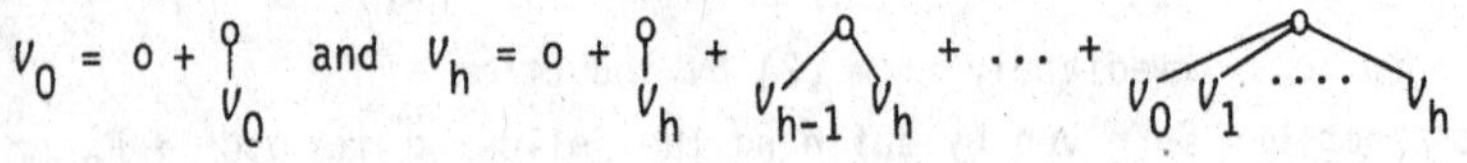

and thus

$$V_0 = \frac{z}{1-z}, \quad V_h = z + zV_h(1 + V_{h-1} + V_{h-1}V_{h-2} + \ldots + V_{h-1}\cdots V_0).$$

From this it is an easy induction to show that

$$V_0 = z/(1-z) \quad \text{and} \quad V_h = z/(1-V_{h-1}).$$

Since $V_0 = P_1$, a comparison with (2) finishes the proof.

We also present a proof by establishing a bijection $\varphi: V_h \to P_{h+1}$. The first step maps a tree with v-height $\leq h$ and n nodes onto a binary tree with h^*-height $\leq h$ and n-1 nodes. This is done recursively:

$$o \overset{\varphi}{\mapsto} o \,,$$

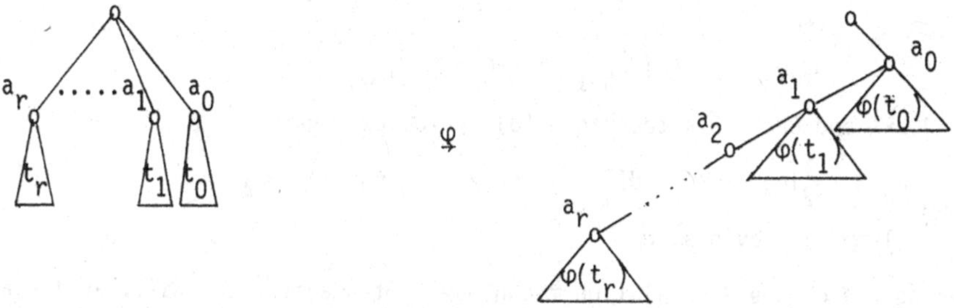

Having performed this recursive operation, the root is to be deleted; this is the first step of our bijection. Regard that in fact φ is a version of the inverse of the "rotation correspondence" [7]. The second step is the classical version of this correspondence between binary trees with h^*-height $\le h$ and $n-1$ nodes and planted plane trees with ordinary height $\le h+1$ and n nodes. □

So the asymptotics of v_n are immediate from the asymptotics of h_n^* ([1]) and part (b) of the main theorem is proved.

We are now left with the proof of part (c) of the main theorem. While in the proofs of (a) and (b) our method was to establish an explicit connection with DE BRUIJN, KNUTH and RICE's result for the ordinary height of planted plane trees, another approach seems to be necessary to achieve (c). The more function theoretic approach was stimulated by the pioneering treatment of the problem of the average height of binary trees by FLAJOLET and ODLYZKO [3].

LEMMA 5. With $\varepsilon=\sqrt{1-4z}$ and $f_h(z) = y(z)-W_h(z)$,

$$f_h^2 + (\varepsilon+z)f_h - zf_{h-1} = 0.$$

Proof. We have

$\omega_0 = o$ and $\omega_h = o +$ 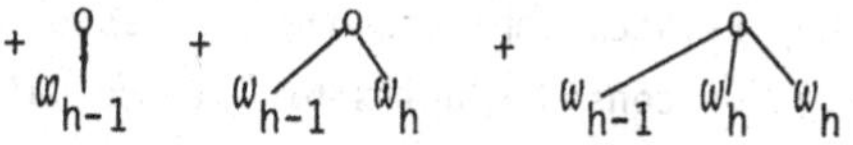 $+ \dots ,$

whence

$$W_0 = z \text{ and } W_h = z + zW_{h-1}/(1-W_h)$$

from which the result follows by some easy manipulations. □

LEMMA 6. $\sum_{h\ge 0}(y-W_h) = -\frac{1}{8}\log\varepsilon + K + O(|1-4z|^{\nu})$ for $z \to \frac{1}{4}$ and for all $\nu < \frac{1}{4}$.

Proof. Because of the complexity of a complete treatment we omit the details and only stress the main steps:

Solving the quadratic equation of Lemma 5 and expanding the square root it follows that

$$f_h = \frac{z}{\varepsilon+z} f_{h-1} \left(1 - \frac{z}{(\varepsilon+z)^2} f_{h-1}\right) + \dots$$

With the substitution $g_h = \frac{z}{(\varepsilon+z)^2} f_h$,

$$g_h = \frac{z}{\varepsilon+z} g_{h-1} (1 - g_{h-1} + \dots) + \dots$$

Since $\frac{z}{\varepsilon+z} = 1 - 4\varepsilon + O(\varepsilon^2)$ it turns out that the behaviour of Σg_h is asymptotically equivalent to ΣG_h, with

$$G_h = (1-4\varepsilon)\, G_{h-1}\, (1 - G_{h-1}).$$

Adopting FLAJOLET and ODLYZKO's technique [3] it follows that

$$\sum_{h\geq 0} G_h = -\frac{1}{2}\log\varepsilon + K' + O(|\varepsilon|^{\nu}) \text{ for } z \to \frac{1}{4} \text{ and all } \nu < \frac{1}{4}$$

from which the lemma is obvious. □

Again making use of the "translation technique" cited above we finally arrive at part (c) of the main theorem.

We finish this section with some results related to the material from above.

Let $h_k(t)$ denote the maximal number of nodes of outdegree k in a chain connecting the root with a leaf. Furthermore let $H_{k,h}(z)$ be the generating function of the trees t with $h_k(t) \leq h$. Then we get

$$H_{k,h} = \frac{z}{1-H_{k,h}} - z\, H_{k,h}^{k} + z\, H_{k,h-1}^{k} .$$

With $e_{k,h}(z) = y(z) - H_{k,h}(z)$ we get in a similar way as above

$$e_{k,h} = e_{k,h-1}\,\left(1 - \frac{2^{k+2}}{k}\, e_{k,h-1}\right) + \ldots$$

and therefore

$$\sum_{h\geq 0} e_{k,h} = -\frac{k}{2^{k+3}}\log\varepsilon + K_k + O(|\varepsilon|^{\nu}),$$

so that the average value of the "height" $h_k(t)$ for trees t of size n is asymptotically equivalent to

$$\frac{k}{2^{k+1}}\sqrt{\pi n}\ . \tag{5}$$

A slightly different but related topic is now discussed: Following POLYA [8], resp. FÜRLINGER and HOFBAUER [5], we consider pairs of lattice paths in the plane, each path starting at the origin and consisting of unit horizontal and vertical steps in the positive direction.

Let $L_{n,j}$ be the set of such path-pairs (π,σ) with the following properties:

(i) both π and σ end at the point $(j,n-j)$

(ii) π begins with a unit vertical step and σ with a horizontal

(iii) π and σ do not meet between the origin and their common endpoint.

The elements of $L_n = \bigcup_{j=1}^{n} L_{n,j}$ are polygons with circumference 2n, and it is well known that $|L_n| = \frac{1}{n}\binom{2n-2}{n-1}$, $n \geq 2$; $|L_1| = 0$.

We define now the height $d(\pi,\sigma)$ of a path-pair (π,σ) to be the maximal length of a "diagonal" parallel to y=-x between two lattice points on the path-pair, e.g.

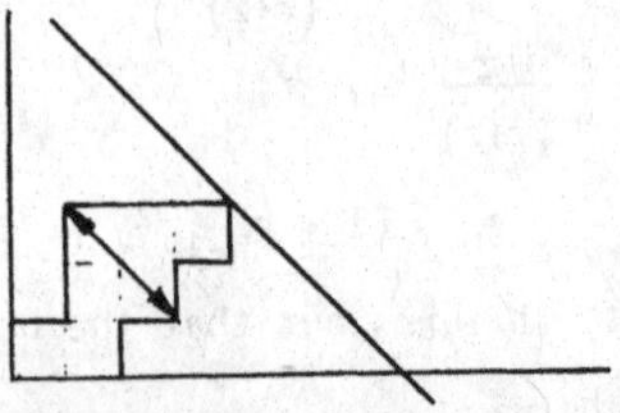

has $d(\pi,\sigma) = 2$.

Let $D_h(z)$ denote the generating function of path-pairs (π,σ) with $d(\pi,\sigma) \le h$.

LEMMA 7. $D_h(z) = P_{2h}'(z) - z$.

Proof. We use the bijection between L_n and "Catalan" words in $\{0,1\}^*$ described in [5]: Represent a path-pair $(\pi,\sigma) \in L_n$ as a sequence of pairs of steps: let v be a vertical step and h a horizontal step. The pair (π,σ) with $\pi = a_1 \dots a_n$, $\sigma = b_1 \dots b_n$ where each a_i and b_i is a v or h, is represented as the sequence of step-pairs $(a_1,b_1) \dots (a_n,b_n)$. To encode the sequence of step-pairs as a Catalan word the following translation is used:

$$(v,h) \to 00 \qquad (v,v) \to 10$$
$$(h,v) \to 11 \qquad (h,h) \to 01$$

Omitting one "0" at the beginning and one "1" at the end a Catalan word is derived.

[For example: The path-pair (π,σ) from above is represented by the sequence

$$(v,h),(h,h),(v,v),(v,h),(h,v),(h,h),(h,v)$$

and encoded as the word 001100011011.]

The Catalan word is now represented in the well known way as a planted plane tree $t(\pi,\sigma)$ of size n.

[In the example 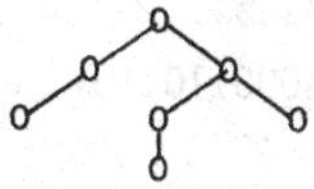 .]

We study now the influence of a step-pair (a_i,b_i) of the path-pair (π,σ) on the height of the corresponding nodes of the planted plane tree $t(\pi,\sigma)$:

If we had arrived at a node of height k before attaching the part of the tree corresponding to (a_i,b_i) the next two nodes will have heights

$$\begin{array}{ll} k-1,k & \text{if } (a_i,b_i) = (v,v) \leftrightarrow 10 \\ k+1,k+2 & \text{if } (a_i,b_i) = (v,h) \leftrightarrow 00 \\ k-1,k-2 & \text{if } (a_i,b_i) = (h,v) \leftrightarrow 11 \\ k+1,k & \text{if } (a_i,b_i) = (h,h) \leftrightarrow 01 \end{array} .$$

On the other hand the "local" diagonal distance l between the path-pairs develops as follows:

$$\begin{array}{ll} l & \text{if } (a_i,b_i) = (v,v) \leftrightarrow 10 \\ l+1 & \text{if } (a_i,b_i) = (v,h) \leftrightarrow 00 \\ l-1 & \text{if } (a_i,b_i) = (h,v) \leftrightarrow 11 \\ l & \text{if } (a_i,b_i) = (h,h) \leftrightarrow 01 \end{array} .$$

So it is an easy consequence that the set of all path-pairs (π,σ) with $d(\pi,\sigma) \le h$ corresponds to the set of trees t of size n with height of t equal to 2h-1 or 2h. Thus we have $D_h - D_{h-1} = P_{2h} - P_{2h-2}$, $h \ge 1$, with $D_0(z) = 0$. Summing up we get

$$D_h(z) = P_{2h}(z) - P_0(z) = P_{2h}(z) - z. \square$$

PROPOSITION. The average value of $d(\pi,\sigma)$ for path-pairs in L_n is

$$h_n - u_n = \frac{1}{2}\sqrt{\pi n} - \frac{1}{2} + O(n^{-1/2}).$$

Proof. Let $l(z) = y(z) - z$ denote the generating function of all path-pairs. Then, regarding Lemma 7 and Lemma 1,

$$\sum_{h\geq 0}(l-D_h) = \sum_{h\geq 0}(y-P_{2h}) = \sum_{h\geq 0}(y-P_h) - \sum_{h\geq 0}(y-U_h)$$

from which the result is immediate. □

In [5] there is another interesting bijection between path-pairs and planted plane trees. Let $(\pi,\sigma) \in L_{n,j}$ be a path-pair with steps $\pi = a_1\dots a_n$, $\sigma = b_1\dots b_n$ (a_i, $b_i \in\{v,h\}$). We decompose now π resp. σ in the following way:

For

$$\pi = v^{s_1}h\,v^{s_2}h\dots v^{s_j}h\,,\quad s_i \geq 0$$

$$\sigma = h\,v^{t_1}h\,v^{t_2}\dots h\,v^{t_j}\,,\quad t_i \geq 0$$

we consider the "Catalan" word

$$0^{s_1}1^{t_1+1}0^{s_2+1}1^{t_2+1}\dots 1^{t_{j-1}+1}0^{s_j+1}1^{t_j}$$

which again corresponds to a planted plane tree as usual.

[In our example from above (π,σ) is encoded as 010001101101 and corresponds to

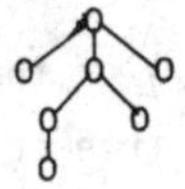

.]

It is easily seen that the height of the i-th leaf from the left of the tree constructed as indicated equals the area of the i-th vertical rectangle of width 1 from the left between π and σ.

[In our example the sequence of areas is 1,3,2,1, corresponding to

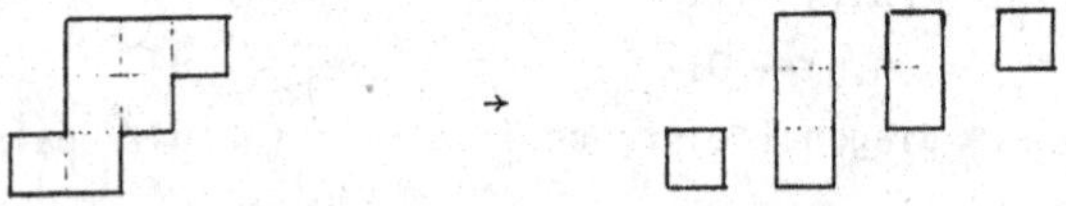

and 1,3,2,1 is also the sequence of heights of the leaves of the tree 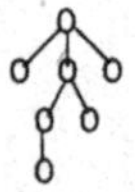 .]

REFERENCES

[1] N.G. DE BRUIJN, D.E.KNUTH and S.O.RICE, The average height of planted plane trees, in "Graph Theory and Computing" (R.C.Read ed.), 15-22, Academic Press, New York, 1972.

[2] P.FLAJOLET, Analyse d'algorithmes de manipulation d'arbres et de fichiers, Cahiers du BURO, 34-35 (1981), 1-209.

[3] P.FLAJOLET and A.ODLYZKO, The average height of binary trees and other simple trees, J.Comput.Syst.Sci. 25 (1982), 171-213.

[4] P.FLAJOLET, J.C.RAOULT and J.VUILLEMIN, The number of registers required to evaluate arithmetic expressions, Theoret.Comput.Sci. 9 (1979), 99-125.

[5] J.FÜRLINGER and J.HOFBAUER, q-Catalan numbers, preprint, Universität Wien, 1983.

[6] R.KEMP, The average number of registers needed to evaluate a binary tree optimally, Acta.Inf. 11 (1979), 363-372.

[7] D.E.KNUTH, "The Art of Computer Programming: Fundamental Algorithms", Addison-Wesley, Reading, Mass., 1968.

[8] G.POLYA, On the number of certain lattice polygons, J.Comb.Theory 6 (1969), 102-105.

[9] H.PRODINGER, The height of planted plane trees revisited, Ars Combinatoria, to appear, 1984.

PERFORMANCE ANALYSIS OF SHAMIR'S ATTACK ON THE BASIC MERKLE-HELLMAN KNAPSACK CRYPTOSYSTEM

(Extended Abstract)

J. C. Lagarias

AT&T Bell Laboratories

Murray Hill, New Jersey

0. Abstract

This paper gives a performance analysis of one variant of Shamir's attack on the basic Merkle-Hellman knapsack cryptosystem, which we call Algorithm S. Let $R = \dfrac{\text{\# plain text bits}}{\text{maximum \# cipher text bits}}$ denote the rate at which a knapsack cryptosystem transmits information, and let n denote the number of items in a knapsack, i.e. the block size of plaintext. We show that for any *fixed* R Algorithm S runs to completion in time polynomial in n on all knapsacks with rate $R_o \geq R$. We show that it successfully breaks at least the fraction $1 - \dfrac{c_R}{n}$ of such knapsack cryptosystems as $n \to \infty$, where c_R is a constant depending on R.

1. Introduction

In 1978 Merkle and Hellman [11] proposed public key cryptosystems based on the knapsack problem. The simplest of these cryptosystems, the *basic knapsack cryptosystem*, works as follows. The *public information* is a set of nonnegative integers $\{a_i: 1 \leq i \leq n\}$ which are called *knapsack weights*. Messages are encrypted by first being broken into blocks $(x_1, \ldots, x_n)$ of n binary digits. A block is encrypted as the integer E given by

$$a_1x_1 + \ldots + a_nx_n = E; \quad \text{all } x_i = 0 \text{ or } 1 . \tag{1.1}$$

The problem of solving (1.1) for $(x_1, \cdots, x_n)$ when given *arbitrary* $\{a_1, \cdots, a_n, E\}$ is known to be NP-hard. However in the basic Merkle-Hellman cryptosystem the knapsack items $\{a_i: 1 \leq i \leq n\}$ have a special structure which allows (1.1) to be solved easily; this structure is concealed by a *trapdoor*. The trapdoor information is any *decryption pair* (W,M) of integers satisfying the following conditions:

(i) $1 \leqslant W < M$ and $(W,M) = 1$.

(ii) $M > \underset{i}{MAX}\{a_i\}$.

(iii) The sequence $\{s_i : 1 \leqslant i \leqslant n\}$ defined by $0 \leqslant s_i < M$ and

$$s_i \equiv Wa_i \ (mod\ M)$$

is *superincreasing*, i.e.

$$s_1 + ... + s_i < s_{i+1} \text{ for } 1 \leqslant i \leqslant n-1 .$$

(iv) The *size condition.* $s_1 + ... + s_n < M$ holds.

Given a decryption pair (W,M) a ciphertext E is decrypted by finding

$$E^* \equiv WE \ (mod\ M); \quad 0 \leqslant E^* < M \tag{1.2}$$

and solving the 0–1 integer programming problem

$$s_1x_1 + ... + s_nx_n = E^*; \quad \text{all } x_i = 0 \text{ or } 1 . \tag{1.3}$$

Under the conditions (i)–(ii) equations (1.1) and (1.3) have the same solution when E and E^* are related by (1.2). The equation (1.3) is easily solved in linear time using the superincreasing property of the $\{s_i\}$.

In order to produce knapsacks $\{a_i : 1 \leqslant i \leqslant s_n\}$ having such a trapdoor, Merkle and Hellman proceed as follows. Given an *expansion factor* $d \geqslant 1$ and a *block size* n, they pick an integer M with

$$2^{dn} < M < 2^{dn+1} . \tag{1.4}$$

Next they pick a "random" superincreasing sequence $\{s_i, ..., s_n\}$ such that $s_1 + ... + s_n < M$. Finally they draw W^* from $1 \leqslant W^* < M$ with $(W^*,M) = 1$ using the uniform distribution and set

$$a_i \equiv W^* s_i \ (mod\ M) ; \quad 1 \leqslant a_i < M .$$

It is easy to verify that (i)–(iv) hold in this case, provided W is determined by $1 \leqslant W < M$ and by

$$WW^* \equiv 1 \ (mod\ M) .$$

After the knapsack items $\{a_i : 1 \leq i \leq n\}$ are produced, Merkle and Hellman scramble their order using a permutation $\sigma \in S_n$, so that the *public keys* are $\{a_{\sigma(i)} : 1 \leq i \leq n\}$. In this case the permutation σ is also part of the trapdoor information.

The interpretation of the *expansion factor d* is that it is a measure of how much longer ciphertext messages are than plaintext messages, i.e.

$$d \cong \frac{\log_2(nM)}{n} \cong \frac{\text{maximum \# } \textit{bits in ciphertext E}}{\textit{\# bits in plaintext block}}$$

The inverse quantity $R = d^{-1}$ is a measure of the average number of bits of plaintext transmitted per bit of ciphertext, i.e. R is the *information rate*.

Merkle and Hellman's hope was that it would not be easily possible to recover the trapdoor information. However in 1981 Adi Shamir [13] discovered a strong attack on the basic Merkle-Hellman cryptosystem. He showed that his attack runs in time polynomial in n as $n \to \infty$ when the modulus $M \leq 2^{dn}$ and d is *fixed*. (This running time is however, at least exponential in d.) He analyzed the performance of the key step in his attack (Step 2 following), assuming an unproved but plausible assumption (Hypothesis U in Section 3B) and showed that this step succeeded with high probability provided $1 < d < 2$. As we indicate in Section 3B and [6], this key step depends on a rational vector constructed from the public keys having an "unusually good" simultaneous Diophantine approximation. The unproved assumption is that the "unusually good" simultaneous Diophantine approximation arising from superincreasing sequences behave similarly to "random" rational vectors having an "unusually good" simultaneous Diophantine approximation. Shamir also presented heuristic arguments that his attack works in general for $1 \leq d < \infty$. (The condition $d \geq 1$ is required in order that encrypted messages be uniquely decipherable.)

The object of this paper is to outline a performance analysis of Shamir's attack that considers all steps in his attack, assumes no improved hypothesis, and which applies to all expansion rates d with $1 \leq d < \infty$. In particular it asserts that a version of Hypothesis U is true. The result contrasts with a similar heuristic put forward by Adleman [1] in connection with an attack on iterated knapsack cryptosystems, which does not seem to hold on numerical examples (c.f. [3]).

Some of the methods here can be applied to the analysis of other knapsack cryptosystems, c.f. [2], [4], [6], [8], [12].

2. Shamir's Attack on Basic Knapsack Cryptosystems

The object of Shamir's attack is to find a *decryption pair* (W^*, M^*), which need not be the same as the pair (W,M) used by the encrypter. This is possible because any basic knapsack cryptosystem has *infinitely many* decryption pairs: any pair with $\frac{W^*}{M^*}$ sufficiently close to $\frac{W}{M}$ will work.

Shamir's attack proceeds in several steps, which we sketch here.

Algorithm S.

Step 1. Estimate modulus M by $\tilde{M} = \max_{1 \leqslant i \leqslant n} \{a_i\}$ and estimate the expansion factor d by $d^* = \frac{1}{n} \log_2 (n^2 \tilde{M})$.

Step 2. Set $g = d^* + 2$ or $g = 5$, whichever is larger. Guess the correct g knapsack items $(a_1, \ldots, a_g)$ corresponding to the g *smallest* superincreasing elements. (That is, run the following algorithm on all $\binom{n}{g}$ possible g-tuples.) Solve the integer program (I.P.)

$$|x_i a_1 - x_1 a_i| \leqslant B \; ; \; 2 \leqslant i \leqslant g \, , \tag{2.2}$$

$$1 \leqslant x_1 \leqslant B-1 \, , \tag{2.3}$$

where

$$B = [2^{-n+g} M^*] \, . \tag{2.4}$$

If a solution $(x_1^{(0)}, \ldots, x_1^{(0)})$ is found, create two new integer programs by replacing (2.3) by the constraints

$$1 \leqslant x_1 < x_1^{(0)}$$

and

$$x_1^{(0)} < x_1 \leqslant B-1 \, ,$$

respectively. Solve these two I.P.'s and for each solution found, create two new I.P.'s by continuing to subdivide the x_1 regions according to the values of $x_1^{(i)}$ found. Do this until either $n \log_2 n$ distinct solutions are found, with at most $2n \log_2 n$ I.P.'s examined, or else until the process halts before this with a set of I.P.'s with no further solutions.

Step 3. For each solution $(x_1^{(i)}, \ldots, x_n^{(i)})$ found in Step 2, examine the n^7 rationals

$$\theta_j^{(i)} = \frac{x_1^{(i)}}{a_i} + j \, \frac{1}{n^7 2^n \tilde{M}} \; ; \quad 1 \leqslant j \leqslant n^7 \, . \tag{2.5}$$

Find $\theta_j^{(i)} = \frac{W_j^*}{M_j^*}$ in lowest terms using the Euclidean algorithm. Check if (W_j^*, M_j^*) is a decryption pair for $\{a_1, \ldots, a_n\}$. If so, the algorithm *succeeds*. If not, continue. □

The rationale for this procedure is as follows. The decryption congruence

$$W\, a_i \equiv s_i \ (mod\ M) \tag{2.6}$$

is equivalent to the equality

$$Wa_i - M\, k_i = s_i \tag{2.7}$$

for some non negative integer k_i. Then (2.7) gives:

$$\frac{W}{M} - \frac{k_i}{a_i} = \frac{s_i}{Ma_i}\,. \tag{2.8}$$

Hence we obtain

$$\frac{k_i}{a_i} - \frac{k_1}{a_1} = \frac{s_1}{Ma_1} - \frac{s_i}{Ma_i}\,, \tag{2.9}$$

so that

$$k_i a_1 - k_1 a_i = \frac{1}{M}\,(s_1 a_i - s_i a_1)\,. \tag{2.10}$$

Since any superincreasing sequence $\{s_i\}$ with $\sum_{i=1}^{n} s_i < M$ has

$$0 \leqslant s_i \leqslant 2^{-n+i}\, M\,, \tag{2.11}$$

the bounds (2.10), (2.11) yield for $1 \leqslant i \leqslant g$ that

$$|k_i a_1 - k_1 a_i| \leqslant 2^{-n+g}\, \tilde{M}\,. \tag{2.12}$$

So in this case the integer program (2.2) and (2.3) has at least one solution $(x_1, \ldots, x_g) = (k_1, \ldots, k_g)$. It turns out that for $g \geqslant d^* + 2$, a "random" integer program of the form (2.2), (2.3) can be expected to have no integer feasible solution; in this sense our particular I.P. is "unusual" in having a solution. The condition $d^* \geqslant 5$ is a technical one.

Now suppose Step 2 succeeds in finding a solution $(x_1^{(i)}, \ldots, x_n^{(i)})$ with $x_1^{(i)} = k_1$. Then (2.8) and (2.11) give

$$0 \leqslant \frac{W}{M} - \frac{k_1}{a_1} \leqslant \frac{1}{2^{n+1}a_1} . \tag{2.13}$$

Also suppose that

$$\frac{1}{n^2} M \leqslant a_1 \leqslant M . \tag{2.14}$$

Then (2.13) becomes

$$0 \leqslant \frac{W}{M} - \frac{k_1}{a_1} \leqslant \frac{n^2}{2^n M} . \tag{2.15}$$

In this case Step 3 is bound to find a pair $\frac{W_j^*}{M_j^*}$ with

$$\left| \frac{W_j^*}{M_j^*} - \frac{W}{M} \right| \leqslant \frac{1}{n^5 2^n M} . \tag{2.16}$$

Set (W^*,M^*) equal to this (W_j^*,M_j^*). Then if λ is defined by $M^* = \lambda M$, we have

$$W^* = \lambda(W + \epsilon)$$

where (2.16) gives

$$|\epsilon| \leqslant n^{-5}2^{-n} . \tag{2.17}$$

Hence

$$\begin{aligned} W^* a_i - M^* k_i &= \lambda [(Wa_i - Mk_i) + \epsilon a_i] \\ &= \lambda (s_i + \epsilon a_i) , \end{aligned}$$

where

$$|\epsilon a_i| \leqslant n^{-5}2^{-n} M . \tag{2.18}$$

It turns out that

$$s_i^* = s_i + \epsilon a_i \tag{2.19}$$

will be a superincreasing sequence for "almost all" superincreasing sequences (Corollary 3.6) and hence (W^*,M^*) will then be the desired decryption pair.

This rationale indicates that Algorithm S can only fail in the following ways:

(1) The bound $\frac{1}{n^2} M \leqslant a_1 \leqslant M$ can fail to hold.

(2) Step 2 may fail to find a solution $(x_1^{(i)}, \ldots, x^{(1)})$ with $x_1^{(i)} = k_1$.

(3) Step 3 may fail for all j because all sequences $\{s_i^*\}$ given by (2.19) aren't superincreasing.

We analyze these possibilities in Section 3.

Before proceeding we bound the running time of Algorithm S. The integer programs encountered in Step 2 all have g variables, which we regard as fixed while the number of items $n \to \infty$. Such I.P.'s can be solved in polynomial time in the input length L using an algorithm of H. W. Lenstra, Jr. [10]. The running time bound of Lenstra's algorithm has (apparently) the form $O(L^{F(g)})$ where $F(g)$ grows exponentially in g. Kannan ([5], Theorem 1) has announced a faster algorithm, which runs in time $O(g^{9g} L \log L)$. Using Kannan's algorithm, it is easy to obtain the following results.

Lemma 2.1. Algorithm S runs to completion in time $0(n^{g+10} L \log L)$ *where* $L = g \log \tilde{M}$.

Note here than when the information rate $R_o \leqslant R$ then the expansion factor $d^* \leqslant d \leqslant R^{-1}$ is bounded above. Hence $g = d^* + 2$ is fixed and Lemma 2.1 gives a bound for the running time which is polynomial in the input length L.

3. Performance Analysis

We assume the following probablistic model. The modulus M is *fixed*. The multiplier W is drawn uniformly from the set of all W with $1 \leqslant W \leqslant M$ with $(W,M) = 1$. The superincreasing sequence $\{s_i, \ldots, s_n\}$ drawn uniformly from all superincreasing sequences with $\sum_{i=1}^{n} s_i < M$. We *define* d by $M = 2^{dn}$. Let $G(n,M)$ denote the number of choices for $(W; s_1, \ldots, s_n)$. Our main result is:

Theorem 3.1 For any fixed information rate R with $O < R < 1$ *there is a constant* c_R *such that for fixed M Algorithm S fails on at most* $(1 - \frac{c_R}{n})\, G(n,M)$ *choices* $(W; s_1, \ldots, s_n)$, *provided* $M = 2^{dn}$ *with* $1 \leqslant d \leqslant R^{-1}$.

We now indicate the main steps in the proof, corresponding to the three types of failure mentioned at the end of Section 2.

A. Bounding the knapsack item a_1

In this step we consider the smallest element s_1 of the superincreasing sequence as fixed. Now $Wa_1 \equiv s_1 \ (mod\ M)$ so that

$$W^* s_1 \equiv a_1 \ (mod\ M) \ . \tag{3.1}$$

where $WW^* \equiv 1 \ (mod\ M)$. There are $\phi(M)$ choices for W^* with $(W^*,M) = 1$ and we want to show that at most $O\left(\frac{1}{n}\phi(M)\right)$ such choices give $|a_1| \leqslant \frac{1}{n^2} M$, provided $M \geqslant 2^n$. We use:

Lemma 3.2. Let $B(M,T) = |\{x : (x,M) = 1$ *and* $1 \leqslant x \leqslant T\}|$.
Then

$$B(M,T) \leqslant \frac{T}{M}\phi(M) + O\left(M^{\frac{c_0}{\log\log M}}\right) .$$

This suffices if $(s_1,M) = 1$ and in fact gives $O\left(\frac{1}{n}\phi(M)\right)$. There are some complications if $(s_1,M) > 1$. We may assume $(s_1,M) \leqslant n$ since the fraction of superincreasing sequences with $(s_1,M) > n$ is $O\left(\frac{1}{n}\right)$ of the total, as can be inferred using Theorem 3.5 below.

B. Bounding failure in Step 2

This is done in two stages. First, we show that for a fixed K the *expected* number of solutions of a "random" integer program of the form (2.2), (2.3) having a solution $(x_1^{(0)}, \ldots, x_g^{(0)})$ with $x_1^{(0)} = K$ is bounded above by a constant depending on g (but not on n). Second, we show that the set of all sequences $(W, s_1, \ldots, s_n)$ mapping onto a *fixed* a_1 have images $(a_2, \ldots, a_g)$ hitting at least a positive fraction (depending on g) of all "random" I.P.'s of the form (2.2), (2.3). Consequently the expected number of solutions to such "special" integer programs is bounded above by a (larger) constant depending on g.

Shamir's analysis avoided this second stage by assuming:

Hypothesis U. The integer programs of the form (2.2), (2.3) *arising from basic knapsack cryptosystems have, up to a multiplicative constant depending on g, the same expected number of solutions* as a *"random" integer program* (2.2), (2.3) *having at least one solution.*

The first stage is handled by:

Theorem 3.3. *(a) Let a_1 and K be fixed. Let $a_1 = \lambda M$ with $\frac{1}{n^2} \leqslant \lambda \leqslant 1$. The number $(a_2, \ldots, a_g)$ of integer programs*

$$|a_i x_1 - a_1 x_i| \leqslant \lambda 2^{-n+g} a_1 ; \quad 2 \leqslant i \leqslant g ,$$

with $0 \leqslant a_i < a$, having at least one solution $(x_1^{(0)}, \ldots, x_g^{(0)})$ with $x_1^{(0)} = K$ is bounded above by a constant depending on g times $\lambda^g 2^{(g-1)dn}$.

(b) *The expected number of solutions to such an integer program is bounded above by a constant depending on g but not on n, provided $g \geqslant d + 2$ and $g \geqslant 5$.*

This is proved by reformulating it as the equivalent $(g-1)$-dimensional simultaneous Diophantine approximation problem

$$\left| \frac{a_i}{a_1} - \frac{x_i}{x_1} \right| \leqslant \frac{2^{-n+g}}{x_1} , 2 \leqslant i \leqslant g$$

and applying the results of [7]. Here (a) uses an easy counting argument and (b) is difficult to prove.

The second stage is supplied by the following lemma.

Lemma 3.4. *Let a_1 be fixed, with $a_1 = \lambda M$ for $\frac{1}{n^2} \leqslant \lambda \leqslant 1$. The number of distinct $(a_2, \ldots, a_g)$ (mod a_1) arising as the image of some $(W, s_1, \ldots, s_g)$ with $W a_1 \equiv s_1 \pmod{M}$ is either zero or at least a constant depending on g times $\lambda^g 2^{(g-1)dn}$.*

To prove this we hold W and s_1 fixed and vary $s_2, \ldots, s_g$, using the bounds on the number of superincreasing sequences given in Theorem 3.5 below. We also need the result that the number of ways of extending a given superincreasing sequence $(s_1, \ldots, s_g)$ with $s_i < 2^{-n+i} M$ to a superincreasing sequence $(s_1, \ldots, s_n)$ with $\sum_{i-1}^{n} s_i \leqslant M$ is roughly a constant for "almost all" $(s_1, \ldots, s_g)$, c.f. Corollary 3.6.

C. Bounding failure in Step 3

Here we use good estimates for the number of superincreasing sequences with various restrictions on their elements $(s_1, \ldots, s_n)$. Let $S_n(M)$ denote the number of superincreasing sequences with $\sum_{i=1}^{n} s_i < M$. If we set

$$d_i = s_i - (s_1 + \ldots + s_{i-1}) ; \quad 1 \leqslant i \leqslant n .$$

then

$$s_1+...+s_n = 2^{n-1}d_1 + 2^{n-2}d_2+...+2d_{n-1} + d_n$$

we find $S_n(M)$ is the number of integer solutions to

$$d_i > 0 \ ; \quad 1 \leqslant i \leqslant n \ , \tag{3.1}$$

$$M > 2^{n-1}d_1+...+2d_{n-1} + d_n \ .$$

The system (3.1) cuts out a simplex $\Omega_n(M)$ in $\mathbf{R}^n$ with volume $\frac{2^{-\binom{n}{2}}}{n!} M^n$. Consequently this is about the number of integer points we expect to satisfy (3.1) for large enough M.

Theorem 3.5. $S_n(M) = \frac{2^{-\binom{n}{2}}}{n!} M^n + O\left(\frac{2^{-\binom{n}{2}}}{n!} M^n \left(\frac{2^n n^4}{M}\right)\right)$

In order to make Step 3 successful, we want relatively large perturbations ϵa_i in (2.19) to not ruin the superincreasing property. This is equivalent to requiring that all the d_i in (3.1) be "large." Now the integer program

$$d_i > B \ ; \quad 1 \leqslant i \leqslant n \ ,$$

$$M \geqslant 2^{n-1}d_1+...+2d_{n-1} + d_n \ .$$

has the same number of integer feasible solutions as

$$d_i^* > 0 \ ; \quad 1 \leqslant i \leqslant n \ ,$$

$$M-(2^n-1)B > 2^{n-1}d_1^*+...+2d_{n-1}^* + d_n^* \ ,$$

which has $S_n(M-(2^n-1)B)$ solutions. Hence as long as

$$S_n(M-2^nB) \sim S_n(M) \tag{3.2}$$

as $M = 2^{dn}$ with $n \to \infty$, we have "almost all" superincreasing sequences have all $d_i \geqslant B$. The following Corollary of Theorem 3.5 shows that we may choose $B = n^{-2}2^{-n}M$.

Corollary 3.6. If $M = 2^{dn}$ with $d > 1$ then as $n \to \infty$ at most $0(\frac{1}{n} S_n(M))$ superincreasing sequences with $\sum_{i-1}^{n} s_i < M$ and $d_i = s_i - (s_1+...+s_{i-1})$ have some

$$d_i < n^{-2}2^{-n}M \ . \tag{3.3}$$

Now the bounds (2.19) and (2.17) give

$$|\epsilon a_i| \leqslant n^{-5} 2^{-n} M \tag{3.4}$$

Comparing this with (3.3) we easily check that "almost all" superincreasing sequences remain superincreasing when perturbations of size $n^{-5}2^{-n}M$ are allowed.

References

[1] L. Adleman, On Breaking Generalized Knapsack Cryptosystems, Proc. 15th Annual ACM Symposium on Theory of Computing, 1983, pp. 402-412.

[2] E. Brickell, Solving Low Density Knapsacks, in: *Advances in Cryptology, Proceedings of Crypto-83* (D. Chaum, Ed.), Plenum Publ. Co., New York 1984.

[3] E. Brickell, J. C. Lagarias and A. M. Odlyzko, Evaluation of Adleman's Attack on Multiply Iterated Knapsacks (Abstract), *Advances in Cryptology Proceeding of Crypto-83* (D. Chaum, Ed.), Plenum Publ. Co., New York 1984.

[4] Y. Desmedt, J. Vandewalle, R. Govaerts, A Critical Analysis of the Security of Knapsack Public Key Cryptosystems, preprint.

[5] R. Kannan, Improved Algorithms for Integer Programming and Related Lattice Problems, Proc. 15th Annual ACM Symposium on theory of Computing, 1983, pp. 193-206.

[6] J. C. Lagarias, Knapsack Public Key Cryptosystems and Diophantine Approximation (Extend Abstract), *Advances in Cryptology, Proceedings of Crypto-83* (D. Chaum, Ed.), Plenum Publ. Co., New York, 1984, pp. 3-24.

[7] J. C. Lagarias, Simultaneous Diophantine Approximation of Rationals by Rationals, preprint.

[8] J. C. Lagarias and A. M. Odlyzko, Solving Low Density Subset Sum Problems, Proc. 24th IEEE Symposium on Foundations of Computer Science, 1983, pp. 1-10.

[9] A. K. Lenstra, H. W. Lenstra, Jr. and L. Lovasz, Factoring polynomials with rational coefficients, Math. Annalen. 261 (1982), pp. 515-534.

[10] H. W. Lenstra, Jr., Integer programming with a fixed number of variables, Math. of Operations Research, to appear.

[11] R. Merkle and M. Hellman, Hiding Information and Signatures in Trapdoor Knapsacks, IEEE Trans. Information Theory IT-24 (1978), pp. 525-530.

[12] A. M. Odlyzko, Cryptanalytic attacks on the multiplicative knapsack cryptosystem and on Shamir's fast signature scheme, IEEE Trans. Information Theory, to appear.

[13] A. Shamir, A polynomial time algorithm for breaking the basic Merkle-Hellman cryptosystem, Proc. 23rd Annual Symposium on Foundations of Computer Science, 1982, pp. 145-152.

MEASURES OF PRESORTEDNESS AND OPTIMAL SORTING ALGORITHMS

Extended abstract

Heikki Mannila
Department of Computer Science, University of Helsinki
Tukholmankatu 2, SF-00250 Helsinki 25, Finland

Abstract

The concept of presortedness and its use in sorting are studied. Natural ways to measure presortedness are given and some general properties necessary for a measure are proposed. A concept of a sorting algorithm optimal with respect to a measure of presortedness is defined, and examples of such algorithms are given. An insertion sort is shown to be optimal with respect to three natural measures. The problem of finding an optimal algorithm for an arbitrary measure is studied and partial results are proven.

1. Introduction

The question of identifying in some sense "easy" cases of a computational problem and utilizing this easiness has considerable interest. In sorting, easiness is can be identified with existing order. Indeed, when discussing sorting, it is customary to note that the input can be almost in order or at least have some existing order (see e.g. /Knu73, p. 339/, /Sed75, p.126/, /Dij82, p. 223/ and /Her83, p. 165/).

In this paper we study the use of presortedness in sorting. We do this by trying to answer three questions:

- How can the existing order (presortedness) of a sequence be measured?
- What does it mean that an algorithm utilizes the presortedness of input (measured in some way)?

- Do there exist algorithms utilizing presortedness (in the sense of the answers to the previous questions)?

Our questions can be seen as special cases of a more general problem: how can the structure of the input be used in sorting? For structure different from presortedness, this problem has been analyzed in e.g. /HPS75/, /Fre75/ and /ElS81/.

We start in Section 2 by discussing the first question. We present four natural ways to measure presortedness, review briefly their properties and then give general conditions which any measure of presortedness should satisfy.

In Section 3 we tackle the second question. We give a definition of an m-optimal algorithm, where m is a measure of presortedness. The definition is similar to the optimality criteria used in /Me79b/ and /GMPR77/ in the case of a particular measure of presortedness. We give two justifications for the definition: one information-theoretic, and the other based on the behaviour of m-optimal algorithms under various probability distributions.

Section 4 moves to the third question and gives examples of m-optimal algorithms for various natural choices of the measure m. In particular, we are able to exhibit an algorithm which is optimal with respect to three natural measures, is intuitively simple and has a reasonably straightforward implementation.

Section 5 studies the existence of optimal algorithms for arbitrary measures. While we cannot exhibit concrete algorithms, we can still show that for any measure m there exists an almost m-optimal sequence of comparison trees; i.e. we are able to give non-uniform algorithms. If the measure is computable in linear time, then we get truly optimal trees. The result is based on a search technique of Fredman (/Fre76/).

In Section 6 we discuss the results and outline some possible extensions.

If A is a set, then $|A|$ denotes its cardinality; for a sequence X the notation $|X|$ means the length of X. The notation log means logarithm in base 2.

2. Measures of presortedness

2.1. Natural measures

Let $X = \langle x_1, \ldots, x_n \rangle$ be the input to be sorted. For simplicity, we assume that the x_i's are distinct integers. We consider ascending order to be the correct one.

Inversions

Let

$$inv(X) = |\{(i,j) \mid 1 \leq i < j \leq n \text{ and } x_i > x_j\}|$$

be the number of pairs in the wrong order (inversions). Then $0 \leq inv(X) \leq n(n-1)/2$ for all X, the smallest value occurring in the case of an already sorted list, and the largest value in the case of a list in descending order. Inv(X) indicates how many exchanges of adjacent elements are needed to sort X (in e.g. bubble sort).

This quantity has been used as a measure of presortedness in /Me79b/ and /GMPR77/. The drawback with it is that inputs of the type

$(n+1, n+2, n+3, \ldots, 2n, 1, 2, 3, \ldots, n)$

have a quadratic number of inversions, even though such sequences are intuitively almost in order and are also easy to sort using merging. The next measure handles this case very well.

Runs

Define

$$runs(X) = |\{i \mid 1 \leq i < n \text{ and } x_{i+1} < x_i\}| + 1.$$

Then runs(X) is the number of ascending substrings of X, i.e. the number of runs at the beginning of the so called natural merge sort (/Knu73, p. 161/). For an already sorted list we have runs(X) = 1, and for a sequence in reverse order runs(X) = n.

This measure is quite natural: a small number of ascending runs clearly indicates a high degree of presortedness. The drawback with this measure is opposite to the one of inversions: local disorder, as in $\langle 2,1,4,3,\ldots,2n,2n-1 \rangle$, produces a lot of runs, even though the sequence is intuitively quite ordered and is certainly easy to sort using e.g. bubblesort.

Longest ascending subsequence

Define

$$las(X) = \max \{t \mid \exists\ i(1),\ldots,i(t) \text{ such that } 1 \leq i(1) < \ldots < i(t) \leq n \text{ and } x_{i(1)} < \ldots < x_{i(t)}\}.$$

Thus las(X) is the length of the longest ascending subsequence of X; therefore $1 \leq las(X) \leq n$. The direction of growth of this quantity is opposite to the previous ones. Therefore we rather use the quantity rem(X) = n-las(X), which indicates how many elements have to be removed from X to leave a sorted list. So rem(X) = 0, if X is sorted, and rem(X) attains its maximum value n-1 for a list in reverse order. This quantity can be defined operationally as the least number of data movements needed to sort X.

As a measure of presortedness rem is a little less intuitive than the previous two. A long ascending run guarantees a quite low value of rem; so does little local disorder. Thus rem seems to be to a certain degree immune to the deficiencies of the previous measures.

The number rem(X) has been used as a measure of presortedness in an empirical study investigating the applicability of usual sorting algorithms for nearly sorted lists (/CoK80/). Algorithms for calculating rem(X) or las(X) have been given in /Dij80/ and /DMS82/.

Number of exchanges

Define

exc(X) = the smallest number of exchanges of arbitrary elements needed to bring X into ascending order.

Obviously exc(X) = 0 for a sorted list X, and exc(X) $\leq$ inv(X) for all X. To find the maximum value of exc, we use the following somewhat surprising result:

$$exc(X) = n - \text{the number of cycles in the permutation of } \{1,\ldots,n\} \text{ corresponding to } X.$$

(see /Knu73, Ex. 5.2.2-2/). As every permutation has at least one cycle, we have $exc(X) \leq n-1$ for all X. An X realizing this upper bound is $\langle n,1,2,\ldots,n-1\rangle$. If X is in reverse order, then $exc(X) = \lfloor n/2 \rfloor$.

This measure indicates how many exchange operations we have to perform in a sorting algorithm based solely on this method of arranging the input. Actually finding sorting methods realizing this bound and using comparisons efficiently seems to be quite difficult.

The operational definition of exc is simple and corresponds to some intuitive idea of presortedness. On the other hand, the largest value of exc is obtained for a permutation X one certainly would think of as possessing a high degree of presortedness. In fact, according to the three previous measures X is almost in order.

2.2. General properties of measures

In this section we list some general conditions which a measure of presortedness should satisfy.

We first fix the functionality of measures. A measure m is a function $N^{<N} \to N$, where $N^{<N}$ denotes the set of all finite sequences of (distinct) integers; thus we consider only integer-valued measures.

The first two conditions state that a sorted list has zero disorder, and that the value of a measure m depends only on the order of its argument:

(1) $m(X) = 0$, if X is in ascending order;

(2) if $X = \langle x_1,\ldots,x_n\rangle$, $Y = \langle y_1,\ldots,y_n\rangle$ and $x_i < x_j$ if and only if $y_i < y_j$ for all i and j, then $m(X) = m(Y)$.

Thus we consider only comparison-based algorithms.

Conditions (1) and (2) do not restrict the allowed measures much. The following additional conditions are, in our opinion, necessary for a measure:

(3) if X is a subsequence of Y, then $m(X) \leq m(Y)$;

(4) if $X < Y$, i.e. every element of X is smaller than every element of Y, then $m(XY) \leq m(X) + m(Y)$;

(5) for all a we have $m(\langle a \rangle X) \leq |X| + m(X)$.

We will next outline why these conditions are necessary for a measure of presortedness.

Two approaches to the concept of presortedness or disorder are

(a) disorder is quantified by the number of operations of a given type which are needed to order the input (concrete approach)

(b) disorder is quantified by how much information of the form $x_i < x_j$ is needed to identify the sequence, using a given way of collecting the information (information-theoretic approach).

Both these approaches lead to measures of disorder satisfying properties (3), (4) and (5). For approach (a), we have to assume that the set of allowed operations is closed under subsequences. If we can sort a supersequence of X by a certain number of operations, then the restrictions of these operations to X will sort X; if $X < Y$, then XY can be sorted by first sorting X and then sorting Y, in a total of $m(X) + m(Y)$ operations; and sorting $\langle a \rangle X$ can be done by sorting X in $m(X)$ operations and inserting a into its place, for which there are $|X|$ possibilities different from the original position of a. For approach (b), if we have enough information to identify a supersequence of X, then the same information identifies X; if $X < Y$, then XY is identified by identifying X and Y; and $\langle a \rangle X$ is identified by identifying X and then locating the place of a.

The measures presented in Section 2.1 are easily seen to satisfy properties (1) - (5), once they have been scaled to have value 0 for a sorted list. Examining the definitions of inv, runs, rem and exc we see that they in fact satisfy the conditions for approach (a) needed in the above reasoning.

3. The concept of an optimal algorithm

We turn now to our second question: What does it mean that an algorithm utilizes presortedness?

Let m be a measure of presortedness and z an integer. Define

$$\text{below}'(z,X,m) = \{Y \mid Y \text{ is a permutation of } \{1,\ldots,|X|\} \text{ and } m(Y) \leq z\}\ .$$

where $m(X) \leq z$, and

$$\text{below}(X,m) = \{Y \mid Y \text{ is a permutation of } \{1,\ldots,|X|\} \text{ and } m(Y) \leq m(X)\}\ .$$

These sets are non-empty for all X and m, as the permutation of $\{1,\ldots,n\}$ order-isomorphic to X belongs to them.

Consider algorithms having as input not only the sequence X but also an upper bound z on the quantity m(X). Let z be given, and analyze the comparison tree (see /Knu73, p. 182-183/) for input length $|X|$ of such an algorithm restricted to the cases where $m(X) \leq z$. This subtree must have at least $|\text{below}'(z,X,m)|$ leaves, as the number of possible inputs is at least this; so the height of the tree and the running time of the algorithm are at least $\log |\text{below}'(z,X,m)|$. Thus we could require that an algorithm utilizing presortedness in the sense of m would work in time $O(\log |\text{below}'(z,X,m)|)$. But below'(z,X,m) can be a very small set and this can lead to a sublinear time requirement. However, it seems reasonable to give at least linear time to any sorting algorithm.

So we have the following definition. An algorithm S, which uses $T_S(X,z)$ steps on inputs X and z, is <u>weakly</u> <u>m-optimal</u>, if for some $c > 0$ and for all X we have

$$T_S(X,z) \leq c \max\{|X|, \log |\text{below}'(z,X,m)|\}.$$

What if an upper bound z on m(X) is not available? We strengthen the definition by assuming that z is always given as the best possible one, i.e. $z = m(X)$ always, with the following definition as a result.

Let m be a measure of presortedness, and S a sorting algorithm, which uses $T_S(X)$ steps on input X. We say that S is <u>m-optimal</u> (or optimal with respect to m), if for some $c > 0$ we have for all X

$$T_S(X) \leq c \max\{|X|, \log |\text{below}(X,m)|\}.$$

This is the definition of optimality from /Me79b/ and /GMPR77/ generalized to arbitrary measures.

The definition can be related to probability distributions on the input. Let p(X) be the probability that an input of length $|X|$ is X; then $\Sigma\{p(X) \mid |X| = n\} = 1$ for all n. Consider the comparison tree for an algorithm for input length n. Labelling the left branch of each comparison node with 0 and the right branch with 1, the tree gives a binary code for the set of permutations. The code word for permutation q is obtained by traversing the path from the root to the leaf corresponding to q. From the noiseless coding theorem of Shannon (see /Ash65, p. 36/) we know that the average code length for the set of permutations is at least

$$\Sigma\ p(X) \log (1/p(X)).$$

Thus no sorting method can have better average case number of comparisons than this.

By our definition the average time used by an m-optimal algorithm for distribution p is at most

$$c\ \Sigma\ p(X) \max\{|X|, \log |\text{below}(X,m)|\}.$$

So if

$$\log (1/p(X)) \geq \max\{|X|, \log |\text{below}(X,m)|\}$$

for all X, then an m-optimal algorithm comes within a constant factor of c from the theoretical minimum. This condition simplifies to

$$p(X) \leq \min\{2^{-|X|}, |\text{below}(X,m)|^{-1}\}.$$

This restricts the allowed distributions in two ways: no input can have a very large weight, and, more importantly, inputs X with large below(X,m) sets must have small weights.

As trivial examples of optimal algorithms consider the measures m_0 and m_{01} defined by

$m_0(X) = 0$ for all X;

$m_{01}(X) = 0$, if X is sorted,

$m_{01}(X) = 1$, otherwise.

These functions satisfy the conditions (1) - (5) imposed on measures. Any sorting algorithm having O(n log n) worst case (e.g. heapsort) is m_0-optimal, and an algorithm which first checks whether the input is in order and uses heapsort only if it is not, is m_{01}-optimal.

4. Examples of optimal algorithms

We start this section by a result showing that natural merge sort is optimal with respect to the number of runs. Next we review an insertion sort algorithm given by Mehlhorn /Me79b/, which is optimal with respect to the number of inversions. We then give results showing that by a suitable choice of data structure a modified insertion sort can be made to be simultaneously optimal with respect to inv, runs, and rem. The algorithm can be implemented using e.g. level-linked 2-3 or 2-4 trees (/BrT80/, /HuM82/).

Generally, proofs of m-optimality of an algorithm S consist of two parts: calculating the running time of S for sequences Y with $m(Y) \le z$, and estimating the size of the corresponding below-set.

Natural merge sort (see /Knu73, p. 161/) is a sorting method which starts from the runs present in the input and as a first phase merges them pairwise. Pairwise merging of the resulting longer runs is continued until there is only one run.

<u>Theorem 1</u>. Natural merge sort is optimal with respect to the number of runs. (Proofs can be found in /Man84/.)

We now turn to algorithms optimal with respect to other measures. Consider the following skeleton for insertion sorting of $X = \langle x_1, \ldots, x_n \rangle$:

for i:=1 to n do
    insert x_i to its proper place among the elements of
    the sorted list formed by the elements $x_1, \ldots, x_{i-1}$.

Depending on the implementation of the sorted list used to represent $x_1, \ldots, x_{i-1}$ this skeleton gives different algorithms.

If we use a data structure for sorted lists allowing insertions at distance h from the end of the list in time $O(1 + \log(h+1))$, we arrive at algorithms described in /Me79b/ and /GMPR77/. Insertion sort implemented in this way is optimal with respect to the number of inversions. This result is more surprising than the optimality of natural merge sort with respect to the number of runs: the insertion sort does not appear to have anything to do with the number of exchanges of adjacent elements needed to sort the list.

This insertion sort algorithm is not optimal with respect to the number of runs: among the inputs with two runs the sequence X = <n+1,n+2,...,2n,1,2,...,n> makes the algorithm use O(n log n) time. There are, however, only $O(2^{2n})$ inputs of length 2n with two runs, and therefore an optimal algorithm should sort them in linear time.

The smoothsort algorithm of Dijkstra /Dij82/ gives an example of an algorithm which, despite its claimed 'smoothness', is not optimal with respect to the number of inversions, as recently shown by Hertel /Her83/.

Local insertion sort

Suppose now that we have a data structure for representing sorted lists which is capable of making insertions in time O(1 + log (d+1)), where d is the distance from the previous element inserted. We call an insertion sort algorithm implemented using such a data structure local insertion sort.

The data structure applicable here is e.g. the finger tree of /GMPR77/ or /Kos81/. Simpler alternatives, however, are the level-linked 2-3 and 2-4 trees of Brown & Tarjan /BrT80/ and Huddleston & Mehlhorn /HuM82/. These structures are simple enough to make local insertion sort quite practical; their disadvantage is the large amount of space needed. Actually, these structures achieve the O(1 + log(d+1)) bound only in the amortized sense, i.e. averaged over a sequence of searches. This is, however, quite sufficient for our purposes.

Theorem 2. Local insertion sort is optimal with respect to the measures inv, runs and rem.

5. The existence of optimal algorithms

The previous section showed that for certain measures m there exist m-optimal algorithms. In this section we address the problem of finding optimal algorithms for arbitrary measures. As the conditions imposed on measures are weak, we cannot expect to find concrete algorithms. We rather direct our attention to the existence of comparison trees.

The existence proofs are based on a result of Fredman (/Fre76/) showing that for the sorting type problem the information-theoretic bound on the number of comparisons is tight. For similar use of Fredman's result see /Me79a/.

Theorem 3. For any measure of presortedness m there exist weakly m-optimal comparison trees. If m is such that for some $c > 0$ and for all X the value of m(X) is computable in

$$c \max \{|X|, \log |below(X,m)|\}$$

comparisons, then there exist m-optimal comparison trees.

6. Concluding remarks

We have studied the use of presortedness in sorting by trying to give different explications of the notion of presortedness, by defining optimality with respect to a measure, by giving examples of optimal sorting algorithms and by studying the existence of m-optimal algorithms for arbitrary measures m.

Different measures have totally different behaviour, and for practical considerations it would be important to know what kind of presortedness can be expected (if any). If this information is not available, but some presortedness is expected, then the use of a sorting algorithm optimal with respect to many measures (e.g. local insertion sort) could be useful.

The properties (1) - (5) necessary for a measure are quite weak. In trying to strengthen the results of section 5 additional properties could be useful, as the proofs of the results in that section do not use the nontrivial properties (3), (4) and (5) at all. A possible extension is indeed to try to find necessary and sufficient conditions for the existence of m-optimal algorithms.

One can also ask whether for any algorithm with worst case O(n log n) and best case O(n) (e.g. smoothsort) there exists a measure m (different from m_0 and m_{01}) such that the method is m-optimal.

Acknowledgement

I would like to thank Kari-Jouko Räihä and Esko Ukkonen for useful comments.

References

/Ash65/ R. Ash: Information theory. Interscience Publishers, 1965.

/BrT80/ M.R. Brown & R.E. Tarjan: Design and analysis of a data structure for representing sorted lists. SIAM Journal on Computing 9, 3 (Aug. 1980), 594-614.

/CoK80/ C.R. Cook & D.J. Kim: Best sorting algorithm for nearly sorted lists. Communications of the ACM 23, 11 (Nov. 1980), 620-624.

/DMS82/ R.B.K. Dewar, S.M. Merritt & M. Sharir: Some modified algorithms for Dijkstra's longest upsequence problem. Acta Informatica 18 (1982), 1-15.

/Dij80/ E.W. Dijkstra: Some beautiful arguments using mathematical induction. Acta Informatica 13 (1980), 1-13

/Dij82/ E.W. Dijkstra: Smoothsort, an alternative to sorting in situ. Science of Computer Programming 1 (1982), 223-233.

/ElS81/ M.H. Ellis & J.M. Steele: Fast searching of Weyl sequences using comparisons. SIAM Journal on Computing 10, 1 (Feb. 1981), 88-95.

/Fre75/ M.L. Fredman: Two applications of a probabilistic search technique: sorting X+Y and building balanced search trees. In: Proceedings of the 7th Annual ACM Symposium on Theory of Computing, 1975, p. 240-244

/Fre76/ M.L. Fredman: How good is the information theory bound in sorting? Theoretical Computer Science 1 (1976), 355-361.

/GMPR77/ L.J. Guibas, E.M. McCreight, M.F. Plass & J.R. Roberts: A new representation of linear lists. In: Proceedings of the 9th

Annual ACM Symposium on Theory of Computing, 1977, p. 49-60.

/HPS75/ L.H. Harper, T.H. Payne, J.E. Savage & E. Straus: Sorting X+Y. Communications of the ACM 18, 6 (June 1975), 347-349.

/Her83/ S. Hertel: Smoothsort's behaviour on presorted sequences. Information Processing Letters 16 (1983), 165-170.

/HuM82/ S. Huddleston & K. Mehlhorn: A new data structure for representing sorted lists. Acta Informatica 17 (1982), 157-184.

/Knu73/ D.E. Knuth: The Art of Computer Programming, Vol. III: Sorting and Searching. Addison-Wesley, 1973.

/Kos81/ S.R. Kosaraju: Localized search in sorted lists. In: Proceedings of the 11th Annual ACM Conference on Theory of Computing, 1981, p. 62-69.

/Man84/ H. Mannila: Measures of presortedness and optimal sorting algorithms. Report C-1984-14, Department of Computer Science, University of Helsinki, 1984.

/Me79a/ K. Mehlhorn: Searching, sorting and information theory. In: Mathematical Foundations of Computer Science 1979, J. Becvar (ed.), Springer-Verlag, 1979, p. 131-145.

/Me79b/ K. Mehlhorn: Sorting presorted files. In: 4th GI Conference on Theoretical Computer Science, Springer-Verlag, 1979, p. 199-212.

/Sed75/ R. Sedgewick: Quicksort. Ph.D. Thesis, Stanford University, 1975.

LANGUAGES AND INVERSE SEMIGROUPS.

S.W. Margolis and J.E. Pin

INTRODUCTION

The theory of recognizable - or regular-languages is well known to be deeply connected to the theory of semigroups. For instance powerful new tools for studying recognizable languages have been provided by Eilenberg in his theory of varieties of languages and semigroups. Also a lot of classical examples of context-free languages are defined as the kernel of a morphism from the free monoid into a certain monoid. In this way free groups define Dyck language D_n^*, polycyclic monoids define restricted Dyck languages $D_n'^*$, etc... We could also mention numerous theoretical questions dealing with semigroup such as word problems, associative rewriting systems, non-counting languages, limitness problem and restricted star-height, etc.

On the other hand a simple look at Mathematical Reviews show that a substantial part of the literature on semigroups is dedicated to inverse semigroups. But surprisingly there was until recently only a few number of papers [5, 13, 14] dealing with languages and inverse semigroups. In particular although a great number of results give a description of the recognizable languages whose syntactic monoids belong to a given variety of finite monoids, no such result was known for the variety Inv generated by all finite inverse monoids. In 1983, two papers by Margolis [6] and T. Hall [4] established that the variety of language $\mathcal{I}$nv (corresponding to Inv via Eilenberg's theorem) can be described by its finite biprefix codes. Even more recently, Pecuchet [8] has found a very nice connection between two-way automata and inverse monoids.

The aim of this paper is to show that the relationship between languages and inverse semigroups is real and deeper than was expected. Our first result gives a new construction of the free inverse semigroup. Contrary to the previous constructions of [7,15], our construction is symmetric. The ingredients of this construction are just the free group and the transduction that associates to a word w the set of all pairs (u,v) such that uv = w. Second we give three new descriptions of the variety of languages $\mathcal{I}$nv. The statement of the more symmetric version is quite simple : the syntactic monoid of a recognizable language L is in Inv iff L belongs to the boolean closure C of the languages of the form L_1aL_2 where a is a letter and L_1,L_2 are group-languages. Third we "relativize" the result of Margolis and Hall mentioned above as follows. Instead of considering the whole variety Inv, we consider the subvariety consisting of all finite monoids of Inv whose groups are elements of a given variety of groups, such as commutative, nilpotent, solvable groups, etc. We show that the corresponding varieties of languages are still described by their biprefix codes. The reader may have the feeling that such relativization results are quite automatic but this is not the case. For instance we show that Inv is generated by all finite monoids which are extensions of a group by a semilattice. This result is not trivial - it requires Simon's Lemma on graph congruences - and cannot be relativized. More precisely we exhibit an inverse monoid all of whose groups are commutative - in fact trivial - and which is not in the variety generated by extensions of a commutative group by a semilattice. This type of result is important with respect to the following open problem. Given a finite monoid M, is there an algorithm to decide whether or not M belongs to Inv. This is equivalent to ask if one can decide whether a given recognizable language belongs to the boolean algebra defined above. We conjecture that such algorithms exist and in fact quite simple.

Conjecture A finite monoid M is an element of Inv iff the idempotents of M commute.

It is easy to see that the variety Inv is contained in the variety of monoids whose idempotents commute, but the reverse inclusion appears to be a difficult problem of semigroup theory. However we prove the following particular case : if M is a finite monoid and if idempotents of M commute with any element of M, then M belongs to Inv.

No proofs - except short ones - are given in this extended abstract.

1. PRELIMINARIES

Let S be a semigroup. The elements x and y of S are inverses if xyx = x and yxy = y. S is said to be regular if every element of S has an inverse. S is an inverse semigroup if every element of S has a unique inverse. It is well known that S is an inverse semigroup iff S is a regular semigroup whose idempotents commute [2] . A semilattice is a commutative and idempotent semigroup.

Let S be a semigroup and let M be a monoid with 1 as an identity. To decongest notation we write S additively, without assuming that S is commutative. A left action of M on S is a mapping $\begin{cases} M \times S \to S \\ (m,s) \to ms \end{cases}$ satisfying for all $s,s_1,s_2 \in S$ and $m,m_1,m_2 \in M$

(1) $m(s_1+s_2) = ms_1+ms_2$

(2) $m_1(m_2s) = (m_1m_2)s$

(3) $1s = s$

This action is used to form a semigroup S*M on the set S x M with multiplication

$$(s,m)(s',m') = (s+ms',mm')$$

S*M is called a semidirect product of S and M.

Dually a right action of M on S defines a reverse semidirect product $M*_r S$ defined on the set M x S by (m,s)(m',s') = (mm',sm'+s'). If M is a group the following result shows that there is no difference between semidirect and reverse semidirect product.

Proposition 1.1. Let S be a semigroup and let G be a group. Then every semidirect product $S*G$ is isomorphic to a reverse semidirect product $G*_r S$.

Proof Given a left action of G on S, define a right action of G on S by setting $s.g = g^{-1}s$. A simple calculation now shows that the function $\varphi : S*G \to G*_r S$ defined by $(s,g) = (g,g^{-1}s)$ is an isomorphism.

The Schützenberger product of two monoids was introduced by Schützenberger in his study of the concatenation product. Let M and N be two monoids. The Schützenberger product $\Diamond(M,N)$ is the set of all matrices of the form $\begin{pmatrix} m & P \\ 0 & n \end{pmatrix}$ where $m \in M$, $n \in N$, and P is a subset of $M \times N$, with multiplication given by

$$\begin{pmatrix} m & P \\ 0 & n \end{pmatrix} \begin{pmatrix} m' & P' \\ 0 & n' \end{pmatrix} = \begin{pmatrix} mm' & mP' \cup Pn' \\ 0 & nn' \end{pmatrix} \quad \text{where } mP' = \{(mx,y) \mid (x,y) \in P'\} \quad \text{and}$$

$$Pn' = \{(x,yn') \mid (x,y) \in P\}$$

If M and N are groups we have

Proposition 1.2. [3] Let G and H be two groups. Then $\Diamond(G,H)$ is isomorphic to a semidirect product $S*(G \times H)$ where S is the semilattice of subsets of $G \times H$ under union.

If M is a monoid we denote by $\mathcal{P}(M)$ (resp. $\mathcal{P}_f(M)$) the monoid of (finite) subsets of M under multiplication given by $XY = \{xy \mid x \in X \text{ and } y \in Y\}$.

A variety of finite semigroups (monoids) is a class of finite semigroups (monoids) closed under taking subsemigroups, quotients and finite direct products. If $\underline{V}$ and $\underline{W}$ are two varieties of monoids, we denote by $\underline{V}*\underline{W}$ (resp. $\underline{V}*_r\underline{W}$, $\Diamond(\underline{V},\underline{W})$) the variety generated by all semidirect products $M*N$ (resp. reverse semidirect product $M*_r N$, Schützenberger products $\Diamond(M,N)$) where $M \in \underline{V}$ and $N \in \underline{W}$

$\underline{G}$ denotes the variety of all finite groups.

$\underline{J}_1$ denotes the variety of all finite semilattices.

$\underline{A}$ denotes the variety of all finite aperiodic (or group-free) monoids.

$\underline{I}$ denotes the trivial variety of monoids consisting of the monoid 1 only.

Let S and T be two semigroups. A relational morphism $\tau : S \to T$ is a relation from S to T such that

(1) For all $s \in S$, $s\tau \neq \emptyset$

(2) For all $s,t \in S$ $(s\tau)(t\tau) \subset (st)\tau$

Let $\underline{V}$ be a variety of semigroups. A relational morphism $\tau : S \to T$ is a relational $\underline{V}$-morphism if for all subsemigroups T' of T, $T' \in \underline{V}$ implies $T'\tau^{-1} \in \underline{V}$. A relational $\underline{A}$-morphism is also called a relational aperiodic morphism. If $\underline{V}$ is a variety of semigroups and $\underline{W}$ is a variety of monoids, $\underline{V}^{-1}\underline{W}$ denotes the variety of all monoids M such that there exists a relational $\underline{V}$-morphism $\tau : M \to N$ with $N \in \underline{W}$.

We refer the reader to [3,9,12] for basic results on varieties of semigroups and varieties of languages. In particular we assume familiarity with the variety theorem of Eilenberg. Recall that a <u>group-language</u> is a recognizable language whose syntactic monoid is a group.

2. FREE INVERSE MONOIDS AND CONCATENATION PRODUCT

In this section we give a new presentation of the free inverse monoid over a finite set X. Similar results have been found independantly by Birget and Rhodes [16].

Let A be a finite alphabet and let $\tau : A^* \to A^* \times A^*$ be the transduction defined by $w\tau = \{(u,v) \mid uv = w\}$. It is not difficult to see that τ is a rational transduction realized by the following nondeterministic transducer $\mathcal{C}$ (see the book of Berstel [1, chap. 3] for the definition of a transduction).

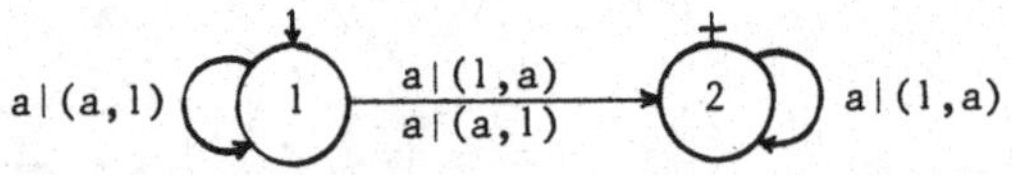

for all $a \in A$

A slightly different presentation is obtained by using the matrix representation of $\mathcal{C}$. Let $K = \mathcal{P}_f(A^* \times A^*)$ be the semiring of finite subsets of $A^* \times A^*$: union is the addition and the multiplication of subsets (as defined in section 1) is the multiplication. Now let $\mu : A^* \to K^{2x2}$ be the morphism (from A^* into the multiplicative monoid of 2x2 matrices with entries in K) defined by

$$a\mu = \begin{pmatrix} \{(a,1)\} & \{(a,1),(1,a)\} \\ 0 & \{(1,a)\} \end{pmatrix} \quad \text{for all } a \in A.$$

Clearly this is just another way to represent the transducer $\mathcal{C}$ and thus we have for all $u \in A^*$

$$u\tau = (u\mu)_{12}$$

Now assume that $A = X \cup \bar{X}$ where $\bar{X}$ is a disjoint copy of X and let $F(X)$ be the free group over X. Then $F(X)$ is isomorphic to $A^*/\sim$ where $\sim$ is the congruence generated by the relations $x\bar{x} = \bar{x}x = 1$ for all $x \in X$. Thus we have a canonical morphism $\pi : A^* \to F(X)$ which can be extended to a morphism $\pi \times \pi : A^* \times A^* \to F(X) \times F(X)$. Now the composite transduction $\sigma = \tau(\pi \times \pi) : A^* \to F(X) \times F(X)$ also admits a matrix representation. Let k be the semiring of all finite subsets of $F(X) \times F(X)$ and let $\nu : A^* \to k^{2x2}$ be the monoid morphism defined by

$$a\nu = \begin{pmatrix} \{(a,1)\} & \{(a,1),(1,a)\} \\ 0 & \{(1,a)\} \end{pmatrix} \quad \text{for all } a \in X \cup \bar{X}$$

More explicitely, we have for all $u \in (X \cup \bar{X})^*$

$$u\nu = \begin{pmatrix} \{(u\pi,1)\}\{(u_1\pi,u_2\pi) \mid u_1u_2 = u\} \\ 0 \qquad \{(1,u\pi)\} \end{pmatrix}$$

Then we have

Theorem 2.1 The free inverse monoid on X is isomorphic to the submonoid $A^*\nu$ of k^{2x2}.

If we identify the diagonal entries of $u\nu$ to $u\pi$, the elements of $A^*\nu$ have the form

$\begin{pmatrix} g & P \\ 0 & g \end{pmatrix}$ where $g \in F(X)$ and P is a finite subset of $F(X)x\, F(X)$

Example If $X = \{a,b\}$ $A = \{a,b,\bar{a},\bar{b}\}$, we have

$$(ab\bar{b}a\bar{b})\nu = \begin{pmatrix} aa\bar{b} & \{(1,aa\bar{b}),(a,a\bar{b}),(ab,\bar{b}a\bar{b}),(aa,\bar{b})\} \\ 0 & aa\bar{b} \end{pmatrix}$$

By construction $A^*\nu$ is embedded in the Schützenberger product $\lozenge(F(X),F(X))$. Therefore

Theorem 2.2. The free inverse monoid over X is a submonoid of $\lozenge(F(X), F(X))$.

3. THE VARIETY GENERATED BY FINITE INVERSE MONOIDS.

We first give an algebraic description of this variety.

Theorem 3.1 The equalities $\underline{Inv} = \underline{J}_1 * \underline{G} = \underline{G} *_r \underline{J}_1$ hold.

This means that Inv is generated by semidirect products (or reverse semidirect products) of a semilattice by a group. In order to convert this result to one on languages, we need to describe the operation on languages corresponding to the operations $\underline{V} \to \underline{J}_1 * \underline{V}$ (resp. $\underline{V} \to \underline{V} *_r \underline{J}_1$) on varieties of monoids. Thus let $\underline{V}$ be a variety of monoids and let $\mathcal{V}$ be the corresponding variety of languages.

Theorem 3.2 (1) $\underline{J}_1 * \underline{V}$ corresponds to the boolean closure of all languages of the form L or LaA^* where $L \in A^*$ and $a \in A$.

(2) $\underline{V} *_r \underline{J}_1$ corresponds to the boolean closure of all languages of the form L or A^*aL where $L \in A^*$ and $a \in A$.

It follows now from 3.1 and 3.2

<u>Corollary 3.3.</u> Let L be a recognizable language over A. The following conditions are equivalent :

(1) The syntactic monoid of L is in <u>Inv</u>.

(2) L is in the boolean closure of all languages of the form KaA^* where K is a group language and $a \in A$.

(3) L is in the boolean closure of all languages of the form A^*aK where K is a group language and $a \in A$.

Note that the previous characterizations are somewhat asymmetric. In fact a symmetric characterization is possible, but requires some further algebraic tools. We first describe the operation on languages corresponding to the operation $\Diamond(\underline{V},\underline{W})$ on varieties of monoids. Let $\underline{V}$ and $\underline{W}$ be two varieties of finite monoids and let $\mathcal{V}$ and $\mathcal{W}$ be the corresponding varieties of languages.

<u>Theorem 3.4</u> To $\Diamond(\underline{V},\underline{W})$ corresponds the boolean closure of all languages of the form K, L or KaL where $K \in A^*\mathcal{V}$, $L \in A^*\mathcal{W}$ and $a \in A$.

It follows immediately from 3.2 and 3.4.

<u>Corollary 3.5</u> For any variety of monoids $\underline{V}$, $\underline{J}_1 * \underline{V} = \Diamond(\underline{V},\underline{I})$ and $\underline{V} *_r \underline{J}_1 = \Diamond(\underline{I},\underline{V})$.

Notice that a direct (but messy!) algebraic proof of this result is possible. We consider now the case of a variety of groups $\underline{H}$.

<u>Theorem 3.6</u> For any variety of groups $\underline{H}$, the following equalities hold

$$\underline{J}_1 * \underline{H} = \underline{H} *_r \underline{J}_1 = \Diamond(\underline{I},\underline{H}) = \Diamond(\underline{H},\underline{I}) = \Diamond(\underline{H},\underline{H})$$

<u>Proof</u> By proposition 1.1., every semidirect product $S*G$ of a semigroup by a group is isomorphic to a reverse semidirect product $G *_r S$. The equality $\underline{J}_1 * \underline{H} = \underline{H} *_r \underline{J}_1$ follows. Now by 3.5 we have $\underline{J}_1 * \underline{H} = \underline{H} *_r \underline{J}_1 = \Diamond(\underline{I},\underline{H}) = \Diamond(H,I) \subset \Diamond(\underline{H},\underline{H})$.
Moreover by proposition 1.2 every Schützenberger product of the form $\Diamond(G_1,G_2)$ -where G_1 and G_2 are groups- is isomorphic to a semidirect product $S*(G_1 \times G_2)$ where S is a semilattice. It follows $\Diamond(\underline{H},\underline{H}) \subset \underline{J}_1 * \underline{H}$ and this concludes the proof.

We can now reuse theorem 3.4 in the opposite direction to obtain the desired symmetric result.

<u>Corollary 3.7</u> Let L be a recognizable language over A. The following conditions are equivalent :

(1) The syntactic monoid of L is in <u>Inv</u>

(2) L is in the boolean closure of all languages of the form KaK' where K,K' are group-languages and $a \in A$.

4. BIPREFIX CODES AND INVERSE MONOIDS.

The results above were obtained by viewing inverse monoids as semidirect products of semilattices and groups or as Schützenberger products of groups. There have been alternative descriptions of the languages corresponding to Inv and various subvarieties by viewing inverse monoids as monoids of partial one-to-one maps [5,13,14]. These descriptions use the theory of codes. Here we extend a result of [6.4].

Let A be a finite alphabet. A subset X of A^+ is a code if X^*, the submonoid of A^* generated by X, is free with base X. X is a prefix code if, for all $u,v \in A^*$, $u, uv \in X$ implies $v = 1$. Dually, X is a suffix code if, for all $u,v \in A^*$, $u, vu \in X$ implies $v = 1$.
A biprefix code is a set that is both a prefix and a suffix code. Notice that, as suggested by the terminology, a prefix (resp. suffix, biprefix) code is a code.

The following result, which improves a result of [11], shows that any monoid of Inv can be, in some sense, approximated by a syntactic monoid of the form $M(P^*)$ where P is a finite prefix code.

Theorem 4.1 Let $M \in$ Inv be a finite monoid. Then there is an (effectively constructable) finite biprefix code P such that :
(1) M divides $M(P^*)$
(2) $M(P^*) \in$ Inv
(3) There is an aperiodic relational morphism $\tau : M(P^*) \to M$

Now let $\underline{H}$ be a variety of groups and let $\bar{\underline{H}}$ be the variety of monoids all of whose subgroups belong to $\underline{H}$. We then have :

Corollary 4.2. Let $M \in \bar{\underline{H}} \cap$ Inv be a monoid. Then there is an (effectively constructable) finite biprefix code P such that
(1) M divides $M(P^*)$
(2) $M(P^*) \in \bar{\underline{H}} \cap$ Inv

Proof. Let P be the finite biprefix code given by theorem 4.1. Then M divides $M(P^*)$ and $M(P^*) \in$ Inv. Moreover $M \in \bar{\underline{H}}$ by hypothesis and there exists an aperiodic relational morphism $\tau : M(P^*) \to M$. Therefore $M(P^*) \in \underline{A}^{-1}\bar{\underline{H}} = \bar{\underline{H}}$.

We say that a variety of monoids $\underline{V}$ is described by a class $\mathcal{C}$ of codes if the variety $\underline{V}$ is generated by the syntactic monoids $M(P^*)$ for $P \in \mathcal{C}$. In particular we say that $\underline{V}$ is described by its finite biprefix codes if $\underline{V}$ is described by the class of all finite biprefix codes P such that $M(P^*) \in \underline{V}$. We can now state

Theorem 4.3 For any variety of groups $\bar{\underline{H}}$, the variety $\bar{\underline{H}} \cap$ Inv is described by its finite biprefix codes.

5. A DECIDABILITY PROBLEM

In section 3 we have given a number of algebraic descriptions of the variety Inv(theorems 3.1 and 3.6). However none of these descriptions gives a criterion for the membership problem for Inv. That is, given the multiplication table of a finite monoid M, decide whether or not $M \in$ Inv.

It is easy to see that the class of all finite monoids whose idempotents commute is a variety, denoted by Ecom. The conjecture mentioned in the introduction can be now restated as follows.

Conjecture Inv = Ecom

Since idempotents commute in an inverse monoid, we have Inv $\subset$ Ecom and thus the conjecture is equivalent to show that Ecom is contained in Inv. For the discussion of this conjecture we need some non trivial algebraic results. If T is a semigroup we denote by $E(T)$ the set of idempotents of T.

Theorem 5.1. Let $T \in$ Ecom and let G be a group. Then the following conditions are equivalent

(1) There is a relational morphism $\tau : T \to G$ such that $1\tau^{-1} = E(T)$

(2) T divides a semidirect product $S*G$ where S is a semilattice.

We just prove the easy part, namely (2) implies (1). If T divides $S*G$ there exists an injective relational morphism $\tau : T \to S*G$ (see [12, chap 3]). Let $\pi : S*G \to G$ be the morphism defined by $(s,g)\pi = g$. Then $\tau\pi : S \to G$ is a relational morphism. Moreover $1\pi^{-1} = \{(s,1) | s \in S\} = E(S*G)$ and $(E(S*G))\tau^{-1} = E(T)$. Thus $1(\tau\pi)^{-1} = E(T)$ as required.

The proof that (1) implies (2) is more involved and requires Simon's theorem on graph congruences [3, chap 9].

In terms of varieties we have

Corollary 5.2 For any variety of groups $\underline{H}$, $\underline{J}_1^{-1}\underline{H} = \underline{J}_1 * \underline{H}$. In particular

$$\text{Inv} = \underline{J}_1 * \underline{G} = \underline{J}_1^{-1}\underline{G}$$

Theorem 5.1 permits to relate our conjecture to some classical objects of the theory of inverse monoids called E-unitary monoids. We will not develop this point of view in this abstract. It also leads to a new formulation of the conjecture.

Conjecture For any finite monoid M whose idempotents commute there exists a relational morphism $\tau : M \to G$ onto a group G such that $1\tau^{-1} = E(M)$.

Thus we may try to prove the conjecture as follows. Take a finite monoid M whose idempotents commute and try to find a relational morphism onto a group G such that $1\tau^{-1} = E(M)$. Now can we bound the size or the "complexity" of G ? In particular if groups in M are all commutative, can we assume that G is commutative ? Unfortunately the answer is no. Let Gcom be the variety of all finite commutative groups.

Theorem 5.3 Let M be the syntactic monoid of the language ab^*aba^*b on the alphabet $A = \{a,b\}$. Then M is a finite inverse monoid all of whose groups are trivial. However M is not in the variety $\underline{J}_1^{-1}\underline{Gcom}$.

Let us conclude on a more positive statement that solves the conjecture in a particular case.

Theorem 5.4 Let M be a monoid whose idempotents commute with any element of M. Then M is an element of $\underline{Inv}$.

Sketch of the proof

Step 1 Denote by U(M) the group of units of a monoid M. Let $\underline{V}$ be the variety of all monoids M whose idempotents commute with every element of M. Then $\underline{V}$ is generated by all monoids M such that $M \setminus U(M)$ is a nilpotent semigroup.

Step 2 Let M be a monoid such that $S = M \setminus U(M)$ is nilpotent and let $\kappa = (\text{Card } S + 1)^2 + 1$. Then there exists a semidirect product $G = Z_k * U(M)$ (Z_k denotes the cyclic group of order k) and a relational morphism $\tau : M \to G$ such that $1\tau^{-1} = E(M)$

Step 3 Steps 1 and 2 show that $\underline{V}$ is contained in $\underline{J}_1^{-1}\underline{G}$.
But $\underline{J}_1^{-1}\underline{G} = \underline{Inv}$ by Corollary 5.2.

Appendix : Examples of languages whose syntactic monoid is in $\underline{Inv}$.
One can use one of the following properties

a) If a language L is recognized by an automaton whose transitions are partial one-to-one functions, then L is recognized by an inverse monoid. For instance ab^*aba^*b and $(a(ab)^*b)^*$ are recognized by inverse monoids:

b) Corollaries 3.3. and 3.7. For instance, for $A = \{a,b\}$
$L = A^*a(A^2)^* \cap (b^3)^*a(b^5)^*$ is recognized by a monoid of $\underline{Inv}$

c) Every finite (or cofinite) language is recognized by a monoid of $\underline{Inv}$ (which is not an inverse monoid in general). This follows from theorem 5.4.

REFERENCES

[1] J. Berstel, Transductions and Context-free languages. Teubner (1979).

[2] A.H. Clifford and G.B. Preston, The algebraic theory of semigroups, Math. Surveys 7, Amer. Math. Soc., Providence, Vol. 1 (1961), Vol 2 (1967).

[3] S. Eilenberg, Automata, Languages and Machines, Academic Press, Vol. B (1976)

[4] T.E. Hall, Biprefix codes, inverse semigroups and syntactic monoids of injective automata. To appear.

[5] M. Keenan and G. Lallement, On certain codes admitting inverse semigroups as syntactic monoids, Semigroup Forum 8, (1974), 312-331.

[6] S.W. Margolis, On the syntactic transformation semigroup of a language generated by a finite biprefix code, Theoretical Computer Science 21, (1982), 225-230.

[7] W.D. Munn, Free inverse semigroups, Proc. London Math Soc. 3, 29, (1974), 385-404.

[8] J.P. Pécuchet, Automates boustrophédons, semigroupe de Birget et monoide inversif libre, to appear.

[9] G. Lallement, Semigroups and Combinatorial applications, Wiley, New York, (1979)

[10] J.E. Pin, Arbres et hiérarchies de concaténation, 10th ICALP, LNCS 154, (1983), 617-628.

[11] J.E. Pin, On varieties of rational languages and variable length codes, J. Pure and Applied Algebra 23, (1982), 169-196.

[12] J.E. Pin, Variétés de langages formels. Masson (1984).

[13] J.F. Perrot, Codes de Brandt, in Théorie des codes, actes de la 7ème Ecole de Printemps d'Informatique Théorique, édités par D. Perrin, (1979), 177-183.

[14] Ch. Reutenauer, Une topologie du monoide libre, Semigroup Forum 18, (1979), 33-49.

[15] H.E. Scheiblich, Free inverse semigroups, Proc. Amer. Math. Soc. 38, (1973), 1-7.

[16] J.C. Birget et J. Rhodes, Group theory via global semigroup theory, to appear.

S.W. Margolis
Computer Science
Votey Building
Burlington Vermont
USA

J.E. Pin
Université Paris VI et CNRS
Tour 55-65
4 place Jussieu
75230 Paris Cedex 05

AREA-TIME OPTIMAL VLSI INTEGER MULTIPLIER

WITH MINIMUM COMPUTATION TIME

K. Mehlhorn and F. P. Preparata

Abstract: According to VLSI theory, $[\log n, \sqrt{n}]$ is the range of computation times for which there may exist an AT^2-optimal multiplier of n-bit integers. Such networks were previously known for the time range $[\Omega(\log^2 n), O(\sqrt{n})]$; in this paper we settle this theoretical question, by exhibiting a class of AT^2-optimal multipliers with computation times $[\Omega(\log n), O(n^{1/2})]$. Our designs are based on the DFT on a Fermat ring, whose elements are represented in a redundant radix-4 form to ensure O(1) addition time.

1. Introduction

Research on efficient integer multiplication schemes, potentially suitable for direct circuit implementation, has been going on for some years. Investigations have focussed on both the realization of practical (and possibly suboptimal) networks, and on the more subtle question of the existence of optimal networks. Optimality is defined with respect to the costumary AT^2 measure of complexity, which is central to the synchronous VLSI model of computation [T79 , BK81]. Here A is the area of the multiplier chip, while T is the computation time, i.e., the time elapsing between the arrival of the first input bit and the delivery of the last output bit. As is well-known [AA80 , BK81], any multiplier of two n-bit integers must satisfy $AT^2 = \Omega(n^2)$, $A = \Omega(n)$, $T = \Omega(\log n)$. These three lower bounds indicate that $[\log n, \sqrt{n}]$ is the range of computation times for which there may exist an AT^2-optimal multiplier.

The search for an AT^2-optimal integer multiplier began with the suboptimal design of Brent-Kung [BK81], for which $AT^2 = O(n^2 \log^2 n)$. Subsequently, Preparata-Vuillemin [PV81a], proposed a class of optimal designs whose computation time could be selected in the range $[\theta(\log^2 n), \theta(\sqrt{n})]$. More recently, Preparata [P83] exhibited an optimal mesh-connected multiplier achieving $T = O(\sqrt{n})$. An intriguing feature of all the above optimal designs is the explicit recourse to the Discrete Fourier Transform (DFT), as the device used for computing convolutions. However, none of these optimal designs achieves the minimum computation time $T = O(\log n)$. On the

---

This work was supported by the National Science Foundation under Grants MCS-81-05552 and ECS-81-06939; additional support was provided by Deutsche Forschungsgemeinschaft SFB 124, VLSI - Entwurf und Parallelität.

other hand there are well-known multiplication algorithms which achieve optimum computation time T = O(logn), e.g. the Wallace tree [W64] and Dadda counting [D65]. Both algorithms are not easily embedded into silicon because of their irregular interconnection pattern. More recently, there have been proposals of optimum computation time and nearly optimum AT^2-measure designs [V83], [B82], [LV83], [LM83]. Moreover, some of these designs are eminently practical. We refer the reader to [LV83] for a detailed discussion. All of these designs are based on divide-and-conquer techniques and achieve their speed by the use of a redundant operand representation, which results in O(1) addition time. The most efficient of these designs [LV83, LM83] achieves $T = O(\log n)$ and $AT^2 = O(n^2(\log n)^2)$.

In this paper we shall exhibit a class of optimal, i.e. $AT^2 = O(n^2)$, designs realizing any computation time in the range $[\Omega(\log n), \theta(n^{1/2})]$ thereby realizing the first AT^2-optimal O(logn)-time multiplier. More generally, the new design settles, at least theoretically, the problem of integer multiplication: There are AT^2-optimal circuits for all possible computation times. Our new design incorporates ideas of many of the papers cited above. Not unlike previous optimal designs, it makes essential use of the DFT over a finite ring G which we choose as a Fermat ring. In contrast to previous papers, a low order DFT is used to achieve fast computation time. More precisely, in order to achieve computation time O(T) we will resort to a T-point DFT over a ring of $2^{O(n/T)}$ elements. In [PV81a] and (n/logn)-point DFT over a ring of $2^{O(\log n)}$ elements is used for all achievable values of T. Since we compute a DFT in a large ring of $2^{O(n/T)}$ elements, efficient implementations of the ring operations and of the data transfer between computing elements are crucial. We borrow from [P83] the idea of computing the DFT on a mesh of processing elements. Only communication between adjacent processing elements is required in this case and hence we can provide for a large communication bandwidth without paying too high a penalty in area. Each processing element of the mesh has the ability to do additions-subtractions over G and multiplications by power of the root of unity. We choose a redundant representation for ring elements and thus achieve O(1) addition/subtraction time in a small area. Since ring G is a Fermat ring, i.e., the set of integers modulo $m = 2^p+1$ for some p, and since the root of unity used in the DFT is a power of two, multiplication by a power of the root of unity can be essentially reduced to a cyclic shift and a small number of additions/subtractions. We implement cyclic shifts by means of a cube-connected-cycle network [PV81b] . Finally, general multiplications in G are realized by one of the fast, suboptimal designs referred to above. Since only O(T) general multiplications of ring elements (which are essentially O(n/T)-bit numbers) are required we will stay within the limits of time and area.

2. The AT^2-optimal Integer Multiplier

Figure 1 shows the general structure of the integer multiplier. We realize integer multiplication via polynomial multiplication and

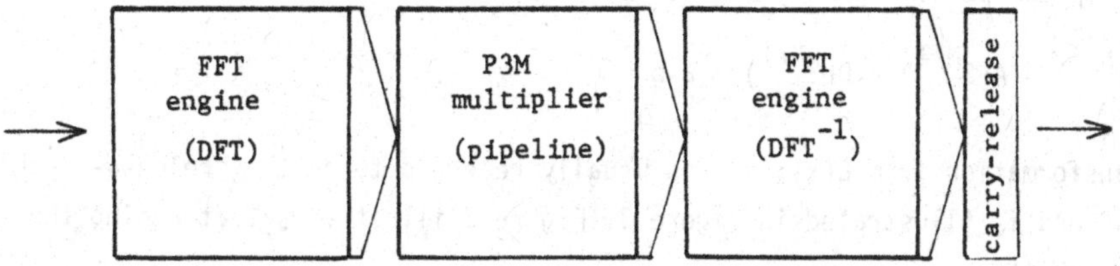

Figure 1. General Scheme of the Multiplier

carry release . The polynomial multiplication is carried out by evaluation/pairwise multiplication of function values/interpolation, a strategy already used in [SS71]; evaluation and interpolation are performed by the FFT and FFT^{-1} - engines and the pairwise multiplications are performed in the pipelined - 3 - multiplication (P3M) network. We will now discuss the various components in turn.

Let $a = \sum_{i=o}^{N-1} a_i 2^i$ and $b = \sum_{i=o}^{N-1} b_i 2^i$ be two N/2 - bit integers, i.e. $a_{N/2} = \ldots = a_{N-1} = b_{N/2} = \ldots b_N = 0$ and let $c = \sum_{i=o}^{N=1} c_i 2^i$ be their product. Let $T \in [\log N, \sqrt{N}]$ be a power of 2 that divides N. We will describe a multiplier which operates in time $O(T)$ and uses area $O(N^2/T^2)$.

We divide a and b into T chunks of N/T bits each which we denote $A_o, \ldots, A_{T-1}$, $B_o, \ldots, B_{T-1}$ respectively. (cf. figure 2).Then $0 \le A_i, B_i \le 2^{N/T}$. Let polynomials

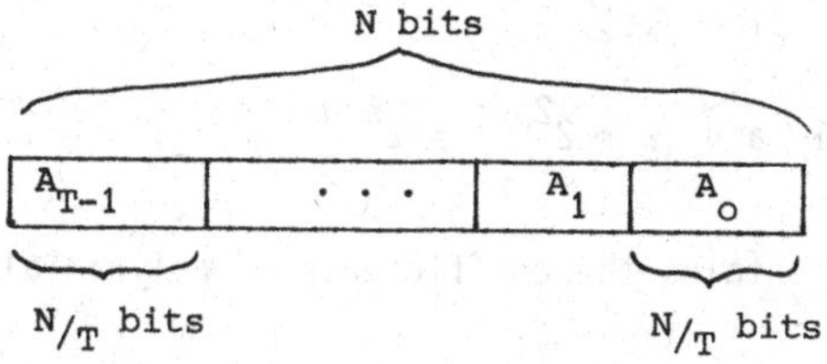

Figure 2. An N bit integer and its decomposition into chunks.

$A(x), B(x)$ be defined by $A(x) = \sum_{i=o}^{T-1} A_i x^i$, $B(x) = \sum_{i=o}^{T-1} B_i x^i$ (note that $A(x)$ and $B(x)$ have degree $T/2$) and let $C(x) = A(x) \cdot B(x) = \sum_{i=o}^{T-1} C_i x^i$ be their product. Then $0 \le C_j \le T2^{2N/T} \le N/T2^{2N/T} \le 2^{3N/T}$ and hence the A_i, B_i and C_i can be represented using $3N/T$ bits each. Also,

$$C(2^{N/T}) = A(2^{N/T}) \cdot B(2^{N/T}) = a \cdot b = c \quad .$$

The transformation from $C(x)$ to c is usually referred to as the "release-of-the-carries" and is illustrated in figure 3. Figure 3 illustrates that adding the suitably shifted

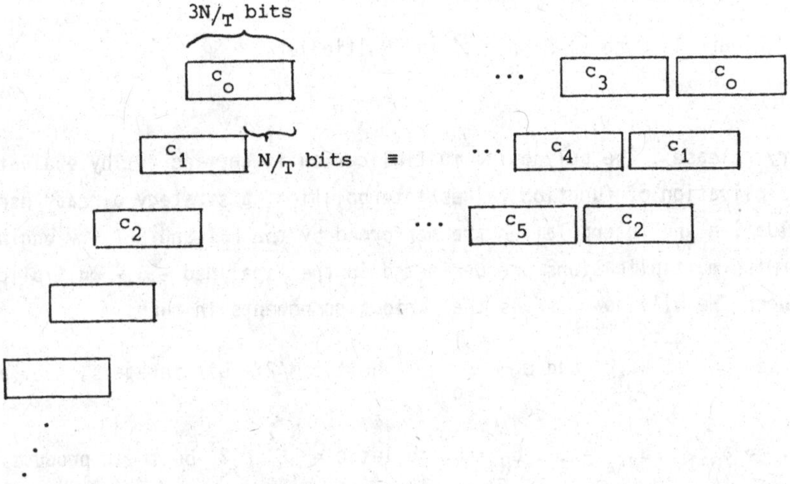

Figure 3. release of the carry

$C_i^{'}s$ is tantamount to adding three N-bit integers. The addition of N-bit integers can be performed in time $O(T)$ and space $O(N^2/T^2)$ as has been shown in [BK81]. It is taken care of in the carry-release component.

The multiplication of polynomials $A(x)$ and $B(x)$ is done by evaluation, pairwise multiplication, and interpolation. Let

$$p = 3\lceil N/T^2 \rceil T \ , \ m = 2^p+1 \quad \text{and} \quad w = 2^{2p/T} = 2^{6\lceil N/T^2 \rceil} \quad .$$

Then $\mathbb{Z}_m$ is a ring which contains the coefficients of polynomials $A(x)$, $B(x)$ and $C(x)$. We have

Fact 1 (see [AHU74] , p. 266, Theorem 7.5): Let r and w be powers of 2 and let $m = w^{r/2}+1$. Then r and w have multiplication inverses in $\mathbb{Z}_m$ and w is a primitive r-th root of unit in $\mathbb{Z}_m$. $\mathbb{Z}_m$ is usually referred to as a Fermat ring.

We infer from Fact 1 that w is a T-th root of unit in $\mathbb{Z}_m$ and that w and T have ultiplicative inverses in $\mathbb{Z}_m$ for our particular choice of m,w, and T. The complete trategy for multiplying A(x) and B(x) is given by

) (Discrete Fourier Transform): Compute $u_i := A(w^i)$ and $v_i = B(w^i)$ for $0 \le i < T$

) (Pairwise Multiplication): Compute $z_i = u_i \cdot v_i \bmod m$ for $0 \le i < T$

) (Inverse Discrete Fourier Transform): Let C(x) be the unique polynomial of degree at most T-1 with $C(w^i) = z_i$ for $0 \le i < T$.

Steps 1 and 3 correspond to the Discrete Fourier Transform and its inverse. They an be realized using basically the same network and therefore we will only discuss the FT-engine below.

In step 2 we have to multiply T pairs (u_i, v_i) of ring elements. For these multilications we interpret ring elements as integers, multiply the integers and then reuce the result mod m. The reduction mod m is essentially an addition/subtraction and an certainly be carried out in the desired time and area. Our method for multiplying he T pairs (u_i, v_i) of 3N/T-bit integers is based on

act 2 (see [LM83] or [LV83]): There is a VLSI-chip which multiplies T pairs of n-bit ntegers in time O(T+logn) and area $O(n^2)$.

The multiplier described in [LM83] or [LV83] implements the Karazuba/Offman [KO62] ethod for integer multiplication. It multiplies one pair in time O(logn) because a edundant number representation is used to represent intermediate results and it is ipelinable and hence multiplies T pairs in time O(T+logn).

We apply fact 2 with n = 3N/T. This allows us to carry out step 2 in area $O(n^2)$ = (N^2/T^2) and time O(T+logn) = O(T).

It remains to describe the DFT-engine. The DFT-engine consists of T macro-modules rganized as a $\lfloor\sqrt{T}\rfloor \times \lceil\sqrt{T}\rceil$ mesh (see figure 4)

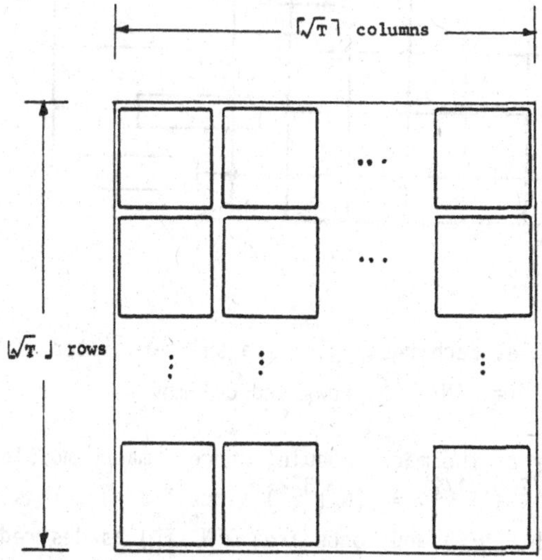

Figure 4. Architecture of the FFT engine.

Each macro-module stores a ring element. It has been shown in [P83] how a mesh-connected architecture of $s \times s$ modules can be used to compute the DFT of s^2 elements in $O(s)$ "parallel exchange steps" and $O(\log s)$ "parallel butterfly steps", where an exchange step involves the exchange of the operands of two adjacent macro-modules and the butterfly step involves a multiplication by a power w^i of the principal root and an addition-subtraction. Therefore each macro-module must have the following capabilities:

1) Transfer its operand to a neighboring module (or exchange operands with a neighboring module);
2) Add/subtract two operands;
3) Multiply an operand by w^i, $0 \leq i < T$.

We treat capability 1 first. An operand, i.e. a ring element, consists of $\theta(N/T)$ bits. We store an operand in $\theta(N/T^{3/2})$ fragments of $\ell = \theta(T^{1/2})$ bits each. The exact value of ℓ will be determined later. Each fragment is contained in a shift register. A macro-module is then organized as shown in figure 5. The shift register in row i starts at a distance

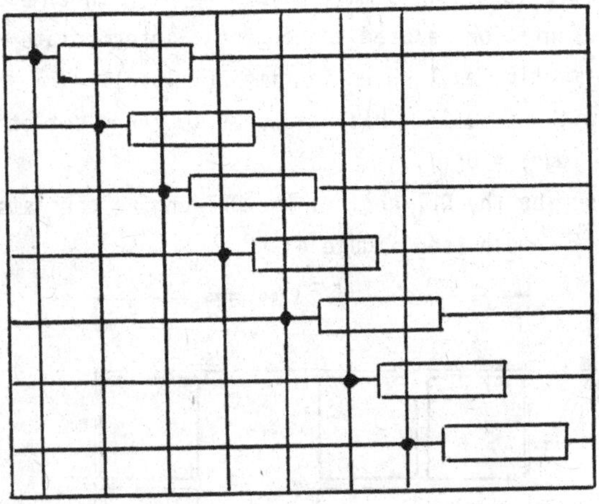

Figure 5. A macro-module. Each rectangle is a shift-register of length $\theta(T^{1/2})$ bits. There are $\theta(N/T^{3/2})$ rows and columns

$\theta(i)$ from the left boundary of the macro-module. Hence a macro-module has height $\theta(N/T^{3/2})$ and width $\theta(N/T^{3/2} + T^{1/2}) = \theta(N/T^{3/2})$ since $T \leq \sqrt{N}$. Thus the entire DFT-engine has height and width $\theta(N/T)$ and hence area $O(N^2/T^2)$ as desired.

An exchange of operands between neighboring macro-modules is performed as follows: The contents of all shift registers are exchanged in parallel and each single shift register is exchanged bit-serially. Hence the time for a single exchange is $O(T^{1/2})$ and thus the time for all exchanges is $O(T^{1/2} \cdot T^{1/2}) = O(T)$ as desired.

It remains to treat the arithmetic operations. We represent operands in a <u>redundant radix 4 form</u> . More precisely, let $R := [-4^L+1, 4^L-1] \supseteq \mathbb{Z}_m$ where $L = p/2+1$. An element $x \in R$ is written as $x = \sum_{i=o}^{L-1} x_i 4^i$ where $x_i \in \{-3,-2,-1,o,+1,+2,+3\}$. Note that this representation is redundant.

Let us discuss addition and subtraction first. Let $x = \Sigma\, x_i 4^i$ and $y = \Sigma\, y_i 4^i \in R$. Since $-y = \Sigma(-y_i)4^i$ subtraction reduces trivially to addition. Suppose now that we want to compute z such that $z \in R$ and $z = x+y \bmod m$. For $0 \le i < L$, compute pair (s_i, c_{i+1}) from (x_i, y_i) according to the following table:

x_i+y_i	-6	-5	-4	-3	-2	-1	0	1	2	3	4	5	6
s_i	-2	-1	0	1	-2	-1	0	1	2	-1	0	1	2
c_{i+1}	-1	-1	-1	-1	0	0	0	0	0	1	1	1	1

Notice that $x_i+y_i = 4c_{i+1}+s_i$, $|c_{i+1}| \le 1$ and $|s_i| \le 2$. Let $c_o = 0$ and let $z_i = c_i+s_i$ for $0 \le i < L$. Then $-3 \le z_i \le 3$ and $x+y = \Sigma\, z_i 4^i + c_L 4^L$.

If $c_L = 0$ then $z = \Sigma\, z_i 4^i \in R$ and we are done. So let us assume that $c_L = \pm 1$. Note first that $4^L = 2^{p+2} = -4 \bmod m$. Hence if $|c_L+z_1| \le 3$ then we only have to replace z_1 by c_L+z_1 and are done. So let us finally assume that $|c_L+z_1| = 4$. We then perform the addition z+c where $z = \Sigma\, z_i 4^i$ and $c = -4c_L$ as described above and observe that $c_L+z_1 = 4\bar{c}_2+\bar{s}_1$ with $\bar{s}_1 = 0$. Thus the "umpleasant" wrap-around cannot happen again.

We infer from this discussion that addition/subtraction takes time O(1) and that it requires only local interactions. Hence we can equip macro-modules with the capability of performing addition/subtraction in $\mathbb{Z}_m$ by increasing the area by only a constant factor.

Multiplication by a power of the root of unity. We discuss more generally multiplication and division by a power of 4. (Note that $w = 2^{6\lceil N/T^2 \rceil}$ is a power of 4). Let $x = \Sigma\, x_i 4^i$ and consider the product $x4^s \bmod m$ for some integer s. We have:

$$x4^s \bmod m = \sum_{j=0}^{L-1} x_j 4^{j+s} \bmod m = \left(\sum_{h=s}^{L-1} x_{h-s} 4^h + \sum_{h=L}^{L-1+s} x_{h-s} 4^h \bmod m \right) \bmod m$$

$$= \left(\sum_{h=s}^{L-1} x_{h-s} 4^h + \sum_{i=0}^{s-1} x_{L-s+i} 4^i (-4) \right) \bmod m$$

since $4^L \bmod m = -4$. Thus multiplication by 4^s is equivalent to:

(i) cyclically shifting to the left the L-digit string by s digit positions;

(ii) changing the sign of the s least significant digits of the string obtained in (i) and shifting them one position to the left;

(iii) adding the two resulting numbers with the method described above.

In the DFT we need the multiplications by $4^{3\lceil N/T^2 \rceil i}$, $0 \leq i \leq T-1$, i.e. we have to realize all cyclic shifts of operands (= strings of $L = p/2-1 = 3\lceil N/T^2 \rceil T/2-1$ digits) by $3\lceil N/T^2 \rceil i$ positions, $0 \leq i < T-1$.

In order to simplify the discussion we assume $3\lceil N/T^2 \rceil \geq T^{1/2}$, i.e. $T \leq O(N^{2/5})$, from now on. We will come back to the case $T \geq N^{2/5}$ at the end. To realize the cyclic shifts we organize the macro-module into T micro-modules. Each micro-module holds a super-fragment of exactly $3\lceil N/T^2 \rceil$ bits; it consists of $3\lceil N/T^2 \rceil / \ell = \theta(N/T^{5/2})$ consecutive shift registers. ($\ell = \theta(N^{1/2})$ has to be chosen such that ℓ divides $3\lceil N/T^2 \rceil$). The T micro-modules are organized as a cube-connected-cycles network (CCC) [PV81b]. More precisely, we have 2^{t-r} cycles of common length 2^r where $T = 2^t$. The structure of the CCC requires $2^r \geq t-r$. We choose $r = \lceil 1/2 \log T - \log\log T + c \rceil$ where $c \simeq 1.308$. Note that this CCC has cycles of length $O(T^{1/2}/\log T)$ and is capable of performing any of the T prescribed shifts in $O(T^{1/2}/\log T)$ steps. A step is the (parallel) exchange of super-fragments between micro-modules. We show below how to embed the CCC of micro-modules into a macro-module such that an exchange takes time $O(T^{1/2})$. Then any single shift takes time $O(T^{1/2} \cdot T^{1/2}/\log T)$ and since the total number of arithmetic steps is $O(\log T)$ the total time for the arithmetic is $O(T)$, as desired.

It remains to describe a layout for the CCC. As we noted above each micro-module consists of $\theta(N/T^{5/2})$ consecutive shift registers. If we conceptually shrink each micro-module to a single node then a macro-module shrinks to a T by T grid with the micro-modules on the diagonal. It is now easy to embed the CCC connections in the shrunken graph. We use the main diagonal for the forward cycle connections, while the lower-left portion of the grid is used for the return connections of the cycles, and the upper-right portion of the grid is for the intercycle lateral connections. The scheme is illustrated for a 4 by 4 CCC in figure 6.

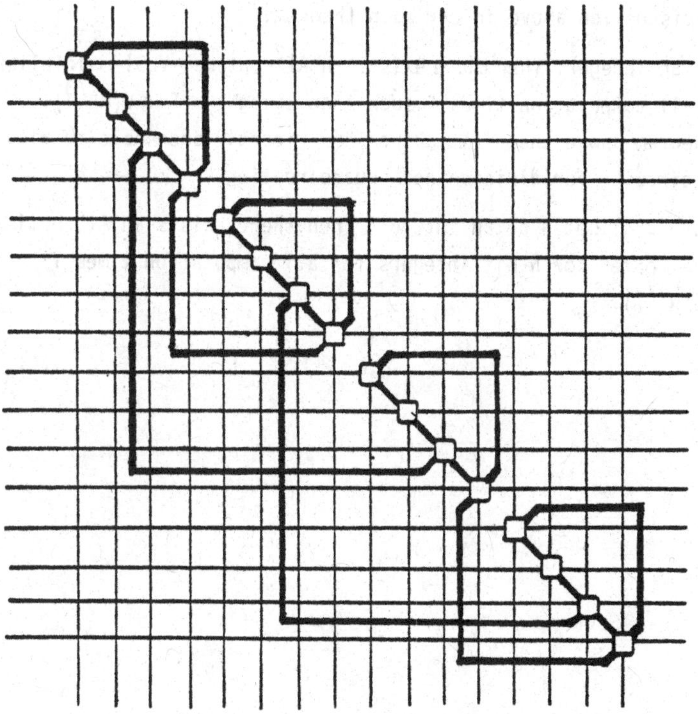

Figure 6. Embedding of a 4 x 4 CCC into a 16-element macro-module.

t is now easy to reverse the shrinking process and to embed the CCC with connections f the required bandwidths by expanding the area of the macro-module by a constant actor.

This essentially finishes the description of the DFT engine. We leave it to the eader to show that the communication between the major components (DFT,P3M,DFT^{-1}) can e performed in time O(T).

We close our discussion with a short comment on the case $T \geq N^{2/5}$. If $T \geq N^{2/5}$ hen we realize a CCC with $\theta(N/T^{3/2})$ nodes, each shift register being a node. A shift y $\lceil 3\,N/T^2\rceil\, i = c\ell+d$ with $d < \ell$ for some integers c,d is performed in two steps. We irst perform a shift by $c \cdot \ell$ positions using the CCC and then perform a shift by d ositions by connecting the shift registers to a single cyclic shift register. Thus he time needed for a shift is $O(T/\log T + T^{1/2}) = O(T/\log T)$ by appropriate choice of he cycle length of the CCC (cycle length $T^{1/2}/\log T$ will do) and hence the total ost of all arithmetic steps is O(T).

We summarize the discussion above in our main theorem.

Theorem: Let N be an integer. Then there exists an AT^2-optimal VLSI-multiplier for N-bit integers for all computation times T such that $\Omega(\log N) \leq T \leq O(N^{1/3})$.

Using the theorem above the first author has recently been able to also construct AT^2-optimal VLSI-circuits for division and square rooting.

Theorem: ([Mehlhorn 83]) Let N be an integer. Then there exists an AT^2-optimal VLSI-divider and square rooter for N-bit integers for all computation times T such that $\Omega((\log N)^2) \leq T \leq O(N^{1/2})$.

References

[AA80] H. Abelson and P. Andreae, "Information transfer and area-time trade-offs for VLSI-multiplication," Communications of the ACM, vol. 23, n. 1, pp. 20-22, Jan. 1980.

[AHU74] A. V. Aho, J. E. Hopcroft and J. D. Ullman, The Design and Analysis of Computer Algorithms, Addision-Wesley, Reading, MA, 1974.

[B83] B. Becker, "Schnelle Multiplizierwerke für VLSI - Implementierung," Technical Report, Uni. des Saarlandes, 1982.

[BK81] R. P. Brent and H. T. Kung, "The chip complexity of binary arithmetic," J. Ass. Comp. Mach., vol. 28, pp. 521-534, July 1981.

[D65] L. Dadda, "Some schemes for parallel multipliers," Alta Frequenza, vol. 34, pp. 343-356, 1965.

[KO62] A. Karazuba und Y. Ofman, "Multiplication of multidigit numbers on automata," Doklady Akademija Nauk SSSR, vol. 145, pp. 293-294, 1962.

[LM83] Th. Lengauer und K. Mehlhorn, "VLSI complexity theory, efficient VLSI algorithms and the HILL design system," in The International Professorship in Computer Science: Algorithmics for VLSI, Ed. Trullemans, Academic Press, to appear.

[LV83] W. K. Luk and J. E. Vuillemin, "Recursive implementation of optimal time VLSI integer multipliers," VLSI83, Trondheim, Norway, September 1983

[M83] K. Mehlhorn, AT^2-optimal VLSI-circuits for integer division and integer square rooting, submitted for publication.

[PV81a] F. P. Preparata and J. Vuillemin, "Area-time optimal VLSI networks for computing integer multiplication and Discrete Fourier Transform," Proceedings of I.C.A.L.P., Haifa, Israel, July 1981, pp. 29-40.

[PV81b] F. P. Preparata and J. Vuillemin, "The Cube-Connected-Cycles: A versatile network for parallel computation," Communications of the ACM, vol. 24, n. 5, pp. 300-309, May 1981.

[SS71] A. Schönhage and V. Strassen, "Schnelle Multiplikation grosser Zahlen," Computing 7, pp. 281-292, 1971.

[T79] C. D. Thompson, "Area-time complexity for VLSI," Proc. of the 11th Annual ACM Symposium on the Theory of Computing (SIGACT), pp. 81-88, May 1979

[V83] J. E. Vuillemin, "A very fast multiplication algorithm for VLSI implementation," Integration, VLSI Journal, vol. 1, n. 1, pp. 33-52, 1983.

[W64] C. S. Wallace, "A suggestion for a fast multiplier," IEEE Transactions on computers, vol. EC-13, n. 2, pp. 14-17, 1964.

ON THE INTERPRETATION OF INFINITE COMPUTATIONS IN LOGIC PROGRAMMING

M.A. Nait Abdallah
Department of Computer Science
University of Waterloo
Waterloo, Ontario
Canada N2L 3G1

Abstract

We study in this paper the operational and greatest fixpoint semantics of infinite computations in logic programming. We show their equivalence in the case of fair derivations, and generalize to infinite computations some important results about finite ones.

1. Introduction:

We first recall some basic definitions [5]. A logic program is a finite set of definite clauses. A definite clause is a quantifier-free first order formula of the form:

$$A \leftarrow B_1 \wedge \ldots \wedge B_m \qquad m \geq 0$$

where A, B_1, ..., B_m are atoms. An atom has the form $p(t_1,\ldots,t_k)$, where p is a k-ary relation symbol and $t_1,\ldots,t_k$ are terms. A term is a variable, a constant, or has the form $f(t_1,\ldots,t_n)$, where f is a n-ary function symbol and $t_1,\ldots,t_n$ are terms.

A goal clause is a formula of the form:

$$\leftarrow B_1 \wedge \ldots \wedge B_m \qquad m \geq 0$$

where $B_1,\ldots,B_m$ are atoms. A goal clause where m = 0 is called an empty clause, denoted by □. A Horn clause is either a definite clause or a goal clause.

The computation technique used for logic programs is a special kind of resolution [10]. As an example the execution of the following logic program:

1. sum $(0,x,x) \leftarrow$
2. sum $(s(x),y,s(z)) \leftarrow sum(x,y,z)$ together with the goal clause
3. $\leftarrow$ sum $(s^2(0),u,v)$ yields:
4. $\leftarrow$ sum $(s(0),u,v_1)$ — $v = s(v_1)$, by 2.,3.,Modus Toller
5. $\leftarrow$ sum $(0,u,v_2)$ — $v_1 = s(v_2)$ 2,4 Modus Tollens
6. □ — $u = x = v_2$, 1,5, Modus Tollens

The result of the above computation is the answer substitution θ =

$\{v \to s^2(u)\}$, which is obtained by composing the sequence of most general unifiers used in the execution, and restricting the result of this composition to the variables of the first goal clause.

This execution has two components: a logical component given by the sequence of clauses, which may be read backwards as a proof in the first order predicate calculus, and a computational component, which is given by the sequence of most general unifiers used, and which gives the result of the computation from a programming point of view. However, this computation result makes only sense when the last clause of the execution is the empty clause; in particular the computation should be finite.

However, there are cases where the computation is infinite (and thus the empty clause is never reached), but where the sequence of most general unifiers still makes sense, at least intuitively.

Consider the sequence of Fibonacci numbers:

$$F_0 = F_1 = 1 \quad , \quad F_{n+2} = F_{n+1} + F_n$$

This sequence can be coded into an infinite list F, where the n-th atom of the list is the n-th Fibonacci number:

$$F = 1.1.2.3. \ldots$$

If x is an infinite list of numbers:

$$x = x_0.x_1.x_2. \ldots$$

then u.x will denote the list obtained by inserting atom u at the head of list x:

$$u.x = u.x_0.x_1.x_2. \ldots$$

Addition of infinite lists is defined componentwise:

$$(x_0.x_1.x_2. \ldots) + (y_0.y_1.y_2. \ldots) = (z_0.z_1.z_2. \ldots)$$

$$\text{iff } \forall i \in \mathbb{N} \quad x_i + y_i = z_i$$

Now by definition the list coding the Fibonacci sequence verifies the following fixpoint equation:

$$0.0.F + 1.F = F \qquad (*)$$

Addition of infinite lists may be formalized by the following

Horn clause:

1. lsum (a.x, b.y, c.z) $\leftarrow$ sum (a,b,c) $\wedge$ lsum (x,y,z)

where "lsum (x,y,z)" means "infinite list z is the sum of infinite lists x and y", and "sum (a,b,c)" means "a + b = c" and has been defined earlier. Equation (*) can be formalized by the goal clause

2. $\leftarrow$ lsum (0.0.f,1.f,f)

clauses 1., 2., together with the above definition of sum, yield the infinite computation:

3. $\leftarrow$ lsum (0.f,f,f_1) $\wedge$ sum (a_1, b_1, c_1) $a_1 = 0$, $b_1 = 1$, $f = c_1 f_1$

4. $\leftarrow$ lsum (0.f,f,f_1) f = 1.f_1 (after execution of sum

5. $\leftarrow$ lsum (f,f_1,f_2) $a_2 = 0$, $b_2 = 1 = c_2$, f_1 = 1.f_2

6. $\leftarrow$ lsum (f_1,f_2,f_3) f_2 = 2.f_3

etc.

(Execution of calls to sum has been abbreviated, and numbers are designated by their usual names.)

This infinite computation yields successive approximations of the Fibonacci sequence:

1.f_1

1.1.f_2

1.1.2.f_3

etc.

and every Fibonacci number will eventually be produced by the computation.

Similarly consider the difference equation:

$$y_{n+4} - 4y_{n+3} + 5y_{n+2} - y_{n+1} + 4y_n = 4 \quad (**)$$

with the initial conditions $y_0 = 5$, $y_1 = 0$, $y_2 = -4$, $y_3 = -12$. A solution of this equation may be coded as an infinite list of numbers:

$$\bar{y} = \bar{y}_0 . \bar{y}_1 . \bar{y}_2 . \; \cdots \; . \bar{y}_n . \; \cdots$$

Now if we define the predicate:

$$\varphi(a,b,c,d,e) \Leftrightarrow a-4b+5c-d+4e = 4$$

and the infinite list:

$$\bar{y} = 5.0.(-4).(-12).y$$

then coding the above equation into the clauses:

1. $\Phi(a.X,\ b.Y,\ c.Z,\ d.U,\ e.V) \leftarrow \varphi(a,b,c,d,e) \wedge \Phi(X,Y,Z,U,V)$

2. $\leftarrow \Phi(y,(-12).y,(-4).(-12).y,0.(-4).(-12).y,5.0.(-4).(-12).y)$

and executing these clauses will yield one particular solution of difference equation (**). The computation will be an infinite one.

More generally, using Prolog as an assembly language for a Personal Inference Machine as some authors advocate [8], leads also into considering infinite computations as relevant.

Infinite logic programming computations are not taken into account in the classical semantics of logic programming. Indeed, in [6] it is shown that the least Herbrand model of a logic program P is the least fixpoint $\bigcup_n T^n(\phi)$ of the set-theoretic transformation T: $\mathcal{P}(H_b) \rightarrow \mathcal{P}(H_b)$ associated to this program (H_b denotes the Herbrand base here). This links the model-theoretic semantics of a logic program with its Scott-Stratchey semantics. In [1] the authors show that the complementary set of the intersection $\bigcap_n T^n(H_b)$ in the Herbrand base H_b, is exactly the finite failure set of P, i.e., the set of all elements $a \in H_b$ such that there exists a finite SLD-tree for $P \cup \{\leftarrow a\}$ which contains no success branch. Little is known about the difference set $\bigcap_n T^n(H_b) - \bigcup_n T^n(\phi)$. All these results concern the <u>finitary</u> case, and the characterization of infinite computations remains an open question.

We present in this paper some tools for solving this question, and expound our results in this direction. We generalize Herbrand models to <u>continuous Herbrand models</u> by introducing a distance in the Herbrand base and taking the metric completion, as in [2]. We give a partition of the <u>completed Herbrand base</u> into atoms which are the result of finite successful computations, those which are finitely failed, and those which are the result of infinite fair computations. We show that the greatest fixpoint of the transformation T associated to a logic program P is $\bigcap_{n\in\mathbb{N}} T^n(\overline{H}_b)$. We finally show that the notion of fair derivation is sound and complete in the present setting.

II. Continuous Herbrand interpretations:

Let P be a finite logic program.

Let $F = \bigcup_{i\in\mathbb{N}} F_i$ be the set of function symbols occurring in P, where $f\in F_i \Leftrightarrow$ arity (f) = i. Let $R = \bigcup_{i\in\mathbb{N}} R_i$ be the set of relation symbols occurring in P, where $r\in R_i \Leftrightarrow$ arity (r) = i.

Let H_u be the Herbrand universe generated by F (i.e., the set of all terms constructed from F), and H_b be the Herbrand base generated by F and R (i.e., the set of all atoms constructed from F and R). In fact H_b is the free R-algebra generated by H_u.

The set of trees H_u can be equipped with the following distance:

$$d(t,t') = 0 \quad \text{if } t = t'$$
$$2^{-\inf\{n:\ \alpha_n(t) \neq \alpha_n(t')\}} \quad \text{otherwise}$$

where $\alpha_n(t)$ denotes the cut at height n of tree t. The completed metric space of infinite trees constructed from H_u will be denoted $\overline{H}_u$. Since P is finite, $\overline{H}_u$ is compact [2].

The very same process, when applied to H_b yields a compact metric space $\overline{H}_b$ which will be the completed Herbrand base. One easily verifies that $\overline{H}_b$ is the free R-algebra generated by $\overline{H}_u$. We define $2^{\overline{H}_b}$ as the set of nonempty closed subsets of $\overline{H}_b$.

A continuous Herbrand interpretation I for a formula φ is defined as follows:

(i) the domain of interpretation is $\overline{H}_u$

(ii) constants in φ are assigned to themselves

(iii) $\forall f\in F_n$ occurring in φ, the interpretation of f is the uniformly continuous function $I(f): \overline{H}_u^n \to \overline{H}_u,\ (t_1,\dots,t_n) \to f(t_1,\dots,t_n)$

(iv) $\forall r\in R_n$ occurring in φ, $I(r):\ \overline{H}_u^n \to \{tt,\ ff\}$ where tt denotes true, and ff denotes false, is semi-continuous in the following sense:

$\forall$ every Cauchy sequence $\{u_p\}_{p\in\mathbb{N}}$ in $\overline{H}_u^n$ such that $I(r)(u_p) = tt$ for almost every p, we have $I(r)(\lim_p u_p) = tt$.

Lemma 2.1: There is a canonical bijection between continuous Herbrand interpretations and closed subsets of $\bar{H}_b$. □

III. Derivations:

We now come to the study of *SLD-derivations*. Since no other derivations will be considered, the prefix SLD will be omitted. From now on, an *infinitary atom* will be an element of the algebra $M(R,M(F,V\cup\bar{H}_u))$.

A *substitution* θ is a function θ: $V \to M(F,V\cup\bar{H}_u)$ whose domain $D(\theta) = \{x\in V: \theta(x) \neq x\}$ is finite. A *ground substitution* is a substitution which maps every variable onto an element of $\bar{H}_u$. If t is an atom, then we define its *ground closure* [t] by:

$$[t] = \{t\theta: \ \theta \text{ ground substitution}\}$$

A *variable-pure* substitution is a substitution whose image contains only variables.

A substitution θ is a *unifier* for two atoms t_1 and t_2, iff $t_1\theta = t_2\theta$. A unifier θ for t_1,t_2 is a *most general unifier* (*mgu*) iff for every unifier σ of t_1,t_2 there exists a substitution γ such that $\sigma=\theta\gamma$.

If $a \leftarrow b_1\wedge\dots\wedge b_m$ is a definite clause, then a *rule variant* of this clause is any rewriting rule $A \to B_1\wedge\dots\wedge B_m$ where $A = a\theta$, $B_1 = b_1\theta,\dots$, $B_m = b_m\theta$ for some variable-pure substitution θ.

A *goal* is any conjunction of atoms. *Occurrences* in goals are defined in the usual way, $(t{\downarrow}\sigma)$ denotes the atom of occurrence σ in t.

A *derivation step* from a goal t is a triple $\langle\sigma,r,\theta\rangle$ where σ is an occurrence of an atom in t, r is a rule variant with no variable in common with t and whose left-hand side unifies with the atom selected by σ, and θ is a most general unifier for this unification. If $t = u_1\wedge\dots\wedge u\wedge\dots\wedge u_p$, where u is the atom of occurrence σ in t, and if $r = A \to B_1\wedge\dots\wedge B_m$ is a rule variant with no variable in common with t and if $\theta = mgu(u,A)$, then the *yield* $\langle\sigma,r,\theta\rangle(t)$ of derivation step $\langle\sigma,r,\theta\rangle$ is by definition:

$$\langle\sigma,r,\theta\rangle(t) = (u_1\theta)\wedge\dots\wedge\underbrace{(B_1\theta)\wedge\dots\wedge(B_m\theta)}_{\text{replaces occurrence } \sigma}\wedge\dots\wedge(u_p\theta)$$

In the case $r = A \to$, nothing replaces occurrence σ. If σ is not an occurrence in t, this definition is extended to $\langle\sigma,r,\theta\rangle(t) = t$.

Lemma 3.1 (square lemma): Let t be a goal i.e., a conjunction of atoms

$\in M(R,M(F,V\cup\overline{H}_u))$, $\delta = \langle\sigma,r,\theta\rangle$ a derivation step from t, and $\delta_1=\langle\sigma_1,r_1,\theta_1\rangle$ a derivation step from $\delta(t)$ such that $(\delta(t)\downarrow\sigma_1)$ has not been introduced by the replacement performed by δ in t. Assume that u and the rule variants r: $A \to B$ and r_1: $A_1 \to B_1$ (resp. v, r, r_1) have pairwise no variable in common, and let:

$$\theta = mgu(A,v) \text{ where } v = (t\downarrow\sigma)$$

$$\theta_1 = mgu(A_1,u\theta) \text{ where } u = (t\downarrow\sigma_1)$$

then there exist two derivation steps δ^*, δ_1^* such that:

$\delta^* = \langle\sigma_1,r_1,\theta^*\rangle$ is a derivation step from t

$\delta_1^* = \langle\sigma,r,\theta_1^*\rangle$ is a derivation step from $\delta^*(t)$

where $\theta^* = mgu(A_1,u)$, $\theta_1^* = mgu(A,v\theta^*)$ and two variable-pure substitutions σ and γ s.t.

$$yield(\delta,\delta_1) = yield(\delta^*,\delta_1^*)\sigma$$

$$yield(\delta^*,\delta_1^*) = yield(\delta,\sigma_1)\gamma \qquad \square$$

The above lemma intuitively means that derivation steps may be permuted around, as long as they are completely independent of each other.

A finite derivation from t is a finite sequence $\Delta = t_0,\delta_1,t_1,\ldots,\delta_n,t_n$ such that:

$t_0 = t$

$\delta_i = \langle\sigma_i,r_i,\theta_i\rangle$ is a derivation step from t_{i-1}

$t_i = \delta_i(t_{i-1})$ $i = 1,2,\ldots,n$

t_0 is called the root of derivation Δ. A finite derivation is successful iff it eventually yields an empty goal i.e., the constant true.

Lemma 3.2 (Rectangle lemma): For every derivation $\Delta = G\theta,\delta_1,\ldots,\delta_n, U\theta_n$, there exists a derivation $\Delta' = G,\delta_1',\ldots,\delta_n' V\sigma_n$ and a substitution γ_n such that:

$$U\theta_n = V\sigma_n\gamma_n \qquad \square$$

The set $[\Delta(t)]$ computed by a finite derivation $\Delta=(t_0=t,\delta_1,t_1,\ldots,\delta_n,t_n)$ from a atom t, is by definition the ground closure

$$[\Delta(t)] = [t\theta_1\theta_2\ldots\theta_n] \quad .$$

An infinite derivation Δ from t is an infinite sequence

$$\Delta = t_0,\delta_1,t_1,\ldots,\delta_n,t_n,\ldots$$

such that

$$t_0 = t$$

$$\delta_i = \langle\sigma_i,r_i,\theta_i\rangle \text{ is a derivation step from } t_{i-1}$$

$$t_i = \delta_i(t_{i-1}) \quad \forall i > 0 \ .$$

If Δ is an infinite derivation, then $\Delta|_j$ is the finite derivation obtained by taking the first j steps of Δ:

$$\Delta|_j = t_0,\delta_1,\ldots,\delta_j,t_j \quad .$$

The set $[\Delta(t)]$ computed by an infinite derivation Δ from an atom t, is by definition:

$$[\Delta(t)] = \bigcap_{j\in\mathbb{N}} [\Delta|_j(t)]$$

because $\bar{H}_b$ is metric and complete, this set is never empty.

A derivation Δ from t is fair up to $q\in\mathbb{N}$ $q > 0$, iff intuitively every atom u of t is eventually replaced by some step δ of Δ, and for each atom v thus introduced by step δ, the subderivation of Δ starting from v is fair up to q - 1. Every derivation is fair up to 0.

As a consequence, every successful derivation is fair up to q, $\forall q\in\mathbb{N}$.

An infinite derivation Δ is fair iff $\forall q\in\mathbb{N}\ q>0\ \exists j\in\mathbb{N}\ \ \Delta|_j$ is fair up to q. (The notion of fairness was introduced in [7]). Fair derivations generalize successful derivations.

If P is a logic program, then we define the subset transformation T associated with P:

$$T: S \mapsto \{a\theta\in\bar{H}_b : (a \leftarrow b_1\wedge\ldots\wedge b_m)\in P;\ b_1\theta,\ldots,b_m\theta\in S;\ \theta \text{ substitution}\}.$$

Lemma 3.3: Transformation T maps elements of $2^{\overline{H}_b}$ into elements of $2^{\overline{H}_b} \cup \{\phi\}$. □

Lemma 3.4: Let t be an atom, $\Delta = t_0, \delta_1, t_1, \ldots, \delta_n, t_n$ a finite derivation fair up to q, q > 0. Then $[\Delta(t)] \subseteq T^q(\overline{H}_b)$. □

Lemma 3.5: Let t be an atom; then:

$$[t] \cap T^q(\overline{H}_b) \subseteq \cup\{[\Delta(t)]: \Delta \text{ finite derivation fair up to } q\}. \ \square$$

From the above two lemmae we deduce the following theorem which is given in [9]:

Theorem 3.6: For every atom $t \in M(R, M(F, V \cup \overline{H}_u))$,

$$[t] \cap \left(\bigcap_{q \in \mathbb{N}} T^q(\overline{H}_b) \right) = \cup\{[\Delta(t)] : \Delta \text{ fair derivation}\}. \quad \square$$

IV. Canonical partition of $\overline{H}_b$:

We have the following partition of the complete Herbrand base $\overline{H}_b$, which generalizes and completes the partition given in [1] in the finitary case.

Theorem 4.1: $a \in \overline{H}_b$ begins a successful derivation, ⇔ a is an element of the least fixpoint $\bigcup_n T^n(\phi)$ of transformation T: $P(\overline{H}_b) \rightarrow P(\overline{H}_b)$. □

Let P be a logical program, and G a goal. An SLD-tree for $P \cup \{\leftarrow G\}$ is the set of all derivations from G arranged as a tree by coalescing all common initial subsequence. In such a tree, a node n' is the son of a node n iff n' is the yield of some derivation step δ from n, i.e., n' = δ(n).

A finite SLD-tree is failed [1] iff no path in the tree is a successful derivation.

Theorem 4.2: $a \in \overline{H}_b$ is the root of a finite and failed SLD-tree ⇔ $a \notin \bigcap_{q \in \mathbb{N}} T^q(\overline{H}_b)$. □

And finally:

Theorem 4.3: $a \in \overline{H}_b$ is the root a fair derivation ⇔ $a \in \bigcap_{q \in \mathbb{N}} T^q(\overline{H}_b)$. □

V. Greatest fixpoint theorem:

Lemma 5.1: If t_0 is an atom $\in \overline{H}_b$, and if $\Delta = t_0, \delta_1, t_1, \Delta'$ is a derivatio here Δ' denotes the remainder of the derivation, then:

$$\{t_0\} = [\Delta(t_0)] \subseteq T(\cup\{[\Delta'(t_1^i)]: t_1^i \text{ is an atom of } t_1\}) \qquad \square$$

From this lemma and theorem 3.6, we deduce the following fixpoint heorem:

heorem 5.2: $\bigcap_{q\in\mathbb{N}} T^q(\overline{H}_b)$ is the greatest fixpoint of T. □

There is a more direct, and more topological way of obtaining this heorem. The set $2^{\overline{H}_b}$ of non-empty closed subsets of $\overline{H}_b$ can be equipped ith Hausdorff distance:

$$d(A,B) = \inf\{\varepsilon: A \subseteq \nu_\varepsilon(B),\ B \subseteq \nu_\varepsilon(A)\}$$

here

$$\nu_\varepsilon(A) = \{y\in\overline{H}_b: \exists x\in A \ \ d(x,y) < \varepsilon\}$$

here $d(x,y)$ denotes the distance of $\overline{H}_b$. We may also define on $2^{\overline{H}_b}$ imits in the Kuratowski-Painlevé sense. For any sequence $(S_n)_{n\in\mathbb{N}}$ f 2^{H_b},

$$x\in \underset{n}{LI}\,(S_n) \Leftrightarrow \forall \text{ open neighbourhood } V(x) \text{ of } x\ \exists N>0\ \forall p \geq N \quad V(x)\cap S_p \neq \phi$$

$$x\in \underset{n}{LS}\,(S_n) \Leftrightarrow \forall \text{ open neighbourhood } V(x) \text{ of } x\ \forall N>0 \quad \exists p \geq N\ \ V(x)\cap S_p \neq \phi.$$

Define an atom t as being normal iff $t \notin \overline{H}_b$ and for no variable x, contains more than one occurrence of x. Example: q(x,y,z) is normal, hereas p(y,y) is not.

emma 5.3: (i) If b is a normal atom, and κ: a ← b is a definite lause, then the transformation T_κ: $2^{\overline{H}_b} \to 2^{\overline{H}_b}\cup\{\phi\}$, $S \to \{a\theta\in\overline{H}_b: b\theta\in S\}$ hen restricted to $\{S\in 2^{\overline{H}_b}: T_\kappa(S) \neq \phi\}$ is uniformly continuous for the ausdorff distance. (ii) Let κ: a ← $b_1\wedge\ldots\wedge b_m$ m≥0 be a definite clause hen for any Cauchy sequence $(S_n)_{n\in\mathbb{N}}$ of $2^{\overline{H}_b}$, whenever $\lim_n T_\kappa(S_n)$ exists, e have $\lim_n T_\kappa(S_n) \subseteq T_\kappa(\lim_n S_n)$. □ □

emma 5.4: Let P be a logic program.

i) For any sequence of $2^{\overline{H}_b}$ $\underset{n}{LS}\ T_P(S_n) \subseteq T_P(\underset{n}{LS}(S_n))$.

ii) For any Cauchy sequence $(S_n)_{n\in\mathbb{N}}$ of $2^{\overline{H}_b}$, $\underset{n}{LI}\ T_P(S_n) \subseteq T_P(\underset{n}{LI}(S_n))$ □

Theorem 5.5: Let P be a logic program. (i) For every Cauchy sequence $(S_n)_{n\in\mathbb{N}}$ of $2^{\bar{H}_b}$, if $\lim_n T_P(S_n)$ exists, then $\lim_n T_P(S_n) \subseteq T_P(\lim_n S_n)$.

(ii) For every decreasing sequence $(S_n)_{n\in\mathbb{N}}$ of $2^{\bar{H}_b}$, $T_P(\bigcap_n S_n) = \bigcap_n T_P(S_n)$.

(iii) $\bigcap_n T_P{}^n(\bar{H}_b)$ is the greatest fixpoint of T_P. □

VI. Soundness and completeness of fair derivation:

A computation rule R is a function from a set of goals to a set of atoms, such that the value of the function for a goal is always an atom in that goal. The atom thus selected will be the atom to be rewritten in that goal.

A computation rule is fair iff for any derivation Δ it generates, either Δ is fair or Δ is finite and non-successful. In the latter case the yield of Δ contains an atom which is not true and cannot be further rewritten.

Let P be a logic program, $G = A_1 \wedge \ldots \wedge A_m$ be a goal, and R a computation rule.

An answer substitution [1] for $P \cup \{\leftarrow G\}$ is a substitution whose domain is the set of variables of G.

A continuous Herbrand model for P is proper iff it contains no atom which is the root of a finite and failed SLD-tree. An answer substitution θ is consistent iff $P \cup \{A_1\theta \wedge \ldots \wedge A_m\theta\}$ has a proper model. (This generalizes to infinite derivations the notion of correct answer substitution [1] which was defined for finite derivations.)

An R-computed answer substitution for $P \cup \{\leftarrow G\}$ is the substitution obtained by restricting the (possibly infinite) composition (in fact limit in the sense of simple convergence):

$$\theta_1\theta_2\ldots\theta_n\ldots = \lim_n(\theta_1\theta_2\ldots\theta_n)$$

to the variables of G, where $(\theta_n)_{n\in\mathbb{N}}$ is the sequence of mgu's used in a fair derivation from G via R.

We now generalize to infinite derivations results from [1].

Theorem 6.1 (Soundness): Let P be a program, G a goal, R a fair computation rule. Then every R-computed answer substitution for $P \cup \{\leftarrow G\}$ is a consistent answer substitution.

Theorem 6.2 (Completeness): For every consistent answer substitution θ for $P \cup \{\leftarrow G\}$, there exists a fair computation rule R, an R-computed nswer substitution $\sigma = \lim_n \sigma_n$ for $P \cup \{\leftarrow G\}$, and an effectively constructed equence of substitutions (γ_n) such that $\lim_n(\sigma_n\gamma_n) = \theta$. □

II. An example: We now illustrate what the above results mean by onsidering "Hamming's problem" as discussed in Dijkstra [3]: construct he sorted list of all natural numbers $\neq 0$ containing as prime factors nly 2, 3 and 5.

This question can be solved by using a data flow program formalized y a logic program. We first give our notation:

.x	is the list resulting from inserting atom u at the beginning of list x (cf. Introduction)
, >	are 2-ary relation symbols with their usual notation (infix notation is used here)
rod (a,b,c)	means a * b = c
(x,n,y)	means "list y is obtained by multiplying all elements of list x by n" (scalar multiplication)
(x,y,z)	means "sorted list z is obtained by merging without repetition sorted lists x and y".

rom this follows the following logic program P together with goal q(x,1.x):

. $F(a.x, n, b.y) \leftarrow Prod(a,n,b) \wedge F(x,n,y)$

. $M(u.x, u.y, u.z) \leftarrow M(x,y,z)$

. $M(x_1.x, y_1.y, x_1.z) \leftarrow (x_1 < y_1) \wedge M(x,y_1.y,z)$

. $M(x_1.x, y_1.y, y_1.z) \leftarrow (y_1 < x_1) \wedge M(x_1.x, y,z)$

. $Eq(x,y) \leftarrow F(y,3,u) \wedge F(y,5,v) \wedge M(u,v,w) \wedge F(y,2,z) \wedge M(w,z,x)$

. $\leftarrow Eq(x,1.x)$

The desired infinite list, which is computed by fair derivations:

$\ell = 2.3.4.5.6.8.9.10.12.15.16.18.20.24. \ldots$

erfifies $Eq(\ell,1.\ell) \in \bigcap_{n\in\mathbb{N}} T^n(\bar{H}_b)$ i.e.

$\forall n\in\mathbb{N}\ Eq(\ell,1.\ell) \in T^n(\bar{H}_b)$

here $\bar{H}_b$ is the completed Herbrand base associated with the above rogram.

The proof is as follows: for n = 0, it is obvious. Let $n \neq 0$. o make the proof simple let us assume that <, > and Prod produce their esults "instantaneously". We may remark that $\forall q\in\mathbb{N}$, $q > 0$

$(\{F(\vec{\alpha}.\vec{u},m,\vec{\beta}.\vec{v}): \vec{\alpha}, \vec{u}, \vec{\beta}, \vec{v} \text{ lists}, |\vec{\alpha}| = |\vec{\beta}|, \vec{\alpha} = m*\vec{\beta}\} \subseteq T^q(\bar{H}_b))$

From this we deduce, if $(\ell/_{n+1})$ denotes the initial segment of length n+1 of list ℓ, that

$$\{Eq((\ell/_{n+1}).\vec{u},\ 1.(\ell/_{n+1}).\vec{v}):\ \vec{u},\ \vec{v}\ \text{lists}\} \subseteq T^{n+1}(\bar{H}_b)$$

by applying the fifth clause once. Whence $Eq(\ell,1.\ell) \in T^{n+1}(\bar{H}_b)$.

We also have:

$$[Eq(x.1.x)] \cap (\bigcap_n T^n(\bar{H}_b)) = \{Eq(\ell,1.\ell)\}$$

which is an occurrence of theorem 3.6.

Acknowledgements:

This research was supported by the Canadian NSERC under grant #A2484. Partial support was also provided by Laboratoire de Recherche Informatique, Orsay. The author is indebted to Maarten van Emden for many helpful discussions.

References

[1]. K.R. Apt, M.H. van Emden: Contributions to the theory of logic programming, JACM 29, 3 (1982), pp. 841-862.

[2]. A. Arnold, M. Nivat: The metric space of infinite trees. Algebraic and topological properties, Fundamenta Informaticae 3, 4 (1980), pp. 445-476.

[3]. E.W. Dijkstra: A discipline of programming, Prentice Hall, (1976

[4]. F. Hausdorff: Set theory, Chelsea Publishing Company, New York (1962).

[5]. R.A. Kowalski: Logic for problem solving, Elsevier North Holland New York, (1979).

[6]. R.A. Kowalski, M.H. van Emden: The semantics of logic as a programming language, JACM 23, 4 (1976), pp. 733-742.

[7]. J.L. Lassez, M.J. Maher: Closure and fairness in the semantics of logic programming, T.C.S. (to appear).

[8]. T. Moto-Oka: Overview of the fifth generation computer project, SIGARCH Newsletter 11(3), 1983, pp. 417-422.

[9]. M.A. Nait-Abdallah, M.H. van Emden: Algorithm theory and logic programming, (draft manuscript).

[10]. J.A. Robinson: A machine-oriented logic based on the resolution principle, JACM 12, 1 (1965), pp. 23-41.

A Linear Time Algorithm to Solve the Single Function Coarsest Partition Problem

Robert Paige[1]
Dept. of Computer Science
Rutgers University
New Brunswick, NJ 08903/USA

and

Robert E. Tarjan
AT&T Bell Laboratories
600 Mountain Avenue
Murray Hill, NJ 07974/USA

Abstract

The problem of finding the coarsest partition of a set S with respect to another partition of S and one or more functions on S has several applications, one of which is the state minimization of finite state automata. In 1971 Hopcroft presented an algorithm to solve the many function coarsest partition problem for sets of n elements in O(n log n) time and O(n) space. Aho, Hopcroft, and Ullman later presented an algorithm that solves the special case of this problem for only one function. Both these algorithms use a negative strategy that repeatedly refines the original partition until a solution is found. We present a new algorithm to solve the single function coarsest partition problem in O(n) time and space using a different, constructive approach.

Introduction

The single function coarsest partition problem accepts as input a set S of n elements, a partition $B = \{b_1,\ldots,b_k\}$ of S, and a function f:S-->S. The problem is to form a new partition $Q=\{q_1,\ldots,q_m\}$ of S in which each set q_i in Q is a subset of some set b_j in the original partition B, and each image set $f[q_i]$ is a subset of some set q_k in the new partition. Furthermore, we want Q to be the coarsest partition (i.e., with the fewest number of sets) that satisfies the problem constraints.

The problem is illustrated in Figure 1, where S is a set of numbers on the real line, B is a partition of S that results from dividing the line into intervals, and Q is a partition of S that results from further subdivision of these intervals.

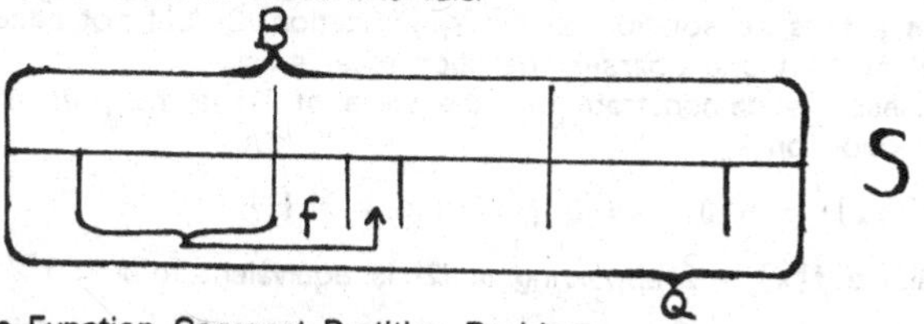

Figure 1. The Single Function Coarsest Partition Problem

A generalization of this problem with more than one function was solved by Hopcroft in 1971 with an O(n log n) algorithm, where n is the number of elements in S [5]. The simpler

---

[1] Part of this work was done while this author was visiting Yale University on Sabbatical from Rutgers University, and is partly based upon work supported by the National Science Foundation under Grant No. MCS-8212936

problem for one function was discussed by Aho, Hopcroft, and Ullman [1], who presented algorithms that run in O(n**2) and O(n log n) steps and O(n) space. These algorithms work by repeatedly refining the original partition B using a negative strategy. One reason that these algorithms are nonlinear is that an element of S can belong to a set in B that is refined several times.

In this paper we present a new, more efficient algorithm that solves the single function coarsest partition problem. Our algorithm uses a positive strategy that constructs the final partition directly and is O(n) in both time and space. Of particular importance, it exploits properties of the function f that permit each element x in S to be placed into a set of the Q partition based only on the sets in the B partition that contain x, f(x), f(f(x)), etc.

Throughout the paper several notational conventions will be used. We use the notation f^{-1} to denote the inverse of the function f, and say that $f^{-1}\{x\}$ is the preimage set $\{y \in S \mid f(y) = x\}$ The cardinality operation #Q denotes the number of elements contained in a set, tuple, or string valued variable Q. If x is a set, the image set operation f[x] denotes the union of all the image sets f{y} for all y belonging to x. Finally, we use the notation

the Q partitionof S | K(Q) minimizing #Q

to denote the coarsest partition Q (i.e., Q has the fewest number of sets) over the set S that satisfies the predicate K. If there are no such partitions or the solution is not unique, the expression is undefined.

The Problem

A formal, abstract but still computable, specification of the single function coarsest partition problem is,

(1) the Q = $\{q_1, \ldots, q_m\}$ partitionof S | ($\forall$ x $\in$ Q | ($\exists$ y $\in$ B | x $\subset$ y) and ($\exists$ z $\in$ Q | f[x] $\subset$ z)) minimizing #Q

The following theorem states that the problem specification (1) is well defined.

Theorem 1: If B is any partition of a finite set S, and f:S-->S is any total function, then there always exists a unique coarsest partition Q that satisfies the specification (1).

Proof:) We define a relation *subpartitionof* over the set of all partitions of S as follows. Let Q and B be partitions of S. We say that Q subpartitionof B iff $\forall$ x $\in$ Q | ($\exists$ y $\in$ B | x $\subset$ y). Based on the definition of subpartitionof, we can rewrite the specification (1) equivalently as

(2) the Q subpartitionof B | ($\forall$x $\in$ Q | $\exists$z $\in$ Q | f[x] $\subset$ z) minimizing #Q

Consider the space U of subpartitions of B. (U,subpartitionof) forms a lattice with B as the unique maximum element and the partition $\{\{x\}: x \in S\}$ as the unique minimum element. Since the lattice is finite, it has both a finite ascending and descending chain condition. Moreover, because the minimum element is a feasible solution to the specification (2) (but not necessarily the coarsest solution), we know that at least one coarsest partition must exist.

To show uniqueness we demonstrate that the value of (2) is the greatest fixed point of the following monotone function on U:

$$g(Q) = \{ x \cap f^{-1}[z]: x \in Q, z \in Q \mid f[x] \cap z \neq \{\}\}$$

Observe that the predicate $f[x] \subset z$ appearing in (2) is equivalent to $x \subset f^{-1}[z]$, which can also be expressed as $x \cap f^{-1}[z] = x$. This allows us to transform the universal quantifier within (2) into:

(3) $Q = \{x \in Q \mid \exists z \in Q \mid x \cap f^{-1}[z] = x\}$

But the equality, (3), is just the same as

(4) $Q = \{x \cap f^{-1}[z]: x \in Q, z \in Q \mid f[x] \cap z \neq \{\}\}$

Consequently, we can rewrite the specification (2) in the following fixed point form:

(5) the Q subpartitionof B | Q = g(Q) minimizing #Q

which proves uniqueness■

Based on a theorem due to Tarski [2], we can calculate the coarsest partition (1), which is the greatest fixed point of the monotone function g, by performing the following steps

```
(6)      Q := B;                $ Initialization
         Repeat until Q does not change:
           Q := g(Q);         $ Refinement step
```

Starting from the naive algorithm just above the two more efficient algorithms found in [1] can be derived. To obtain the $O(n^2)$ algorithm, we first replace the refinement step appearing in (6) with the following code:

```
For each set x ∈ Q
  Replace x by the sets x ∩ f⁻¹[z], ∀z ∈ Q such that f[x] ∩ z ≠ {}
```

Further transformation to the actual algorithm is straightforward.

To obtain the strategy of the more complicated $O(n \log n)$ algorithm, we replace the refinement step in (6) with,

```
Choose any z ∈ {u ∈ Q | {x ∈ Q| f⁻¹[u] ∩ x ≠ {} and x ⊄ f⁻¹[u]} ≠ {}}
For each x ∈ Q such that f⁻¹[z] ∩ x ≠ {} and x ⊄ f⁻¹[z]
  Replace x by the sets x ∩ f⁻¹[z] and x - f⁻¹[z]
```

Further transformations by the techniques of finite differencing [8] and storage structure selection [9] can be used to derive the algorithm described in [1].

While the two algorithms reported in [1] determine the coarsest partition as the greatest fixed point of a monotone function, our algorithm conceptually finds the same solution as a least fixed point of a monotone function. Our initial partition can be regarded as the bottom element of the partition lattice described in the proof of Theorem 1. This initial partition is repeatedly augmented until the coarsest partition is obtained.

In explaining the algorithm it is convenient to represent the elements of S by consecutive integers from 1 to n. Also, the sets in the input partition B and the sets in the transitional partition Q will each be identified by consecutive integers; for any element x in S, B(x) and Q(x) are the integers that identify the sets in the B and Q partitions containing x. From this perspective our algorithm finds a Q-labeling (i.e., defines the Q function on S) that represents the coarsest partition of S with respect to B and f. The following Lemma, which is a direct consequence of the formal specification (1), gives a formula for assigning Q-labels based entirely on B-labels:

Lemma 1: Let $f^0(x)=x$ and $f^i(x)=f(f^{i-1}(x))$, $i>0$. Then for all $x,y \in S$, $Q(x)=Q(y)$ iff $B(f^i(x))=B(f^i(y))$, $i=0,1,2...$ Also, $Q(x)=Q(y)$ iff $B(x)=B(y)$ and $Q(f(x))=Q(f(y))$.

The Strategy

Interesting properties of the structure of the problem specification are essential to the algorithm. In particular, we will exploit the fact that the function f:S-->S represents a directed graph of outdegree one. This allows us to think of the function as a set of edges. From this perspective the function can contain paths and cycles. If x and y are elements of S, we say that y is *reachable* from x if there is path in f from x to y. The following lemma states the consequences of the graph structure of f.

Lemma 2:

i. f must have at least 1 cycle;
ii. all paths end in a cycle;
iii. no path entering a cycle can leave the cycle;
iv. no path leads from one cycle to another cycle;
v. all paths outside of cycles form trees whose roots are in cycles.

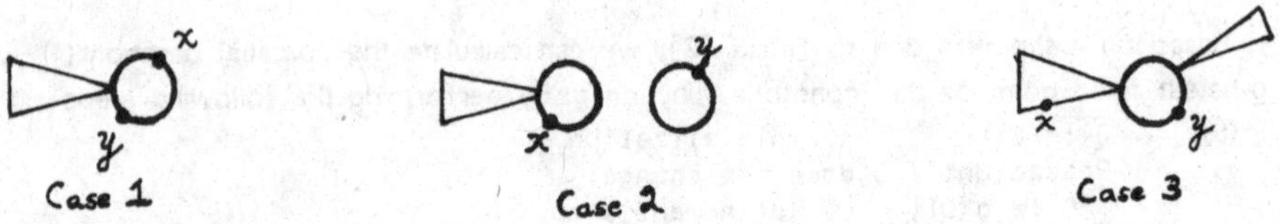

Figure 2. The Structure of f

Lemma 1 implies that the Q-label for a vertex x depends only on the B-labels of vertices reachable along paths in f from x. Making reference to Figure 2, we see three distinct cases in which two vertices x and y can be given the same Q-label according to Lemma 1.

i. When x and y are within the same cycle, the decision to give them the same Q-labels depends entirely on B-labels for vertices within that cycle.

ii. When x and y are on two different cycles, the decision is based only on B-labels for vertices in those two cycles.

iii. For the case when at least one of the two vertices x and y is a tree vertex, the fact that there is always a path from a tree vertex to a cycle makes the Q-labels for x and y depend on B-labels for both tree and cycle vertices reachable from x and y.

It is useful to consider separately the coarsest partition problem restricted to each of these three cases. We first consider the coarsest partition problem for a function whose graph representation is a single cycle with no trees leading in.

Definition: If str is any string, let str^i denote a string of i repetitions of str.
For example, $(abc)^3$ = abcabcabc.

Definition: The *smallest repeating prefix* of a string str is the smallest prefix x of str for which x^k = str.

For example, the smallest repeating prefix of $(abc)^3$ = abc.

Definition: If x is a vertex on a cycle C of k vertices, an *x-rotation* of C is a string $(x, f(x), f^2(x), \ldots, f^{k-1}(x))$.

See Figure 3 below for an example.

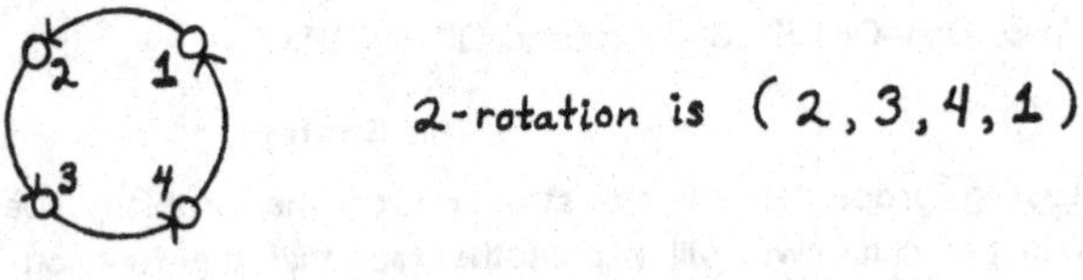

Figure 3. X-Rotation Example

The following lemma, which is a consequence of Lemmas 1 and 2, states that the equivalence classes representing the coarsest partition of a cycle C of k elements are completely determined by the smallest repeating prefix of the string $(B(x), B(f(x)), B(f^2(x), \ldots, B(f^{k-1}(x))$, where x is an arbitrary vertex of C.

Lemma 3: Let x be an arbitrary element of a cycle C of k elements, and let p be the smallest repeating prefix of the string $(B(x), B(f(x)), B(f^2(x)), \ldots, B(f^{k-1}(x))$. Then the coarsest partition of C with respect to f and B is the set of #p equivalence classes defined according to the following rule:

(7) For $j=1..\#p,\ i=1..k/\#p - 1,\ Q(f^{j-1}(x)) = Q(f^{i*\#p+j-1}(x))$

Figure 4 below illustrates the coarsest partition of a single cycle, where numbers identify vertices, letters represent B-labels, and vertices incident to broken edges belong to the same set in the coarsest partition.

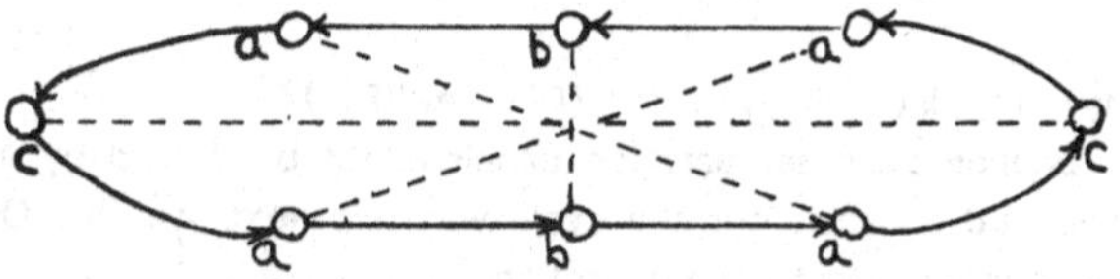

Figure 4. The partition consists of four sets with two vertices each.

To solve the coarsest partition problem for two different cycles, it is useful to state a few additional definitions.

Definition: Let < be a total ordering on a finite alphabet E. The lexicographical ordering lex< is a total ordering over strings of characters in E and is defined according to the following rule for comparing two strings ([1], p.78):

$$(x_1,\ldots,x_n) \text{ lex<= } (y_1,\ldots,y_m) \text{ iff:}$$

1. $\exists\, j \mid x_j < y_j$ and $x_i = y_i$, $i=1..j-1$; or
2. $n <= m$ and $x_i = y_i$, $i=1..n$.

Definition: Let C be a cycle with k vertices. An x-rotation of C is said to be a *lexicographically least rotation* with respect to B if there are no y-rotations of C such that

$$(B(y), B(f(y)), \ldots, B(f^{k-1}(y))) \text{ lex< } (B(x), B(f(x)), \ldots, B(f^{k-1}(x)))$$

Lexicographically least rotations are illustrated in figure 5 below.

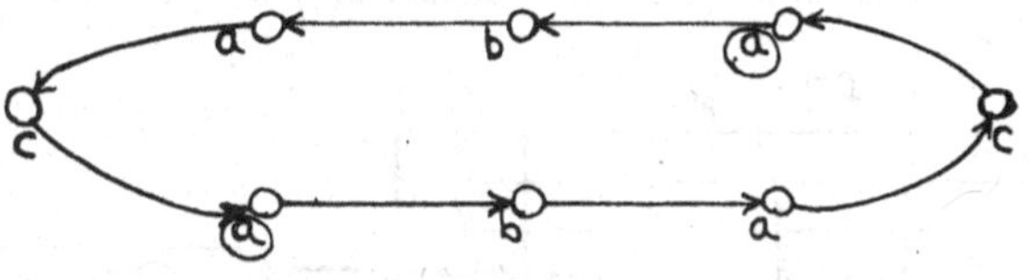

Figure 5. The two lexicographically least rotations begin at vertices with circled labels

The next lemma, which is a consequence of Lemmas 1 and 2, states that the coarsest partition for vertices in two different cycles is determined by the smallest repeating prefixes of strings formed from B-labelings of the lexicographically least rotations of the two cycles.

Lemma 4: Let the vertices x and y respectively begin lexicographically least rotations relative to B-labels of two different cycles C_1 and C_2. Then there exists an equivalence class that can contain vertices of both C_1 and C_2 iff the smallest repeating prefix of $(B(x), B(f(x)), \ldots, B(f^{\#C_1 - 1}(x)))$ equals the smallest repeating prefix of $(B(y), B(f(y)), \ldots, B(f^{\#C_2 - 1}(y)))$. When p is the same smallest repeating prefix for both cycles, the equivalence classes representing the coarsest partition of vertices in both C_1 and C_2 are determined by the following rule:

(8) For $j=1..\#p$, $Q(f^{j-1}(x)) = Q(f^{j-1}(y))$

It is easy to see that rule (8) can be extended to solve the coarsest partition problem for any number of cycles all of whose smallest repeating prefixes of a lexicographically least rotation with respect to B-labels are identical. Such cycles are called *similar*. From Lemma 4 it follows that the coarsest partition for a function f with only cycles and no trees is just the union of coarsest partitions of maximal groups of similar cycles in f.

Finally, we consider the coarsest partition problem for unrestricted functions, which have both trees and cycles. Based on Lemmas 1, 2, and 4 no two vertices can have the same Q-labels unless they lead to similar cycles. Thus, the coarsest partition for a function f is the uniion of the coarsest partitions of maximal groups of connected components of f that contain similar cycles. Q-Labels for tree vertices are determined by a closure process in accordance with the Lemma 1 rule:

$$Q(x)=Q(y) \text{ iff } B(x)=B(y) \text{ and } Q(f(x))=Q(f(y))$$

Thus, the single function coarsest partition problem can be solved by splitting the problem into two parts. First, we find Q-labels for the cycle vertices; next, we find Q-labels for the tree vertices. The details are discussed in the next section.

The Algorithm

The algorithm consists of three main steps:

1. Find all the cycles and all the tree roots;
2. Find Q-labels for the cycle vertices;
3. Find Q-labels for the tree vertices.

STEP 1. Finding the Cycles and Roots.

The following lemma is based on Lemma 2, and states that the cost of gathering all cycles and roots is O(n).

Lemma 5: Because n = #domain f = #f, we can find all the disjoint prime cycles and the roots of all the trees in O(n) time and space.

The procedure to find all cycles and roots makes use of the main data structure shown in Figure 6. This data structure is an array of size n in which the i-th component is a 5-tuple storing information about the i-th vertex in S; i.e., it stores the value f(i), a pointer $f^{-1}\{i\}$ to a list of predecessors of i, a field for the predecessor of i, c_pred(i), on the cycle containing i (This field is undefined when i is not on a cycle.), the label B(i) of i, and a field for the label Q(i) to be determined.

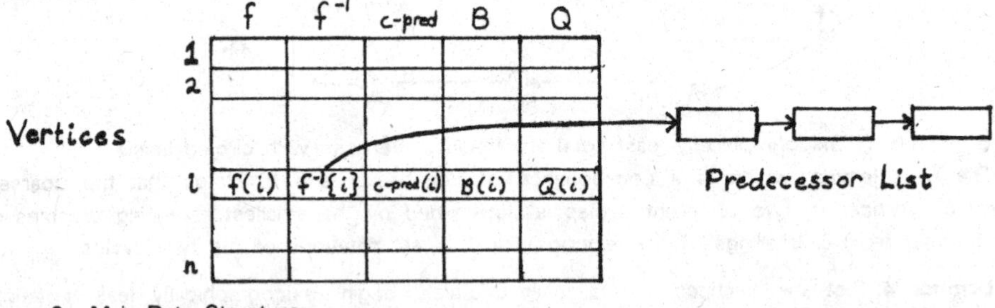

Figure 6. Main Data Structure

Before the algorithm is presented it is useful to give a formal specification of this subproblem. Those vertices that lie on cycles are defined by the following expression

$$\text{cycle\_vertices} = \text{the } T \subset \text{domain } f \cup \text{range } f \mid (\forall x \in T \mid f^{-1}\{x\} \cap T \neq \{\}) \quad \text{maximizing } \#T$$

which denotes the largest subset T of the vertices such that every element of T has a predecessor in T. This specification is implemented by initializing T to the set of vertices, and then repeatedly removing an arbitrary element x from T that has no predecessor y belonging to both $f^{-1}\{x\}$ and T.

To obtain an efficient algorithm, we maintain two invariants while T is being repeatedly diminished. These are

i. a set of reference counts

$$\text{numpred}(i) = \#\{ y \in f^{-1}\{i\} \mid y \in T\}$$

for each vertex i, and

ii. a set

minset = {x ∈ T | numpred (x) = 0}

of elements that can be removed from T in the next iteration.

The algorithm can be made to run in O(n) time and space by using the main data structure (see Figure 6) and an array of size n that stores T, numpred, and minset. For each vertex i=1..n, the i-th component of the array represents T by a bit field which has the value 1 when i belongs to T, and 0 otherwise; a field for numpred(i) is also present. Minset is embedded in the array as a queue.

A procedure to determine the cycle vertices and the tree roots is given by the following steps:

```
i.  initialize T to the set of all vertices, and compute numpred and minset;
ii. while minset ≠ {} repeat the following steps
        a.  remove an arbitrary element 'a' from minset;
        b.  if numpred(f(a)) = 1 then
                add f(a) to minset
            end if
        c.  decrement numpred(f(a))
        d.  delete a from T
iii. cycle_vertices := T
iv.  roots := {x ∈ cycle_vertices | #f⁻¹{x} > 1};
```

It is then a straightforward matter to assign the c__pred field in the main data structure, and to decompose the set of cycle vertices into a list of cycles, where each cycle is stored as a list of vertices reflecting an arbitrary rotation.

STEP 2. Q-Labeling the Cycle Vertices.

The procedure to label the cycle vertices is given just below:

```
i.   Find the lexicographically least rotation with respect to B-labels
        for each cycle.
ii.  Find the smallest repeating prefix of each of these rotations with
        respect to B-labels.
iii. Lexicographically sort the prefixes with respect to B-labels.
iv.  In a single pass through the prefixes sorted in the previous step,
        use rules (7) and (8) to define Q-labels within similar cycles.
        At the same time construct the equivalence classes in a data
        structure diagrammed in Figure 7.
```

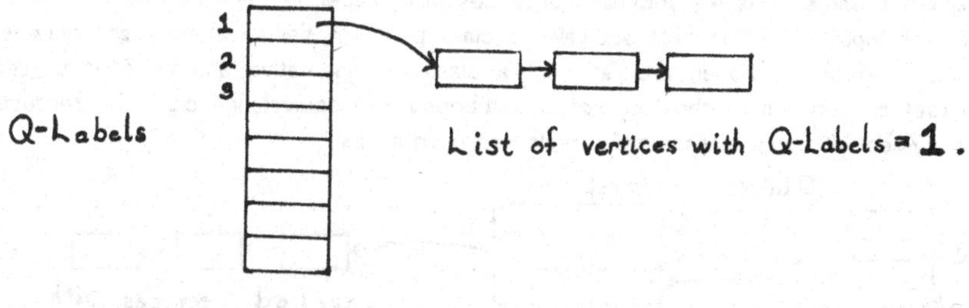

Figure 7. Equivalence classes

The following lemmas are used to show that the preceding steps can be achieved in linear time and space.

Lemma 6: The problem of finding the lexicographically least rotation in a cyclic string of k elements over an alphabet of m <= k elements can be solved in O(k) time and space.

Proof) see either Booth [3] or Shiloach [10] ■

Lemma 7: The problem of finding the smallest repeating prefix of a string of length k can be solved in O(k) time and space.

Proof) Let str be a string of length k. Use the fast string matching algorithm due to Knuth, Pratt, and Morris [6] to find the first occurrence of the substring str in the string str^2. The smallest repeating prefix is the prefix of str^2 up to the character just before the match. ■

Lemma 8: The problem of lexicographically sorting varying length strings over an alphabet of m elements can be solved in O(m) time and space, where the total number of symbols contained in all of the strings is O(m).

Proof) see Aho, Hopcroft, and Ullman [1], pp. 78-84 ■

Theorem 2: The single function coarsest partition problem can be solved for problem instances with no trees in O(n) time and space.

STEP 3. Q-Labeling the Tree Vertices.

After Q-labels have been determined for the cycle vertices, vertices within trees are either given completely new Q-labels, or they are given the same Q-labels assigned to other vertices in previous steps. This procedure is a straightforward closure process with a slight complication that arises when tree vertices are added to the equivalence classes containing cycle vertices. The essential idea for assigning Q-labels for tree vertices in an incremental way is based on the following lemma:

Lemma 9: Let u be an element of S such that $f^{-1}\{u\}$ is empty. If there exists an element x in S such that $x \neq u$, $Q(f(x)) = Q(f(u))$, and $B(x) = B(u)$, then $Q(u) = Q(x)$; otherwise no element of S different from u has the label Q(u).

Proof) Immediate from Lemma 1. ■

Lemma 9 leads to the following inefficient but perspicuous Q-labeling procedure for the tree vertices. Assume that C is the set of all cycles of f, and that Q is the coarsest partition of the function $f|_C$ restricted to C. Then iterate the following two steps until all of the tree vertices have been labeled:

```
i.  Pick an edge [u,v] ∈ f | v ∈ C and u ∉ C.²
ii. Assign a Q-label to u based on Lemma 9, and add u to C.
```

A much more efficient procedure is described as follows. The main data structure supporting this procedure is a dynamic workset of equivalence classes, each containing tree vertices that have the same Q-labels and have predecessors deeper in the tree that have not yet been Q-labeled (see Figure 8). For each equivalence class p, if any vertex in the class resides on a cycle, one such vertex is chosen arbitrarily as a class representative and denoted c_rep(p). Initially the workset contains all of the tree roots partitioned into equivalence classes. Because all roots reside on cycles, all these classes have cycle representatives.

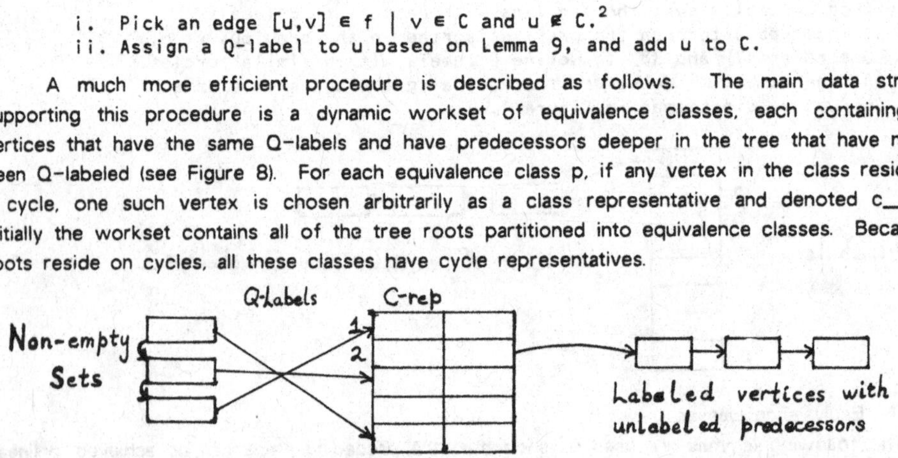

Figure 8. Workset of Equivalence Classes.

The algorithm proceeds by repeatedly performing the following steps until the workset is empty.

```
i. select and remove an equivalence class p from workset;
ii. partition the predecessors (deeper inside the tree) of vertices in p
```

---

[2] Recall that the graph representation of the function f is set of edges.

into groups with common B-labels;

iii. for each such group, if p has no cycle representative, or if p has a cycle representative but the unique B-label for the cycle predecessor of the representative is different from the B-label for vertices in the group, then perform substep a.; otherwise, perform substep b.

a. all vertices in this group will belong to a new equivalence class with a Q-label 1 greater than the largest current Q-label; these new Q-labels are added to the main data structure (fig. 3), and the list of vertices in this group are added to the Q data structure (fig. 7); this list is also added to the workset (fig. 8);

b. all vertices in this group will be added to the equivalence class of the cycle predecessor of the cycle representative of p; the Q-labels for these vertices in the main data structure are set to Q(c_pred(c_rep(p))), and these vertices are appended to the end of the appropriate list entry within the Q data structure; finally, if the equivalence class to which these vertices belong is represented in the workset, append them to the list within the workset; otherwise, insert them into the workset, and assign c_pred(c_rep(p)) as their cycle representative.

Theorem 3: The procedure just outlined to determine Q-labels for the tree vertices costs O(n) in time and space.

Conclusion

The algorithm just presented solves the single function coarsest partition problem in linear time and space. The best previous solution required O(n log n) steps and linear space. Because the many function coarsest partition problem has several important applications including state minimization of finite automata [5] and congruence closure [7, 4], it would be important to see whether our algorithm can be extended to solve the general problem in linear time and space.

References

1. Aho, A., Hopcroft, J., Ullman, J.. *Design and Analysis of Computer Algorithms*. Addison-Wesley, 1974.

2. Birkhoff, G.. *Lattice Theory*. American Mathematical Society, Providence, 1966.

3. Booth, K. S. "Lexicographically Least Circular Substrings." *IPL 10*, 4,5 (July 1980), 240-242.

4. Downey, P., Sethi, R., and Tarjan, R. "Variations on the Common Subexpression Problem." *JACM 27*, 4 (Oct 1980), 758-771.

5. Hopcroft, J.E. An n log n Algorithm for Minimizing States in a Finite Automaton. In *Theory of Machines and Computations*, Kohavi, and Paz, Ed.,Academic Press, New York, 1971, pp. 189-196.

6. Knuth, D.E., Morris, J.H., Pratt, V.R. "Fast Pattern Matching in Strings." *SIAM J. Computing 6*, 2 (1977), 323-350.

7. Nelson, G., and Oppen, D. "Fast Decision Procedures Based on Congruence Closure." *JACM 27*, 2 (Apr 1980).

8. Paige, R., and Koenig, S. "Finite Differencing of Computable Expressions." *ACM TOPLAS 4*, 3 (July 1982), 402-454.

9. Schwartz, J.T. "Automatic Data Structure Choice in a Language of Very High Level." *CACM 18*, 12 (Dec 1975), 722-728.

10. Shiloach, Y. "Fast Canonization of Circular Strings." *Journal of Algorithms 2* (June 1981), 107-121.

COMPLEXITÉ DES FACTEURS DES MOTS INFINIS ENGENDRÉS PAR MORPHISMES ITÉRÉS

JEAN-JACQUES PANSIOT
Université Louis-Pasteur
Centre de Calcul de l'Esplanade
7, rue René-Descartes
67084 Strasbourg Cédex, France

RÉSUMÉ. — EHRENFEUCHT, LEE et ROZENBERG ont montré que la complexité des facteurs des D0L langages (et donc des mots infinis engendrés par morphismes itérés) était majorée par cn^2 (resp. $cn \log n$, cn) suivant que le morphisme est quelconque, croissant ou uniforme. Nous introduisons une classe intermédiaire dont la complexité est majorée par $cn \log\log n$. De plus, nous montrons que tout mot infini engendré par morphisme a une complexité en $O(n^2)$, $O(n \log n)$, $O(n \log\log n)$, $O(n)$ ou $O(1)$ suivant la nature du morphisme.

ABSTRACT. — EHRENFEUCHT, LEE and ROZENBERG have shown that the subword complexity of D0L languages (hence for infinite words obtained by iterated morphisms) is bounded by cn^2 (resp. $cn \log n$, cn) if the morphism is arbitrary (resp. growing, uniform). We introduce a new class with complexity bounded by $cn \log\log n$. Moreover we show that every infinite word generated by morphism has a complexity in $O(n^2)$, $O(n \log n)$, $O(n \log\log n)$, $O(n)$ or $O(1)$ according to the type of the morphism.

1. Introduction et préliminaires.

La *complexité des facteurs* d'un mot infini S (resp. d'un langage L) est la fonction $f(n)$ égale au nombre de facteurs distincts de longueur n de S (resp. des mots de L). Un *D0L système* (*cf.* [RS]) est la donnée d'un triplet $\langle X, g, \alpha \rangle$, où X est un alphabet fini, g un morphisme de X^*, et α un mot de X^* appelé axiome. Le D0L langage engendré par un tel système est $L = \{g^i(\alpha), i \geq 0\}$. EHRENFEUCHT, LEE ET ROZENBERG [ELR] ont étudié la complexité des facteurs des D0L langages en fonction des propriétés de g (voir aussi [ER81a], [ER82], [ER83a], [ER83b], [R]). Un morphisme g est *croissant* (resp. *uniforme* de module $m \geq 2$) si $|g(x)| \geq 2$ pour tout x (resp. $|g(x)| = m$). Il est montré dans [ELR] que la complexité des facteurs d'un D0L langage est majorée par cn^2 (resp. $cn \log n$, cn) suivant que le morphisme à itérer est quelconque, croissant ou uniforme. De plus, il existe des langages atteignant ces bornes.

Dans ce travail, nous donnons des bornes inférieures pour la complexité des facteurs. Nous nous plaçons dans le cadre des mots infinis engendrés par itération de morphisme, qui permet des preuves plus simples que pour les D0L langages.

Soit g un morphisme *prolongeable* en x_0, c'est-à-dire tel que $g(x_0) = x_0u$. Alors $g^{i+1}(x_0)$ commence par $g^i(x_0)$, $i \geq 0$ et la suite $g^i(x_0)$, $i \geq 0$, converge vers un mot unique en général infini que l'on note $g^\omega(x_0)$.

RÉSULTAT. — *Soit $S = g^\omega(x_0)$ un mot infini. Alors il existe des constantes c_1 et c_2, $0 < c_1 \leq c_2$ telles que la complexité $f(n)$ des facteurs de S vérifie $c_1c(n) \leq f(n) \leq c_2c(n)$ où $c(n)$ est l'une des fonctions* 1, n, $n \log\log n$, $n \log n$, *ou* n^2.

En particulier, la complexité de S ne peut pas croître comme $n^{3/2}$, $n(\log n)^2$ ou $n \log^3 n$.

Le comportement asymptotique de la complexité dépend essentiellement d'un critère: la vitesse relative de croissance des images itérées des lettres. On sait (*cf.* [SS], chap. III.7), que $|g^n(x)|$ est soit bornée, soit croissante comme $n^{a_x}b_x^n$ appelé *ordre de x* pour un entier $a_x \geq 0$, et un nombre $b_x \geq 1$.

DÉFINITION. — Un morphisme g est *quasi-uniforme* si toutes les lettres ont le même ordre de croissance, de la forme b^n. Il est *polynomialement divergent* si toute lettre x a un ordre de la forme $n^{a_x}b^n$, avec $b > 1$ et certains a_x non nuls. Finalement, il est *exponentiellement divergent* s'il existe des lettres x et y d'ordre $n^{a_x}b_x^n$ et $n^{a_y}b_y^n$ avec $1 < b_x < b_y$, et $b_z > 1$ pour tout z.

REMARQUES.

a) Nous utiliserons une définition des morphismes croissants un peu plus large que celle de [ELR] : un morphisme est croissant si toute lettre a un ordre de croissance non borné. Ceci entraîne qu'une puissance suffisante de ce morphisme est croissante au sens de [ELR].

b) Un morphisme est croissant si et seulement s'il est soit quasi-uniforme, soit polynomialement ou exponentiellement divergent.

Nous pouvons alors préciser le résultat ci-dessus comme suit.

THÉORÈME. — *Soit $S = g^\omega(x_o)$ un mot infini non ultimement périodique, de complexité $f(n)$.*

(i) Si g est croissant alors $f(n)$ croît comme n, $n \log\log n$, $n \log n$ *suivant que g est quasi-uniforme, polynomialement ou exponentiellement divergent.*

(ii) Si g est non croissant, alors, ou bien $f(n)$ croît comme n^2 ou bien S est l'image par un morphisme non effaçant d'un mot infini S' engendré par un morphisme croissant g'. Dans ce dernier cas, la complexité de S croît comme celle de S', c'est-à-dire comme n, $n \log\log n$, $n \log n$ *suivant le type de g'.*

Dans le paragraphe 2 nous donnons un lemme général permettant d'établir des bornes inférieures sur la complexité. Au paragraphe 3 nous traitons des morphismes croissants, et au paragraphe 4 des morphismes non croissants.

2. Résultat général sur les bornes inférieures pour la complexité.

Soit S un mot infini et $f(n)$ sa complexité. Appelons *biprolongeable* un facteur u de S tel qu'il existe des lettres x et y, $x \neq y$ avec ux et uy facteurs de S. Soit $b(n)$ le nombre de facteurs biprolongeables de S de longueur n. En tenant compte du fait que tout facteur se prolonge d'au moins une façon, on obtient

$$f(n+1) \geq f(n) + b(n) \qquad \text{et} \qquad f(n) \geq \sum_{i=0}^{n-1} b(i).$$

Il suffit donc de minorer $b(n)$ pour minorer la complexité.

LEMME 2.1. — *Soit $S = \alpha_0 x \beta_0 = \alpha_1 x \beta_1 = \cdots = \alpha_i x \beta_i = \cdots$ une suite infinie de factorisations de S et des fonctions $p(n)$, $s(n)$, telles que*

(i) le plus long préfixe p_i commun à β_i et β_{i+1} vérifie p_i ne contient pas x, $|p_i| < |p_{i+1}|$ et $|p_i| \leq p(i)$

(ii) le plus long suffixe s_i commun à α_i et α_{i+1} vérifie $|s_i| \geq s(i)$.

Alors $b(n)$ est minoré par le nombre d'entiers i vérifiant

$$1 + p(i) \leq n \leq 1 + p(i) + s(i). \tag{1}$$

Démonstration. — Soit α un suffixe de s_i. Alors $\alpha x p_i$ est biprolongeable puisque $s_i x p_i$ se prolonge différemment dans $\alpha_i x \beta_i$ et dans $\alpha_{i+1} x \beta_{i+1}$ (sinon p_i ne serait pas maximal). Pour chaque n et chaque i vérifiant $|xp_i| \leq n \leq |s_i x p_i|$ on a donc un mot biprolongeable de longueur n. De plus, pour n fixé et i variable, tous ces mots sont distincts, puisque la dernière occurrence de x apparaît à distance $|p_i|$ de la fin du mot et $i \neq i'$ entraîne $|p_i| \neq |p']i|$ d'après (i). Pour n fixé le nombre de mots est donc bien minoré par le nombre de i vérifiant (1). ∎

Pour différents choix de $p(n)$ et $s(n)$ on obtient les minorations suivantes :

COROLLAIRE 2.2. — *Il existe des constantes positives c et d telles que*

(a) Si $p(n) = k_1 n$ et $s(n) = k_2 n$, $k_1 > 0$, $k_2 > 0$, alors

$$b(n) \geq cn, \quad f(n) \geq dn^2.$$

(b) Si $p(n) = b_1^n$ et $s(n) = b_2^n$, $1 < b_1 < b_2$, alors

$$b(n) \geq c \log n, \quad f(n) \geq dn \log n.$$

(c) Si $p(n) = n^{a_1} b^n$ et $s(n) = n^{a_2} b^n$, $a_1 < a_2$, alors

$$b(n) \geq c \log \log n, \quad f(n) \geq dn \log \log n.$$

Démonstration.

(a) Le nombre de i vérifiant $1 + k_1 i \leq n \leq 1 + k_1 i + k_2 i$ est

$$\left[(n-1)\left(\frac{1}{k_1} - \frac{1}{k_1 + k_2}\right)\right] + 1$$

et on a bien $b(n) \geq cn$, et $f(n) \geq c \sum_{i=1}^{n-1} i \geq dn^2$.

(b) Le nombre de i vérifiant $1 + b_1^i \leq n \leq 1 + b_1^i + b_2^i$ est minoré par le nombre de i vérifiant $1 + i \log b_1 \leq \log n \leq 1 + i \log b_2$ et donc par $c \log n$. D'autre part, $\sum_{i=1}^{n-1} c \log i \geq dn \log n$.

(c) Le nombre de i vérifiant $1 + i^{a_1} b^i \leq n \leq 1 + i^{a_1} b^i + i^{a_2} b^i$ est minoré par le nombre de i vérifiant $1 + i \log b + a_1 \log i \leq \log n \leq 1 + i \log b + a]2 \log i$, soit $(1/\log b)(\log n - 1 - a_2 \log i) \leq i \leq (1/\log b)(\log n - 1 - a_1 \log i$. En minorant a_1 par 0 et $\log i$ par $\log(\log n / \log b)$ on obtient bien $b(n) \geq c \log\log n$ et $f(n) \geq \sum_{i=2}^{n-1} c \log\log i \geq dn \log\log n$. ∎

Nous allons maintenant appliquer ce résultat aux différents types de morphismes.

3. Morphismes croissants.

Pour obtenir des bornes inférieures non triviales, on remarque que tout mot infini S a une complexité $f(n) \leq n$ si et seulement si S est ultimement périodique. Dans ce cas, il existe des constantes c_1 et c_2, $0 < c_1 < c_2$ telles que $c_1 \leq f(n) \leq c_2$, et S peut être engendré par morphisme uniforme. Tout mot infini $S = g^\omega(x_0)$ non ultimement périodique avec g uniforme vérifie donc $c_1 n \leq f(n) \leq c_2 n$, $1 \leq c_1 \leq c_2$, d'après [ELR, théorème 6].

Néanmoins il existe des mots $S = g^\omega(x_0)$ où g n'est pas uniforme, mais où la complexité est linéaire, comme par exemple le mot de Fibonacci engendré par $\varphi : a \mapsto ab$, $b \mapsto a$. Nous allons caractériser la classe des morphismes engendrant des mots de complexité linéaire.

Remarquons qu'un morphisme uniforme de module b est quasi-uniforme, avec des lettres d'ordre b^n. De même, si pour tout couple (x, y) il existe i tel que $g^i(x)$ contienne y, alors x et y ont le même ordre et g est quasi-uniforme (l'inverse n'est pas vrai en général). Ainsi le morphisme de Fibonacci est quasi-uniforme car $\varphi(a)$ contient b et $\varphi(b)$ contient a.

LEMME 3.1. — *Tout mot infini non ultimement périodique $S = g^\omega(x_0)$ où g est quasi-uniforme a une complexité $f(n)$ vérifiant $c_1 n \leq f(n) \leq c_2 n$, $1 \leq c_1 \leq c_2$.*

Démonstration. — La borne inférieure est déjà établie. Pour la borne supérieure, $f(n) \leq c_2 n$, nous allons adapter la preuve de [ELR] pour le cas uniforme. Soit $u = u_0$ un facteur de S de longueur n. Soit u_1 le plus court facteur de S *couvrant* u_0, c'est-à-dire tel que u_0 soit un facteur de $g(u_1)$. Un tel u_1 existe puisque u_0 est facteur de $S = g(S)$. On construit ainsi une suite $u_0, u_1, \ldots, u_k$ où u_{i+1} couvre u_i. Comme g est croissant, on note que si $|u_i| \geq 4$, alors $|u_i| > |u_{i+1}|$. Il existe donc un plus petit k tel que $|u_k| \leq 3$, $|u_{k-1}| \geq 4$. Soit $u_{k-1} = x_1 v x_2$. On a donc $|g^{k-1}(v)| < n$. Soit k_n le plus grand k tel qu'il existe v, $|v| \geq 2$ avec $|g^{k-1}(v)| < n$. Soit l_0 tel que $g^{l_0}(x_0)$ contienne tous les facteurs de longueur au plus trois de S (il en existe un puisque $g^{j+1}(x_0)$ commence par $g^j(x_0)$). Soit $v_0 = g^{l_0}(x_0)$. Alors tout facteur de longueur n de S apparaît dans $g^{k_n}(v_0)$. Le morphisme g étant quasi-uniforme il existe c et c', $0 < c \leq c'$ tels que $cb^n \leq |g^n(x)| \leq c'b^n$, $n \geq 0$. Donc $|g^{k_n}(v_0)| \leq c|v_0|b^{k_n}$. D'autre part $|g^{k_n-1}(v)| < n$ donc $n > c'|v|b^{k_n-1} > c'b^{k_n-1}$. Le nombre de facteurs de longueur n de $g^{k_n}(v_0)$ est majoré par $|g^{k_n}(v_0)| - n + 1 \leq c|v_0|b^{k_n} - n + 1 \leq (c|v_0|/c')bn - n + 1 \leq c_2 n$. ∎

REMARQUE. — Un langage $L \subset X^*$ a une *distribution constante* s'il existe une constante c et un sous-alphabet $Y \subset X$ tels que l'ensemble des lettres apparaissant dans un facteur quelconque de L de longueur c soit exactement Y. Dans [ER 81b], il est montré qu'un D0L langage à distribution constante a une complexité au plus linéaire. Dans le cas d'un D0L langage de la forme $\{g^i(x_0)\}$, g prolongeable en x_0, on observe que nécessairement $Y = X$, et g est quasi-uniforme. La complexité est donc bien linéaire par le théorème ci-dessus.

Nous allons voir que pour un morphisme croissant non quasi-uniforme la complexité des facteurs croît au moins comme $n \log\log n$. Pour un morphisme croissant, la complexité est donc linéaire si et seulement si le morphisme est quasi-uniforme mais non périodique.

LEMME 3.2. — *Pour tout mot infini $S = g^\omega(x_0)$ où g est polynomialement divergent il existe des constantes c_1 et c_2 telles que la complexité $f(n)$ vérifie*

$$c_1 n \log\log n \leq f(n) \leq c_2 n \log\log n.$$

Démonstration. — Montrons tout d'abord la majoration. Soit g un morphisme polynomialement divergent, et $b^n, nb^n, \ldots, n^a b^n$ l'ordre de croissance de ses lettres, $a \geq 1$ (*cf.* [SS, chap. III.7]). En particulier, il existe des constantes c'_1 et c'_2 telles que pour tout u on a $c'_1 b^n |u| \leq |g^n(u)| \leq c'_2 n^a b^n |u|$. Soit u_0 un mot de longueur n facteur de $S = g^\omega(x_0)$. Il est couvert par un facteur u_1 et on peut construire une suite $u_0, u_1, \ldots, u_k$, comme dans la démonstration du Lemme 3.1, avec $|u_k| \leq 3$ et $|u_{k-1}| \geq 4$. Il y a un nombre fini de possibilités pour u_k. Il suffit donc de majorer le nombre de u_0 provenant d'un $u = u_k$ fixé. On a $g(u) = x_1vx_2$ et $g^{k-1}(v)$ est un facteur de u_0, lui-même facteur de $g^{k-1}(x_1vx_2)$. Pour k fixé, il y a au plus $n - |g^{k-1}(v)| + 1$ possibilités, soit au plus n. Pour u et n fixés comptons maintenant le nombre de valeurs possibles pour k. On a $|g^{k-1}(v)| < n < |g^{k-1}(x_1vx_2)|$, soit $|v|c'_1b^{k-1} \leq n \leq |x_1vx_2|c'_2(k-1)^ab^{k-1}$. Le nombre de k vérifiant cette inégalité est donc majoré par $c''_2 \log\log n$. Pour chaque k il y a au plus n valeurs de u_0 possible. On a donc bien $f(n) \leq c_2 n \log\log n$.

Pour la minoration, on considère une lettre x d'ordre maximum n^ab^n. Alors pour i assez grand, $g^i(x)$ contient au moins deux lettres d'ordre n^ab^n, donc S contient une infinité de telles lettres. Il existe alors un facteur $x_1u_1x'_1$, où x_1 et x'_1 sont d'ordre n^ab^n, et les lettres de u_1 sont d'ordre au plus $n^{a-1}b^n$. Soient $g(x_i) = v_{i+1}x_{i+1}u_{i+1}$, $g(x'_i) = u'_{i+1}x'_{i+1}v'_{i+1}$, où x_{i+1} et x'_{i+1} sont d'ordre n^ab^n, et les lettres de u_{i+1} et u'_{i+1} sont d'ordre inférieur. En considérant la suite

$$x_1u_1x'_1, x_2u_2g(u_1)u'_2x'_2, \dots, x_iu_ig(u_{i-1})\dots g^{i-2}(u_2)g^{i-1}(u_1)g^{i-2}(u'_2)\dots u'_ix'_i$$

on observe que les suites x_i, $i \geq 0$ et x'_i, $i \geq 0$ sont ultimement périodiques. En prenant une puissance appropriée de g, on peut donc supposer qu'il existe un facteur xu_0x' de S avec $g(x) = vxu$, $g(x') = u'x'v'$ où x et x' sont d'ordre n^ab^n, et u, u_0, u' sont d'ordre inférieur.

Considérons maintenant la suite de factorisations de $S = \alpha_1x\beta_1 = \alpha_2x\beta_2 = \dots = \alpha_ix\beta_i = \dots$, où β_1 commence par u_0x' et où $\alpha_i = g(\alpha_{i-1})v$, $\beta_i = ug(\beta_{i-1})$. Soit p_i le plus long préfixe commun à β_i et β_{i+1}. Si u est non vide, il croît strictement. Si u est vide, il faut remplacer g par une de ses puissances telle que le plus long préfixe commun à $g^i(u_0)$ et $g^{i+1}(u_0)$ soit strictement croissant. Il est clair que p_i qui ne contient que des lettres d'ordre inférieur à n^ab^n ne peut contenir x. Finalement, on a

$$\begin{aligned} |p_i| &\leq |ug(u)\dots g^{i-1}(u)g^i(u_0)g^{i-1}(u')\dots g(u')u'| \\ &\leq c'_2|uu'|\sum_{j=0}^{i-1} j^{a-1}b^j + c'_2|u_0|i^{a-1}b^i \\ &\leq ci^{a-1}b^i. \end{aligned}$$

D'autre part, le plus long suffixe s_i commun à α_i et α_{i+1} croît au moins comme $c'i^ab^i$, d'où le lemme d'après le Corollaire 2.2. ∎

EXEMPLE. — Soit g le morphisme défini par $x \mapsto xyxy$, $y \mapsto yy$. Alors on a $|g^n(y)| = 2^n$ et $|g^n(x)| = (n+1)2^n$. Le morphisme g est donc polynomialement divergent, et il engendre un mot infini de complexité en $O(n \log\log n)$.

LEMME 3.3. — *Pour tout mot infini $S = g^\omega(x_0)$ où g est croissant exponentiellement divergent, il existe des constantes c_1 et c_2 telles que la complexité $f(n)$ de S vérifie $c_1 n \log n \leq f(n) \leq c_2 n \log n$.*

Démonstration. — La borne supérieure est donnée dans [ELR, théorème 4]. Pour la borne inférieure on applique le même raisonnement que pour le cas polynomialement divergent. On considère un facteur $x_1 u_1 x'_1$ tel que x_1 et x'_1 soient d'ordre maximal ($n^{a_1} b^n$ et $n^{a_2} b^n$) et les lettres de u_1 sont d'ordre au plus $n^a b'^n$, $b' < b$. On obtient cette fois les relations $|p^i| \leq c'_1 n^a b'^n \leq c''_1 b''^n$, avec $b' \leq b'' \leq b$ et $|s_i| \geq c'_2 b^n$, d'où le lemme par le Corollaire 2.2. ∎

Les trois lemmes précédents peuvent se résumer dans le théorème qui suit:

THÉORÈME 3.4. — *Soit $S = g^\omega(x_0)$ un mot infini non ultimement périodique, où g est croissant. Alors il existe des constantes c_1 et c_2 telles que la complexité $f(n)$ de S vérifie*

$$c_1 c(n) \leq f(n) \leq c_2 c(n)$$

où $c(n) = n$ (resp. $n \log \log n$, $n \log n$) si et seulement si g est quasi-uniforme (resp. polynomialement, exponentiellement divergent).

4. Morphismes non croissants.

Soit g un morphisme non croissant. Il existe donc une lettre x telle que $|g^n(x)|$ soit bornée. Soit B l'ensemble des lettres bornées et C l'ensemble des lettres croissantes.

THÉORÈME 4.1. — *Soit $S = g^\omega(x_0)$ un mot infini non ultimement périodique où g est non croissant. Alors l'une (et une seule) des deux propriétés suivantes est vraie:*

(i) S contient des facteurs arbitrairement longs dans B^*, et sa complexité $f(n)$ vérifie $c_1 n^2 \leq f(n) \leq c_2 n^2$, $c_1 > 0$.

(ii) Les facteurs de S dans B^* sont de longueur bornée, il existe un alphabet Y, un morphisme croissant $g' : Y^* \to Y^*$, $y_0 \in Y$ et un morphisme non effaçant $h : Y^* \to X^*$, tels que $S = h(S')$ où $S' = g'^\omega(y_0)$.

Dans le second cas, la complexité de S croît asymptotiquement comme celle de S', c'est-à-dire en $O(n \log n)$, $O(n \log \log n)$, ou $O(n)$ suivant que g' est exponentiellement divergent, polynomialement divergent ou quasi-uniforme.

EXEMPLE 1. — Soit $X = \{a, b, c\}$ et g défini par $a \mapsto ab$, $b \mapsto bc$, et $c \mapsto c$. La lettre c est non croissante, et le mot infini

$$S = g^\omega(a) = abc^0bc^1bc^2b\ldots bc^ib\ldots$$

contient des facteurs de c^* non bornés. Ce mot a donc une complexité quadratique.

EXEMPLE 2. — Soit $X = \{a, b, c\}$ et g défini par $a \mapsto acb$, $b \mapsto bca$, et $c \mapsto c$. Seule la lettre c est non croissante, et le mot infini $S = g^\omega(a)$ a seulement ϵ et c comme facteurs de c^*. En fait $S = h(S')$ où S' est le mot infini de Thue-Morse, engendré par $g' : a \mapsto ab$, $b \mapsto ba$, et où $h : a \mapsto ac$, $b \mapsto bc$ (*cf.*[P]). La complexité de S est donc linéaire comme celle de S'.

Pour prouver le Théorème 4.1 nous allons utiliser le lemme suivant:

LEMME 4.2 . — *Soient S et S' deux mots infinis et h un morphisme non effaçant tel que $h(S') = S$. Alors il existe des constantes positives a , b telles que les complexités $f(n)$ et $f'(n)$ de S et S' vérifient $f(n) \le af'(n+b)$.*

Démonstration. — Soit f'' le nombre de facteurs de longueur n de S de la forme $h(u)$, où u est facteur de S'. Si $|h(u)| = |h(v)| = n$, $h(u) \ne h(v)$ alors u ne peut être un préfixe de v. Donc u et v se prolongent en deux facteurs distincts de longueur n de S' ,et $f''(n) \le f'(n)$. Soit $K = \max\{|h(x)|\}$ et u un facteur de longueur n de S. Alors u est un facteur d'un mot de la forme $h(v)$, où $n \le |h(v)| \le n + 2K - 2$, et v est facteur de S'. Donc $f(n)$ est majorée par

$$f''(n)+2f''(n+1)+\cdots+Kf''(n+K-1)+(K-1)f''(n+K)+\cdots+f''(n+2K-2).$$

Comme f' est croissante on a bien le résultat avec $a = K^2$ et $b = 2K - 2$. ∎

Démonstration du théorème 4.1. — Soit $x \in B$. Il existe donc i et j tels que $g^i(x) = g^j(x)$. Quitte à remplacer g par une de ses puissances, on peut supposer que $g^i(x) = g(x)$, $x \in B$, $i \ge 1$.

Premier cas. — Le mot S contient des facteurs arbitrairement longs dans B^*. Soit $g(x_0) = x_0\alpha$. Nécessairement α contient une lettre croissante, sinon $g^\omega(x_0) = x_0\alpha g(\alpha)\dots g^i(\alpha)\dots = x_0\alpha(g(\alpha))^\omega$, et S serait ultimement périodique. Le mot S contient donc une infinité de lettres croissantes. Pour que les facteurs de S dans B^* soient non bornés, il faut qu'il existe une lettre croissante x et un entier i tels que $g^i(x) = vxu$ (ou uxv) avec $v \in X^*$, $u \in B^+$. Quitte à remplacer g par une de ses puissances, il existe donc un facteur xu_0x' de S avec $g(x) = vxu$, $g(x') = u'x'v'$ où u_0, $u' \in B^*$, $u \in B^+$. Considérons la suite de factorisations $S = \alpha_0 x\beta_0 = \cdots = \alpha_i x\beta_i = \dots$, où β_0 commence par u_0x', et où $\alpha_{i+1} = g(\alpha_i)v$, $\beta_{i+1} = ug(\beta_i)$. Le plus long préfixe commun p_i à β_i et β_{i+1} vérifie

$$\begin{aligned}|p_i| &\le |ug(u)\dots g^{i-1}(u)g^i(u_0)g^{i-1}(u')\dots g(u')u'|\\ &\le |u(g(u))^{i-1}g(u_0)(g(u'))^{i-1}u'|\\ &\le k_1 i.\end{aligned}$$

Considérons maintenant le plus long suffixe s_i commun à α_i et α_{i+1}. Si $g(v) \neq \epsilon$ alors α_i se termine par $(g(v))^{i-1}v$ donc $|s_i| \geq k_2 i$. Si $g(v) = \epsilon$, on considère la dernière lettre croissante z dans $\alpha_0 = \alpha'_0 z w_0$, $w_0 \in B^*$, et on peut supposer que $g(z) = tzw$, $w \in B^*$. Alors s_i se termine par $(g(w))^{i-1} g(w_0)v$ si $g(w)$ est non vide, et par $g^{i-1}(t) \ldots g(t)tzwg(w_0)v$ sinon. Dans les deux cas on a bien $|s_i| \geq k_2 i$, et $c_1 n^2 \leq f(n) \leq c_2 n^2$ d'après le Corollaire 2.2 pour la minoration et [ELR, théorème 2] pour la majoration.

Deuxième cas. — Les facteurs de S dans B^* sont bornés. Soit $S = x_0 \alpha_0 x_1 \ldots$, où x_0, $x_1 \in C$, $\alpha_0 \in B^*$. Soit Y l'alphabet composé de tous les symboles $[x\alpha x']$ où $x\alpha x'$ est un facteur de S, avec $\alpha \in B^*$, $x, x' \in C$. Cet alphabet est fini par hypothèse. On définit le morphisme g' de Y^* par

$$g'([x\alpha x']) = [z_1 \alpha_1 z_2][z_2 \alpha_2 z_3] \ldots [z_k \alpha_k z_{k+1}],$$

où $g(x\alpha) = \alpha_0 z_1 \alpha_1 z_2 \ldots \alpha_{k-1} z_k \alpha_k'$ et $g(x')$ commence par $\alpha''_k z_{k+1}$, avec $\alpha'_k \alpha''_k = \alpha_k$, $\alpha_i \in B^*$, $z_i \in C$. Il est clair que l'ordre de croissance de $[x\alpha x']$ pour g' est le même que celui de x pour g, et g' est donc croissant. On définit le morphisme h de Y^* dans X^* par $[x\alpha x'] \mapsto x\alpha$. En posant $S' = g'^{\omega}([x_0 \alpha_0 x_1])$ on a alors $g^i(x_0)$ préfixe de $h(g'^i([x_0 \alpha_0 x_1]))$, $i \geq 1$, et $S = h(S')$. Par le Lemme 4.2 on a la relation $f(n) \leq af'(n+b)$ entre les complexités de S et de S'. Par ailleurs on observe que si $u_1 y_1$ et $u_2 y_2$ sont deux facteurs de S' de longueur n, $u_1 \neq u_2$, et y_1, y_2 des lettres alors $h(u_1 y_1)$ et $h(u_2 y_2)$ se prolongent en deux facteurs distincts de S de longueur Kn ($K = \max\{|h(y)|, y \in Y\}$). Donc $f'(n-1) \leq f(Kn)$ et $f(n) \leq af'(n+b)$, d'où le théorème. ∎

REMARQUE. — Nous avons vu que si la complexité d'un mot infini $S = g^{\omega}(x_0)$ est en $O(n^2)$, alors il existe un facteur u non vide tel que u^i soit facteur de S, $i \geq 1$. Il en découle immédiatement que si S est sans carré, et plus généralement sans $k^{ième}$ puissance, $k \geq 2$, alors la complexité de S est au plus en $O(n \log n)$ et au moins en $O(n)$. Ceci est à rapprocher des résultats sur les D0L langages sans carré (*cf.*[ER 81a],[ER 83b]).

RÉFÉRENCES

[ELR] EHRENFEUCHT (A.), LEE (K.P.) and ROZENBERG (G.). — Subword complexities of various classes of deterministic developmental languages without interaction, *Theoretical Computer Science*, t. **1**, 1975, p. 59–75.

[ER81a] EHRENFEUCHT (A.) and ROZENBERG (G.). — On the subword complexity of square-free D0L-languages, *Theoretical Computer Science*, t. **16**, 1981, p. 25–32.

[ER81b] EHRENFEUCHT (A.) and ROZENBERG (G.). — On the subword complexity of D0L-languages with a constant distribution, *Information Processing Letters*, t. **13**, 1981, p. 108–113.

[ER82] EHRENFEUCHT (A.) and ROZENBERG (G.). — On subword complexities of homomorphic images of languages, *R.A.I.R.O. Informatique Théorique*, t. **16**, 1982, p. 303–316.

[ER83a] EHRENFEUCHT (A.) and ROZENBERG (G.). — On the subword complexity of locally catenative D0L-languages, *Information Processing Letters*, t. **16**, 1983, p. 7–9.

[ER83b] EHRENFEUCHT (A.) and ROZENBERG (G.). — On the subword complexity of m-free D0L-languages, *Information Processing Letters*, t. **17**, 1983, p. 121–124.

[P] PANSIOT (J.-J.). — Hiérarchie et fermeture de certaines classes de tag-systèmes, *Acta Informatica*, t. **20**, 1983, p. 179–196.

[R] ROZENBERG (G.). — On the subword complexity of formal languages, *Fundamentals of Computation Theory* [Proc. FCT Conf., Szeged, Hungary. 1981], p. 328–333. — Berlin, Springer-Verlag (*Lecture Notes in Computer Science*, **117**, 1981).

[RS] ROZENBERG (G.) and SALOMAA (A.). — *The Mathematical Theory of L-systems.* — New York, Academic Press, 1980.

[SS] SALOMAA (A.) and SOITTOLA (M.). — *Automata Theoretic Aspects of Formal Power Series.* — New York, Springer-Verlag, 1978.

AUTOMATES BOUSTROPHEDON, SEMI-GROUPE DE BIRGET ET MONOIDE INVERSIF LIBRE.

J.P Pécuchet, LITP, Laboratoire d'Informatique,
Faculté des Sciences et des Techniques, BP 67,
76130 Mont-Saint-Aignan, France.

Abstract : The power of two-way automata is showed to be unaltered by various recognition rules. Some properties of the rational sets in the Birget's semigroup and the free inverse monoide are deduced.

Résumé : On montre que la puissance des automates boustrophédon reste inchangée pour divers modes de reconnaissance. On en déduit certaines propriétés des parties rationnelles du semi-groupe de Birget et du monoïde inversif libre.

PROBABILISTIC BIDDING GIVES OPTIMAL DISTRIBUTED RESOURCE ALLOCATION†

John Reif
Aiken Computation Laboratory, Harvard University
Paul Spirakis
Courant Institute of Mathematical Sciences, New York University

ABSTRACT

In this paper we consider a fundamental problem of *resource allocation* in a distributed network. Each user's demands for resources may change dynamically and the processors speeds can vary dynamically. Let v be the maximum number of users competing for a particular resource at any time instant. Let k be the maximum number of resources that a user is willing to get, at any time instant. This problem was previously formulated in [Lynch, 1980]. It has application (1) to two-phase locking in databases (2) to generalized dining philosophers, and (3) to the implementation of a novel extension of the CSP language, called Social-CSP and to many other applications to concurrent programming.

Informally we say that an algorithm for this problem is *real time* if its response time is upper bounded by a function which does not depend on any global measure of the system of processes and resources, except k and v. [Reif, Spirakis, 1982b] gave the first known real time algorithms to the problem, with (mean) response time of $O(v^k)$. This response time may be too long, however, in applications where k has a large value.

In this paper we provide new algorithms whose response time is *polynomial* to v and k. Our most efficient new algorithm has expected response time $O(vk)$. Moreover, our constant factors appear to be small enough for practical applications.

Unlike our previous probabilistic algorithms of [Reif, Spirakis, 1982b], we do not use random delays as means of avoiding process starvation and of achieving probabilistic fairness. Instead, our new algorithm utilizes a method of *probabilistic bidding*, to resolve contention of users for resources. This technique is essential in our achievement of polynomial response time.

We furthermore prove that our solution is *optimal* with respect to the average response to a user's request. In particular we provide matching *lower bounds* for any distributed algorithm for resource allocation, and these bounds are within a constant factor of the response time of our own algorithms.

We also provide a suboptimal algorithm which is useful for improving the throughput rate of resource allocation in systems where the majority of users is willing to get only a few resources. This suboptimal algorithm does use random waits combined with probabilistic bidding. These techniques employ limited parallelism within each process, together with the probabilistic bidding. (This limited parallelism is useful in achieving optimal response time, though we would still get polynomial response time without limited parallelism.)

1. INTRODUCTION

1.1 Resource Granting Systems. In this paper, we consider a resource allocation problem previously described in [Lynch, 1980] and generalized in [Reif, Spirakis, 1982b]. The system has potentially an infinite set of processes π and each process has an integer name. There is a potentially infinite set of resources ρ in the system. Let $R \subseteq \pi$ be the set of processes which control resources. The set of user's processes is $U = \pi - R$. Each resource $\rho(j) \in \rho$ is controlled by a distinct granting process j. This process has the responsibility of granting each resource to a distinct user process in U, so no two different processes in U may use the same resource at the same time. We assume that there is a global time which totally orders events, but processes may not have access to the global time. User processes communicate only with those granting processes for which they request resources.

A system as above is called a *Resource Granting System* (RGS); see [Reif, Spirakis, 1982b]. The goal of an RGS is to satisfy dynamically changing user requests for resource allocation, in a distributed way, by only a local communication between granting and requesting processes.

†This work was supported in part by the National Science Foundation Grants NSF-MCS79-21024 and NSF-MCS-8300630, and the Office of Naval Research Contract N00-14-80-C-0647.

The set of possible schedules of processes actions is determined by an "adversary" oracle $\mathcal{A}$ which has the power to set actions in the worst possible way to increase the response time. $\mathcal{A}$ has also the capability to select at time $t=0$ the schedule of speeds of all processes at all times $t \geq 0$. In addition, at each time $t \geq 0$, the requests by user processes U are specified by $\mathcal{A}$. The adverse oracle $\mathcal{A}$ is restricted, to allow users to keep asking for their resources until they are granted. In practice, no such $\mathcal{A}$ may exist but coincidence of worst case situations may replace its action.

Let a process be *tame* during a time interval Δ, if for any interval Δ' which intersects Δ and is a single step of the process, then $|\Delta'| \in [r_{min}, r_{max}]$ where r_{min}, r_{max} are fixed real constants with $0 < r_{min} \leq r_{max}$. We do not require processes to be tame at all times. However, our proof that our techniques are real time makes use of the assumption that processes are tame. Finally, we assume that processes are *reliable* in the sense that they perfectly execute their programs. See Sections 1.2 and 1.3 for further details of this model and for precise definition of response time. (Sections 1.2 and 1.3 may be skipped in a first reading of the paper.)

1.2 The RGS Model. A process *step* consists of either an assignment of a variable, a test, a logical or arithmetic operator or a no-op. A step is considered to be a finite time interval Δ in which a single primitive instruction is executed just at the last moment of Δ, and no other instructions are executed within Δ. Let a process be *tame* during a time interval Δ, if for any interval Δ' which intersects Δ and is a single step of the process, then $|\Delta'| \in [r_{min}, r_{max}]$ where r_{min}, r_{max} are fixed real constants with $0 < r_{min} \leq r_{max}$. We will not require processes to be tame at all times. However our proof that our algorithms are real time makes an assumption that processes are tame. We assume that processes are *reliable* in the sense that they perfectly execute their programs. The rate of execution varies dynamically. We require that, at no time, any granting process $i \in R$ simultaneously grant the resource $\rho(i)$ to more than one requesting process. We also require that, as soon as a process $j \in U$ has got all its required resources, then it can keep them only for a time interval whose length is upper bounded by a fixed parameter δ (containing at most $\mu = \delta/r_{min}$ steps, if the process is tame). Let $\text{resource}_t(i)$ be the set of resources that process i is requesting at time instant t. Let $k_{i,t}$ be $|\text{resources}_t(i)|$. Let $\text{askers}_t(j)$ be the set of user processes requesting $\rho(j)$ for $j \in R$ at time t. Let $v_{j,t}$ be $|\text{askers}_j(t)|$. We assume that at all times $t \geq 0$, $v_{j,t}$ and $k_{i,t}$ are upper bounded by constants v,k respectively and that $k \leq v$. (This does not necessarily imply any bounds on $|\bigcup_{t=0}^{\infty} \text{resources}_t(i)|$ or $|\bigcup_{t=0}^{\infty} \text{askers}_t(j)|$ for any i in U or j in R.

With respect to interprocess communication we assume (1) that each resource allocator $j \in R$ has a set S_j available to it of size at most v, containing the names of those processes willing to get the resource. As in [Lynch, 1980] we assume this to be a primitive of our system (it could be implemented by a queued message system, for example) (2) that synchronization must be done by special variables, called *flags*, each of which is written only by one process and read by at most one other process. Read-write conflicts on flags are excluded by our process step semantics and by our notion of global time. Flags seem to be the simplest primitives for synchronization and lead to an easy implementation (in contrast to distributed shared variables of multiple readers and writers).

1.3 Implementations and Complexity of an RGS. An *implementation* of an RGS determines the synchronization algorithms that the processes run. As stated above, the synchronization algorithms use only flags to implement the synchronization between processes. We consider a time-varying hypergraph H_t, with node set π and time-varying hyperedge set $E_t = \{\{i\} \cup \text{resource}_t(i) \mid i \in U\}$, i.e., where a hyperedge at time instant t is the set of nodes of π consisting of a single process i in U and the granting processes of the resources i is willing to get at t. An RGS implementation dynamically achieves distributed matchings in the hypergraph H_t.

For each adverse oracle $\mathcal{A}$, let the *response time* of the RGS implementation by the random variable $\gamma_{\mathcal{A},k}$ which is the length of the smallest interval Δ required for any process $i \in U$ to have k resource request simultaneously granted, given that i requested these resources during the entire interval Δ and assuming that, i and all allocators of the resource requested by i within Δ, are tame within Δ.

Let the *mean response* $\bar{\gamma}_k$ be the $\max\{\text{mean}\{\gamma_{A,k}\}$ over all oracles $A\}$. Let the ε-*response* be the minimum $\gamma_k(\varepsilon)$ such that for every oracle $\mathcal{A}$ $\text{prob}\{\gamma_{A,k} \leq \gamma_k(\varepsilon)\} \geq 1-\varepsilon$. The RGS implementation is *real time* if $\forall \varepsilon \in (0,1], \gamma_k(\varepsilon) > 0$ and upper bounded by a function independent of any *global measure* of the network. (Note: A *global measure* of the network is any positive function g of $h = |\pi|$ such that $\lim_{h\to\infty} \frac{v}{g(h)} = 0$). Hence if an RGS implementation is real time, then the mean response $\bar{\gamma}_k$ is also upper bounded by a function independent of any global measure of the network.

1.4 Previous Work. [Rabin, 1980a] first applied probabilistic choice to synchronization problems in distributed systems and provided a solution to the dining philosophers problem which, with probability 1, is deadlock free and starvation free. [Rabin, 1980b] applied probabilistic coordination methods to synchronize access to processes to a critical resource in a space-efficient manner. [Frances and Rodeh, 1980] and [Itai and Rodeh, 1981] also proposed probabilistic techniques for synchronization and leader election problems, respectively.

[Lynch, 1980] first posed the localized resource allocation problem as a formal synchronization problem. Let the resource graph G be the graph whose nodes are the resources and two resources are connected by an edge if there is ever a user process requesting both of them, maybe at different times. Let $\chi(G)$ be the chromatic number of G. The implementation proposed by Lynch was a deterministic one in which processes should know the color of each resource in a coloration of G. The response time achieved in [Lynch, 1980] is of the order of $\chi(G)v^{\chi(G)}\cdot\tau$ where τ is the time necessary for interprocess communication. This was not a real time implementation since $\chi(G)$ is $\Omega(|\pi|)$ in general.

[Reif, Spirakis, 1982b] provided the first real time RGS implementation, with mean response time $O(kv^{k+2}\log v)$. In that previous work, we used the techniques of probabilistic selection of processes by resource allocators and random waits to avoid adverse schedules of speeds which might be set up by the oracle. Although this was a real time implementation, it was still exponential in k.

1.5 The New Results of This Paper. We shall present (in Section 3) a probabilistic implementation of an RGS, with mean response $O(kv)$. To achieve this response, we make essential use of the probabilistic bidding technique, together with use of limited parallelism within each user process and each resource allocator. In our *uniform bidding* algorithm, we do not use random waits to achieve probabilistic fairness. Instead we use only the probabilistic bidding technique. In particular, we slice the time of each process into rounds. In each round each user process tries to get all the wanted resources. It has to get all of them in the same round. The users deny the allocation of resources to them, unless all the required resources are offered to be allocated in a small number of steps. At the end of the round, users release their allocated resources (if any) and make a fresh start. User rounds have the same length in steps for all users and this length is a parameter of the algorithm. In contrast, resource rounds are not of the same length and their length in steps is not fixed in advance, but adjusts to the conditions of the algorithm. We conjecture that this is essential in avoiding exponential growth of the response with k.

We also prove lower bounds of $\Omega(kv)$ for the worst case and average response time of any algorithm for the local resource allocation problem. Thus our proposed technique is of optimal performance within a constant factor. We also provide a *priority bidding* algorithm which has mean response time polynomial in k (however not optimal) and is useful for improving the throughput rate of resource allocations in the network. In particular, it allows user processes which demand less than k resources to have higher probability of being assigned. This algorithm has the property that if a user $i \in U$ has a request of at most $k_i \leq k$ resources, then it has mean response $O(vk_i \log k \log(k_i v))$.

1.6 Applications. *Example 1: Social CSP.* An extension of CSP, defined and discussed in [Francez, Reif, 1984], has an efficient implementation by our real time RGS. Social-CSP has the following new commands:

(1) *Extended Output Command:* $(p_{j_1},\ldots,p_{j_k})!(u_1,\ldots,u_k)$ in which the sender process simultaneously sends the value u_ℓ to proces p_{j_ℓ}, $\ell=1,\ldots,k$. Here, "simultaneously" means that the receipt of a value by a process named in the output command does not affect in any way the receipt of the values by other processes named in the output command. Note that (1) can be considered as the generalization of a broadcast command.

(2) *Extended Input Command:* $(p_{i_1},\ldots,p_{i_k})?(x_1,\ldots,x_k)$ where the receiver process simultaneously gets a value for its variable x_ℓ from process p_{i_ℓ}, $\ell=1,\ldots,k$.

Although these extended input and output commands can, in theory, be simulated in Hoare's CSP, it is not clear how to provide an efficient simulation. The power of the new constructs of Social-CSP can be demonstrated by the simplicity they give to a program solving the k-fork philosophers problem. In contrast, it is not known how to solve the k-fork philosophers problem by the conventional CSP constructs. (See also our Example 2, below.)

Social-CSP commands can be directly implemented by our RGS real time implementation, by considering the sender in the output command (respectively the receiver in the input command) as a user process and the processes $p_{j_1},\ldots,p_{j_k}$ (respectively $p_{i_1},\ldots,p_{i_k}$) as resource granting processes. Note that our implementation of Social-CSP allows for unspecified or computed targets of communication, since the identities of the resources a user wants may change dynamically. (This is useful in case of routing protocols and was first considered in [Francez, 1982].)

Example 2: k-fork Philosophers. As a simple example of the usefulness of RGS, consider a generalization of the dining philosophers problem to the case where each philosopher requires k-forks to eat. (This problem was first considered in [Lynch, 1980]). We extend it to the case where the identities of the forks required by each philosopher change dynamically. Let the set of "forks" be $R = \{r_1,\ldots,r_n\}$ and the set of "philosophers" be $U = \{u_1,\ldots,u_n\}$ and let $\text{resources}_t(u_i) = \{r_i, r_{(i+1)\bmod n},\ldots,r_{(1+k-1)\bmod n}\}$ and $\text{askers}_t(r_i) = \{u_{(i-k+1)\bmod n},\ldots,u_{(i-1)\bmod n},u_i\}$ for all t. Our new resource allocation algorithm achieves mean response time $O(k^2)$. In contrast, our previous results achieved mean response time $O(k^{k+3})$, (see [Reif, Spirakis, 1982b]).

Example 3: Two-Phase Locking in Databases. Two-phase locking is a concurrency control method in databases; for a survey see [Bernstein, Goodman, 1980]. It has the feature that as soon as a transaction releases a lock, it never obtains additional locks. A very efficient static implementation of two-phase locking can be achieved by our methods. Our assumption is that transactions are allowed to act on the data only if they got all the locks requested. In the context of such a database system, let the users in U be called *transaction modules* and the processes of R be called *data modules*. If the readsets of the transactions are of cardinality at most k at each time instant and if at most v transactions can compete for a lock at a time instant t, then our optimal RGS will result in an $O(vk)$ mean response time per transaction. Our suboptimal RGS achieves an even smaller mean response time when $|\text{readset}_i(t)| = O(k)$. In this case, if a transaction wants to lock k_i data items at a time, it has a mean response $O(vk_i \log(vk_i)\log k)$. (However, this becomes $O(vk \log(vk)\log k)$ when $|\text{readset}_i(t)| = k$). Our implementations of two phase locking proposed in this paper are asymptotically more efficient than the static locking method proposed in [Reif, Spirakis, 1982b], which had a mean response $O(kv^{k+2})$. This our new algorithm becomes advantageous in cases of database systems with small granularity of locking and hence very large cardinality of transaction readsets. In those cases other known algorithms are impractical since they have response time exponential in k.

2. AN $\Omega(kv)$ LOWER BOUND FOR THE LOCAL RESOURCE ALLOCATION PROBLEM

THEOREM 1. *For* $k > 0$ *and* $v \geq k$, *there is a network in which at least one user process has to have a response time of at least* $(kv-1)\mu$ *steps.*

Proof. Consider a network with a set of resources R such that $|R| = k$ and a set of users U such that $|U| = kv$. Let $\mathcal{A}$ be an oracle such that all processes are equispeed, synchronous and such that $\forall t \geq 0$, $\forall j \in U$, $|\text{resources}_t(j)| \geq (k/2)+1$. Then, only one user process can be granted all its resources at each time instant t. To see this, assume for sake of contradiction that at least two users j_1, j_2 are granted all their resources at time t. Each resource has to be granted to only one user at a time, thus forming a bipartite matching of the hypergraph H_t, as defined previously in Section 1.3. Hence we conclude that the number of allocated resources at time t is

$$|\text{resources}_t(j_1)| + |\text{resources}_t(j_2)| \geq k+2 > k \qquad \text{for all} \quad j \geq 0 \ .$$

This implies that resources will be allocated to processors *serially*, hence the last process of the serial order will have a response time of at least $(kv-1)\mu$ steps. The above holds independently of the synchronization technique. □

COROLLARY. *Our probabilistic bidding algorithm of Section 2 has optimal mean response within a constant factor.*

Proof. By Theorem 1 and by the fact that given any multiset of serial orders of kv elements, there is at least one element whose *average* position (over the multiset of orders) is at least $\lfloor kv/2 \rfloor$. □

3. OUR DISTRIBUTED UNIFORM PROBABILISTIC BIDDING ALGORITHM

We assume that the requesting processes communicate only to the resource allocators whose resources they want (or have been allocated), and that each granting process j is willing to communicate only to the requesting processes in the set S_j (as defined in Section 1.2). The actions of the requesting and granting processes are time-sliced in *rounds*, each round being a repetition of a basic set of actions. Processes use independent sequences of probabilistic choices as the basic construct to counteract adverse speed schedules and adverse resource demands set up by the oracle $\mathcal{A}$. We assume that $\mathcal{A}$ cannot affect or foresee the results of these probabilistic choices. We allow each user in V and each resource allocator in R to have a set of synchronous parallel subprocesses, which aid in our algorithms. The use of local parallelism here is not actually essential in achievement of polynomial response time.

3.1 An Informal Description of the Rounds.

a. *The User's Round*. A user's round starts with the user drawing (with equal probability) a random number in the set $\{1,2,\ldots,\beta kv\}$ where $\beta \geq 1$ is an integer. If the number drawn was less than βkv, the user remains nonactive, until the end of the rounds. (All users' rounds take a predetermined number of steps.) Else, the user immediately notifies (by the use of at most k parallel synchronous subprocesses) all the resource allocators of the resources he wants, that he is a winner. Then, the user's parallel subprocesses collect answers from the resources for a period which is bounded by a constant number of steps. During this period some of the resources may declare that they agree to be allocated to the particular user. However, if at that time, any other resource requested by that user is denied, then that user does not utilize the resources which agreed to be allocated to him, but he continues to report that he is a winner to all of his requested resources and repeats the algorithm (without drawing again), until the user's round ends. If all of the wanted resources agree to be allocated at the same period (in which the user collects answers), then the user utilizes them for μ steps (μ is a small integer constant, as in Section 2.1) and then he releases these resources. This is done in parallel, by explicitly notifying the granting processes of the release, using his k subprocesses. Note that a communication with all the k resource allocators takes only r_{max} time due to the limited parallelism and tameness of processes.

b. *The Resource Allocator's Round*. The round of resource allocator j starts with a *monitoring period* of a constant number of steps during which at most v parallel synchronous subprocesses continuously monitor the users of the set S_j, looking for winners. Let M_j be the set of winners detected during the monitoring period. If M_j contains more than one winner, then all the elements of M_j are notified in parallel that they have been denied, and the round ends. However, if M_j has a unique winner, then the granting process notifies the winner that it agrees to be allocated. If the winner does not accept the agreement then the rounds ends. If the winner accepts, then the round enters an *allocation period*. During this period, the parallel subprocesses of the resource allocator deny all appearing winners. The round now ends by receipt of the notification by the user that the resource has been released.

c. *Additional Remarks*. Note that communication with all v of the user processes and all set operations in a resource allocator's round take only a constant (independent of v and k) number of steps due to the parallelism employed. Note also that the following holds with certainty:

A resource decides to be allocated to a *unique* winner, only after the resource allocator agrees to allocate the resource and the winner accepts the agreement. Thus, no resource can be allocated to more than one user at the same time, by our bidding algorithm.

3.2 A Detailed Description of the Uniform Bidding Algorithm.

a. *Detailed Description of Variables and Constants Used*. In the following, we set

$$\beta = 1 + \frac{r_{max}}{r_{min}}\ , \qquad c = (2(2+\mu)+1)\left(\frac{r_{max}}{r_{min}}\right)^2$$

$$\lambda_2 = \mu , \qquad \lambda_1 = 2\,\frac{r_{max}}{r_{min}}$$

The users use the following flags: For user i, the flag $W_{ij} = 1$ iff i is a winner and is willing to get resource $\rho(j)$. The flag $A_{ij} = 1$ iff user i *accepts* the allocation of the resource $\rho(j)$. Both flags are 0 else. The flag N_{ij} is initially 0, it becomes 1 when user i *releases* resource j.

The resource allocators j use the following flags: $E_{ji} = 0$ if the resource is denied and 1 if j agrees that its resource is allocated to i. Each allocator j has also a *shared* (for its parallel subprocesses) variable M_j which allows concurrent reads, and, in case of multiple writes of the same value, their sum modulo 3 is recorded. This can be done in constant (3 steps) parallel time by using the concurrent read-exclusive write model and a summation binary tree of depth 3. M_j is used to count winners during the monitoring period.

Each user i uses also a *shared* (for all its parallel subprocesses) variable L_i. It allows concurrent reads and concurrent writes of the same value. L_i is used to identify situations in which all wanted resources have been proposed to be allocated to user i, at the same time.

The counters $counter_i$, $counter_j$ count steps of respectively i,j in a round. Note also that every time a user (or resource allocator) p (1) modifies a flag and then (2) reads a flag of a resource allocator (or user) q to see its answer, we allow for $\lambda_1 = (r_{max}/r_{min})\cdot 2$ steps between the two actions of p (these steps allow for at least 2 steps of process q so that q can read the asking flag and answer back).

We now present formally the rounds of a user i and a resource allocator j. Note that, in the code which follows, the section of code between cobegin, and coend is executed (in a synchronous fashion) by all the parallel subprocesses of the process to which the cobegin-coend block belongs.

b. *The User's Round for User i.* (Initially $W_{ij} = A_{ij} = N_{ij} = 0$ $\forall j = 1,\dots,k$ and $L_i = 1$)

```
start round
L_i ← 1
choose x randomly uniformly from {1,2,...,βkv}
if x ≠ βkv then do c-1 no-ops; go to finish
repeat: cobegin {comment in parallel for j = 1,...,k}
            W_ij ← 1; do λ_1 no-ops; if E_ji = 0 then L_i ← 0
        coend
    if L_i = 1 AND counter_i < c-μ then
        begin
            cobegin {comment All resources allocated}
                A_ij ← 1 {comment accept}
                use resource ρ(j) for μ steps
                N_ij ← 1 {comment release resource}
            coend
            N_ij ← 0; A_ij ← 0; wait until counter_i = c; go to finish
        end
    else
        begin
            cobegin A_ij ← 0 {comment deny allocation} coend
            if counter_i < c - μ - 2 then go to repeat else wait until counter_i = c
        end
finish: end round
```

c. *The Resource Allocator's Round for Allocator j.* (Initially $M_j = 0$, $E_{ji} = 0$, $a_{ij} = 0$)

```
local a_ij
start round
begin
    cobegin
      do until (counter_j = λ_2  or  M_j > 0)
      if W_ij = 1  then  (M_j ← (M_j + 1)mod 3; a_ij ← 1)
      if counter_j < λ_2  then (do no-op until  counter_j = λ_2)
    coend
    cobegin
      if (M_j = 0  or  M_j = 2)  then
         begin  E_ji ← 0;  go to finish end
      else
         begin
           if  a_ij = 1  then
              begin
                 E_ji ← 1;  wait for  λ_1  steps
                 if A_ij = 0  then  begin  (E_ji ← 0;  go to finish) end
                 else
                    begin
                       do no-op until  N_ij = 1
                       {comment:  Resource allocated.  Await release by user}
                       E_ji ← 0
                       go to finish
                    end
              end
           else (repeat  E_ji ← 0  until resource deallocated)
         end
    coend
finish:  end round
```

3.3 PROPERTIES OF THE UNIFORM BIDDING ALGORITHM

In the following we assume all processes tame.

PROPOSITION 1. *If a particular user* i *is a winner (i.e. selects* $x = \beta kv$*) in its current round, then its* k *parallel synchronous subprocesses will, at least once in its current round, report at the same time that* i *is a winner when all requested resources are in a monitoring period.*

Proof. Assume that user i has just been declared a winner in its current round because i got as an outcome $x = \beta kv$ in the probabilistic selection. Within one of its steps (at most r_{max}/r_{min} of a resource allocator's steps) all resource allocators are notified. If some resource allocator is in an allocating period at the time of notification, then it is going to enter a monitoring period by at most a number of its steps equal to the allocating period. If a resource allocator was in a monitoring period at the time of notification, then it shall continue being in such a period (since his resource cannot be allocated to another winner, due to the presence of inner i). So, by at most a number of steps equal to an allocating period from the time i decided that i is a winner (i.e., by $\leq (2+\mu)(r_{max}/r_{min})^2$ steps of i), all i's resources are going o be notified, at the same time, within their monitoring period, that i is a winner. □

ROPOSITION 2. *Given that a particular user* i *is a winner in its current round, the probability hat* i *stays a unique winner for all its wanted resources during the whole round, is lower bounded y a constant, independent of* k *or* v.

roof. We need the following definition:

EFINITION. Let a *draw* by a user be a random independent selection of one of the numbers $\{1,2,\ldots,\beta kv\}$.

First we prove Lemma 1

EMMA 1. *During a round of user* i, *any other distinct user* j, *competing for the same resource cannot draw for more than* $\beta = r_{max}/r_{min} + 1$ *times.*

roof of Lemma 1. The maximum number of rounds of user j, overlapping with the round of user i, is $r_{max}/r_{min}+1$ (because the maximum ratio of speeds cannot exceed r_{max}/r_{min} and j may have drawn t most once in each round). The "plus 1" is to take into account the fact that a round of user j ay partially overlap the beginning of the round of user i. □

Now, given that user i is a winner, the probability that i remains a *unique* winner during his urrent round is equal to the probability that none of the competing users manages to be a winner ithin i's round. The number of the competing users is at most kv (at most v competitors per ach of the k resources asked by user i) and each competing user can draw for at most β times ithin i's round (by Lemma 1). The probability of each draw failing to win is $1 - 1/\beta kv$, hence he probability that i stays a unique winner during his current round is at least

$$\left(1 - \frac{1}{\beta kv}\right)^{\beta kv} > \frac{1}{2e} \quad , \qquad \text{where } e = 2.73\ldots \quad .$$ □

HEOREM 2. *The probability that a user is allocated all his wanted resources in its current round is pper bounded by* $1/\beta kv$ *and lower bounded by* $1/2e\beta kv$, $e = 2.73\ldots$

roof. The probability $\underline{p}(\Gamma_t, A)$, for oracle $\mathcal{A}$ and history Γ_t, that a user i is llocated all its wanted resources in his current round starting at t, never exceeds $1/\beta kv$ due to he fact that prob{user i chooses to be a winner in his current round} = $1/\beta kv$. Given that user i hooses to be a winner, if i remains a unique winner during all of his current round, i is going o be allocated all of his resources (due to Proposition 1) with certainty. Multiplying probabilities iven by Proposition 2, we get that

$$\underline{p}(\Gamma_t, A) \geq \frac{1}{\beta kv}\,\frac{1}{2e} = \frac{1}{2e\beta kv} \quad .$$ □

HEOREM 3. *Our uniform bidding algorithm has* ε*-response* $O(kv \log(1/\varepsilon))$ *and mean response* $O(kv)$.

roof. Let u be the number of rounds required for user i to be granted all its k resources in ome round, given that i starts requesting them at time t_1 and also assuming any history of the ystem up to t_1 and any oracle $\mathcal{A}$. Let round i start at time t_i $i \leq n$. We have by Baye's ormula $\text{Prob}(u{=}m) = (1 - \underline{p}(\Gamma_{t_1}, A))\ldots(1 - \underline{p}(\Gamma_{t_{m-1}}, A))\cdot\underline{p}(\Gamma_{t_m}, A)$. By use of Theorem 2, we get

$$\text{Prob}(u=m) \leq \left(1 - \frac{1}{2e\beta kv}\right)^{m-1} \frac{1}{\beta kv} .$$

If $u(\varepsilon)$ is the least number such that $\text{Prob}\{u > u(\varepsilon)\} \leq \varepsilon$, then

$$u(\varepsilon) \leq \frac{\log\left(\frac{\varepsilon}{\beta}\right)}{\log\left(1 - \frac{1}{2e\beta kv}\right)}$$

Since $\log\left(1 - \frac{1}{2e\beta kv}\right) > -2e\beta kv$ we get $u(\varepsilon) \leq 2e\beta kv \log\left(\frac{\beta}{\varepsilon}\right)$. Each allocation part of a resource's round takes $2+\mu$ steps. So, it is enough for the length of the user's round to be equal to $c = (2(2+\mu)+1)(r_{max}/r_{min})^2$, by the proof of Proposition 1. This implies that the duration of a user's round is at most cr_{max} and so (for μ independent of k,v) $\text{Prob}\{\gamma_{\mathcal{A},k} \leq cr_{max} \cdot u(\varepsilon)\} \geq 1-\varepsilon$. Hence $\gamma_k(\varepsilon) = O\left(kv \log\left(\frac{1}{\varepsilon}\right)\right)$. □

Note: Theorems 2 and 3 imply, with probability 1, that our algorithms never deadlock, no process starves, and our algorithm is probabilistically fair, in the sense that each willing user, gets its resources infinitely often in an infinite time interval, with probability 1.

4. THE PRIORITY BIDDING ALGORITHM

4.1 Motivation. Theorem 1 provided lower bounds for systems which are saturated with requests. In practice, systems will not continuously have so many requests at all times. This section provides an algorithm which gives good response time in the case in which the system is not saturated, (though it is not asymptotically efficient for saturated systems, as the algorithm of Section 3).

4.2 Description of the Priority Bidding Algorithm.

a. *Round for User i.* The round starts with the user waiting for a randomly chosen number of steps, uniform in an interval upper bounded by a constant $c_1 = (2(2+\mu)+1)(r_{max}/r_{min})^3$ steps. Note that c_1 is chosen in such a way that $c_1 \cdot r_{min}$ is greater than the maximum possible duration of the useful part of the round. The rest of the round is the same as in our uniform bidding algorithm.

b. *Round for Resource Allocator j.* Each round of process j is split into a sequence of $\lceil \log k \rceil$ intervals. For each $m = 0,\ldots,\lceil \log k \rceil$, in each interval Δ_m only the users i for which $k_i \in [\lfloor k/2^{m+1} \rfloor, \lceil k/2^m \rceil]$ are monitored. Process j proceeds to the next interval Δ_{m+1} only if all user processes which demand k_i resources, $k_i \in [\lfloor k/2^{m+1} \rfloor, \lceil k/2^m \rceil]$ have been allocated their resources. Within each Δ_m, the resource allocator goes through a sequence of "small rounds", each small round being exactly as a round of a resource allocator in our uniform bidding algorithm of Section 3.

4.3 Probabilistic Analysis of the Priority Bidding Algorithm. Let us consider a time interval Δ_m. Let u' be the number of rounds required for user i with $k_i \in [\lfloor k/2^{m+1} \rfloor, \lfloor k/2^m \rfloor]$, and also for all users competing with user i, to have all resources allocated. The number of those users is $\leq k/2^m \cdot v$. Let u be the number of rounds (within Δ_m), required just for user i. Let $u(\varepsilon')$ be such that $\text{Prob}\{u \leq u(\varepsilon')\} > 1-\varepsilon'$. Then, $\text{Prob}\{u' \leq u(\varepsilon')\} \geq (1-\varepsilon')^{kv/2^m}$, because users take independent actions and due to the random waits. Let us set $\varepsilon' = (\varepsilon/kv)\cdot 2^m$. Then

$$\text{Prob}\left\{u' \leq u\left(\frac{\varepsilon\cdot 2^m}{kv}\right) \geq \left(1-\frac{\varepsilon\cdot 2^m}{kv}\right)^{\frac{kv}{2^m}} \geq 1-\varepsilon\right\}$$

But, from the analysis of the uniform bidding algorithm (Theorem 3) and from the fact that, within each Δ_m, the algorithm looks exactly like the uniform bidding algorithm, we get

$$u\left(\frac{\varepsilon 2^m}{kv}\right) = O\left(\frac{k}{2^m} v \log\left(\frac{kv}{2^m}\cdot\frac{1}{\varepsilon}\right)\right)$$

leading to a mean response of $O\left(\frac{kv}{2^m}\log\left(\frac{kv}{2^m}\right)\right)$ for the interval Δ_m. This determines probabilistic upper bounds on the length of the interval Δ_m. Since there are $\lceil\log k\rceil$ such intervals, the ε-response for a user with $k_i \in [\lfloor k/2^{m+1}, k/2^m\rfloor]$ will be

$$O\left(\frac{kv}{2^m}\log\left(\frac{kv}{\varepsilon\cdot 2^m}\right)\log k\right) \quad \text{implying a mean response of} \quad O\left(\frac{kv}{2^m}\log k \log\left(\frac{kv}{2^m}\right)\right) .$$

For users with small demands (i.e., when $k/2^m = o(k)$) the above mean response is better than the mean response of the uniform bidding algorithm of Section 3. E.g., for $2^m = \theta(k)$ we get a mean response $O(v \log k \log v)$. We hence conclude:

THEOREM 4. *Our priority bidding algorithm has the following property: For users* i *with demands* k_i *in* $[\lfloor h_{m/2}, h_m\rfloor]$ *and* $h_m = k\cdot 2^{-m}$, *the* ε*-response is*

$$O\left(h_m v \log k \log\left(\frac{h_m v}{\varepsilon}\right)\right)$$

and the mean response is $\bar{\gamma}_{h_m} = O(h_m v \log k \log(h_m v))$. □

REFERENCES

Andrews, G., "Synchronizing Resources," *ACM Trans. on Programming Languages and Systems*, 3(4), 405-430 (1981).

Angluin, D., "Local and Global Properties in Networks of Processors," *12th Annual Symp. on Theory of Computing*, Los Angeles, CA, 82-93 (April 1980).

Arjomandi, E., M. Fischer, and N. Lynch, "A Difference in Efficiency Between Synchronous and Asynchronous Systems," *13th Ann. Symp. on Theory of Computing*, (April 1981).

Bernstein, A.J., "Output Guards and Nondeterminism in Communicating Sequential Processes," *ACM Trans. on Programming Languages and Systems*, 2(2), 234-238 (1980).

Bernstein, P. and N. Goodman, "Fundamental Algorithms for Concurrency Control in Distributed Database Systems," CCA Tr. Contract No. F30603-79-0191, Cambridge, MA (1980).

Dennis, J.B. and D.P. Misunas, "A Preliminary Architecture for a Basic Dataflow Processors," *Proc. 2nd Annual Symp. on Computer Architecture, ACM IEEE*, 126-132 (1974).

Fisher, M.J., N.A. Lynch, J.E. Burns, and A. Borodin, "Resource Allocation with Immunity to Limited Process Failure," *19th FOCS*, 234-254 (1979).

Francez, N., "Extended Naming Conventions for Communicating Processes," *9th ACM Symp. on Principles of Programming Languages*, Albuquerque, New Mexico, (Jan. 1982).

Francez, N. and J. Reif, "A Social CSP," to appear.

Francez, N. and Rodeh, "A Distributed Data Type Implemented by a Probabilistic Communication Scheme," *21 Ann. Symp. on Foundations of Computer Science*, Syracuse, New York, 373-379 (Oct. 1980).

Hart, S. and M. Sharir, "Termination of Probabilistic Concurrent Programs," *9th Ann. SCM Symp. on Principles of Prgramming Languages*, Albuquerque, New Mexico, (Jan. 1982).

Hoare, C.A.R., "Communicating Sequential Processes," *Com. of ACM*, 21 (8), 666-677 (1978).

Itai, A. and M. Rodeh, "Symmetry Breaking in Distributive Networks," *22nd Annual Symp. on Foundations of Computer Science*, Nashville, Tennessee, Oct. 1981, 120-158.

Lehmann, D. and M. Rabin, "On the Advantages of Free Choice: A Symmetric and Fully Distributed Solution to the Dining Philosophers' Problem," to appear in *8th ACM Symp. on Principles of Programming Languages*, (Jan. 1981).

Lipton, R. and F.G. Sayward, "Response Time of Parallel Programs," Research Reprot #108, Dept. of Comp. Science, Yale University, (June 1977).

Lynch, M.A., "Fast Allocation of Nearby Resources in a Distributed System," *12th Ann. Symp. in Theory of Computing*, Los Angeles, CA, 70-81 (April 1980).

Rabin, M., "N-Process Synchronization by a 4 $\log_2 M$-Valued Shared Variable," *21st Ann. Symp. on Foundations of Comp. Science*, Syracuse, NY, 407-410 (Oct. 1980).

Rabin, N., "The Choice Coordination Problem," Mem. No. UCB/ERL MBO/38, Electric. Research Laboratory, University of California, Berkeley, (Aug. 1980).

Reif, J.H. and P. Spirakis, "Distributed Algorithms for Synchronizing Interprocess Communication Within Real Time," *13th Ann. Symp. on Theory of Computation*, Wisconsin, 133-145 (1981); also as "Real-Time Synchronization of Interprocess Communications," to appear in *Transactions on Programming Languages*, 1984.

Reif, J.H. and P. Spirakis, "Unbounded Speed Variability in Distributed Communications Systems," *9th ACM Symp. on Principles of Programming Languages*, Albuquerque, New Mexico (1982a), also to appear in *SIAM Journal of Computing*, 1984.

Reif, J.H. and P. Spirakis, "Real Time Resource Allocation in Distributed Systems," *ACM SIGACT-SIGOPS Symp. on Principles of Distributed Computing*, Ottawa, Canada, (Aug. 1982b).

Schwarz, J., "Distributed Synchronization of Communicating Sequential Processes," DAI Research Report No. 56, University of Edinburg, (1980).

artial Order Semantics versus Interleaving Semantics for CSP-like Languages and its Impact on Fairness

Wolfgang Reisig
RWTH Aachen
Büchel 29 -31
D-5100 Aachen
West Germany

. Introduction

sually operational semantics of both sequential and nonsequential programs in describ-
d as sequences of global states and action occurrences. In case of nonsequential pro-
rams, local states (i.e. those of single sequential tasks or processes) are considered
s parts of global states; hence local command executions affect given global program
tates. If in one state a set of mutually independend commands is enabled, they are
ither interleaved i.e. executed in arbitrary order (as e.g. in [12]) or, what is less
ommon, they are executed in one step (as e.g. in [2]).

evertheless it has been discussed [7] or at least mentioned [12] that it might be worth-
hile to consider independend command executions of a nonsequential program as being
artially ordered rather than to inforce a total order by interleaving them or to assume
heir coincident execution. Petri Net Theory takes this idea of partial ordering as a
asic concept [11]. This idea meets exactly what [1] requires by refusing any assump-
ions about speed ratios of independent processes.

n this paper we give an operational semantics for CSP-like languages with partially
rdered command executions. Technically this might look more difficult than usual oper-
tional semantics since a notion of global state does not exist. What we gain by this
emantics is a sharp distinction between nondeterminism and nonsequentialism (as the
atter is no longer considered as a special case of the former). Furthermore we gain
nsights into the nature of fairness concepts and fairness properties, which are prob-
ly new.

is paper is organized as follows: In Chapter 2 we give some examples in order to show
e intuition of partial order semantics and its impact on the distinction of nondeter-
nistic and nonsequential behaviour. A formal definition of the language we consider
oughly CSP without nesting of parallel commands and without distributed termination)
d of its partial order semantics, is given in Chapter 3. In order to compare partial
der semantics with the usual interleaving semantics, we give, in Chapter 4, an inter-
aving semantics and state some relationships between the two concepts. In Chapter 5
discuss fairness properties in the light of partial order semantics.

Intuitive Concepts of Partial Order Semantics

assume the reader to be familiar with the basic concepts of CSP (a formal syntax will be given in Chapter 3.1). Our kind of semantics is heavily influenced by Plotkin's suggestions of structural induction for the specification of semantics [12]. Roughly this means to consider configurations which consist of the actual state (i.e. the values of variables) and the program code still to be executed. Labelled relations indicate the elementary commands to be executed next and thus lead to follower configurations. Radically different from Plotkin's approach is the absence of global configurations. Instead, transition relations concern only single processes or, in case of communication, pairs of them.

As an example, let $C_1 = \underline{do}\ b_1 \rightarrow A; P_2!e\ \underline{od}$

$C_2 = \underline{do}\ b_2 \rightarrow P_1?x\ \underline{od}$

$C_3 = B$

and let $Pr_1 = P_1::C_1 \| P_2::C_2 \| P_3::C_3$,

where A and B are assignments, b_1 and b_2 are Boolean expressions, x is a variable and e any expression.

The semantics of Pr_1 is given by $[Pr_1]$ =

$(C_1, s_{10}) \rightarrow skip \rightarrow (A; P_2!e; C_1, s_{10}) \rightarrow A \rightarrow (P_2!e; C_1, s_{11}) \searrow$ x:=e $\nearrow (C_1, s_{11}) \rightarrow skip \rightarrow$

$(C_2, s_{20}) \rightarrow skip \rightarrow (P_1?x; C_2, s_{20}) \nearrow$ x:=e $\searrow (C_2, s_{21}) \rightarrow skip \rightarrow$

$(C_3, s_{30}) \rightarrow B \rightarrow (end, s_{31})$

This construction is straightforward: Separately for each process P_i we construct a sequence of configuration and action occurrences, beginning with its initial state s_{i0} as if $P_i::C_i$ were sequential programs. The evaluation of the guards b_1 and b_2, and the execution of the assignments A and B depend only on the actual states of their corresponding processes. The execution of the synchronized commands $P_2?x$ and $P_1!e$, however, depends on the actual states of two processes, P_1 and P_2 (and changes the actual configurations of both). This is indicated by two arcs ending and two arcs beginning at the action x:=e . Hence the execution of synchronized commands $P_2!e$ and $P_1?x$ in the local state s of P_1 results in a synchronized assignment action x:=e which affects only the actual state of P_2, but depends on the actual state of P_1.

$[Pr_1]$ is infinite if both b_1 and b_2 remain true forever. Otherwise either both P_1 and P_2 terminate with an end-configuration (end,s), or only one of them terminates with an end-configuration, and the other is blocked in a configuration where no synchronization command can be executed.

The process P_3 operates completely independently from P_1 and P_2, terminating after execution of the command B .

$[Pr_1]$ may be considered as a partially ordered set of (instances of) configurations and actions. The order is given by the transitive closure $\rightarrow^+$ of the $\rightarrow$-relation in $[Pr_1]$: a<b iff a must occur before b .

Pr_1 is a nonsequential, but deterministic program. This is obvious, as $[Pr_1]$ represent ne and <u>the only one</u> computation which Pr_1 can execute. Usual interleaving semantics efines - in general infinitely - many computations for Pr_1.

e turn now to the general case of programs, which are both nonsequential and nondeter- inistic.

$$\text{Let } C_1 = \underline{\text{do}}\ b_1 \to A_1 \,[\!]\, P_2?x \to B_1\ \underline{\text{od}}$$
$$C_2 = \underline{\text{do}}\ b_2 \to A_2 \,[\!]\, P_1!e \to B_2\ \underline{\text{od}}$$
$$\text{and let } Pr_2 = P_1::C_1 \,\|\, P_2::C_2 \,,$$

here A_i and B_i are assignments, b_i are Boolean expressions, x is a variable and e ny expression. The semantics of Pr_2 is given by

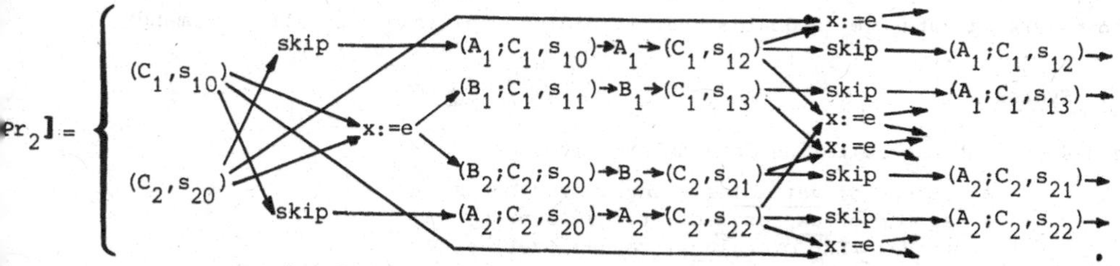

n order to construct $[Pr_2]$ we start with the initial configurations and construct eparately for each process all feasable local actions and configurations. Synchronized uards and commands depend on configurations of <u>two</u> processes, and corresponding actions nd configurations are constructed for each pair of concurrent configurations φ_i, φ_j. otice that synchronized guards give rise to (synchronized) assignments, just as syn- hronized commands do.

oncurrency of configurations x,y can be tested by inspecting the set $\overleftarrow{x,y}$ of those lements which are smaller than both of them ($x<y$ iff there exists a sequence of arrows rom x to y). x an y are <u>concurrent</u> if $\overleftarrow{x,y}$ has no configuration as a maximal lement (such a configuration would imply an alternative between x an y) and if either $x<y$ nor $y<x$. As an example, the first occurrences of the configurations (C_1, s_{12}) and (C_2,s_{21}) in $[Pr_2]$ have (C_1,s_{10}) as a maximal joint predecessor. So (C_1,s_{12}) nd (C_2,s_{21}) are not concurrent. For such pairs of configurations no follower nodes re to be constructed.

enote a configuration or action <u>backward branched</u> (<u>forward branched</u>, respectively) if t is target (source, respectively) of more than one arc. It is obvious that branching nfigurations represent nondeterminism, whereas branching actions deal with nonse- uential behaviour.

s Pr_2 is nondeterministic, many different computations can be performed. Two of them e

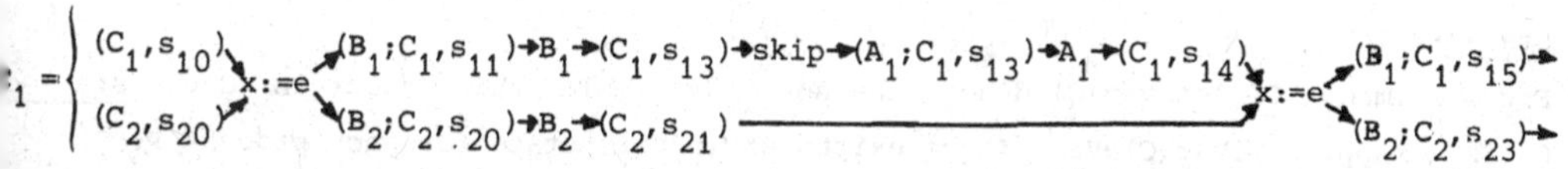

and

$$PC_2 = \left\{ \begin{array}{l} (C_1,s_{10}) \longrightarrow \searrow \\ (C_2,s_{20}) \to skip \to (A_2;C_2,s_{20}) \to A_2 \to (C_2,s_{21}) \nearrow \end{array} \right. x:=e \begin{array}{l} \nearrow (B_1;C_1,s_{14}) \to B_1 \to (C_1,s_{15}) \searrow \\ \searrow (B_2;C_2,s_{22}) \to B_2 \to (C_2,s_{23}) \nearrow \end{array} x:=e \begin{array}{l} \nearrow \\ \searrow \end{array}$$

A computation of Pr_2 is a subset of Pr_2 without branched configurations. The semantics $[\![Pr_2]\!]$ may be considered as an example for an event structure in the sens of [9].

3. The Language

We define a CSP-like language in the style of [5] and [12]. As we stress the aspects of synchronization, our language slightly deviates from original CSP. We allow both inputs P?x outputs P!e in guards, but we exclude nesting of parallel commands.

3.1 Syntax

We assume that the following domains are given:

- A set Var of variables, ranged over by x
- A set Exp of expressions, ranged over by e
- A set Val ⊂ Exp of values, ranged over by v
- A set Bexp ⊂ Exp of Boolean expressions, ranged over by b
- A set Tval = {true, false} ⊂ Bexp of truthvalues
- A set Lab of process labels, ranged over by P .

For expressions e we assume that substitution of expressions e' for variables x in e makes sense, giving expressions e[e'∖x].

The syntax of our language can be specified by a little grammar; adopting the above domains:

Guards	$G ::= b \mid b \wedge P?x \mid b \wedge P!e$
Commands	$C ::= x{:=}e \mid P?x \mid P!e \mid C_1;C_2 \mid$ do $G_1 \to C_1 [\!] \ldots [\!] G_n \to C_n$ od
Programs	$Pr ::= P_1::C_1 \parallel \ldots \parallel P_m::C_m$

We assume the labels P_i to be all different and P_i not to occur in C_i. In case b = tru we allow as shorthands P?x and P!e for b∧P?x and b∧P!e, respectively.
A command is either an assignment (x:=e) or it is synchronized (P?x, P!e) or it is composed ($C_1;C_2$, do...od). Assignments and synchronized commands are elementary or indivisible (they will be executed in one step). $P_i::C_i$ is a process.
We do not specify any branching command like B := if...$[\!]G_1 \to C_i$...fi , as a command of this type would not contribute to that what we want to emphasize.

3.2 Partial Order Semantics

Here we define the semantics of processes adopting the technique of defining relations by structural induction, as introduced in [5] and [12].

States

For a command C let Var(C) denote the set of variables which occur in C . A state c C is a mapping S:Var(C)→Val. There exists an initial state for each process P::C.

Given a state s, let s[v/x] denote the state s after substituting v for x. For expressions e and b let es and bs be the result of substituting s(x) for each variable x in e and b, respectively; es and bs are instances of closed expressions (i.e. they contain no variables). We assume that closed expressions e',b' have values [e'], [b'] in Val and Tval, respecitvely.

Actions

Roughly, an action is a command which is supposed to be executed in a state:

Actions a ::= x:=e | P?xv | P!e | skip

Notice that input commands P?x are supplemented by a value v to become executable in a local state s of a process.

Guards

With respect to a given process P::C, let GUARDS be the set of guards occurring in C and let STATES be the set of states of C.

For each action a, let $\hat{a}$: GUARDS × STATES ---→ STATES ∪ {fail} be the smallest partial function such that

$$\left.\begin{array}{ll}\widehat{skip}\ (b,s) & = s\\ \widehat{P?xv}\ (b\wedge P?x,s) & = s[v/x]\\ \widehat{P!e}\ (b\wedge P!e,s) & = s\end{array}\right\}\ \text{iff } [bs] = \underline{true} \qquad \left.\begin{array}{ll}\widehat{skip}\ (b,s) & = fail\\ \widehat{skip}\ (b\wedge P?x,s) & = fail\\ \widehat{skip}\ (b\wedge P!x,s) & = fail\end{array}\right\}\ \text{iff } [bs] = \underline{false}$$

The labels a of the functions $\hat{a}$ allow one to trace the actions which are performed upon evaluating guards.

Commands

Given a process P::C, let COM be the (inductively given) set of commands C consists of, augmented by the termination command end. CONF = COM × STATES are the configurations of P.

For each action a let $\underset{\rightarrow}{a}$ ⊆ CONF × CONF be the least relation such that

(i) $(x:=e,s) \xrightarrow{x:=e} (\underline{end}, s[[es]/x])$

(ii) $(P?x,s) \xrightarrow{P?xv} (\underline{end}, s[v/x])$

(iii) $(P!e,s) \xrightarrow{P!e} (\underline{end}, s)$

(iv) if $\forall i\in[m]$ $\widehat{skip}(G_i,s)$ = fail then $(\underline{do}\ G_1\rightarrow C_1 [] \ldots [] G_n\rightarrow C_n\ \underline{od},s) \xrightarrow{skip} (\underline{end}, s)$

(v) if $(C_1,s) \underset{\rightarrow}{a} (\underline{end},s')$ then $(C_1;C_2,s) \underset{\rightarrow}{a} (C_2,s')$

(vi) if $\exists i\in[m]$ $\hat{a}(G_i,s) = s'$ then $(\underline{do}\ G_1\rightarrow C_1 [] \ldots [] G_n\rightarrow C_n\ \underline{od},s) \underset{\rightarrow}{a} (C_i;\underline{do}\ldots\underline{od},s')$.

Programs

We define the semantics [Pr] of a program Pr as a partially ordered set, the elements of which are instances of configurations and instances of assignment- and skip-actions. It should not be confusing if our notion will not distinguish configurations and actions from their corresponding instances.

In the sequel, φ will denote a variable ranging over configurations and their instances.

Let $Pr = P_1::C_1 \| \ldots \| P_m::C_m$ be a program with initial states s_i of P_i. We define inductively the semantics [Pr] of Pr as the smallest set of configuration instances and action instances, together with a relation → over this set as the smallest relation such that

(i) the transitive closure of → is a partial order on [Pr], denoted < .

(ii) $\{(C_1,s_1),\dots,(C_m,s_m)\} \subseteq$ [Pr].

(iii) If $\varphi \in$ [Pr] and if a is an elementary action (assignment or skip) and if $\varphi \xrightarrow{a} \varphi'$ then there exists in [Pr] an action instance a and a configuration instance φ' such that $\varphi \rightarrow a \rightarrow \varphi'$.

(iv) If in [Pr] there exist configuration instances $\varphi_i = (C,s)$ of P_i and φ_j of P_j such that

(a) each maximal element x such that $x \leq \varphi_i$ and $x \leq \varphi_j$ is an action and

(b) $\varphi_i \xrightarrow{P_j!e} \varphi'_i$ and $\varphi_j \xrightarrow{P_i?x[es]} \varphi'_j$ then there exists in [Pr] an action instance x:=e and instances of the configurations φ'_i and φ'_j such that

$$\begin{array}{ccccc} \varphi_i & \searrow & & \nearrow & \varphi'_i \\ & & x:=e & & \\ \varphi_j & \nearrow & & \searrow & \varphi'_j \end{array} .$$

The action instances in [Pr] denote the execution of guards and of elementary commands. In (iii), skip denotes the execution of a Boolean guard, and assignments x:=e denote executions of local assignment commands x:=e. In (iv) x:=e denotes either the execution of synchronized guards b∧P?x and b'∧P!e or the execution of synchronized commands P?x and P!e. This kind of assignment is called synchronized.

For all action instances a in [Pr] it is obvious from their surrounding configuration the executions of which guard or command they represent. These guards or commands will sometimes also be denoted a .

Notice that we make no attempt at modelling the distributed termination convention of [6].

The →-relation is to be conceived as describing the causal dependencies of Pr. In $a_1 \rightarrow \varphi \begin{array}{l} \nearrow a_2 \\ \searrow a_3 \end{array}$ the occurrence of action a_1 causes an instance of the configuration φ. This instance is changed by the occurrence of either a_2 or a_3. In $\begin{array}{ccccc} \varphi_1 & \searrow & & \nearrow & \varphi'_1 \\ & & a & & \\ \varphi_2 & \nearrow & & \searrow & \varphi'_2 \end{array}$ the action a occurs, as both local configurations φ_1 and φ_2 are present. The occurrence of a transforms φ_1 to φ'_1 and φ_2 to φ'_2 .

Generally, each two elements x,y of [Pr] are related in exactly one of the following three ways:

(i) x and y are ordered, i.e. x<y or y<x. In this case they are causally dependent; if x<y, x is a predecessor of y .

(ii) x and y are not ordered and all maximal elements z which are smaller than both x and y , are action occurrences. In this case x and y are concurrent. This means that they can both occur mutually independently in one process.

(iii) x and y are not ordered and the set of maximal elements which are smaller than both x and y , contains a configuration occurrence. In this case, x and y are alternative. They can never both occur in one process.

:he concept of these three relations has been introduced in [9].

3.3 Computations and Behaviours

'he semantics $[\![Pr]\!]$ of a program Pr describes the joint potential behaviour of all pro-
:esses. It is easy to seperate single computations, or the behaviour of single processes.

A (partial order) computation PC of a program Pr is a maximal subset of $[\![Pr]\!]$ such that (i) PC is left closed (i.e. $\forall x,y\in[\![Pr]\!]\; x\in PC \wedge y<x \Rightarrow y\in PC$) and (ii) each configuration of PC has at most one successor in PC.
xamples have been discussed in Chapter 2.

he behaviour $[\![P_i]\!]$ of a process P_i of Pr is the subset of $[\![Pr]\!]$ which consists of all onfiguration- and action-instances of P_i. (Remember that synchronized assignments elong to two processes.)
s an example, the behaviour $[\![P_1]\!]$ of P_1 in Pr_2 is given by

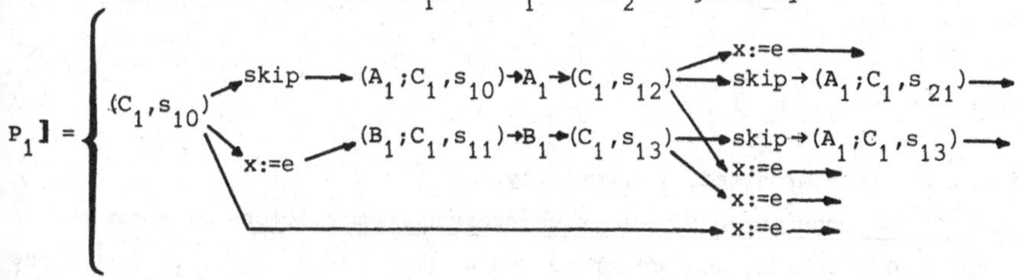

. Partial Order Semantics versus Interleaving Semantics

n this chapter we consider the usual interleaving semantics for nonsequential programs nd relate it to partial order semantics as defined above.

.1 Interleaving Semantics

nterleaving semantics is the usual technique to define an operational semantics for onsequential programs and particularly for CSP like languages. A step of a single pro-
ess is described as a step of the whole system, changing some global state. A com-
utation is defined as a sequence of such global steps.
iven a program $Pr = P_1::C_1 \| \ldots \| P_n::C_n$, let CONF denote the Cartesian product of the ets of the local configurations of the processes P_i. Given $\tau\in CONF$, τ_i denotes the pro-
ection of τ onto the component of P_i.
ased on the relations $\underset{\rightarrow}{a}$ of 3.2.d we define global next state relations $\underset{\Rightarrow}{a} \subseteq CONF \times CONF$ s the smallest relations such that for $\tau,\tau'\in CONF$

f $\tau_i \underset{\rightarrow}{a} \tau_i'$ then $\tau \underset{\Rightarrow}{a} \tau'$ and if $\tau_i, \tau_j \rightarrow x{:=}e \rightarrow \tau_i', \tau_j'$ then $\tau \underset{\Rightarrow}{x:=e} \tau'$.

t is easy to verify that this semantics corresponds to Plotkin's [12] in that for a iven program they rise equal steps.

.2 Decomposition and Total Ordering of Po Computations Related to Il Computations

bviously, both kinds of semantics yield different computations for a given program.

Nevertheless, as a computation describes a distinguished execution of a program, one may ask for partial order computations and interleaving computations which describe the same execution, whatever this means.

A <u>slice</u> of a po computation is a maximal subset of pairwise unordered configurations. Given two slices C and C' and an action a of a po computation PC, the triple (C,a,C') is an <u>elementary subcomputation</u> of PC if $C \overset{a}{\Rightarrow} C'$, where $\overset{a}{\Rightarrow}$ denotes the global next state relation as defined in 4.1 and C,C' are conceived as global configurations.

In po computations, elementary subcomputations are represented

by figures like

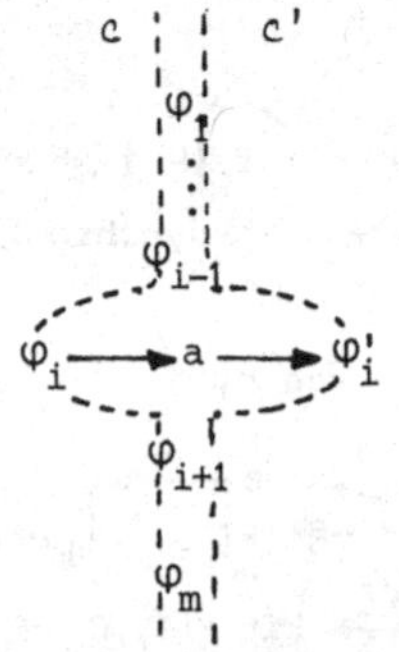

or

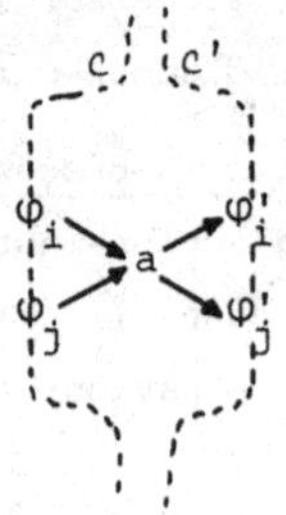

if a is elementary or synchronized, respectively.

<u>A decomposition of a po computation PC into elementary subcomputations</u> is a maximal sequence $C_0 a_1 C_1 a_2 \dots$ of slices C_i and actions a_i such that for $i = 1,2,\dots$ (C_{i-1},a_i,C_i) is an elementary subcomputation of PC.

As an example, the following describes the decomposition of the computation PC_1 into elementary subcomputations:

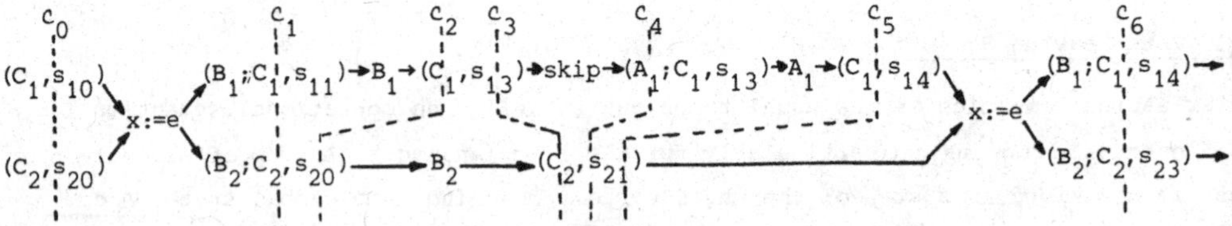

Obviously, il computations and decompositions of po computations coincide, as global configurations of il computations are equal to slices of po computations.

<u>Theorem</u> A sequence of configurations and actions is an il computation of some program Pr iff it is a decomposition of a po computation of Pr.

This is easily proved by induction on the length of this sequence.

The above considerations suggest to characterize il computations by extending the partial order of po computations to total orders. Vice versa, a po computation may be constructed from an il computation by weakening its total ordering. Howver, one has to be careful when linearizing an infinite partial order. As an example, the action occurrence in the (unique) computation of the program Pr_1 can be totally ordered as follows (assuming b_1 and b_2 never fail):

(*) $skip_1 < A < skip_2 < x{:=}e < skip_1 < A \dots \dots < B$

here $skip_i$ denotes an occurrence of skip in C_i and ... ...denotes an infinity of kip-, A- and x:=e-occurrences. This order does not correspond to any decomposition r to any il computation because B is an element in this order which is not reachable y finitely many steps. However, if we consider only those elements of (*) which have finite set of predecessors, we obtain indeed the ordered action occurrences of a ecomposition: There exist slices C_i such that

$$(**) \quad C_0 \Rightarrow skip_1 \Rightarrow C_1 \Rightarrow A \Rightarrow C_2 \Rightarrow skip_2 \Rightarrow C_3 \Rightarrow x{:=}e \Rightarrow C_4 \Rightarrow skip_1 \Rightarrow C_5 \Rightarrow A \Rightarrow \ldots$$

s a decomposition of the computation under consideration, (written as il computation).

o the relationship of po computations and il computations is in general given as fol- ows:

iven a po computation PC, consider the partially ordered set (A,<) of its action occur- ences. Let (A,<') be a total ordering of A which includes < and let $(\underset{\sim}{A},<'')$ be the estriction of (A,<') to its founded elements. Then there exists an il computation IC uch that its action occurrences and their order coincide with $(\underset{\sim}{A},<'')$. We denote PC, A,<') and IC to correspond.

n this way, each po computation corresponds to an il computation and vice versa, each l computation corresponds to a po computation. These correspondencies, however, are n general not unique.

s an example, the (unique) po computation of Pr_1 corresponds to the total order (*) nd to the il computation (**).

n element x of an order is foundend iff the set of its predecessors if finite. The ounded restriction of an order is the restriction to its founded elements. As an kample, the founded restriction of (*) is (**). A completion of a partial order < s a total order which contains <.

ieorem A set (A,<) of action occurrences corresponds to an il computation IC iff (A,<) is the founded restriction of a completed ordering of the action occur- rences of some po computation.

) prove this theorem, it is - with the above Theorem - sufficient to show that each composition of a po computation into elementary subcomputations corresponds to the unded restriction of one of its completed orderings. This, however, is obvious.

Justice and Well Orders

ccording to [8] we define an il computation IC = $C_0 \Rightarrow a_1 \Rightarrow C_1 \ldots$ as unjust to a guard a command a iff IC is infinite, contains a finitely often, and for some $n \in \mathbb{N}$ l configurations C_{n+i} activate a. IC is just to a iff IC is not unjust to a.

eorem Let IC be an il computation and let a be a guard or an assignment. IC is unjust to a $\Leftrightarrow$ there exists a total order (A,<) corresponding to IC such that a is the smallest nonfounded element of (A,<).

oof "$\Leftarrow$" Let P be a po computation which corresponds to IC and (A,<). Clearly a is an element of P . So there exists a local configuration φ in P which activates a . As a is the smallest nonfounded element of (A,<), there exists a global configuration c_n in IC which contains φ. As a is no element of IC, all global configurations c_{n+i} contain φ:

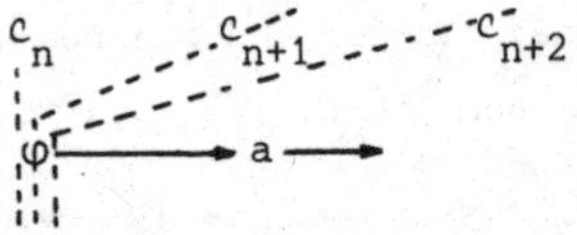

So, all configurations which are greater than c_n, activate a and hence IC is unjust to a .

"⇒" by definition of justice there exists an index n such that all global configurations c_{n+1} activate a . Hence there exists a slice of some computation PC, corresponding to IC, which activates a . Furhtermore IC may be chosen in such a way that a is contained in PC.

Obviously, it is possible to include a as the first element of some corresponding order , preceded by the elements of IC. ■

As a consequence of this theorem we obtain that the il computation (**) in Section 4.2 is unjust to B .

Based on this theorem we can characterize justice in terms of well orders. As usual, call an order a <u>well order</u> iff all its elements are founded.

<u>Corollary</u> An il computation IC is just iff all total orders corresponding to IC are well orders.

<u>Corollary</u> Let PC be a po computation and let IC be a corresponding just il computation. The set of elements (i.e. local configuration occurrences and action occurrences of PC is equal to the set of elements of IC (where local configurations are elements of global configurations).

<u>Corollary</u> An il computation is just iff its action occurrences are equal to the action occurrences of all corresponding po computations.

<u>Proof</u> If the action occurrences are equal, the corresponding total orders are well founded. ■

<u>Corollary</u> To each po computation there corresponds a just il computation.

<u>Proof</u> It is possible to extend the partial order of each po computation to a total well order. ■

Justice requirements denote the absence of infinite delay for activated guards and commands in il computations. One may be interested in comparable properties of po computations. The inductive definition of po semantics implies that each process proceeds whenever a guard or a command is activated. So infinite delays cannot occur in po computations and each po computation is - intuitively - just. To say it in other words: delay of one process is in il semantics caused by propagation of other processes. Mutual independency in po semantics exludes such delays.

6. Conclusion

The idea of partial order semantics is not at all new. Petri Net Theory is based on the absence of central clocks [11]. [1] calls it "penny wise and pound foolish" if one relays on speed ratios. Further arguments given in [7]. [9] describes the unfolding of Petri nets to what is called "occurrence nets". These unfolding are quire close to our partial order semantics.

[10] gives some good reasons to consider weak fairness, i.e. justice (rather than "strong fairness"), as the appropriate constraints to use. Notice that in po semantics there does not exist something like unjust computations: Every guard or command which is permanently activated will eventually be executed due to the maximality requirement for computations. We showed that justice is a problem due to interleavings, and not due to nonsequential behaviour.

References

[1] Dijkstra, Esger, W.: Co-Operating Sequential Processes in F. Genyus (ed.): Programming Languages, Academic Press (1968)

[2] Elrad, Tzilla; Frances, Nissam: Decompositions of Distributed Programs into Communication - Closed Layers Science of Computer Programming 2, 155-173 (1982)

[3] Francesz, Nissam; Hoare, C.A.R.; Lehman, Daniel; de Roever, William P.: Semantics of Nondeterminism, Concurrency and Communication Journal of Computer and System Sciences 19, pp. 290-308 (1979)

[4] Francesz, N.; Lehmann, D.; Pnueli, A.: A Linear History Semantics for Distributed Languages (Extended Abstract) 21. Conference on Foundations of Computer Science IEEE 143-151 (1980)

[5] Hennessy, Matthew; Li, Wei; Plotkin, Gordon: A First Attempt at Translating CSP into CCS Proceedings of the 2nd International Conference on Distributed Computing Systems Paris, France, April 8-10, 1981, IEEE, Computer Society Press pp. 105-114 (1981)

[6] Hoare, C.A.R.: Communicating Sequential Processes Communications of the ACM Vol. 21, No. 8, pp. 666-677 (1978)

[7] Lamport, Leslie: Time, Clocks and the Ordering of Events in a Distributed System Communications of the ACM Vol. 21, No. 7, pp. 558-564 (1978)

[8] Lehmann, D.; Pnueli, A.; Stavi, J.: Impartiality, Justice and Fairness: The Ethics of Concurrent Termination Lecture Notes in Computer Science 115, 264-277 (1981)

[9] Nielsen, M.; Plotkin, G.; Winskel, G.: Petri Nets, Event Structures and Domains, Part I Theoretical Computer Science 13, 85-108 (1981)

[10] Park, David: A Predicate Transformer for Weak Fair Iteration The University of Warwik Report No. 36 (1981)

[11] Petri, Carl-Adam: Non-Sequential Processes Internal Report ISF-77-5, Gesellschaft für Mathematik und Datenverarbeitung Bonn (Germany) (1977)

[12] Plotkin, Gordon.: An Operational Semantics for CSP in: Formal Description of Programming Concepts-II, D. Bjørner (ed.) North Holland Publishing Company, IFIP pp. 199-223 (1983)

CANCELLATION, PUMPING AND PERMUTATION IN FORMAL LANGUAGES

Antonio Restivo
Istituto di Matematica, Università di Palermo
Via Archirafi 34, Palermo (Italy)

Christophe Reutenauer
LITP
Institut de Programmation, 4 Place Jussieu, 75005 Paris

I. INTRODUCTION

Cancellation and pumping are well known properties of regular languages. These properties follows from the fact that a finite automaton accepting long strings must repeat twice some internal state: this implies that the corresponding portion of the input string may be cancelled or pumped without affecting acceptance or rejection by the automaton. In [2] Ehrenfeucht, Parikh and Rozenberg proved that a certain property, which they called the cancellation property, is a necessary and sufficient condition for languages to be regular.

Our first result is another characterization of regular languages, which has a formal analogy with the previous one, but which uses, instead of cancellation, transposition and periodicity. Roughly speaking, a language has the transposition property if in each word it is possible to transpose two consecutive blocks such that the two words are together in the language or out of it. For a regular language this property follows naturally from the fact that a finite automaton accepting a long string must repeat three times the same internal state, so that the two corresponding portions of the string may be interchanged. However, it is easy to see that a language having the transposition property is in general not regular. Periodicity is a property which is closely related to pumping (see [3]). A classical problem in language theory is to find under what condition a periodic language is regular. This problem is closely related to the Burnside problem for semigroups (see [7]). We prove that a language is regular if and only if it is periodic and has the transposition property (Theorem2.2).

A weaker property than transposition is the permutation property: instead of transposing two blocks in the given word, one permutes some blocks in it. According to [1], a language is Parikh-bounded if it contains some bounded language having the same image under the Parikh mapping. We show that, if a language has the permutation property, then it is Parikh-bounded (Theorem 3.2). In fact, to establish theorems 2.2 and 3.2, we use the notion of n-divided words, as introduced by Shirshov (see e.g. [6]). He shows that each long word either is n-divided or contains some p-th power (Theorem 2.3). From this we derive that a language is bounded if and only if for some integer n it does not contain any n-divided word (Theorem 3.1).

The rest of the paper is devoted to the study of languages that are support of rational power series (a natural generalization of regular languages). First we show, as a consequence of theorem 3.2, that each support is Parikh-bounded (Theorem 4.1). For this we must show that each support satisfies the permutation property (Lemma 4.1), which is proved by using polynomial identities of matrices. Then we solve a conjecture quoted in [11] : if two supports are complementary languages, then they are regular (Theorem 4.2). For this we introduce a weak cancellation property and show that each support has this property (Lemma 4.2); the proof is then obtained as a consequence of the characterization of regularity throught the cancellation property of Ehrenfeucht et al. Finally we show that each support verifies the Ehrenfeucht conjecture on finite test set (Theorem 4.3). For this we establish a more delicate cancellation property of supports (Lemma 4.3), which allows us to prove the Ehrenfeucht conjecture in a similar way as for regular languages.

2. A CHARACTERIZATION OF REGULARITY

In [2] Ehrenfeucht et al. introduced a property of languages as follows: a language $L \subset A^*$ has the cancellation property if there exists an integer $n \geqslant 1$ such that for any words $w,u,v,x_1,\dots,x_n$ satisfying $w = ux_1\dots x_n v$ there exist i,j, $1 \leqslant i \leqslant j \leqslant n$, such that

$$w \in L \quad \text{iff} \quad ux_1\dots x_{i-1}x_{j+1}\dots x_n v \in L .$$

They proved the following theorem.

Theorem 2.1 (Ehrenfeucht, Parikh, Rozenberg [2]) A language is regular if and only if it has the cancellation property.

We introduce here a property of languages which has a formal analogy with the cancellation property. We say that a language $L \subset A^*$ has the transposition property if there exists an integer $n \geq 1$ such that for any words $w, u, v, x_1, \dots, x_n$ satisfying $w = ux_1 \dots x_n v$, there exist i, j, k, $1 \leq i < j < k \leq n$, such that

$$(2.1) \qquad w \in L \iff ux_1 \dots x_{i-1} x_j \dots x_{k-1} x_i \dots x_{j-1} x_k \dots x_n \in L$$

(the right member word is obtained by interchanging in w the consecutive blocks $x_i \dots x_{j-1}$ and $x_j \dots x_{k-1}$).

Note that each regular language L has the transposition property: indeed, let m = twice the number of states of some finite deterministic automaton recognizing L; let q_o be the initial state and $w = ux_1 \dots x_m v$. Then in the sequence of m+1 states $q_o u$, $q_o ux_1$, $q_o ux_1 x_2$, ..., $q_o ux_1 \dots x_m$ there is one state, say q, which appears at least three times. This implies that one can interchange the two corresponding blocks in w, obtaining a word w' such that $w \in L \iff w' \in L$. Hence L has the transposition property.

Recall that the syntactic congruence of a language L is the congruence of A^* defined by: $x \sim y$ if and only if for any words u and v, $uxv \in L \iff uyv \in L$. The syntactic monoid of L is the quotient monoid $A^*/\sim$, see [3]. A monoid is periodic if any element of it is periodic, i.e. generates a finite submonoid. We call a language periodic if its syntactic monoid is periodic. Note that for any finite cyclic monoid generated by an element x, there exists a positive integer p such that $x^{2p} = x^p$. Hence a language L is periodic if and only if for each word x there exists a positive integer p satisfying, for any words u and v,

$$(2.2) \qquad ux^p v \in L \iff ux^{2p} v \in L .$$

Note also that each regular language is periodic because, by Kleene's theorem, its syntactic monoid is finite. We come now to the converse.

Theorem 2.2 A language is regular if and only if it is periodic and has the transposition property.

In order to prove the theorem we use a combinatorial result established by

Shirshov (see [6] or [10]) in the context of problems concerning algebras with polynomial identities. He introduced the notion of n-divided word as follows. Let A be a totally ordered and finite alphabet. In the free monoid A^* generated by A words of equal length are ordered lexicografically (from left to the right); the order is denoted by $\leqslant$ and $u < v$ means that $u \leqslant v$ and $u \neq v$. Let w be a word in A^*. An n-division of w is a factorization $w = ux_1 \dots x_n v$ such that for any permutation σ of $\{1,\dots,n\}$, $\sigma \neq id$, one has

$$w < ux_{\sigma(1)} \dots x_{\sigma(n)} v .$$

We say that a word is n-divided if it admits at least one n-division. The following theorem is due to Shirshov. A proof may be found in [6] or [10] .

Theorem 2.3 (Shirshov) For any integers $k,p,n \geqslant 1$ such that $p \geqslant 2n$, there exists an integer N(k,p,n) such that each word of length at least N(k,p,n) on an alphabet of cardinality k either is n-divided or contains a p-th power of a word of length at most n-1.

(We say that a word w contains a p-th power of a word x if x is nonempty and if w may be written $w = ux^p v$ for some words u and v).

Proof of theorem 2.2 (i) We use a particular case of Ramsey's theorem. For each set X, denote by X[3] the set of subsets of X of cardinality 3. Then: for each $m \geqslant 1$, there exists an integer n(m) such that, for each set X, card(X) $\geqslant$ n(m), and each partition $X[3] = I \cup J$, there is some subset Y of X, card(Y) = m, such that

$$Y[3] \subset I \quad \text{or} \quad Y[3] \subset J \tag{2.3}$$

see [4] th.1.7.1 .

(ii) Note that if L is a periodic language and W a finite set of words, then it is possible to find p such that (2.2) holds for all $x \in W$; moreover p may be chosen arbitrarily large. Denote by $\mathcal{L}_{m,p}$ the set of languages on the given alphabet A which have the transposition property for m and which are periodic, with the property that all word x of length at most n(m) verify (2.2). By the previous remark, each periodic language having the transposition property is in some $\mathcal{L}_{m,p}$ with $p \geqslant n(m)$.

(iii) Let $\mathcal{L} = \mathcal{L}_{m,p}$ with $p \geqslant n(m)$. It will suffice to show that $\mathcal{L}$ is finite: indeed $L \in \mathcal{L}$ implies that $a^{-1}L = \{w/\ aw \in L\} \in \mathcal{L}$ for each letter a, and one applies Nerode's criterion (see [3] th.III.8.1). Let n = n(m) and N = N(k,2p,n) defined as in th.2.3, with k=card(A). Then each word of length at least N is either n-divided or contains a (2p)-th power of some word of length at most n-1.

(iv) Let L , $L' \in \mathcal{L}$ such that for each word w, $|w| < N$: $w \in L \Leftrightarrow w \in L'$. We show that this implies $L = L'$ (hence $\mathcal{L}$ is finite). For this order A^* : $u \prec v$ means either that $|u| < |v|$ or that $|u| = |v|$ and $u > v$ (lexicographic order). We show by induction on this order that for each word w, $w \in L \Leftrightarrow w \in L'$. This is true if $|w| < N$. Let $|w| \geq N$. Suppose w contains a (2p)-th power of a word x, $|x| \leq n-1$: $w = ux^{2p}v$. Then because L , $L' \in \mathcal{L}_{m,p}$, one has by (2.2) and induction:
$w \in L \Leftrightarrow ux^{p}v \in L \Leftrightarrow ux^{p}v \in L' \Leftrightarrow w \in L'$.

Suppose now that w contains no such (2p)-th power: then w admits an n-division

(2.4) $$w = ux_1 \ldots x_n v .$$

Let $X = \{1,2,\ldots,n\}$ and define a subset I of $X[3]$ by: for $1 \leq i < j < k \leq n$,
$\{i,j,k\} \subset I \Leftrightarrow ux_1 \ldots x_{i-1}x_j \ldots x_{k-1}x_i \ldots x_{j-1}x_k \ldots x_n v \in L$.

Note that, because is (2.4) an n-division and by induction, I remains unchanged if L is replaced in the above definition by L'. Let $J = X[3] \setminus I$. Then, by Ramsey's theorem, there exists $Y \subset X$, card(Y) = m , such that (2.3) holds.

Let $w = u'y_1 \ldots y_m v'$ be the subfactorization of (2.4) corresponding to Y. Because L has the transposition property, there exist i,j,k with $1 \leq i < j < k \leq n$ such that
$w \in L \Leftrightarrow u'y_1 \ldots y_{i-1}y_j \ldots y_{k-1}y_i \ldots y_{j-1}y_k \ldots y_m v' \in L$.

Hence if $w \in L$, then there is some $\{i,j,k\}$ in $Y[3]$. By (2.3) this implies that $Y[3] \subset I$. Conversely if $Y[3] \subset I$, then by the transposition property of L one has $w \in L$. Hence $w \in L \Leftrightarrow Y[3] \subset I$. A previous remark and the transposition property of L' also imply $w \in L' \Leftrightarrow Y[3] \subset I$. Thus $w \in L \Leftrightarrow w \in L'$ and the theorem is proved.

3. PARIKH-BOUNDED LANGUAGES

Recall that a language is <u>bounded</u> if for some words $u_1,\ldots,u_q$, it is contained in $u_1^* \ldots u_q^*$. The following theorem gives a characterization of bounded languages in terms of n-divided words. Its proof may be found in [8].

<u>Theorem 3.1</u> A language is bounded if and only if for some integer n it contains no n-divided words.

Following [1] we say that a language L is <u>Parikh-bounded</u> if it contains some bounded language L' such that $p(L) = p(L')$, where $p : A^* \longrightarrow N^k$ is the Parikh mapping and $k = \mathrm{card}(A)$. In [1] is shown that each context-free language is Parikh-bounded. We consider now a weaker property than transposition. A language L has the <u>permutation property</u> if there exists an integer $n \geqslant 1$ such that, for any words $w, u, v, x_1, \ldots x_n$ satisfying $w = ux_1 \ldots x_n v \in L$, there exists some permutation σ of $\{1,2,\ldots,n\}$, $\sigma \neq id$, such that $ux_{\sigma(1)} \ldots x_{\sigma(n)} v$ is still in L. We prove the following theorem.

<u>Theorem 3.2</u> A language having the permutation property is Parikh-bounded.

<u>Proof</u>. Let $L_n = \{w \,/\, w \text{ is not n-divided}\}$ .Let $L' = L \cap L_n$. By theorem 3.1 , L' is bounded and $p(L') \subset p(L)$. It remains to show that $p(L) \subset p(L')$. Let $w \in L$. Then either $w \in L_n$, hence $w \in L'$ and $p(w) \in p(L')$, or $w \notin L_n$: then w is n-divided

$$w = ux_1 \ldots x_n v \; .$$

By hypothesis there is some permutation σ of $\{1,2,\ldots,n\}$ such that $w' = ux_{\sigma(1)} \ldots x_{\sigma(n)} v$ is still in L . Then $|w'| = |w|$ and $w' > w$: hence by induction $p(w) = p(w') \in p(L')$. Thus $p(L) \subset p(L')$.

Since, by th.2.2, a regular language satisfies the permutation property, theorem 3.2 gives a new proof for the fact that each regular language is Parikh-bounded. Unfortunately this proof does not work for context-free languages, because they do not satisfy in general the permutation property (for example, the set of palindrome words).

4. SUPPORTS

In this section we study <u>supports</u>, that is languages which are supports of rational power series (see [12]) ; they are a natural generalization of regular languages. Recall that a language L is support of a rational power series exactly when there exists a monoid homomorphism $\mu : A^* \longrightarrow k^{n \times n}$ (the multiplicative monoid of n by n matrices over a field k) and a linear mapping $\varphi : k^{n \times n} \longrightarrow k$ such that

$$L = \{ w \in A^* \mid \varphi(\mu w) \neq 0 \} \quad , \tag{4.1}$$

see [12], where is also proved the classical fact that each regular language is a support .

Lemma 4.1 Any support has the permutation property.

Proof Let L be a language defined as by (4.1). By the theorem of Amitsur-Levitzki (see [10] th.1.4.1), for any matrices $m_1,\dots,m_{2n}$ in $k^{n\times n}$, one has

$$\sum_{\sigma\in\mathfrak{S}_{2n}} (-1)^{\sigma}\, m_{\sigma(1)}\cdots m_{\sigma(2n)} = 0$$

where $(-1)^{\sigma}$ is the signature of the permutation σ. Let $w = ux_1\dots x_{2n}v \in L$. Then

$$\sum_{\sigma} (-1)^{\sigma}\, \mu(ux_{\sigma(1)}\dots x_{\sigma(2n)}v) = 0 .$$

Apply φ to this equality. Because $\varphi(\mu(ux_1\dots x_{2n}v)) \neq 0$, there is some σ such that $\varphi(\mu(ux_{\sigma(1)}\dots x_{\sigma(2n)}v)) \neq 0$, hence $ux_{\sigma(1)}\dots x_{\sigma(2n)}v \in L$.

As a consequence of theorem 3.2 and lemma 4.1, we obtain the following theorem.

Theorem 4.1 Any support is Parikh-bounded.

In analogy with the cancellation property of Ehrenfeucht et al. (see section 1) we say that a language L has the weak cancellation property if there exists an integer n such that, for each word w in L such that $w = xu_1\dots u_n y$ for some words $x,u_1,\dots,u_n,y$, there exist i,j, $1\leq i\leq j\leq n$ such that $xu_1\dots u_{i-1}u_{j+1}\dots u_n y$ is in L (the weak property is obtained from the strong one by replacing $\Leftrightarrow$ by $\Rightarrow$).

By theorem 2.1 we can deduce the following corollary.

Corollary Let L_1, L_2 be two complementary languages. If they have both the weak cancellation property, then they are regular.

The proof of the following lemma may be found in [9].

Lemma 4.2 Any support has the weak cancellation property.

As a consequence of corollary and lemma 4.2 we obtain the solution of a conjecture quoted in [11].

Theorem 4.2 Let L_1, L_2 be two complementary languages which are supports of rational power series. Then they are regular languages.

The following conjecture is due to Ehrenfeucht, see [5]:

Let $L \subset A^*$ be a language. Then there exists a finite subset K of L such that, for any alphabet B and any homomorphisms $f, g : A^* \rightarrow B^*$, the condition $f|K = g|K$ implies $f|L = g|L$.

In other words, to test whether two homomorphisms coincide on L it is enough to do the test on some finite subset of L (depending only on L). This conjecture was proved in the case where L is context-free or when A has only two letters (see [5]).

Theorem 4.3 The Ehrenfeucht conjecture is true for supports

In order to prove theorem 4.3 we need a lemma which gives another cancellation property of supports (for a proof see [9]).

Lemma 4.3 Let L be a support. Then there exists an integer N such that each word w in L of length at least N admits a factorization w = xuyvz such that $u,v \neq 1$ and xyvz , xuyz , xyz $\in$ L .

The proof of theorem 4.3 can then be obtained by previous lemma in a similar way as for regular languages. Moreover this proof shows that a finite test set may effectively be constructed.

REFERENCES

[1] M.Blattner,M.Latteux, Parikh-bounded languages, 8-th Int.Colloquium on Automata, Languages and Programming, Acre (Israel), Lecture notes in Computer Science 115 (1981) 316-323.

[2] A.Ehrenfeucht,R.Parikh,G.Rozenberg, Pumping lemmas for regular sets, SIAM J. of Computing 10 (1981) 536-541.

[3] S.Eilenberg, Automata, languages and machines, Vol.A, Academic Press (1974).

[4] M.Harrison, Introduction to formal language theory, Addison-Wesley (1978).

[5] K.Culik,A.Salomaa, Test set and checking words for homomorphisms equivalence, J.Comp.System Science 19 (1980) 379-395.

[6] M.Lothaire, Combinatorics on words, Addison-Wesley (1983).

[7] A.Restivo,C.Reutenauer, On the Burnside problem for semigroups, J.of Algebra (to appear).

[8] A.Restivo,C.Reutenauer, Some applications of a theorem of Shirshov to language theory, Information and Control (to appear).

[9] A.Restivo,C.Reutenauer, On cancellation properties of languages which are support of rational power series, J. of Computer and System Science (to appear).

[10] L.H.Rowen, Polynomial identities in ring theory, Academic Press (1980).

[11] A.Salomaa, Formal power series in noncommuting variables, Proc.Scandinavian Math. Congress, Aarhus 1980, Prog.Math. 11 (1981).

[12] A.Salomaa,M.Soittola, Automata theoretic aspects of formal power series, Springer Verlag (1978).

A Hardware Implementation of the CSP Primitives and its Verification

by

Dorit Ron*, Flavia Rosemberg* and Amir Pnueli*

Abstract

A design for a hardware interface that implements CSP-like communication primitives is presented. The design is based on a bus scheme that allows processes to "eavesdrop" on messages not directly addressed to them. A temporal logic specification is given for the network and an outline of a verification proof is sketched.

1. Introduction

This work reports the design and formal verification of a hardware implementation of a communication protocol. The unit designed serves as an interface between a host process (or set of processes) and a bus-based local network. The services that it provides are synchronous message passing modelled after Hoare's CSP language [H].

More precisely, the host submits to the designed unit, which we call IPL (short for Inter Process Level), a list of alternatives (AC). Each alternative consists of (i) the name of a process which is the candidate partner for the corresponding communication, (ii) an indication as to whether the associated request is for input or output, and (iii) in the case of an output command, the data that is to be sent to the corresponding partner. The IPL is supposed to perform one of the alternatives and eventually report to the host which of them was actually performed. In the case of an input command it also delivers to the host the data that was received.

The protocol presented here is one of three variants given in [Ros]. In this version we strongly utilize the following property of carrier-sense communication system: when node i sends a message to node j, actually every other node in the system listens and receives this message and may perform some internal actions as a result of this "eavesdropping". We also make some strong simplifying assumptions about the possible failures of the system, and the *eventual reliability* of the communication medium. Some of the other variants reported on in [Ros] are more robust and make much weaker assumptions about the reliability of the network.

After presenting the basic algorithm for the designed IPL we use temporal logic in order to verify its correctness. The main new tool that has been added to the verification techniques of, say [MP1], is the treatment of an *eventually reliable* channel, as a special fairness construct. The application of this device to verification of other protocols is also reported on in [R].

The contribution of this work to the programming languages area is the presentation of a hardware implementation of the CSP primitives that is based on a carrier-sense based network, and its formal verification using temporal logic. The success of the

*Department of Applied Mathematics, Weizmann Institute, Rehovot, 76100 Israel.

verification illustrates the usefulness of temporal logic for the analysis of implementations on a most detailed level.

2. The Use of Temporal Logic

The temporal language and proof system that we use here is taken from [MP2]. In addition we use the following eventuality rule:

Generalized Eventuality Rule—GEVNT
Let φ, χ and ψ be three state formulas.
A. $\vdash P$ leads from $\varphi \vee \chi$ to $\varphi \vee \chi \vee \psi$
B. $\vdash \varphi \supset (\Diamond \chi \vee \Diamond \psi)$
C. $\vdash \Box \Diamond \chi \supset \Diamond \psi$

$\vdash (\varphi \vee \chi) \supset (\varphi \vee \chi) \mathcal{U} \psi$

We can use this rule to establish: $\vdash (\varphi \vee \chi) \supset \Diamond \psi$. The GEVNT rule is very useful for proving eventuality (liveness) properties under the assumptions that a communication channel is eventually reliable. A channel is defined to be eventually reliable if, whenever one process that is connected to it wishes to send a message, there could be only finitely many failed attempts (or rejections), before a message by this process is eventually accepted by the channel, and delivered successfully to all of its destinations.

Typically, φ represents a situation from which we wish to exit to ψ. The assertion χ represents a state (or some states) within φ in which an attempt to communicate is made. If the attempt is successful then χ leads to ψ, otherwise it goes back to φ. Premise A states that as long as we do not exit to ψ, $\varphi \vee \chi$ continues to hold. Premise B states that from φ we either exit to ψ directly or get to χ trying to communicate. Premise C is usually the guarantee given from outside (by the hardware manufacturer) about the eventual reliability of the communication medium. It states that if we make an infinite number of attempts to communicate, then eventually one of them will succeed.

3. The Communication Protocol

The structure of the processes (Host's Level) and the interfaces (Inter Process Level—IPL) taking part in the communication is as follows:

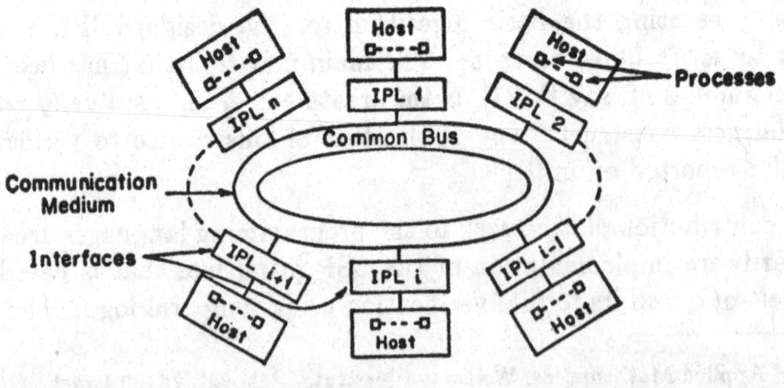

As mentioned earlier, the host submits to the IPL a list of communication alternatives. In case the host runs a CSP program it is its own responsibility to identify alternatives whose boolean guard part is true and to submit only those to the IPL. The host may also choose to perform any local alternative, i.e. one that does not involve communication, and not submit any list in this case. Note that the case of I/O commands not in guards can be represented as an AC with precisely one alternative. ACs presented to the IPL contain a finite number of I/O alternatives which have the following format:

command type	source	destination	other details

The type of a command can be either an input request (IREQ) or an output request (OREQ). Output alternatives are submitted together with the data that should be sent in case this alternative is selected. The data message associated with an OREQ is referred to as DMSG. The source is always that process from which the IPL gets the AC. The destination is a process connected to another IPL that is the intended partner for this communication. Each IPL has the following structure:

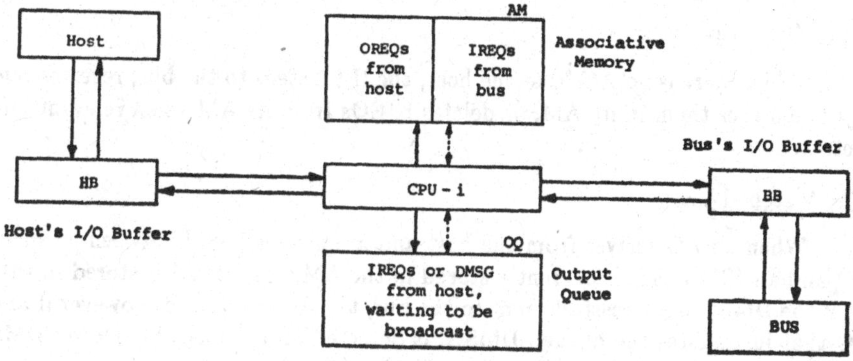

The Host's I/O Buffer (HB) stores the AC available to the CPU until one of the alternatives is successfully performed and this fact reported back to the host. An I/O alternative is successfully completed when a communication occurs between two processes, i.e., it is delayed until the other process is ready with the corresponding answer. For this reason, each IPL contains an Associative Memory (AM) which is divided into two logical parts for storing the relevant IREQs received from the bus separately from the OREQs submitted by the host. The Bus's I/O Buffer (BB) which is a single-element buffer stores the message which comes from the bus until the CPU receives it.

The algorithm we present here is asymmetric in the way it treats IREQs and OREQs: only IREQs are sent to other processes, while OREQs are stored in the AM until a compatible IREQ is received from the bus. When an IPL gets an AC from the host it checks in its AM to see whether there is already a matched IREQ for one of the AC's OREQs. If a match is found the DMSG—which includes the information to be interchanged, is stored in the Output Queue (OQ) and, if possible, submitted to the bus. If no match is found all IREQs are stored in the OQ, while all OREQs are stored in the AM. In this case a match might take place between an IREQ that comes from the bus and one of the OREQs in the AM, or between an IREQ that was sent earlier and an

OREQ which belongs to another IPL. A special delay is provided by the hardware after an IREQ message is received. This delay allows the recipient to respond immediately by a DMSG that matches the IREQ, if one is available. In this case a successful transmission with no contention is guaranteed.

When a match occurs and the relevant DMSG is sent, it means that one communication alternative has been successfully completed and the rest of the AC should be deleted. It is straightforward for the sender to delete all the IREQs left in the OQ, and all the OREQs in the AM. The question is who will delete all the IREQs that the sender has sent to all of the alternate candidates for communication? In our algorithm we use the "eavesdropping" principle by which any process j that hears on the bus a DMSG being directed from i to k, updates its own tables. Updating of the tables deletes all previous IREQs that have been received at j from either i or k, since the fact that i and k have communicated successfully invalidates all such previous IREQs. Similarly, if j has already prepared a response to a request from either i or k, and has stored this response in its OQ, the response should be deleted as soon as a DMSG from i to k is seen on the bus. We summarize the possible operations of the IPL:

A. <u>The Idle Case</u>

While there is no AC from the host, the IPL listens to the bus, receives relevant IREQs and stores them in its AM, or deletes IREQs from its AM when relevant DMSGs are detected.

B. <u>The Matched Case</u>

When an AC arrives from the host and a match is found between an incoming OREQ and an IREQ that is currently stored in the AM, the DMSG is stored in the OQ. Then, if the DMSG is successfully sent to the bus, the AC is satisfied, however if another DMSG that invalidates the queued DMSG, is detected on the bus, the queued DMSG is cancelled and the AC is compared again with the AM.

C. <u>The Unmatched Case</u>

When an AC has no match with the IREQs in the AM, all its IREQs are delivered to the OQ to be sent, and all its OREQs are stored in the AM. A match might occur either between an IREQ from the bus and an OREQ in AM, or when an IREQ finds a match in another IPL. In this case, a DMSG will arrive as an answer to one of the IREQs that were sent by the IPL.

The code for the protocol of IPL$_i$ is given below.

<u>idle</u>:

```
      loop
τ0^i: if HB_i ≠ Λ then match;
      handle-input
      end loop
```

match:

loop

τ_4^i: *if* $OQ_i = \Lambda \wedge \forall k[(OREQ,i,k,m) \in HB_i \supset (IREQ,k,i) \notin AM_i]$
then $[OQ_i := HB_i.IREQ;\ AM_i := AM_i \cup HB_i.OREQ;$ unmatch; *exit*$]$

τ_5^i: *else if* $OQ_i = \Lambda \wedge (OREQ,i,k,m) \in HB_i \wedge (IREQ,k,i) \in AM_i$
then $OQ_i := (DMSG,i,k,m)$;

if $OQ_i = (DMSG,i,k,m)$ *then* try-send $(DMSG,i,k,m)$

τ_6^i: *on* success *do* [report_sent$_i(k)$; $OQ_i := \Lambda$; $HB_i := \Lambda$;
$AM_i := AM_i - \{(IREQ,k,i)\}$; *exit*];

handle-input

end loop

unmatch:

loop

if $OQ_i = (IREQ,i,k)*\alpha$ *then* try-send $(IREQ,i,k)$

τ_7^i: *on* success *do* $OQ_i := \alpha$;

τ_8^i: *if* $BB_i = (IREQ,j,i) \wedge (OREQ,i,j,m) \in AM_i$ *then*
[send $(DMSG,i,j,m)$; report_sent$_i(j)$; $BB_i := \Lambda$;
$OQ_i := \Lambda$; $HB_i := \Lambda$; $AM_i := AM_i - \{OREQs\}$; *exit*]

τ_9^i: *else if* $BB_i = (DMSG,j,i,m)$ *then*
[report_rec$_i(j,m)$; $BB_i := \Lambda$; $OQ_i := \Lambda$; $HB_i := \Lambda$;
$AM_i := AM_i - \{OREQs\}$; *exit*];

handle-input

end loop

handle-input:

τ_1^i: *if* $BB_i = (IREQ,j,k) \wedge k \neq i$ *then* $BB_i := \Lambda$

τ_2^i: *else if* $BB_i = (IREQ,j,i) \wedge \forall m(OREQ,i,j,m) \notin AM_i$
then $[AM_i := AM_i \cup \{(IREQ,j,i)\};\ BB_i := \Lambda]$

τ_3^i: *else if* $BB_i = (DMSG,j,k,m) \wedge k \neq i$ *then*
$[AM_i := AM_i - \{(IREQ,j,i),(IREQ,k,i)\};$
$OQ_i := OQ_i - \{(DMSG,i,j,-),(DMSG,i,k,-)\};\ BB_i := \Lambda]$

In this program $HB_i.IREQ$ and $HB_i.OREQ$ present the lists of IREQs and OREQs in HB_i, respectively. Notice that a 'send' operation always terminates and thus is used for describing the immediate response in τ_8^i. A try-send operation may be rejected in mid-communication because of a collision. The messages sent back to the host are either report_sent$_i(k)$ or report_rec$_i(k,m)$, where the first reports of a successful transmission of a DMSG to process k, and the second reports reception of the DMSG m from process k.

This algorithm may also be presented in the following transitions diagram form:

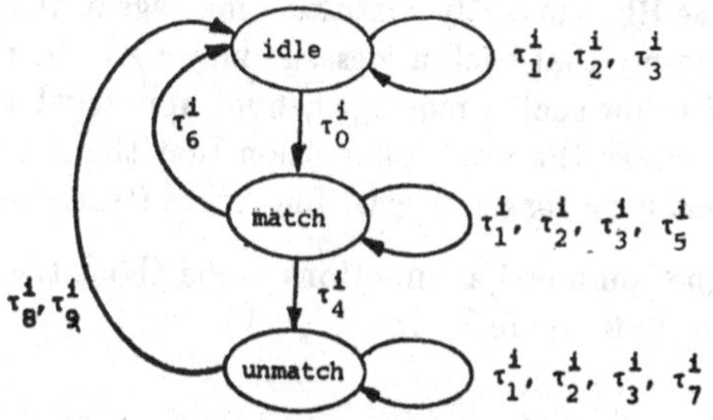

Since in the original algorithm the alternatives out of each label are scanned in sequential order, we may assume in the diagram representation that the alternate transitions are chosen with justice, i.e. each transition that is continuously enabled must eventually be chosen. An even stronger assumption should be made about τ_4^i and τ_5^i. Namely that if continually one of them is enabled, then eventually one of them must be taken. This is because their conditions are complementary and they are tested one after the other in the algorithm. Note also that the enabling condition for the transitions τ_6 and τ_7 is both the boolean condition and success of sending the message onto the bus.

4. Assumptions Made About the System

The algorithm for gaining control of the bus is similar to that of an Ethernet, i.e., if an IPL attempts to send a message there are two possibilities: either everybody else is silent and will remain so until the IPL finishes sending, or some other IPL sends a message interrupting the first IPL's operation. In this case everybody stops sending and some contention resolution phase takes place. It is guaranteed that with probability 1 every process that has a message will eventually get to send it. Rejections in our algorithm above refer to the detection of a collision or a busy bus when trying to send.

There are certain assumptions about the behavior of the bus that are crucial to the correctness of the algorithm. They may be summarized as follows:

(BL1) There exists a delay $\delta_1 > 0$ such that from the instant an IPL_i successfully places a message on the bus, it appears within δ_1 units in the bus buffer BB_j of each IPL_j, $j \neq i$.

(BS1) There exists a second delay $\delta_2 > 0$, such that from the instant an IPL_i successfully places a message on the bus, no other message may be placed on the bus (the bus will be considered busy) within the next $\delta_1 + \delta_2$ units.

The requirement (BL1) is a liveness property of the bus, while (BS1) is a safety property. A second liveness property is given by:

(BL2) If a certain IPL_i is continually trying to place the message m on the bus then eventually it will succeed.

The two bus properties (BL1) and (BS1) allow each IPL_j the time delay δ_2 in which to remove the current contents of the buffer BB_j, before a new message can be placed on the bus. When we examine the algorithm, we see that if BB_j is currently loaded with any message, it will be read and the message removed within at most 4 transitions or steps performed by IPL_j. The only case this is not immediately clear is when IPL_j is at *idle* or at *match* and the BB_j currently contains a message of the form (DMSG, i, j, m). The algorithm seems to imply that such a message may never be removed. However, as we prove in statement I7 below such a message cannot appear while IPL_j is at *idle* or at *match*. Consequently we make the vital assumption that the minimal speed of each of the processors is such that it performs at least four steps (transitions) in δ_2 units.

As a result of the combined assumptions made about the bus and the speed of the processor we may conclude the following:

(C1) A message m deposited in the BB_j buffer is eventually read by IPL_j and no new message will be placed on the bus until m is removed from BB_j.

We may now use this conclusion to model the system consisting of the bus and the local BB_j buffers in a more convenient and compact way. Instead of a single bus transmitting the message to every process, we consider a net of disjoint lines, providing a direct connection C_{ij} between each two nodes IPL_i and IPL_j. The line C_{ij} is disjoint from the line C_{ji}. The broadcasting of the message m by IPL_i causes m to appear simultaneously on each C_{ij} line, $j \neq i$. Then IPL_j may read a message from any of the C_{kj}, $k \neq j$ and remove it from there.

We can easily modify the program to refer to the $\{C_{ij}\}$ convention by replacing each test of the form $BB_k = (x, i, j)$ by the test $C_{ik} = (x, i, j)$ where x is one of the message types IREQ, OREQ or DMSG.

Listed below are the precise assumptions that we make now about the $\{C_{ij}\}$ network that represent the behavior of the low level transmission system.

F1: $(C_{ij} = x) \supset [\bigcirc(C_{ij} = x)]\,\mathcal{U}\,(P_j \text{ reads } C_{ij})$

Here a read operation is equivalent to taking τ_ℓ^j for $\ell \in \{1, 2, 3, 8, 9\}$. This property states that once a message is placed on the line, it will eventually be removed by the process at the end of the line and will not be modified until then. This corresponds to the conclusion (C1) above.

Other consequences of (C1) are that at a certain time only one message can be contained anywhere in the $\{C_{ij}\}$ network.

F2: $(C_{ij} \neq \Lambda) \supset (\forall \ell, k \neq i)(C_{k\ell} = \Lambda)$

F3: $[(C_{ij} = x) \wedge (C_{k\ell} = y)] \supset [(x = y) \wedge (k = i)]$

F4: $(C_{ij} = \Lambda) \supset (C_{ij} = \Lambda)\ U\ [\exists x \forall k (C_{ik} = x)]$

The statement F4 describes the "broadcasting" character of the bus. It says that whenever a message x appears on one of the lines—C_{ij}, it simultaneously appears on all the other lines, C_{ik}, originating from the same source. In F4 we have used the ***unless*** operator U which is the weak form of the ***until***. A formula pUq states that p must hold until q happens, but it may also be the case that q never happens and then p must hold continually.

The next two properties represent the eventual reliability assumption of the bus, previously stated in (BL2).

F5: $\square\Diamond[(P_i \text{ at } \mathit{match}) \wedge (OQ_i = C)] \supset \Diamond[(P_i \text{ at } \mathit{idle}) \wedge (OQ_i = \Lambda) \wedge (\forall j \neq i)(C_{ij} = C)]$

F6: $\square\Diamond[(P_i \text{ at } \mathit{unmatch}) \wedge (OQ_i = C{*}\alpha)] \supset \Diamond[(P_i \text{ at } \mathit{unmatch}) \wedge (OQ_i = \alpha) \wedge (\forall j \neq i)(C_{ij} = C)]$

As can be seen in the protocol, these statements refer to τ_6^i and τ_7^i, respectively. It assures us that if infinitely often IPL_i wishes to send a message, then eventually it will find all the C_{ij}s not busy for every $j \neq i$, and the transmission will be successfully completed.

5. Correctness of the Implementation

A specification of the presented network design should state that the network, consisting of the bus and the algorithms for the IPLs, correctly implements the CSP primitives. Such a specification may be formulated using temporal logic and will then consist of several statements. These statements can be partitioned into safety and liveness statements. We choose to express the specification by relating the following events:

$\text{submit}_i(\text{AC})$- This event describes the submission of the AC by host_i to its IPL.

$\text{report\_sent}_i(j)$- This event corresponds to IPL_i reporting to its host a successful sending of a DMSG to IPL_j. In our algorithm it corresponds to one of the transitions τ_6^i, τ_8^i.

$\text{report\_rec}_i(j, m)$- This event corresponds to IPL_i reporting to its host of a DMSG m received from node IPL_j.

The three events above are externally observable since they describe interchanges between the network, represented by the IPLs, to the environment, represented by the hosts. We found it convenient to add the following internal event:

$\text{SD}(i, j, m)$- This corresponds to the DMSG m being sent from IPL_i to IPL_j in a way that ensures its eventual acceptance by IPL_j. In our program it is representable by one of the transitions τ_6^i, τ_8^i.

5.1 Safety Properties

Following is a list of the safety properties of the network. We use the following abbreviations:

$\textit{submit}_i = (\exists\, \text{AC})\ \text{submit}_i(\text{AC})$ - The host submits some AC to IPL_i

$\textit{report}_i = (\exists\, j, m)\ (\text{report\_sent}_i(j) \vee \text{report\_rec}_i(j, m))$

$SD_i = (\exists\, j, m)\ (\text{SD}(i, j, m) \vee \text{SD}(j, i, m))$

The first two properties are immediate consequence of the definitions of the events:

(S1) $\text{submit}_i(\text{AC}) \supset [(HB_i = \Lambda) \wedge \bigcirc(HB_i = \text{AC})]$

(S2) $\textit{report}_i \supset [(HB_i \neq \Lambda) \wedge \bigcirc(HB_i = \Lambda)]$

The next three properties relate the events to the current contents of the HB_i buffer:

(S3) $\text{SD}(i, j, m) \supset [((IREQ, j, i) \in HB_j) \wedge ((OREQ, i, j) \in HB_i)]$

(S4) $(HB_i = \Lambda) \supset [\bigcirc(HB_i = \Lambda)]\ \mathcal{U}\ \textit{submit}_i$

(S5) $(HB_i = \text{AC}) \supset [\bigcirc(HB_i = \text{AC})] \; U \; \textit{report}_i$

Property (S4) states that if HB_i is currently empty it will remain empty until the next $\textit{submit}_i$ event. Property (S5) states that if HB_i is currently full it will retain its current contents until the next $\textit{report}_i$ event. Both properties use the *unless* operator U that does not guarantee that the $\textit{submit}_i$ and $\textit{report}_i$ actually happen.

The next several properties dictate necessary ordering between the events.

(S6) $\textit{submit}_i \supset [(\exists m) \, \text{SD}(i,j,m) \; P \; \text{report\_sent}_i(j)]$

Property (S6) states that a $\text{report\_sent}_i(j)$ event must be preceded by an $\text{SD}(i,j,m)$ event for some m.

(S7) $\textit{submit}_i \supset [\text{SD}(j,i,m) \; P \; \text{report\_rec}_i(j,m)]$

Similarly property (S7) states that a $\text{report\_rec}_i(j,m)$ must be preceded by an $\text{SD}(j,i,m)$ event.

(S8) $SD_i \supset \bigcirc[\textit{submit}_i \; P \; SD_i]$

Property (S8) ensures that only one SD_i may result from a single $\textit{submit}_i$ event. It states that following an SD_i event, the next SD_i event must be preceded by a new submission.

5.2 Liveness Properties

There are two liveness properties that the network should guarantee:

(L1) $\text{SD}(i,j,m) \supset (\Diamond \, \textit{report}_i \wedge \Diamond \, \textit{report}_j)$

This property assures that if a message has been sent from i to j then this fact would eventually be reported to both hosts.

(L2) $\sim \Box[((IREQ,i,j) \in HB_i) \wedge ((OREQ,j,i) \in HB_j)]$

This is the main liveness property of the network. It forbids the possibility that from a certain point on IPL_i and IPL_j continually hold a pair of matching requests and yet fail to communicate.

6. Verification

In this section we present an outline of the proof that the designed network meets its specification. The full proof is included in [RRP]. Due to space limitations we will concentrate on the proofs of the liveness properties (L1) and (L2). For detailed proofs of the other properties we refer again to [RRP].

We begin by presenting a list of invariants that are necessary for the liveness proof. The main one—I7 states that it is possible for P_i to receive a (DMSG,k,i,m) only while being in the *unmatch* state. In fact, this (DMSG,k,i,m) is a response to an (IREQ,i,k) sent before. Such an invariant that restricts the possible states of P_i

while P_k sends a DMSG to it, is proved as a part of a set of invariants that are verified simultaneously.

I1: $[\exists \ell(C_{j\ell} = (DMSG, j, i, m))] \supset$
$(\forall k \neq i, k \neq j)[(C_{jk} = (DMSG, j, i, m)) \vee ((IREQ, \binom{j}{i}, k) \notin AM_k)]$

I2: $[C_{ik} = (IREQ, i, k)] \supset (P_i \text{ at } unmatch)$

I3: $[(IREQ, i, k) \in AM_k] \supset \{(P_i \text{ at } unmatch) \vee$
$\exists m[(C_{ik} = (DMSG, i, j, m)) \vee (C_{jk} = (DMSG, j, i, m))]\}$

I4: $[((IREQ, i, k) \in AM_k) \wedge (C_{ik} \neq (DMSG, i, j, m)) \wedge$
$(C_{jk} \neq (DMSG, j, i, m))] \supset (P_i \text{ at } unmatch)$

I5: $[(P_k \text{ at } match) \wedge (OQ_k = (DMSG, k, i, m))] \supset [(IREQ, i, k) \in AM_k]$

I6: $[(P_k \text{ at } idle) \wedge (C_{ki} = (DMSG, k, i, m))] \supset (P_i \text{ at } unmatch)$

I7: $[C_{ki} = (DMSG, k, i, m)] \supset (P_i \text{ at } unmatch)$.

In addition we present two invariants that list the possible states of an IPL according to the contents of its HB.

I8: $[(IREQ, i, j) \in HB_i] \supset \{(P_i \text{ at } match) \vee$
$\{(P_i \text{ at } unmatch) \wedge [((IREQ, i, j) \in OQ_i) \vee (C_{ij} = (IREQ, i, j))$
$\vee ((IREQ, i, j) \in AM_j) \vee (\exists k, m)((DMSG, k, i, m) = C_{ki})]\}\}$

I9: $[(OREQ, j, i) \in HB_j] \supset \{(P_j \text{ at } match) \vee$
$[(P_j \text{ at } unmatch) \wedge ((IREQ, i, j) \notin AM_j)]\}$.

The proof of these invariants is conducted by checking all the transitions that may potentially falsify any of the statements, i.e., those transitions which may cause an antecedent to become true and those which may falsify a consequence.

The verification of L1 is almost trivial. The event $report_i$ occurs in the same transition as SD(i, j, m) (τ_6^i or τ_8^i), which sets $C_{ij} = (DMSG, i, j, m)$. By F1 and I7 it is guaranteed that P_j receives that DMSG while being at *unmatch*. This is done by taking τ_9^j which also includes the $report_j$ event.

Instead of proving L2 we verify an equivalent Theorem that states that if processes i and j have a matched pair of IREQ and OREQ in their HBs then at least one of them will eventually have a communication with some process:

$$\textbf{Theorem:} \vdash [((IREQ, i, j) \in HB_i) \wedge ((OREQ, j, i) \in HB_j)] \supset$$
$$\Diamond[P_i \text{ takes } (\tau_6^i, \tau_8^i, \tau_9^i) \vee P_j \text{ takes } (\tau_6^j, \tau_8^j, \tau_9^j)]$$

The three transitions τ_6, τ_8 and τ_9 signify a successful completion of a communication after which HB is erased. Consequently their taking ensures that the corresponding HB does not retain its value continually.

Proof: The proof is based on the diagram presented earlier. It proceeds by negation. Assume to the contrary that:

φ: $[((IREQ,i,j) \in HB_i) \wedge ((OREQ,j,i,m) \in HB_j)] \wedge$
$\Box[\sim \text{taken } (\tau_6^i, \tau_8^i, \tau_9^i; \tau_6^j, \tau_8^j, \tau_9^j)]$

From this hypothesis, since $HB \neq \Lambda$, it is clear that neither IPL$_i$ nor IPL$_j$ are ever in the *idle* case:

N1: $\varphi \supset \Box[(\sim P_i \text{ at } idle) \wedge (\sim P_j \text{ at } idle)]$

Another conditional invariance we establish is:

N2: $[\forall m(C_{i\ell} \neq (DMSG,i,k,m)) \wedge \Box(\sim P_i \text{ at } idle)] \supset$
$\Box(\forall m)[(C_{i\ell} \neq (DMSG,i,k,m)) \wedge (C_{kr} \neq (DMSG,k,i,m))]$

The first part of the consequence is proved by checking all relevant transitions. The second is proved by negation using I7 and contradicting the antecedent of N2 that states $\sim$(P$_i$ at *idle*).

By the liveness property of the bus F1, every message is eventually read off the bus. Consequently for every ℓ eventually $C_{i\ell} = \Lambda$. We thus may conclude:

N3: $\varphi \supset \Diamond \psi$

where $\psi = \Box[(\sim P_i \text{ at } idle) \wedge (\sim P_j \text{ at } idle) \wedge \forall m(C_{i\ell} \neq DMSG(i,k,m))$
$\wedge \forall m(C_{kr} \neq DMSG(k,i,m))]$

This statement ensures the obvious fact that if P$_i$ never gets back to *idle* then neither a DMSG issued by P$_i$ nor a DMSG directed to P$_i$ should be observed on the bus from a certain point on. Consequently it is sufficient to prove:

$$\psi \supset \Diamond[P_i \text{ takes } (\tau_6^i, \tau_8^i, \tau_9^i) \vee P_j \text{ takes } (\tau_6^j, \tau_8^j, \tau_9^j)]$$

Consider now the different states in which P$_i$ may be under the assumption of $(IREQ,i,j) \in HB_i$. According to I8 there are five different cases:

Case 1: $(\exists k,m)[(DMSG,k,i,m) = C_{ki}]$

This case contradicts ψ and hence is impossible.

Case 2: $((IREQ,i,j) \in AM_j)$

By I9 P$_j$ must currently be at *match*. Since $(OREQ,j,i,m) \in HB_j$ transition τ_5^j is continually enabled (τ_4^i being disabled) causing P$_j$ to repeatedly load OQ$_j$ with some DMSG. According to ψ, P$_j$ will never see a DMSG relevant to P$_i$ that will cause it to remove (IREQ,i,j) from AM$_j$. Consequently, P$_j$ is infinitely many times ready to take τ_6 and send some DMSG to the bus. By the GEVNT rule and F5 P$_j$ will eventually take τ_6.

Case 3: $(C_{ij} = IREQ,i,j)$

Since by F1 P$_j$ must eventually read (IREQ,i,j) off the C_{ij} line, there are two locations where the request may be read. If it is read while P$_j$ is at *match* it is done via τ_2 and we get back to case 2 in which P$_j$ at *match* and $(IREQ,i,j) \in AM_j$. If on the other hand it is read while P$_j$ is at *unmatch*, it must be done via τ_8 since $(OREQ,j,i,m) \in HB_j.OREQ \subseteq AM_j$. Thus taking τ_8 is directly guaranteed.

Case 4: (P_i at *unmatch*) $\wedge$ $((IREQ, i, j) \in OQ_i)$

This case ensures that $OQ_i \neq \Lambda$. Since by ψ we assumed (by negation) that τ_8 and τ_9 are never taken, it follows that τ_7 that attempts to send the top of OQ_i is infinitely many times enabled. By F6, the top of OQ_i will in fact be transmitted, and by induction on the position of (IREQ,i, j) in OQ_i, this input request will eventually be sent. Thus, we are ensured of eventually getting to Case 3.

Case 5: (P_i at *match*)

Since by ψ we forbid P_i to ever take τ_6, P_i must either stay at *match* forever or eventually take τ_4 moving to the state described by Case 4 above. The only way it may stay at *match* forever is that it repeatedly finds some (IREQ,k, i) in AM_i matching some (OREQ,i, k) in HB_i. In that case it will repeatedly load OQ_i with the appropriate DMSG and infinitely often attempt to transmit this message. In view of GEVNT and F5 it must eventually succeed and take τ_6 to *idle*. ∎

7. Conclusions

The paper demonstrates that it is plausible and highly recommendable to combine the activity of hardware design, or more generally any implementation design, with temporal verification of the resulting algorithm. The temporal specification forces the designer to formulate precisely what the implementation is expected to accomplish. The verification process points out numerous bugs and oversights some of which are very subtle. It also clarifies and makes explicit the assumptions made about components that are not designed but used as black boxes, such as the lowest level communication protocols assumed in our design.

There is no doubt that a higher standard of confidence in the design and preciseness in its presentation to others is achieved by the combination of design and verification as presented in this paper.

Acknowledgement

The work reported here is part of the M.Sc. thesis of Dorit Ron and the Ph.D. thesis fo Flavia Rosemberg. The latter's thesis is done under the supervision of S. Ruhman whom we wish to thank for support and encouragement.

8. References

[H] C.A.R. Hoare "Communicating Sequential Processes", *Communications of the ACM*, Vol. 21, No. 8, 666–677, August 1978.

[MP1] Z. Manna and A. Pnueli, "Verification of Concurrent Programs: Temporal Proof Principles", *Proc. of the Workshop on Logic of Programs* (D. Kozen, ed.), Yorktown Heights, NY (1981).

[MP2] Z. Manna and A. Pnueli, "Verification of Concurrent Programs: A Temporal Proof System", *Proc. 4th School on Advanced Programming*, Amsterdam, The Netherlands (June 1982).

[R] D. Ron, "Temporal Verification of Communication Protocols", M.Sc. Thesis, Weizmann Institute.

[Ros] F. Rosemberg, "Final Report", Dept. of Applied Mathematics, The Weizmann Institute of Science, July 1983.

[RRP] D. Ron, F. Rosemberg and A. Pnueli, "Verification of a Hardware Implementation of the CSP Primitives". In preparation.

FACTORIZATION OF UNIVARIATE INTEGER POLYNOMIALS BY DIOPHANTINE APPROXIMATION AND AN IMPROVED BASIS REDUCTION ALGORITHM

Arnold Schönhage

Mathematisches Institut
der Universität Tübingen
Auf der Morgenstelle 10
D 74 Tübingen, W-Germany

1. Introduction

We describe an algorithm for factoring univariate integer polynomials f (except for their integer prime factors) with a running time of $O(n^{6+\varepsilon}+n^4(\log|f|)^{2+\varepsilon})$ bit operations (for any $\varepsilon > 0$), where n denotes the degree, and $|f|$ is the norm of f. With classical integer multiplication the bound is $O(n^8+n^5(\log|f|)^3)$, respectively. This improves the corresponding bounds of Lenstra, Lenstra, Lovász [3] plus Kaltofen's refinement [1] by a factor of order n^3.

Our method starts from some real or complex zero z of f and performs a test for $m = 2,4,8,\ldots,n-1$, whether the minimal polynomial of z, say p, is of degree not greater than m. If so, the factor p of f will be found by diophantine approximation of $1,z,\ldots,z^m$. For that an approximation of z with error bound $2^{-\ell}$ is used, where $\ell = O(mn+n\cdot\log|f|)$ turns out to be sufficient.

The diophantine approximation hinges on the basis reduction technique [3]. By simply applying the reduction algorithm as given in [3] we arrive at a time bound $O(n^{7+\varepsilon}+\ldots)$ for factorization. We can, however, save another factor of order n by means of a modified reductio algorithm, which may be of interest in its own right. Meanwhile also A.K. Lenstra has worked out the idea of using diophantine approximation (as mentioned in [3] already) in greater detail [2], but withou improving the bounds of the p-adic approach. In any case a rather fast algorithm for finding some zero of the given polynomial is needed. We refer to the results of our preliminary report [4]. Unfortunately, the final publication of this essential part of the story will take more time.

2. Modified basis reduction

In the sequel familiarity with the basis reduction as presented in [3] is assumed; where possible we will use the same notation. Let $b_1,\ldots,b_n \in \mathbb{Z}^{n'}$ form a basis of an n-dimensional lattice L in $\mathbb{R}^{n'}$, where $n' = O(n)$. In our application to diophantine approximation we will have $n' = n+1$ or $n' = n+2$. Gram-Schmidt orthogonalization determines the associated orthogonal basis $b_1^*,\ldots,b_n^*$ together with the elimination factors $\mu_{i,j} = \langle b_i, b_j^* \rangle / |b_j^*|^2$ such that $\mu_{i,i} = 1$, and $\mu_{i,j} = 0$ for $i < j$. The Gramian determinants $d_i = Gr(b_1,\ldots,b_i)$ $= |b_1^*|^2 \cdots |b_i^*|^2$ are positive integers, and all the components of the b^*'s and all the μ's are integer multiples of $1/d_i$ for some i. In order to control the length of numbers we assume that there is a bound B such that (initially)

(2.1) $\quad |b_i|^2 \le B$, $d_i \le B$ for $1 \le i \le n$, and $2^n \le B$.

Observe that this is different from [3], where $|b_i|^2 \le B$ and $d_i \le B^i$ are used. During the basis reduction process the d_i will never increase, thus always $1 \le d_i \le B$ and

(2.2) $\quad B^{-\frac{1}{2}} \le |b_i^*| \le B^{\frac{1}{2}}$ for $1 \le i \le n$.

We find it useful to distinguish three different meanings of 'reduced'. A vector b_k (or the whole basis) is called <u>reduced in size</u> iff $|\mu_{k,i}| \le \frac{1}{2}$ holds for all $i < k$ (so for all k). This implies $|b_k|^2 \le nB$. A basis is called <u>2-reduced</u> iff $|b_k^*|^2 \le 2|b_{k+1}^*|^2$ for $1 \le k < n$. For many applications, however, a weaker condition will already be sufficient. A basis $b_1,\ldots b_n$ is called <u>semi-reduced</u> iff

(2.3) $\quad |b_r^*|^2 \le 2^{n+s-r}|b_s^*|^2$ for $1 \le r < s \le n$.

In [3] 'reduced' means 2-reduced and reduced in size. 2-reduction steps are followed by size reduction, the latter being the most expensive part of the reduction algorithm.

Each 2-reduction step performs an exchange $b_k \leftrightarrow b_{k+1}$ for some k, provided $|b_{k+1}^*|^2 < \frac{1}{2}|b_k^*|^2$ and $|\mu_{k+1,k}| \le \frac{1}{2}$, thereby decreasing $|b_k^*|^2$ by a factor $q < \frac{3}{4}$ while $|b_{k+1}^*|^2$ is increased by the factor $1/q$. In [3] always the smallest such k is chosen, whereas other choices may be preferable. It is at this crucial point where our modification comes in. Things can be arranged such that many 2-reduction steps can be performed locally, i.e. with k varying in a rather small interval, while only once in a while a global size reduction pass will be required. A detailed study of this idea (sections 3. and 4.) yields the following result.

Theorem 2.1. There exists an algorithm which, for any given basis $b_1,\ldots,b_n$, will achieve semi-reduction (and final size reduction) by performing at most $O(n^2 \log B)$ arithmetic operations with integers of length $O(\log B)$, where B is an upper bound for the $|b_i|^2$, also for the Gramians d_i, and $B \geq 2^n$. Thus at most $O(n^2(\log B)^{2+\varepsilon})$ bit operations are needed.

This form of our result is well suited for later use in section 6. With other applications it may happen that only some $B_o \geq |b_i|^2$ is known and nothing better than $d_i \leq B_o^n$ can be used. Then the bounds are $O(n^3 \log B_o)$ operations with numbers of length $O(n \log B_o)$, which still amounts to an improvement of the corresponding bound in [3] by a factor $O(n)$.

3. Block-wise reduction

Our semi-reduction algorithm keeps stored the vectors $b_1,\ldots,b_n \in \mathbf{Z}^{n'}$, the integers $d_1,\ldots,d_n$, and the vectors $b_1^*,\ldots,b_n^*$ (practically, of course, the integer vectors $d_{i-1}b_i^*$ can be used, instead). Progress will be made by successively performing basis reduction (in the sense of [3]) within blocks. Such a block is determined by the data b_j, d_j, b_j^* for $p-m \leq j \leq p$ with some $p \leq n$, $p \geq 2$, and $1 \leq m \leq p-1$. Its reduction will be prepared by previous size reduction of $b_{p-m},\ldots,b$ in the course of which also the $\mu_{k,i}$ for $i < k \leq p$ are computed. Whence the local basis vectors

$$u_k = \sum_{j=p-m}^{k} \mu_{k,j}\, b_j^* \qquad (p-m \leq k \leq p) \tag{3.1}$$

can be computed. Then basis reduction in the sense of [3] is performed on these block data, in such a way, however, that only the μ's of thi block are shuffled around, without any change of the u's. Instead, a unimodular $(m+1)\times(m+1)$ matrix H is maintained (initially set to I_{m+} in which all column operations performed on the μ's are recorded. Only after the block is reduced completely, updating of the global information is done by means of two $n'\times(m+1)\times(m+1)$ matrix multiplications, namely

$$\begin{aligned}(b_{p-m},\ldots,b_p) &\leftarrow (b_{p-m},\ldots,b_p)H\,,\\ (v_{p-m},\ldots,v_p) &\leftarrow (u_{p-m},\ldots,u_p)H\,.\end{aligned} \tag{3.2}$$

From these v's, and by means of the new μ's, also the new

$b^*_{p-m},\dots,b^*_p$ can be computed.

It is a crucial fact that H never becomes too large.

Lemma 3.1. During block reduction H always satisfies

(3.3) $$|H|_1 \le (m+1)^2(3/2)^m B .$$

Hereby we can show that in our whole reduction algorithm only numbers of length $O(\log B)$ will occur.

Proposition 3.2. Block reduction of $b_{p-m},\dots,b_p$ with t exchange steps of 2-reduction requires at most $O(tm^2)$ arithmetic operations plus an overhead of $O(mn^2)$ operations with integers of length $O(\log B)$.

Proofs. Size reduction of $b_{p-m},\dots,b_p$ preceding the block reduction will have produced (modified) b's satisfying

(3.4) $$|b_j|^2 \le nB \quad \text{for} \quad p-m \le j \le p .$$

In addition, we have the upper triangular $(m+1)\times(m+1)$ matrix M of the μ's with ones in its diagonal and $|\mu_{k,j}| \le 1/2$ for $p-m \le j < k \le p$. Thereby (3.1) becomes

(3.5) $$(b^*_{p-m},\dots,b^*_p)M = (u_{p-m},\dots,u_p) .$$

A similar matrix equation will hold for the modified data after an arbitrary sequence of 2-reduction steps has been performed in the course of this block reduction, namely

(3.6) $$(c^*_{p-m},\dots,c^*_p)N = (v_{p-m},\dots,v_p) = (u_{p-m},\dots,u_p)H .$$

Observe that only the ν's of N and the elements of H are subject to the intermediate computations. Exchange steps of the columns $H_j \longleftrightarrow H_{j+1}$ leave the norm $|H|_1 = \max|H_j|_1$ unchanged. Size reduction of a column N_j makes all $|\nu_{j,i}| \le 1$, Thus $|N_j|_1 \le m+1$. By (3.5) and (3.6), the corresponding new column H_j can be expressed as

$$H_j = M^{-1}\left(\frac{\langle b^*_i, c^*_k\rangle}{|b^*_i|^2} \;\middle|\; \begin{matrix} p-m \le i \le p \\ p-m \le k \le p \end{matrix}\right) N_j .$$

Thus the estimates $|M^{-1}|_1 \le (3/2)^m$ and $|c^*_k|/|b^*_i| \le B$ from (2.2) yield (3.3) in Lemma 3.1.

For the proof of Prop. 3.2 we have to show that all numbers occurring in these computations are bounded by $B^{O(1)}$. To begin with, the components of $d_{i-1}b^*_i = (g_{1,i},\dots,g_{n',i})^T \in \mathbb{Z}^{n'}$ fulfil

$$\sum_j g^2_{j,i} = d^2_{i-1}|b^*_i|^2 = d_{i-1}d_i \le B^2 .$$

A similar bound holds for the u's and v's in (3.5), (3.6), since their components are multiples of $1/d_{p-1}$. After completion of the block reduction the b's subject to (3.4) are updated by (3.2). Due to Lemma 3.1 the new b's are then bounded according to

$$(3.5)\qquad |b_k| \le (nB)^{1/2}|H|_1 \le n^{5/2}(3/2)^{n-1}B^{3/2} ,$$

where we have used $m+1 \le n$ in order to obtain a general bound $|b_k| \le B_1$ for all k. It is only during a pass of size reduction on b_k that this bound will temporarily be exceeded. As in [3], size reduction on b_k is only performed under the hypothesis $|\mu_{i,j}| \le 1/2$ for $j < i < k$. Our algorithm using an intermediate integer vector b, is:

$b_k \to b$,
<u>for</u> $j = k-1, k-2, \ldots, 1$ <u>do</u> $\langle b, b_j^*\rangle/|b_j^*|^2 \to \rho_j$,
$\lfloor \rho_j + 0.5 \rfloor \to r_j$,
$b - r_j b_j \to b$, $\rho_j - r_j \to \mu_{k,j}$;

finally, $b \to b_k$.

By observing $|r_i| \le 2|\rho_i|$ and the identity

$$\rho_j = \langle b_k, b_j^*\rangle/|b_j^*| - \sum_{i=j+1}^{k-1} r_i\, \mu_{i,j} ,$$

we can derive bounds recursively; then (2.2) yields the estimates

$$|r_j| \le |b_k|\cdot 2^{k-j}B^{1/2} \quad \text{and always} \quad |b| \le 2^k|b_k|\cdot B^{1/2} .$$

The operation count of Proposition 3.2 includes the overhead caused by the fact that $m+1$ of the b's, previously reduced in size, will now require size reduction again. The above algorithm performs at most $\mathcal{O}(n^2)$ operations for each b_k, whence a total of $\mathcal{O}(mn^2)$. The other steps (3.1) and (3.2) take only $\mathcal{O}(m^2 n)$.

4. The semi-reduction algorithm

Progress of the reduction process is related to the quantity

$$\prod_{i=1}^{n-1} d_i = \prod_{j=1}^{n-1} |b_j^*|^{2(n-j)}, \quad \text{resp.} \quad \lambda = \sum_j (n-j)\log|b_j^*|^2 .$$

This logarithm is bounded by $0 \le \lambda \le (n-1)\log B$, and each 2-reduction step decreases λ by at least $\log(4/3)$. Thus the total number of exchange steps in all the block reductions is bounded by $\mathcal{O}(n\cdot\log B)$. This part of our algorithm will therefore contribute not more than $\mathcal{O}(n^2\cdot\log B)$ arithmetic operations, provided $m^2 = O(n)$, which will be achieved by restricting the block size to $m = O(\sqrt{n})$.

In order to obtain a similar bound on the extra cost caused by the overhead of each block reduction we consider the numbers

$$\beta_j = j + \log|b_j^*|^2 = j + \log d_j - \log d_{j-1} .$$

Lemma 4.1. Block reduction of $b_{p-m},\dots,b_p$ will decrease the value of λ to some λ' such that

(4.1) $$\lambda - \lambda' \geq S_{p,m} = \sum_{i=0}^{m} (i - \tfrac{m}{2})\beta_{p-i} .$$

Proof. By block reduction the numbers $\beta_{p-m},\dots,\beta_p$ will be changed into new $\beta'_{p-m},\dots,\beta'_p$, such that $\sum_i(\beta_{p-i}-\beta'_{p-i}) = 0$, since $|b^*_{p-m}|^2\dots|b_p^*|^2 = d_p/d_{p-m-1}$ remains unchanged. Therefore

$$\lambda - \lambda' = \sum_{j=p-m}^{m} (n-j)(\beta_j-\beta'_j) = \sum_{i=0}^{m} (i - \tfrac{m}{2})(\beta_j-\beta'_j) \geq S_{p,m} ,$$

because completed 2-reduction implies $\beta'_{p-m} \leq \dots \leq \beta'_p$.

The main idea behind our algorithm is now to compare the overhead costs of $O(mn^2)$ operations with the minimum λ decrease guaranteed by (4.1). Restricting block reduction to those cases, where $S_{p,m} > \tau mn$ holds (with some constant $\tau > 0$), will imply that we have only overhead costs $O(n)$ per unit of λ decrease, whence an overall bound of $O(n^2 \log B)$ arithmetic operations as claimed in Theorem 2.1. This approach is justified by the following lemma, the proof of which will be given below.

Lemma 4.2. For given $n \geq 4$ let $\tau > 0$, $m_o \leq n-2$ be such that

(4.2) $$\tau\left(4 + \frac{12(n-m_o-2)}{(m_o+1)(m_o+2)}\right) \leq 1$$

holds. Then any basis $b_1,\dots,b_n$ satisfying $S_{p,m} \leq \tau mn$ for all admissible pairs p,m with $m \leq m_o$ is semi-reduced (see (2.3)).

A suitable choice of these parameters is $m_o = \lceil\sqrt{3n+1} - 3\rceil$ with $\tau = 1/8$ (e.g. $n = 40$, $m_o = 8$), whence $m \leq m_o = O(\sqrt{n})$. Other choices may turn out to be preferable in practice.

After all these theoretical considerations we now give a brief outline of our semi-reduction algorithm:

A0: Compute all d_i, b_i^* and set $1 \to p$;
A1: $p+1 \to p$;
A2: perform size reduction on b_p and store the $\mu_{p,i}$;
A3: for $m = 1,2,\dots,\min(m_o,p-1)$ do
  if $S_{p,m} > \tau mn$ then
  perform block reduction on $b_{p-m},\dots,b_p$,
  set $p-m \to p$ and goto A2 ;
A4: if $p < n$ then goto A1 ;

The initialization A0 and one global pass of size reduction A2 for all p requires not more than $\mathcal{O}(n^3)$ operations which is $\mathcal{O}(n^2 \log B)$, due to our assumption $B \geq 2^n$. The extra A2 costs that are caused by the set-backs of p under A3 are covered by Proposition 3.2 already.

Proof of Lemma 4.2. With regard to (4.1) we introduce 'weight' functions $w_{p,m}$ on the integers defined by

$$(4.3) \quad w_{p,m}(p-i) = \tfrac{2}{m}(i-\tfrac{m}{2}) \text{ for } 0 \leq i \leq m, \quad w_{p,m}(j) = 0 \text{ otherwise.}$$

In particular, $w_{p,m}(p-m) = 1$, $w_{p,m}(p) = -1$, and $\sum_j w_{p,m}(j) = 0$. Thus the supposition $S_{p,m} \leq \tau mn$ of Lemma 4.2 can be rewritten as

$$(4.4) \quad \sum_j w_{p,m}(j)\beta_j \leq 2\tau n \text{ for all } p,\, m \text{ with } m \leq m_o.$$

For any fixed pair $r < s$ the inequality (2.3) similarly takes the for

$$(4.5) \quad \sum_j f(j)\beta_j \leq n, \quad \text{where } f(j) = \delta_{r,j} - \delta_{s,j}.$$

Our goal is to prove (4.5) by superposition of suitable instances of (4.4), i.e. we have to represent f as a suitable positive linear combination of $w_{p,m}$'s. For $s-r = 1$ or $s-r = 2$ we simply have $f = w_{s,1}$ or $f = w_{s-1,1} + w_{s,1}$, respectively, since $\tau \leq 1/4$. For $s-r \geq 3$ let $M = \min(m_o, s-r-1)$. Then (4.2) implies

$$(4.6) \qquad 4\tau n + 12\tau n \cdot \frac{s-r-M-1}{(M+1)(M+2)} \leq n.$$

With respect to sums like $w_{p,M} + w_{p+1,M} + \dots$ we furthermore introduce functions

$$W_a(k) = c \cdot \sum_{p \geq a} w_{p,M}(k) = c \cdot \sum_{j \leq k} w_{a,M}(j),$$

where c is chosen such that $\sum_k W_a(k) = 1$ holds (observe that $W_a(k) = 0$ for $k < a-M$ or $k \geq a$). An easy calculation gives $c = 6/((M+1)(M+2))$. By multiplying (4.4) with c and adding up these for $r+M+1 \leq p < s$ we therefore obtain

$$(4.7) \quad \sum_j W_{r+M+1}(j)\beta_j - \sum W_s(j)\beta_j \leq 12\tau n \cdot \frac{(s-r-M-1)}{(M+1)(M+2)}.$$

The remaining problem is to alter these W-sums into $\delta_{r,j}$ and $\delta_{s,j}$ (cf. (4.5)). There exist unique coefficients $\gamma_m > 0$ for $1 \leq m \leq M$ such that (for all j)

$$w_{r+M+1}(j) + \sum_{m=1}^{M} \gamma_m w_{r+m,m}(j) = \delta_{r,j} \ , \ \sum_{m=1}^{M} \gamma_m w_{s,m}(j) - W_s(j) = -\delta_{s,j} \ ,$$

and $\gamma_1 + \ldots + \gamma_M = 1$. Combining this with (4.7) leads to the expression on the left-hand side of (4.6), and thereby we get (4.5) which completes the proof of Lemma 4.2.

5. Zeros anf factors of f

We discuss the factorization of primitive polynomials $f(x) = c_n x^n + \ldots + c_o \in \mathbb{Z}[x]$ with $c_o c_n \neq 0$. We assume that some (real or complex) zero z of f with rather high precision can be found sufficiently fast, and that $|z| \leq 1$ holds (otherwise we could factor the reversed polynomial $x^n f(1/x)$). More precisely z (and its powers) shall be specified by real numbers $\sigma_j, \tau_j \in 2^{-\ell}\mathbb{Z}$ such that

(5.1) $\qquad |\sigma_j - \mathrm{Re}\, z^j| < 2^{-\ell}, \ |\tau_j - \mathrm{Im}\, z^j| < 2^{-\ell} \quad \text{for } 0 \leq j \leq n ,$

where ℓ is at least of order $n \cdot \log|f|$. For our final time bound it suffices to compute these numbers in time $O(n^3 \ell^{1+\varepsilon})$. By our splitting circle method (cf. [4], Thm. 19.2) this amount of time would already be enough to compute all zeros of f , while a single zero can even be found in time $O(n^2 \ell^{1+\varepsilon})$.

Let $p(x) = p_o + p_1 x + \ldots + p_k x^k \in \mathbb{Z}[x]$ with $p_k > 0$ denote the minimal polynomial of z , which is an irreducible factor of f . With regard to the vectors $s = (\sigma_o, \ldots, \sigma_m)^T$, $t = (\tau_o, \tau_1, \ldots, \tau_m)^T$, $p = (p_o, p_1, \ldots, p_k, 0, \ldots)^T$ in case of $k \leq m$ we have

(5.2) $\qquad |\langle p,s\rangle| < 2^{-\ell}|p|_1 \ , \ |\langle p,t\rangle| < 2^{-\ell}|p|_1 \ ,$

where $|p|_1 = |p_o| + |p_1| + \ldots + |p_k|$ is bounded by

(5.3) $\qquad |p|_1 \leq 2^{k-\frac{1}{2}}|f| \quad \text{with } |f|^2 = c_o^2 + \ldots + c_n^2 .$

In case of $t \neq 0$ (5.1) implies $z \notin \mathbb{R}$; we call this the complex case, where $\bar{z}$ is a further zero of p . Otherwise we speak of the real case (though possibly $z \notin \mathbb{R}$).

6. How to find the minimal polynomial

We test $m = 2,4,8,\ldots,n-1$ whether $k \leq m$ holds, where $k = \deg(p)$. For fixed m we use a fixed value of the precision parameter ℓ (to be suitably specified below) and consider the $(m+1)$-dimensional lattice $L = M(\mathbb{Z}^{m+1}) \subseteq \mathbb{R}^{m'}$, where M denotes the integer $(m+3)\times(m+1)$ matrix

$$M = \begin{pmatrix} 1 & & & \bigcirc \\ & 1 & & \\ & \bigcirc & \ddots & \\ & & & 1 \\ 2^{\ell}\sigma_0 & 2^{\ell}\sigma_1 & \cdots & 2^{\ell}\sigma_m \\ 0 & 2^{\ell}\tau_1 & \cdots & 2^{\ell}\tau_m \end{pmatrix}$$

and $m' = m+3$ in the complex case; in the real case we choose $m' = m+$
and omit the last row of M. Starting from the basis formed by the columns of M this lattice L is now semi-reduced by the algorithm described in 3. and 4. By Theorem 2.1 the running time is $\mathcal{O}(m^2\ell^{2+\varepsilon})$, due to the following bounds (to be proved below).

<u>Lemma 6.1.</u> For the initial basis $b_o = Me_o, \ldots, b_m = Me_m$ all the Gramian determinants are bounded by

$$B = (1+2^{2\ell}(m+1))^2 \quad \text{in the complex case,}$$

$$B = 1 + 2^{2\ell}(m+1) \quad \text{in the real case.}$$

<u>If $k \leq m$</u>, then the lattice L contains a short vector,

(6.1) $|Mp|^2 = |p|^2 + |\langle p,s\rangle|^2 \cdot 2^{2\ell} + |\langle p,t\rangle|^2 \cdot 2^{2\ell} \leq 3|p|_1^2 \leq 3\cdot 2^{2k-1}|f|^2$.

The same bound holds for the shifted versions $xp(x), x^2p(x), \ldots, x^{m-k}p($
which are linearly independent. For the semi-reduced basis $b_o, \ldots, b_m$ this implies that one of these polynomials corresponds to a $\mathbb{Z}$-combination $c_ob_o + \ldots + c_sb_s$ with some $s \geq m-k$ and $c_s \neq 0$, therefore

$$3\cdot 2^{2k-1}|f|^2 \geq |b_s^*|^2.$$

Moreover (2.3) then yields $|b_i^*|^2 \leq 3\cdot 2^{2k-1+(m+1)+s-i}|f|^2$ for $i \leq m-k$, and by $|\mu_{j,i}| \leq 1/2$ finally

(6.2) $|b_j|^2 \leq 3\cdot 2^{4m}|f|^2$ for $0 \leq j \leq m-k$.

<u>Reversely</u>, if in the reduced basis (6.2) holds for $0 \leq j \leq r$, then there exist $r+1$ linearly independent primitive polynomials $g_o, \ldots, g$
of degree m at most such that

(6.3) $|g_j| \leq \beta$ with $\beta = \sqrt{3}\cdot 2^{2m}|f|$,

(6.4) $|g_j(z)| \leq 2^{-\ell}\cdot\sqrt{2m+2}\,\beta$

are fulfilled for all $j \leq r$. The first of these inequalities is immediate from (6.2), i.e. from

(6.5) $|g_j|^2 + 2^{2\ell}\langle g_j,s\rangle^2 + 2^{2\ell}\langle g_j,t\rangle^2 \leq \beta^2$.

In order to prove (6.4) for any j, let $g_j(x) = \gamma_o + \ldots + \gamma_m x^m$. The

$$|g_j(z)| = \left|\sum_{\nu=0}^{m}\gamma_\nu z^\nu\right| \le \sum_{\nu=1}^{m}|\gamma_\nu|\cdot|z^\nu-(\sigma_\nu+i\tau_\nu)|+|2^\ell\langle g_j,s\rangle|\cdot 2^{-\ell}+|2^\ell\langle g_j,t\rangle|\cdot 2^{-\ell}.$$

Here we use Schwarz's inequality with (6.5) and $|z^\nu-(\sigma_\nu+i\tau_\nu)|\le\sqrt{2}\cdot 2^{-\ell}$ from (5.1).

Lemma 6.2. (6.3) and (6.4) imply that the minimal polynomial p of z divides g_j, provided

(6.6) $\ell \ge 3mn + (m+n)\cdot\log|f| + 2n+2$

in the real case; in the complex case (6.6) shall hold for 2ℓ instead of ℓ.

With such a choice of ℓ we therefore obtain that $p = \gcd(g_0,\dots,g_r)$ and $r = m-k$. (A similar argument was used in [3], by the way.) The computation of this gcd is possible in time $O(m^{5+\varepsilon}+m^4(\log|f|)^{1+\varepsilon})$.

Proof of Lemma 6.1. For simplicity let us consider the real case. By means of the vectors $s_q = (\sigma_0,\dots,\sigma_q)^T$ we can evaluate the Gramian determinants for the columns of M as

$$Gr(b_0,\dots,b_q) = \det F_q, \text{ where } F_q = I_{q+1}+2^{2\ell}s_q s_q^T.$$

This positive definite matrix F_q has the q-fold eigenvalue 1 with eigenvectors orthogonal to s_q and the further eigenvector s_q itself with the eigenvalue

$$\det F_q = 1+2^{2\ell}|s_q|^2 \le 1+2^{2\ell}(m+1),$$

because $|z|\le 1$ implies $|s_q|^2 \le q+1 \le m+1$.

The complex case can be handled in a similar way.

Proof of Lemma 6.2. If $g = g_j$ has a common zero with the minimal polynomial p, then p will divide g. Therefore we will show that $g(z_i) \neq 0$ for all zeros z_i of p is impossible, provided ℓ is large enough. For that purpose we introduce the resultant polynomial

(6.7) $$h(y) = \mathrm{res}_x(p(x),y-g(x)) = p_k^{\bar m}\prod_{i=1}^{k}(y-g(z_i))$$
$$= h_0 + h_1 y + \dots + h_k y^k,$$

where $\bar m = \deg(g) \le m$. Expanding this resultant as a huge sum of determinants and Hadamard's inequality together with $|g| \le B$ lead to the bound

(6.8) $|h_\nu| \le \binom{k}{\nu}B^{k-\nu}|p|^m$ for $\nu \le k$.

Assuming $g(z_i) \neq 0$ for all z_i we get $h_0 \neq 0$, and $|h_0| \ge 1$, since h_0 is an integer. On the other hand $\eta = |g(z)|$ is small according to (6.4). In this way we find from $h(g(z)) = 0$

$$1 \le |h_o| \le |h_1|\eta + |h_2|\eta^2 + \ldots + |h_k|\eta^k ,$$

$$1 + \frac{1}{|p|^m \beta^k} \le \left(1 + \frac{\eta}{\beta}\right)^k \qquad \text{(by (6.8))},$$

$$\eta \ge \left(\left(1 + \frac{1}{|p|^m \beta^k}\right)^{1/k} - 1\right)\beta \geqq \frac{1}{2k} \cdot \frac{\beta}{|p|^m \beta^k} .$$

Inserting the bounds from (6.3), (6.4) and (5.3) with $k \le n$ finally yields (after some calculation)

$$\ell \le \frac{1}{2} \log(2m+2) + \log(2n) + m(n-\frac{1}{2}) + (m+n)\log |f| + 2mn + \frac{n}{2} \log 3 ,$$

but this is not compatible with (6.6).

With regard to the asymptotic bounds mentioned in the Introduction this part of the proof is already sufficient. The refinement for the complex case that half the value of ℓ will do is based upon the observation that for $z \notin \mathbb{R}$ also $\bar{z}$ is a zero of p , whence the resultant $h(y)$ has two linear factors $(y-g(z))(y-g(\bar{z}))$, i.e. two small zeros of size η . - We skip the further details.

7. Conclusion

All steps described in the preceding section for fixed m are certainly covered by the rather crude bound of $O(m(n^{5+\varepsilon}+n^3(\log|f|)^{2+\varepsilon}))$ bit operations. For a factor p of degree $k \le \frac{n}{2}$ this bound applies for $m = 2,4,\ldots$ until some m with $m/2 < k \le m$ is reached. The sum of the corresponding time bounds is therefore $O(k(n^{5+\varepsilon}+n^3(\log|f|)^{2+\varepsilon}))$. Further factors are found in the very same way, dealing with f/p , etc. There is at most one factor of degree $k > n/2$ (possibly f itself), thus the final time bound $O(n^{6+\varepsilon}+n^4(\log|f|)^{2+\varepsilon})$ is obtained.

It should be observed that the distinctions between the real and complex case in Lemma 6.1 and in Lemma 6.2 nicely match such that in both cases $\log B \sim 6mn + 2(m+n)\log|f|$. Due to the estimation (6.1) sometimes shortcuts in the reduction process may be possible. As soon as $|b_m^*|^2$ becomes greater than $3\cdot 2^{2m-1}|f|^2$, b_m can be eliminated from the reduction, etc.

It is conceivable that further (mainly theoretical) improvements of our algorithm are possible, for instance by exploiting fast matrix multiplication, or by iterating the block reduction technique.

References

[1] E. Kaltofen: On the complexity of finding short vectors in integer lattices. Proc. EUROCAL '83, Lecture Notes Comp. Sci.

[2] A.K. Lenstra: Polynomial factorization by root approximation. Preprint, mathem. centrum, Amsterdam 1983.

[3] A.K. Lenstra, H.W. Lenstra, Jr., L. Lovász: Factoring polynomials with rational coefficients. Math. Ann. 261 (1982), 515-534.

[4] A. Schönhage: The fundamental theorem of algebra in terms of computational complexity. Preliminary Report, Math. Inst. Univ. Tübingen, 1982.

ROBUST ALGORITHMS:
A DIFFERENT APPROACH TO ORACLES[†]

(Extended Abstract)

Uwe Schöning
Institut für Informatik
Universität Stuttgart
D7000 Stuttgart 1
West Germany

Introduction

Typical algorithms for computationally hard problems like NP-complete problems usually involve backtrack search techniques to find a solution in a tree of exponential size (in the size of the input). Here we consider the situation that the algorithm is allowed to query an oracle to receive information that might lead to a faster search for the solution. On the other hand, we do not allow the algorithm to rely on the oracle information such that changing the oracle set would result in changing the set that the algorithm computes. We consider here algorithms which are <u>robust</u> with respect to the oracle, i.e. the algorithm always computes the same set independent of what the oracle set is. The oracle only serves to possibly speed up the computation. Using various oracles for such robust algorithms is comparable with using various branching strategies or dominance relations in branch-and-bound algorithms (cf. [9, 7].)

We show that nondeterministic computations do not gain more computational power by receiving "help" (in the above sense) from some oracle. Further, if we consider the class of polynomial functions as feasible running times then our main result states that the class of problems that can be feasibly computed by robust deterministic algorithms with the "help" of some oracle information is exactly $NP \cap co\text{-}NP$. We will prove this in a little more general setting without explicitly refering to polynomial running times.

[†] This research was supported by Deutsche Forschungsgemeinschaft

Notation

All our sets are languages over some fixed alphabet Σ such that $|\Sigma| \geq 2$. For a string $w \in \Sigma^*$ we denote by $|w|$ its length.

Let $L(M)$ denote the set accepted by Turing machine M, and let $L(M, A)$ be the set accepted by oracle Turing machine M using oracle set A.

For a class of functions F on the natural numbers define

$$DTIME(F) = \{ L(M) \mid M \text{ is deterministic and operates in time } f \text{ for some } f \in F \}.$$

Define $NTIME(F)$ analogously for nondeterministic machines.

For a deterministic oracle machine M and oracle set A define the function $time_{M,A} : \Sigma^* \to N \cup \{\infty\}$ as

$$time_{M,A}(x) = \text{number of steps in the (unique) computation of } M \text{ on input } x \text{ when using oracle } A.$$

We can extend this definition also to nondeterministic machines M if we let $time_{M,A}(x)$ be the minimum length of an accepting computation of M on input x using oracle A, provided $x \in L(M, A)$. We let $time_{M,A}(x) = 0$ for $x \notin L(M, A)$.

For a set $A \subseteq \Sigma^*$ let $\bar{A} = \Sigma^* - A$ denote its complement, and for a class of sets C over Σ let co-C denote the set of complements of the sets in C, co-$C = \{A \mid \bar{A} \in C\}$.

A function $f : N \to N$ is <u>time constructible</u> if there is a deterministic Turing machine which on inputs of size n halts after exactly $f(n)$ steps.

Further we assume that $\langle\cdot,\cdot\rangle$ is a standard pairing function on strings.

Main Results

We consider the situation that the influence of an oracle set to an oracle machine is not so strong that it influences the accepted set.

<u>Definition 1</u>. An oracle machine M is <u>robust</u> iff for each oracle set A, $L(M, A) = L(M, \emptyset)$.

The only influence of the oracle to the machine that we allow is to possibly speed up the computation. In the following we let F be a class of functions on the natural numbers. The intuition behind this is that F is a class of running times that we consider as tolerable.

One important such class F is the class of polynomial functions.

Definition 2. An oracle set A F-helps a robust oracle machine M iff for some $f \in F$ and each input x, $time_{M,A}(x) \leq f(|x|)$.

Now we define the class of sets which can be computed by robust oracle machines that can be F-helped by a given oracle set A.

Definition 3. (i) $DTIME_{help}(F, A) = \{ L(M, A) \mid M$ is a robust deterministic oracle machine and A F-helps $M \}$,

(ii) $NTIME_{help}(F, A) = \{ L(M, A) \mid M$ is a robust nondeterministic oracle machine and A F-helps $M \}$.

Now we have our first result which states that nondeterministic algorithms do not gain more computational power when receiving "help" (in the above sense) from an oracle.

Theorem 1. $\bigcup_A NTIME_{help}(F, A) = NTIME(F)$.

Proof. It suffices to show that for each oracle set A, $NTIME_{help}(F, A) \subseteq NTIME(F)$. Let $L \in NTIME_{help}(F, A)$, hence there is a robust nondeterministic oracle machine M and some $f \in F$ such that $L(M, A) = L$ and $time_{M,A}(x) \leq f(|x|)$ for each $x \in \Sigma^*$.

Define a Turing machine M' which on input x behaves like M on input x except that M' treats each oracle query of M as a nondeterministic guess. By the robustness of M it follows that $L(M') = L$ and because $time_{M,A}(x) \leq f(|x|)$ it follows that M' operates in time f. Hence M' witnesses that $L \in NTIME(F)$. □

The following theorem shows that for robust deterministic oracle machines being F-helped by some oracle set, the computational power might be greater than for a machine without oracle (provided $DTIME(F) \neq NTIME(F) \cap co\text{-}NTIME(F)$.)

Theorem 2. Let F be a class of functions satisfying the following conditions:

(i) each $f \in F$ is time constructible,

(ii) if $f, g \in F$ then $\max(f, g) \in F$,

(iii) for each $f \in F$ and each constant c there is a $g \in F$ such that for each n, $c \cdot f(n) \leq g(n)$.

Then $\bigcup_A \ \mathrm{DTIME}_{help}\ (F, A) = \mathrm{NTIME}\ (F) \cap \text{co-NTIME}\ (F)$.

roof. The forward inclusion follows from Theorem 1 and the observation hat for each A and F,

$$\mathrm{DTIME}_{help}\ (F, A) \subseteq \mathrm{NTIME}_{help}\ (F, A) \cap \text{co-NTIME}_{help}\ (F, A).$$

Conversely, let $L \in \mathrm{NTIME}\ (F) \cap \text{co-NTIME}\ (F)$. Hence there are non-eterministic Turing machines M_1, M_2 accepting L and $\overline{L}$, respectively. y clause (ii) there is a function $f \in F$ bounding the running times f both M_1 and M_2. Since by clause (i) f is time constructible, is recursive. Therefore, there exists a deterministic Turing machine 3 which halts on each input and accepts L.

Now consider the deterministic oracle machine M described by the ollowing program:

```
begin
  input x ;
  z := e ;  {the empty string}
  while |z| ≤ f(|x|) do
    if <x, z0> ∈ oracle then z := z0
                         else z := z1 ;
  if z encodes an accepting computation of M1 on x
     then halt and accept ;
  if z encodes an accepting computation of M2 on x
     then halt and reject ;
  simulate M3 on input x ;
end.
```

Clearly M halts on each input and it always accepts the set L, ıdependent of what the oracle set is. Hence M is robust. Now, define ıe following specific oracle set A:

A = {<x, y> | $x \in \Sigma^*$ and the string $y \in \{0,1\}^*$ can be extended to a string that describes an accepting computation of M_1 or of M_2 on input x }.

M uses this oracle set A, then M on input x always halts either the first or the second if-statement after the while-loop. By the .me constructibility of f and because the while-loop is executed $(|x|)$ times, it follows $\mathrm{time}_{M,A}\ (x) = O(f(|x|))$. Hence by clause (iii) ıere is a function $h \in F$ such that $\mathrm{time}_{M,A}\ (x) \leq h(|x|)$. This proves ıat $L \in \mathrm{DTIME}_{help}\ (F, A)$. □

Discussion

The most obvious application of Theorems 1 and 2 is to let F = poly the class of polynomial functions. Then Theorems 1 and 2 state that

$$\bigcup_A \text{NTIME}_{\text{help}}(\text{poly}, A) = \text{NP}, \text{ and}$$

$$\bigcup_A \text{DTIME}_{\text{help}}(\text{poly}, A) = \text{NP} \cap \text{co-NP}.$$

This means that the question whether in a polynomial time computation "help" from an oracle (in our sense) can always be eliminated is connected to the question $P =?\ NP \cap co\text{-}NP$. Note that $P =?\ NP \cap co\text{-}NP$ is an important question in cryptography. If polynomial time computable one-way functions exist, then $P \neq NP \cap co\text{-}NP$ (see [2] and [4].)

From the proof of Theorem 2 it can be seen that the oracle set A can be taken to be in NTIME (F), hence

$$\bigcup_{A \in \text{NTIME}(F)} \text{DTIME}_{\text{help}}(F, A) = \text{NTIME}(F) \cap \text{co-NTIME}(F),$$

or in particular,

$$\bigcup_{A \in \text{NP}} \text{DTIME}_{\text{help}}(\text{poly}, A) = \text{NP} \cap \text{co-NP}.$$

This suggests to consider the outcome of our definition when we restrict the oracle to other classes. We state one such example. Let ZPP and BPP be the classes recognized by probabilistic, polynomial time Turing machines with zero- or bounded error probability, resp. (for the exact definitions, please see [5].) The following observation is due to Dave Russo (Santa Barbara):

$$\bigcup_{A \in \text{BPP}} \text{DTIME}_{\text{help}}(\text{poly}, A) \subseteq \text{ZPP}.$$

A seemingly similar notion of "helping" appears in a paper by Karp and Lipton [8]. The authors consider algorithms which on inputs of size n receive "advice", that is a string concatenated to the input which is bounded in length by some function $h \in F$ and which depends only on n, not on x. This model is essentially equivalent to the usual oracle machine model where the function class F determines the degree of "sparcity" of the oracle. But since there is no robustness restriction, this model is essentially different from ours.

There is a certain connection of our notion to the recent "positive relativization" results by Book et al. [10, 3]. Since Baker, Gill and Solovay [1] have shown that there exist oracles A and B such that $P(A) = NP(A)$, but $P(B) \neq NP(B)$, many authors tried to give explanations for this phenomenon -- even by reaching to independence issues (cf. [6]. A restriction imposed on oracle machines is called a "positive relatiization" [10, 3] of the P =? NP question if the following is true:

P = NP iff for each oracle set A, $P_r(A) = NP_r(A)$.

ere $P_r(\ )$ ($NP_r(\ )$) means a relativization with respect to this restricted kind of oracle machine. Now, a trivial consequence of Theorems and 2 above is that

P = NP iff for each oracle set A, $DTIME_{help}$(poly, A) = $NTIME_{help}$ (poly, A).

ence the robustness-restriction provides a positive relativization of he P =? NP question, but it is a very severe restriction. It might be nteresting to consider weaker versions of robustness which still yield ositive relativizations.

References

. T. Baker, J. Gill and R. Solovay, Relativizations of the P=?NP question, SIAM J. Comput. 4 (1975), 431-441.

. L. Berman and J. Hartmanis, On isomorphisms and density of NP and other complete sets, SIAM J. Comput. 6 (1977), 305-322.

. R.V. Book, T.J. Long and A.L. Selman, Quantitative relativizations of complexity classes, SIAM J. Comput., to appear.

G. Brassard, S. Fortune and J. Hopcroft, A note on cryptography and NP∩co-NP - P, Techn. Report TR78-338, Cornell University 1978.

J. Gill, Computational complexity of probabilistic Turing machines, SIAM J. Comput. 6 (1977), 675-695.

J. Hartmanis and J. Hopcroft, Independence results in computer science, SIGACT News 8 (1976), 13-24.

T. Ibaraki, The power of dominance relations in branch-and-bound algorithms, Journal of the ACM 24 (1977), 264-279.

R.M. Karp and R.J. Lipton, Some connections between nonuniform and uniform complexity classes, Proc. 12th ACM Sympos. Theory of Comput., 1980, 302-309.

C.H. Papadimitriou and K. Steiglitz, Combinatorial optimization, Prentice-Hall, 1982.

. A.L. Selman, Xu Mei-Rui and R.V. Book, Positive relativizations of complexity classes, SIAM J. Comput. 12 (1983), 565-579.

Node Weighted Matching

Thomas H. Spencer*
Ernst W. Mayr †
Computer Science Department,
Stanford University

Introduction.

In this paper we study matching problems where the vertices are assigned weights. The weight of a vertex corresponds to the value of matching that vertex. The problem is to find a matching that maximizes the sum of the weights of the matched vertices. We show that the complexity of this problem is closely tied to that of the unweighted matching problem.

Node weighted matching problems have only rarely been discussed in the literature before. If we assign to every edge the sum of the weights of its endpoints we will get a traditional edge weighted matching problem, which can be solved by the methods of Edmonds [1] or Galil and Micali [2]. We are thus interested in whether the node weighted matching problem is any easier than the general edge weighted matching problem. This paper shows that the complexity of the node weighted matching problem is close to that of the unweighted matching problem. In fact, if an algorithm for the maximum cardinality matching problem (CMP) runs in $U(n,m)$ time, with U convex, then the node weighted matching problem can be solved in $O(U \log n)$ time. Hopcroft and Karp [3] have shown that the unweighted matching problem can be solved in $O(n^{1/2}m)$ time for bipartite graphs. Micali and Vazirani [5] have extended this result to general graphs. The running time $U(n,m) = cn^{1/2}m$ is convex so the node weighted matching problem can be solved in $O(n^{1/2}m \log n)$ time.

The algorithm presented here uses divide and conquer. The subproblems that are generated are not necessarily small. Instead, each subproblem has a nonobvious parameter which is initially $O(n)$ and is halved in every recursive call. When this parameter has the value 1, the node weighted matching problem is easy.

We first discuss the bipartite positive node weighted matching problem (BPMP). Then we reduce the positive node weighted matching problem (PMP) on general graphs to the BPMP. Finally, the node weighted matching problem (MP) with general weights is shown to reduce to the PMP.

The Bipartite Positive Node Weighted Matching Problem.

Here we solve the BPMP by divide and conquer. Thus, we will often want to talk about subgraphs of the input graph. It is convenient to designate a subgraph by its vertex set V. It is understood that the edges of this graph are all edges in the input graph with both endpoints in V.

* Partially supported by the National Science Foundation under grant MCS-83-00984 and by a United States Army Research Office Program fellowship DAAG29-83-G0020.

† Partially supported by an IBM Faculty Development Award

We will make the technical assumption that no two vertices have the same weight. If several vertices have the same weight, we sort them by nonincreasing weight and declare that vertices that are earlier in the order are heavier than vertices that are later in the order.

First we will show that we can assume that the maximum weight matching has maximum cardinality and that the weight of all of the vertices in T is 0. Then a method of dividing the BPMP into two disjoint subproblems will be discussed. These subproblems are not necessarily small. Therefore, next a way of making the algorithm run quickly in spite of this fact will be discussed.

Simplifying the Problem

The most important consequence of the assumption that all of the weights are nonnegative is that we can assume that we are looking for a maximum cardinality matching.

Lemma 1: There is a solution to the PMP that is a maximum cardinality matching.

Proof: If a maximum weight matching does not have maximum cardinality, then it can be extended to a maximum cardinality matching as follows: take its symmetric difference with any maximum cardinality matching and switch the matching within every connected component of the symmetric difference whenever this increases the cardinality of the matching. This process does not decrease the weight of the matching, since no matched vertex becomes unmatched. ∎

Hence, we will use the phrase "maximum weight matching" to refer to a maximum cardinality maximum weight matching.

To solve the BPMP we first determine which vertices are to be matched, and then find a perfect matching of these vertices. Finding this matching is relatively easy. Also, since the input graph $B(S,T,E)$ is bipartite, it is possible to determine which vertices are to be matched separately for S and T. To see this, suppose that M_T is a maximum weight matching if the weights of all vertices in S are set to zero, and M_S is a maximum weight matching if the weights of the vertices in T are set to zero. A matching M that matches all of the vertices in T (respectively S) that M_T (respectively M_S) does certainly is a maximum weight matching if it exists. The existence of such a matching was first proved by Mendelson and Dulmage [4] in a somewhat different context. The same ideas are used in the proof given here.

Lemma 2: Given maximum cardinality matchings M_T and M_S of a bipartite graph $B(S,T,E)$, there is a maximum cardinality matching M that matches all of the vertices in T (respectively S) that M_T (respectively M_S) does.

Proof: The matching M can be constructed as follows: All edges in $M_T \cap M_S$ are in M. To find the other edges of M consider the symmetric difference $M_T \oplus M_S$. Each connected component C of $M_T \oplus M_S$ is either a simple path or a simple cycle. If C is a cycle then $M_S \cap C$ and $M_T \cap C$ match the same vertices, so (arbitrarily) the edges in $C \cap M_S$ are added to M. Each component C also contains as many edges from M_T as from M_S, so, if it is not a cycle, it contains an odd number of vertices. If a component C contains more vertices in S (respectively T) then the edges from $M_S \cap C$ (respectively $M_T \cap C$) are included in M. The matching M matches the desired vertices. ∎

Given M_S and M_T, M can be found in $O(n)$ time, where n is the number of vertices in the graph. Thus, we may also assume, without loss of generality, that the weights of the vertices in T are zero. An instance of the BPMP where all of the weights of the vertices in T are zero is an

function $BPMP(B(S,T,E)$: **graph**; l : **integer**) : **matching**;
{ *BPMP* finds a maximum weight matching on B. }
begin
Set the weights of all of the vertices in T to 0;
$M_S \leftarrow RBPMP(B(S,T,E),|S|)$;
{ The function *RBPMP* solves the RBPMP and will be defined later. }
Restore the weights of the vertices in T;
Set the weights of all of the vertices in S to 0;
$M_T \leftarrow RBPMP(B(T,S,E),|T|)$;
$S^* \leftarrow$ the set of vertices in S that are matched by M_S;
$T^* \leftarrow$ the set of vertices in T that are matched by M_T;
$BPMP \leftarrow$ a perfect matching on $S^* \cup T^*$
end;

Figure 1. The function *BPMP*.

instance of the *restricted bipartite matching problem* (RBPMP). Figure 1 shows how the BPMP can be solved by an algorithm that solves the RBPMP.

The Division Strategy.

Furthermore, to solve the RBPMP we need only identify which vertices in S are to be matched, or equivalently, which vertices in S are to be left unmatched by the maximum weight matching.

First note that any vertex in S that is matched by every maximum cardinality matching must be matched by the maximum weight matching that is computed. All other vertices in S are candidates to be left unmatched by the maximum weight matching. Hence they are called *candidate* vertices. It is convenient to consider any vertex in T that is adjacent to a candidate vertex (in S) to be a candidate vertex as well, because of the following lemma:

Lemma 3: Given a maximum cardinality matching M, the set of vertices reachable via an alternating path starting at an unmatched vertex in S is the same as the set of candidate vertices.

Proof: Suppose that some vertex v is reachable via an alternating path P that starts at an unmatched vertex in S. Note that this implies that v is matched by M. Then if $v \in S$, it is not matched by $M \oplus P$, a maximum cardinality matching. Alternatively, if $v \in T$, then it is adjacent to the previous vertex on P, which is a candidate vertex. Conversely, if $v \in S$ is not matched by some maximum cardinality matching N, then it is in some connected component of $M \oplus N$. This connected component is an alternating path (with respect to M) starting at an unmatched vertex x in S. Similarly, if $w \in T$ is adjacent to v, the alternating path going from x to v can be extended to w. ∎

Thus, the candidate vertices can be identified in $O(m)$ time, where m is the number of edges in the graph, once a maximum cardinality matching has been constructed.

An important consequence of Lemma 3 is that the non-candidate vertices in S can all be matched with non-candidate vertices in T. Therefore, only the candidate vertices need to be considered.

Lemma 4: Let F be the subgraph of non-candidate vertices. There is a matching M on F that matches all of the vertices in $F \cap S$.

Proof: Let M' be a maximum cardinality matching on the whole graph. Let v be a vertex in $F \cap S$, and let e be the edge in M' that is incident to it. Let u be the other endpoint of e. If u was a candidate vertex then, by Lemma 3, there would be an alternating path (with respect to M') from an unmatched vertex in S to u. This path could be extended to v by adding e. So v would not be in F, contrary to our assumption. Therefore, the restriction of M' to F matches all of the vertices in $F \cap S$. ▮

The candidate vertices in T act much like the non-candidate vertices in S.

Lemma 5: Let C be the subgraph of candidate vertices. Then any maximum cardinality matching M_C of C matches all of $C \cap T$.

Proof: Let M_F be a maximum cardinality matching on the non-candidate vertices. Then $M = M_C \cup M_F$ is a maximum cardinality matching on the whole graph. Suppose that $v \in T$ was a candidate vertex that is not matched by M. Then, by Lemma 3, v would be reachable via an alternating path P starting at an unmatched vertex in S. The matching $M \oplus P$ would then contain more edges than M, which is impossible. Therefore, M, and hence M_C, match all of $C \cap T$. ▮

Intuitively, the matched vertices should be as heavy as possible. Informally, the basis of our algorithm is the observation that which of the heavy vertices and which of the light vertices are to be matched can be determined independently. The heavy vertices are the k heaviest vertices, for some k. The choice of k will be made later.

Let S' be the set of heavy vertices. Let H the subgraph determined by the candidate vertices of $S' \cup T$. Recall that if v is adjacent to a vertex in $H \cap S$, then $v \in H$. Let L be the subgraph determined by the set of candidate vertices of the whole graph that are not in H. Suppose that maximum weight matchings M_H and M_L on H and L have been found recursively. Let $M = M_H \cup M_L$. The matching M is a maximum weight matching on the graph of candidate vertices. To see why this is so, the following lemma is useful.

Lemma 6: Let S_k be the k heaviest vertices, for some k. If there is a matching N that matches all of S_k, then any maximum weight matching M matches all of S_k.

Proof: Suppose to the contrary that M does not match $v \in S_k$. Then there is some connected component C of $M \oplus N$ that contains v. This component is a simple path with one end at v and the other at some vertex $u \in S$. Since $u \notin S_k$, it is lighter than v. Thus, $M \oplus C$ is a heavier matching than M, which is impossible. Therefore, M matches all of S_k. ▮

Lemma 7: If

i) $S' \subset S$, such that all of the vertices in S' are heavier than any vertex in $S - S'$;
ii) H is the set of candidate vertices for $S' \cup T$;
iii) L is the set of candidate vertices for the whole graph that are not in H;
iv) M_H is a maximum weight matching on H; and
v) M_L is a maximum weight matching on L;

then $M = M_H \cup M_L$ is a maximum weight matching on $H \cup L$.

Proof: The idea behind the proof is to examine all possible augmenting paths with respect to M and to show that none exist. Any augmenting path must start at an unmatched vertex in S.

Observe that any alternating path that starts at an unmatched vertex in S can not leave H. If such a path were to leave H, the last vertex on the path in H could not be in S, since every vertex adjacent to a vertex in $H \cap S$ is in H. The last vertex in H could also not be in T, since the next edge would have to be matched, and by construction, there are no edges in M that have one endpoint in H and the other in L.

Furthermore, since M_H and M_L are maximum weight matchings, an augmenting path P must contain vertices from both H and L. Therefore, it starts in L, enters H, and ends in H. It can not end in $H \cap T$, since, by Lemma 5, all of these vertices are matched by M_H.

Since P is an augmenting path, its starting (unmatched) vertex is heavier than its ending (matched) vertex. Because of condition i), P starts at a vertex in $S'' = S' \cap L$. Note that S'' is the set of non-candidate vertices in S of $S' \cup T$. Hence, by Lemma 4, there is a matching N of $S' \cup T$ that matches all of the vertices in S''. Therefore, by Lemma 6, M_L matches all of S''. Thus, P can not be an augmenting path, and M has maximum weight. ∎

Making the algorithm go fast.

Now we want to choose k so that the algorithm will run quickly. If we blindly put half of the vertices of S into S', then H will possibly be empty, and we will make no progress. By Lemma 6, however, if we know that we can match the l heaviest vertices, they will be matched by any maximum weight matching. We call such vertices *processed.* A vertex in S that is not processed is *unprocessed.*

If we chose S' to contain all of the processed vertices and half of the unprocessed vertices, then the algorithm can be made to run quickly. Of course, it is necessary to distinguish the processed from the unprocessed vertices. Therefore, another parameter l is added to the recursive calls to the algorithm. It is the number of unprocessed vertices.

When the algorithm calls itself recursively to find a maximum weight matching on H, the unprocessed vertices are the unprocessed vertices in H. When a maximum weight matching on L is to be found, however, the processed vertices are all of the vertices in $S' \cap L$. Figure 2 contains a listing of the recursive procedure *RBPMP*.

Now we want to see that this works.

Lemma 8: The function *RBPMP* computes a maximum weight matching, if the initial call is $RBPMP(B, s)$, where s is the number of vertices in S.

Proof: First, when *RBPMP* is called, there is a matching N that matches all but the l lightest vertices in S. We will prove this fact by induction on the level of recursion. Initially, $l = |S|$, so the base case is trivial. There are two recursive calls to *RBPMP*, $RBPMP(H, l_1)$ and $RBPMP(L, l_2)$.

Consider the call $RBPMP(H, l_1)$ first. Let $S_p = S - S_u$, where S_u is the set of the l lightest vertices in S. That is, S_u is the set of initially unprocessed vertices and S_p is the set of processed vertices. All but the l_1 lightest vertices in $H \cap S$ are in S_p. By induction, there is a matching N' on B that matches all of S_p. The restriction of this matching to H matches all of $S_p \cap H$.

Now consider the recursive call $RBPMP(L, l_2)$. All but the l_2 lightest vertices in $L \cap S$ are in S'. Since H is the set of candidate vertices of $S' \cup T$, by Lemma 4, there is a matching N' on $(S' \cup T) - H$ that matches all of the vertices in S' that are not in H. The restriction of N' to L matches all but the l_2 lightest vertices in $L \cap S$. Therefore, the invariant condition for l is always satisfied.

Now we wish to see that if $l = 1$, M is a maximum weight matching. If a matching that matches all of $B \cap S$ exists, it is a maximum weight matching. If it does not, then a matching M'

```
function RBPMP(B(S,T,E) : graph; l : integer) : matching;
{ RBPMP finds a maximum weight matching on B, where l is the number of unprocessed
vertices in B. }
    begin
    if l = 1 then
        begin
        v ← the lightest vertex in S;
        if there is a matching that matches all of B ∩ S
          then RBPMP ← such a matching
          else RBPMP ← a maximum cardinality matching on B − {v};
            { In the second case all of S − {v} will be matched. }
        return
        end;
    S_u ← the l lightest vertices in S;
    S'' ← the ⌈l/2⌉ lightest vertices in S;
    S' ← S − S'';
    H ← the graph on the set of candidate vertices for S' ∪ T;
    l_1 ← the number of vertices in S_u ∩ H;
    M_H ← RBPMP(H, l_1);
    L ← the rest of the candidate vertices for B;
    l_2 ← the number of vertices in S'' ∩ L;
    M_L ← RBPMP(L, l_2);
    M_R ← a maximum cardinality matching on the non-candidate vertices for B;
    RBPMP ← M_R ∪ M_L ∪ M_H
    end;
```

Figure 2. The function *RBPMP*.

that matches all of $B \cap S$ except the lightest vertex is a maximum weight matching, if it exists. By the previous paragraphs there is a matching M' that matches all of $S - \{v\}$. In either case M is a maximum weight matching.

Hence, by Lemma 7, if $l > 1$, $M_H \cup M_L$ is a maximum weight matching on $H \cup L$. Since, by Lemma 4, M_R matches all of the non-candidate vertices in S, M is a maximum weight matching. Therefore, *RBPMP* calculates a maximum weight matching. ▮

The analysis of the running is based on the following observation.

Lemma 9: In the procedure *RBPMP* if $l > 1$ then $l_1, l_2 \leq \lceil l/2 \rceil$. ▮

Note that most of the time required by the above algorithm is spent calculating maximum cardinality matchings. Thus, the running time of the algorithm should depend on the running time of the algorithm used to calculate the maximum cardinality matchings. Let F and H be disjoint subgraphs of G. A reasonable algorithm that solves the CMP will take at least as long to find a maximum cardinality matching on G as it will to find maximum cardinality matchings on F and then H. Any algorithm with this property has a *convex* running time. As long as the running time for the CMP algorithm is convex only an additional $O(\log n)$ factor is required to solve the BPMP.

Theorem 1: If there is an algorithm to solve the CMP in time $U(n,m) = \Omega(m)$ and $U(n,m) \geq U(n_1,m_1) + U(n_2,m_2)$ for any n_1, n_2, m_1, and m_2 which could be the sizes of disjoint subgraphs of a graph with n vertices and m edges, then the BPMP can be solved in $O(U(n,m)\log n)$ time.

Proof: If we let $T(n,m,l)$ be the running time of the function *RBPMP*, where n, m, and l are the number of vertices in the graph, the number of edges in the graph, and the number of unprocessed vertices, respectively, then T satisfies

$$T(n,m,l) \leq \max_{n_1,n_2,m_1,m_2} \{O(U(n,m)) + T(n_1,m_1,\lceil l/2 \rceil) + T(n_2,m_2,\lceil l/2 \rceil)\},$$

where (n_1,m_1) and (n_2,m_2) are required to describe disjoint and possibly empty subgraphs of a graph with n vertices and m edges. It is easy to show by induction that $T(n,m,n) = O(U(n,m)\log n)$. ▮

Corollary : The BPMP can be solved in $O(n^{1/2} m \log n)$ time. ▮

General Graphs.

The general PMP can be reduced to the BPMP. The idea is to make the input graph bipartite by collapsing all of the blossoms with respect to some maximum cardinality matching. Blossoms were first introduced by Edmonds [1].

Definition: A *flower* is a subgraph of a graph with a matching, M, consisting of two parts, the *stem* and the *blossom*. The *blossom*, C, is a odd length (simple) cycle containing r edges from M and $r+1$ other edges, for some r. There will be exactly one vertex in C which does not have an edge from $M \cap C$ incident to it. This vertex is called the *base* of the blossom. The *stem* is an alternating path from an unmatched vertex, which is called the *root* of the flower, to the base of the blossom. The stem of a flower may be empty.

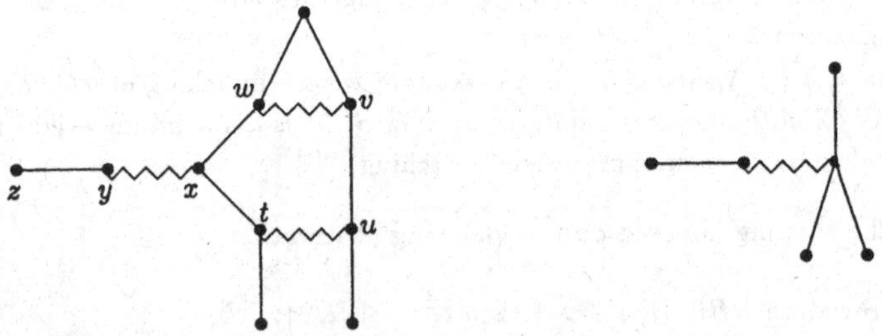

Figure 3. (a) A flower (b) After the blossom has been collapsed.

In Figure 3, a matched edge is denoted by a zig-zag line while an unmatched edge is denoted by a straight line. Figure 3a depicts a flower, where z is the root; the stem consists of the edges (z,y) and (y,x); x is the base of the blossom; and the blossom consists of the edges (x,w), (w,v), (v,u), (u,t), and (t,x). The result of collapsing the blossom is shown in Figure 3b.

Once the blossoms have been collapsed, the resulting graph is called G'. All of the nodes in G' that are an even distance along an alternating path from an unmatched vertex are put in a set S. Similarly, all of the vertices that are an odd distance along an alternating path are put in another set T. Only the edges with one endpoint in S and one in T are retained. The result is then a bipartite graph B. This fact is proved later. The vertices of B that are collapsed blossoms are given a weight equal to the weight of the lightest vertex belonging to the blossom.

```
function PMP(G(V,E) : graph) : matching;
{ PMP finds a maximum weight matching on G. }
    begin
    M' ← a maximum cardinality matching on G;
    while there is a blossom b do
        begin
        w ← the weight of the lightest node belonging to b;
        Collapse b to a single node v_b;
        Make w the weight of v_b
        end;
    S ← the set of all nodes that are an even distance along an alternating path from an
    unmatched node;
    T ← the set of all nodes that are an odd distance along an alternating path from an
    unmatched node;
    M_R ← the restriction of M to those vertices not in S ∪ T;
    E' ← the set of edges with one endpoint in S and the other in T;
    Call the resulting graph B;
    M ← BPMP(B(S,T,E'));
    for each collapsed blossom v_b in the reverse order in which they were created do
        begin
        Expand v_b into the blossom b;
        if v_b was matched by some e ∈ M
            then v ← the endpoint of e in b
            else v ← the lightest node in b;
        Add a perfect matching of b − {v} to M
        end;
    PMP ← M ∪ M_R
    end;
```

Figure 4. The function *PMP*.

A maximum weight matching on B can then be found as discussed above. A maximum weight matching on the original graph G can be found by expanding the blossoms as in [1] taking care that if a collapsed blossom is unmatched then the unmatched vertex in that blossom is the lightest vertex in the blossom. This procedure is summarized in Figure 4.

We want to see that *PMP* is correct. First the call to *BPMP* is well formed.

Lemma 10: When *PMP* calls *BPMP*, $B(S,T,E')$ is a bipartite graph.

Proof: It is enough to show that the sets S and T are disjoint. If it were the case that $v \in S \cap T$, then there would be alternating paths P_1 and P_2 from an unmatched vertex to v of odd and even length respectively. If P_1 and P_2 were disjoint (except for v) then $P_1 \cup P_2$ would be an alternating path between two unmatched vertices. This is impossible since M' is a maximum cardinality matching. Alternatively, if P_1 and P_2 share another vertex, then parts of the two paths would form a blossom, which is also impossible. Thus, $S \cap T = \emptyset$ and B is bipartite. ∎

The reason why *PMP* calculates a maximum weight matching is that augmenting paths in G correspond to augmenting paths in B. Let us make this correspondence precise. Consider a path P in G. For each $v \in P$, let $b(v)$ be the node that v belongs to in G', the graph formed from G by collapsing all of the blossoms wit respect to M'. Then, if we ignore consecutive repeated nodes, the image $b(P)$ is a (not necessarily simple) path in G'.

Lemma 11: If P is an alternating path (with respect to M, the matching returned by *PMP*) starting at an unmatched vertex v, then $b(P)$ is an alternating path (with respect to M'', the matching returned by the call to *BPMP*) in the subgraph B of G'.

Proof: Let us make some observations about the relationship between B and G. First, all nodes that result from collapsed blossoms are in S, since the stem of a flower must have even length. Second, the only vertices that are not matched by the final value of M (subsequently referred to as M) belong to nodes in S. Let M'' be the matching that is returned by *BPMP*. Since M' matches every vertex in T and M'' is a maximum cardinality matching, M'' also matches all of T. The matching M_R matches every vertex that is not in $S \cup T$. Therefore the only vertices that are not matched by M belong to nodes in S.

Therefore, P contains an unmatched vertex v belonging to a node in S. Let us think of P as starting at v. If $b(P)$ is not an alternating path in B with respect to M'', then either there are two consecutive unmatched edges in $b(P)$ or there is some edge that is not in B and is in $b(P)$. Let e be the first edge in $b(P)$ that is either the second of two consecutive unmatched edges in $b(P)$ or an edge in $b(P)$ but not B. Also let u be the first node of e in $b(P)$.

Suppose that $u \in T$. Then u did not result from the collapse of a blossom, so the edges incident to u in $b(P)$ are consecutive edges in P. Hence, e is matched, and, the other end of e is in S, contradicting both possibilities above.

Alternatively, u could be in S. In this case, the edge in $b(P)$ before u is in M'', if it exists. Therefore, in either case, there are not two consecutive unmatched edges incident to u. Moreover, $e \notin M''$. Since $u \in S$, it is an even distance along an alternating path Q from an unmatched (by M') node. The path Q can be extended by adding e. Hence, the other end of e is in T, contrary to our assumption. Therefore, $b(P)$ is an alternating path that is entirely in B. ∎

The correctness of *PMP* follows from Lemma 11.

Lemma 12: The final value of M produced by *PMP* is a maximum weight matching of G.

Proof: To prove the lemma, it is enough to show that here are no augmenting paths (with respect to M). Suppose that P is an augmenting path. It must contain an unmatched vertex v, and $b(v)$ is unmatched (by M''). Then, by Lemma 11, $b(P)$ is an alternating path (with respect to M''). Let u be the other end of P, so $b(u)$ is the other end of $b(P)$. Since M'' has maximum weight, $b(u)$ is matched and the weight of $b(u)$ is at least the weight of $b(v)$. Since every vertex belonging to $b(u)$ is matched, u is matched. Furthermore, the weight of u is at least the weight of $b(u)$, since the weight of a collapsed blossom b is the weight of the lightest vertex belonging to b. and the weight of v is equal to the weight of $b(v)$. Therefore, the weight of u is at least the weight of v, and P is not an augmenting path. Therefore, M is a maximum weight matching ∎

Theorem 2: The PMP can be solved as quickly as the more difficult of the BPMP and the CMP for general graphs if one of these problems requires at least $\Omega(m + n\alpha(n))$ time.

Proof: Transforming the graph G into G' can be done as a post phase of the Micali-Vazirani algorithm [5]. This requires at most $O(m + n\alpha(n))$ time, where $O(n\alpha(n))$ is the time required to do $O(n)$ operations on the union-find data structure of Tarjan [6]. The sets S and T can be found in $O(m)$ time by a depth first search. The transformation of G' to B is trivial. The time required to expand a blossom is proportional to its size. Therefore only $O(n)$ time is spent expanding blossoms and transforming M'' into the final value of M. Thus, the two most time consuming steps of this process are finding the original maximum cardinality matching M' and solving the BPMP on B. ∎

Corollary : The PMP can be solved in $O(n^{1/2}m\log n)$ time. ∎

Negative weights.

We have seen that the PMP is almost as easy as the CMP. If the weights are allowed to be negative, however, then there might be some vertices which should not be matched.

Suppose that some vertex v has weight $-a$, where $a > 0$. For every such vertex, we add a new vertex v' to the graph which is adjacent only to v. If v is matched with some vertex other than v' then v' can not be matched. Thus, the matching is penalized the weight of v'. So the transformation gives v' the weight a and changes the weight of v to be zero. The only effect of this transformation will be to increase by a the weight of all matchings that match v.

Since this transformation at most doubles the size of the graph, the MP is no harder than the PMP.

The procedure is shown in Figure 5.

```
function MP(G(V,E) : graph) : matching;
{ MP finds a maximum weight matching on G. }
    begin
    for each vertex v_i with weight w(v_i) < 0 do
        begin
        Add a new vertex v'_i to V;
        Add an edge between v_i and v'_i to E;
        w(v'_i) ← −w(v_i);
        w(v_i) ← 0
        end;
    MP ← PMP(G(V,E))
    end;
```

Figure 5. The function *MP*.

Conclusions.

We have shown that maximum node weighted matchings can be found almost as quickly as maximum cardinality matchings. This was done by reducing the problem to the bipartite positive weighted case. There the properties of maximum cardinality matchings allowed an efficient divide and conquer algorithm.

Note that our algorithm for the BPMP does not use the weights except to identify the k heaviest vertices, for various values of k. Thus, only the order of the weights matters. This fact may explain why the MP appears to be easier than the edge weighted matching problem.

The obvious way to test this hypothesis is to change the problem so that the weights are no longer totally ordered. Thus we are lead to consider the vector weighted matching problem (VMP), "given a graph G with d-dimensional weights attached to the vertices, is there a matching M such that the (vector) sum of the weights of the matched vertices is greater than some given target vector?" The VMP turns out to be weakly NP-complete even for $d = 2$ and complete bipartite graphs. If d is allowed to be an input parameter, the problem is NP-complete, even if all of the components of the weights are required to be 0 or 1.

Another interesting problem is to determine whether or not the $\log n$ is necessary in the running time. If the graphs H and L could be guaranteed to be small, then the recurrence would telescope and the $\log n$ factor would disappear. There is an algorithm that usees binary search to find a value for S' such that the graphs H and L contain no more than half the edges. For this algorithm, a $\log n$ factor is not necessary for the recursion, but one is necessary for the binary search. Perhaps these approaches can be combined to yield a faster algorithm.

References.

[1] Edmonds, J.: Paths, Trees, and Flowers. *Canad. J. Math.* **17** (1965), pp. 449-467.

[2] Galil, Z., Micali, S., Gabow, H.: Priority Queues with Variable Priority and an $O(EV \log V)$ Algorithm for Finding a Maximal Weighted Matching in General Graphs. Proc. 23rd Annual Symposium on Foundations of Computer Science, (1982), pp. 255-261.

[3] Hopcroft, J. E., Karp, R. M.: An $n^{5/2}$ Algorithm for Maximum Matchings in Bipartite Graphs. *SIAM J. on Comput.* **2** (1973), pp. 225-231.

[4] Mendelson, N. S., Dulmage, A. L.: Some generalizations of the problem of distinct representatives. *Canad. J. Math.* **10** (1958) pp.230-241.

[5] Micali, S., Vazirani, V. V.: An $O(\sqrt{|V|}|E|)$ Algorithm for Finding Maximum Matchings in General Graphs. Proc. 21st Annual Symposium on Foundations of Computer Science, (1981), pp. 17-27.

[6] Tarjan, R. E.: Efficiency of a Good But Not Linear Set Union Algorithm. JACM **22** (1975), p. 215-225.

The Propositional Mu-Calculus is Elementary

Robert S. Streett
Computer Science Department
Boston University
Boston, MA 02215
USA

E. Allen Emerson
Computer Sciences Department
University of Texas
Austin, TX 78712
USA

ACKNOWLEDGEMENT: The work of the second author was supported in part by NSF grant MCS-8302878.

ABSTRACT: The propositional mu-calculus is a propositional logic of programs which incorporates a least fixpoint operator and subsumes the Propositional Dynamic Logic of Fischer and Ladner, the infinite looping construct of Streett, and the Game Logic of Parikh. We give an elementary time decision procedure, using a reduction to the emptiness problem for automata on infinite trees. A small model theorem is obtained as a corollary.

1. Introduction

First-order logic is inadequate for formalizing reasoning about programs; concepts such as termination and totality require logics strictly more powerful than first-order (Kfoury and Park, 1975). The use of a least fixpoint operator as a remedy for these deficiencies has been investigated by Park (1970, 1976), Hitchcock and Park (1973), deBakker and deRoever (1973), deRoever (1974), Emerson and Clarke (1980), and others. The resulting formal systems are often called mu-calculi and can express such important properties of sequential and parallel programs as termination, liveness, and freedom from deadlock and starvation.

Propositional versions of the mu-calculus have been proposed by Pratt (1981) and Kozen (1982). These logics use the least fixpoint operator to increase the expressive power of Propositional Dynamic Logic (*PDL*) of Fischer and Ladner (1979). Kozen's formulation captures the infinite looping construct of Streett (1982) and subsumes Parikh's Game Logic (1983a, 1983b), whereas Pratt's logic is designed to express the converse operator of *PDL*. The filtration-based decision procedure and small model theorem obtained for *PDL* extend to Pratt's mu-calculus, but the ability to express infinite looping renders the filtration technique inapplicable to Kozen's version.

Kozen (1982) and Vardi and Wolper (1984) have obtained exponential time decision procedures for fragments of Kozen's mu-calculus. Both fragments can expresses all of *PDL*, but are not strong enough to capture the infinite looping construct of Streett (1982). Kozen and Parikh (1983) have shown that the satisfiability problem for the full propositional mu-calculus can be reduced to the second-order theory of several successor functions (*SnS*). By results of Rabin (1969) this supplies a decision procedure for the propositional mu-calculus, but one which runs in non-elementary time, i.e., time not bounded by any fixed number of compositions of exponential functions. Meyer (1974) has shown that this is the best that can be achieved using a reduction to *SnS*.

2. Syntax and Semantics

The formulas of the propositional mu-calculus are:

(1) Propositional letters $P, Q, R, \ldots$

(2) Propositional variables $\ldots, X, Y, Z$.

(3) Ap, where A is a member of a set of program letters $A, B, C, \ldots$ and p is any formula,

(4) $\neg p$,

(5) $p \vee q$,

(6) $\mu X.f(X)$, where $f(X)$ is any formula syntactically monotone in the propositional variable X, i.e., all occurrences of X in $f(X)$ fall under an even number of negations.

A sentence is a formula containing no free propositional variables, i.e., no variables unbound by a   operator. Mu-calculus sentences are satisfied in Kripke structures, which interpret propositional letters as subsets of states and program letters as binary relations on states. The formula Ap is true in a state when there is an A edge to a state satisfying p. In the formula $\mu X.f(X)$, f denotes a monotone operator on sets of states, and $\mu X.f(X)$ is interpreted as the least fixpoint of this operator, i.e., the least set of states X such that $f(X) = X$.

Examples: The sentence $\mu X.P \vee AX$ is true at a state x if there is a chain (possibly empty) of A edges leading from x to a state satisfying P. It is equivalent to the sentence $\langle A^*\rangle P$ of Propositional Dynamic Logic (*PDL*). The sentence $\mu X.P \vee A(\ Y.X \vee BY)$ is equivalent to the *PDL* sentence $\langle (AB^*)^*\rangle P$.

It is convenient to reduce the problem of satisfiability over the general models described above to satisfiability over a special class of models, the tree models.

Definition: A deterministic model is a Kripke structure in which the relations corresponding to the programs are partial functions; for each state x and program A there is at most one A edge from x. A tree model is a deterministic model whose universe of states is the set of words over an alphabet of program letters. Each program is interpreted as a binary relation in the obvious way: there is an A edge from x to xA.

Proposition 1. There is a translation of mu-calculus

sentences such that a sentence is satisfiable if and only if its translation is satisfied in a tree model.

Outline of Proof: Kozen and Parikh (1983) establish a Lowenheim-Skolem theorem for the propositional mu-calculus; if a sentence is satisfiable, then it has a countable model. These countable models can be further restricted to be deterministic; this is accomplished by translating Ap as $A(\mu X.p \vee BX)$, where B is a new program, a technique due to Parikh (1978). It is not difficult to expand and unwind the resulting models into tree models.

In a tree model, any sentence can be put into a special positive form, by using the following DeMorgan-like laws to move negations until they are only applied to propositional letters.

(1) $\neg\neg p \rightarrow p$,
(2) $\neg(p \vee q) \rightarrow (\neg p) \,\&\, (\neg q)$,
(3) $\neg Ap \rightarrow A(\neg p)$,
(4) $\neg(\mu X.f(X)) \rightarrow \nu X.\neg f(\neg X)$.

The formula $\nu X.f(X)$ represents the greatest fixpoint of the monotone operator f.

Examples: The sentence $\mu X.P \vee (AX \,\&\, BX)$ is true when there is a finite binary tree of A and B edges with a frontier of states satisfying P. The sentence $\nu X.P \,\&\, (\mu Y.BX \vee AY)$ is true when there is an infinite $AB*$ chain of states satisfying P.

In what follows we shall assume that all sentences are in positive form and that all models are tree models.

3. Ordinal Ranks and Signatures

By the Tarski-Knaster theorem, $\mu X.f(X)$ can be defined by transfinite induction, i.e., $\mu X.f(X) = \cup_\alpha f^\alpha(false)$, where

$$f^0(false) = false$$
$$f^{\alpha+1}(false) = f(f^\alpha(false))$$
$$f^\lambda(false) = \cup_{\alpha<\lambda} f^\alpha(false),\ \lambda \text{ a limit ordinal.}$$

A mu-sentence $\mu X.f(X)$ has rank α at a state x if $f^\alpha(false)$ is true at x. Since a mu-sentence can contain other mu-sentences as subsentences, it is useful to associate a sequence of ordinal ranks to a sentence. Bounded length sequences of ordinals can be well-ordered lexicographically.

Definition. The mu-height of a sentence is the depth of nesting of mu-subsentences of the sentence.

Example: The sentence $\mu X.P \vee A(\mu Y.X \vee BY)$ has mu-height 1, since the subformula $\mu Y.X \vee BY$ is not a sentence.

Given a sentence p of mu-height n and a sequence of ordinals $s = \alpha_1 \cdots \alpha_n$, we let $p{:}s$ denote the sentence obtained by replacing each mu-subsentence $\mu X.f(X)$ of p by $f^{\alpha_i}(false)$, where i is the mu-height of $\mu X.f(X)$. A sentence p has signature s at a state x if $p{:}s$ is true at x.

Examples: Consider $\mu Y.(\mu X.P \vee A(\mu Z.X \vee BZ)) \vee BY$, equivalent to the PDL sentence $\langle B*\rangle\langle(AB*)*\rangle P$. This sentence has mu-height 2, and if P is true at a state $xBABABBBBB$, then this sentence has signature 3-2 at x, 3-1 at xB, 2-2 at xBA, 2-1 at $xBAB$, 1-6 at $xBABA$, and so on down to 1-1 at $xBABABBBBB$. Infinite ordinals can arise in signatures through the interaction of mu-sentences and nu-sentences. Consider $\nu X.(\mu Y.(P \vee BY) \& AX)$, equivalent to the PDL sentence $[A*]\langle B*\rangle P$. In a tree model in which the states satisfying P are precisely $A^n B^n$, for $n \geq 0$, the signature of this sentence at the root will be ω.

Lemma: The following rules hold of signatures:

(1) if $p \vee q$ has signature s at x, then either p or q has signature s at x.
(2) if $p \& q$ has signature s at x, then both p and q have signature s at x.
(3) if Ap has signature s at x, then p has signature s at xA.
(4) if $\mu X.f(X)$ has signature s at x, then $f(\mu X.f(X))$ has signature t at x, where t lexicographically precedes s.
(5) if $\nu X.f(X)$ has signature s at x, then $f(\nu X.f(X))$ has signature s at x.

Proof (for case 4 only): Suppose $\mu X.f(X)$ has mu-height n. The mu-subsentences of $f(\mu X.f(X))$ can be divided into three classes:

(1) The proper mu-subsentences of $\mu X.f(X)$, with mu-height $< n$.
(2) $\mu X.f(X)$ itself, with mu-height n.
(3) Mu-sentences properly containing $\mu X.f(X)$, with mu-height $> n$.

If $\mu Y.g(Y)$ is in the first class and can be replaced by $g^{\alpha}(false)$ within $\mu X.f(X)$ at x, then it can be similarly replaced within $f(\mu X.f(X))$ at x. If $\mu X.f(X)$ has rank α at x, then $\mu X.f(X)$ can be replaced by $f^{\beta}(false)$, for $\beta < \alpha$, within $f(\mu X.f(X))$ at x. Hence if $\mu X.f(X)$ has signature $s = \alpha_1 \cdots \alpha_n$ at x, then $f(\mu X.f(X))$ will have signature $t = \alpha_1 \cdots \alpha_{n-1} \beta_n \beta_{n+1} \cdots \beta_m$ at x, where $\beta_n < \alpha_n$, so that t lexicographically precedes s.

Example: Consider $\mu X.(\mu Y.P \vee CY) \vee A(\mu Z.X \vee BZ)$, equivalent to the PDL sentence $\langle(AB*)*\rangle\langle C*\rangle P$. In a model in which P is true at $xABBBACCCC$, this sentence has signature

5-3 at x, indicating that P can be reached via two $(AB*)$'s and four C's. The derived sentence, equivalent to the *PDL* sentence $\langle C*\rangle P \vee \langle A\rangle\langle B*\rangle\langle (AB*)*\rangle\langle C*\rangle P$, has signature 5-2-4 at x, indicating that, from xA, P can be reached via three B's, one $AB*$, and four C's .

4. The Decision Procedure

Given a sentence p, we will construct a finite automaton on infinite trees (Rabin, 1969; Hossley and Rackoff, 1972) which recognizes the tree models of p. This automaton will evaluate a given sentence in a candidate tree structure by recursive descent, i.e., by recursively evaluating its consequences. At a disjunction $q \vee r$ contained within a mu-sentence it is necessary to make a careful choice of which disjunct to evaluate. Consider the formula $\mu X.P \vee AX$, equivalent to the PDL sentence $\langle A*\rangle P$, which is satisfied in a tree structure when the formula P is satisfied somewhere along the path of A's. Consistently choosing the disjunct AX of $P \vee AX$ will cause tree structures in which p is false along the path of A's to be mîstakenly regarded as models of $\mu X.P \vee AX$.

A choice function for a model is a function which chooses, for every disjunction, one of the disjuncts. Ordinal signatures can be used to define a choice function which selects the true disjunct with lexicographically least signature.

Any choice function over a tree structure determines a derivation relation between occurrences of sentences.

(1) A disjunction, $q \vee r$, derives the disjunct chosen by the choice function,
(2) A conjunction, $q \& r$, derives both conjuncts,
(3) A program sentence, Aq, occurring at a state x, derives q at Ax.
(4) A mu-sentence, $\mu X.f(X)$, derives $f(\mu X.f(X))$.
(5) A nu-sentence, $\nu X.f(X)$, derives $f(\nu X.f(X))$.

Definition. A sentence p at x generates q at y if p at x derives q at y in such a way that q is a subsentence of every derivation step. In particular, note that q must be a subsentence of p, so that a sentence can only generate its subsentences.

Example: $\mu X.P \vee A(\mu Y.X \vee BY)$ at x can derive, but not generate, $\mu Y.((\mu X.(P \vee A(\mu Y.X \vee BY)) \vee BY)$ at xA.

Definition. A mu-sentence $\mu X.f(X)$ is regenerated from state x to state y if an occurrence at x generates an occurrence at y.

Example: $\mu Y.((\mu X.(P \vee A(\mu Y.X \vee BY)) \vee BY)$ can be regenerated from x to xB, but from x to xA. A derivation from x to xA is possible, but requires $\mu X.P \vee A(\mu Y.X \vee BY)$ as a derivation step.

If we start with a tree model and construct a choice function based on ordinal signatures, then by the Lemma of Section 3 the regeneration relations for mu-sentences will always decrease signature and hence be well-founded. Conversely, if a candidate tree structure can be supplied with a choice function which make the regeneration relations well-founded, it will in fact be a model.

In particular, if the regeneration relations are well-founded, then each occurrence of a mu-sentence is associated with an ordinal, the well-ordering ordinal of the regeneration relation from that occurrence. It is then possible to calculate a signature $s = \alpha_1 \cdots \alpha_n$ for every sentence q at state x, via the definition:

$$\alpha_i = \text{l.u.b.}(\alpha : q \text{ at } x \text{ generates mu-sentence } r \text{ at } y, \; r \text{ has mu-depth } i, \text{ and } r \text{ at } y \text{ has regeneration ordinal } \alpha).$$

We have therefore shown:

Proposition 2. A sentence p is satisfiable if and only if there is a tree model with an attached choice function over which the regeneration relations for mu-sentences are well-founded.

It is then a exercise in automaton programming to show:

Proposition 3. Given a sentence p, we can effectively construct an automaton which expects as input a tree structure with attached choice functions and accepts precisely when the choice function guarantees that the structure is a model of p. The size of this automaton (and the time required to construct it) can be kept elementary in the length of the formula.

Proof: Given a candidate tree structure, the desired automaton checks that the structure is both locally and globally consistent. A structure is locally consistent when no state contains both a propositional letter and its negation, or contains a disjunction without one of its disjuncts, etc. Global consistency consists of the well-foundedness of the regeneration relation for mu-sentences derived from p. It is straightfoward to construct an automaton on infinite strings which, when run down a single path of a tree structure, nondeterministically searches for an infinite descending chain in the regeneration relations. A complement construction then supplies an automaton which, when run down every path of a tree structure, checks global consistency.

Combining Propositions 1, 2, and 3, we have reduced the

satisfiability problem for the propositional mu-calculus to the emptiness problem for finite automata on infinite trees. Since this last problem is elementarily decidable, the mu-calculus is also. The methods of Streett (1981) can be used to show that the decision procedure runs in triple exponential time. As a corollary, we obtain a small model theorem. For if the set of tree models is automaton recognizable, then there must be a finitely generable tree model, i.e., one obtained by unwinding a finite graph. This graph will be a finite model.

5. References

deBakker, J., and deRoever, W. P. (1973), A Calculus for Recursive Program Schemes, in "First International Colloquium on Automata, Languages, and Programming", 167-196.

deRoever, W. P. (1974), "Recursive Program Schemes: Semantics and Proof Theory", Ph. D. thesis, Free University, Amsterdam.

Emerson, E. A., and Clarke, E. C. (1980), Characterizing Correctness Properties of Parallel Programs Using Fixpoints, in "Seventh International Colloquium on Automata, Languages, and Programming", 169-181.

Fischer, M. J., and Ladner, R. E. (1979), Propositional Dynamic Logic of Regular Programs, *Journal of Computer System Science 18*, 194-211.

Hitchcock, P., and Park, D. M. R. (1973), Induction Rules and Termination Proofs, in "First International Colloquium on Automata, Languages, and Programming", 225-251.

Hossley, R., and Rackoff, C. W. (1972), The Emptiness Problem for Automata on Infinite Trees, in "Thirteenth IEEE Symposium on Switching and Automata Theory", 121-124.

Kfoury, A. J., and Park, D. M. R. (1975), On Termination of Program Schemes, *Information and Control 29*, 243-251.

Kozen, D. (1982), Results on the Propositional Mu-Calculus, in "Ninth International Colloquium on Automata, Languages, and Programming", 348-359.

Kozen, D., and Parikh, R. J. (1983), A Decision Procedure for the Propositional Mu-Calculus, to appear in "Second Workshop on Logics of Programs".

Meyer, A. R. (1974), Weak Monadic Second Order Theory of Successor is not Elementary Recursive, *Boston Logic Colloquium, Springer-Verlag Lecture Notes in Mathematics 453*.

Parikh, R. J. (1979), A Decidability Result for a Second Order Process Logic, in "Nineteenth IEEE Symposium on the Foundations of Computing", 177-183.

Parikh, R. J. (1983a), Cake Cutting, Dynamic Logic, Games, and Fairness, to appear in "Second Workshop on Logics of Programs".

Parikh, R. J. (1983b), Propositional Game Logic, to appear in "Twenty-third IEEE Symposium on the Foundations of Computer Science".

Park, D. M. R. (1970), Fixpoint Induction and Proof of Program Semantics, *Machine Intelligence 5*, Edinburgh University Press.

Park, D. M. R. (1976), Finiteness is Mu-Ineffable, *Theoretical Computer Science 3*, 173-181.

Pratt, V. R. (1982), A Decidable Mu-Calculus: Preliminary Report, in "Twenty-second IEEE Symposium on the Foundations of Computer Science", 421-427.

Rabin, M. O. (1969), Decidability of Second Order Theories and Automata on Infinite Trees", *Transactions of the American Mathematical Society 141*, 1-35.

Streett, R. S. (1981), "Propositional Dynamic Logic of Looping and Converse", MIT LCS Technical Report TR-263.

Streett, R. S. (1982), Propositional Dynamic Logic of Looping and Converse is Elementarily Decidable, *Information and Control 54*, 121-141.

Vardi, M., and Wolper, P. (1984), Automata Theoretic Techniques for Modal Logics of Programs, to appear in "Sixteenth ACM Symposium on the Theory of Computing".

AVL-trees for Localized Search

Athanasios K. Tsakalidis

FB 10, Informatik, Universität des Saarlandes
D-6600 Saarbrücken, West Germany

bstract: We present a data structure based on AVL-trees which allows to erform an insertion or a deletion in time O(log d) where d is the disance of the position searched for from the finger which points to the nd of the file. Moving a finger costs O(log d). This result demonstrates he power of the oldest basic data structure, the AVL-tree. A special ase of interest is an efficient implementation of searchable priority ueues such that Deletemin requires only constant time.

. Introduction:

In the seventies many balanced trees (AVL-trees, B-trees, BB[α]-trees) ere developed having a worst case behavior of O(log n) for the operaions Search, Insert, Delete in a file of size n. From 1978 on the aplications of the balanced trees began to be more interesting and we got he results of [2] that the total number of rotations and double rotaions after m arbitrary insertions and deletions in a BB[α]-tree is (m) then, the results of [7] showed that the total number of rebalaning operations after m arbitrary insertions and deletions in a weak -tree is O(m). But it is important to have results about an individual nsertion or deletion, since there are applications as in sorting preorted files [10,11] and in finger trees [3,5] where the search time an be o(log n). Additionally in parallel processing it is important to now that a rebalancing operation does not need much time after an nsertion or deletion.

In [5] and [9] data structures are given where every insertion and eletion can be performed in time O(search time). More precisely, the perations Search-Insert-Delete can be performed in time O(log d), here d is the distance of the position searched for from the finger. moving of a finger can be performed in time O(log d) in [9], but it eeds time O(log n) in [5]. L. Guibas et. al. [5] use (m/3,m)-trees, ith m=24 and some complex regularity conditions on the finger path. ne data structure of Kosaraju in [9] is complicated too. It consists f a forest of (2,3)-trees with some regularity conditions (monotoicity, multiplicity, gap property). Both structures have the disadvanage that they are complicated and they use costly operations.

Since such an elementary problem is solved by complicated data structures the natural question arises, if the usual basic data structures can solve this problem by simple modifications. S. Huddleston [6] gives an affirmative answer to this question for the class of the small-order B-trees, but his simple modifications change the basic data structure substantially. R.E. Tarjan [12] gives an elegant solution for (2,6)-trees.

The main result of this paper is a new implementation of the usual AVL-tree which directly answers the question above positively for the case of an AVL-tree without changing it substantially and demonstrates the power of this oldest basic data structure.

An application of the result provides a searchable priority queue implemented by an AVL-tree, where the operations Min and Deletemin can be performed in constant time and an insertion or a search in time O(log n) where n is the current size of the queue.

2. Definitions

AVL-trees were defined by Adelson-Velskii, G.M. Landis in [1]. Results about their behavior can be found in [4,8,11]. We use the following definitions for a binary tree.

1) Height(v) is the length of the longest path from v to a leaf.
2) For every node v we define its height balance hb(v) as:

   $hb(v) = \text{Height}(\text{right son}(v)) - \text{Height}(\text{left son}(v))$.
3) A binary tree T is called AVL-tree if for every node v of T holds: $|hb(v)| \leq 1$.
4) Let $v_o, v_1, \ldots, v_k$ be a path from a root v_o to a leaf v_k of an AVL-tree. Let i be minimal such that $hb(v_i)=hb(v_{i+1})=\ldots=hb(v_{k-1})=0$. Then node v_{i-1} is called the critical insert node (CIN) $(i\geq 1)$ and $v_i,\ldots,v_k$ is called the critical insert path.

   Let v_s be a node on the search path with $\text{Height}(v_s)=2$. Then the critical delete node (CDN) is v_s, if $hb(v_s)=0$, otherwise the node v_{j-1}, where j is minimal such that:

   $$hb(v_t) = \begin{cases} +1, & \text{if right son}(v_t) \text{ lies on the search path} \\ -1, & \text{if left son}(v_t) \text{ lies on the search path} \end{cases}, \text{ for } j\leq t\leq s \text{ if such a t exists,}$$

   or the father (v_s), if such a t does not exist.
5) T_v denotes the subtree rooted at v.

3. Elementary Operations

We use the elementary operations as given in [8]. In the following figures a node contains its height balance and a subtree is represented by its height h.

a) INSERT:

Let v be the CIN with hb(v)=+1, as in figure a.o. We explore the case in which the node x will be inserted into the right subtree of v, thus increasing the height of the latter.

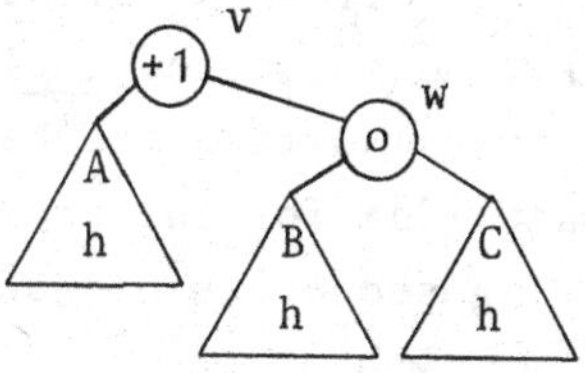

figure a.o

a.1 Single rotation (rot): insertion into C;

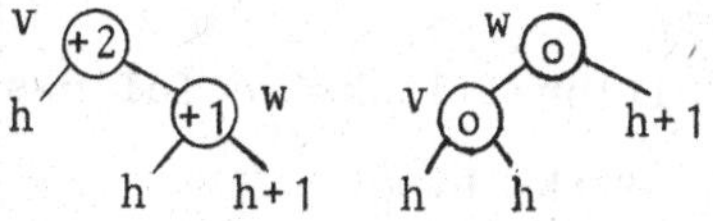

a.2 Double rotation (drot): insertion into B

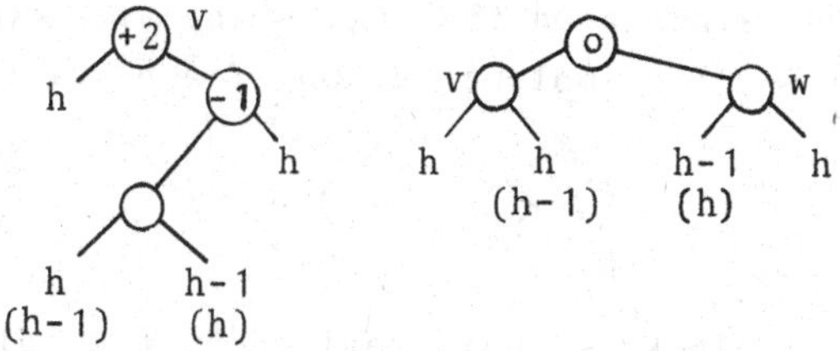

Remark a: In both cases the rebalanced subtree does not change its height. Its root takes the height balance 0.

b) DELETE:

Let v be the CDN with hb(v)=+1. We explore the case where a deletion causes a height decrease of the left subtree of v. If hb(v)=0 we have absorption.

b.1 Terminating rotation: hb(w)=0

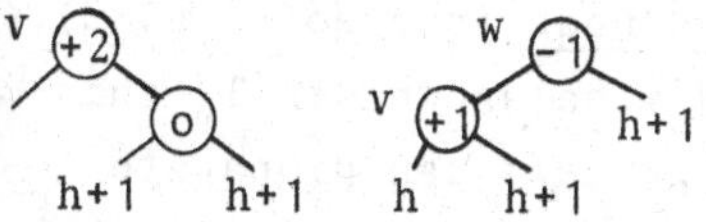

Remark b.1: The height of the rebalanced subtree does not change, and after the rotation the following holds: hb(v)=-hb(w)≠0.

b.2 Propagating rot: hb(w)=+1;

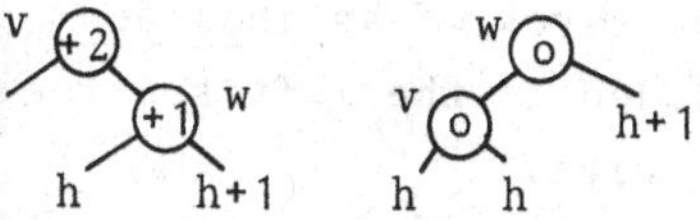

b.3 Propagating drot: hb(w)=-1

b.3.1: hb(k)=+1

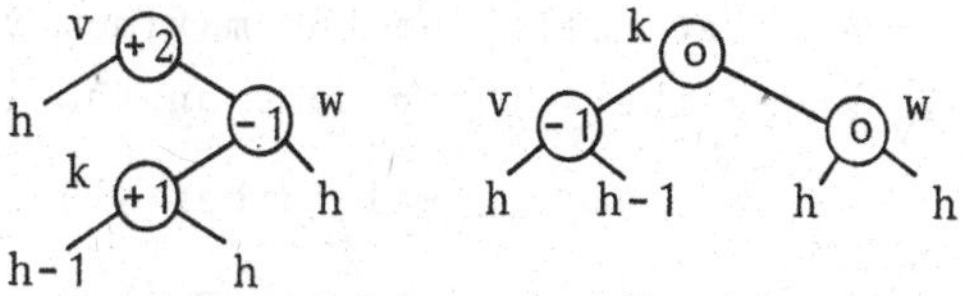

b.3.2: hb(k)=0, then we get hb(k)=0, hb(v)=0, hb(w)=0

b.3.3: hb(k)=-1, " " " " " ,hb(w)=+1

Remark b.2,3: In the cases b.2 and b.3 the rebalanced subtree decreases its height by one and the rebalancing will propagate higher up. The new root of this subtree takes balance 0 and v takes hb(v)≠+1.

4. Inclined AVL-tree and the informal algorithms

We use the following definitions and implementations:

1) An AVL-tree is called inclined AVL-tree, if the nodes on the left spine can also take the height balance +2.
2) The main idea for the implementation of such a tree is to keep the following sequences of nodes on the left spine in a block structure:

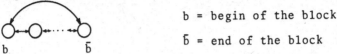

2.1) (o)—(o)...(o)	called critical insert block	(o)
2.2) (-1)—(-1)·····(-1)	called critical delete block	(-1)
2.3) (some (+1)—nodes)	called critical rebalancing block	(CRB)

3) The nodes on the left spine are doubly linked.
4) For the implementation of a block we use additional links as follows:

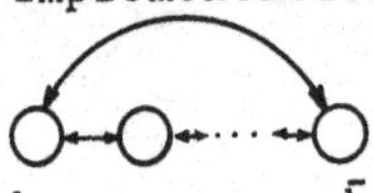

b = begin of the block

$\bar{b}$ = end of the block

5) A block is characterized by the balance of its b node. (i.e., the balance of the first node determines the balance of the nodes in the block).
6) If the b node of CRB takes the balance of +2, then we call it guilty block. The meaning of such a definition is that these nodes must be rotated or doubly rotated if they are reached during the search process.
7) (+2) denotes a guilty block which consists of one node.

Remark 1: For the definition of (CRB) we use some special nodes with balance +1. Such a special node is called bad-node (see def. in§ 5) and has the property that after deleting and rebalancing in T_v this subtree can decrease its height by one; this process can propagate higher up than to v.

Let d be the distance of the element x from the finger f which points to the left end of a file stored in the leaves of an inclined AVL-tree, let val(v) be the maximum value included in the left subtree of T_v and y the turning node on the left spine with:

$$\text{val}(v) < x \leq \text{val}(\text{father}(y))$$

Then the situation is as given in figure 1.

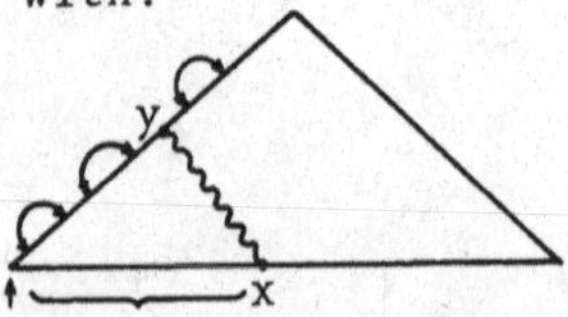

fig.1

The algorithm is based on the following idea:

1) We search from f upwards in direction of the root up to the turning node y. During this search we clean all the guilty blocks we meet. Then we search downwards to the leaves. After inserting or deleting x we execute all the necessary operations for balance changes and rebalancing on the nodes which belong into T_y, and above y we perform at most a constant number of the necessary rebalancings. The remaining ones of them generate a guilty block.
2) During this process we try to keep the following invariant * valid on the nodes of the left spine.

   *.1) There are no adjacent guilty blocks

   *.2) There are no sequences like

   a) 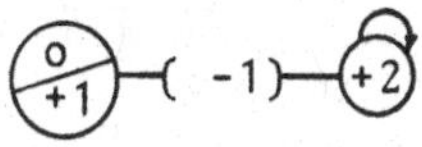

   or b) 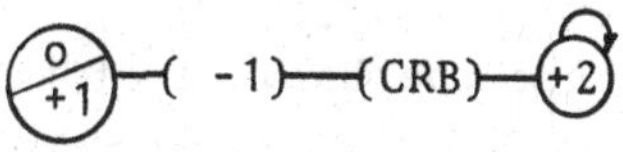

Next we informally give the operations Insert(x) and Delete(x) using the auxiliary procedures Isubseq(v) and Dsubseq(v) with the following functions:

Isubseq(v) executes all the subsequent operations after the height increase of T_ℓ of one, where ℓ=left son(v).
Dsubseq(v) does the same after the height decrease of T_ℓ of one.

The operation Search(x) will be executed as follows before any of the operations Insert(x) and Delete(x):

```
proc Search(x);
          co Let y be the turning node if it exists, or the father
             of the left most leaf otherwise;
    Search upwards to y and use rotations and double rotations to
       clean the guilty blocks; i.e., whenever a node v with balance
       +2 is encountered, we rebalance it. Note that this might
       change the balance of v's father to +2 (+3 is impossible be-
       cause of invariant *.1). We continue with this process until
       node y is reached;
    Search downwards up to the leaf position of x;
end.

proc Insert(x) [Delete(x)];
    Insert [Delete] x in the conventional manner (see Knuth);
    Execute all the necessary rot/drot and balance changes up to the
    turning node y (including y);
```

ID: Save the invariant *.2 on y or on a descendant v of y;

<u>if</u> T_y increased [decreased] its height by one
<u>then</u> Isubseq(father(y)) [Dsubseq(father(y))] <u>fi</u>
<u>end</u>.

We have to distinguish between "good" and "bad" (+1)-nodes. A (CRB) consists of <u>bad</u>-nodes. The meaning of these nodes is the following: After decreasing the height of the left subtree of a node v the rebalancing of a good node v does <u>not</u> change the height of T_v (i.e.,the process <u>terminates</u>) and the rebalancing of a <u>bad</u> node v decreases the height of T_v by one (i.e., the process propagates).

<u>proc</u> Isubseq(v);
<u>co</u> The left subtree T_ℓ of v has increased its height by one;
Change the balance of v;
<u>if</u> $(v,\bar{v})$ was a (o)-block change it into a (-1)-block;
if $(v,\bar{v})$ was a guilty block change it into a (CRB)-block;
otherwise execute the proper rot/drot;
<u>end</u>.

For the next procedure we additionally need a special operation shrink$(v,\bar{v})$ which executes a rebalancing on v and terminates without changing the height of T_s, where s=father(v).

<u>proc</u> Dsubseq(v);
<u>co</u> Let w=father$(\bar{v})$ and L(v)=length of a block $(v,\bar{v})$;
Change the hb(v);
A: <u>if</u> v was a (-1)-block <u>then</u> change it into (o)-block and execute Dsubseq(w);
B: <u>if</u> v was a good node <u>then</u> rebalance T_v and terminate;
C: <u>if</u> $(v,\bar{v})$ was a (CRB) <u>then</u> make it <u>guilty</u> and save invariant *.1; terminate either by shrinking or execute Dsubseq(father(w)) if L(w)=1;
D: <u>if</u> $(v,\bar{v})$ was a guilty block <u>then</u> we have hb(v)=+3 and we terminate either by shrinking $(v,\bar{v})$ or we execute Dsubseq(father(v)) if L(v)=1;

5. The Special Operations for Dsubseq(v)

In addition to the elementary operations given in § 3 we use some <u>special</u> operations for Dsubseq(v). These operations first handle the rebalancing of a (+3)-node v (i.e. hb(v)=+3) which arises for a moment either on the left spine or not.

Secondly, they replace the terminating rotation b.1 on the left spine. This replacement is necessary since b.1 executed on the left spine provides a new node on the left spine with balance -1, and this can be dangerous for the preserving of the invariant *.2. The operations d.1, d.2, d.3, executed instead of b.1 lead to a usefull configuration on the left spine (see Remark 3).

Let w=right son(v). If a node v becomes hb(v)=+3 and hb(w)≠0 then we perform the respective operations of b.2 and b.3 (called c.2 and c.3).

<u>Remark 2</u>: The operations c.2 and c.3 each decrease the height of the rebalanced subtree by one and yield the configuration (+1)—(o) or (o)—(+1) on the left spine.

<u>:.4 Propagating and terminating rot:</u> hb(w)=0 (compare with b.1)

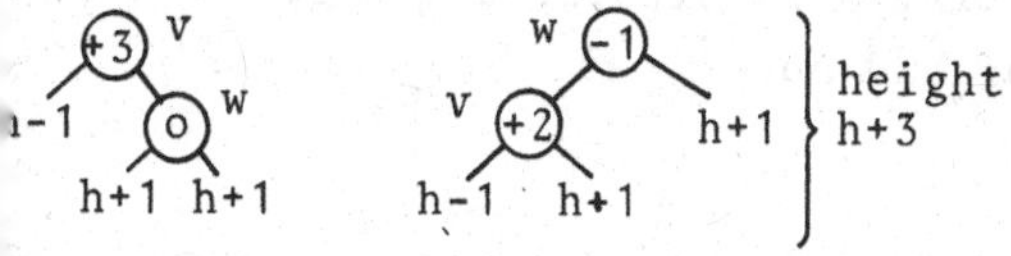

After rebalancing on v with hb(v)=+2 we get a subtree T_w with height either h+3 (terminating) or h+2 (propagating).

This operation applied only to nodes which do not belong to the left spine is used only as part of the following operation d.3.

The next operations d.1, d.2, d.3 are performed in the case where hb(v)=+2 and hb(w)=0 and lead us to partition the (+1)—nodes on the left spine into <u>good</u> and <u>bad</u> nodes as mentioned in § 4 **(see Remark 1).**

Let T_v have height h+3 and k=left son(w):

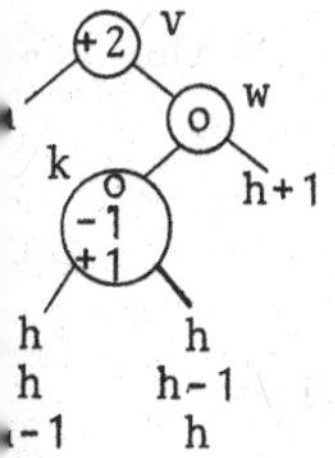

<u>case d.1</u>: hb(k)=0 , we take

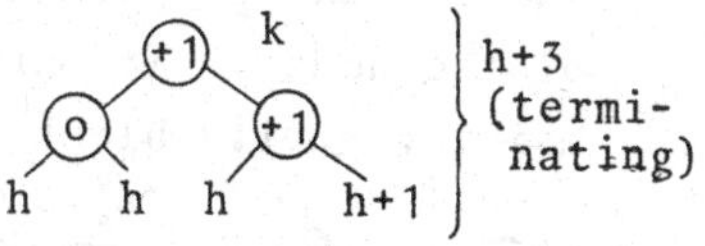

<u>case d.2</u>: hb(k)=-1, we take

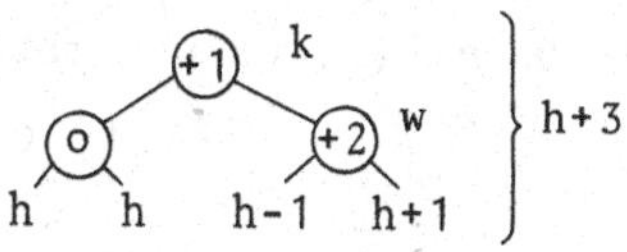

Rebalancing T_w either decreases the height of T_k or not. The resulting configuration is (o)—(+1) for the terminating case and (o)—(o) for the propagating ones.

<u>ase d.3</u>: hb(k)=+1

et s=right son(k)

irst we rebalance, making s the new root of T_v. The cases with b(s)≠-1 leave w with hb(w)=+2. After rebalancing w T_s becomes either eight h+3 with configuration (o)^v—(+1)^s or height h+2 with ^{v}(o)—^{s}(o).

(see detailed operations in [13]).

In the case with hb(s)=-1 we get hb(w)=+3. This will be handled by the operations c.2, c.3 or c.4. But in all the cases we have the same effect on T_s as in the case above.

The last operations lead us to the following definitions:

Definitions:

1) An operation of the d.1, d.2 or d.3 is called terminating, if, after performing it, the rebalanced subtree does not change its height. Otherwise it is called propagating if it decreases its height.
2) The above terminating or propagating operations lead us to partition conceptually the (+1)— nodes on the left spine into "good" and "bad" nodes respectively. Thus good nodes are those nodes v which are handled by the operations d.1 and the terminating ones of d.2 and d.3, and bad are those which are handled by the operations b.2, b.3, and the propagating ones of d.2, and d.3.
3) The (CRB)-block consists only of bad nodes.

Now we can state an important remark:

Remark 3: The terminating operations d.1, d.2, and d.3 yield the configuration (0)—(+1) on the left spine, and the propagating ones yield (0)—(0).

Now we define the shrinking operation mentioned in § 4.

Def: Let $(v,\bar{v})$ be a guilty block, i.e., a block of the form:

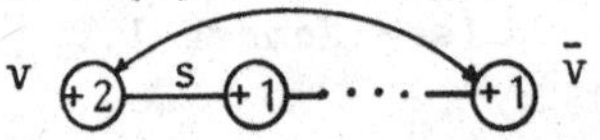

The shrinking operation is an operation executed after rebalancing of the node v; it makes the father(v) to the first node of the remaining guilty block. Thus we take:

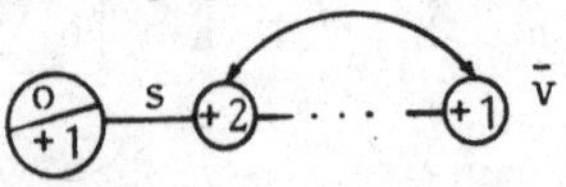

For the point ID of Insert(x) or Delete(x) we use the following procedure:

```
proc save-*.2(y)
          Let z be a node as in fig. 2
          and y the turning node;
    if *.2 is violated for y or for a
          descendant v of y
    then execute the proper propagating
          operation or b.2 or b.3 on z.
          Dsubseq(father(z));
end
```

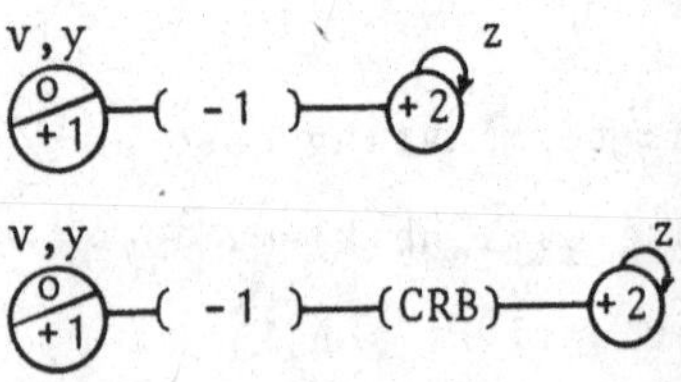

fig. 2

Remark 4: The procedure save-*.2 always causes a height decrease of the subtree of a (+2)–node.

6. The Complexity

In this section we show that the operations used keep the invariant * valid, and that this is sufficient to exclude some bad sequences and to guarantee the O(log d) time for an insertion or deletion.

Lemma 1: The invariant *.2 implies that the sequences

i) ^{v}(+2)—(-1)—(+2) and ii) ^{v}(+2)—(-1)—(CRB)—(+2)

cannot arise after an execution of Insert(x) or Delete(x).

Proof: The sequence i) can arise only from the sequence ^{v}(+1)—(-1)—(+2) after a height decrease of the left subtree T_v. The sequence ii) can arise according to the same reason from the sequence:

^{v}(+1)—(-1)—(CRB)—(+2). Since *.2 excludes the generating sequences the claim is true.

□

Next we present some lemmata with short proofs. For details we refer to [13].

Lemma 2: If the invariant * is valid then both the shrinking operation and the terminating operations on the left spine terminate immediately, thus keeping the invariant valid.

Proof: The shrinking operation yields the configuration (o)—(+2) or (o)—(+1)—(+2) (see b.2,3 or c.2,3) without violating any invariant. The terminating operations yield a sequence ^{v}(o)—(+1) (Remark 3); since invariant *.2 was valid before they cannot violate any invariant.

Since these operations do not change the height of the rebalanced subtree they terminate immediately.

□

Lemma 3: The invariant * stays valid after the execution of Isubseq(v)

Proof: We have no creation of a new guilty block. Because of Lemma 1 a height increase of the left subtree of T_v cannot produce sequences which could violate *.2.

□

Lemma 4: The invariant * stays valid after the execution of Dsubseq(v).

Proof: This procedure includes operations which preserve the invariants. □

Lemma 5: The invariant * stays valid after the execution of Search(x), Insert(x) and Delete(x).

Proof: At the moment that the searching operations are performed on y we have: all the descendants of y on the left spine (including y) have balance ∈ {-1,0,+1}; also all invariants are valid;

This can be seen as follows:

if y's father has not changed its balance or its new balance is not +2 then claim is obvious. If its new balance is +2 then situation before must be seen as in fig. 3 is given. Thus father (y) is element of a guilty block before and after. Thus invariants still hold true. Lemma 3 and 4 show this for Insert(x) and Delete(x).

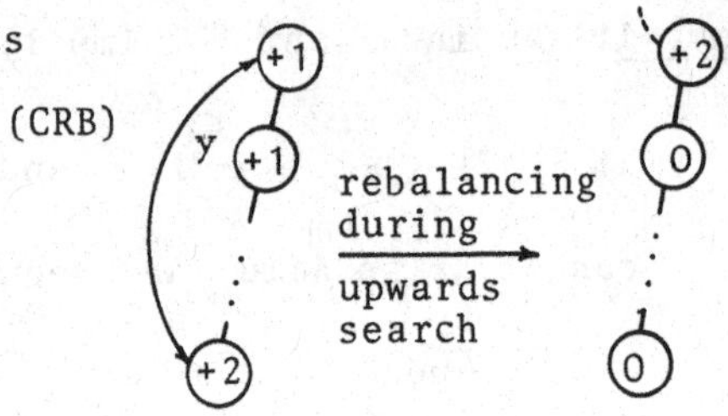

fig. 3

□

Now we can state our main result:

Theorem 1: Let d be the distance of the position of x from the finger f which points on the left end of the file stored at the leaves of an inclined AVL-tree. Then each one of the operations Search(x), Insert(x) and Delete(x) can be performed in O(log d) steps.

Proof: The search path has length O(log d). The critical node for an insertion or deletion can be localized in constant time because of the implementation given. All operations for organizing the blocks can be performed in O(1) steps. Both for an insertion and for a deletion we have a calling of Dsubseq(v) which can be recursive. Next we will show that only a constant number of calls of Dsubseq(v) is possible for every insertion or deletion.

Lemma 5 guarantees that the invariant * is valid during the whole process. Because of Lemma 2 we know that shrinking and terminating operation terminate immediately; Thus we only have to explore the rebalancing of a (+2)-node v and the subsequent calling of Dsubseq. First (case 1) we handle the direct rebalancing of v, and secondly (case 2) the case that v got balance +3.

Let w=father(v) and r be the new root after rebalancing T_v.

<u>case 1</u>: (it appears during save $*.2(v)$).

After rebalancing T_v we get $hb(r)=0$.

<u>case 1.1</u>: $hb(w)=0$; Dsubseq(w) provides $hb(w)=+1$; and we take the sequence ^{r}(0)—^{w}(+1) without height decrease of T_w, and we <u>terminate</u> immediately since $*.2$ was valid on w before.

<u>case 1.2</u>: w is a good node; Dsubseq(w) terminates immediately (see Lemma 2).

<u>case 1.3</u>: w is a bad node. This case cannot arise since $L(v)=1$, w and v should belong to a common block.

<u>case 1.4</u>: $hb(w)=-1$

After calling Dsubseq(w) we have $hb(w)=0$, and we here explore the propagation of height decrease of T_w. The next guilty block which could cause an operation either to save $*.1$ or to rebalance a (+3)-node must have length at least 2 (see Lemma 1), since v is a (+2)-node according to our assumption. Thus we get <u>immediate</u> termination by shrinking this block (see Lemma 1).

The invariant $*.1$ guarantees that we have explored all the cases.

<u>case 2:</u> $hb(v)=+3$ (step D)

Rebalancing on T_v is executed by the opeations c.2, c.3, and by the respective operations d.2 and d.3 for the <u>bad</u> nodes. In all cases we take either the configuration (+1)—^{r}(0) or (0)—^{r}(+1) or (0)—^{r}(0) on the **left** spine. Then we execute Dsubseq(w); it terminates immediately as in case 1 since $hb(w)\neq+2$, according to the invariant $*.1$.

The step A <u>cannot</u> be repeated immediately during the recursive calling of Dsubseq(w) since $hb(w)\neq-1$, and it cannot immediately yield $hb(w)=0$ which is necessary for the step A. Hence Dsubseq(v) terminates in O(1) steps. □

<u>7. The moving operation and the multiple fingers</u>

We have considered the case that the finger points to the left end of the file. Now we consider the operation moving the finger to a distance d and the case of multiple fingers.

<u>Theorem 2:</u> Inclined AVL-trees allow to perform a moving of the finger f to a distance d in time $O(\log d)$. If we have k fingers then the dictionary operations can be performed in $O(\log k + \log d)$ steps, where d is the distance of the element worked at from the nearest finger.

<u>Proof:</u> We cut the tree into two parts L and R. L has as root the turning node y. We always keep $hb(\text{grand father}(y))\neq+2$. Then we handle this cut-

ting as a height decrease. We reorganize additionally the right spine of the subtree L, and f will be replaced by two fingers f_1 and f_2 where f_1 points to the right end of L and f_2 to the left end of R. Figure 5 shows this process:

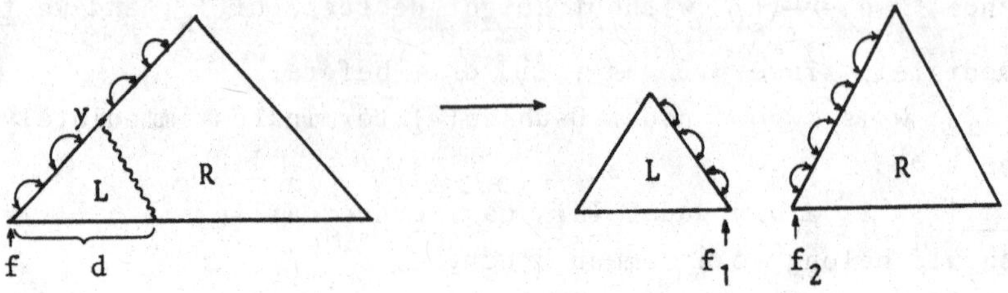

fig. 5

The reorganisation needs O(log d) steps. For the k fingers we use 2k inclined AVL-trees; first performing a binary search on these fingers we need O(log k + log d) time for the dictionary operations, where d is the distance of the element worked at from the nearest finger. □

Acknowledgement

The author would like to thank Kurt Mehlhorn and Norbert Blum for their helpful remarks.

References

[1] ADELSON-VELSKII, G.M. LANDIS, "An Algorithm for the organisation of information" (in Russian), Dokl.Ak.Nauk SSSR Vol. 146, p. 263-266 (1962)

[2] N. BLUM and K. MEHLHORN, "On the average number of rebalancing operations in weight-balanced trees" TCS 11, p. 303-320 (1980)

[3] M.BROWN and R.TARJAN, "Design and analysis of a data structure for representing sorted lists", SIAM J. Computing Vol 9, p. 594-614 (1980)

[4] C.C. FOSTER, "Information storage and retrieval using AVL-trees" ACM 20th National Conference, p. 192-205 (1965)

[5] L. GUIBAS, E. MC.CREIGHT, M. PLASS, J. ROBERTS, "A new representation of linear lists" 9th STOC, p. 49-60 (1977)

[6] Sc. HUDDLESTON, " An efficient scheme for fast local updates in linear lists", University of California at Irvine (1981)

[7] S. HUDDLESTON and K. MEHLHORN, " A new data structure for representing sorted lists" Acta Informatica 17, p. 157-184 (1982)

[8] D. KNUTH, "The art of computer programming", Vol 3, Sorting and Searching. Addison Wesley Reading Mass. (1973)

[9] S.R. KOSARAJU, "Localized search in sorted lists" 14 STOC, p. 62-69 (1981)

[10] K. MEHLHORN, "Sorting presorted files", 4th GI-Conference on Theoretical Computer Science, Aachen LNCS Vol. 67, p. 199-219 (1979)

[11] K. MEHLHORN and A.TSAKALIDIS, "AVL-trees, refined analysis and application to sorting presorted files", Technischer Bericht A82/05, FB 10 Universität des Saarlandes (1982)

[12] R.E. TARJAN, private communication

[13] A. TSAKALIDIS, "AVL-trees for localized Search", Technischer Bericht A 83/13, FB 10, Universität des Saarlandes (1983)

The Simple Roots of Real-Time Computation Hierarchies*

(Preliminary version)

Paul M.B. Vitányi

Centre for Mathematics and Computer Science (C.W.I.), Amsterdam†

SUMMARY

A BLAH machine is any memory device that can be simulated in real-time by a multitape Turing machine and such that a multiBLAH machine can real-time simulate a pushdown store. A multiBLAH machine consists of a finite control connected to an input terminal and an output terminal and one or more copies of the BLAH memory unit. It is shown that a $(k+1)$-BLAH machine is more powerful in real-time than a k-BLAH machine, for each k. Thus the hierarchies, within the real-time definable computations, are *proper* and *smooth*, that is, adding a device *always* increases power. It also turns out that all real-time hierarchy results in this vein are simple corollaries of a single root: the real-time hierarchy of multipushdown store machines. As examples of such new results we mention that in real-time, $k+1$ tape-units with a fast rewind square are more powerful than k such units; that $(k+1)$-head tape-units with fast rewind squares are more powerful than k-head tape-units with fast rewind squares; that $(k+1)$-dequeue machines are more powerful than k-dequeue machines; and that $(k+1)$-concatenable-dequeue machines are more powerful than k-concatenable-dequeue machines.

1. Introduction

It is known that $(k+1)$-tape Turing machines cannot be simulated in real-time by k-tape Turing machines [Aa, Pa]. We shall show that the same property holds for types of memory units, other than single-head tape units, if they satisfy the following condition.

(*) *Proper Power Increase.* For each assemblage of k units there is a finite number l such that an assemblage of $k+l$ units is more powerful in real-time than the assemblage of k units.

Hierarchy results concerning #tapes, #heads, with and without head-to-head jumps have been demonstrated in [Aa, Vi, PSS] and elsewhere. They are all corollaries to Theorem 1 below which in its turn rests on the exploitation of the (*) observation.

Theorem 1. *Let a k-BLAH machine consist of k copies of BLAH connected to a common finite control which is attached to an input- and output terminal. Let a BLAH be a memory device which can real-time simulate a pushdown store (or is such that a multiBLAH machine can real-time simulate a pushdown store) and which in its turn can be real-time simulated by a multitape Turing machine. In real-time,* $(k+1)$*-BLAH machines are more powerful than k-BLAH machines.*

Note that Limited Random Access Turing machines [FR], deques, concatenable dequeues, single-head tapes, multihead tapes, multihead tapes with head-to-head jumps, stacks, and what have you, are BLAH machines. Consequently, we first list some immediate *new* corollaries of Theorem 1 which represent hitherto unknown hierarchies. The reader may think of a few others on his own.

Limited Random Access Turing machines were introduced in [FR]. They consist of a multitape Turing machine with *fast rewind squares*. That is, the machine can drop a marker on a scanned square and henceforth can reset the head concerned in one step to the marked tapesquare, regardless of the distance in between. It is shown in [FR] that such machines are not more powerful than multitape Turing machines in real-time. In fact, 14 tapes suffice to simulate 1 fast rewind tape unit in real-time. Since additional tapes increase power (follows trivially from the 14 versus 1 relation above together with that according to [Aa] $14k+1$ tapes are more powerful in real-time than $14k$ tapes, $k \geq 0$) we satisfy (*). More in particular, as required by Theorem 1 the devices are capable of real-time simulating a pushdown store and a finite number of pushdown stores is capable of simulating the device. Hence,

---

* This work was supported by the *Stichting Mathematisch Centrum*.

† Full Address: Centre for Mathematics and Computer Science (C.W.I.), Kruislaan 413, 1098 SJ Amsterdam, The Netherlands.

Corollary. $(k+1)$-tape Turing machines with fast rewind squares are more powerful in real-time than k-tape Turing machines with fast rewind squares. Similarly, $(k+1)$-head Turing machines with fast rewind squares are more powerful in real-time than k-head Turing machines with fast rewind squares.

A *dequeue* is a double-ended queue, and at least as powerful as a pushdown store, see e.g. [LS, Ko]. A multidequeue machine with the additional option of instantaneous concatenation of any current dequeue contents onto another dequeue's contents, thus emptying the first dequeue in a single step, is called a multi*concatenable* dequeue machine. Such machines can be real-time simulated by multitape Turing machines [Ko]. Consequently we have, by Theorem 1,

Corollary. $(k+1)$-dequeue machines are more powerful in real-time than k-dequeue machines. Also, $(k+1)$-concatenable dequeue machines are more powerful in real-time than k-concatenable dequeue machines.

2. The smoothness of real-time memory hierarchies

Theorem 1 establishes many real-time hierarchies within the real-time definable computations (computations which can be performed in real-time by multitape Turing machines), a small sample of which was exhibited in the Corollaries above. The novelty of the present approach is that the arguments used are surprisingly simple and uniform for a great variety of Turing machine like models. It will also appear that there is a master problem here.

Master Problem. For each k there exists an l such that $(k+l)$-pushdown store machines are more powerful in real-time than k-pushdown store machines.

> If we find a simple proof for this master problem (as opposed to the complicated proofs [Aa, PSS] for seemingly stronger problems) then this proof implies all real-time hierarchies by the simple argument below. The proofs in [Aa, PSS] have the appearance, possibly misleading, of the use of a sledge hammer to kill a fly. Thus, using the intricate arguments more effectively, [Pa] has strengthened the consequences of the methods in [Aa] to a nonlinear lower bound on the on-line simulation time required to simulate the effect of an additional tape.

For definitions of the considered devices we direct the reader to the references. For convenience, we consider the machines as transducers; the results can then be transferred to language recognizers at will. To lead up to the general statement we first discuss some lemma's. It will be at once apparent to the reader that (the proof of) Lemma 1 is a particular instance of a general argument applicable to virtually any transducer whatever. Lemma 2 is another such instance. Rather than confusing the issue by unnecessary definitions and formalisms we give representative instances and trust that the general case is self-evident.

Lemma 1. *Let k be an integer greater than 0. Either $(k+1)$-pushdown store machines are more powerful in real-time than k-pushdown store machines or, for all $i \geq 1$, $(k+i)$-pushdown store machines are equally powerful in real-time as k-pushdown store machines.*

Proofsketch. Suppose the Lemma is false for some k. Then there exists an l, l minimal and $l > k+1$, such that l-pushdown store machines are more powerful in real-time than k-pushdown store machines. Let M_l be any l-pushdown store machine. Decompose M_l in a $(l-1)$-pushdown store machine M_{l-1} and a separate pushdown store P. Multiplex the input of M_{l-1} with the current top symbol on P and the resulting output of M_{l-1} with the replacing new top string on P. More precisely, if M_l contains a transition

$$\text{(input, state,topsymbol store 1, \ldots, topsymbol store } l)$$

$$\rightarrow \text{(newstate, topstring store 1, \ldots, topstring store } l\text{, output)}$$

then M_{l-1} has the corresponding transition

$$\text{((input, topsymbol store } l\text{), state,topsymbol store 1, \ldots, topsymbol store } l-1)$$

$$\rightarrow \text{(newstate, topstring store 1, \ldots, topstring store } l-1\text{, (output, topstring store } l)) .$$

In M_{l-1} we have an $(l-1)$-pushdown transducer which transforms transductions from the input (over a new input alphabet) to output (over a new output alphabet). By the contradictory assumption we can replace M_{l-1} by a k-pushdown transducer M_k performing the same transduction from the relevant strings in $(I \times T)^*$ into $(O \times T^*)^*$, where I is the input alphabet, T is the stack alphabet and O is the output alphabet of the original M_l. Replacing the transducer M_{l-1} by the transducer M_k, in the combination M_{l-1} and P, makes no difference. The resultant combination however, viewed as a transducer, is a $(k+1)$-pushdown transducer M_{k+1} performing the same transduction as the original M_l. Since by the contradictory assumption (viz., the minimality of l) it follows that $(k+1)$-transducers are equally powerful in real-time as k-transducers, we can replace M_{k+1} by a k-transducer M'_k, performing the same transduction as the original M_l, which yields the required contradiction. □ □

Corollary. If, for each k there is an l, $l>k$, such that l-pushdown machines are more powerful in real-time than k-pushdown machines, then $(k+1)$-pushdown machines are more powerful in real-time than k-pushdown machines, for each k.

Lemma 2. *Analogous results to Lemma 1 plus Corollary, with "-pushdown store machines" replaced by "-tape Turing machines", can be derived with M_{l-1} performing the obvious transduction from $(I \times T)^*$ into $(O \times T \times M)^*$ where I and O are as before, T is the tape alphabet and M* = {left, nomove, right}.

Theorem 2 below establishes a particular instance of a wide variety of equivalences between real-time hierarchies within the class of real-time definable computations.

Theorem 2. *If, for all $k \geq 0$ we can find an $l>k$ such that l-pushdown store machines are more powerful in real-time than k-pushdown store machines then $(t+1)$-tape Turing machines are more powerful in real-time than t-tape Turing machines for all $t>0$. The same statement holds with "-pushdown store machines" and "-tape Turing machines" interchanged.*

Proof. It is obvious that by breaking each tape of a t-tape Turing machine around the head position we can simulate such machines by $2t$-pushdown store machines in real-time. If the condition in the Theorem is satisfied then $(2t+1)$-pushdown store machines are more powerful than $2t$-pushdown store machines by Lemma 1. The former, in their turn, are trivially simulatable in real-time by $(2t+1)$-tape Turing machines. So $(2t+1)$-tape Turing machines are more powerful in real-time than t-tape Turing machines, which gives the required result by Lemma 2. The second statement in the theorem follows because if l-tape Turing machines are more powerful in real-time than k-tape Turing machines $(l>k)$ then $2l$-pushdown store machines are more powerful than k-pushdown store machines in real-time, which gives the result by Lemma 1. □

The argument is quite general and is used for the proof below.

Proof of Theorem 1. Let it be established that there is no k such that $(k+l)$-pushdown store machines are equally powerful to k-pushdown store machines for all $l \geq 1$, e.g. [Aa]. Let a BLAH be a memory unit which can simulate a pushdown store in real-time (or such that a multiBLAH machine can real-time simulate a pushdown store) and can itself be simulated by a multitape Turing machine in real-time. If k-BLAH machines can be simulated in real-time by $f(\text{BLAH},k)$-pushdown store machines then we can also assume that $f(\text{BLAH},k)$ is minimal. By assumption, there is an $l_{\text{BLAH},k}$ such that $(f(\text{BLAH},k)+l_{\text{BLAH},k})$-pushdown store machines are more powerful in real-time than $f(\text{BLAH},k)$-pushdown store machines and therefore more powerful than k-BLAH machines. Also by assumption, a c-BLAH machine can real-time simulate a pushdown store, $c \geq 1$, so there is a minimal integer m such that m-BLAH machines are more powerful in real-time than k-BLAH machines. Either $m=k+1$ and we have established what we want or $m>k+1$. In the latter case a $(m-1)$-BLAH machine can be simulated in real-time by a k-BLAH machine and, following the method of proof of Lemma 1, we show that an m-BLAH machine can be real-time simulated by a k-BLAH machine: contradiction. Therefore, $(k+1)$-BLAH machines are more powerful in real-time than k-BLAH machines. □

The situation is slightly more general. If we have a transducer of type X, which can be real-time simulated by a multitape Turing machine transducer, and we plug in an extra memory unit of type BLAH satisfying the conditions of Theorem 1, then we obtain a new transducer type Y which is more powerful in real-time than transducers of type X.

It follows from the above that the unsatisfactory complicated proofs for the real-time tape hierarchy in [Aa, PSS] may possibly be replaced by a proof for the fact that for no k we have that $(k+l)$-pushdown store machines are equally powerful to k-pushdown store machines for all $l \geq 1$. This is the *master* problem for the real-time hierarchies and finding a neat proof for it would simplify a great deal.

Different tape architectures and computation modes. The main result established is Theorem 1 which follows, in the realm of real-time definable computations, from [Aa] together with Lemma 1. We like to point out, however, that the principle enunciated in Lemma 1 has a far larger scope. The argument, and the Lemma, seems to hold for all types of transducers. Thus, like intuition tells us, the real-time computation hierarchies are *smooth*. For various reasons people like to consider tape *architectures* which are not linear lists but trees, more dimensional arrays or graphs. *Mutatis mutandis* Lemma 1 holds for each such class of machines too. A useful *computation mode* which is often considered is that of an *oblivious* computation. A computation is *oblivious* if the sequence of accessed storage cells is a fixed function of time, independent of the inputs to the machine. See e.g. [PF]. One of the attractive features of oblivious Turing machine computations is that they can be simulated by combinational logic networks at the cost in logic gates of the latter in the order of the time complexity of the former. Oblivious *real-time* computations translate in combinational logic networks with a response time of O(1) in between processing the i-th input at the i-th input port and producing the i-th output at the i-th output port, which enables the $i+1$-th input port. The oblivious real-time computations are the computations which can be performed by oblivious real-time multitape Turing machines. Notice that *linear* oblivious computations, that is, those performed by oblivious linear time multitape Turing machines, may translate in combinational logic networks with an *unbounded* response time. Other computation modes are *nondeterminism* or *alternation*. As a general, intuitively clear statement, Lemma 1 does hold for all BLAH-transducers in BUH mode, and not just for pushdown transducers in deterministic mode, using the same proof outline in each case. Thus, each transducer hierarchy either stops at some point or proceeds by proper inclusion according to computing power with *each* added unit.

REFERENCES

Aa Aanderaa, S.O., On k-tape versus $(k-1)$-tape real-time computation. In: *SIAM-AMS Proceedings, Vol. 7 (Complexity of Computation)*, 1974, 75 - 96.

FMR Fischer, P.C., A.R. Meyer and A.L. Rosenberg, Real-time simulation of multihead tape-units, *J. Ass. Comp. Mach.* **19** (1972) 590 - 607.

FR Fischer, M.J., and A.L. Rosenberg, Limited random access Turing machines, Proceedings 9-th IEEE Conference on Switching and Automata Theory, 1968, 356 - 367.

Ko Kosaraju, S.R., Real-time simulation of concatenable double-ended queues by double-ended queues. Proceedings 11-th ACM Symposium on Theory of Computing, 1979, 346 - 351.

LS Leong, B., and J.I. Seiferas, New real-time simulations of multihead tape units, Proceedings 9-th ACM Symposium on Theory of Computing, 1977, 239 - 248.

Pa Paul, W.J., On-line simulation of $k+1$ tapes by k tapes requires nonlinear time. Proceedings 22-nd IEEE Conference on Foundations of Computer Science, 1982, 53 - 56.

PSS Paul, W.J., J.I. Seiferas and J. Simon, An information-theoretic approach to time bounds for on-line computation. Proceedings 12-th ACM Symposium on Theory of Computing, 1980, 357 -367.

PF Pippenger, N., and M.J. Fischer, Relations among complexity measures, *Journal ACM* **26** (1979) 361 - 384.

Vi Vitányi, P.M.B., On the power of real-time Turing machines under varying specifications. Proceedings of the 7-th International Colloquium on Automata, Languages and Programming, *Lecture Notes in Computer Science* **85**, Springer Verlag, Berlin, 1980, 658 - 671.

COMPUTATIONAL COMPLEXITY OF AN OPTICAL DISK INTERFACE*

(extended abstract)

Jeffrey Scott Vitter

Department of Computer Science
Brown University
Providence, RI 02912
USA

Abstract. The notion of an I/O interface for optical digital (write-once) disks is introduced that is quite different from earlier research in this area. The purpose of an I/O interface is to allow existing operating systems and application programs that use magnetic disks to use optical disks instead, with minimum difficulty. The interface is especially geared to applications that are not update-intensive or that require access to previous versions of records. We define what it means for an I/O interface to be *disk-efficient*. We demonstrate a disk-efficient interface and show that its I/O performance in many cases is *optimum*, up to a constant factor, among all disk-efficient interfaces. The basis of the interface is a data structure we call *offset trees*, which stores information about intervals with dynamically changing coordinates. Since this complexity model is based on practical concerns, these theoretical results translate nicely into an efficient implementation.

1. INTRODUCTION

The development of high-capacity, low-cost optical digital disks is having a major impact on information storage and retrieval (e.g. [Goldstein, 82], [Copeland, 82], [O'Lear and Choy, 82]). Optical disks provide "orders of magnitude" more storage density and cost performance than conventional magnetic disks, at roughly the same access rate. The tradeoff is that optical disks are "write-once": a binary 1 is represented by a hole burned by a laser in the disk medium, and a binary 0 is represented by the absence of a hole; once burned, the hole cannot be mended. Thus, optical disks are ideal for archival storage and for applications that do not require the updating of records.

The problem of how to use optical disks in situations with update provides theorists with interesting new problems that call out for solutions. Some methods for applications with little update are given in [Maier, 82]. Very clever techniques have been devised in [Rivest and Shamir, 82] for allowing a k-bit number to be updated m times in $o(km)$ space. In the process, the former values of the number are lost. The model assumes that the entire memory consists of 0-bits originally and that 0-bits can be changed to 1-bits, but not vice-versa.

A problem with these techniques is that the underlying model does not take into account the large overhead involved in manipulating individual bits on the disk. For example, in one product, each data sector on the disk requires roughly 80 bytes of overhead information, which is used for head synchronization and error detection and correction. If we allow individual bits to be manipulated, only a small fraction of the disk would be useable for data storage, the rest taken up for overhead.

---

* Some of this research was done while the author was consulting for the IBM Palo Alto Scientific Center. Support was also provided in part by NSF Grant MCS-81-05324, by an IBM research contract, and by ONR and DARPA under Contract N00014-83-K-0146 and ARPA Order No. 4786.

One can argue that it is a mistake to try to make an optical disk "behave" like a magnetic disk in situations where update is frequent, since the device is inherently not geared to such applications. We can turn this argument around and argue that optical disks should be used for those applications in which magnetic disks have been a severe disadvantage. For example, optical disks can give database systems the ability to keep around all previous versions of a record, not just the current version. This ability is crucial in some new database systems, such as in [Arnold et al, 81]. Such important applications were often unheard of with magnetic disks, due to the very high storage cost.

In this paper we introduce a storage model different from that in [Rivest and Shamir, 82]. Each rewrite of an R-byte record onto the optical disk requires $R + G$ bytes of space, where G is the "gap" space for overhead. Previous versions of the record are not destroyed. Special-purpose algorithms have been developed for B-trees and other access methods (e.g. [Vitter, 83a], [Rathmann, 84]), which can be viewed as time- and space-efficient implementations in this model.

The blind development of special-purpose algorithms, in the author's opinion, is a mistake. In response to this, we introduce the notion of an I/O interface that allows operating systems and applications which currently use magnetic disks to use optical disks instead. This interface can be implemented as a software layer that manages I/O buffers and that handles memory mapping between internal memory and secondary storage. In order to be effective, the interface must be *disk-efficient*; that is, the amount of disk space used and the I/O time must be optimum, up to a constant factor. This concept is defined in the next section.

The important difference between our approach and the one in [Rivest and Shamir, 82] is that we seek to exploit the features of optical disks, rather than use them as a mere substitute for magnetic disks. Our philosophy is that applications which have frequent updating and which require access to only the current versions of records are inherently unsuited for optical disks, and thus should not be expected to make efficient use of optical technology.

The complexity model and the basic definitions are given in the next section. In Section 3 we give a simple I/O interface in order to illustrate the general concepts. A fast and disk-efficient I/O interface, based on a data structure we call *offset trees*, is discussed in Section 4. The interface has tremendous potential for a very large number of applications. In fact, the standard B-tree algorithms run with this interface perform as well on optical disks as do special-purpose algorithms that have been developed! The analysis is given in Section 5. In Section 6, we derive lower bounds on the average CPU time per I/O required by any disk-efficient interface. Our I/O interface is optimum, up to a constant factor, in many situations and can be shown to be globally optimum in some models of computation. Conclusions are given in Section 7.

2. THE COMPLEXITY MODEL

The goal of this study is to devise provably efficient I/O interfaces so that operating systems and applications that use magnetic disks can use optical disks instead. For notational purposes, we will refer to the basic unit of data transfer between the CPU and the magnetic disk as a *block*. A block contains B bytes; for simplicity we assume that a byte contains $\log_2 B$ bits and can be processed by the CPU in constant time. When a block on the magnetic disk is accessed, it is paged (*input*) by a separate I/O processor into internal memory and stored in a block buffer. This buffer might be modified several times before the I/O processor writes the new version of the block onto the magnetic disk (which is called an *output*). Output is done by rewriting the entire block buffer onto the corresponding locations on the magnetic disk, thus erasing the former contents. The problem is how to simulate this I/O process when an optical disk is used instead of a magnetic disk.

One naive (and inefficient) I/O interface for using an optical disk to replace a magnetic disk is to write an entire new copy of the block onto the optical disk during each output. If the block contains B bytes and there are R I/Os, then $\Omega(BR)$ bytes of storage are required on the optical disk, which is excessive. In order to develop a quantitative notion of what it means for an I/O interface to be efficient, first let us define exactly what an interface is supposed to do.

Definition 1. An I/O interface is a layer of software that supports the following three basic update operations on the block buffers in internal memory:

insert ℓ *data* s
write ℓ *data* s
delete ℓ s

The **insert** operation writes the ℓ bytes of information contained in *data* starting at buffer address s, bumping everything in locations s, $s+1$, $s+2$, ...to the right by ℓ bytes. The **write** operation is similar except that no bumping is done, so the original data in locations s, $s+1$, ..., $s+\ell-1$ is written on top of and destroyed. The **delete** operation effectively deletes the ℓ bytes in locations s, $s+1$, ..., $s+\ell-1$ by bumping everything in locations $s+\ell$, $s+\ell+1$, ...over to the left by ℓ bytes; null values are written into the ℓ locations at the end. The **write** operation can be implemented as a **delete** followed by an **insert**, but it is convenient to have an explicit **write** operation.

An example of possible operations that can be added to an I/O interface to make it more powerful are

swap $\ell 1$ $s1$ $\ell 2$ $s2$
copy1 ℓ $s1$ $s2$
copy2 ℓ $s1$ $s2$

The **swap** command exchanges the $\ell 1$ bytes starting at buffer address $s1$ with the $\ell 2$ bytes starting at address $s2$. It is assumed that $\ell 1, \ell 2 \geq 0$ and that $s1 + \ell 1 - 1 < s2$; that is, the two ranges of data being exchanged are assumed to be distinct. The data in the block between the two ranges is bumped $\ell 2 - \ell 1$ bytes, where a positive value means that the bumping is "to the right" and a negative value means "to the left." The **copy1** command duplicates the ℓ bytes starting at buffer address $s1$ and inserts them (with bumping) starting at buffer address $s2$. The **copy2** command is identical except that no bumping is done.

Definition 2. The terms *input*, *output*, and *I/O* are used to denote the "logical" operations being simulated by the optical disk; each I/O operation may consist of several individual read/writes on the optical disk. Similarly, the term *block* refers to the "logical" unit of transfer and storage being simulated by the optical disk. Storage is allocated dynamically on the optical disk $O(B)$ contiguous bytes at a time.

Definition 3. The term *round* refers to the time period beginning with an input of a block, followed by updates to the block buffer, and ending with an output of the block.

Definition 4. An I/O interface is *disk-efficient* if the following three conditions hold continously:

1. The amount of space used on the optical disk to store a logical block is $O(S)$, where

$$S = O + \sum_{\text{each round}} (U_i + N_i);$$

$O =$ the amount of data (in bytes) originally in the block;
$U_i =$ the number of updates to the block during round i;
$N_i =$ the net amount of data (in bytes) added to the block during round i;

2. The amount of data (in bytes) transferred during each I/O is $O(B + \log^2(S/B))$. and
3. The number of read/write operations on the optical disk per I/O is $O(1 + \log^2(S/B))$.

For all practical purposes, we can regard $\log^2(S/B)$ as a constant. The term N_i is the amount of data added during the ith round by **insert**, **write**, **copy1**, and **copy2** (but not **swap**) operations *that is not deleted by subsequent* **deletes** *during the same round*. Intuitively, N_i is the minimum amount of data that must be stored on the optical disk after each round in order to record the changes made to the former version of the block. The naive interface mentioned at the beginning of the section is not disk-efficient, because the amount of space used BR can be $\Omega((O + \sum_i (U_i + N_i))^2)$, which is far too much. The measure of performance we use to compare disk-efficient I/O interfaces is the amount of CPU overhead per I/O.

Definition 5. We define CPU_{input} to be the CPU time used to input a block. We define CPU_{output} to be the CPU time used during the current round to output a block; it includes any time spent processing the update operations, except for the actual manipulations of the block buffer required for implementing the update operations.

For the naive inefficient interface discussed above, assuming that the disk indexes reside in internal memory and can be accessed in constant time, CPU_{input} and CPU_{output} are bounded by a constant, since a separate I/O processor manages the transfer of data. The I/O time is $O(B)$, which is linear in the amount of data transferred.

3. A SIMPLIFIED I/O INTERFACE

In this section and the next, we describe I/O interfaces that are disk-efficient, at the expense of an increase in CPU time over the naive interface mentioned earlier. The simple scheme described in this section, which uses $O(B^2)$ CPU time per I/O, serves as an introduction to the concepts needed for discussing the more sophisticated I/O interface given in Section 4. The latter interface uses a data structure called *offset trees* and requires $O(B \log B)$ CPU time per I/O.

Our simple I/O interface works as follows: Whenever one of the update operations (`insert`, `write`, `delete`, `swap`, `copy1`, or `copy2`) is performed on the block buffer in internal memory, an entry is appended to the *block log*. Each block buffer has its own block log, which is also kept in internal memory. The entry to the log is in the same format as the operation performed, except that in the case of `insert` and `write` operations, the data field is not included. This means that each entry into the block log is very short (roughly 2–4 bytes) regardless of the amount of data inserted or written.

When the operating system or application program desires to output the block buffer onto the disk, what is usually written is an optimized list of the updates made during that round. This optimized list is called an *update list* and is formed by processing the block log. Each block has associated with it a region containing $B + \Omega(B)$ bytes of contiguous space on the optical disk, which store the initialized version of the block and a sequence of update lists. A special situation arises when the space for the block on the optical disk runs out; in that case a new contiguous region is allocated on the optical disk and the former region is linked to it. What is written into the new region is either the update list for the round or else the full contents of the block buffer. We refer to the writing of the contents of a block buffer onto the optical disk as *initialization* of the block on the disk. In either case, the total amount of space used for the block is still $O(S)$. Simplified algorithms for the output process are discussed in Section 3.2.

In order to perform an I/O, the location of the block's most recently allocated region on the optical disk must be determined. If all indexes and pointers reside in internal memory, then when a new region is allocated, it might be possible to update the pointer entries to point to the new region, so that the lookup time is fast. A more general approach is to store pointers in the ith allocated region to regions $i+1$ and $2i$; the most recently allocated region can then be accessed in $O(1+\log^2(S/B))$ time using binary search. This might be handled by the I/O processor. We shall treat the lookup time as a constant, since it is insignificant in reasonable applications.

Input is done by reading in the initialized data for the block as well as all subsequent update lists. The current contents of the block are reconstructed in internal memory from these items. The simplified method for this is discussed in Section 3.1.

3.1. INPUT (from the Optical Disk into Internal Memory)

Each logical block on an optical disk consists of the data that was written during initialization, followed by a sequence of *update lists*, one for each round since initialization. The format of an update list is as follows: The length of the updated block buffer (at the end of the round) appears at the beginning. Next is a sequence of records, each having one of the two types:

`new` *len data*
`old` *len start*

The records in the update list express the contents of the block buffer at the end of the round in terms of its contents at the beginning of the round (immediately after input). For example, the update list that begins with

```
1000
old 20 0
new 15 "D*KI?V+A!?QZ/.J"
old 4 20
old 26 124
new 7 "JEFFREY"
   etc.
```

means that the updated version of the block (at the end of the round) consists of 1000 bytes. The first 20 bytes (bytes 0–19) are the same as the 20 bytes starting at location 0 in the former version of the block (at the beginning of the round). The next 15 bytes (bytes 20–34) are new and are represented above in the update list in character form "D*KI?V+A!?QZ/.J". The next four bytes (bytes 35–38) are the same four bytes starting at location 20 in the former version of the block. The next 26 bytes (bytes 39–64) are the same 26 bytes beginning at location 124 in the former version of the block. The next seven bytes (bytes 65–71) are new and appear above in character form "JEFFREY". And so on.

For the case in which there is only one update list, it is easy to see that when the original block and the update list are input into internal memory, the block can be converted into its correct updated form with a minimum number of move instructions.

This process can be extended to handle multiple update lists as well, which arises when there is more than one round between initializations of the block on the optical disk. The update lists can be processed sequentially and combined into one grand update list. This grand update list can then be used to reconstruct the updated version of the block from its initial version, as described in the preceding paragraph. The combining of the update lists can be done in $O((\sum_{i>i_0} U_i)^2)$ time, where round i_0 is the last round in which the block was initialized on the optical disk. If we let I be the amount of initialized data ($I \leq B$), the total CPU time for input can be expressed as $CPU_{\text{input}} = O(I + (\sum_{i>i_0} U_i)^2 + \sum_{i>i_0} N_i)$. As a preview, the interface described in Section 4 yields $CPU_{\text{input}} = O(I + (\sum_{i>i_0} U_i) \log(\sum_{i>i_0} U_i) + \sum_{i>i_0} N_i)$ time.

3.2. OUTPUT (from Internal Memory onto the Optical Disk)

What remains is to show how to convert the block log into an optimized update list. The simple algorithm we discuss in this section maintains a linked-list data structure and requires CPU time $CPU_{\text{output}} = O(U_j^2 + N_j)$ for the jth round, except when the block on the optical disk is reinitialized; in that case, we have $CPU_{\text{output}} = O(1)$. By contrast, in Section 4 we demonstrate a much faster interface that uses offset trees in place of linked-lists; the resulting CPU time is $CPU_{\text{output}} = O(U_j \log U_j + N_j)$ without reinitialization and $CPU_{\text{output}} = O(1)$ otherwise.

The update entries in the block log are processed sequentially in chronological order. As each entry is processed, the data structure contains the length of the block buffer (reflecting all the update entries processed so far) followed by a linked list of records. Each record has one of the following forms:

new *len*
old *len start*

The interpretation is the same as for the update list we discussed in Section 3.1, except that the *data* field in the **new** record is implicit.

The basic idea of the algorithm is that for each entry in the block log, its *address* in the linked list is found by walking through the linked list, adding up the field lengths, until the record that *spans* the desired address is found. Next the affected records in the linked list are modified, with possibly some new records added and others deleted. Each of the U_i entries in the block log during the ith round may require the entire list to be traversed while looking for its address in the list, so this algorithm requires $O(U_i^2)$ time.

For example, let us consider the linked list pictured at left below. The meaning of these records is identical to the example in the Section 3.1. If the next entry processed in the block log is "**insert** 6 42" (which stands for the insertion of 6 bytes starting at address 42), the linked list is updated as shown below on the right:

	1006
1000	old 20 0
old 20 0	new 15
new 15	old 4 20
old 4 20	old 3 124
old 26 124	new 6
new 7	old 23 127
etc.	new 7
	etc.

The inserted data at address 42 causes the "old 26 124" record to be "split" in two, since that record spans addresses 39–64. If the next log entry is "**delete** 50 25" (which stands for the deletion of 50 bytes starting at address 25), the linked list can be modified in one of two ways:

956		956
old 20 0	or	old 20 0
new 5		new 8
new 3		etc.
etc.		

The latter is preferred, since it reduces the size of the data structure. As a final example, if the next block log entry is "**swap** 10 15 0 3" (which stands for the swap of the 10 bytes starting at location 15 into the locations starting at address 3, bumping locations 3–14 to the right by 10 bytes), the linked list becomes

956
old 3 0
old 5 15
new 5
old 12 3
new 3
etc.

3.3. ROLLBACK AND HISTORY

Optical disks are particularly well-suited to database applications in which access is desired to all versions of a given record, not just the most recent version. The interface described above (and similarly the one described in Section 4) can be modified easily to keep track of when each block is reinitialized and when each update list is written onto the optical disk. This would allow fast access to previous versions of a record that existed at the time of an output.

If access must be given to the versions of records that existed *between* I/Os, then each entry in the block log should be timestamped, and the block log (rather than the optimized update list) should be appended to the optical disk at the end of a round. The formation of the update list would be done during input rather than during the output. The definition of N_i should be modified to be "the amount of new information added during the round" rather than "the net amount added." This allows disk-efficient I/O interfaces to use more space on the optical disk, which is necessary in this application. The I/O and CPU time would increase slightly.

4. A FAST I/O INTERFACE USING OFFSET TREES

In this section we introduce a data structure we call *offset trees* that allows us to reduce the CPU time per I/O from $O(B^2)$ (for the linked list data structure in the last section) to $O(B \log B)$. In practical situations, this amount of processing time is negligible compared to the I/O time. It is also negligible compared to the CPU time required to implement the actual update operations, which can be $\Omega(U_i B)$ for the ith round. We shall discuss the topics of input and output in the opposite order as before: output is covered in Section 4.1, followed by input in Section 4.2.

4.1. OUTPUT (from Internal Memory onto the Optical Disk)

Let us describe how the block log is converted to the update list during output. Instead of keeping the records in a linked list, as in Section 3.2, we store them as nodes in an offset tree. Each node in the offset tree has the following format:

offset
either `new` or `deleted`
len
start (present if the second field has value `new`)
left
right

Fields 2–4 have the same interpretation as before. The fields *left* and *right* store the left son and right son pointers. The nodes are not in a linear order, so the addresses of the update operations cannot be computed by adding up the field lengths as in Section 3.2. Instead, the *offset* field is used to determine the span of each node (i.e., its starting address and ending address) as the offset tree is traversed. The length of the span for a node is given by the value of its *length* field. The starting address for the root node is equal to its *offset* field value. For each remaining node, its starting address is equal to its *offset* value plus the starting address of its father.

For example, a possible offset tree representation of the example at the beginning of Section 3.2 is pictured in Figure 1. To process the entry "`insert 6 42`" in the block log, the tree node spanning the target address 42 must be found. The function call *lookup*(*root*, 0, 42) returns a pointer to the desired node, which in this case is the "`old 26 124`" node. The formal parameters to *lookup* have the following interpretation: *p* points to the root of the subtree to be searched, *p_address* is the start address of the first node in symmetric order in the subtree, and *target_address* is the sought-after address. We assume that $0 \le target\_address < current\_buffer\_length$.

```
function lookup(p: node_ptr; p_address, target_address: integer): node_ptr;
begin
while true do
      begin p_address := p_address + p↑.offset;
      if target_address < p_address then p := p↑.left
      else if p_address + p↑.len ≤ target_address then p := p↑.right
      else break loop
      end;
lookup := p
end;
```

Balanced search trees (such as self-adjusting binary trees ([Sleator and Tarjan, 83]), RB trees ([Guibas and Sedgewick, 78]), AVL trees ([Adel'son-Vel'skiĭ and Landis, 62]), and 2-3 trees ([Aho, Hopcroft, and Ullman, 74])) can be used to guarantee logarithmic search times. The offset values have to be modified in order to preserve their semantic interpretation each time the tree is rebalanced, since rebalancing typically involves rotations in which subtrees are exchanged among nearby nodes. Top-down self-adjusting trees offer an especially elegant implementation, since all manipulations to the tree occur in the vicinity of the root. There are no explicit balancing conditions, but rather certain rotations are done automatically. Any sequence of n operations on a self-adjusting tree (initially empty) takes $O(n \log n)$ time. The following implementation of *lookup* is the algorithm *simple_top-down_splay* given in [Sleator and Tarjan, 83], modified to handle offsets. The node that spans *target_address* is made the root of the subtree rooted at *p*↑, and a pointer to the new root is returned.

```
function lookup(p: node_ptr; p_address, target_address: integer): node_ptr;
var l, r, dummy, temp: node_ptr; l_address, r_address: integer;
begin
new(dummy); dummy↑.left := dummy↑.right := nil;
l := r := dummy; l_address := r_address := 0;
target_address := target_address − p_address; p_address := p↑.offset;
while true do
    begin
    if target_address < p_address then
        begin  {The target address is in the left subtree}
        if target_address < p_address + p↑.left↑.offset then rotate_right;
        link_right end
    else if p_address + p↑.len ≤ target_address then
        begin  {The target address is in the right subtree}
        if p_address + p↑.right↑.offset + p↑.right↑.len ≤ target_address then rotate_left;
        link_left end
    else break loop
    end;
assemble; lookup := p  {The node p↑, which spans the target address, is the new root}
end;
```

The macros *rotate_left*, *link_left*, and *assemble* are specified below. The definitions of macros *rotate_right* and *link_right* are symmetric to those for *rotate_left* and *link_left*.

```
rotate_left ≡ begin temp := p↑.right; p↑.right := temp↑.left; temp↑.left := p;
              if p↑.right ≠ nil then p↑.right↑.offset := p↑.right↑.offset + temp↑.offset;
              p↑.offset := −temp↑.offset; p_address := temp↑.offset := temp↑.offset + p_address;
              p := temp end
  link_left ≡ l↑.right := p; l := p; p := p↑.right; l↑.right := nil; l↑.offset := l↑.offset − l_address;
              l_address := p_address; p_address := p↑.offset := p↑.offset + p_address
 assemble ≡ if r ≠ dummy then begin
                 if p↑.right ≠ nil then begin r↑.left := p↑.right;
                      r↑.left↑.offset := r↑.left↑.offset + p_address − r_address end;
                 p↑.right := dummy↑.left; p↑.right↑.offset := p↑.right↑.offset − p_address end;
              if l ≠ dummy then begin
                 if p↑.left ≠ nil then begin l↑.right := p↑.left;
                      l↑.right↑.offset := l↑.right↑.offset + p_address − l_address end;
                 p↑.left := dummy↑.right; p↑.left↑.offset := p↑.left↑.offset − p_address end
```

During the search for *target_address*, the tree is partitioned into three parts for purposes of rebalancing: a left tree, a middle tree, and a right tree. The variable *p* points to the current node in the binary search, which is always at the root of the middle tree. The left tree contains all the nodes whose span is known to precede *target_address* as a result of the previous comparisons in the search, and the right tree contains all the nodes whose span is known to follow *target_address*. The variable *l* points to the last node in symmetric order in the left tree; the node's start address is stored in *l_address*. Similarly, *r* points to the first node in symmetric order in the right tree; the node's start address is stored in *r_address*. The left and right trees are stored as the right and left subtrees, resp., of the node *dummy*. At the end of *lookup*, the macro *assemble* combines all the pieces into one tree by inserting the left tree and right tree into the left subtree and right subtree of the middle tree. The pointer *p* to the new root is returned.

Using this new version of *lookup*, the function call *root* := *lookup*(*root*, 0, 42) rearranges the data structure as shown in Figure 2. The processing of the "`insert` 6 42" operation is completed by replacing the root node in Figure 2 by the three nodes pictured in Figure 3.

Deletion operations can be handled in a very elegant way. The operation "`delete` 50 25" is processed by first executing $root := lookup(root, 0, 25)$, which brings the node spanning the start target address 25 to the root. Then $root\uparrow.right := lookup(root\uparrow.right, root\uparrow.offset, 74)$ is executed, which makes the node spanning the end target address 74 the right son of the root, as shown in Figure 4. The processing is completed by updating the root and its right son and by deleting the nodes in between, as illustrated in Figure 5. Of course, there are several special cases to consider, such as the case in which a single node spans both the start and end target addresses and the case in which the start (end) target address coincides with the start (end) address of the node that spans it. The details are omitted.

4.2. INPUT (from the Optical Disk into Internal Memory)

Let us assume that round i_0 was the last round in which the block was initialized on the optical disk. Inputting the block from the optical disk to internal memory requires the combination of the update lists (one per round) into one grand list, which expresses the version of the block after round j in terms of the version of the block after round i_0. The combination is done sequentially. When the update list for the ith round is being processed, the update lists for the preceding rounds have already been combined into a cumulative update list in the form of an offset tree. The entries in the update list for the ith round are processed iteratively; each entry requires the lookup of its address(es) in the cumulative update list. A new cumulative update list is formed by pasting in sections from the old cumulative list.

5. ANALYSIS OF THE I/O INTERFACE

In this section we show that the I/O interface proposed in the last section, which uses offset trees with the self-adjusting mechanism, is both disk-efficient and fast.

Theorem 1. *The I/O interface using offset trees discussed in the last section is disk-efficient, as specified in Definition 4. The worst-case CPU times for input and output during the jth round are*

$$CPU_{\text{input}} = O\Big(I + \sum_{i>i_0} U_i \log \sum_{i>i_0} U_i + \sum_{i>i_0} N_i\Big);$$

$$CPU_{\text{output}} = \begin{cases} O(U_j \log U_j + N_j), & \text{if } \sum_{i>i_0}(U_i + N_i) = o(B); \\ O(1), & \text{otherwise,} \end{cases}$$

where j is the number of the current round, i_0 is the number of the last round in which the block was initialized on the optical disk, $I \leq B$ is the amount of data written during the last initialization, and B, U_i, and N_i are as defined in Section 2.

Proof. The input process is described briefly in Section 4.2. Each entry in the update list for the ith round requires the lookup of its address(es) in the cumulative update list, which requires $\log \sum_{i>i_0} U_i$ amortized processing time. The total time required is thus $(\sum_{i>i_0} U_i) \log(\sum_{i>i_0} U_i)$ plus the $O(N_i)$ time required to move the data fields.

During output, either the block on the optical disk is reinitialized, which takes constant CPU time, or else the block log must be converted into an optimized update list by using the offset tree data structure described in Section 4.1. Each modification to the offset tree requires $O(\log U_j)$ amortized time. An `insertion` at address s, which causes a portion of the block to be bumped to the right, is processed by searching for the node that spans address s (which brings that node to the root of the tree), by changing the *offset* value for the right son, and by "splitting" the root node, if necessary. A `deletion` requires the lookup in the offset tree of the nodes spanning the target start and end addresses; these two nodes are updated appropriately, and the nodes in

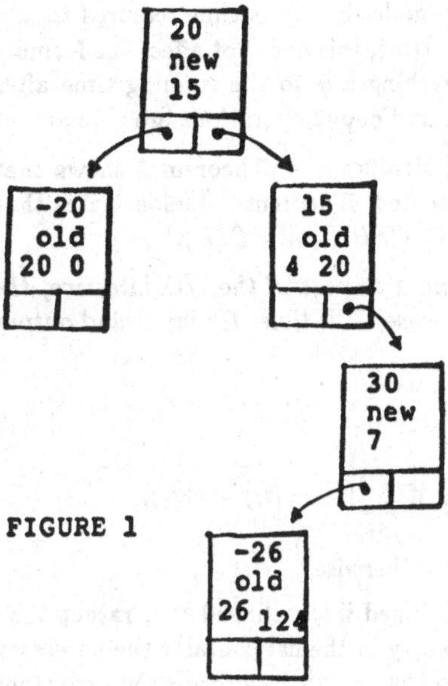

FIGURE 1

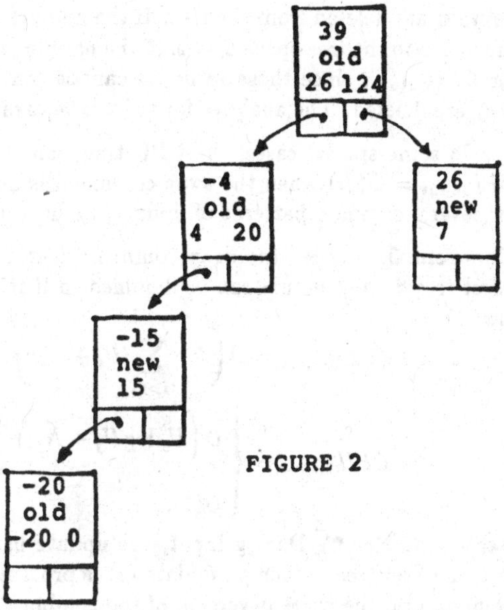

FIGURE 2

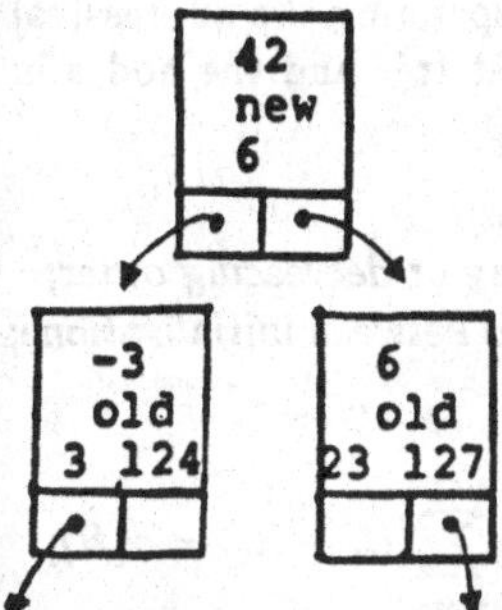

FIGURE 3

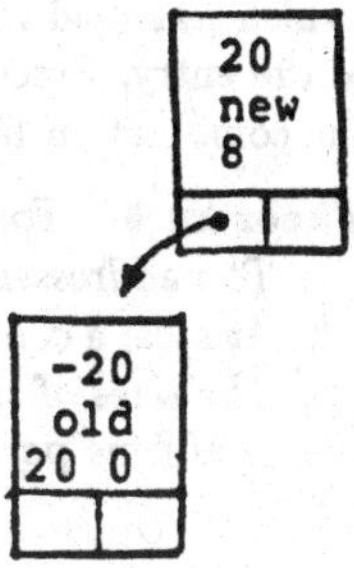

FIGURE 5

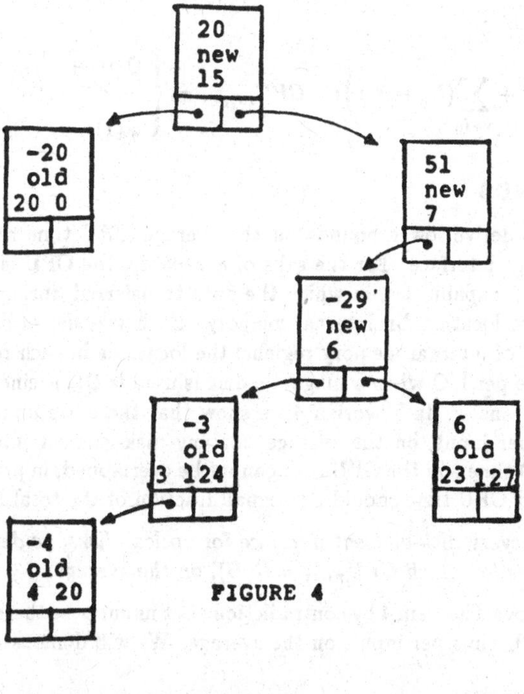

FIGURE 4

between are deleted from the tree. If the number of deleted nodes is m, the time required to add the nodes to the free-space list using the naive algorithm is $O(m)$; this does not affect the formula for CPU_{output}, since those m nodes cannot contribute anything else to the running time after they are deleted. The analyses for the **write**, **swap**, **copy1**, and **copy2** operations are similar. ∎

In some special cases, the CPU time can be reduced significantly. Theorem 2 shows that $CPU_{\text{input}} = O(B)$ when the **swap** command is not implemented. Theorem 3 demonstrates that for several common patterns of update, we have $CPU_{\text{input}} = CPU_{\text{output}} = O(B)$.

Theorem 2. *When the* **swap** *command is not implemented as part of the I/O interface, the offset tree data structure can be modified so that the worst-case CPU times for input and output are*

$$CPU_{\text{input}} = O\Big(I + \sum_{i>i_0}(U_i + N_i)\Big);$$

$$CPU_{\text{output}} = \begin{cases} O\Big(U_j \log U_j + N_j + \sum_{i>i_0} U_i\Big), & \text{if } \sum_{i>i_0}(U_i + N_i) = o(B); \\ O(1), & \text{otherwise.} \end{cases}$$

Sketch of Proof. During input, the update lists are combined into a linked list, rather than into an offset tree. When an update list is processed, each entry in the list contains the necessary pointers into the current version of the combination list so that it can be processed in constant time. These pointer values were computed during the output in the preceding round as follows: The entries in the offset tree were processed sequentially; for each entry, the combination list (which was read in earlier during input) is searched to find the node(s) spanning the address(es) of the entry. Since there are no **swap** operations, the entries in the offset tree and the nodes in the combination list can be processed left-to-right without backtrack. ∎

Theorem 3. *For the each of the following common patterns of updates:*

1. *The addresses of the updates between initializations are in increasing or decreasing order;*
2. *At most a constant number of nodes span the addresses of the updates between initializations;*
3. *The sizes of the offset trees are always $O(B/\log B)$,*

the CPU time per I/O is

$$CPU_{\text{input}} = O\Big(I + \sum_{i>i_0}(U_i + N_i)\Big); \quad CPU_{\text{output}} = \begin{cases} O(U_j + N_j), & \text{if } \sum_{i>i_0}(U_i + N_i) = o(B); \\ O(1), & \text{otherwise.} \end{cases}$$

6. LOWER BOUNDS

In this section we derive lower bounds on the average CPU time required per I/O operation for any disk-efficient interface. For the sake of generality, the CPU is assumed to have "scatter read—gather write" capabilities, in which the data transferred during I/O can come from or go into nonconsecutive locations in internal memory. Each transfer of data can involve at most a constant number s of internal memory regions; the locations in each region must be contiguous.

The CPU time per I/O when a magnetic disk is used is $O(1)$. since a separate I/O processor handles the data transfer. In Theorem 4 we show that there are update sequences that require $\Omega(B)$ CPU time per input, on the average, for any disk-efficient interface. Theoretically, this means that the I/O time and the CPU time cannot be overlapped; in practical situations, however, the non-overlapped CPU time should be a small fraction of the total I/O time.

Theorem 4. *For every disk-efficient interface for optical disks, as defined in Section 2, there is sequence of updates for which $CPU_{\text{input}} = \Omega(B)$, on the average.*

Proof. We will prove Theorem 4 by contradiction. Let us suppose there is a disk-efficient interface that uses $o(B)$ CPU time per input, on the average. We will demonstrate a sequence of updates that forces the amount of space used on the optical disk to be excessive, which will contradict the assumption that the interface is disk-efficient. The theorem will then follow.

We assume that before any updates occur, each byte of the original data on the optical disk has a unique value. Let $U(B)$ be an unbounded sublinear function of B, say, $U = \sqrt{B}$. The sequence of updates we construct is made up of $R = B/U$ rounds; each round consists of 1) input from the optical disk, 2) U `insert` operations, each consisting of two bytes, and 3) output to the optical disk. By the definition of disk-efficiency, the total amount of space used on the optical disk must be $O(B+UR) = O(B)$, the amount of data transferred from the optical disk to the CPU during each round must be $O(B)$, and the transferred data in each round must consist of at most c_1 regions on the optical disk, for some constant c_1.

Our assumption that $CPU_{\text{input}} = o(B)$ means that for an arbitrary constant $0 < c_2 < \frac{1}{3}$, we can choose B large enough so that the average value of CPU_{input} among the R rounds is $< c_2 B$. For at least half the R rounds, we have $CPU_{\text{input}} < 2c_2 B$. This means that at most $2c_2B$ bytes of data can be rearranged in the CPU during each of these $R/2$ rounds; the remaining $(1-2c_2)B$ bytes of data must be fetched by "scatter reads," as discussed at the beginning of the section. WLOG, the scatter reads can be assumed to take place before any data is rearranged by the CPU. The total number of "scatters" per round is at most sc_1, where s is the maximum number of scatters allowed for each transfer from the optical disk, and where c_1 is the maximum number of transfers allowed per input.

The U `insert` operations during a round are chosen in order to break up the at most sc_1 scatters of that round into regions of size $\leq B/U$ bytes. The data inserted by each `insert` is a two-byte value, distinct from any two-byte sequence currently on the optical disk or in internal memory. Intuitively, the `inserts` prevent each large scatter from being used effectively in more than one round. Let us make B larger, if necessary, so that $sc_1 B/U < c_2 B$; we are able to do this because U is an unbounded sublinear function of B. The amount of data transferred in each round in scatters of size $\leq B/U$ bytes is at most $sc_1 B/U < c_2 B$ bytes; thus, in $R/2$ rounds at least $(1-3c_2)B$ bytes of data must be transferred in scatters of size $> B/U$ bytes. The `inserts` guarantee that no byte of data on the optical disk need be part of a scatter larger than B/U bytes in more than one round. This accounts for at least $(1-3c_2)B$ unique bytes of data on the optical disk in each of $R/2 = B/(2U)$ rounds, for a grand total of $(1-3c_2)B^2/(2U) = \omega(B)$ bytes. This contradicts the assumption of disk-efficiency; hence, the theorem holds. ∎

By Theorems 2 and 4, the CPU time per input required by the offset tree interface when the `swap` command is not implemented is optimum, up to a constant factor. In the general case, when `swap` is implemented, the interface is optimum, except when $\sum_{i \geq i_0} U_i$ is $\omega(B/\log B)$ and $o(B)$ and when $\sum_{i \geq i_0} N_i$ is $o(B)$, where i_0 is the last round in which the block was initialized on the optical disk. We can show in the comparison model of computation using a similar argument as above that for any disk-efficient interface, there are update sequences that require $\Omega(B \log B)$ CPU time per I/O, on the average. We can also get the $\Omega(B \log B)$ result if we assume that the underlying data structure is a tree which stores the update list. We conjecture that this result remains true even in the general RAM model of computation. This would mean that the offset tree interface is optimum among all disk-efficient interfaces, up to a constant factor.

It is important to note that if we modify the definition of CPU_{ouput} to "count" the CPU time required to process the update commands, then it is easy to see that there are update sequences for which we must have $CPU_{\text{output}} = \Omega(U_i B)$ in the ith round. In other words, the CPU time required to perform the updates typically is much larger than the overhead for the interface. The extra time required by the interface is, thus, often negligible.

7. CONCLUSIONS AND OPEN PROBLEMS

This paper presents a practical approach for allowing operating systems and applications programs that currently use magnetic disks to use optical disks instead. The I/O interface we propose uses a data structure called offset trees. B-tree algorithms obtained by using the standard disk algorithms applied to this interface are roughly as efficient as the special-purpose algorithms that have been developed. We have defined a model of complexity for this problem and have shown that the proposed I/O interface is optimum in many cases among all disk-efficient implementations. We can show that the interface is optimum under weaker models of computation; we conjecture that it is optimum under the general RAM model.

A future goal is to implement this in connection with a real product. The general methods presented in this paper will have to be modified in order to conform to the specifications of a particular device. For example, if the optical disk has a fixed-record format, the data that is written to disk has to be partitioned into one or more record blocks. Space is wasted when the amount of data written is not an even multiple of the record size. Issues of fault tolerance, which we have not considered in this paper, must also be handled.

It would also be interesting to compare the performance of the self-adjusting implementation of offset trees to other balanced tree implementations and to non-balanced implementations. Non-balanced offset tree algorithms might be faster when the locations of updates are fairly random, since they do not have the added overhead of rotating nodes in the tree.

A variant of this offset tree data structure can be combined with the clever data structures given in [Fischer and Ladner, 79] to provide fast lookup by location in text editors. This combined data structure can also resolve object references in text editor environments, which arise in certain Undo/Redo packages, like linear undo/redo (e.g. COPE, PECAN) and US&R ([Vitter, 83b]).

Acknowledgements. The author thanks Dick Arnold, Malcolm Easton, Gene Lindstrom, Don Knuth, and John Savage for interesting discussions and helpful comments.

REFERENCES

1. G. M. Adel'son-Vel'skiĭ and E. M. Landis. An Algorithm for the Organization of Information. An English translation appears in *Soviet Mathematics, 3*, 5 (July 1962), 1259–1263.
2. A. V. Aho, J. E. Hopcroft, and J. D. Ullman. *The Design and Analysis of Computer Algorithms*, Addison-Wesley, Reading, MA (1974).
3. R. F. Arnold, G. R. Hogsett, R. W. Holliday, and P. J. Friedl. STAR, A Data Base System Architecture—Concepts and Facilities. Technical Report ZZ20-6452, IBM Palo Alto Scientific Center (February 1981).
4. G. Copeland. What if Mass Storage Were Free? *Computer, 15*, 7 (July 1982), 27–35.
5. M. J. Fischer and R. E. Ladner. Data Structures for Efficient Implementation of Sticky Pointers in Text Editors, Technical Report 79-06-08, University of Washington (June 1979).
6. C. M. Goldstein. Optical Disk Technology and Information. *Science, 215*, 4534 (Feb. 1982), 862-868.
7. L. J. Guibas and R. Sedgewick. A Dichromatic Framework for Balanced Trees. *Proc. 19th Annual IEEE Symposium on Foundations of Computer Science*, Ann Arbor, MI (October 1978), 8–20.
8. D. Maier. Using Write-Once Memory for Database Storage. *Proc. 1st Annual ACM Symposium on Principles of Database Systems*, Los Angeles, CA (March 1982), 239–246.
9. B. T. O'Lear and J. H. Choy. Software Considerations in Mass Storage Systems. *Computer, 15*, 7 (July 1982), 36–44.
10. P. Rathmann. Dynamic Data Structures on Optical Disks. *Proc. IEEE Computer Data Engineering Conference*, Los Angeles, CA (April 1984).
11. R. L. Rivest and A. Shamir. How to Reuse a "Write-Once" Memory. *Proc. 14th Annual ACM Symposium on Theory of Computing*, San Francisco, CA (May 1982), 105–113.
12. D. D. Sleator and R. E. Tarjan. Self-Adjusting Binary Search Trees. A summary appears in *Proc. 15th Annual ACM Symposium on Theory of Computing*, Boston, MA (April 1983), 235–245.
13. J. S. Vitter. Search Mechanisms for Optical Disks. Internal Memo, IBM Palo Alto Scientific Center (March 1983).
14. J. S. Vitter. US&R: A New Framework for Redoing. *Proc. ACM Symposium on Practical Software Development Environments*, Pittsburgh, PA (April 1984).

ENCODING GRAPHS BY DERIVATIONS AND IMPLICATIONS FOR THE THEORY OF GRAPH GRAMMARS

Emo Welzl[1)]

Inst. of Appl. Math. and Comp. Sci.
University of Leiden
2300 RA Leiden, The Netherlands

INTRODUCTION

A typical (notion of a sequential) graph grammar G consists of a finite set of abels Σ, a set of terminal labels Δ, ($\Delta \subseteq \Sigma$), a finite set of productions of the orm $Y_1 \rightarrow Y_2$, where Y_1 and Y_2 are graphs (with labels from Σ), and a start graph (or finite set of start graphs). A derivation step in G is performed as follows.

Given a graph X and a production $Y_1 \rightarrow Y_2$ from G, one locates a subgraph of X iso-orphic to Y_1 and "replaces" it by a subgraph Y_2' isomorphic to Y_2. The crucial part f the replacement is to establish connections between Y_2' and the remainder of X. he way that the connections are established is specified by the so-called embedding-echanism which may be unique for the whole grammar or intrinsic to each of the pro-uctions. This embedding mechanism is really "the heart of G". Often also application onditions are added to the productions in G - roughly speaking, they specify which ubgraphs of X that are isomorphic to Y_1 may be replaced.

The language generated by G is the set of all graphs labeled by terminal labels nly which can be derived from a start graph in one or more steps. (See Rosenfeld & ilgram, 1972; Della Vigna & Ghezzi, 1978; Nagl, 1979; Ehrig, 1979; or Janssens & ozenberg, 1980, 1982, for examples of different types of graph grammars and embed-ing mechanisms.)

We give here a somewhat informal presentation of a very simple idea which is ell applicable to (almost) every graph grammar concept independently of the embedding echanism used. Given a graph X in a graph language generated by a graph grammar G, e encode this graph by encoding its derivation. In general, such an encoding will be ore "complex" than the standard representation of X by its nodes, edges, and labels. owever, if the derivation of the graph is "reasonably short", then this encoding utperforms the standard representation.

This simple observation has a number of implications for normal forms of graph rammars. In particular, we show that a graph grammar which generates all graphs (la-eled by some arbitrary but fixed set of labels) cannot be essentially growing.

) On absence from: Institutes for Information Processing, IIG, Technical University of Graz and Austrian Computer Society, A-8010 Graz, Austria.
This research has been supported by the Austrian "Fonds zur Förderung der wissenschaftlichen Forschung".

(Informally speaking, essentially growing means that every production has a right hand side with at least as many nodes as its left hand side, and if the right hand side has the same number of nodes as the left hand side, then the nodes of the right hand side cannot be replaced in a subsequent derivation step.) Hence, for example, a node replacing graph grammar without "chain-rules" cannot generate all graphs (labeled by an arbitrary but fixed set of labels).

Growing normal forms play an important role in the considerations of the complexity of the parsing of graph languages generated by graph grammars, because they seem to indicate the border-line between PSPACE-complete and NP-complete membership complexity, see Brandenburg (1983).

DEFINITIONS AND EXAMPLES

Because of limitations on the size of this paper, all definitions and notions are introduced rather informally.

The underlying objects of our considerations are finite node and edge labeled directed graphs, (possibly with loops). For a set Σ of labels, a <u>graph</u> X over Σ is described by a system $X = (V_X, E_X, \varphi_X)$, where V_X is a finite set (of <u>nodes</u>), E_X is a set (of <u>edges</u>) of ordered pairs (x,y) of (not necessarily distinct) nodes x,y in V_X, and φ_X is a (<u>labeling</u>) <u>function</u> from $V_X \cup E_X$ into Σ. The set of all graphs over Σ is denoted by G_Σ. Clearly, edge (and/or node) unlabeled graphs as well as undirected graphs can be considered as special cases of the above notion. Moreover, graphs with parallel edges of different labels can be described in this scheme simply by replacing parallel edges with labels $a_1, a_2 \ldots a_k$ by an edge labeled by $\{a_1, a_2, \ldots, a_k\}$, i.e., we use 2^Σ instead of Σ as set of labels.

A <u>graph production</u> p <u>over</u> Σ is a 4-tuple $p = (Y, \bar{Y}, \gamma, \varepsilon)$, where $Y, \bar{Y} \in G_\Sigma$, γ is an <u>application condition</u>, and ε is an <u>embedding mechanism</u>. The set of all graph productions over Σ is denoted by P_Σ. The application condition and the embedding mechanism are used in the process of the application of a graph production $p = (Y, \bar{Y}, \gamma, \varepsilon) \in P_\Sigma$ to a graph $X \in G_\Sigma$. This is done as follows.

(1) Locate a subgraph Y' of X which is isomorphic to Y and which satisfies the application condition γ, Y' is referred to as the <u>replaced graph</u>, (γ could be, for example, (i) "The replaced graph is an induced subgraph of X" or (ii) "There are at least five nodes of X that are not in the replaced graph, but which are adjacent to a node in the replaced graph.")

(2) Delete this subgraph Y' and all edges incident to nodes in Y'. The graph induced by $V_X - V_Y$ is called the <u>remainder of</u> X.

(3) Add a graph $\bar{Y}'$ isomorphic to $\bar{Y}$ disjointly to the remainder of X. $\bar{Y}'$ is

'eferred to as the embedded graph.

(4) Apply the embedding mechanism ε which "inserts" edges between (some) nodes f the remainder of X and (some) nodes of the embedded graph. The embedding mechanism ay still make use of the position of the replaced graph in X. (ε could be, for examle, (iii) "Insert edges (x,y) between all nodes x in the remainder of X which were djacent to nodes of the replaced graph and all nodes y in the embedded graph" or iv) "Insert edges (y,x) between nodes y of the embedded graph and nodes x of the reainder of X in such a way that every node in the embedded graph has eventually at east degree 4.")

Let Z be the graph obtained by steps (1)-(4). Then we write

$$X \Rightarrow^{p}_{(Y',\bar{Y}')} Z.$$

If no application condition is imposed on a graph production p, then p is speciied in the form $p = (Y,\bar{Y},-,\varepsilon)$.

A graph production p is deterministic if after performing steps (1)-(3) above he resulting graph Z is uniquely determined, that is, $X \Rightarrow^{p}_{(Y',\bar{Y})} Z'$ implies that $Z' = Z$. learly, this definition reflects the "deterministic character" of the involved emedding mechanism.

A graph grammar G is a 4-tuple $G = (\Sigma,\Delta,P,S)$ where Σ is a finite set of labels. is a nonempty subset of Σ (set of terminal labels), P is a finite subset of P_Σ (set f productions) and S is a finite subset of G_Σ (set of start graphs). A graph grammar $= (\Sigma,\Delta,P,S)$ is called production deterministic, pd for short, if all graph producions in P are deterministic.

A graph X directly derives a graph Z in G, in symbols $X \underset{G}{\Rightarrow} Z$, if there is a prouction, $p \in P$ and graphs $X',\bar{Y}',Z'$ such that $X \Rightarrow^{p}_{(Y',\bar{Y}')} Z'$ and Z' is isomorphic to Z. omewhat informally, we refer to "$X \Rightarrow^{p}_{(Y',\bar{Y}')} Z'$" as a concrete derivation step in G f $p \in P$. $\overset{*}{\underset{G}{\Rightarrow}}$ is the reflexive transitive closure of $\underset{G}{\Rightarrow}$. The language, L(G), of G is efined as $L(G) = \{Z \in G_\Delta \mid X \overset{*}{\underset{G}{\Rightarrow}} Z \text{ for some } X \in S\}$.

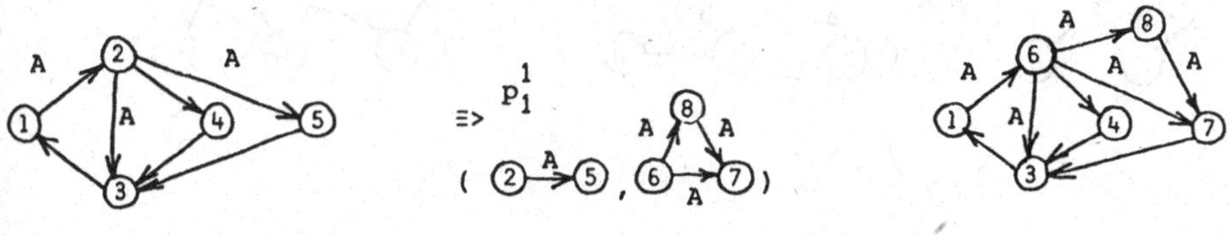

Fig. 1. A concrete derivation step in the graph grammar G_1 of Example 1.

Example 1. (Context-free graph grammars with edge replacement, see Habel &
Kreowski, 1983; A special case of the algebraic approach, see Ehrig, 1979). The underlying objects are directed edge labeled (but node unlabeled) graphs. Let
$G = (\{A,\lambda\},\{\lambda\},P_1,S_1)$, where the graph of S_1 is the directed cycle of length 3 with
edges labeled by A. P_1 consists of the following two productions. (As customary, the
label λ is used to indicate no label at all and so in drawing labeled graphs the label λ is not shown at all.)

$p_1^1 = (\bullet \xrightarrow{A} \bullet, \; \text{[triangle with } A \text{]}, \; - \;,\varepsilon),p_2^1 = (\bullet \xrightarrow{A} \bullet, \; \bullet \rightarrow \bullet, \; - \;,\varepsilon)$, where ε is the following
embedding mechanism: "Let x be the node with outgoing edge in the replaced graph,
let y be the node with incoming edge, in the replaced graph, let x' be the node
of the embedded graph with outgoing edges only, and let y' be the node of the
embedded graph with incoming edges only. Then, for a node z of the remainder of
the graph to be rewritten, we insert edges (x',z) ((z,x'),(y',z),(z,y')), whenever (x,z) ((z,x),(y,z),(z,y) respectively) was present in the graph to be rewritten.

Fig. 1 gives an example of a concrete derivation step in G_1. In this figure we use the
standard convention of using positive integers as nodes - hence ⓘ in a drawing represents the node $i \in \mathbb{N}$. Note that the set of underlying undirected graphs of graphs
in $L(G_1)$ is exactly the set of so-called 2-trees (see, e.g. Proskurowski, 1980).

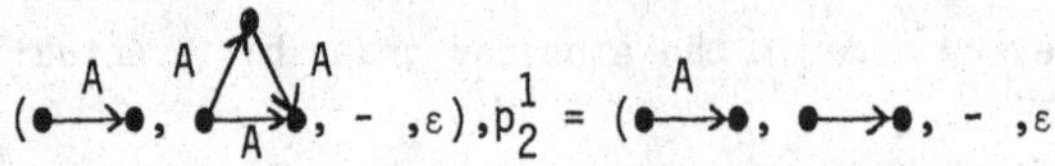

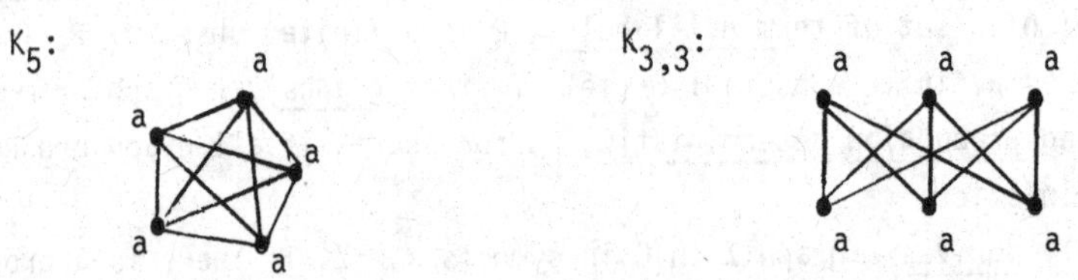

Fig.2. Two start graphs of the graph grammar G_2 in Example 2.

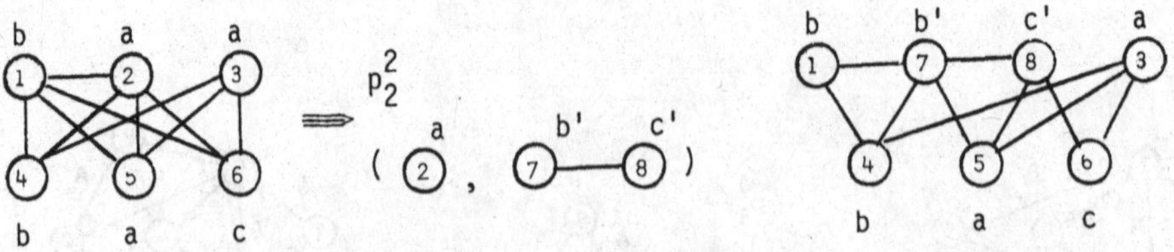

Fig.3. A concrete derivation step in the graph grammar G_2 of Example 2.

Example 2. (Nonplanar graphs by node label controlled (NLC) graph grammars. NLC grammars have been introduced by Janssens & Rozenberg, 1980). The underlying objects are undirected node labeled (but edge unlabeled) graphs. Let $G_2 = (\{a,b,c,a',b',\lambda\},\{\lambda\},P_2,S_2)$, where S_2 consists of the two graphs from Fig. 2 , and all graphs which can be obtained from $K_{3,3}$ in Fig. 2 by adding edges. For all productions from P_2 we have the same embedding mechanism ε which is described as follows: "Connect all a-,b-,c-, and λ-labeled nodes of the embedded graph to all neighbors of the replaced node and connect all b'-labeled (c'-labeled) nodes of the embedded graph to all a-,b-,b'- or λ-labeled (a-,c-,c'- or λ-labeled, respectively) neighbors of the replaced node." P_2 consists of the following productions:

$$p_1^2 = (\bullet^{a}, \bullet^{b}, - ,\varepsilon),\ p_2^2 = (\bullet^{a}, \bullet^{b'}\!\!-\!\!\!-\!\!\!-\!\!\bullet^{c'}, - ,\varepsilon),\ p_3^2 = (\bullet^{a}, \bullet , - ,\varepsilon)$$

$$p_4^2 = (\bullet^{b},\bullet^{c}, - ,\varepsilon),\ p_5^2 = (\bullet^{c},\bullet^{a}, - , \varepsilon),$$

$$p_6^2 = (\bullet^{b'},\bullet^{b}, - ,\varepsilon),\ p_7^2 = (\bullet^{c'},\bullet^{c}, - ,\varepsilon) .$$

Fig. 3 depicts a concrete derivation step in G_2. Note that all productions in P_2, except for p_2^2, amount to simple "relabeling" without changing edges while p_2^2 can be seen as the inverse of an edge contraction. By this observation and by the characterization of planar graphs in Wagner (1937) or Harary & Tutte (1965), (see Harary, 1969,page 113) it can be shown that $L(G_2)$ consists of all connected nonplanar graphs.

Example 3. (Tutte's characterization of 3-connected graphs.) The underlying objects are unlabeled undirected graphs. A wheel is a graph which consists of a cycle (of length at least 3) and an additional node adjacent to all nodes in the cycle. Let $G_3 = (\{\lambda\},\{\lambda\},P_3,S_3)$, where S_3 contains only the wheel on 4 nodes (which is the complete graph on 4 nodes) and P_3 consists of the following productions:

$p_1^3 = (\bullet, \bullet\!\!-\!\!\!-\!\!\bullet, \gamma_1,\varepsilon_1)$, where γ_1: "The replaced node is a node of degree 3 in a wheel," and ε_1:" Connect one node of the embedded graph to a neighbor of degree 3 of the replaced node, the other node of the embedded graph to a different neighbor of degree 3 of the replaced node, and moreover, connect both nodes to the third (remaining) neighbor of the replaced node."

$p_2^3 = (\bullet\ \ \bullet, \bullet\!\!-\!\!\!-\!\!\bullet, - , \varepsilon_2)$, where ε_2: "Connect one node of the embedded graph to all neighbors of the replaced graph and the other node to the other's neighbors."

$p_3^3 = (\bullet, \bullet\!\!-\!\!\!-\!\!\bullet, \gamma_3,\varepsilon_3)$, where γ_3: "The replaced node has degree at least 4," and ε_3: "Every neigbbor of the replaced node is connected to exactly one node of the embedded graph, such that in the resulting graph the nodes of the embedded graph have degree at least 3."

Note that using p_1^3 several times, one can first generate a wheel (of arbitrary size) and that p_2^3 amounts to the addition of a new line. Thus, (see Tutte, 1961, or also Harary, 1969, page 46), $L(G_3)$ is the set of 3-connected graphs. Observe that G_3 is not a pd graph grammar.

ENCODING GRAPHS BY DERIVATIONS

Let $G = (\Sigma,\Delta,P,S)$ be a pd graph grammar and let X be a graph in L(G). Then there is a sequence $\mathcal{D}$ of concrete derivation steps in G (from now on called concrete derivation in G)

$$(+)\quad \mathcal{D}:\ X_0 \overset{p_1}{\Rightarrow}_{(Y_0,\bar{Y}_1)} X_1 \overset{p_2}{\Rightarrow}_{(Y_1,\bar{Y}_2)} X_2 \cdots \overset{p_n}{\Rightarrow}_{(Y_{n-1},\bar{Y}_n)} X_n,$$

$n \geq 0$, where X_n is isomorphic to X, $X_0 \in S$, and $p_i \in P$ for all i, $1 \leq i \leq n$. If we want to encode a concrete derivation step in $\mathcal{D}$

$$X_i \overset{p_i}{\Rightarrow}_{(Y_i,\bar{Y}_{i+1})} X_{i+1}, \qquad \text{for some } i,\ 1 \leq i \leq n,$$

then we observe that such a derivation step is uniquely specified by X_i, p_i, and $(Y_i,\bar{Y}_{i+1})$. (Recall that G is production deterministic.) This means actually that the graph $X_0 \in S$ together with the sequence

$$(*)\quad p_1,(Y_0,\bar{Y}_1);\ p_2,(Y_1,\bar{Y}_2);\ \ldots\ p_n,(Y_{n-1},\bar{Y}_n)$$

defines $\mathcal{D}$, hence it defines X_n, and, consequently, it defines X (up to isomorphism). Observe that (i) (even with p_i given) we have to specify Y_i, because there might be several isomorphic instances of Y_i in X_i, (ii) (additionally to specifying $(Y_i,\bar{Y}_{i+1})$) we have to specify p_i, because G may contain two productions $p = (Y,\bar{Y},\gamma,\varepsilon)$ and

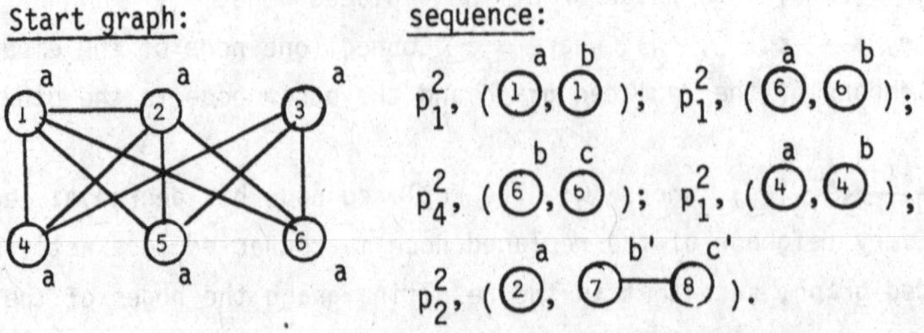

Fig. 4. Encoding the right hand side graph in Fig. 3 by its derivation in G_2.

' = $(Y',\bar{Y}',\gamma',\varepsilon')$ with Y isomorphic to Y' and $\bar{Y}$ isomorphic to $\bar{Y}'$, but $\varepsilon \neq \varepsilon'$, and iii) finally, we have to specify $\bar{Y}$, since we have to refer to its nodes in a subse-uent step. Fig. 4 depicts an example of such an encoding of the right hand side graph n Fig. 3. Note that we are "reusing" the names (integers) of replaced nodes, but in way that does not cause any ambiguity.

In order to analyse the space needed for sequences of the form (*) we need the ollowing definitions. The <u>length</u>, $lgth(\mathcal{D})$,of a concrete derivation $\mathcal{D}$ is the number of oncrete derivation steps in $\mathcal{D}$, and the <u>workspace</u>, $ws(\mathcal{D})$, of a concrete derivation $\mathcal{D}$ s the maximum number of nodes among all graphs involved in $\mathcal{D}$. So for (+) above we ave $lgth(\mathcal{D}) = n$ and $ws(\mathcal{D}) = \max\{\#X_i \mid 0 \leq i \leq n\}$. (For a graph X, #X denotes the number f nodes in V_X.)

Let G be an arbitrary but fixed pd graph grammar. For encoding a concrete deri-ation $\mathcal{D}$ in G, we need a constant number of bits for the start graph, a constant num-er of bits for specifying a production, and order $\log_2 ws(\mathcal{D})$ bits for specifying the eplaced and embedded graphs of the concrete derivation steps in $\mathcal{D}$. his amounts to the following bound.

THEOREM 1. For every pd graph grammar G there exists a positive integer constant c such that: If $\mathcal{D}$ is a concrete derivation of a graph X in L(G), then $\mathcal{D}$ (and hence X) can be encoded by a number of bits not exceeding $c \cdot lgth(\mathcal{D}) \cdot \log_2 ws(\mathcal{D})$.

A graph grammar $G = (\Sigma,\Delta,P,S)$ is <u>monotone</u>, if, for every production = $(Y,\bar{Y},\gamma,\varepsilon) \in P$, $\#Y \leq \#\bar{Y}$ holds.

COROLLARY 2. For every monotone pd graph grammar G there exists a positive integer constant c such that: If $\mathcal{D}$ is a concrete derivation of a graph X in L(G), then $\mathcal{D}$ (and hence X) can be encoded by a number of bits not exceeding $c \cdot lgth(\mathcal{D}) \cdot \log_2 \#X$.

A graph grammar $G = (\Sigma,\Delta,P,S)$ is <u>essentially growing</u>, if it is monotone, and when-ver, for $p = (Y,\bar{Y},\gamma,\varepsilon) \in P$, $\#Y = \#\bar{Y}$ holds, then there is no node $y \in \bar{Y}$ such that there xists a production $p' = (Y',\bar{Y}',\gamma',\varepsilon') \in P$ and a node $y' \in Y'$ with $\varphi_{\bar{Y}}(y) = \varphi_{Y'}(y')$. Intuitively speaking, this means that no node $y \in \bar{Y}$ can be replaced by a production in .)

COROLLARY 3. For every essentially growing pd graph grammar G there exists a posi-tive integer constant c such that: If $\mathcal{D}$ is a concrete derivation of a graph X in L(G) then $\mathcal{D}$ (and hence X) can be encoded by a number of bits not exceeding $c \cdot \#X \cdot \log_2 \#X$.

Thus we have seen that graphs containing at most n nodes from a graph language enerated by an essentially growing pd graph grammar can be encoded in $O(n \cdot \log_2 n)$ bits.

IMPLICATIONS FOR THE THEORY OF GRAPH GRAMMARS

The encoding which we have obtained in Corollary 3 for essentially growing pd graph grammars is considerably better than the standard representation of a graph by its nodes, labels and edges, where we need order n^2 bits for a graph on n nodes. On the one hand, there cannot be a general graph encoding for all graphs (over some fixed alphabet) that needs less than order n^2 bits, since there are more than C^{n^2} nonisomorphic unlabeled and undirected graphs with n nodes, for a suitable constant C. On the other hand, this means that there are at most $2^{c \cdot n \cdot \log_2 n}$ distinct (nonisomorphic) graphs with n nodes in a graph language generated by an essentially growing pd graph grammar. We formalize these ideas using the following definition.

For a graph language L, the positive integer function $numb_L$ is defined by[1)]

$numb_L(n) = \#\{X \in L \mid \#X \leq n\}, \quad n \geq 1.$

THEOREM 4. For every essentially growing pd graph grammar G there is a constant number c, such that $numb_{L(G)}(n) \leq 2^{c \cdot n \cdot \log_2 n}$ for all $n \geq 1$.

This theorem immediately implies the following result.

THEOREM 5. Let F be a family of pd graph grammars which includes a grammar $G \in F$ such that, for every constant c, there is an integer n with $numb_{L(G)}(n) > 2^{c \cdot n \cdot \log_2 n}$. Then there exists no essentially growing normal form for F.

In Rosenfeld & Milgram (1972) it was shown that there is a Web grammar which generates all connected (edge unlabeled undirected) graphs over some arbitrary but fixed alphabet.

COROLLARY 6. There is no essentially growing normal form for Web grammars.

In Janssens (1983) an example of an NLC grammar is given which generates all (edge unlabeled undirected) graphs over arbitrary but fixed alphabet. NLC languages are known to be NCE languages (see Janssens & Rozenberg, 1982).

COROLLARY 7. There is no essentially growing normal form for NCE grammars. In particular, there is none for NLC grammars.

---

1) For a finite set U, #U denotes its cardinality.

It is not too difficult to prove that there is an essentially growing normal orm for "context-free graph grammars", as they were defined by Della Vigna & Ghezzi 1978). Thus we get here a result of different type.

COROLLARY 8. For every context-free graph grammar G (Della Vigna & Ghezzi, 1978), there is a constant c, such that $\mathrm{numb}_{L(G)}(n) \leq 2^{c \cdot n \cdot \log_2 n}$ for $n \geq 1$.

We conclude this section with an improvement of Theorem 5 for a special class f pd graph grammars which replace nodes only.

A graph grammar $G = (\Sigma, \Delta, P, S)$ is a <u>(normalized) node replacing graph grammar</u>, if or every production $p = (Y, \bar{Y}, \gamma, \varepsilon) \in P$, we have $\#Y = 1$, and, moreover, $\varphi_Y(y) \notin \Delta$, here $Y = \{y\}$.

A typical feature of graph grammars is that even for node replacing graph gramars, the order of applying productions to the nodes in a graph can affect the resuling graph. Consider for example the following two graph productions for node labeled ndirected graphs

$$p' = (\overset{a}{\bullet},\ \overset{c}{\bullet}\!\!-\!\!\!-\!\!\overset{d}{\bullet}, -, \varepsilon),\quad p'' = (\overset{b}{\bullet},\ \overset{e}{\bullet}, -, \varepsilon),$$

here ε: "Connect all nodes of the embedded graph to all a- or e-labeled neighbors of he replaced graph". Then Fig. 5 illustrates the above mentioned fact.

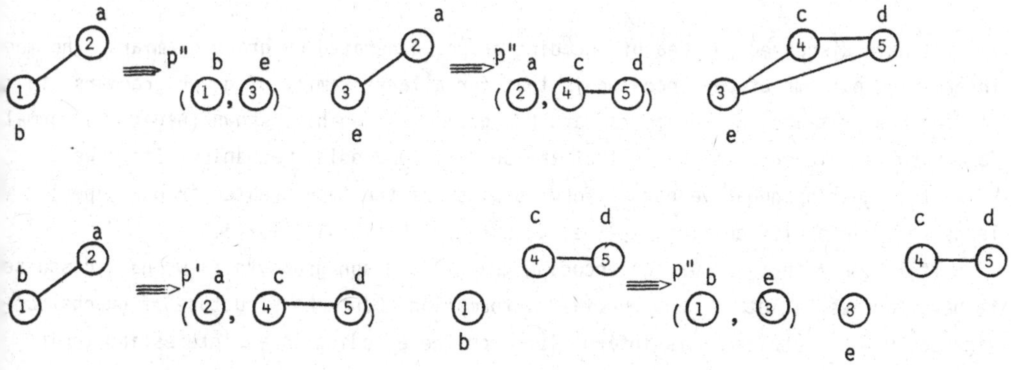

Fig. 5. An example how the order of applying productions can affect the resulting graph.

A node replacing graph grammar which does not allow such phenomena is called derivation commutative (see e.g. Church-Rosser NLC grammars, Ehrig et al., 1982; Neighbourhood-uniform NLC grammars, Janssens & Rozenberg, 1983 or Boundary NLC grammars, Rozenberg & Welzl, 1984). A more formal definition of this property (related to the finite Church Rosser property) is omitted here.

In a derivation commutative node replacing graph grammar, we can impose an ordering on the nodes of a graph and define a notion similar to that of a "left-most derivation" for context free string grammars. In such a "left-most derivation" in every step the node to be replaced is determined, (i.e., the first node in order which has no terminal label). Because of this one gets a more efficient encoding of derivations in such grammars.

THEOREM 9. For every essentially growing derivation commutative node replacing pd grammar G there is a constant c such that: For every graph $X \in L(G)$, there is a concrete derivation $\mathcal{D}$ of X in G, which can be encoded by a number of bits not exceeding $c \cdot \# X$.

COROLLARY 10. For every essentially growing derivation commutative node replacing pd grammar G there is a positive constant c such that $numb_{L(G)}(n) \leq 2^{c \cdot n}$ for all $n \geq 1$.

CONCLUSION

We have discussed an idea of encoding graphs generated by graph grammars. The most interesting outcome of our encoding is that for a large family of graph grammars (including Web grammars, NLC grammars, and NCE grammars), we have shown (negative) normal form results which are independent of the specific embedding mechanism. It is well known that getting negative normal form results (of the type treated in our paper) leads to various difficulties, see, e.g., Ehrenfeucht et al. (1984).

It is clear that the way of encoding graphs in graph grammars as we have discussed it here carries "a lot of constructive" information about the structure of graphs considered. How to retrieve this information from the encoding is an interesting topic of further research.

Acknowledgement. I thank Professor Grzegorz Rozenberg for discussion and for introducing graph grammars to me.

REFERENCES

Brandenburg, F.-J. (1983), On the complexity of the membership problem for graph grammars, in "Proceedings of the WG'83" (Nagl, M. & Perl, J., Eds.), Universitätsverlag Trauner, Linz, pp. 40-49.

Della Vigna, P. & Ghezzi, C. (1978), Context-free graph grammars, Inform. and Control 37, pp. 207-233.

Ehrenfeucht, A., Main, M.G. & Rozenberg, G. (1984), Restrictions on NLC graph grammars, to appear in Theoret. Comput. Sci.

Ehrig, H.,(1979), Introduction to the algebraic theory of graph grammars (a survey), Lecture Notes in Computer Science 73, pp. 1-69.

Ehrig, H.,Janssens, D., Kreowski, H.-J. & Rozenberg, G. (1982), Concurrency of node label controlled graph transformations, University of Antwerp, Report 82-38.

Habel, A. & Kreowski, H.-J. (1983), On context-free graph languages generated by edge replacement, Lecture Notes in Computer Science 153, pp. 143-158.

Harary, F. (1969), "Graph Theory", Addison Wesley, Reading, Massachusetts.

Harary, F. & Tutte, W.T. (1965), A dual form of Kuratowski's theorem, Canad Math. Bull. 8, pp. 17-20.

Janssens, D. (1983), "Node Label Controlled Graph Grammars," Ph.D. Thesis, University of Antwerp.

Janssens, D. & Rozenberg, G. (1980), On the structure of node label controlled graph languages, Inform. Sci. 20, pp. 191-216.

Janssens, D. & Rozenberg, G. (1982), Graph grammars with neighbourhood-controlled embedding, Theoret. Comp. Sci. 21, pp. 55-74.

Janssens, D. & Rozenberg, G. (1983), Neighbourhood uniform NLC grammars, in "Proceedings of the WG'83" (Nagl,M. & Perl, J., Eds.), Universitätsverlag Trauner, Linz, pp. 114-124.

Nagl, M. (1979), "Graph Grammatiken",Vieweg, Braunschweig.

Proskurowski, A. (1980), Centers of 2-trees, Ann. Discrete Math. 9, pp. 1-5.

Rosenfeld, A. & Milgram, D. (1972), Web automata and web grammars, Machine Intelligence 7, pp. 307-324.

Rozenberg, G. & Welzl, E. (1984), Boundary NLC grammars: Basic definitions and normal forms, in preparation.

Tutte, W.T. (1961), A theory of 3-connected graphs, Indag. math. 23, pp. 441-455.

Wagner, W. (1937), Über eine Eigenschaft der ebenen Komplexe, Math. Ann. 114, pp. 570-590.

Sampling Algorithms for Differential Batch Retrieval Problems (Extended Abstract)

Dan E. Willard

SUNY Albany Campus, Albany, New York 12222

and consultant to Bell Communications Research

Goal of Paper:

In many computing applications, there are several equivalent algorithms capable of performing a particular task, and no one is the most efficient under all statistical distributions of the data. In such contexts, a good heuristic is to take a sample of the data base and use it to guess which procedure is likely to be the most efficient. This paper defines the very general notion of a differentiable query problem and shows that the ideal sample size for guessing the optimal choice of algorithm is $O(N^{2/3})$ for all differential problems involving $\leq N$ executing steps. Our result is applicable to an extremely large number of different computing applications, and several computer scientists seem to now agree that some version of this result should become a standard part of a graduate student curriculum in computer science. Section 4 of this paper explains the relevance of this result to the new RCS data base theory.

1. Introduction

A query control problem is an ordered pair $\{Q,A\}$ where Q is a family of query states whose individual members are denoted as $q_1 q_2 \ldots$, and A is family of (usually batch search) algorithms $a_1 a_2 \ldots$ such that each procedure $a \in A$ can solve each problem-state $q \in Q$ in an amount of time henceforth denoted as $q(a)$. A query control problem is called nontrivial iff there is no one algorithm $a \in A$ which is optimal for all query states $q \in Q$. For instance, $\{Q,A\}$ would certainly be nontrivial if for each a_1 and a_2 in A, there existed different query states q_1 and q_2 such that $q_1(a_1) < q_1(a_2)$ and $q_2(a_1) > q_2(a_2)$.

An algorithm-assignment procedure is defined as a (possibly randomized) procedure, henceforth denoted as α, which maps each query state q onto an algorithm $a \in A$. The symbol $\alpha(q)$ will henceforth denote the particular algorithm which α assigns to q, and the "ideal" assignment procedure, henceforth denotes as α^*, will be that assignment procedure satisfying $q(\alpha^*(q)) = \text{MIN}[q(a) \mid a \in A]$.

A common problem in computing applications is that the ideal assignment procedure may have major hidden costs because it requires a great deal of overhead to decide which $a \in A$ is optimal. A natural solution, especially applicable to data base batch query problems, is to take a small random sample s of the query state q, and use that sample s to guess which $a \in A$ is likely to be the most efficient solution algorithm. This type of solution requires that the sampling size be chosen carefully so that its overhead is not very large while the sample is still large enough to guarantee a high probability of guessing an efficient algorithm. This paper introduces the new notions of a differentiable query problem and the complexity measure OSCOR, and proves the rather surprising result that the optimal sample size is $O(N^{2/3})$ in nearly all differentiable applications of size N, with $O(N^{2/3})$ also characterizing the difference in costs between the unrealistic ideal assignment procedure α^* and the most reliable approximation to this ideal.

Our result will refine some of the results in [As76,BG83,Go75,Ha77,KTY83,PK82,Ul82,Wie82,Wi83a,Wi84a], among other articles about databases. The next section introduces one example of a differentiable control problem together with the formal definitions of OSCOR and of general differentiable query problems. Then Section 3 will state and prove the main Theorems. These two sections will also survey the previous literature on statistical optimization of data bases and explain our formalism's relevance. In this section we make only the following observation.

A fairly straightforward consequence of the theory of statistics is that if the cost of drawing a sample is proportional to its size and if the cost of incorrectly guessing the number of elements with a certain property is linearly proportional to the size of the error then the optimal sample size is $O(N^{2/3})$. These observations do not imply our main theorem because our cost model is a step function having one level for each element of the last paragraph's set A, a set which typically has small cardinality. Indeed, a Bayesian estimate of the optimal sample size for typical sets A would be $\ll N^{2/3}$. Our main theorem follows despite these facts because OSCOR is a "frequentist" rather than a Bayesian measure whose worst-case distribution needs $O(N^{2/3})$ sampling.

The surprising fact is that none of the main textbooks on algorithms or data bases mention the importance of drawing samples of size $N^{2/3}$, and the author also could not find a partial analog to his newly discovered theorem in seven of the probability and statistics textbooks, he consulted or in some cases skimmed [B68, BD77,Bi62,De70,Fe68,GH81,GOS77]. Eventually, a partial analog concerning the linear cost model mentioned in the previous paragraph was found in [Co77] as one of several seemingly obscure exercises for the reader. [DS77]applies this idea to advertising surveys. Neither the computer scientists nor the statisticians seem to have realized that the dropping cost of computer memory will soon make a previously fairly obscure idea in statistics into a key programming concept when it is expanded into the form outlined in the next two chapters. The Bayesian cost model is unlikely to become as practical because it makes assumptions about the probability distribution that are poor for computer applications, and these assumptions at best can only reduce the size of a sample which often is already adequately small.

A reader should examine some of Willard's other recent paper on batch retrieval (references in Section 4) to appreciate the scope of applications (to relational data bases). The only prior article in the literature using samples of size $N^{2/3}$ for even one computer application appears to be [FR75]'s algorithm for finding the median element of a set. The generality of our theorem will be described in simple enough form to be understood by computer scientists with little background in statistics. We will also explain some generalizations which justify drawing samples of sizes different from $N^{2/3}$.

2. Notation and an Example

Throughout this paper, $|q|$ will denote the number of records associated with the query state q. Every query control family Q will be assumed to be associated with an integer M_Q such that all $q \in Q$ satisfy $|q| = M_Q$. No other information about q will be initially known to the assignment procedure α. All other information inferred by α will come from the randomly drawn sample s. The size of this sample is often denoted as $|s|$.

The symbol r will denote a particular record belonging to either the sample s or to the state q. Thus s and q can be thought of as a set of records satisfying the set inclusion inequality $s \subseteq q$. Note q has four different interpretations under the notation introduced in this paragraph and the previous section. Its four interpretations are:

i) as a set of records defining a particular query problem.

ii) as a member of the set Q defining all conceivable query states.

iii) as a function q(a) which maps each particular algorithm $a \in A$ onto its time q(a) for processing the state q.

iv) and as an argument of the (possibly randomized) assignment function α which maps each state q onto one algorithm $a = \alpha(q) \in A$.

For instance, if A is a family of algorithms for sorting a set of M_Q different records then the notation would have:

1) q denote a possible input set for the sort algorithm,

2) Q denote the set of all conceivable inputs,

3) q(a) designate the time which a needs to sort q, and

4) $\alpha(q)$ designate a procedure which guesses which $a \in A$ most efficiently sorts q.

Throughout this paper, $b_i(r)$ will denote a particular function which maps each record r onto the boolean value of TRUE or FALSE, and B will denote a family of such functions. The symbols $f_i(q)$ and $f_i(s)$ will denote the fractions of the sets q and s that satisfy the boolean condition b_i. These fractions will be called frequencies. F will denote a family of frequency functions defined over q and s. Obviously, the randomly selected sample s satisfies f(s)=f(q) when $|s|=|q|$; the law of large numbers [Fe68] states that these two quantities are unlikely to differ by a large amount when the size of the random sample is sufficiently large.

In our discussion, $g(t)$ will denote the cost of taking a sample s of size $|s|=t$. In most of this paper we will simply assume:

$$g(t) = t \text{ (or equivalently } |s| \text{)} \tag{2.1}$$

Larger samples s thus have greater sampling costs but cause $f(s)$ to be a better guess of $f(q)$'s actual value.

Since sampling is our only method for deciding which algorithm from the collection A is the most efficient, our analysis will need to carefully balance the disadvantages of large sample sizes against their advantages.

Now, we offer an example of a particular query control problem $\{Q_0,A_0\}$ which illustrates this formalism in much more detail. Suppose q is a set of M_{Q_0} records, Let r_j denote the j-th record in this set. Suppose r_j has two fields, denoted as $r_j.1$ and $r_j.2$. Define $b_i(r_j)$ to be the boolean value $r_j.i \neq 0$. Then $f_i(q)$ will denote the fraction of records in q which satisfy $r.i \neq 0$.

Our example will illustrate a family A of two algorithms, a_1 and a_2, which list the subset of q that satisfy the conjunction $r.1 \neq 0 \wedge r.2 \neq 0$. For i=1 or 2, define a_i to be the following four-step procedure.

1) INITIALLY SET j=1
2) IF $r_j.i = 0$ THEN GO TO STEP 4
3) IF $r_j.(3 - i) \neq 0$ THEN LIST (r_j)
4) IF $j = M_Q$ THEN algorithm terminates ELSE GO BACK TO STEP 2 with $j \leftarrow j + 1$.

It is transparent that the procedures a_1 and a_2 above are correct. Assume the four steps of these procedure consume one unit of time each. Then under the last section's notation, the total time consumption of a_i will be:

$$q(a_i) = 1 + 2\, M_Q + M_q \cdot f_i(q). \tag{2.2}$$

Thus, a_1 is the more efficient procedure when $f_1(q) < f_2(q)$, and a_2 the more efficient procedure when this inequality is reversed.

The purpose of the algorithm-assignment procedure α will be to choose with a high probability the more efficient among the two procedures for a particular state q. The symbol α_t will denote that assignment procedure which takes a sample s of size $|s|=t$, and then selects to execute a_1 when $f_1(s) \leq f_2(s)$, and a_2 otherwise. Let $Prob_t(a_i,q)$ denote the probability that α_t will choose a_i for resolving the query state q. Let $G(\alpha_t,q)$ denote the <u>combined</u> expected cost for taking the sample s and then applying the algorithm $\alpha_t(q)$ for resolving the query problem q. The notation from the previous four paragraphs then implies the query control problem $\{Q_0,A_0\}$ is characterized by the following cost function:

$$\dot{G}(\alpha_t,q) = g(t) + \sum_{i=1}^{2} \text{Prob}_t(a_i,q) \cdot q(a_i) \tag{2.3}$$

An interesting aspect of Equation (2.3) is that its term g(t) grows with t while the summand decreases when t increases. An algorithm which optimizes cost would thus try to balance these two opposite effects and find the t which intuitively minimizes the total cost.

Much of the notation in the rest of this paper will be a generalization of the example $\{Q_0,A_0\}$ above. In that discussion, α_t will denote an assignment procedure that takes a sample of size t and uses its information to assign an algorithm $a \in A$ to the problem state $q \in Q$. $\text{Prob}_t(a,q)$ will denote the probability of the event $\alpha_t(q) = a$; that is, it denotes the probability that the randomized algorithm α_t assigns a to q. Also $G(\alpha,q)$ will denote the combined cost for taking the sample s and executing the procedure $a = \alpha_t(q)$. The function $G(\alpha_t,q)$ will satisfy Equation (2.4), by a generalization of the previous paragraph's justification of (2.3):

$$G(\alpha_t,q) = g(t) + \sum_{q \in Q} \text{Prob}_t(a_i,q) \cdot q(a_i) \tag{2.4}$$

Throughout this paper, $T_\alpha(q)$ will denote that t which minimizes $G(\alpha_t,q)$ in Equation (2.4). As an example, let us calculate the value of T_α for three states q_1,q_2 and q_3 belonging to Q_0 which have the respective frequencies:

i) $f_1(q_1) = 0$ and $f_2(q_1) = 1$

ii) $f_1(q_2) = 1$ and $f_2(q_2) = 0$

iii) $f_1(q_3) = f_2(q_3)$.

The frequencies above imply that a_1 is the optimal algorithm for executing q_1, a_2 the optimal algorithm for executing q_2, and the two procedures are equally efficient for q_3. Obviously, a sample s of even one element is unjustified for q_3 since $q_3(a_1) = q_3(a_2)$. Therefore, $T_\alpha(q_3) = 0$. On the other hand, a sample size of precisely one element will cause α to choose the optimal algorithm for the states q_1 and q_2, implying $T_\alpha(q_1) = T(q_2) = 1$.

Now we will explain the main theme of this paper. Given an arbitrary query control problem {Q,A}, our goal will be to find the optimal size of the sample used by the assignment algorithm α. This problem is hard because the optimal sample size $T_\alpha(q)$ varies with the particular state q as we have seen in the example in the above paragraph. Many engineering applications are characterized by the fact that one does not know which $q \in Q$ characterizes the system and the question then arises of what sample size to choose. At first, it may appear that Bayesian statistics [De70] provides a solution. Let P(q) denote the probability that the system is in the state q. Then, it might at first appear that the optimal sample size t is that value which minimizes:

$$\sum_{q \in Q} P(q) \cdot G(\alpha_t, q). \tag{2.5}$$

The problem with this solution is that it assumes the probability function $P(q)$ is known. In many computing applications, one does not begin with <u>even</u> enough solid information to <u>guess</u> at $P(q)$'s distribution! A formalism is needed that shows how to solve the many real-world problems where the probability distribution $P(q)$ is this vague!

A common alternative used by statisticians, called the minimax solution, chooses that t which minimizes the cost $MAX(G(\alpha_t,q) \mid q \in Q)$. This solution may be reasonable for some query control problems, but it is not for most others. It is evident that the optimal sample size under this measure is zero for many query control problems, including the problem (Q_0,A_0)! Straightforward minimax solutions are often expensive. For instance, the textbook [De70] spends only 2 pages discussing them.

Throughout the rest of this paper, α^* will denote the unrealistic but ideal assignment procedure which maps each state q onto the optimal algorithm for resolving that state. In Section 1's notation, this is equivalent to stating $a^* = \alpha^*(q)$ if and only if $q(a^*) = MIN\{q(a) \mid a \in A\}$. Thus, $q(a^*) = q(\alpha^*(q))$ is the ideal although possibly unrealistic time for resolving the state q. The symbol $DIFF(q,\alpha_t)$ will be used in this paper to denote the difference between α_t's time-cost $G(\alpha_t,q)$ and this ideal. That is, Equation (2.6) formalizes this concept:

$$DIFF(q,\alpha_t) = G(\alpha_t,q) - q[\alpha^*(q)]. \tag{2.6}$$

Our goal will be to find that sample size t_Q which minimizes the quantity $MAX[DIFF(q,\alpha_t) \mid q \in Q]$. This number t_Q will be called the <u>optimal sample size</u> (OSS) and the resulting complexity $MAX[DIFF(q,\alpha_{t_Q}) \mid q \in Q]$ will be called the <u>optimal sample's cost over-run</u> (OSCOR). This measure is analogous to minimization of worst-case loss in the frequintist school of statistics, and our thesis is that it is especially relevant to data base problems.

For instance, the next section will prove $OSCOR < O(M_{Q_0}^{2/3})$ for the example of the query problem $\{Q_0,A_0\}$. The ideal (but unrealistic) complexity $q[\alpha^*(q)]$ for this problem is $MIN[q(a_1), q(a_2)]$, a quantity which is $> 2\, M_{Q_0}$, by Equation (2.2). Therefore, the cost over-run of our algorithm will be an insignificant increment over the time needed by the unrealistic ideal algorithm. For instance, if $M_{Q_0} = 10^6$, our procedure will differ from the unrealistic ideal by only 1% of the full cost. The perhaps main point is that this reasoning generalizes to a very broad class of problems which include many examples from the computing literature. Nearly all data base batch query problems of size N have complexities OSCOR and OSS lying within $O(N^{2/3})$, and we write this paper primarily because this very useful principle of statistics is not noted in any of the major computer textbooks on data bases or algorithms.

The remainder of this section will define the notions of a differentiable query problem and state the main theorem proven in this paper. In our discussion, F will denote a family of j different frequencies $f_1\ f_2 \ldots f_j$. The symbol F(q) will denote the j-tuple $(f_1(q),\ f_2(q) \ldots f_j(q))$, and N will denote a <u>rough estimate</u> of the number of steps needed by an algorithm $a \in A$ to process a query $q \in Q$. For each $a \in A$, assume there also exists a function H_a which maps R^j into R such that the algorithm a's precise cost q(a) satisfies the equality

$$q(a) = N \cdot H_a[F(q)]. \tag{2.7}$$

Then the problem {Q,A} will be said to be a <u>differential query control problem</u> bounded by the ordered pair (N,K) <u>iff</u> each function H_a satisfies the inequality

$$\left| d \frac{H_a}{df} \right| < K. \tag{2.8}$$

For instance, the query problem $\{Q_0, A_0\}$ is a differentiable batch problem.

In our discussion, X will denote a j-tuple $(x_1\ x_2 \ldots x_j)$, and ALG(X) will denote a function which maps X onto one $a \in A$ which minimizes $H_a(X)$. Then the <u>natural assignment procedure</u> α_t <u>induced by ALG(X)</u> will be defined to be an assignment algorithm which first takes a sample s of size t from the initial state q, and then chooses the procedure $a = ALG(f_1(s), f_2(s) \ldots f_j(s))$ for processing this state. For instance, our much discussed example of the problem $\{Q_0, A_0\}$ was characterized by a function $ALG(f_1(s), f_2(s))$ that produced the value a_1 when $f_1(s) \leq f_2(s)$ and otherwise produced a_2. This paper proves that the asymptote $O(N^{2/3})$ characterize the optimal sample size (OSS) and the optimal sample's cost over-run (OSCOR) for the natural assignment procedure of differentiable batch query problems and that better results are impossible in these complexity measures when g(t) is linear.

Our formalism also suggests two generalizations of the theorem above which lack of space do not allow us to prove. These are as follows: First assume the function g(t) specifying the cost of drawing a sample of size t is $O(t^x)$ rather than the linear asymptote from equation (2.1) for some fixed $0 < x \leq 1$. Then the optimal sample size is $\cong \mathrm{Min}(N^{2/(1+2x)}; N)$. Next suppose u is an uniform probability distribution defined over a K-dimensional cube in the frequency space of length $O(N^{-y})$ for some fixed $0<y<1$, and we wish to use Bayesian analysis to calculate the optimal sample size for the worst possible density u defined over the frequency space F. Such a decision problem parametrized by x and y has an optimal sample size proportional to the minimum of the previous quantity and $N^{2y} \log N$. In all cases, the cost over-run is $\cong [OSS]^x$. These results correspond to classical bayesian analysis when y=0 and to our previous OSCOR measure in the alternate extreme case where y=1. The proofs of the four statements made in this paragraph are fairly straightforward generalizations of the next section's analysis.

Section 3 of this paper outlines our formal proof of the $N^{2/3}$ sampling theorem and explains the background literature. Section 4 illustrates a very important application which warrants the readers attention even if he skips Section 3.

3. Main Proof and Background Literature

Some examples of articles in database science which would benefit from our rule of thumb $N^{2/3}$ for sampling include [As77, BG83,GO75,Ha77,KTY82, Pk82,Ul83,Wie82,Wi83a,Wi84a]. An interesting question therefore is why it was that none of the main textbooks or articles in algorithms and data bases did not introduce such a useful rule. After discovering this principle, we started to investigate the extent to which statisticians have known about similar principles to the proof which follows in this section. To our surprise, no mention of this principle was found in [De70], which dismissed minimax decision making in two pages of discussion, and there was also no discussion in several other text books we consulted or skimmed [Be68,Bi62,BD77,Fe68,GH81,GOS77]. The first several consulted statisticians and operations research scientists also did not recall seeing a similar principle, but eventually a partial analog was found in Cochran's textbooks [Co77] in an exercise for the reader not deemed important enough to be mentioned in the main text. Using the fact that $E(|f(s) - f(q)|) \cong 1/\sqrt{s}$, it noted that $cN^{2/3}$, where the value of c depends on f(q), is the optimal sample size for minimizing the expected value of $|s|+|f(s)-f(q)|N$. This result can be generalized to show $O(N^{2/3})$ upper bounds the optimal sample sizes for any differentiable query problems, but it does not imply the complementing lower bound; the latter in fact is false if the complexity measure is changed from the minimax OSCOR criterias to a Bayesian estimate. The literature in management science has noted the importance of $N^{2/3}$ sampling for selecting the most effective advertising campaign [DS77], and Floyd and Rivest have noted the use of an analogous principle for finding the median element [FR75]. However, its widespread use for every differentiable query problem in computer science has not been noted, and this principle appears to be very practical.

The discussion which follows is divided into two parts. The remainder of this section offers a proof sketch, and the next section explains how this principle has a major application to Willard's other work on RCS data base theory. Our proof will again begin with a discussion of the simple problem $\{Q_0,A_0\}$ and then present the results in greater generality. Bear in mind that the fairly simple theory discussed in this section is important because of its application.

<u>Theorem 1</u>: The query control problem $\{Q_0,A_0\}$ satisfies the following matching upper and lower bounds:

A) Let $t = M_{Q_0}^{2/3}$. Then there exists a constant C_1 whose value is independent of M_{Q_0} and q such that all q satisfy the upper bound $DIFF(q,\alpha_t) < C_1 \cdot M_{Q_0}^{2/3}$.

B) There exists a constant C_2 such that if $M_{Q_0} >> 1$, then some $q \in Q_0$ will satisfy the lower bound $DIFF(q,\alpha_t) > C_2 \cdot M_{Q_0}^{2/3}$.

Proof Sketch: Let $a_1, a_2, f_1, f_2, \alpha_t$ and $Prob_t(a,q)$ have the same definitions as in Section 2; and α^* again denote the ideal but unrealistic assignment procedure. Assume with no loss of generality that the state q is characterized by $f_1(q) \leq f_2(q)$. Then a straightforward analysis implies:

$$DIFF(\alpha_t,q) = t + Prob_t(a_2,q) \cdot [f_2(q) - f_1(q)]\, M_{Q_0}. \tag{3.6}$$

The remainder of our proof will calculate upper and lower bounds for the right side of (3.6) by bounding its term $Prob_t(a_2,q)$.

Proof Sketch for Assertion A: Since $f_1(q) < f_2(q)$ and since α_t is allowed to choose a_2 only when $f_1(s) \geq f_2(s)$, its choice of a_2 will occur only when either $f_1(s) \geq [f_1(q) + f_2(q)]/2$ or $f_2(s) \leq [f_1(q) + f_2(q)]/2$. From a variation of the central limit theorem, we may then infer that $Prob_t(a_2,q) \leq 2/[(f_2(q) - f_1(q)) \sqrt{t}]$. Substituting this inequality into (3.6) and using the fact $t = M_{Q_0}^{2/3}$, we obtain assertion A. Q.E.D.

Proof Sketch of Assertion B: It is trivial to verify Assertion B when $t \geq M_{Q_0}^{2/3}$, since $DIFF(q,\alpha_t)$ is always $\geq t$ and the latter quantity exceeds $M_{Q_0}^{2/3}$. Therefore, the remainder needs only verify that Assertion B is valid in the alternate case where $t < M_{Q_0}^{2/3}$. Consider a state q where a randomly drawn record's probability of satisfying $b_1(r)$ and $b_2(r)$ is independent and where f_1 and f_2 satisfy $f_1(q) = 1/2 - M_{Q_0}^{-1/3}/3$ and $f_2(q) = 1/2 + M_{Q_0}^{-1/3}/3$. A variation of the central limit theorem will then imply the existence of a lower bounding constant K such that $Prob_t(a_2,q) > K$ for the values of t under consideration. Assertion B then follows by substituting the last 3 inequalities into Eq. (3.6). Q.E.D.

Corollary 2. The Optimal Sampling Cost Over-Run (OSCOR) and the Optimal Sample Size (OSS) for the problem $\{Q_0,A_0\}$ are both proportional to $M_{Q_0}^{2/3}$.

Proof Sketch: The upper and lower bounds from Theorem 1 indicate $OSCOR(Q_0,A_0) \cong M_{Q_0}^{2/3}$. A simple consequence of the proof of Part B is that if either the sample size t satisfies $t >> M_{Q_0}$ or $t << M_{Q_0}$ then $DIFF(q,\alpha_t) >> M_{Q_0}^{2/3}$ for some $q \in Q_0$, implying $OSS(Q_0,A_0)$ is also proportional to $M_{Q_0}^{2/3}$. Q.E.D.

Three further definitions are needed to generalize the results above to an arbitrary differentiable retrieval problem. The symbol R_a will denote the standard topological closure of the set $ALG^{-1}(a)$, induced by the inverse of the function ALG.

If X and Y denote the j-tuples $(x_1 x_2 \dots x_j)$ and $(y_1 y_2 \dots y_j)$ then the "distance" between these two j-tuples will be defined as the quantity:

$$D(X,Y) = \sum_{i=1}^{j} |x_i - y_i|. \tag{3.8}$$

Finally, if X is a j-tuple and if $a \in A$ then the "distance" between these two entities is defined to be $D(X,a) = \text{MIN}\{D(X,Y) \mid Y \in R_a\}$ Our Proof of Theorem 5 requires two preliminary lemmas whose proofs are omitted for the sake of brevity.

Lemma 3. Suppose {Q,A} is a differentiable query problem of order (N,K). Then every j-tuple X and every $a \in A$ satisfy $H_a(X) - H_{ALG(X)}(X) \leq 2K \cdot D(X,a)$

Lemma 4. Let F denote a family of j frequencies and F(s) and F(q) denote the j-tuples $(f_1(s), f_2(s), \dots, f_j(s))$ and $(f_1(q), f_2(q), \dots, f_j(q))$, respectively. Then a sample s of size t must satisfy $\text{PROB}\{D(F(q), F(s)) > \epsilon\} \leq j/(2\epsilon\sqrt{t})$.

Theorem 5. Suppose {Q,A} is a differentiable query problem bounded by the ordered pair (N,K) and that the sampling cost g(t) is again characterized by Equation (2.1). Let |A| denote the number of algorithms in the family A, and j designate the number of frequencies in F. Then this problem's OSCOR and OSS are asymptotically $O(N^{2/3})$ (with a coefficient that depends on K, |A| and j).

Proof Sketch. Let α_t denote the natural assignment algorithm associated with the problem {Q,A}, and let $\text{Prob}_t(a,q)$ denote the probability that α_t assign a to q. The first half of the Proof of Theorem 5 is much the same as the justification of Theorem 1. In particular, Equation (3.10) is the natural generalization of (3.6):

$$\text{DIFF}(\alpha_t, q) \leq t + N \sum_{a \in A} \{\text{Prob}_t(a,q)[H_a(F(q)) - H_{ALG(F(q))}(F(q))]\} \tag{3.10}$$

Since α_t cannot choose a without $D(F(q), F(s)) \geq D(F(q), a)$, the probabilities of these events must certainly satisfy

$$\text{Prob}_t(a,q) \leq \text{PROB}[D(F(q), F(s)) \geq D(F(q),a)]. \tag{3.11}$$

Substituting the last inequality into Equation (3.10) and then applying Lemmas 3 and 4 to bound the summand, we conclude

$$\text{DIFF}(\alpha_t, q) \leq t + N \sum_{a \in A} Kj/\sqrt{t} \leq t + NKj|A|/\sqrt{t}. \tag{3.12}$$

Thus if $t = N^{2/3}$ then every $q \in Q$ satisfies $\text{DIFF}(\alpha_t, q) \leq O(N^{2/3})$ with a coefficient depending on K, j and |A|. The same remark also applies to OSCOR(Q,A) and OSS(Q,A), since they are always $\leq \text{MAX}\{\text{DIFF}(\alpha_t, q) \mid q \in Q\}$. Q.E.D.

Comment 6. It is impossible to develop an asymptote tighter than Theorem 5 for general differentiable query problems. Such an upper bound would violate the lower bound $M_{Q_0}^{2/3}$ which Theorem 1B established for the example of the query problem $\{Q_0,A_0\}$. To be sure, improvements are possible for some special differentiable query problems, but these tend to be fairly isolated examples. For instance, Corollary 2 and the Proof of Part B of Theorem 1 generalize to show that the bound $O(N^{2/3})$ is the optimal OSCOR and OSS for any differentiable problem where $N \ll M_Q^{3/2}$ and where there exists a point $X \in R^j$ and a vector direction v in this space such that $H_{a_1}(X) = H_{a_2}(X) = H_{ALG(X)}(X)$ and $dH_{a_1}/dv \neq dH_{a_2}/dv$, for some a_1 and a_2. Nearly all nontrivial differentiable query problems in batch data base applications can be shown to satisfy these two conditions, and that is why we suspect Theorem 5 touches upon a very fundamental principle to computer science.

Comment 7. For the sake of simplicity, this paper has studied only the asymptotic value of OSCOR and OSS. The coefficients could be improved with a more elaborate presentation. The most notable improvement is that the asymptote $O(N^{2/3})$ in Theorem 5 does not need a coefficient with a value depending on $|A|$. We also remind the reader that the second to last paragraph in section 2 defined alternate although perhaps less realistic complexity measures which enabled us to justify sample sizes $\neq N^{2/3}$.

4. Further Discussion

Chapter 1 noted our rule of thumb $O(N^{2/3})$ is a fairly straightforward consequence of classical probability theory, although one which the computer science and statistics textbooks have not recognized as having such major implications for the new emerging electronic technology. Our algorithm is suboptimal under the Bayesian cost model, but it should probably be taught in computer science classes and be used by some applications programs because there is certainly merit to a method which is optimal in some cost models, which guarantees that an application program can never exceed the cost of an ideal program by a factor of $> N^{-1/3}$, and which also has a simple proof. One motive for writing this paper was thus to advocate that Theorem 5 work its way into the standard textbooks and curriculum in computer science, as well as into some application programs.

A second motive was that these methods appear to have major implications for relational calculus theory. The relational calculus was proposed by Codd in the early 1970's as a set-theoretic data base language whose existential and universal quantifier primitives would provide the commercial user with a friendly interface for requesting data. The disadvantages of Codd's proposal was that relational calculus optimization is NP-hard, and his language allows users to casually make some requests which consume unacceptable amounts of resources. Accordingly, we proposed in [Wi78a,Wi83a,Wi83b,Wi84a] a modified calculus language, now called RCS, whose purpose was to be broad enough to include most of the requests likely to come from commercial user queries while narrow enough to exclude the ones that should not be allowed because of their inefficiency.

Our language and initial statement of results appeared as early as 1978 in Theorem 7.5L of [Wi78a], but the memory space there was inefficient. (The purpose of Theorem 7.5L was only to guarantee good time.) In 1983, Edelsbrenner and Overmars [EO83] generalized a memory saving technique from [Be80,BS77] that is relevant to many decomposable data structure theories [Fr81,LW80,OL82,Wi78a,Wi78b]. As a result of the latter memory savings, our new papers [Wi83a,Wi83b,Wi84a] report that all RCS queries over a database of M elements can be processed in time $O(M \log^d M)$ and space $O(M)$ for a constant d that depends on the particular query and whose value is usually ≤ 1. The only disadvantage of the proposals in [Wi83a,Wi83b,Wi84a] is that the coefficient associated with the time $O(M \log^d M)$ varies with the query and with the statistical distribution of the data. The work reported in this manuscript is relevant to RCS control theory because there are actually several different available $O(M \log^d M)$ algorithms for executing each particular RCS expression, and sampling is the only good method for finding that algorithm which is most efficient for a particular statistical distribution. The particular sampling method in Theorem 5 appears more suited for RCS applications than traditional Bayesian decision theory because its assumptions about the probability distribution are less stringent and because its sampling cost is still small compared to the database query costs.

If you wish to learn more about RCS, we suggest you read [Wi84a] first, then [Wi83a] and finally [Wi83b]. The first paper is an intuitive introduction possibly useful for classroom presentation. The second article is adequate to fully prove the RCS theorem in conjunction with [Wi84a]. The final paper [Wi83b] is the unabridged version of our article; it is more subtle than [Wi84a] because it lowers the exponent d in the time $O(M \log^d M)$. These articles appear to be seminal, and you may wish to examine at least their theorem statement.

Acknowledgements:

The realization that no article in the previous data base literature had studied the trade-off between sample size and the accuracy of α dawned first on me in the Winter of 1981. At that time, I asked Larry Kerschberg and Shlomo (Dick) Tsur whether they concurred with this conclusion, and I thank them both for their careful consideration to this question. I also thank my Bell Labs supervisor, B. Gopinath, for patiently waiting for this article as I further refined my concepts over the last year.

References (with titles omitted to save journal space):

[As76]Astrahan, et al., ACM's TODS 1(1976), 97-137.
[AU79]Aho & Ullman, ACM's TODS, 4(1979), 435-454.
[BD77]Bickel & Doksum, Mathematical Statistics, Basic Ideas and Topics, 1977.
[Be80]Bentley, CACM 23(1980), 214-228.
[BG83]Batore & Gottlieb, ACM's TODS, 7(1982), 509-540.
[Bi62]Birnbaum, Introduction to Probability and Mathematical Statistics, 1962.
[BKS68]Bechover, Kiefer & Sobel, Sequential Ident. & Ranking Procedures, 1968.
[Bo79]Bolour, JACM, 26(1979), 196-210.
[BS77]Bentley & Shamos, 15-th Allerton Conf. (1977), 193-201.
[BS80]Bentley & Saxe, J.Alg. 1(1980), 301-358.
[Co77]Cochran, Sampling Algorithms, John Wiley Sons, New York, 1977.
[De70]DeGroot, Optimal Statistical Decisions, McGraw Hill Inc., N.Y., 1970.
[DS77]Dalal & Srinivasan, Mangement S. 23(1977), 1284-1294.
[EO83]Edelsbrenner & Overmars, "Batch Solutions ..." 1983, U. Utrecht RUU-CS-83-8.
[Fe68]Feller, Introduction to Probability Theory and Its Applications, v.1, 1968.
[FR75]Floyd & Rivest, CACM 18(1975), 165-172.
[Fr81]Fredman, JACM 28(1981), 696-706.
[GH81]Guptat Huang, Lecture Notes in Statistics, 1981.
[GOS77]Gibbons, Olkin & Sobel, Selecting & Ordering Popul., 1977.
[GRG80]Gonnet et al., Acta Inf., 13(1), 1980, 39-52.
[Go75]Gottlieb, 1975 ACM SIGMOD Conference.
[Ha77]Hannai, CACM, 20(1977), 344-347.
[KTY83]Kerschberg et al., ACM's TODS 7(1982), 678-712.
[LW80]Lee & Wong, ACM's TODS, 5(1980), 339-347.
[OL82]Overmars & von Leeuvwen, Acta Inf. 17(1982), 267-286.
[PK82]Paige & Koenig, ACM's TOPL, 1982, 402-454.
[PR77]Pearl & Reingold, IPL, 6(1977), 219-222.
[PIA78]Pearl, Itai & Avni, CACM 21(7), 1978, 550-554.
[Ul82]Ullman, Principles of Database Systems, Computer Science Press, 1982.
[Wie82]Wiederhold, Database Design, McGraw Hill, New York, 1982.
[Wi78a]Willard, Predicate-Oriented Database Search Algorithms, Ph.D. Thesis, Harvard University, 1978. Also in Outstanding Dissertations in Computer Science, Garland Publishing, New York, 1979. The Garland copies are priced as hard-cover books; you can save money by asking your librarian to purchase a copy.
[Wi78b]_____, "New Data Structure for Orthogonal Queries," first draft was Harvard TR-22-78 (1978), second draft in 1982 Allerton Conference, third draft to appear in SIAM J. Comp, Feb. or May, 1985.
[Wi81]_____, "Searching Nonuniformly Generated Files in Log Log N Runtime," extended abstract in Proc. of the ORSA-TMS Conf. on Applied Probability - Computer Science Interface, 1981; full length paper to appear in SIAM J. Comp.
[Wi83a]_____, 21-st Allerton Conf. on Comm. Contr. and Comp., 1983, 663-675.
[Wi83b]_____, "Predicate Retrieval Theory," SUNY Albany, TR 83-3, Aug., 1983.
[Wi83c]_____, 21-st Allerton Conf. on Comm. Contr. and Comp., 1983, 656-662.
[Wi83d]_____, Inf. Proc. Lett., 24(1983), 81-84.
[Wi84a]_____, paper on relational calculus, at ACM's 1984 SIGMOD Conference.
[Wi84b]_____, JCSS, June 1984.
[Wi84c]_____, ACM 1984 Symp. on Theory of Comp.
[WL83]Willard & Lueker, "Adding Range Restriction Capability to Dynamic Data Structures," to appear in Journal of ACM.
[YY76]Yao & Yao, 17th IEEE FOCS, 1976, 173-177.

Author Index

ol. 142: Problems and Methodologies in Mathematical Software roduction. Proceedings, 1980. Edited by P.C. Messina and A. Murli. I, 271 pages. 1982.

ol. 143: Operating Systems Engineering. Proceedings, 1980. Edited y M. Maekawa and L.A. Belady. VII, 465 pages. 1982.

ol. 144: Computer Algebra. Proceedings, 1982. Edited by J. Calmet. IV, 301 pages. 1982.

ol. 145: Theoretical Computer Science. Proceedings, 1983. Edited y A.B. Cremers and H.P. Kriegel. X, 367 pages. 1982.

ol. 146: Research and Development in Information Retrieval. roceedings, 1982. Edited by G. Salton and H.-J. Schneider. IX, 1 pages. 1983.

ol. 147: RIMS Symposia on Software Science and Engineering. roceedings, 1982. Edited by E. Goto, I. Nakata, K. Furukawa, . Nakajima, and A. Yonezawa. V. 232 pages. 1983.

ol. 148: Logics of Programs and Their Applications. Proceedings, 980. Edited by A. Salwicki. VI, 324 pages. 1983.

ol. 149: Cryptography. Proceedings, 1982. Edited by T. Beth. VIII, 02 pages. 1983.

ol. 150: Enduser Systems and Their Human Factors. Proceedings, 983. Edited by A. Blaser and M. Zoeppritz. III, 138 pages. 1983.

ol. 151: R. Piloty, M. Barbacci, D. Borrione, D. Dietmeyer, F. Hill, nd P. Skelly, CONLAN Report. XII, 174 pages. 1983.

ol. 152: Specification and Design of Software Systems. Proceedgs, 1982. Edited by E. Knuth and E. J. Neuhold. V, 152 pages. 1983.

ol. 153: Graph-Grammars and Their Application to Computer cience. Proceedings, 1982. Edited by H. Ehrig, M. Nagl, and . Rozenberg. VII, 452 pages. 1983.

l. 154: Automata, Languages and Programming. Proceedings, 83. Edited by J. Díaz. VIII, 734 pages. 1983.

ol. 155: The Programming Language Ada. Reference Manual. pproved 17 February 1983. American National Standards Institute, c. ANSI/MIL-STD-1815A-1983. IX, 331 pages. 1983.

ol. 156: M.H. Overmars, The Design of Dynamic Data Structures. I, 181 pages. 1983.

ol. 157: O. Østerby, Z. Zlatev, Direct Methods for Sparse Matrices. II, 127 pages. 1983.

ol. 158: Foundations of Computation Theory. Proceedings, 1983. dited by M. Karpinski, XI, 517 pages. 1983.

ol. 159: CAAP'83. Proceedings, 1983. Edited by G. Ausiello and Protasi. VI, 416 pages. 1983.

ol. 160: The IOTA Programming System. Edited by R. Nakajima d T. Yuasa. VII, 217 pages. 1983.

l. 161: DIANA, An Intermediate Language for Ada. Edited by Goos, W.A. Wulf, A. Evans, Jr. and K.J. Butler. VII, 201 pages. 83.

l. 162: Computer Algebra. Proceedings, 1983. Edited by J.A. n Hulzen. XIII, 305 pages. 1983.

l. 163: VLSI Engineering. Proceedings. Edited by T.L. Kunii. II, 308 pages. 1984.

l. 164: Logics of Programs. Proceedings, 1983. Edited by E. Clarke d D. Kozen. VI, 528 pages. 1984.

l. 165: T.F. Coleman, Large Sparse Numerical Optimization. V, 5 pages. 1984.

l. 166: STACS 84. Symposium of Theoretical Aspects of Computer ience. Proceedings, 1984. Edited by M. Fontet and K. Mehlhorn. 338 pages. 1984.

l. 167: International Symposium on Programming. Proceedings, 84. Edited by C. Girault and M. Paul. VI, 262 pages. 1984.

Vol. 168: Methods and Tools for Computer Integrated Manufacturing. Edited by R. Dillmann and U. Rembold. XVI, 528 pages. 1984.

Vol. 169: Ch. Ronse, Feedback Shift Registers. II, 1-2, 145 pages. 1984.

Vol. 171: Logic and Machines: Decision Problems and Complexity. Proceedings, 1983. Edited by E. Börger, G. Hasenjaeger and D. Rödding. VI, 456 pages. 1984.

Vol. 172: Automata, Languages and Programming. Proceedings, 1984. Edited by J. Paredaens. VIII, 527 pages. 1984.